SMITHSONIAN INS
BUREAU OF AMERICA
BULLETIN 84

# VOCABULARY OF
# THE KIOWA LANGUAGE

BY

## JOHN P. HARRINGTON

UNITED STATES
GOVERNMENT PRINTING OFFICE
WASHINGTON
1928

# LETTER OF TRANSMITTAL

SMITHSONIAN INSTITUTION,
BUREAU OF AMERICAN ETHNOLOGY,
*Washington, D. C., September 16, 1924.*

SIR: I have the honor to submit the accompanying manuscript, entitled "Vocabulary of the Kiowa Language," by John P. Harrington, and to recommend its publication, subject to your approval, as a bulletin of this Bureau.

Respectfully,

J. WALTER FEWKES,
*Chief.*

Dr. CHARLES D. WALCOTT,
*Secretary of the Smithsonian Institution.*

# CONTENTS

# ILLUSTRATION

# VOCABULARY OF THE KIOWA LANGUAGE

## By JOHN P. HARRINGTON

## INTRODUCTION

The present paper is a reconnaissance report on the language of the Καεguα, or Kiowa Indians, a small and distinct tribe which history traces from an original habitat in what is now western Montana to their present home about Anadarko, Okla. It is based on field work done in 1918 at Anadarko, and the willing informants who were found in Mr. Enoch Smoky [1] and Mr. Paul McKenzie made it possible to gather more material during the time devoted to this language than would otherwise have been the case. I found what seemed a more than usual amount of intelligent interest on the part of the Kiowas in the writing of their language, and it is with Kiowa speakers in mind that the orthography of the present vocabulary has been shaped. The writing of such a language is difficult at best, and can not be simplified beyond a certain point without omitting essential features of pronunciation. An outline of the phonetics, pronoun tables, and a brief text have been included, as well as Tanoan etymologies taken from the Tewa dialect spoken at San Juan Pueblo near Santa Fe, New Mexico. The writer also has in preparation a paper showing the surprisingly smaller number of structural and lexical resemblances which Aztec shares with these languages, yet some of these resemblances striking, and appearing to one who has developed a sprachgefühl as features inherited from unity in the remote past.

In addition to the principal informants, Mr. Delos Lonewolf, adopted son of the famous Kiowa chief, Lonewolf, Mrs. Laura D. Pedrick, sister of the present head chief of the Kiowa, and Mr. James Waldo also rendered valuable assistance. I wish also to acknowledge my indebtedness to Superintendent C. V. Stinchecum, of the Kiowa

---

[1] Mr. Smoky was an enthusiastic informant. He would work until late at night, running up the hours and thus increasing his earnings. He put the money into fixing up his car preparatory to a trip to those other Kiowas in New Mexico known as the Taos. He would dictate sitting, standing, pacing, and lying on his cot.

1

Indian Agency, who took the kindest interest in the work and assisted it in many ways; to Mrs. George Laird; and to Mr. F. W. Hodge, former ethnologist in charge, and Dr. J. Walter Fewkes, present Chief of the Bureau of American Ethnology, for active and sympathetic interest in the long-looked-forward-to project of making an examination of the language of the Kiowa.

## PHONETICS

### § 1. GENERAL REMARKS

Six vowel qualities and twenty-two consonants are found in Kiowa (see the mouth-map, fig. 1). The Kiowa system is very normal in that its sounds are also found in neighboring stocks; it contains no sounds as peculiar for the region, as for instance Omaha bδ or the Kiowa Apache laterals. The vowels occur unnasalized and nasalized, the voiceless clusives have also glottalized and aspirated varieties. As one of the striking features of the phonetics we might point out not the occurrence of an unusual sound but the lack of w (see §10) and of v.

### §§ 2–9. VOWELS

### § 2. VOWELS AND DIPHTHONGS

Kiowa has two a-sounds: α as in Eng. water, and н as in Eng. land, both short, of course, in Kiowa unless marked long. Frequently the less extreme positions in Fr. basane (bazan), sheepskin, are heard. In loanwords, Eng. α is Kio. α; Eng. н is Kio. н; thus 'αdlαmoubiнdl, automobile; k'нp, cap. In Tewa the sound of α occurs, as in Engl. father, the articulatory position of which lies perhaps midway between α and н.

ou, ei are false diphthongs, pronounced as in Eng. soul, eight, and can also be written ow, ey. When ou, ei occur as the final element of true diphthongs (see below) their spelling has been reduced to o, e, but the final w or y is retained in the pronunciation and can be preglottalized or preaspirated; e. g. kue'y, wolf, written kue'; 'ouseitн'ęhyoudl, to kill by choking, for 'ouseitн'ę-houdl. Kio. ou, ei regularly represent Eng. ou, ei in loanwords. Kio. ou, ei are probably also the regular representatives of Eng. u, i, although some examples show Kio. iн for Eng. ı. Thus t'oubeitsei, two bits; tseidlei, chile (but 'αdlαmoubiнdl, automobile, as given above).

u, i occur only as first element of the diphthongs uα, ue, iн. The second element of the diphthongs uα, iн is frequently elided; thus gu(α)dl, to be red; ki(æ)dl, to dwell. Examples also occur of the elision of the second element of the diphthong iн in word auslaut before 'н-; thus hн'gi(н) 'ń- łα'dei', they must be staying somewhere;

bǫŋgi(H) 'ȟ-dǫ̧ŋgyHe, I smelled something rotten.  ŋ, apparently
without a following diphthong element, occurs in 'ǫ̧m-hy̧ŋ'm-dei, right
(dexter), but the form is probably contracted from *'ǫ̧m-hy̧ŋ(ȩ)'m-
dei (see p. 25).  It should be noticed that while 'iH begins a few
words, 'uₐ or 'uₑ has not been found as an initial syllable.

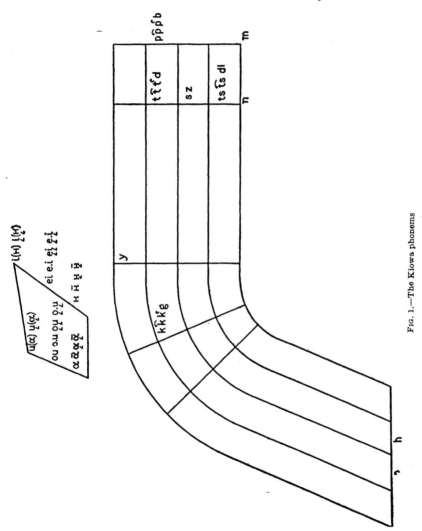

FIG. 1.—The Kiowa phonems

The true diphthongs, as they may be termed to distinguish them,
from the diphthongized vowels ou, ei, have been listed as follows.
Glottalized forms, with the glottal clusive falling between the two
elements, have been included in the list.  Examples have been
found only for part of the possibly occurring diphthongs.

(1) αe: k'αe, skin.
    α'e: tα'tα'e, my father.
    αe̜: 'α'pαe̜, otter.
    ą'e̜:

(2) oue: poue, prohibitive particle.
    ou'e: tou'e, room.
    ou̯e̜: bou̯e̜, transparent.
    ou̯'e̜:

(3) uα: hąn 'é̜i-guαgu'αdα', you will not hit me.
    u'α: hąn 'é̜i̯-guαgu'αdα', you will not hit me.
    u̯ą:
    u̯'ą:

(4) ue: k'uep'ḥ, wagon.
    u'e:
    u̯e̜: -hyu̯e̜, tpl. form of -hi̜ḥ, real.
    u̯'e̜: toubyu̯'e̜, camp-circle.

(5) нe: k̑yнtнekiн, chief.
    н'e: 'α'zн'e, udder.
    нe̜: t̑ḥe̜, to be white.
    ḥ'e̜: 'ouseit̑ḥ'e̜hyoudl, to kill by choking.

(6) iн: k̑iнgyн, to throw.
    i'н: k'i'нbα', to move off, fly away.
    i̜ḥ: 'α'pi̜ḥ, fish.
    i̜'ḥ: hi̜'ḥgyн, he died.

The loanword form t'нαn-gyн, in town, shows a diphthong different from any listed above, imitating Eng. "ow" as pronounced in the Southern States.

oue sounds dissyllabic in certain forms; e. g. 'ou-ei-dei, that one.

Glide ʷ, ʸ are developed in the diphthongs uα, iн respectively; e. g. gu(ʷ)αdl, to be red; ki(ʸ)нdl, to dwell, as, e. g., in Russian pri ʸétix, near these, for pri étix. In the glottalized forms of uα, iн the glottal clusive falls before the glide; e. g. k̑yн̜hi̜'(ʸ)ḥ, man.

For iн equal to yн in syllable inlaut see § 10.

### § 3. VOWEL LENGTH

Long α, н, largely recorded as glottalized, have their length indicated by the macron; e. g. pн̄'gα, one. Short glottalized open final α, н sometimes sounded lengthened before a following word; e. g. tou-yα' 'н̄-tsн̜n, tou-yᾱ' 'н̄-tsн̜n, I came from the house.

Examples of rhetorical lengthening were obtained and may be indicated by placing a colon after the overlengthened sound; e. g. tα'dei he̜igyн dα'me̜i' gα sαt нн:'oue k̑iнgyн tsн̜nheidl I heard that he was away for a long time and that he came back way afterward; 'o:ue, way over there, equals 'o:uhiн.

Forms of ou, ei in non-final syllables in which the second element of the diphthong was heard with prominence have been written by placing a period between the two elements; thus gyн̇-bo.u-boụnmœ, I see him all the time.

### § 4. GLOTTALIZATION OF VOWELS AND DIPHTHONGS

(a) œ', н', in narrow transcription œ'œ, н'н, have a resumed fragment of the preceding vowel quality after the glottal clusive, as if the vowel had been doubled. Both short and long glottalized forms of these two vowels were recorded. Thus bœ'dlœ', butter (fr. Eng.); k̑œ' gyн̇-pн̑'deidœ', I am going to sharpen my knife; 'н̇-t̑н'dl, break it in two (the string)!; k̑yн'dlei, to call, summon; k'œ'm, to call, name.

(b) In the false diphthongs ou', ei', the glottal clusive falls before the u, i respectively, yielding what in narrow transcription would be written o'ᵘ, e'ⁱ, or o'ʷ, e'ʸ. Thus dou', to hold, have; houdldн gyн̇t-dou'dœ', I am going to put on my coat; doụ'm, down; toụneị', he said; zнedei bн̑-peị'n, let us butcher half!

(c) In the true diphthongs, a glottal clusive appears to fall between the two constituent elements of the diphthong. This glottal clusive appears to be (1) the initial ' of the etymological element forming the second part of the diphthong; e. g. in such a form as tœ'tœ'e, my father, our father; or (2) a glottal hardening; as in -hị'н, real, which alternates for reasons not yet discovered with an unglottalized form, -hiн.

For ' derived from syllabically final t̑, p̑ after vowels and diphthongs, see § 11.

### § 5. NASALIZATION OF VOWELS AND DIPHTHONGS

Nasalization is indicated by placing the Polish hook beneath letters.

The nasalization of many syllables is induced by that of contiguous syllables; thus postpound -k̑iн, man, but independent k̑yн-hị'н, man, for k̑yн-hị'н; dœ'-mœ', was not, for dœ'-mœ'.

### § 6. VOWEL MUTATIONS

Frequently observed vowel mutations are: ou —— uœ, ei —— iн. Thus goup, to hit —— guœdœ, fut.; heị'm, to die —— hị'нheidl, inferential.

### § 7. VOWEL SANDHI

#### (1) ELISION OF VOWELS

The following elisions have been noted:

(a) Elision of second element of iн in word auslaut before 'н- (see § 2).

(b) Elision of initial glottal clusive and vowel or diphthong of certain verbal prefixed pronouns; e. g. hꞔyн' m-hou'ꞔ'zọ̣unheidl, they traveled off somewhere, for hꞔyн' 'ẹ̣im-hou'ꞔ'zọ̣unheidl.

(2) ASSIMILATION AND ELISION OF VOWELS

Clear examples were obtained of the assimilation of the vowels of gα and nα̨, both meaning and, to the quality of the first syllable of following heigα, then. Thus pн' t̓αþp'нdl houdlheidl geigα pẹinheidl, he killed a buffalo bull and butchered it, for gα heigα; 'н̓-houdldα' gei heigα m-t'ọ̣up'н̨t̓α', if you kill him, they'll get you, for gα heigα; nẹigα, and then, frequent for nα̨ heigα; sat̓ tsн̨n nẹi 'ẹim-tsou 'ȩ̀im-k'uαt, he came here just now and went out this way, for nα̨ 'ẹim-tsou.

§ 8. VOWEL INSERTION BETWEEN HETERO-ORGANIC NASALS

A short vowel was heard inserted between n and m in bọ̣un(α̨)mα̨, curs. of bọ̣u, to see; bн̨n(н̨)mн̨, curs. of bн, to go. The inserted vowel exhibits harmony with the other vowels of the word.

§ 9. PITCH ACCENT

The writer has in progress and well advanced a study of the Kiowa pitch accent. In the present vocabulary only high and low pitch of the verbal prefixed pronouns is indicated and has been written by placing the acute over high, the grave over low syllables.

§§10–16. CONSONANTS

§10. SEMIVOWELS

Except as second element of the diphthong ou and as a glide in the diphthongs uα and ue, w does not occur in Kiowa. Regression of initial ' , h of a following syllable to precede the second element of ou was not noted. Glide ʷ is preceded by ' in the glottalized diphthong u'(ʷ)α (§ 2).

In addition to its occurrence as second element of the diphthong ei and as a glide in the diphthong iн, y is found at the beginning of syllables, both alone and preceded by certain consonants. y is, therefore, the only sound, with exception of s in the affricative ts, which makes syllabically initial consonantal clusters (unless the glottalization and aspiration of clusives is to be regarded as forming such clusters). Syllabically initial y and y-clusters, together with vowel or diphthong following, are listed below. Some of the forms are produced by the retrogression of initial ' , h of the following syllable to precede the second element of the diphthong ei (§15), and are so analyzed in the list. Glide ʸ is also preceded by ' in the glottalized diphthong i'(ʸ)α (§ 2). Nasalized and glottalized vowels and diphthongs have been grouped with unnasalized and unglottalized to simplify the list.

(1) y-

    yɑ: yɑmgɑ, to tremble.

    yu: yūh, interj. of fright.

    yн: y§̂- (varying with y{н-), verbal prefixed pron., they tpl. inan. coll. —— for me.

    yнe: yнebн, to go to play.

    yiн: yiн, two.

(2) 'y-

    'you: 'e'youguɑ'ei, rice, for 'ei-'ouguɑ'ei.

    'yue: 'yue, tpl. children.

    'ʸн: k'į̇'(ʸ)н, to blossom.

(3) hy-

    hyɑ: k'uehyɑ', to drag, for k'ue-hɑ'.

    hyou: k̯yṇhyoup, tpl. men.

    hyu: 'ɑmhyy̨'mdei, right (dexter).

    hyue: tęįhyy̨'ę, sinew.

    hyн: hyн, interj. used in calling to a person.

    hyei: '§̇į-tɑ'tɑ'ehyęį'm, my father died, for '§̇į-tɑ'tɑ'e-hęį'm.

    hyiн: 'ę̇įm-t'нhyi'нdɑ', I am going to accompany you, for 'ę̇įm-t'нe-hi'нda'.

(4) ky-

    kyн: kyнboudliн, sheep.

    kyнe: kyнedɑ, enemy.

    kyue: kyy̨ę, tpl. long ones.

(5) k̯y-

    k̯you: k̯youp, k̯oup, knob, mountain.

    k̯yн, k̯iн: -k̯yн, man.

(6) k'y-

    k'yue: k'yy̨'ę, shield.

    k'yн, k'iн: k'yнdl-dɑ, to be wet.

(7) gy-

    gyн, giн: gyн̇-, giн̇-, verbal prefixed pronoun, I —— him.

(8) sy-

    syɑ: syɑndei, a little.

    syн, siн: syн̨n, to be small.

(9) ny-

    nyн, niн: niннyн, two by two.

(10) py-

    pyн, piн: 'ɑ'-pyн̨'dɑ, tpl. fishes.

(11) by-

    byue: toubyy̨'ę, camp-circle.

yiн varies with yн in the pronunciation of yịн-, yн-, verbal prefixed pronoun, and in several other forms.   yiн also may appear as
yi, with regular elision of the н of the iн diphthong (§ 2); e. g. yi(н)-
kɑ'douk'ịн, two hundred.

you was heard after clusives of the k-group in certain words but
an alternative pronunciation omits the y; thus ƙyoup, ƙoup, knob,
mountain.

After syllabically initial k, ƙ, k', g the vowel н appears only as
yн practically amounting to palatalization of the preceding dorsal,
varying with iн; e. g. -ƙyн, -ƙiн, man.   So apparently also after
n, for н appears after n in the recorded material only in the loanword Nнbнhou-ƙiн, Navaho man, whereas elsewhere we have yн,
iн.   But after syllabically initial s simple н occurs as well as yн
varying with iн; e. g. sнdl, to be hot, beside syн̥n, sịн̥n, small.   The
long correspondent of this yн or iн is yн'; e. g. syн̥'da, tpl. small
ones (an.).   The glottalized form of yн, iн has been written i'н.

When a vowel or diphthong forming a syllable with y is nasalized,
the y of course shares the nasalization.

### §11. CLUSIVES AND AFFRICATIVES

The glottal clusive or " hard attack," written by the apostrophe, ',
regularly introduces words not beginning with any other consonant.
But in word inlaut elements are found both with and without initial',
e. g. sɑ-'e, to be swift [sɑ-=Tewɑ cá, to be swift; -'ei, formative
element with initial '], but sɑ-e, to seat [sɑ- as in Tewa só-gè, to seat;
-ei, causative postfix, here with initial ' absent or elided].

' at the beginning of a word or syllable does not have a glottalizing
effect on the t, dl or p closing a preceding syllable, but is slurred out.
The elision of the ' may be indicated by writing beneath the apostrophe an inferior breve, the sign of elision, or by omitting the apostrophe.   Thus 'ou'kɑt-ʾн', pole mattress, not *'ou'kat̂н'; toudl-ʾɑ̨,
to be savory; 'ę̣i-toµt'нe nɑ̨ 'ɑ̨'kadl ʾнdl gyн̀-t'oµt'нe, when he
spoke to me, I spoke to him.   Some medial and final syllables of
words occur nowhere in the material, obtained in such position as
to show the initial ', e. g. the second syllable of 'нdl-ʾɑ'-gɑ, s. wild
plum fruit; this amounts to dl opening syllables in word inlaut.

In word inlaut after n, m, syllabically initial ' regularly has a
glottalizing effect, tending to fall before the nasal (see § 15).   But
certain other syllables in such position are without initial ', e. g.
-ɑ' in goµm-ɑ̨', in the back.

The glottal clusive also occurs largely as a glottalizer of vowels
and diphthongs; and as simultaneous element of the glottalized
clusives ƙ, t̂, t̂s, p̂, the opening of the glottis coming after the s in
the glottalized affricative.

k, t, ts, p are without following aspiration, and sound exactly the same as the unaspirated, unvoiced lenis g, d, ds, b in Mandarin Chinese kŏu, dog; tǐŋ, top; tsɑi-lǐ, inside; Pěi-tcīŋ, Peking.

ƙ, ṱ, t͡s, ƀ, are simultaneously glottalized and are therefore written by the very suggestive and correct device of tipping the apostrophe, the symbol for the laryngeal clusive, back over the symbols representing the buccal closure. Kiowa shares these sounds with many surrounding languages. The buccal release precedes the laryngeal, thus producing a click like that of suddenly opening a chamber of partial vacuum, like the sound of pulling a cork from a bottle, the buccal consonant retaining of course its characteristic resonance. In glottalized t͡s the laryngeal opening comes after the s, not between the t and the s.

Like the sounds of the glottalized series just discussed, those of the aspirated series, k', t', p' are also immersed, not in a glottal clusive but in an aspiration. They are exactly the sounds of Mandarin k'ȁn, to see; t'óu, head; p'ò, amber; or, to give more familiar examples, of Irish-English K-hate, T-him, P-hat (adopting Mr. Dooley's orthography!). English k, t, p are taken as being of this series in loanwords, e. g. k'ǫmeisei, commissioner (fr. Eng.). The corresponding aspirated form of ts was not found. The spelling k', etc., instead of kh, was adopted to avoid confusion with the heterosyllabic kh, etc., resulting from juxtaposition of syllables, in e. g. 'ɑthʜ'dɑ, to cry, wail, i. e. 'ɑt-hʜ'dɑ.[2]

g, d, b are pronounced as in English. They vary with the unaspirated surd series (§16). The present vocabulary also varies g, d, b somewhat irregularly with k, t, p in word inlaut.

dl is the counterpart of the r or l of other languages and is derived from t, with which it alternates (§16).

Only ', t, p, h ('), dl, n, m, and t, p, dl, n, m preceded by ', can close syllables (see § 14). Glottalized and aspirated series of buccal clusives do not occur as syllable closers. t, p in syllable and word auslaut are little aspirated and unprominent, e. g. the p in ƙoup, knob, mountain. t, p when followed by initial buccal clusive, fricative, voiceless affricative, or nasal (i. e. by k, ƙ, k', g, t, ṱ, t', d, s, z, ts, t͡s, n, p, ƀ, p', b, m) of a following syllable or word are changed to ' and have been written ṱ, ᵱ. Thus in ƙyʜᵱt'ɑ, old man, the lips do not close for the ᵱ. ṱ may represent t or dl of ordinary syllabic auslaut. Final t of the verbal prefixed pronouns was also clearly observed to undergo change to ' before initial ' of the next syllable (see examples given below). A couple of instances are noted below of t becoming ' in absolute auslaut. And t seems to

---

[2] The same reason that led to the distinguishment of double-looped and unlooped h in the writing of Hindūstānī.

disappear before final p, e. g. in tou-p, stick, for *tou-t̓-p̓; cp. tou-dl, dpl. The glottal clusive derived from syllabically final t, p, coming as it does after a vowel, gives the effect of a glottalized vowel, and some of the glottalized vowels recorded in the present vocabulary are of this origin. The change was observed both within words and between words. Examples follow.

(a) Within words:

'ɑdl-, head-hair, head: 'ɑ'-k̄ɑ'gɑ't, scalp, written 'ɑt̓-k̄ɑ'gɑ't.

bʌ̀t-, verbal pronoun: t̄sou bʌ̀'-bǫ, you saw the tpl. stones, written t̄sou bʌ̀t̓-bǫ.

goup, plant: gou'-t'ǫubɑ, stem, written goup̓-t'ǫubɑ.

t̄ɑ'-'iʜyʜ'mḥ, a bird sp., written t̄ɑ'-'iʜyʜt̓mḥ.

gyʌ̀t-, verbal pronoun: hɑ', gyʌ̀'-'ǫupeidldou' dèi-'ɑ'dɑ'dei, yes, I like to gamble, written gyʌ̀t̓-'ǫupeidldou'.

(b) Between words:

tsʜt, door: tsʜ' béi-'ɑ'm, close the door! written tsʜt̓ béi-'ɑ'm.

heit, hortatory particle; bʌ̀t-, verbal pronoun: hei' bʌ̀'-'œe'yɑ'm, you fix it up again! written heit bʌ̀t̓-'œe'yɑ'm, heit bʌ̀t̓-'œe-'ɑ'm.

k'ougyʜp, body: k'ougyʜ' nèịn-bǫ, I saw his body, written k'oukyʜp̓ nèịn-bǫ.

(c) In absolute auslaut:

p'ɑ-'ʜt̓-bʜ, temple (anat.):=p'ɑ-'ʜ'.

t'ʜt̓-gyʜ, several severed: t'ʜ', to sever several.

### § 12. FRICATIVES

h in some forms appears as an alternation of k', t' (§ 16).

h occurs as a syllabically final aspiration in some interjections, e. g. yūh, interj. of fright.

z interchanges with ts, not with s (§ 16).

### § 13. NASALS

The nasals are n and m. ŋ does not occur. Palatalized n is approximated in such a word as niʜnyʜ, two by two.

In certain forms a nasal disappears before a clusive. The examples show lengthening and glottalization of the preceding vowel. Thus mɑ̨'dɑ, hand, dpl. mǫn, hands; 'ʜt̄ɑ̨ẹyɑ̨'bɑ, carpenter's plane, from *'ʜ't̄ɑ̨ẹ-'ɑ'm-bɑ.

### § 14. CONSONANTAL STRUCTURE OF SYLLABLES

A syllable can be opened (a) by any consonant except dl (for dl opening syllables in word inlaut see § 11); (b) by the groups, ts, t̄s, and by groups with y as second element (see § 10).

A syllable can be closed by ', t, p, h (only in certain interjections), dl, n, m; also by 't, 'p, 'dl, 'n, 'm.

## § 15. RETROGRESSION OF LARYNGEALS

Syllabically initial ' in certain recorded forms jumps backward (a) to a position before syllable-closing dl, n, m; e. g. 'ę̄į'mħ, come here! for 'ę̄įm-'ħ; (b) to a position before the closing i (i. e., y) of ei (§ 2) (the diphthong ou, however, did not appear to show this phenomenon); e. g. 'e'youguɑ'ei, rice, for 'ei-'ouguɑ'ei; 'ħ-'ɑdl-k'ɑe'yǫų, I am crazy, for 'ħ-ɑdlk'ɑe-'ǫų (i. e. 'ħ-'ɑdlk'ɑei-'ǫų). If the preceding sound is already glottalized ('dl, 'n, 'm, ei'), the two glottal clusives coincide.

Similarly, the ' of the diphthongs u'(ʷ)ɑ, i'(ʸ)ħ jumps back to a position before the developed glide (as already stated, § 2). This doubtless also tends to occur in the diphthongs ou'e, u'e.

Syllabically initial h in certain recorded forms jumps backward to a position before the closing i of ei; unlike the glottal clusive, h appears to be retroinserted only when ei plays the rôle of second member of a diphthong. Thus k'uehyɑ', to drag, for k'ue-hɑ'; tsħehyħp, one who asks many questions, for tsħe-hħp; 'ę̄į-tɑ'tɑ'e-hyę̄į'm, my father died, for 'ę̄į-tɑ'tɑ'e-hę̄į'm; 'ousei-t̂ħ'ęhyę̄į'm, to die from choking, for ·'ousei-t̂ħ'ę-hę̄į'm; 'ousei-t̂ħ'ęhyoudl, to kill by choking, for 'ousei-t̂ħ'ę-houdl.

## § 16. HARD AND SOFT FORMS OF CONSONANTS

As in the Tanoan languages, several of the consonants have a hard and a soft form. The correspondencies noted are:

(a) Surd clusive to sonant clusive:

  k - - - - g: kuɑt, to be painted, painted thing - - - - guɑt, to paint.

  t - - - - d: tǫųbħ-tou'-k̂iħ, bugle man - - - - dou', to hold.

  p - - - - b: pǫų-k̂iħ, inspector, lit. seeing-man - - - - bǫų, to see.

(b) Surd clusive to sonant affricative:

  t - - - - dl: guɑt, to paint - - - - guɑdl, red.

(c) Surd affricative to sonant fricative:

  ts - - - - z: bout-k'ue-tsǫųn, fish spear, lit. belly-puller - - - - k'ue-zǫųn, to pull out.

(d) Laryngealized buccal surd clusive to its laryngeal accompaniment (i. e. debuccalization):

  k̄ - - - - ': k̄ou-dl, neck - - - - 'ou-sei, throat.

  t̄ - - - - ': t̄ɑn, to be mean - - - - 'ɑ̄'-dei, mean.

  p̄ - - - - ': p̄ɑ', river - - - - 'ɑ̄'-pįħ, fish.

  k' - - - - h: k'ɑ̄'-bħ, to go to get - - - - hɑ̄'giħ, to get.

  t' - - - - h: t'ħ'bei, carrier off - - - - hħ'bɑ, to carry off.

t̓ varies with t‘ in t̓ʜ-t, to sever one, t‘ʜ’, to sever several; and with t‘ and h in t̓ʜ’-dou’, one is erect, t‘ʜ’-dou’, several are erect, hʜ’, to stand up (the t‘ - - - - h change as in section d above).

## KIOWA-ENGLISH VOCABULARY

The alphabetic order is α ɑ ǫ ꞯ ʜ ʜ ʜ̣ ʜ̣ b d ei ęi̥ g h iʜ i̥ʜ k k̓ k‘ m n ou ǫu̥ p p̃ p‘ s t t̓ t‘ ts t̃s y z. The glottal clusive, ’, is assigned no position as a letter, but vowels followed by glottal hardening are given a position after vowels without such hardening.

The following abbreviations have been used:

| | | | |
|---|---|---|---|
| adj | adjective. | Kio | Kiowa. |
| adv | adverb. | lit | literally. |
| an. maj | animate major. | mg | meaning. |
| an. min | animate minor. | obj | objective. |
| ans | answer. | opp | opposite. |
| app | apparently. | plcn | placename. |
| ch | carefully heard. | poss | possessive. |
| coll | collective. | postf | postfix. |
| Com | Comanche. | postp | postposition. |
| comp | composition. | pref | prefix. |
| compd | compound. | proh | prohibitive. |
| compl | compositional. | pron | pronoun. |
| cp | compare. | prpd | prepound. |
| ct | contrast. | prsn | personal name. |
| curs | cursive. | pspd | postpound. |
| d | dual. | ptc | participle. |
| def | defective. | punct | punctual. |
| dem | demonstrative. | refl | reflexive. |
| dpl | duoplural, referring to two or more. | refer | referential. |
| Eng | English. | s | singular. |
| esp | especially. | sbj | subjective. |
| ev | evidently. | sbord | subordinative. |
| fr | from. | so | singular object. |
| Fr | French. | sp | species. |
| gd | gerund. | spl | singular and plural, referring to one or more. |
| gdv | gerundive. | ss | singular subject. |
| hort | hortative. | stat | static. |
| imm | immediative. | tpl | triplural, referring to three or more. |
| imp | imperative. | tplo | triplural object. |
| inf | informant. | tpls | triplural subject. |
| infer | inferential. | tr | transitive. |
| infn | information. | trbn | tribename. |
| inan. coll | inanimate collective. | vd | volunteered. |
| interr | interrogative. | w | with. |
| intr | intransitive. | | |

All references to Mooney are to his Calendar History of the Kiowa Indians, Seventeenth Annual Report of the Bureau of American Ethnology, 1898.

The entry form for nouns is always the singular. The nouns fall according to gender and plural formation into seven classes, which are shown in the following table together with the forms of the verbal prefixed personal pronoun which would be used with the singular, dual, and triplural number of nouns of each class, viz. (a) transitive series, first person singular subject —— third person object in apposition with singular, dual, and triplural of the noun, (b) subjective (intransitive) series, third person subject in apposition with singular, dual, and triplural of the noun. The verbal pronouns used with a noun were found to be a convenient means for determining the class to which a noun belongs. Animate major gender refers to adult members of the Kiowa tribe and is assigned also to certain other nouns. Animate minor gender refers to adult members of other tribes, dolls, lower animals, many body parts, etc. As regards the inanimate declensions, no helpful rules for remembering the gender class have been determined.

## CLASSES OF NOUNS

| | | | |
|---|---|---|---|
| An. I (animate major, e. g. ḳʏʀhĭ'ʀ, man; ḳʏʀhyoup, tpl.). | {gʏʀ-}, I—him / —, he | nę̄ḭn-, I—them d. / 'ę̀ḭ-, they d. | dę̄ḭ-, I—them tpl. / 'ʀ-, —, they tpl. |
| An. II (animate minor, e. g. tsę̄ḭ, horse; tsę̄ḭgɑ, tpl.). | {gʏʀ-}, I—him / —, he | nę̄ḭn-, I—them d. / 'ę̀ḭ-, they d. | dę̄ḭ-, I—them tpl. / 'ę̀ḭ-, —, they tpl. |
| Inan. I (inanimate direct, e. g. tou, house, spl.). | {gʏʀ-}, I—it / —, it | nę̄ḭn-, I—them d. / 'ę̀ḭ-, they d. | {gʏʀ-}, I—them tpl. / —, they tpl. |
| Inan. Iᵃ (inanimate direct with collective triplural, e. g. ʦou, stone, spl.). | {gʏʀ-}, I—it / —, it | nę̄ḭn-, I—them d. / 'ę̀ḭ-, they d. | {gʏʀ-}, I—them tpl. / they tpl. |
| Inan. II (inanimate reversed, e. g. ḳoup, mountain, spl.). | dę̄ḭ-, I—it / 'ę̀ḭ-, it | nę̄ḭn-, I—them d. / 'ę̀ḭ-, they d. | gʏʀt-, I—them tpl. / —, they tpl. |
| Inan. IIᵃ (inanimate reversed with collective triplural, e. g. zeibɑ̆'t, arrow; zeibʀ, dpl.). | dę̄ḭ-, I—it / 'ę̀ḭ-, it | nę̄ḭn-, I—them d. / 'ę̀ḭ-, they d. | gʏʀt-, I—them tpl. / {gʏʀ-}, they tpl. |
| Inan. III (inanimate collective, e. g. tǫn, gɐp, spl.). | gʏʀt-, I—it | {gʏʀt- / nę̄ḭn-} I—them d. / they d. | gʏʀt-, I—them tpl. / {gʏʀ- / 'ę̀ḭ-} they tpl. |

For the verbs the entry form is the positive punctual or positive static, unless otherwise stated. This is followed by such other parts as were obtained, enclosed in parentheses.

The vocabulary contains the words, stems and affixes which were obtained with exception of the verbal prefixed personal pronouns, which have been presented for convenience in tabular form at the end of the vocabulary, page 237.

## Vocabulary

### a

'ɑ ('ɑ'gu'ɑ, punct. neg.; 'ɑ'guɑ, curs.; 'ɑ'dɑ', fut.; 'ɑ'gu'ɑdɑ', fut. neg.; 'ɑ', imp.), to play (a game), gamble [Tewa 'ɛ́, game].  Cp. 'ɑ'-hнp, 'ɑ'-k̃iн, gambler; 'ɑ'-hi̧'н̧, to be a good gambler; tou-'ɑ, to play the handgame; etc. —— dèi-'ɑ'guɑ, I am gambling. k'iнdeidl dèi-'ɑ'guɑ, I gambled yesterday.  hɑn 'н̧n dèi-'ɑ'gu'ɑ (or kɑdl instead of 'н̧n), I never gamble.  poue (kɑdl) bèi-'ɑ'dɑ', do not gamble!  dèi-'ɑ'houdɑ', I am going to go over to play. bèi-'ɑ', gamble!  poue bнt-'ɑ'н.edɑ', do not go over to gamble! hɑ m-'ɑ'bн̧nmн̧, are you going over to gamble?  hɑ k'iнdeidl bèi-'ɑ'guɑ, did you gamble yesterday?  hɑ̧'nei̧, hɑn 'ei̧-('ɑ')t'ei̧n- dɑ'mɑ̧', no, I do not like to gamble (ans.).  hɑ, gyн̀ntdèi-'ɑ- 'dɑ'dei, yes, I like to gamble (ans.).  béi-'ɑ'hou', let us dpl. go over and gamble!  hɑn k'iнdeidl dèi-'ɑ'gu'ɑ, I did not gamble yesterday.  nɑ̧ dèi-bou-'ɑ'guɑ, I gamble all the time.  'ei̧dei m-'ɑ'guɑ, he gambled.

'ɑ-, dem. stem in 'ɑ-hɑ', there, 'ɑhy-ɑ', there, 'ɑ'-gɑ, there, 'ɑ'-bнhɑ', there, 'ɑ'-dei, that one, there, 'ɑ'-bei, past [cp. 'ɑ-p-, dem. stem].

-ɑ', postp., at, on, from [cp. possibly -hɑ', at]. —— k̃oup-mɑ̧'tsнt-ɑ', at the peak of the mountain. p'iн-mɑ̧'tsнt-ɑ' 'н̀-bн'ïɑ', I am going to go up to the top of the hill. gɑ̧um-ɑ̧' yн́-k'oup, (the small of) my back aches. dɑ̧'m-ɑ̧', (to race) on the ground (not on horseback). 'ɑp̀k'ɑ̧'n-ɑ̧', at the end (or edge) of. ïoudɑ̧'m-ɑ̧' 'н̀-tsн̧n, I came from the north.

'ɑ-'ɑ'-dɑ ('ɑ'ɑ'deip, curs.; 'ɑ'ɑ'dɑ'ïɑ', fut.), to be unable [cp. *'ɑ'dɑ, to think; mɑ-'ɑ'dɑ'mɑ̧', to be unable to do].  Cp. pɑ'-t'н̧'mɑ̧', to be unable. —— yн́m-'ɑ'ɑ'deip, I can not do it. yн́m-'ɑ'ɑ'dɑ, I was unable. k'yн̧'hi̧нgɑ 'нdl yн́m-'ɑ'ɑ'dɑ'ïɑ', tomorrow I shall not be able.

'ɑ-dl-, 'ɑ-t-, prepound form referring to head, hair, in 'ɑdl-t'ei̧'m, head; 'ɑ'-dɑ (for * 'ɑ-t̃-dɑ, a hair of the head; etc. [Tewa p̃ǿ-ɳ, head]. —— 'ɑdl-t'нe, on the head.

'ɑdlɑmoubi(н)dl, automobile [fr. Eng.].  Cp. tsei̧hei̧-kɑ'dнdl and tsei̧hei̧-k'uep'н̧, both meaning horseless wagon.

'ɑdl-dɑ'-guɑn, to dance the scalp dance [to hair kill dance]. dèi-'ɑd̃l-dɑ'-guɑnmɑ̧, I am dancing the scalp dance.

'adl-dɑ'-kuɑn-gyн (inan. III) scalp dance [hair-kill dance, Mooney, p. 391].

’ɑdl-guɑdl (an. II; ’ɑdl-guɑt-dɑ, tpl.; ’ɑdl-guɑdl- in comp.), woodpecker sp.; said to be another name for mɒ̨’-îɑ-ku’ɑ, woodpecker
sp. [red head].   Cp. kyнe-’ɑdl-guɑdl, bird sp.; ’нþþнk̦ų̧e, woodpecker sp.

’.ɑdl-hɑ’bн’-k̂iн (an. I) man who uses ’ɑdl-hɑ’bн style of hairdressing;
see ’ɑ’dɑ.

’ɑdl-hɑ’-, prepound form of ’ɑdl-hɒ̨’-gyн, money.

’ɑdlhɒ̨’-bi̦нmk‘ɑe (inan. IIᵃ) purse [money bag].

’ɑdl-hɒ̨’-gyн (app. inan. IIᵃ; a s.   * ’ɑdl-hɒ̨’-gɑ’t was not recorded;
’ɑdl-hɒ̨’- in comp.), coin, dollar, money; also wampum [hair metal
as explained by Mooney, p. 255, but analyzed by the informants
as head metal, metal with a head stamped on it: cp. hɒ̨’gɑ’t, piece
of metal.  ——— pн’kɑ ’ɑdlhɒ̨’gyн, one dollar (not * pн’kɑ ’ɑdlhɒ̨’-
gɑ’t).   ’ɑdlhɒ̨’-hȩi ’н̇-dɑ, I have no money.   ’ȩi-’ɑe ’ɑdlhɒ̨’kyн, I
have lots of money.   kɑdl ’ȩi-’ɒ̨’ ’ɑdlhɒ̨’gyн, give me some
money!

’ɑdl-hɒ̨’-t‘ǫųn (inan. III) mine [money pit: t‘ǫųn, pit, fr. t‘ǫų, to
dig].

’ɑdl-hн̦-ȩ-mȩi (an. II; ’ɑdl-hн̦-ȩ-mou-p, tpl.), mosquito [’ɑdl-, app.
head; w.-hн̦-ȩmȩi, cp. possibly ’ȩim-hн̦’mȩi, ant].

’Ɑdl-k̂ɑ’-t‘oue-k̂iн (an. I; ’Ɑdl-k̂ɑ’-t‘oue-ga, tpl.; ’Ɑdl-k̂ɑ’-t‘oue- in
comp.), Nez Perce man; see Mooney, p. 391 [said to mean man
with hair cut round across the forehead: k̂ɑ’, to cut; -t‘ou-e-,
unexplained; -k̂iн].

’ɑdl-k‘ɑe, crazy, foolish [’ɑdl-, head; -k‘ɑe, unexplained, app. skin].
Cp. t‘ǫų-’ɑdlk‘ɑe, whisky, lit, crazy water; etc.

’ɑdlk‘ɑe-dɑ, to be crazy, foolish, an outlaw, evil [dɑ, to be].—
’ȩim-’ɑdlk‘ɑe-dɑ, you are crazy.   ’ɑdlk‘ɑe-dɑ, he is crazy.   poue
’ɑþgɑ gyн̇-’ɑdlk‘ɑe-dɑ’dei-’ȩi’m̄ dɑ́-pɑ’hнdɑ’, lead us not into
evil!

’ɑdlk‘ɑe-’ɒ̨mgyн (’ɑdlk‘ɑe-’ɒ̨mdeiheidl, infer.), to go crazy.  ———
’ɑdlk‘ɑe-’ɒ̨mgyн, he went crazy.   ’ɑdlk‘ɑe-’ɒ̨mdeiheidl, they say
he went crazy.

’ɑdlk‘ɑe-’ɒ̨’mȩi, to make crazy, to do wrong.—îoubeiguɑ poue ’ȩiha
hɒ̨ndei bн́-’ɑdlk‘ɑe-’ɒ̨mdɑ’, from now on do not ye tpl. do anything
wrong!

’ɑdlk‘ɑe-gyн (inan. III), craziness, crazy act, sin.—nɒ̨ ’ɑdlk‘ɑegyн,
my sins.   nɒ̨́-ɒ̀dlk‘ɑegyн-’ɑe, I have many sins.   ’ɑdlk‘ɑegyн gyнt-
bǫų, I saw a crazy act.

’ɑdlk‘ɑe-k̂iн (an. I; ’ɑdlk‘ɑe-guɑ, tpl.), crazy man, outlaw, sinner.
——— ’ɑdlk‘ɑė-k̂iн ’н̇-dɑ, I am a sinner.

’ɑdl-k‘ɑe-k̂i(н)-hн’ (with second mg. an. II; ’ɑdl-k‘ɑe-k̂i(н)-hн’-bɑ,
’ɑdl-k‘ɑe-k̂i(н)-hн’-gɑ, tpl.) 1. crest; 2. kingfisher [’ɑdl-, head; the
rest of the word is obscure; the kingfisher is so called· from his
crest].   Cp. ’нîɑhɑ’e, warbonnet; ’Ɑdlt‘ǫų-’ɑdlk‘ɑek̂i(н)hн’-k̂iн,
Ponca man; ’Ɑdlt‘ǫų-(k‘ɑe)k̂i(н)hн’-k̂iн, Flathead man.

'ɑdlk'ɑe-'ǫy, to be crazy, be an outlaw [-'ǫy, intensive]. ——
'ʜ-ɑdlk'ɑe-'ǫy, I am crazy.

'Ɔ́dlk'ɑe-touhɑ' (inan. III) crazy bluff, plcn. Cp. Mooney, p. 391.

'ɑdlk'oup-'ei-gɑ (inan. IIᵃ; 'ɑdlk'oup-'ei, dpl.; 'ɑdlk'oup-'ei- in
comp.), gooseberry fruit [headache fruit; 'ɑdl-, head; k'oup, to
ache; 'eigɑ, fruit; cp. 'ɑdlt'ǫy-k'oup, headache].

'ɑdlk'oup-'ei-p'eip (inan. IIᵃ), gooseberry bush.

'ɑdl-p̄ǫ'ɑ, yucca root used as soap; soap [head washer: -p̄ǫ'ɑ, washer,
fr. p̄ǫ'ɑ-ę, to wash].

'ɑdl-p̄ǫ'ɑ-mʜ (an. I), washwoman, = p̄ǫ'ɑ-mʜ [explained as soap
woman].

'ɑdl-p̄ǫ'-dɑ (inan. II; 'ɑdl-p̄ǫn, dpl.) braid of hair [fr. *p̄ǫ . . . , to
braid].

'Ɔ́dl-p'eip̄-dei, prsn., bushy head, name of man known in Eng. as
Frizzlehead; see Mooney, p. 391 [p'eip̄dei, bushy, fr. p'eip, bush].

'ɑdl-sǫym (an. II; 'ɑdl-sǫy-gɑ, tpl.), hair brush, comb [cp. 'ɑdl-sǫym,
to brush or comb hair]. Cp. hǫ'-'ɑdlsǫym, metal comb; t'ǫy-
'ɑdlsǫym, bone comb.

*'ɑdl-sǫym ('ɑdl-sǫydɑ', fut.), to brush hair, comb hair [*sǫy-m, to
brush]. —— déi-'ɑdlsǫydɑ', I am going to brush my hair.

'ɑdl-t'ʜ', to cut the hair [t'ʜ', to cut several].—gɑ́-'ɑdl-t'ʜ'dɑ', I
am going to cut your hair.

'ɑdl-t'ęį'm (app. inan. IIᵃ; 'ɑdl-t'ǫy, dpl.; 'ɑdl-t'ǫy- in comp.), head
[head bone: t'ęį'm, bone]. —— nǫ 'ɑdl-t'ęį'm, my head. 'ɑdl-
t'ęį'm nǫ́-goup, he hit my head, = nǫ 'ɑdlt'ęim 'ę́į-goup. 'ɑdl-
t'ǫygyʜ 'ę́į-goup, he hit me on the head. 'ɑdl-t'ęį'm gɑ́-guɑdɑ',
I am going to hit you on the head.

'Ɔ́dlt'ęį'm 'Éit-k'uekǫ'ndei Pɑ', plcn., head dragging creek; cp.
Mooney, p. 391 ['ɑdlt'ęį'm, head; 'éit-, they tpl. an. maj. ——
it inan. IIᵃ; k'ue-kǫ'n, to bring dragging; -dei; p̄ɑ', creek].

'Ɔ́dlt'ęį'm-'ɑdlk'ɑek̄i(ʜ) hʜ'-k̄iʜ (an. I; 'Ɔ́dlt'ęį'm-'ɑdlk'ɑek̄i(ʜ) hʜ'-
gɑ (an. I; 'Ɔ́dlt'ęį'm-'ɑdlk'ɑek̄i(ʜ)hʜ'-gɑ, tpl.; 'Ɔ́dlt'ęį'm-'ɑdl-
k'ɑek̄i(ʜ)hʜ'- in comp.), Ponca man; cp. Mooney, p. 392.

Mr. Francis La Flesche informs the writer that this name may
refer to headdresses such as are shown in Fletcher and La Flesche,
The Omaha Tribe, 27th Ann. Rept. Bur. Amer. Ethn., 1911, figs.
40, 98, and pl. 24. [head crest man.]

'Ɔ́dlt'ǫy-'eidl, prsn. big head; see Mooney, p. 392.

'Ɔ́dlt'ǫy-(k'ɑe)k̄i(ʜ)hʜ'-k̄iʜ (inan. I), Flathead man ['ɑdlt'ǫy-, head;
(k'ɑe)k̄i(ʜ)hʜ'- as in 'ɑdlk'ɑek̄i(ʜ)hʜ', crest, and stated by
Mooney, p. 392, to mean " compressed." The name is singularly
like that for the Ponka.]

'ɑdlt'ǫy-k'oup, headache [k'oup, to ache; cp. 'ɑdl-k'oup-'eigɑ,
headache fruit]. —— 'ɑdlt'ǫy-k'oup, headache. But 'ɑdlt'ęį'm
mɑ́-k'oup, I have a headache.

'α-e, to be many. Cp. kǫn, to be many. —— k̓ịṇhyoup 'ɥ-'αe, many
  men. hɐ'oudei t͡sou, how many stones? t͡sou gyɥt-'αe, many
  stones (ans.), =gyɥt-'αe t͡sou.

* '̓α-e-, adverbial stem implied in 'αhy-α', there ['α-, dem. stem;
  -ei]. Cp. 'ouehy-α', 'ouhy-α', there.

'α-e-, adverbial verb prefix, again ['α- as in 'α'-bα', repeatedly; -ei].
  —— 'αe-tsɥn heigα, he came back again already. heit bɥt-'αe-
  'yǫm, you fix it up again, do it again! gyɥ'αe-goup, I hit him again.
  'ệịm-'αe-guαdα', I will hit you again. 'αe-tǫụe, he said again.
  heit bɥt-'αe-'yǫm, nǫ dɥ hǫn 'ệịm-t̓ɥhouguαdα' nǫ̈, you do it
  again and see if I don't whip you. gyɥt-k̓uαt gα gyɥ̀-'αe-tsei,
  I pulled it out and then put it back in. hǫn 'αe-tsɥ̓'nǫ, he never
  came back again.

'α-gα-k̓ou, one (in an old Kiowa count) [unexplained].

'α-hα', adv., there ['α-, dem. stem; -hα', postp., at]. Cp. 'αhy-α',
  there, αp-hα', there. —— 'αhα' 'ɥ̀-tsɥn, I arrived there, I have
  been there, ='αhyα' 'ɥ̀-tsɥn. But 'α'deihα' 'ɥ̀-tsɥn, I have come
  from there. 'αhα 'ɥ̀-bɥnmɥ̈, I am going to go there, ='αphα
  'ɥ̀-bɥnmɥ̈. 'αhα' tseidl, he is there inside. 'αhα' 'ɥ̀-t̂α, I was in
  there.

'αhα'-dei ('αhα'-gα, tpl.), dem. pron. and adv., that one, there
  ['αhα', there; -dei].

'α-hịɥ̈, to be plain ['α-, unexplained; -hịɥ̈, real]. Cp. 'αhịɥbα,
  cedar tree, lit. the plain one. —— gyɥ̀-'αhịɥ̈, it is plainly discern-
  ible (from a distance).

'α-hịɥ̈-bα (iṅan. II; s. also once given as 'α-hịɥ̈-dα; 'α-hịɥ̈, dpl.),
  cedar tree [explained as " the plain one," since the cedar stands
  out plainly among other trees; but cp. possibly Tewa hʉ́, cedar].

'αhy-α' adv., there ['αe-, dem. stem; -hα', postp., at, cp. -α', at;
  'αhyα' and 'ouhyα' are probably to be analyzed as from *'αe-hα'
  and *'oue-hα' respectively]. Cp. 'α-hα', 'αp-hα', and esp. 'ouhy-α',
  'ouehyα', all meaning there. —— 'αhyα' 'ɥ-t̂α, I have been
  there, ='αhyα' 'ɥ̀-tsɥn. gyɥ̀-p̓ɥ̓'ougoup nǫ 'αhyα' sat 'ệịm-
  'αthɐ'dα, but when I hit him the third time, he cried. hɐ'gyɥ
  'ẹigα déi-tseidα', where am I going to put this (tumbler)? 'αhyα'
  hɥegyɥhẹi béi-tsei, oh, just set it there anywhere (ans.)!
  k̓yɥ̈'hịɥgα 'αhyα' 'ɥ̀-bɥnmɥ̈, I am going to go there to-morrow.
  poue 'αhyα' ệịm-tseit̂α, don't you be in there (in the ditch)!
  k̓yɥ̈'hịɥ gyɥ̀-peipeidldou' gα 'αhyα'-dou dèi-'α̈'zǫụn, thinking that
  the man was dead, I went away.

'αhyα'-dei ('αhyα'-gα, tpl.), dem. pron. and adv., that one, there
  ['αhyα', there; -dei]. —— 'αhyα'dei dα, that is the one. 'αhyα'gα,
  they are the ones. nǫ 'αhyα'-dei pe.idou m-t̂α̈'hou'α̈'zǫụnheidl,
  and for that reason they went traveling off mad. 'αhyα'gα
  hɐyɥ' m-hou'α̈'zǫụnheidl, they moved off somewhere.

’α-k̇α-pα̇’-dα, to be spotted (or erupted?) [unexplained; dα]. ——
k‘ougyнp ’н̇-guαdl-’αk̇αpα̇’-dα, my body has little red spots on it.
’α-p-, dem. stem in ’αp-hα’, there, ’α᷍p-k‘ǫn-, referring to end; etc.
[’α-, dem. stem; -p-].
’αp-hα’, adv., there [’α-p-, dem. stem; -hα’, postp., at].   Cp. ’αp-dei,
that one; ’α-hα’, there, ’αhy-α’, there. —— ’αphα’ ’н̇-bн̥nmн̥, I
am going there, = ’αhα’ ’н̇-bн̥nmн̥.   sat tsн̥n neị ’αphα’ ’eịm-k‘uαt,
he came a little while ago but he went out that way.   ’eịhα’
.nǫ ’eịgα ’èi-dα’gα ’αphα’ ’èi-tǫumk‘ị’н̥-tseị ’н̥n ’éit-k‘ǫ̇’mǫ
’α̇’znṫǫ’houp, now we present (people) thus (or that way) when
we speak of them, call them: those who went off offended
because of the udder.
’αphα̇’-dei (’αphα̇’-gα, tpl.), dem. pron. and adv., that one, there
[αphα?, there; -dei].   Cp. ’α᷍p-dei, that one.
’α᷍p-gα, 1. dem. pron., tpl. of ’α᷍p-dei, that one; 2. adv., there [’αp-,
dem. stem; -gα].
’α᷍p-k‘ǫn-, referring to end, in -’α᷍p-k‘ǫn-bн, at the end of; ’α᷍p-
k‘ǫn-heị, without end; -’αp-k‘ǫn-gyн, at the end of; ’α᷍p-k‘ǫ̇’n-ǫ̇’,
at the end of [app. ’α-p-, dem. stem; and an element k‘ǫ-n-, as in
mǫn-k‘ǫn-hα̇’-gyн, to have a handful, hardened form of -hǫ-n,
to finish intr.].
-’α᷍pk‘ǫn-bн, at the end of. —— dǫm-’α᷍pk‘ǫnbн, at the end of
the world.
’α᷍pk‘ǫn-heị, without end, forever.
-’α᷍pk‘ǫn-gyн, at the end of. —— ’oue hụ’ǫn-’a᷍pk‘ǫngyн kiнdl, he
lives at the end of the road.
’α᷍pk‘ǫ̇’n-ǫ̇’, at the end of [-ǫ̇’, at]. —— k̇ǫnǫṫsαp‘ouyiн ’α᷍pk‘ǫ̇’n-ǫ̇’
(or ’outα̇’y-α’ instead of last word) ’н̥’gyн, the fly is (lit. is sitting)
on the edge of the table.
’α᷍p-dei (’α᷍p-gα, tpl.), dem. pron. and adv., that one, there [’αp-, dem.
stem; -dei].   Cp. ’αphα̇’-dei, that one. —— poue ’α᷍pgα gyн̇-
’αdlk‘αe-dα̇’dei-’eị’m dα̇-pα̇’hiнdα’, lead us not into temptation!
’α-t-, prepound form referring to head, hair; see ’αdl-.
’α-t-, prepound form of ’αt-dα, to cry, weep.
-’α-t, in pei-sнdl-’αt, “stays in the hot sand,” bird sp.; deịn-αt-
ṫαt‘ǫ̇’neị, mussel.
’αtα, interj. of admiration or surprise; also tαtα.
’αt-hн̥’dα’, (’αthн̥’dα’ punct. neg.; ’αthн̥’doup, curs.; ’αthн̥’deidα’,
fut.; ’αthн̥’dα̇’dα’, fut. neg.; ’αthн̥’dei, imp.), to cry [’α-t-, to cry,
weep; hн̥’dα, to shout, cry]. —— miнn dèi-’αthн̥’doup, I feel
like crying.   poue bei-’αthн̥’deidα’, don’t cry!   heit bèi-’αthн̥’dei,
let us cry.   poue bei-’αthн̥’deidα, let us not cry.
*’αt-k̇α’, to scalp, implied in ’αt-k̇α’-gα’t, scalp.
’αt-k̇α’-gα’t (inan. II; ’αt-k̇α’-gyн, dpl.), scalp [app. ’αt, hair; k̇α’,
to cut]. —— nǫ ’αtk̇α’gα’t, my war-scalp.

’at-p‘oudl-t‘ɴdliɴ (an. I), crybaby boy, boy who cries easily [’at-, to cry; -p‘oudl-, intensive; t‘ɴdliɴ, boy].

’at-da (’a̱’dliɴ, curs.), to cry, weep. Cp. tou-’atda, to be in mourning for a relative. —— ’a̱’dliɴ, he is weeping. heiga ’ɴ-bou-’a̱’dliɴ, I cry all the time.

’at-t‘ɴt-da (inan. II; ’at-t‘ɴt, dpl.), scalp [’at-, hair; t‘ɴt- as in t‘ɴt-gyɴ, several are cut].

’a-t̑a̱-e̱, (’a-t̑a̱-e̱-ma̱, tpl.), smooth, sleek, in t‘o̱ɴ-’at̑a̱e̱, opossum, lit. smooth tail; t̑soudl-’at̑a̱e̱, devil, lit. smooth wings; sɴ’ne̱i̱-’at̑a̱e̱, whip snake, lit. sleek snake; etc. [-’a-, unexplained; t̑a̱-e̱, smooth].

’a-t‘a̱’-n (’at‘a̱’na̱’, punct. neg.; ’at‘a̱nma̱, curs.; ’at‘a̱nda’, fut.; ’at‘a̱’na̱’da’, fut. neg.; ’at‘a̱’n, imp.), to clear away (vegetation) [’a-, unexplained; w. -t‘a̱’-n cp. possibly t‘ɴ’, to cut down several]. Cp. sɴt-’at‘a̱’n, (snow) melts. —— miɴn gyɴ-’at‘a̱nma̱, I am going to cut the trees down. ’ɴ’ gyɴ-’at‘a̱’n, I cleared away the trees (e. g. for sun dance).

’a-t‘ɴ, salty [unexplained]. —— t‘o̱ɴ-at‘ɴ, salty water. Cp. ’at‘ɴ-t̑ɴe̱ma̱, grain of salt.

’at‘ɴt̑ɴe̱-’a̱’me̱i̱, to salt. —— ha ’ɴ-’at‘ɴt̑ɴe̱-’a̱’me̱i̱, did you salt it? ’ɴ-’at‘ɴt̑ɴe̱-’a̱m, salt it!

’at‘ɴ-t̑ɴe̱-ma̱ (inan. IIᵃ; ’at‘ɴ-t̑ɴe̱, dpl.; ’at‘ɴ-t̑ɴe̱- in comp.) 1. grain of salt, salt; 2. name of a small weed that grows on the prairies, lit. salt [’at‘ɴ, salty; t̑ɴe̱, to be white].

’at‘ɴt̑ɴe̱-’o̱ɴ, to be very salty. —— ’at‘ɴt̑ɴe̱-’o̱ɴ, it is too salty.

a

’a̱’-, app. prepound form of p̱a’, river, water, referring to water in ’a̱’-ga, well; ’a̱’-pa̱-e̱, otter; ’a̱’-pa̱’-ga, tule plant; ’a̱’-pi̱ɴ, fish (app. water fish, assuming that -pi̱ɴ may be related to Tewa pa‘, fish, as p‘iɴ, fire, is to Tewa fa‘, fire); ’a̱’-sei, little creek; ’a̱’-da, island [cp. p̱a’, river; Tewa p̱ō‘, ’ò-, ’ō‘-, water].

’a̱’-, prepound form of k̑a̱’-gyɴ, skin, in ’a̱’-yɴ-t, to skin; ’a̱’-yɴ-e-ba, buckskin thong; ’a̱’-yɴ’-ba, pendule of fringe. Cp. also -k̑a̱ in tɴ’-k̑a̱, eyelid, app. a dim. of k̑a̱’- [Tewa ’ɑ́, buckskin, cloth, ’ɑ́-ŋ, tegument, covering].

’a̱’-, verb prefix, a while, temporarily, in ’a-’a̱, to lend; ’a̱’-k‘oup, to be dizzy; *’a̱’-k̑oup, to store away; *’a̱’-k̑uadl, to be stored away; ’a̱’-k̑uat-tou’e, storeroom; ’a̱’-sa, to store away; ’a̱’-t̑a’, to stay a while.

’a̱-’a̱, to lend [’a̱’-, verb prefix, temporarily; ’a̱, to give].—kadl ’adlha̱’gyɴ gyɴ-’a̱’a̱’da’, I am going to lend you some money.

*’a̱’-’ɴe, to go over to gamble [’ɴe, to run, go]. —— poue bɴt-’a̱’-’ɴeda’, don’t go over to gamble!

’a̱’-ba, adv., repeatedly [cp. ’a-e-, again]. Cp. ’ɴdltɴ-’a̱’me̱i̱, to repeat. —— ’a̱’ba, gyɴt-’a̱’me̱i̱, I did it repeatedly, one time after another.

’ɑ’-bн-hɑ’, adv., there, right there [’ɑ-, dem. stem; -bн-hɑ’, postp.,
　　at]. —— gyн̓-tsei ’ɑ’bнhɑ’, I put it right there.
’ɑ’-bei, adv., past; there [app. ’ɑ-, dem. stem; -bei, postp., at, refer-
　　ring to region; for the mg. past cp. esp. the compounded postp.
　　-bei-gyн, in front of]. —— ’ɑ’bei ’н, he is passing by. ’ɑ’bei
　　k‘uep‘н ’ɑ̓n-houpǫų-’н, we heard the wagon passing. ’ɑ’bei, there,
　　up there.
’ɑ’-bįн (an II; ’ɑ-bįн-gɑ, tpl.; ’ɑ’-bįн- in comp.), 1. paunch (e. g. of
　　buffalo); 2. gizzard (of bird) [’ɑ’-, unexplained, -bįн as in sɑ’-bįн,
　　quiver; cp. bįн-m-k‘ɑ-e, bag]. Cp. sei-t̂нę, tripe.
’ǫ’-dɑ (inan. III), island [possibly ’ɑ’-, water; -dɑ, unexplained].
　　—— gyн̓-’ɑ’dɑ-dɑ, there is an island.
’ɑ’-dɑ (inan. IIb; ’ɑ-dl, dpl.; ’ɑ-dl-, ’ɑ-t- in comp.), a hair of the head;
　　the tpl. is used for head-hair collective. The s. form appears to be
　　collective in ’ouy-ɑ’-dɑ, mane, and in one sentence given below.
　　’ɑ-dl-, ’ɑ-t-, in compounds refers to head as well as hair. Cp.
　　’ɑdl-t‘ęį’m, head, lit. head bone. —— ’ɑ’dɑ dei-bǫų, I saw one
　　hair. ’ɑdl dei-bǫų, I saw the hair (of the head, cȯll.). nǫ̧ ’ɑdl,
　　my hair. nǫ̧ ’ɑdl-dǫų’m, in my hair. ’ɑdl-gyн dèi-p̃ǫ̧’ǫ̧’dɑ’, I am
　　going to wash my hair. Also ’ɑdl-dǫų’m dèi-p̃ǫ̧’ǫ̧’dɑ’, I am going
　　to wash my hair, lit. inside my hair. dei-’ɑdlsǫųdɑ’, I am going
　　to brush my hair, = ’ɑ’dɑ déi-sǫųdɑ’. ’ɑdl-hɑ’-bн, at one side of
　　the head, referring to a style of hairdressing described by Mooney,
　　p. 391; cp. ’ɑdl-hɑ’bн̓’-k̃iн, man who uses this style of hairdressing.
*’ɑ’-dɑ (’ɑ’deip, curs.), to think [cp. possibly ’ɑ-’ɑ’-dɑ’, to be unable;
　　’ǫ̧-n- in ’ǫ̧n-t̂ou-t‘н̓’, to forgive; Tewa ’ɑ̧-ŋ-, referring to thinking].
　　—— yɑ̧-guɑ bн̓-’ɑ’deip, I think I am smart (bн̓-, app. a pronoun,
　　is not clear).
’Ɑ’dɑ’-dei, prsn. of a former head chief of the Kiowas; see Mooney,
　　p. 392 [explained by Mooney, loc. cit., as “Island;” ev. ’ɑ’dɑ,
　　island; -dei].
’ɑ’-dei (’ɑ’-gɑ, tpl.), dem. pron. and adv., that one, right there [’ɑ-,
　　dem. stem; -dei]. —— ’ɑ’dei ’н, he is coming right there.
’ɑ’dei-hɑ’, adv., there [’ɑ’dei, there; -hɑ’, postp., at]. —— ’ɑ’dei-hɑ’
　　’н̓-tsнn, I have come from there.
’ɑ’dei-hɑ’-tsou, adv., there [’ɑ’dei, there; -hɑ’-tsou, at]. —— p‘iн-yɑ’
　　’н̓-t̂ɑ’gɑ ’ɑ’dei-hɑ’tsou ’н̓-tsн̧n, I was staying up on the hill and
　　came (down) from there.
’ɑ’-dou (inan. Iᵃ), biceps [said to be so called because it is roundish;
　　cp. possibly -’н-dl-, -’н-t-, round; dou, unexplained].
’ɑ’-gɑ (inan. I; ’ɑ’-gɑ- in comp.) well [possibly ’ɑ’-, water; -gɑ, noun
　　postfix]. —— ’ɑ’gɑ gyн̓-bǫų, I saw a well of water. yiн ’ɑ’gɑ
　　’-bǫų (or gyн̓-bǫų instead of last word), I saw two wells. ’ɑ’gɑ
　　gyн̓-hiнndɑ’, I am going to dig a well. t̂ǫųdei’iн ’ɑ’gɑ-gyн tseidl,
　　the rat is in the well. ’ɑ’gɑ-dǫųgyн tseidl, he is down in the well.

’ɑ’-ga, 1. dem. pron., tpl. of ’ɑ’dei, that one; 2. adv., there, where, look there [’ɑ-, dem. stem; -gɑ]. Cp. ’ɑ’gɑ-sǫm, window. —— ’ɑ’gɑ tou’e ’ʜ-deiyɑ-dei-’iʜ ’ʜ-he.ibeitɑ’, I am going in where they are standing in the room. hǫn nǫ tsoudlhɑ mʜyiʜ ’eim (hʜ’yʜ’) ’ʜ-tɑ’yɑ’ ’ɑ’gɑ ’ęin-’ɑ’zʜ-’iʜk‘ǫ’heidldei, I did not hear anything like that d. woman quarreled over milkbags. ’ʜ-bʜ ’ɑ’gɑ p̄ɑ’-’eidl k̄ɑ’dei-’eim, I went to where the big river was (lying). ’ʜ-heibʜ ’ɑ’gɑ ’eidlk̄iʜ tou’e tɑ’dei-’iʜ, I went in where the old man was staying inside. ’ɑ’gɑ ’ʜn ’eim-kɑ’tɑp̀dɑ-’iʜ, a swimming place. dɑ́-’ǫntout‘ʜ’ ’eigɑ ’ɑdlk‘ɑegyʜ gyʜ́t-dɑ’dei ’ɑ’gɑ nǫ ’oup̀-tsou ’éi-’ǫntout‘ʜ’ ’ɑ’gɑ ’ɑdlk‘ɑedei dɑ́-’ǫ’meidei, forgive us our sins as we forgive those who sin against us! ’ɑ’gɑ, up there. ’ɑ’gɑ, look there! behold! (used like ’oue, ’oueigɑ in calling attention).

’ɑ’-gɑ- in ’ɑ’gɑ-sǫm, window [app. = ’ɑ’gɑ, there].

’ɑ’gɑ-sǫm (an. II; ’ɑ’gɑ-sǫ’bɑ, tpl.), window [app. looking-place: ’ɑ’gɑ, there, where; -sǫm as in sǫm-dɑ, to look].

’ɑ’gyʜ (inan. III), game [’ɑ, to play, gamble].

’ɑ’gyʜ, stingy (to be) [’ɑ’-, unexplained; -gyʜ]. —— yʜ̀-’ɑ’gyʜ, I am stingy. hǫndei ’ɑ’gyʜhei ’ʜ-dɑ, I am not close.

’ɑ’hʜp, to be a great gambler [’ɑ, to gamble; -hʜ-p, excessive usitative postfix]. Cp. ’ɑ’k̄iʜ, gambler. ——. nǫ ’ʜ-’ɑ’hʜp, I am a gambler, =nǫ ’ɑ’k̄iʜ ’ʜ-dɑ.

’ɑ’hʜp̀-k̄iʜ (an. I; ’ɑ’hʜp̀-gɑ, tpl.), gambler, = ’ɑ’-k̄iʜ.

’ɑ’-hi’ʜ, to be a good gambler [-hi’ʜ, real]. —— yʜ́-’ɑ’hi’ʜ, I am a good gambler.

’ɑ’k̄iʜ, (an. I; ’ɑ’-gɑ, tpl.), gambler, = ’ɑ’hʜp̀-k̄iʜ, gambler [’ɑ, to play].—nǫ ’ɑ’k̄iʜ ’ʜ-dɑ, I am a gambler. ’ɑ’gɑ dèi-bǫu, I saw the tpl. gamblers.

-’ɑ’-k̄ou-bʜ, postp., around, at the edge of [’ɑ’-, app. dem. stem; k̄ou, unexplained; -bʜ, at]. —— k̄yʜhi’ʜ t‘ǫu-’ɑ’k̄oubʜ ’ʜ’gyʜ, the man was sitting on the shore.

’ɑ’-k̄ou-bei, postp., around, at the edge of [-bei, at].—t‘ǫu-’ɑ’k̄oubei gyʜ́t-bǫu, I saw the shore. piʜ’ʜ’-’ɑ’k̄oubei, at the edge of the table. nǫ-’ɑ’k̄oubei mʜ’youp ’ʜ-k̄uɑyɑ, the women were sitting all around me. tǫutou-’ɑ’k̄oubei k̄yʜhyoup tei ’ʜ-dɑ, men were all around (outside) the (agency) office.

*’ɑ’-k̄oup, to store away several, in ’ɑ’-k̄uɑ-sou-dei, hook for hanging things away; etc. [’ɑ’-; k̄oup].

’ɑ’-k̄uɑ-sou-dei (inan. Iᵃ), hook for hanging things away [*’ɑ’-k̄oup, to store away; sou- (?) to insert; -dei]. —— hǫndei ’ɑ’-k̄uɑ-soudei gyʜ̀-bǫu, I saw a hook for hanging things.

’ɑ’-k̄uɑ-tou’e (inan. I), storeroom [*’ɑ’-k̄oup, to store away; tou’e, room].

’ɑ’-k‘ǫ, to be light [unexplained]. —— ’ɑ’k‘ǫ, it is light (not heavy). ’éi-doue-’ɑ’k‘ǫ, it is too light.

*'ɑ'-k'oup ('ɑ'k'ouyн, curs.), to be dizzy [app. 'ɑ'-, temporarily;
k'oup, to pain, be sick]. yɑ̜-'ɑ'k'ouyн, I am dizzy.

'ɑ'pɕ-ẹ, (an. II), otter ['ɑ'-, water; -pɕ-ẹ, unexplained]. Recorded
only from Mr. Lonewolf; the other informants did not know this
word.

'ɑ'pɒ̜'-gɑ (inan. IIª; 'ɑ'-pɕ, dpl.) tule, bulrush ['ɑ'-, possibly water
-pɒ̜'-, unexplained; -gɑ].  ——  'ɑ'pɒ̜'gɑ déi-bọụ.  I saw one tule
plant.  'ɑ'pɕ gyн̓t-bọụ, I saw the tule (coll.).

'ɑ'-pįн (an. II; 'ɑ'-pįн-dɑ, tpl.; 'ɑ'-pįн- in comp.), fish, =t'ọụn-îɑ'-
-p'oudl, fish, lit. split tail [possibly water fish: 'ɑ'-, water; w. -pįн
cp. Tewa pɑ`, fish].

'ɑ'pįн-'нîɑhɑ'e (inan. III), dorsal fin of fish; also without prepound
[fish warbonnet].

'ɑ'pįн-guɑdl, recent prsn., of Enoch Smoky [red fish].  Cp. tsọụ-
t'нdliн, prsn. of Mr. Smoky.

'ɑ'pįн-k'ɕe (inan. IIª), fish skin.

'ɑ'pįн-p'ou-e (inan. II; 'ɑ'pįн-p'ou, dpl.), given as meaning fish line
['ɑ'pįн-, fish; p'ou, trap, fishhook; -ei].

'ɑ'pįн-p'oubн, to go fishing [p'ou-, to catch, trap].

'ɑ'pįн-p'oue (inan. II; 'ɑ'pįнp'ou, dpl.), given as meaning fish line
['ɑ'pįн-, fish; p'ou, trap, fishhook; -ei].

'ɑ'pįн-p'ou-kiн (inan. Iª), fish bait [fish catch meat].

'ɑ'pįн-tнẹ-gɑ (inan. II; 'ɑ'pįн-tнẹ, dpl.) fish net [-tн-ẹ, unexplained;
-gɑ.

'ɑ'-p'н̜ (an. II; 'ɑ'-p'н̜'-gɑ, tpl.), boil (on body) [unexplained].

'ɑ'-sɑ, to store away several ['ɑ'-, temporarily; sɑ to put several in].
Cp. *'ɑ'-k̄oup, to store away.  ——  gyн̓t-'ɑ'sɑ'dɑ', I am going
to store it away.

'ɑ'-sei (inan. I), small creek [app. 'ɑ'-, water; -sei as in sei-kɕ-n,
scum on stagnant water, sei-tsou, lake].  Cp. hiнdl, dry arroyo.

'ɑ'-sọụ ('ɑ'-sọụ-gɑ, tpl.; 'ɑ'-sọụ- in comp.), roan [w. 'ɑ'- cp. Tewa 'ɑ̜́,
to be brown; -sọụ, intensive].  ——  tsẹi-'ɑ'sọụ gyн̓-bọụ, I saw
a roan horse.  tsẹi-'ɑ'sọụgɑ déi-bọụ, I saw tpl. roan horses.

'ɑ'-sọụ-dɑ (inan. IIª; 'ɑ'-sọụn, dpl.:), sweetgrass plant ['ɑ'-, unexplained, distinct from -'ɕ', to be sweet; sọụ-dɑ, grass plant].

'ɑ'-îɑ', to stay a while, temporarily ['ɑ'-, temporarily; îɑ', to stay].
——  nɕ 'н̓-'ɑ'îɑ', I am staying here a little while (in Lawton).

'ɑ'-îн̜'-mɕ, (curs.; 'ɑ'îн̜m- in comp.), to suck ['ɑ'-, unexplained;
îн̜ . . ., to suck].  Cp. 'ọụ-'ɑ'îн̜m-poudl, leech.

'ɑ'îsọụ (an. II; 'ɑ'-îsọụ-gɑ, tpl.), tick [unexplained].

'ɑ'-yнe-bɑ (inan. Iª), buckskin thong, =îɑp̓k'ɕe-yнebɑ ['ɑ'-, skin;
yнe-bɑ, string].  Cp. 'ɑ'-yн̓'-bɑ, pendule of fringe.

'ɑ'yн-houdl-dн (inan. III), buckskin dress (formerly worn by Kiowa
women) [fringe shirt].  Cp. îɑp̓k'ɕe-houdl-dн, buckskin shirt.

'α'yн-sα, to fringe [app. sα, to put several in]. —— dei-'α'yн-sα'dα', I am going to fringe it.

'α'-yн-t ('α'yнdldα', fut.; 'α'yнdlheidl, infer.), to skin, scalp ['α'-, prepound form of k̯α'gyн, skin; -yн-t, unexplained, hardly to be compared to -yн'- in 'α'-yн'-bα, pendule of fringe, because of 'α'-yнebα, explained as buckskin rope]. —— geigα k‘αe-'α'yнdlheidl, and then he skinned it. tseịhịн gyн̀-'α'yнdldα', I am going to skin the dog. k‘yнhịнgα tseịhịн gyн̀-'α'yнt, yesterday I skinned the dog. gyн̀-'α'yн̀dldα, I am going to scalp him.

'α'-yн'bα, 'α'-yiн-bα (inan. II*; 'α'-yiн, 'α'-yн, dpl.; 'α'-yiн- in comp.), pendule of fringe ['α'-, skin; w. yн'-bα cp. yн-e-bα, rope]. Cp. 'α'-yнebα, buckskin thong. —— 'α'yн'bα (or 'α'yiнbα) déibọụ, I saw one pendule of fringe. 'α'yн (or 'α'yiн) gyн̀t-bọụ, I saw the fringe. 'α'yн gyн̀t-'ọmdα', I am going to make fringe. dei-'α'yн-sн'dα', I am going to fringe it.

'α'-zн-'e (app. inan. II*; 'α'-zн-'e, 'α'-zн, d.; 'α'-zн'-dα, 'α'-zн'-gα, tpl.; 'α'-zн'- in comp.), udder, milkbag [unexplained]. Cp. zeip, woman's breast. —— 'α'-zн 'ẹ̣in-dα, her milk-bags, 'α'zн'-gyн, in the milk-bags.

'α̯'zн'-t̯α̯'-hou-k̯iн (an. I; also 'α̯'zн'-t̯α̯'-hou-k̯yнhị'н; 'α̯'zн'-t̯α̯'-hou-p, tpl.; 'α̯'zн't̯α̯'-hou- in comp.), trbn., Udder-angry Traveleroff, man who departed angry because of the udder; see the text, page 252.

α̯

'α̯('α̯'nα̯', punct. neg.; 'α̯'mα, curs.; 'α̯'dα', fut.; 'α̯'nα̯'t̯α', fut. neg.; 'α̯', 'α̯'houp, imp.; 'α̯'nα̯'heidl, infer. neg.), to give, hand [Tewa 'ạ̣-ŋ, to give, hand]. Also in *'α̯'-hα', to bring and give; 'α'-'α̯, to lend; k̯α̯'dα-'α̯, to sell; p‘ọụn-'α̯, to pay. Cp. mн'gα, to give, hand. — yн̣́-'α̯', give it to me! = yн̣́-'α̯'hi'н. poue yн̣́-'α̯'dα', do not give it to me! hн'oue 'ẹ̣i-'α̯'dα', when are you going to pay me back? heit bн̣́t-'α̯', let us give it! poue bн̣́t-'α̯'dα', let us not give it! 'н̀-'α̯', you pay him! t̯sou 'ẹ̣i-'α̯', hand me the stone! nн̣́-'α̯', give it to me! =nн̣́-'α̯'houp. mịн̯n gн̣́-'α̯'mα, I am going to give it to you. poue yн̣́-'α̯'dα', k̯α̯'dei, don't give it to him! he is no good. tei 'н' yн̣́-'α̯', give me all the sticks! ='н' teip‘ae yн̣́-'α̯'! hα̯n 'н̀-'α̯'nα̯', I did not grant, I refused; ct. nα̯ 'н̀-'нdl-'α̯mgyн, I granted, I agreed. 'ẹ̣idei t‘нdliн tseị gyн̣́-'α̯'dα', I am going to give my horse to this boy.

'α̯-, 'α̯'-, 'α̯n-, verb prefix, with the foot, in 'α̯'-zọụn, to walk; 'α̯n-tsн̣-'н, to come on foot; etc. [Tewa 'ạ́-, 'ạ́-ŋ-, verb prefix, with the foot]. Cp. 'α̯n-, prepound form of 'α̯n-sou'e, foot, and of 'α̯n-gyн, foottrack, referring to foot, foottrack.

-'α̯', 'α̯'-, to be sweet, savory, in -'н-'α̯'-, sour (?) (in t‘ọụ-'н'-'α̯'-mα, lemon); 'α̯'-guα-dou'e-gyн, to be savory; t̯oudl-'α̯, to be savory [Tewa 'ạ́-, to be sweet].

, form of the postp. -α' with induced nasalization.

ą-'ą̄'-dei (an. II; 'ą̄-'ą̄'-doup, tpl.), magpie ['ą-'ą̄'-, imitative; -dei; cp. Tewa kwą́'ą̄', magpie].

'ą-m- in 'ąm-hyų'mdei, right; 'ąm-t'ʜmdei, left.

'ąm-hyų'-m-dei, right (dexter) [ev. for *'ąm-hyų'ę-m-dei: 'ą-m- as in 'ąm-t'ʜm-dei, left; -hyų-'ę, -hyų-ę̀, real, right; -m-, -dei]. —— 'ąmhyų'mdei t'ǫųdei, the right leg. 'ąmhyų'mgα mą̄'dα, the right hand. 'ąmhyų'mdei mąn, dpl. right hands.

'ą-m-gyʜ ('ąmgα', punct. neg.; -'ą̄'mʜ̨, curs.; 'ą̄'mʜ̨ęgα', curs. neg.; -'ąmdeihα, curs.; -'αmdeiƚα', fut.; -'ąmgα̅'ƚα', fut. neg.; -'α̅mdα', fut.; -'ąmdei, imp), pass. of 'ą̄'-męį, to make: to be made, be done, to happen, become; pass. or transitional postpound with verbs. Cp. 'αmdα, to be made, and many compound verbs. —— 'ąmgyʜ, it is made, it has been made. 'ąmdeiƚα', it will be made. hąn 'ąmgα', it is not made. heigα ƙyʜtʜeƙiʜ-'ą̄'mʜ̨, he is going to be made a chief. Cp. poue bèi-ƙyʜtʜeƙiʜ-'αmdα', do not make yourself chief, don't be made a chief! k'iʜdeidl gyʜ̀-'ąmgyʜ, yesterday it happened. k'iʜdeidl hąn gyʜ̀-'ąmgα', it did not happen yesterday. miʜn gyʜ̀-'ą̄'mʜ̨ęgα', it is not about to happen. k'yʜ̨̄hįʜ̨gα gyʜ̀-'ąmdeiƚα', tomorrow it will happen. k'yʜ̨̄hįʜ̨gα hαn gyʜ̀-'ąmgα̅'ƚα', tomorrow it is not going to happen. gyʜ̀-kąn-'ąmgyʜ, let it happen. miʜn p'ʜ̨n-'ą̄'mʜ̨, it is about to cloud up. ƥα' syʜn-'ąmdeihα, the moon is waning, growing small. ƥα' syʜ̨n-'ąmdeiƚα', the moon is going to wane. heigα yʜ̨-'ąmdeiƚα', (my work) is going to be finished. pʜ̨hįʜ̨ yʜ̨̀-koudou-k'oup-'ąmgyʜ, I am going to be suffering. heigα tou 'ąmgyʜ, the house is finished now. k'yʜ̨̄hįʜ̨gα heigα tou 'ąmdeiƚα, the house will be finished tomorrow. tou heidα hąn 'ąmgα', the house is not finished yet. k'iʜdeidl tou 'ąmgyʜ, the house was finished yesterday. tou k'yʜ̨̄hįʜ̨gα hąn 'ąmgα̅'ƚα', the house will not be finished tomorrow. tou bei-t'ęį'n-dei 'ąmdeiƚα', the house will never be finished. =tou hąn 'ąmgα̅'ƚα'.

'ąm-dα, to be made, be done. Cp. 'ąm-gyʜ, to be made. —— tou heigα 'ąmdα, the house is already finished, the tpl. houses are already finished. tou heigα 'ę̀į-'ąmdα, the two houses are already finished. tou heigα 'ąmdα̅'-dei gyʜ̨̀-bǫų, I saw the house (or tpl. houses) already built. tsę.įhįʜ̨ tsęįn-dou 'ąmdα̅'-dei gyʜ̀-bǫų, I saw the dog made of mud.

'ąm-dou', to make ['ąm-, to make; dou']. —— gyʜ̀ƚ-kαƥk'ǫų-'ąmdou', I am making a shadow. 'ę̀įm-ƚsoudl-touhα̅'-'ąmdou', he soars, lit. slants his wings.

'ąm-t'ʜ̨m-dei, left ['ąm- as in 'ąmhyų'mdei, right; -t'ʜ̨-m-, unexplained; -dei]. Cp. 'ą̄'-t'ʜ̨-, app. variant form. —— 'ąm-t'ʜ̨mgα mą̄'dα, the left hand.

’ȼ-n (’ȼ’dɑ’, punct. neg.; ’ȼ’deip, curs.; ’ȼnȼɑ’, fut.; ’ȼ’dɑ’ȼɑ’, fut.
neg.; ’ȼ’n, imp.), to sound.  Also in tǫu̯-’ȼn, (thunder) sounds;
’ȼn-kǫu̯’m, to sound.—— béiȼ-’ȼn, (flute, train) sounded.  béiȼ-
’ȼ’deip, it is sounding.  kuɑtou wн’wн’wн’wн’ ’ȼn-’ȼn, the bird
went wн’wн’wн’wн’.  kuɑtou ’ȼn-’ȼn, the bird sɛng.  hȼ’ȼnkʻ-
iнgɑ béiȼ-’ȼn, the train whistled, sounded.

’ɑ-n-, prepound form of ’ȼn-sou’e, foot, and of ’ȼn-gyн, foottrack,
referring to foot, foottrack; for ’ȼn-sou’e, ’ȼn-sou- is also used as
prepound.

’ȼ-n-, verb prefix, with the foot, see ’ȼ-.

’ȼ-n-, possibly in ’ȼn-kɑ-douy-ei-dei, too much; ’ȼn-ƙiн-gɑ, at last.

’ȼ-n-, possibly referring to thinking, in ’ȼn-ȼou-tʻн’, to forgive [cp.
possibly ’ɑ’-dɑ, to think; Tewa ’ȼ-ŋ-, referring to thinking].

-’ȼ-n, in dɑm-’ȼn-tʻǫu̯, ocean; kʻȼ-’ȼn, moccasin; kʻȼ-’ȼn, to be
pitiable; mɑn-’ȼn-’ɑ, to play the arrow-throwing game.

-’ȼ-n in ȼɑm-’ȼn, measure [cp. *ȼɑm-’ȼ’neį, to measure].

’ȼn-bн-boudl-tʻeį’m (inan. II; ’ȼn-bн-boudl-tʻǫu̯, dpl.; ’ȼn-bн-
boudl-tʻǫu̯- in comp.), projecting process of bone at either side of
the ankle [’ȼn-, referring to foot; -bн-; -bou-dl- as in tʻǫu̯-bou-t,
shin; tʻeį’m, bone].

’ȼn-bн-pнdl-kʻae (an. II), rug [lit. foot quilt; explained as “quilt
that makes one’s feet walk easy”; ’ȼn-, referring to foot; -bн-;
pнdl-kʻae, quilt].  Cp. tou-dǫu̯’mdei-kʻɑe, rug.

’ȼn-dɑ (’ȼn-dɑ’mȼ’, punct. neg.), to want [’ȼ-n-, unexplained; app.
dɑ, to be].  Also in pǫu̯-’ȼndɑ, to want to see; etc.  Cp. tʻein-dɑ,
to want.—hн’oudei ’eįm-’ȼndɑ, how much do you want?  ’н-’ȼndɑ,
I want it.  tseį ’н-’ȼndɑ, I want a horse.  kʻiнdeidl tseį ’н-’ȼndɑ,
yesterday I wanted a horse.  kʻyнhiнgɑ tseį ’н-’ȼndɑ’, to-morrow
I shall want a horse.  hȼn ’н-’ȼndɑ’mȼ’ tseį, I did not want a
horse, = tseį hȼn ’н-’ȼndɑ’mȼ.  ’н-pǫu̯-’ȼndɑ’, I want to see
(him), = ’ȼį-pǫu̯-tʻeįndɑ.

’ȼn-dǫu̯-bн (inan. III), sole of foot [’ȼn-, foot; -dǫu̯bн, postp.].
= ’ȼn-dǫu̯bнe.

’ȼn-dǫu̯-bн-e (inan. III), sole of foot, = ’ȼn-dǫu̯bн.

’ȼn-gɑ-dou-y-ei-dei, too much [’ȼ-n-, possibly as in ’ȼn-ƙiн, last;
-gɑ-, unexplained; -dou-y- = dou-e-, verb prefix, excessively; -ei-,
unexplained; -dei].  —— ’ȼngɑdouyeidei bнȼ-kȼ’mȼ, you want
too much.

’ȼn-goup, to kick tr. [to foot hit].  —— gyн-’ȼngoup, I kicked him.

’ȼn-gyн (app. inan. III, but s. usage was not readily approved;
’ȼn- in comp.), foottrack [’ȼn-, prepound form of ’ȼn-sou’e, foot,
and of ’ȼn-gyн, foottrack; -gyн].—’ȼngyн gyнȼ-bǫu̯, I saw the
tracks.  But “I saw the track” was turned to ’ȼn-’ȼn-da nȼ
gyнȼ-bǫu̯, I saw his track.  yȼ-’ȼn-dɑ, my foottrack.  yȼn-’ȼn-bǫu̯,
I saw your foottrack.  yȼ-’ȼn-bǫu̯, you saw my track.  ’oueidei

 k̓n-'ɑn-bǫu̯, I saw his track.   nǫ 'ɑnhɐ'dei yk̓n-'ɑn-bǫu̯, I saw the bear's tracks.   'ɑnhɐ'dei 'ŕ-'ɑn-dɑ, bear's tracks, they are bear's tracks.

*'ǫ̇ᴋ̣ɑ̣ᷟ', to stand up, in 'ɑn-hɐ'-dei, bear ['ɑn-, unexplained, possibly foo̱ᴋ̣ᴧ̣ɴʜ', to stand up].

'ɑn-hɐ'-dei (an. II; 'ǫu-hɐ'-ɗoup, tpL; 'ɑn-hɐ'- in comp.), =seit [explained as meaning he who stands up erect: *'ǫn-hʜ', to stand up; -dei].

'ɑnhɐ'dei-'iʜ (an. II), bear cub [-'iʜ, dim.].

'ɑn-hiʜ-t ('ɑnhiʜ, curs.; 'ɑnhiʜda', fut.; 'ɑnk'iʜ-, prepound), to go (along a road or waterway) ['ɑn-, foot; hiʜt, to ascend].   Cp. hǫ̇'-'ɑnk'iʜ-gɑ, railroad train. —— p̄ɑ' heiga bŕ-'ɑnhiʜ, we are following the river along.   hiʜdl gyŕ-'ɑnhiʜdɑ', I am going to go along the gulch.

'ɑn-kɑ'e (inan. IIᵃ), ankle ['ɑn-, foot]. —— 'ɑn-kɑ'e déi-bǫu̯, I saw the ankle.

'ɑn-kǫu̯'m, to sound [app. 'ɑn, to sound; -kǫu̯'m, to be about]. —— 'k̓n-'ɑnkǫu̯'m, he (a bee) buzzed.   'k̓n-'ɑn-kǫu̯'m-dei, buzzing.

'ɑn-k̄ɑn (an. II; 'ɑnk̄ǫ'dɑ, tpl.; and inan. Iᵃ), hoof ['ɑn-, foot; app. -k̄ɑn, stiff].   Ct. 'ɑn-t̄sǫu̯, toenail.—tsęi-'ɑnk̄ɑn, horse's hoof.   'ɑnk̄ǫ'dɑ déi-bǫu̯, I saw the tpl. hoofs, = 'ɑnk̄ɑn gyŕ-bǫu̯.

'ɑnk̄iʜ-, prepound form of 'ɑn-k̄iʜ-gɑ, at last.

'ɑn-k̄iʜ-gɑ, adv., ('ɑn-k̄iʜ- in comp.), at last, finally ['ɑn-, possibly as in 'ɑn-gɑdouyeidei, too much; -k̄iʜ- as in k̄iʜ-gyʜ, afterward; -gɑ]. —— 'ŕ-bʜnmʜ nę̇i 'ɑnk̄iʜgɑ hɑn 'ŕ-bɐ'mɑ̇', I was going to go, but finally did not go.   'ɑnk̄iʜ-p̄ɑ'-hɑn-dei-'ęi tsʜn, he came back last month (can not substitute -yiʜ- for -hɑn-).   'ɑnk̄iʜ-sɐ'-yiʜ-dei-'ęi tsʜn, he came back last year.   'ɑnk̄iʜ-pɐ'yiʜ-dei-'ęi tsʜn, he came back last summer.

-'ɑn-k'įʜ-gɑ in hǫ̇'-'ɑn-k'įʜ-gɑ, train [that which goes along: nominal form of 'ɑn-hiʜ-t, to go along].

'ɑn-p'ɑ'-gɑ (inan. II; 'ɑn-p'ɑ, dpl.; 'ɑn-p'ɑ- in comp.), heel ['ɑn-, foot; -p'ɑ possibly as in p'ɑ-'ʜtdoup, ball].

'ɑn-sou-'e (inan. II; 'ɑ-n-sou, dpl.; 'ɑn-, 'ɑn-sou- in comp., 'ɑn-serving also as prepound form of 'ɑn-gyʜ, foottrack), foot [w. 'ɑ-n- cp. Tewa 'ǫ́-ŋ, foot; -sou-; unexplained; -'ei]. —— 'ɑnsou-gyʜ, on foot.

'ɑnt̄ɑ' ('ɑnt̄ɑ'- in comp.), five [Tewa p̄ɑ́-nu̇, five]. —— mʜyiʜ 'ɑnt̄ɑ' sɐ'dɑ dɑ', the woman has borne five children.   'ɑnt̄ɑ' k̄yɐhyoup, five men.   'ɑnt̄ɑ' sʜe, five years.   'oueidei 'ɑnt̄ɑ'-k̄oup, yonder is the fifth camp.

'ɑnt̄ɑ'-k'įʜ, fifty.

'ɑnt̄ɑ-t, five by five.

10559°—28——3

’ǫnĩɑ’-dou, in five places. —— ’ǫnĩɑ’-dou déi-bǫy, I saw all five'
them.

’ǫnĩɑt-dei, the fifth.

’ǫnĩɑ’-t‘ɥ, fifteen. —— ’ǫnĩɑ’-t‘ɥ k̸yɳhyoup, fifteen men. ’ǫnĩɑ’-
t‘ɥ ꜱʜe, fifteen years.

’ǫn-ŧou-t‘ɥ’ (’ǫnŧout‘ɳ’mǫ’, punct. neg.; ’ǫnŧout‘ɳ’mǫ, curs.; ’ǫnŧout‘ɳ’ĩɑ’, futλ; ’ǫnŧout‘ɳ’mǫ’ĩɑ’, fut. neg.; ’ǫnŧout‘ɥ’, imp.), to
forgive [w. ’ǫ-n- cp. possibly *’ɑ’-dɑ, to think; Tewa ’d̜-ɳ-, referring
to thinking; -ŧou-, unexplained; -t‘ɥ’ as in k‘ɑ’-t‘ɥ’, to pity; etc.]
—— k‘iʜdeidl gyʜ-’ǫnŧout‘ɥ’, yesterday I forgave him. k‘iʜdeidl
hǫn gyʜ-’ǫnŧout‘ɳ’mǫ’, I did not forgive him yesterday. miʜn
gyʜ-’ǫnŧout‘ɳ’mǫ, I am about to forgive him. k‘yɳhiɳgɑ
gyʜ-’ǫnŧout‘ɳ’ĩɑ’, I am going to forgive him tomorrow. k‘yɳhiɳgɑ
hǫn gyʜ-’ǫnŧout‘ɳ’mǫ’ĩɑ’, I am not going to forgive him tomorrow.
’ʜ-’ǫnŧout‘ɥ’, forgive him! poue ’ʜ-’ǫnŧout‘ɳ’ĩɑ’, don’t forgive
him! heit bʜ́-’ǫnŧout‘ɥ’, let us forgive him. heit poue bʜ́-’ǫnŧout‘ɳ’ĩɑ’, let us not forgive him.

’ǫn-t‘ʜdl (an. II; ’ǫn-t‘ʜt-dɑ, tpl.; also inan. I), toe [’ǫn-, foot; -t‘ʜdl,
app. as in ’ei-t‘ʜt-dɑ, grain of corn; t‘ʜdl, liver, kidney]. —— tei
’ɥm ’ǫn-t‘ʜdl gyʜ-bǫy, I saw all of your toes. ’ǫnĩɑ’ ’ǫn-t‘ʜdl
’d̜i-da, I have five toes (’ǫn-t‘ʜtdɑ can not be substituted in this
sentence). ’ǫn-t‘ɥtdɑ déi-bǫy, I saw the tpl. toes. p‘ɳ’ou
’ǫn-t‘ʜdl, three toes; but p‘ɳ’ou ’ǫn-t‘ʜtdɑ déi-bǫy, I saw three
toes.

*’ǫn-t‘ou-t-, to climb steps, in ’ǫn-t‘out-’ʜ’dɑ, ladder [’ǫn-, foot;
t‘ou-t as in t‘ǫy-pɑ’-t‘out, pump].

’ǫn-t‘out-’ʜ’-dɑ (inan. II; ’ǫn-t‘out-’ʜ’, dpl.), ladder [explained as
climb up steps pole: ’ʜ’-dɑ, pole].

’ǫn-tsɳ’-, verb prepound, going on foot, in ’ǫn-tsɳ’-’ɥ, to come on foot;
’ǫn-tsɳ’-bʜ, to go on foot, walk; ’ǫn-tsɳ’-kiɳniɳ, to be a great
walker; ’ǫn-tsɳ’-sɑ’e, to be a fast walker [’ǫn-, with the foot; w.
tsɳ’-, cp. tsʜ-e-, to go, walk].

’ǫn-tsɳ’-’ɥ, to come on foot [’ɥ, to come]. —— ’ʜ-’ǫntsɳ’-’ɥ, I came
on foot.

’ǫn-tsɳ’-bʜ, to go on foot, walk [bʜ, to go].—Cp. ’ǫ’-zǫyn, to walk.
—— ’ʜ-’ǫntsɳ’bʜ’ĩɑ’, I am going to go on foot, I am going to
walk.

’ǫn-tsɳ’-kiɳniɳ, to be a great walker [kiɳniɳ, to be long]. ——
’ǫntsɳ’-kiɳniɳ, lit. he is a long walker.

’ǫn-tsɳ’-sɑ’e, to be a fast walker [sɑ’e, to be swift]. —— ’ǫntsɳ’-sɑ’e,
he is a fast walker.

’ǫn-ŧsǫy (an. II; ’ǫn-ŧsǫy-gyʜ, tpl.), toenail [’ǫn-, foot; -ŧsǫy, nail,
claw]. Cp. ’ǫn-k̸ǫn, hoof; mǫn-ŧsǫy, fingernail. —— ’ǫn-ŧsǫygyʜ
déi-bǫy, I saw tpl. toenails.

Sorry:
The defect on the previous page was that way in the original book we reproduced.

ꞗ

'ꞗ'-, verb prefix, with the foot, see 'ɑ-.

'ꞗ'-, to be sweet, savory; see -'ɑ'.

'ꞗ'-dei, to be mean [w. 'ꞗ'- cp. t̂ɑn, to be mean; -dei]. —— yɦ̥-'ꞗ'dei, I am mean, cranky. 'ɦ̥n-'ꞗ'dei, he is mean. gyнt-'ꞗ'dei, you and I are mean.

'ꞗ'-deiꝑ-dei ('ꞗ'-deiꝑ-gɑ, tpl.), half ['ꞗ'-dei-p-, unexplained; -dei]. Cp. zнe-dei, half. —— 'н'dɑ 'ꞗ'deiꝑgɑ déi-boṵ, I saw one side of the stick, half of the stick. tsẹ.i̥ 'ꞗ'deiꝑdei gyн̇-boṵ, I saw the other side of the horse. tsẹ.i̥gɑ 'ꞗ'deiꝑgɑ déi-boṵ, I saw the other half of the horses. nɑ kɑ'dei toṵnẹi': 'ꞗ'deiꝑgɑ nɦ́-'ɑ', and the other (chief) said: give me half (the other half)!

'ꞗ'-gɑ, own, frequently replacing independent poss. pron.; self. Cp. k'ou-нe, k'ou-hi̥н, own. —— 'ꞗgɑ 'iн, our own son. 'ꞗgɑ tsẹi̥, our own horse. nɑ 'ꞗgɑ tsẹi̥ 'ẹi-dɑ, it is my own horse. gei heigɑ 'ꞗgɑ-dei k̂yн̥hyoup gɑ mɑ̥youp teip'ɑe 'ẹim-to.udɑ, and his own men and women all he gathered together. nɑ tsẹi̥ dɦ́-dɑ, that is our horse, = 'ꞗgɑ tsẹi̥ dɦ́-dɑ. ꞗgɑ tsẹi̥ 'ẹi-dɑ, it is my own horse. 'ꞗgɑ tsẹi̥ gyɦ-dɑ, it is your own horse. 'ꞗgɑ tsẹi̥ bɦ́-dɑ, that is the horse of ye tpl. 'ꞗgɑ-dei tsẹi̥ 'ɦ-dɑ, it is his horse ('ꞗgɑ would hardly replace 'ꞗgɑ-dei in third pers. s., but would be understood). 'ꞗgɑ dèi-houdl, I killed myself. 'ꞗgɑ béi-hou, let us kill ourselves. 'ꞗgɑ 'ẹim-houdl, he killed himself. 'ꞗgɑ dèi-tɑ'bн', I am looking at myself. 'ꞗgɑ 'ẹim-toṵhɑn, he became silent of his own accord.

'ꞗgɑ-dei, own; see 'ꞗgɑ.

'ꞗgɑ-pi̥н (an. II; 'ꞗgɑ-pi̥н-gɑ, tpl.), buffalo, lit. (our) own food ['ꞗgɑ, own; pi̥н, food]. Cp. kɑdl, kɑdlhi̥н, buffalo.

'ꞗ'-guɑ-dou'e-gyн, to taste good ['ꞗ'-, app. = -'ɑ', to be sweet; -guɑ-, unexplained; app.-dou'e-, excessively; -gyн]. —— yɦ̥-'-'ꞗ'-guɑdou-'egyн, it tastes awfully good to me.

*'ꞗ'-hɑ', to bring and give [app. hɑ', to bring]. Cp. *mɑ̥'-hɑ'. —— yɦ̥-'ꞗ'hi̥'н, give it to me! =yɦ̥-'ɑ', give it to me!

'ꞗ'-kɑ-dl, unreal, potential particle ['ꞗ'-, unexplained; kɑ-dl]. Cp. 'ꞗ'kɑdl-t̂ouꝑdei-k'iн, day before yesterday. —— 'ꞗ'kɑdl tsн̥nt̂ɑ' nɑ heigɑ '-'oubɑhy-ouldɑ', if he had come, I would have killed him (notice 'ꞗ'kɑdl in prot., 'oubɑe- in apod.). 'ꞗ'kɑdl tsн̥n-'ẹi, gyн̇-houdldɑ', if he had come, I would have killed him. 'ꞗ'kɑdl hɑn gyн̇t-k'ouꝑbei-'нe'yɑ'-'ẹi, heigɑ 'ẹi-teidɑ', if I had not run away, he would have caught me. 'èi-toṵt'нe nɑ 'ꞗkɑdl 'нdl gyн̇-toṵt'нe, when he spoke to me, I spoke to him.

'ꞗ'kɑdl-t̂ouꝑdei-k'iн, day before yesterday, = t̂ouꝑdei-k'iн ['ꞗ'kɑdl, app. unreal particle; t̂ouꝑ-dei, before, front; k'iн, day]. —— 'ꞗ'kɑdl-t̂ouꝑdei-k'iн hẹi'm, she died day before yesterday.

'ꞗ'-m-ẹi ('ꞗ'mɑ', punct. neg.; 'ꞗ'mɑ', 'ꞗ'mi̥'н̥gyн', curs.; 'ꞗmdɑ', fut.; 'ꞗ'mɑ'dɑ', fut. neg.; 'ɑ'm, imp.; 'ɑmheidl, infer.; 'ɑm- in comp.), to make; also as causative verb postpound [Tewa -'ǫ̀-ŋ, causative verb postpound, to make]. The passive is 'ǫmgyн, 'ǫmdα, q. v. For prepound form cp. dαe-'ǫm-k̑iн, medicine-man; 'ei-k̑oudl-'ǫm-dα, pear, lit. necked fruit; pįн-'ǫm-tou'e, kitchen; tou-'ǫm-k̑iн, shoemaker. —— hǫndei 'ǫ'mǫ, he is doing something. hǫn yǫ́-нnegα' hǫndei 'ǫ'mį'нgyн', I do not know what he is doing. déi-'ǫ'mei̯, I made it. hǫn déi-'ǫ'mǫ', I did not make it, I am not making it. déi-'ǫ'mǫ, I am making it (here 'ǫ'mǫ, but punct. neg. 'ǫ'mǫ'). heigα miнn déi-'ǫ'mǫ, I am about to make it. dèi-'ǫmdα', I shall make it (in apod. frequently I would make it). hǫn dèi-'ǫ'mǫ'dα', I shall not make it. 'ǫgα béi-'ǫ'm, you make it yourself! poue béit̑-'ǫmdα', don't make it! heit̑ béit̑-'ǫ'm, let us make it! heit̑ poue béit̑-'ǫmdα', let us not make it. k̑yн̑hį'н̑ 'éi-'ǫ'mǫ'-dei gyн̀-bǫu̯, I saw the man who was making it, I saw the man making it. k̑yн̑hi'н̑ 'éi-'ǫmheidl-dei gyн̀-bǫu̯, I saw the man who made it. k̑yн̑hi'н̑ tou 'ǫmheidl-dei gyн̀-bǫu̯, I saw the (s. or tpl.) house(s) which the man had made. k̑yн̑hi'н̑ tou'èi̯-'ǫmheidl-dei nèi̯n-bǫu̯, I saw the two houses which the man had made. k̑yн̑hį'н̑ sα'dei'eidl gyн̀-'ǫ'i̯mei̯-dei gyн̀-bǫu̯, I saw the man who did (or had done, or has done) a great work (it was stated that if the syllable -mei̯- is lengthened, the meaning is changed to "was about to do"). heigα gyн̀t̑-bou'ǫ'mǫ', I make it all the time. zeip̑gα déi-'ǫ'mei̯, I made a bow. tseiguαn tsei̯n-tou 'н́-'ǫmheidl-dei gyн̀-bǫu̯, I saw the dog that they had made of mud. k'oup̑dei 'éi-'ǫ'mei̯, they tpl. (Mexicans) injured (lit. did) me much (by stealing my land). tsнt̑ béi-'ǫ'm, close the door! (tsнt, door; the idiom sounds like "make the door!"), = tsнt̑ béi-t̑sou!

-'ǫ'-n-ei̯ (-'ǫndα', fut.; -'ǫn- in comp.) in *t̑ǫm-'ǫ'nei̯, to measure; t̑oudlǫ'-bн-'ǫ'nei̯, to taste of.

'ǫ'-t't̑н-, app. a variant form of 'ǫm-t't̑нmdei, left.

'ǫ'-zǫu̯n ('ǫ'zǫu̯nǫ', punct. neg.; 'ǫ'zǫu̯ndα', fut.; 'ǫ'zǫu̯nǫ'dα', fut. neg.; 'ǫ'zǫu̯n, imp.; 'ǫ'zǫu̯nheidl, infer.), to walk, go, travel, start [app. 'ǫn-, foot; zǫu̯n, to pull (out). Also in hou-'ǫ'zǫu̯n, to travel (off); etc.] —— heigα 'ei̯m-'ǫ'zǫu̯n (the child or cripple) is already walking. heigα dèi-'ǫ'zǫu̯n, I am already walking. k'yн̑hį'н̑gα yн̑t̑bнhe.igα 'ei̯m-'ǫ'zǫu̯ndα', to-morrow the soldiers are going to go. poue béi-(k'ou)-'ǫ'zǫu̯ndα', 1. let us not go! 2. don't ye tpl. go! heit̑ béi-k'ou-'ǫ'zǫu̯n, let us go, let us walk. dèi-'ǫ'zǫu̯n, I went away, walked off, started off, left.

'н-, prefixed to 2nd and 3rd person possessive forms of certain relationship terms, in 'н-kα'kα, your (spl.) mother; 'н-tsα'dei, his or their mother; 'н-kǫu̯m, your (spl.) friend; 'н-tsн̑yiн, your (spl.) paternal aunt. Cp. -ei, my or our, prefixed to 1st person possessive forms.

'н- in 'н-'нt-dα, lump.

-'н in p'α-'н, temple-lock; îα'-'н, earring.

'н-'н-t-dα (inan. IIª; 'н-'н-dl, dpl.), lump, excrescence ['н-, unexplained; -н-t- as in p'α-'н-t-doup, ball; etc.; -dα]. Cp. mǫ'-н-t-dα,
lump on the nose; 'ou-'н-t-dα, throat lump, etc. —— 'н'нtdα
déi-bǫų, I saw the lump.

'н-dl, additional or adversative particle, more, moreover, also,
either. When used with the particle kαdl (see examples below),
'нdl takes second position [cp. possibly tsн-dl, additional particle;
yн-dl, optative particle]. App. also in 'нdl-dн-, backward,
repeated, again. —— kαdl 'нdl syн̥'dα dα'îα', and she is going
to bear some more children. k'yн̥hį'нgα 'нdl hǫn yн̥-hнegα'îα',
tomorrow I shall not know. hα kαdl 'нdl t'ǫų, do you want some
more water? hα kαdl 'нdl, do you want some more? hǫ'nęi, no
(ans.). 'н̥m 'нdl gyн̥-tн̥'p'iнt, you are one-eyed. hǫn 'ęi-guαgu-
'αdα' nǫ nǫ 'нdl hǫn ęim-guαgu'αdα', if you do not hit me, I
will not hit you. 'ęihαdei dǫ'mgyн 'нdl gyн̥-dα'îα', as on earth.

'н-dl- in 'нdl-dн-, backward, again [app. = 'нdl, additional particle].

'н-dl-, to drive, prepound form of 'н-dl-ei, to chase several, in 'нdl-dou',
to herd; нdl-hα', to drive; 'нdl-he.ibα, to drive in; 'нdl-k'uαt, to put
out; 'нdl-toudα, to round up (cattle); 'нdl-t'eip, to drive out.

'н-dl- in 'нdl-α, to play cards.

'н-dl- in 'нdl-'ǫmgyн, to grant.

-'н-dl-, -'н-t-, -'н', round, in 'н-'нt-dα, lump; dα-'нt-dα, bucket,
kettle; hǫ'-'нt-gyн, buffalo fish; k̄α-'нt-dα, dish p'α-'н', temple;
p'α-'нt-dou-p, ball; etc. [cp. possibly 'α'-dou, biceps].

'нdl-α, to play cards ['нdl-, unexplained; 'α, to play]. Cp. 'нtdα,
playing-card. —— dèi-(t'α'k'αe)-'нdl-'α'dα', I am going to play
cards.

'нdl-α'-gα (s. also 'нdl-α'-bα; inan. II; 'нdl-α', dpl.; 'нdl-α'- in
comp.), wild plum fruit, plum; apple. But can not be applied,
e. g. to peach, orange, etc. [app. 'н-dl-, round; -'α'-, unexplained;
-gα]. Cp. 'нhyнdl-'нdlα'-p'eip, persimmon tree; sęi-'нdlα'ga,
prickly pear fruit. —— 'нdlα'gα déi-bǫų, I saw the apple.

'нdlα'-p'eip (inan. II), wild plum bush [p'eip, bush]. 'нdlα'-t'ǫų,
apple juice, cider [t'ǫų, water, juice].

'нdl-ǫmgyн, to grant ['нdl-, unexplained; 'ǫmgyн] —— poue 'ęim-
'нdl-ǫndeiîα', don't say yes, don't grant it! nǫ 'н-'нdl-'ǫmgyн,
I granted it, I agreed.

'нdl-bα', to drive [bα', to bring].

'нdl-dн-, backward; repeated, again, in p'oue-îeidl-'нdldн̥'-guαn, to
turn somersault; 'нdldн̥-'ǫ'męi, to repeat; 'нdldн̥'-k̄α'tou, a
repeated sun dance [app. 'н-dl, additional particle; -dн̥]. Cp. 'α'-bα,
repeatedly.

'ʜdldʜ-'ǫ'mẹị, to repeat [to do again]. —— 'oueigα gyʜ-
'ʜdldʜ-'ǫ'mẹị, they tpl. repeated it.

'ʜdldʜ'-ƙα'tou (inan. I), a repeated sun dance; see Mooney, p. 279.

'ʜdl-dou', to herd ['ʜdl-, to drive; dou']. —— tsẹịgα déi-'ʜdldou', I
herded the horses.

dl-dou'-'iʜ (an. I), member of the order of 'Hdl-tou'-'yue, the tpl.
form being translated by Mooney, p. 230, as "Young (wild) Sheep"
[app. 'ʜdl-dou', to herd; 'iʜ, child; judging from the explanation
given by Mooney, the word may mean herded lamb, mountain
sheep lamb].

'ʜdl-hα' ('ʜdl-hα'bα' punct. neg.; 'ʜdl-hα'dα', fut.; 'ʜdl-hiʜdα', fut.;
'ʜdl-hiʜguαdα', fut. neg.; 'ʜdl-hα', imp.), to drive ['ʜdl-, to drive;
hα', to bring]. —— k'iʜdeidl déi-'ʜdlhα', I drove them (tpl. cows,
chickens); cp. k'iʜdeidl déi-'ʜdlbα', I drove the cows (home),
brought them in. k'yn̥hị'ʜgα hǫn déi-'ʜdl-hiʜguαdα', to-morrow
I shall not drive them.

'ʜdl-heibα, to drive in ['ʜdl-, to chase several; heibα, to carry in].
—— déi-'ʜdl-heibα, I drove them (the horses) in (into the barn);
but déi-heibα, I carried them (tpl. an. min.) in.

'ʜdl-iʜ-dα (inan. II); 'ʜdl-iʜ, tpl.), bowstring ['ʜ-dl-, unexplained,
but cp. possibly Tewa 'α‘, bow; unexplained; w. -'iʜ cp. possibly
yʜ-e-bα, string; -dα].

'ʜdl-k'uαt ('ʜdl-k'uαdα', punct. neg.; 'ʜdl-k'uαdldα', fut.; 'ʜdl-k'uαdl,
imp.), to put out, refl. go out. ['ʜdl-, to drive; k'uαt, to pull out].
—— gyn̄-'ʜdl-k'uαt, I put him out; 'n̄-'ʜdl-k'uαdl, put him out!

'ʜdl-toudα ('ʜdltoudα', punct. neg.; 'ʜdltoudeidα', fut.; 'ʜdltoudα'dα', fut. neg.; 'ʜdltoudei, imp.), to round up ['ʜdl-, to drive;
toudα, to pick up, gather].

'ʜdl-t'eip ('ʜdl-k'i'αgu'α, punct. neg.; 'ʜdl-k'i'ʜdα', fut.; 'ʜdl-k'i'ʜ,
imp.), to put out, drive out ['ʜdl-, to drive; t'eip, to carry out].
—— k'iʜdeidl gyn̄-'ʜdlt'eip, yesterday I put him out (e. g. dog
out of house, bull out in pasture). k'iʜdeidl hǫn déi-'ʜdlk'i'ʜ-
gu'α, yesterday I did not put them tpl. out. k'yn̥hịʜgα hǫn
déi-'ʜdlk'iʜgu'α, to-morrow I am not going to put them tpl. out.
béit-'ʜdlk'i'ʜ, let us put them out!

-'ʜdl-t'out, in 'ei-p'ʜe-'ʜdlt'out, corn cultivator ['ʜdl-, to drive;
-t'out, unexplained].

'ʜ-e ('ʜyα', punct. neg.; 'ʜegoup, curs.; 'ʜedα', fut.), to run, go
[Tewa 'n̥, to run]. Cp. k'ouþbei-'ʜe, to run; t̑ǫy̨m-'ʜe, to come
as a fugitive; 'outbʜtsʜyiʜ-'ʜe, to swing intr. in a swing; p'ouþ-
t'ʜdl-'ʜe, to tie a knot (in end of thread), gǫp-'ʜe, to swap; t̑sn̥ndei,
to run. —— tsẹịhịn̥ hʜyʜ'yn̥-'ʜe, my dog went off. mn̥mgα
gyʜt-ʜedα', I am going to swing high. dǫy̨'m gyn̄t-ʜedα', I am
going to go down (said by man in airship). koudei gyn̄t-ʜedα, I
am going to run swiftly.

’н-е- in ’не-dẹị’-gɑ, leaf; ’не-p̃iн-’eigɑ, potato; ’не-p̃iн-gɑ, willow sp.

’н-е- in ’не-sẹị, to be smoky [’н- as in ’н’-gyн, smoke; -ei].

’не-’ǫ̃’mẹị, ’н’y-ǫ̃’mẹị, to make run. ——— déi-’н’y-ǫ̃’mẹị, I spun it (the top).

’не-dẹị’-gɑ (inan. II; ’н̦e-dẹị-n, dpl.), leaf [’н-е-, app. as in ’неp̃iн-gɑ, willow sp.; -dẹin, possibly = dẹịn, tongue]. ——— ’неdẹị’gɑ déị-bǫụ, I saw the leaf.

’неp̃iн-’ei-goup (inan. II), potato plant [app. willow fruit plant].

’неp̃iн-’ei-gɑ (inan. II; ’неp̃iн-’ei, dpl.), potato [’неp̃iн-, app. willow sp.; ’ei-gɑ, fruit].

’неp̃iн-’ei-poudl (an. II; ’неp̃iн-’ei-pouț-dɑ, tpl.; ’неp̃iн-’ei-poudl-in comp.), potato bug.

’не-p̃iн-gɑ (inan. II; ’не-p̃iн, dpl.), willow sp. This is a low willow sp. which grows along the banks of creeks [said to mean “goes up and bends over”: app. ’не- as in ’не-dẹị’-gɑ, leaf; w. -p̃iн cp. p̃iн-dei, down, downstream; -gɑ]. Cp. sẹị-’н’dɑ, a larger willow sp.; ’неp̃iн-’eigɑ, potato.

’не-p‘iн-bei-gɑ (inan. II; ’не-p‘iн-bei, dpl.), particle of pollen [’не-, app. as in ’не-dẹị’-gɑ, leaf, or perhaps as in ’не-sẹị-gyн, to be smoky; -p‘iн-bei-, unexplained; -gɑ]. ——— ’не-p‘iнbeigɑ déi-bǫụ, I saw one grainlet of pollen.

’не-sẹị (не-sẹigɑ’, punct. neg.; ’не-sẹidɑ’, fut.; ’не-sẹigɑ’t̂ɑ’, fut. neg.), to be smoky [’н- as in ’н’-gyн, smoke; -ei; sẹị, to smell intr.]. Cp. ’не-sẹị-gyн, smoke; ’н’-gyн, smoke. ——— ’не-sẹị, it is smoky. gyн̀-’неsẹị, it is smoky. hǫn gyн̀-’неsẹịgɑ’, it is not smoky. gyн-’неsẹịdɑ’, it is going to be smoky. hǫn gyн̀-’неsẹịgɑ’t̂ɑ’, it is not going to be smoky. p‘iн gyн̀t̂-’неsẹị, the fire is smoking.

’не-sẹị-’ǫmgyн, to get smoky. ——— heigɑ gyн̀-’неsẹị-’ǫmdeit̂ɑ’, it is going to get smoky.

’не-sẹị-gyн (inan. III; ’не-sẹị- in comp.), smoke [’не-sẹị, to be smoky; -gyн]. ——— ’не-sẹịgyн gyн̀t̂-bǫụ, I saw the smoke. ’неsẹị-k‘oup̃н̦’ẹgyн, in the smoke.

’неsẹị-t̂н’dɑ, to shut in smoke [t̂н’dɑ, to shut in].

’Hhyнdl-’нdlɑ’p‘eip (inan. II), persimmon tree [Arapaho wild plum tree].

*’Hhy-нdl-k̃iн (an. I; ’Hhy-нt̂-dɑ, tpl.; ’Hhyнdl- in comp.), Arapaho man [’не-hнdl-, unexplained; -k̃iн; see discussion by Mooney, p. 393.].

’н-’iн-dei, his or their child. Cp. ’iн, child.

’н-kɑ-e (an. II; ’н-kɑ-e-guɑ, tpl.), hawk sp. [unexplained]. Cp. ’нkɑe-k‘ǫụ-gyн, ’нkɑe-t̂н̦e, hawk sps.

’нkɑe-k‘ǫụ-gyн (an. II; ’нkɑe-k‘ǫụ-gɑ’t, tpl.), a blackish hawk sp. Said to fly about the tops of trees. [dark hawk sp.].

’нkɑe-t̂н̦e (an. II; ’нkɑe-t̂н̦e-mɑ, tpl.), hawk sp. [white hawk sp.].

’ʜ-kɑ’-kɑ, your (spl.) mother. Cp. tsɑ, mother; kɑ’kɑ-’e, my or
our mother; kɑ’, mother, voc.; ’ʜ-tsɑ’-dei, his or their mother
[’ʜ- as in ’ʜ-tsɑ’dei; his or their mother; -kɑ’kɑ as in kɑ’kɑ-’e,
my or our mother]. —— ’ʜkɑ’kɑ gyн́-dɑ, it is your (s.) mother.
’ʜkɑ’kɑ mǵ-dɑ, it is your (d.) mother. ’ʜkɑ’kɑ bǽ-dɑ, it is
your (tpl.) mother.

’н́-’oudl-k̃ɑ’-dei (mę́i-’oudl-k̃ɑ’-dei, d.; béi-’oudl-k̃ɑ’-gɑ, tpl.), whore,
lit. one having a load, one having something attached to her
[’oudl (inan. III), load; k̃ɑ, to lie; -dei].

’ʜb̓-t‘ou (inan. II; ’ʜb̓-t‘ou-gɑ, tpl.), “blackbird” sp. [said to mean
“somewhat faded”].

-’ʜt̓- in dɑ-’ʜt̓-dɑ; etc.; see -ʜdl-.

’ʜt̓-dɑ (inan. IIᵃ; ’ʜ-dl, dpl.; ’ʜ-dl- in comp.), playing card [cp.
’ʜdl-ɑ’, to play cards].

’ʜ-k̃ɑ-hɑ-’e (inan. III). —— 1. war bonnet; 2. dorsal fin of fish (so
called because it stands up like a war-bonnet) [unexplained]. Cp.
’ɑdlk‘ɑek̃i(ʜ)hʜ’, crest. —— hʜ’oudei gyн̓-’ʜîɑhɑ’e-sɑdl, they
tpl. have war bonnets on.

’ʜ-tsɑ’-dei (’ʜ-tsɑ’-gɑ, tpl.), his or their mother. Cp. tsa, mother;
[’ʜ- as in ’ʜ-kɑ’kɑ, your (spl.) mother; tsa, mother; -dei]. ——
’ʜtsɑ’dei ’н́-dɑ, it is his mother. ’ʜtsɑ’dei mę́i-dɑ, it is their (d.)
mother. ’ʜtsɑ’dei béi-dɑ, it is their (tpl.) mother.

’ʜ-tsʜy-iʜ, your (spl.) paternal aunt [’ʜ-, prefixed to 2nd and 3rd
person possessive forms; tsʜy-įʜ, my, our, his or their paternal
aunt].

ʜ

’ʜ’-, prepound form of ’ʜ’-dɑ, stick.

’ʜ’-, prepound form of ’ʜ’-gɑ’-t, feather.

’ʜ’- in ’ʜ’-gyʜ, smoke; ’ʜ’-gyʜ, to be dust-windy; ’ʜ’-dɑ, to be dewy.

’ʜ’- in ’ʜ’-dei, a kind of medicine bag.

’ʜ’- in ’ʜ-’x̧’-, sour (?).

-’ʜ’- in pʜ-’ʜ’-gɑ, in one place.

-’ʜ-’x̧’, sour (?), in t‘ǫu̧-’ʜ-’x̧’-mɑ, lemon [-’ʜ’-, unexplained; -’x̧’-,
ev. to be sweet]. Cp. dęi-sʜdl, to be sour.

’ʜ’-bɑdlhɑ’ (inan. III). —— 1. timbered hill; 2. a plcn., see
Mooney, p. 391 [bɑdlhɑ’, hill].

’ʜ’-bʜ-k̃ų̧ę (an. II; ’ʜ’-bʜ-k̃ų̧ę-dɑ, ’ʜ’-bʜ-k̃ų̧ę-mɑ, tpl.; ’ʜ’-bʜ-k̃ų̧ę-
in comp.), woodpecker sp. [explained as meaning the one that
spirals up a bough; ’ʜ’-, stick, bough, cp. ’ʜ’-bou-gɑ’t, bough;
-bʜ-; -k̃ų̧ę, unexplained]. Cp. ’ɑdl-guɑdl, woodpecker sp.;
kyʜe-’ɑdl-guɑdl, woodpecker sp.

’ʜ’-bou-gɑ’-t (inan. II; ’ʜ’-bou-gyʜ, dpl.), bough or limb of tree [w.
-bou- cp. possibly t‘ǫu̧-bout, shin; -gɑ’t]. Cp. p‘oudl, branch.

'ʜ'-dɑ (inan. II; 'ʜ', dpl.; 'ʜ'- in comp.), stick, stalk, plant, tree, pole, timber, lumber, wood [cp. possibly 'ʜ'-gɑ't, feather].  Cp. k̑iʜ-bɑ, stick of firewood.

'ʜ'-dɑ, to be dewy ['ʜ'-, smoke, misty rain; dɑ, to be].  Cp. pʜ-'ʜ'dɑ, to be mirage. —— gyʜ̀-'ʜ'dɑ, it is dewy.  gyʜ̀-'ʜ'dɑîɑ', it is going to be dewy (tonight).

'ʜ'-dei, a kind of medicine-bag; see Mooney, p. 392 ['ʜ'-, unexplained; -dei].

'ʜ'dei-k̑iʜ (an. I), prsn., medicine-bag man; see Mooney, p. 392 [medicine-bag man].

'ʜ'deik̑iʜ-dei-p̃ɑ', plcn., medicine bag man creek; see Mooney, p. 392 [p̃ɑ', creek].

'ʜ-dl-ei (app. 'ʜdl- in comp., used as prepound meaning to drive with verbs of s. and tpl. object), to chase several.  So. correspondent is tɑ'-ʜ̣.  Cp. 'ʜdl-hɑ', to drive; 'ʜdl-touda, to round up (cattle); 'ʜdl-t'eip, to drive out; etc. —— 'éi-kɑdl-'ʜdlei, he is chasing the buffaloes.  'eît-kɑdl-'ʜdlei, they tpl. are chasing the buffaloes.  But kɑdl-tɑ'ʜ̣, he is chasing the buffalo.

''ʜ-dǫ̀ᴜm-dei-k̑iʜ (an. II; 'ʜ'-dǫ̀ᴜm-gɑ, tpl.), Caddo man, man of tribe from the Gulf States; see Mooney, p. 392 [under timber man].

'ʜ'dǫ̀ᴜn, Kiowa name of Mr. Charles E. Adams, former agent; see Mooney, p. 392 [from Eng. Adams].

'ʜ-'ei-gɑ (inan. II) hackberry fruit [tree berry].

'ʜ'ei-p'eip (inan. II), hackberry tree [tree berry bush].

'ʜ'-gɑ'-t· (inan. II; 'ʜ', dpl.; 'ʜ'- in comp.), feather [cp. possibly 'ʜ'-dɑ, stick].  The feathering of an arrow is spoken of collectively as 'ʜ'.

'ʜ'-goup, quill of feather ['ʜ'-, feather; app. goup, plant].  Cp. 'ʜ'-goup̀-t'ę̂i'm, quill of feather.

'ʜ'-goup̀-t'ę̂i'm (app. inan. II; ʜ'-goup-t'ǫ̀ᴜ, dpl.; 'ʜ'-goup-t'ǫ̀ᴜ- in comp.), quill of feather [t'ę̂i'm, bone].

'ʜ'-gyʜ (inan. III; 'ʜ'- in comp.), smoke [w. 'ʜ'- cp. 'ʜ- in 'ʜ-e-sę̂i, to be smokȳ].  Cp. 'ʜe-sę̂i-gyʜ, smoke. —— gyʜ̀-'ʜ'-dɑ, there was smoke (there where the man shot with black powder).  'ʜ'-houdlgyʜ, in the midst of the smoke.

'ʜ'-gyʜ ('ʜ'hʜ'guɑ, curs.), to be dust-windy ['ʜ'-, smoke; -gyʜ; cp. 'ʜ'gyʜ, smoke]. —— p'ʜ̣ę 'ʜ'gyʜ, the dust is blowing.  miʜn 'ę̂im p'ʜ̣ę 'ʜ'hʜ'guɑ, it is going to be dust-windy.

'ʜ'-gyʜ-dǫ̀ᴜ-gɑ'-t (inan. II; 'ʜ'-gyʜ-dǫ̀ᴜ-gyʜ, dpl.), heart of tree ['ʜ'-, tree; -gyʜ, at; -dǫ̀ᴜ-gyʜ, in, underneath; cp. 'ʜdlɑ'-dǫ̀ᴜgyʜ, inside of the apple, core of apple].

'ʜ-hou', particle, thanks [cp. 'ʜ-k'ou, hello; k'ou-, now].  Cp. gyʜ̀-îʜ'gyʜ, thanks.

’ʜ’-hout-ꭓ, shower comes [’ʜ’-, smoke; hout-ꭓ, to come]. ——
    gyà-’ʜ’-hout-ꭓ, rain is coming, lit. smoke (referring to misty
    appearance) is coming.
’ʜ’-hyꭒę (inan. II; ’ʜ’-hįꭓ, dpl.; ’ʜ’-hįꭓ- in comp.), cottonwood
    tree [real tree].   —— ’ʜ’hįꭓ-gyʜ, at the cottonwood tree.
’Ḧ’-kįꭓnįꭓp͞ɑ’, plcn., tall trees creek; see Mooney, p. 393 [kįꭓnįꭓ,
    long, tall].
’ʜ’-kꭒę’ (an. II; ’ʜ’-kꭒꭓ-dɑ, tpl.), a name which one of the inform-
    ants once heard applied by an old Indian to the old-world lion at
    a circus [translated “stays in the timber,” but -kꭒę’ is app. diminu-
    tive of kue’, wolf].
’ʜ’-k̄ɑ’ʜt-dɑ]̣(inan. II; ’ʜ’-k̄ɑ’ʜdl, dpl.), wooden bowl or dish [k̄ɑ’ʜtdɑ,
    dish].
’ʜ’-k̄ꭓ’p‘oudl (an. II; ’ʜ’-k̄ꭓ’p‘out-dɑ, tpl.), excrescence on tree [wood
    wart].
’ʜ’-k̄ꭓ’dei, small bird sp.  The feathers are blackish and shiny;
    called “swallow” by one informant [bad wood one, said to be so
    called because the bird makes its nest in bad wood].  Cp. toudl-
    k̄ꭓ’dei, bird sp.
’ʜ’-k̄ou-t (’ʜ’-k̄outdɑ, curs.; ’ʜ’-k̄oudlda’, fut.), to smoke tr. [-k̄ou-t,
    unexplained].   ·· heigɑ gyà-’ʜ’-k̄outda, I am smoking him
    right now. gyà-’ʜ’k̄out, I smoked him. gyà-’ʜ-k̄oudldɑ’, I am
    going to smoke him.
’ʜ’-k‘ꭓę (inan. II), bark [tree skin].  Cp. ’ɑchįꭓ-k‘ꭓę, cedar bark.
’ʜ’k‘į’ꭓ-ꭓedęi-gɑ (inan. II; ’ʜ’k‘į’ꭓ-ꭓedęin, dpl.) petal [flower leaf].
’ʜ’-k‘į’ꭓ-gɑ (inan. IIᵃ; s. also ’ʜ’-k‘į’ꭓ-gɑ’t, ’ʜ’-k‘į’ꭓ-bɑ; ’ʜ’-k̄‘į’ꭓ-gyʜ,
    dpl.; ’ʜ’-k‘į’ꭓ- in comp.), flower [app. ’ʜ’-, stick, plant; k‘į’ꭓ, to
    bloom].
’ʜ’k‘į’ꭓ-p‘ɑ’-gyʜ (inan. III), stamen [flower fuzz].
’ʜ’-k‘ou, particle, hello, good-bye, how now [cp. k‘ou-, now; ’ʜ-hou,
    thanks].  —— ’ʜ’-k‘ou, hello (said in greeting to a person who
    arrives).
’ʜ’-k‘yʜ-p‘ꭓ-ę-gyʜ, adv., through the whole night [unexplained;
    -gyʜ].
’ʜ’-pɑ’-dʜ, to be crippled [unexplained].  —— tei k‘ou-toudlk̄yʜ
    ’k̄n-’ʜ’pɑ’dʜ, he is all crippled up.
’Ḧ’-piʜ-t‘ɑ’, prsn. of the present head chief of the Kiowas [unex-
    plained].
*’ʜ’-p‘ɑt-dɑ (inan. II; ’ʜ’-p‘ɑdl, dpl.; ’ʜ’-p‘ɑdl- in comp.), single fiber
    of blade of feather [feather hair].  ’ʜ’-p‘ɑdl is applied to blade of
    feather stripped from quill. déi-’ʜ’p‘ɑdl-dɑegɑ, I stripped blade
    from quill. déi-’ʜ’p‘ɑdl-dɑedeidɑ’, I am going to strip blade from
    quill.
’ʜ’-sahyei-gɑ (inan. II; ’ʜ’-sɑhyei, dpl.; ’ʜ’-sahyei- in comp.), alfalfa
    plant [green plant].  Cp. ’ʜ’sɑhyei-dęiseidl, rag weeds.—’ʜ’-sɑhyei,
    alfalfa (coll.).

'ʜ'sɑhyei-dęįsʜdl (dpl.; s. not obtained), ragweeds; see Mooney,
p. 395 [bitter green plants].

'ʜ'-sʠ'nęį (an. II; 'ʜ'-sʜ'n-ou-p, tpl.). —— 1. bullsnake; 2. bull
(male of cattle), evidently so called from Eng. influence [wood
snake].

*'ʜ'-seisei-gɑ (app. inan. I; 'ʜ'-seisei, tpl.; 'ʜ'-seisei- in comp.),
wooden arrowpoint [wooden arrowhead].

'H'-seisei-p̄ɑ', plcn., wooden arrowpoint creek; see Mooney, p. 395.

'ʜ'-sęį-'ǫu-gɑ't (inan. II; 'ʜ'-sęį-'ǫu-gyʜ, dpl.; 'ʜ'-sęį-'ǫu- in comp.),
plant sp. Described as growing five feet tall and having small
black seeds which the Indians put in their clothing as perfume
[strong smelling plant].

'H'-tɑe-'eit-dei, prsn.; see Mooney, p. 392 [so called because he
lived at 'H'-tɑe-'eitdei P̄ɑ, plcn., q. v.].

'H'-tɑe-'eitdei P̄ɑ, plcn.; see Mooney, p. 392 [explained by Mooney
as " big tree creek; " -tɑe-, unexplained].

'H'-tɑn-p̄ɑ', plcn. timber gap creek; see Mooney, p. 392 [wood gap
creek].

'ʜ'-tʜ'bɑ (inan. IIᵃ; 'ʜ'tʜ, dpl.; 'ʜ'tʜ'- in comp.), drawknife ['ʜ'-,
wood; tʜ' . . ., app. a verb].

'ʜ'-tou (inan. I), wooden house, frame house.

'H'-tou'ʜ'-p̄ɑ', plcn.; see Mooney, p. 392 [timber windbrake creek].

'H'-toubyu'ę, plcn., " a circular opening in the timber," acc. to
Mooney, p. 392 [cp. tou-byu'ę, circular camp circle].

'ʜ'-t̂ɑsʜ'-hǫ'-gyʜ (app. inan. III), wedge [wood split iron: t̂ɑ-sʜ'-,
to split.

'ʜ't̂ɑk'ɑe (an. II; 'ʜ'-t̂ɑ'k'ɑe-ou-p, tpl.), donkey [timber mule].

'ʜ'-t̂ǫę-'ǫ'-bɑ (inan. II; 'ʜ'-t̂ǫę-'ǫm, dpl.), plane [wood smoother:
'ʜ'-, wood; t̂ǫę-'ǫ'męį, to smooth; -bɑ].

'ʜ'-t̂ǫę-t'eidl (inan. III), clearing ['ʜ'-, timber; t̂ǫę, to be smooth;
-t'eidl, unexplained, prob. related to t'ʜ', to cut several].

'ʜ'-t̂ʜę-mǫ (inan. IIᵃ; 'ʜ'-t̂ʜę, dpl.; 'ʜ'-t̂ʜę- in comp.), sycamore tree
[white tree].

'ʜ'-t'ɑt-bʜ-hʜt-dɑ (inan. IIᵃ; 'ʜ'-t'ɑt-bʜ-hʜdl, dpl.; 'ʜ'-t'ɑt-bʜ-hʜdl-
ín comp.), chair [explained as "wood which one sits on": 'ʜ'-, wood;
w. t'ɑ-t- cp. t'ɑ'-dɑ..., to seat; -bʜ-; -hʜ-dl-, unexplained; -dɑ].
—— dèi-'ʜ't'ɑtbʜhʜdl-sɑ'dɑ', I am going to sit on the chair.

'ʜ'-t'ʜt-dɑ (inan. II; 'ʜ'-t'ʜdl, dpl.; 'ʜ'-t'ʜdl- in comp.), auger for
boring wood [wood borer]. Cp. hǫ'-t'ʜtdɑ, drill for metal.

'ʜ'-t'ʜ'-bɑ (inan. IIᵃ; 'ʜ'-t'ʜ', dpl.; 'ʜ'-t'ʜ'- in comp.) saw ['ʜ'-,
wood; t'ʜ', to cut several; -bɑ].

'ʜ'-t'ʜn (inan. II), tassel (of corn) ['ʜ'-, stick, plant; -t'ʜ-n, unex-
plained]. —— 'ʜ'-t'ʜn déi-bǫu, I saw the tassel. 'ʜ'-t'ʜn nèįn-
bǫu, I saw the d. tassels. 'ʜ'-t'ʜn gyʜ̀-bǫu, I saw the tpl. tassels.

'ʜ'-t'ǫu, tree sap [tree water].

'ʜ'-t'ǫ̇ṳ (inan. IIª) wooden club. Cp. hǫ̇'-t'ǫ̇ṳ, tomahawk, lit. metal club.

'ʜ'-tǫ̇ṳ-bɑ̈'-t (inan. II; 'ʜ-tǫ̇ṳ-bʜ, dpl.), wooden flute (made of cedar wood); it was stated that a Kiowa boy named Turkey knows how to make these flutes [tǫ̇ṳ-bɑ̈'t, flute]. Cp. t͡soudlt'ẹi'm-tǫ̇ṳbɑ̈'t, wingbone whistle.

'ʜ'-t'ǫ̇ṳdei (an. II; 'ʜ'-t'ǫ̇ṳ-gɑ, dpl.), 1. wooden leg; 2. wooden-legged [t'ǫ̇ṳ-dei, leg]. —— 'ʜ'-t'ǫ̇ṳdei, wooden-legged man, ='ʜ'-t'ǫ̇ṳdeiḱiʜ. 'ʜ'-t'ǫ̇ṳdei 'ẹi-dɑ, I have a wooden leg.

'ʜ'-t͡sǫ̇ṳ, bulb sp. The bulb, which is described as having a thick rind and a white center, was peeled and eaten raw ['ʜ'-, stick, plant; t͡sǫ̇ṳ, said to be the same as in t͡sǫ̇ṳ-gɑ̈'t, down feather].

'ʜ'-yʜdldʜ, plcn., see Mooney, p. 320 [timber bluff].

'ʜ'-yʜdldʜ-sʜe, timber bluff winter, see Mooney, p. 320 [sʜe, year].

'ʜ'-zout (inan. I), driftwood [zou . . . , current flows].

## ʜ

'ʜ ('ṇ'mɑ̈', punct. neg.; 'ʜnmʜ, 'ṇ'doup, curs.; 'ṇ't͡ɑ', fut.; 'ṇ'mɑ̈'t͡ɑ', fut. neg.; 'ʜ, imp.; ṇ'heidl, infer.), to come [Tewa 'ʜ', to come]. Cp. hʜdl-'ʜ, to be in a hurry; hou-'ʜ, to travel along; hǫ̇ṳ-pǫ̇ṳ-'ʜ, to sound along; ḱiʜ-'ʜ, to come to get firewood; t͡ɑ̈-'ʜ, to feel angry. —— 'ʜ̇-'ʜ, I am coming. 'ʜ̇-'ṇ't͡ɑ', I shall come; k'yṇhį̇ʜgɑ dʜ̇m-'ʜ (for dʜ 'ẹ̇im-'ʜ), you come tomorrow! 'ẹ̇im-'ʜ, come! come here! 'ʜ̇-bou-'ʜnmʜ, I am coming all the time. hǫn 'ʜ̇-'ṇ'mɑ̈'t͡ɑ', I shall not come. poue 'ẹ̇im-'ṇ't͡ɑ', don't come! gue 'ʜ, he is coming behind (us), =gue dɑ̈-ʜ, he is coming behind us.

'ʜ-m, independent personal pronoun, you, your, spl. [Tewa 'ṳʾṳʾ, you s.; 'ṳʾ-ŋ, you dpl.]. —— yiʜdei 'ʜm, you two. tei 'ʜm, all of you. 'ʜm tou gyʜ̇-bǫ̇ṳ, I saw your house.

'ʜ-m, app. a particle. —— 'oueidei dɑ tsẹihįʜ 'ʜm ḱyṇhị'ʜ hɑ̈'gyʜ-dei, that is the dog that the man got. 'oueigɑ 'ẹi-dɑ tsẹ.ihyoup 'ʜm ḱyṇhị'ʜ 'ẹi-hɑ̈'gyʜ-gɑ, those are the tpl. dogs that the man got.

'ʜ-m- in 'ʜm-guɑdl-dɑ̈'dei, a cent.

'ʜm-guɑdl-dɑ̈'dei (inan. I), a cent [explained as meaning " the red one; " 'ʜ-m-, unexplained]. ='ʜ̇n-'ʜ't͡ɑhɑe-sɑdl-dei, a cent.

'ʜ-n, particle, always, at any time; with neg. never. Cp. bei-t'ẹi'n-dei, never. ——ḱyṇhị'ʜ hǫn 'ʜn 'ẹim-dɑ̈'p̌ʜ'egɑ̈'-dei gyʜ̇-bǫ̇ṳ, I saw the man who never sings. 'ʜn 'ẹim-ḱɑtdɑ tsẹ.ihįʜ, he is a dog who is always biting the people. 'ẹit-hẹidei-tǫ̇ṳk'ɑm-tsẹi 'ʜn 'ɑ̈'zʜ't͡ɑ'houp 'ẹit-k'ɑ̈'mɑ, when(ever) we speak of them we call them 'ɑ̈'zʜ't͡ɑ'houp. ḱyṇhị'ʜ 'ʜn tougyʜ bou-t͡ɑ', the man stays at home all the time. 'ʜ̇-t͡ɑ' nɑ yʜebɑ 'ʜn t͡ʜt͡gyʜ-pǫ̇ṳe, I heard the rope break. 'ɑ̈'zʜ't͡ɑ'houp 'ʜn 'ẹim-k'ɑ̈'mɑ, 'ɑ̈'zʜ't͡ɑ'houp they call them. kɑ̈'gɑ 'ʜn 'ɑ̈'zʜ't͡ɑ'houp 'ẹim-k'ɑ̈'mɑ, those others they call Ɑ̄zʜ'Ɪ̨ʗ'houp. 'ꞡ(ʜ)hα 'ʜɴ 'ꞡ̨im-kα'Ɪ̨αꞮ̨α'dα, they swim right here. 'α'gα 'ʜɴ 'ꞡ̨im-kα'Ɪ̨αꞮ̨dα-'ꞡ̨ʜ, a swimming place. hꞑn ('ʜɴ) dèi-guαꞑ̀gα' I never fall down. 'ꞡ̨idei hʜ'tsou 'ʜɴ bʜ́t-k'ꞑ̨'mꞑ, how do you call " stone " (lit. stones) in your language? heigα 'ꞡ̨i-bꞑ̨u-dei heigʜn (for heiga 'ʜɴ) 'ꞡ̨i-tꞑ̨u-t'ʜꞮ̨dα, he spoke to me whenever he saw me.

'ʜ̨n-'ʜ'ꞯ̨αhαe-sαdl-dei (inan. I), a cent [that which has the war bonnet on]. ='ʜm-guαdl-dα'-dei, a cent.

## ʜ̨

'ʜ̨'-, referring to dreaming, sleeping, in 'ʜ̨'-bꞑ̨u, to see in dream; 'ʜ̨-nꞡ̨i, to wake tr.; 'ʜ̨'-yꞡ̨ʜ, dream.

-'ʜ̨'- in p'oudl-'ʜ̨'-hꞡ̨ʜ, cottontail rabbit.

'ʜ̨'-bꞑ̨u, to see in dream, to dream of. —— gꞡ̨ʜ-gyʜ k̓yʜ̨hꞡ̨'ʜ gyʜ-'ʜ̨'bꞑ̨u, last night I dreamt about a man.

'ʜ̨'-gyʜ ('ʜ̨'gα', punct. neg.; 'ʜ̨'gyʜꞮ̨α', fut.; 'ʜ̨'gα'Ɪ̨α, fut. neg.), to sit. Tpl. correspondent of both 'ʜ̨'gyʜ and k̓α, to lie, is k̓uαdl ['ʜ̨'- as in Tewα 'ʜ̨-ŋ, to sit; -gyʜ]. —— 'ʜ̀-'ʜ̨'gyʜ, I am sitting, I am seated. hꞑn 'ʜ̀-'ʜ̨'gα', I am not sitting. k'yʜ̨hꞡ̨ʜgα 'ʜ̀-'ʜ̨'gyʜꞮ̨α', I am going to be seated tomorrow. hꞑn 'ʜ̀-'ʜ̨'gα'Ɪ̨α', I am not going to be seated. poue 'ꞡ̀im-'ʜ̨'gyʜꞮ̨α', don't be sitting down! 'ʜ̨'gyʜ, he is sitting down. hꞑ̨'nꞡ̨i, hꞑn 'ʜ̨'gα', no, he is not seated. Dα'k̓iʜ p'ʜn-mʜ̨' 'ʜ̨'gyʜ, the Great Spirit is in heaven.

'ʜ̨'-n-ꞡ̨i ('ʜndα', fut.), to wake tr. [cp, 'ʜ̨'-, referring to dreaming, sleep]. Cp. tʜe, to wake intr. —— 'ʜm nꞡ̀i-'ʜ̨'nꞡ̨i, you woke me up. 'ʜm mʜ̨'yi(ʜ) yiʜ mꞡ́inꞡ̀i-'ʜ̨nꞡ̨i, ye d. women woke me up. 'oueidei déiꞮ̨-'ʜ̨'nꞡ̨i, he woke us d. up. 'ʜm nꞡ́in-'ʜ̨'nꞡ̨i, I woke you. 'oueidei'ꞡ̀im-'ʜ̨'nꞡ̨i, he woke him.

'ʜ̨'-yꞡ̨ʜ (inan. III), a dream ['ʜ̨'-; -yꞡ̨ʜ, unexplained].

## b

bα' (bꞑ̨'mꞑ', punct. neg.; bꞑnmꞑ, curs.; bα'dα', fut.; bꞑ̨'mꞑ̨'dα', fut. neg.; bα, imp.), to bring [Tewα mꞑ̀, to bring]. Cp. hα', to bring; kꞑ̨'n, to bring. —— heigα gyʜ̀-bα', I brought it (e. g. a book) with me. hꞑn gyʜ̀-bꞑ̨'mꞑ', I did not bring it with me. gyʜ̀-bou-bꞑnmꞑ, I bring it all the time. miʜn gyʜ̀-bꞑnmꞑ, I was thinking about bringing it. 'ʜ̀-bα, bring it! poue 'ʜ̀-bα'dα', don't bring it! heiꞮ̨ poue bʜ-bα'dα', let us not bring it. heigα gὰꞮ̨-bα'dα', we'll bring it to you, =heigα gὰꞮ̨-hiʜdα' (from hα', to bring). gyʜ́-bα'dα', I'll bring it over. Ɪ̄sou gyʜ́-bα', I brought you a rock. Ɪ̄sou 'ꞡ̨i-bα, bring me a rock! Ɪ̄sou 'ʜ̀-bα, hand (me) the stone! 'ꞡ̨idei Ɪ̄sou 'ʜ̀-bα, hand (me) the stone here!

-bα, 1. noun postfix, in 'ʜ'-tʜ'-bα, drawknife; 'ʜ'-ꞯ̨ꞑ̨ę-'ꞑ̨'-bα, plane; 'ʜ'-t'ʜ'-bα, saw; dꞑm-sʜ'-bα, plough; 'eit'ʜdl-'eik̓uα-bα, corn planting machine; etc.; 2. postp., at, in 'ɑ'-bɑ, repeatedly; -t'ɑ'-bɑ, beyond; etc. [cp. -bн].

bɑdl-hɑ' (inan. III), hill, small hill.  Cp. zout-bɑdlhɑ'-hн'guɑ, it has waves; p'iн-gɑ, hill; ƙoup, mountain. —— hн'oudei bɑdlhɑ' gyнt-bọų, I saw several hills.  gyн-bɑdlhɑ', it is a little hill.

bɑ'dlɑ', butter (fr. Eng.).

bɑ'-dн (bɑ'dɑ', punct. neg.; bɑ'deip, curs.; bɑ'deidɑ', fut.; bɑ'dɑ'tɑ, fut. neg.; bɑ'dei, imp.; bɑ'dei-, pɑ'- in comp.), to rise (e. g., of sun).  Cp. bɑ'dei-'н, to come up (of sun); t'ọų-pɑ'-t'out, pump. —— pне bɑ'dн, the sun rose.  pне bɑ'deitɑ', the sun is going to come up (sometime).  k'iнdeidl bɑ'dн, it rose yesterday.  hǫn bɑ'dɑ', it did not rise.  pне bou-bɑ'deip, the sun comes up all the time.  heigɑ hн'oue pне bɑ'deitɑ', the sun will rise sometime.  pнehyǫn (for pне hǫn) bɑ'dɑ'tɑ', the sun will not rise.  pне, 'ẹ̀ịm-bɑ'dei, sun, come up!  pне, poue 'ẹ̀ịm-bɑ'deitɑ, sun, do not rise!  heidɑ hǫn pне bɑ'dɑ' heigɑ dèi-hн', I got up before sunrise.  miнn pне bɑ'deip, the sun is about to come up.  pне bɑ'deip, the sun is rising, is about to rise.  tẹịm 'ẹ̀ịm-bɑ'dei, do your best in the race, lit. rise strongly! = bèi-peidei!

bɑ'dei-'н, to come up, rise hitherward (e. g. of sun) ['н, to come]. —— heigɑ pне bɑ'dei-'н, the sun is coming up right now.

-bɑ'-t, tpl. of -bн.

bн (bн̦'mǫ', punct. neg.; bн̦nmн̦, curs.; bн̦'tɑ', fut; bн̦'mǫ̦'tɑ', fut. neg.; bн, imp.; bн̦'heidl, inf.), to go [Tewa mн̦', to go]. —— k'yнhịнga 'н-bн̦nmн̦, I am going to go to-morrow.  hн'ouei 'ẹ̀ịm-bн̦nmн̦, when are you going?  'н-bн, I went.  hǫn 'н-bн̦'mǫ', I did not go.  'н-bou-bн̦nmн̦, I go all the time.  miнn 'н-bн̦nmн̦, I am about to go.  hн̦yн'-dou 'н-bн̦'tɑ', I may go.  'н-bн̦'heidl, they said that I went.  bн̦-tọųnẹị' 'н-bн̦'heidl, they said that I went.  hǫn 'н-bн̦'mǫ', I am not going.  miнn 'Hннdɑrk'ou-guɑ 'н-pịн-bн̦nmн̦, I am going to go to eat at Anadarko.  'ẹ̀ịm-bн, you go!  poue 'ẹ̀ịm-bн̦'tɑ', don't go!  bн̦-bн, let us go.  poue bн̦-bн̦'tɑ', let us not go.  gue 'н-bн̦'tɑ', I am going to go along behind him.  gue mẹ́ị-bн̦nmн̦, I am following them.  'н-pǫų-bн̦'tɑ', I am going (in order) to see him.  yiнdei bн̦-bн̦nmн̦, we are both going to go.

-bн, 1. noun postfix; -bɑ'-t, tpl. correspondent; 2. tpl. pronoun postfix; 3. postp., beside, on, against, at; 4. with locative force between members of compounds [cp. -bɑ, -bei].  Cp. -bн-bн, -bн-e; -bн-p. —— 1. p'ɑ-'нt-bн, temple; 2. pн̦'-bн, some (tpl.); tei-bн, all (tpl.); 3. tou-bн 'н-dei, I am standing beside the house.  tou-bн 'н-yiн-bн̦'-ƙa, I am leaning against the house.  tou-bн 'н-tsoueigyн, I ran against the house.  zou-bн nẹ́ị-tẹ.ịmǫ, it sticks to my teeth.  p̄ɑ' p'н̦n-bн ƙɑ, the moon is in the sky, = p̄ɑ' ƙɑ' p'н̦n-bн.  pн̦'gɑ tн̦' p'н̦n-bн ƙɑ, one star is in the sky.  yiн tн̦' p'н̦n-bн ƙɑ, two

stars are in the sky. tн̨' p'н̨n-bн̄ k̄uɑdl, the tpl. stars are in the
sky, = tн̨' p'н̨n-bei k̄uɑdl (-bei may be substituted only with tpl.
subject, since it refers to stars extending across the whole sky, so
the informant explained). With p'н̨n-bн̄, in the sky, ct. p'н̨n-mн̨,
way up above the sky-vault. 'ɑ'sei-bн̄, by the little creek.
sн̄'bei-bн̄, on the north side (e. g. of a street). 'н̄-kiнdl k̄ouþ̀-bн̄, I
live on the mountain, = k̄ouþ̀-bн̄ 'н̄-kiнdl. hн̄'-bн̄, where? somewhere. 'ou-bн̄'-hɑ', enough. 4. 'н̄'-bн̄-k̄uę, woodpecker sp., lit.
bough spiraler, he who spirals on boughs; 'н̄'-t'ɑt-bн̄-hнt-dɑ,
chair, lit. what one sits on; 'ɑn-bн̄-boudl-t'ęi'm, ankle process, app.
foot shin bone; 'ɑn-bн̄-pн̄dl-k'ɑe, rug, lit. foot bed blanket; bo̧uę-
bн̄-heiþ̀-gyн̄, lightning; bo̧uę-bн̄-toubн̄-hɑndei-gɑ, strainer; 'eit-ɑ-
bн̄-dou-p, mortar; k'ɑe-bн̄-toudlei, butterfly; mɑ̨'-bн̄-tsнt-ɑ', at
the point of the nose; 'out-bн̄-tsнe-youp, swing; toudlɑ̨'-bн̄-'ɑ'mei,
to taste of tr.; tɑ'-bн̄-k'ɑ, ear wax; tsoudl-k̄ɑn-bн̄-tsнt, wing
feather; zout-bн̄-t'oue-goup, to eddy.

-bн̄-bн̄, postp., beside, near [-bн̄, beside, followed by a second -bн̄].
—— tou do̧ugyн̄ p̄ɑ'-bн̄bн̄ tseidl, the house is down by the creek.
k̄ouþ̀-bн̄bн̄ 'н̄-kiнdl, I live by the mountain. tou'н̄'-bн̄bн̄ 'н̄-dei,
I was standing beside the corral. 'eik̄uɑ-(dɑm-)bн̄bн̄ 'н̄-dei, I am
standing by the field.

-bн̄-e, noun postfix [-bн̄, noun postfix; -'ei]. —— pн̄'gyн̄bei-bн̄e-dou
gyн̄-k̄ɑ', I cut him with edge (cp. pн̄'gyн̄bei-bн̄, edge of knife).

-bн̄-gɑ'-bei, postp., up close to [-bн̄, -bei, postps.; -gɑ'- unexplained].
—— k̄uɑtouhįн̨ p'н̨n-bн̄gɑ'bei p'iнhoutko̧um, the eagle is flying up
close to the sky. But tou-hɑegɑ, close to the house.

-bн̄-hɑ', postp., at, in 'ɑ'-bн̄hɑ', there [-bн̄, postp., right beside; -hɑ',
postp., at].

-bн̄-hei in yн̄t-bн̄-hei-k̄iн̄, warrior soldier.

bн̄'ou-tseiou (an. II; bн̄'ou-tseiou-p, bн̄'ou-tseiou-gɑ, tpl.), domestic
cat [bн̄-'ou-, unexplained; tsei-ou, young of animal, pet].

-bн̄-p, postp., at, -hɑ̄-bн̄-p, on the side of; k̄iн̄hн̄'-bн̄-þ̀-gɑ, occiput
[-bн̄; -p].

-bei, postp., at, in, along, referring to region [cp. -bн̄]. Cp. 'ɑ'-bei,
past; 'ou-bei-hɑ', in that region; -bei-guɑ, to; -bei-gyн̄, in front of;
-bei-bei, at; -bei-yɑ', from; etc. —— to.udɑm-bei, in the north.
tн̨' k̄uɑdl p'н̨n-bei, the tpl. stars are in the sky. zo̧u-bei, on the
teeth, along the teeth.

-bei-bн̄, postp., at, in pн̄'gyн̄-beibн̄, edge [-bei; -bн̄].

-bei-bн̄-e, postp., at, in pн̄'gyн̄-beibн̄e-dou, with the edge [-bei;
-bн̄; -ei].

-bei-bei, postp., at, referring to region [-bei, followed by a second
-bei]. —— tou-beibei, at the face, at the front.

bei-dl-, prepound form of beit-dɑ, external mouth, lip. beidl-
'ɑdlt'ęi'm (inan. II; beidl-'ɑdlt'o̧u, dpl.; beidl-'ɑdlt'o̧u- in comp.),
head of penis.

beidl-gyн (app. an. I), mouth (external, ct. sα'αdl-gyн, the inside
of the mouth [beidl-, prepound form of beit-dα, external mouth,
lip; -gyн]. Cp. beidl-t'ẹi'm, chin. —— nǫ beidlgyн, my mouth,
the region of my lips or mouth. beidlgyн gyн̇-bǫy, I saw the
mouth, = beidlgyн̇ '-bǫy. beidlgyн ḍèi-bǫy, 1. I saw the tpl.
mouths; 2. I saw my own mouth; I saw their mouths is made
nonambiguous by saying: 'oueigα beidlgyн ḍèi-bǫy.

beidl-kiн̇t-gyн (an II; beidl-kiн̇t-gα'-t, tpl.), screech owl (an owl sp.)
[beidl-, mouth; kiα-t-, unexplained; -gyн].

beidl-k'αe (inan. IIª), lip [lip-skin]. Cp. beidl-k'αẹ.

beidl-k'αẹ (inan. IIª), foreskin [dim. of beidl-k'αe, lip].

beidl-mαnkαmdou', to point with the lips [mαnkαmdou', to point].

beidl-p'α'-, pubic hair, in beidlp'α'-ƙiн, white man (app. inan. IIª;
cp. sẹin-p'α'-gα, beard hair).

Beidl-p'α'ƙiн (an. I; beidl-p'α'-gα, tpl.), white man, lit. pubic hair
man, opprobrious term based on Sẹin-p'α'-ƙiα, lit. "beard man."

beidl-sẹi-'н'-dα (inan. IIª), lamb's quarter (plant sp.). The plant
is used for greens when young [pubic smell plant].

beidl-t'ẹi'm (inan. II; beidl-t'ǫy, dpl.), chin [lip (or mouth) bone].

-bei-guα, postp., to (the region of). —— sн'-beiguα, to the north.
pнe-beiguα, to the south.

-bei-gyн, postp., in front of, by [app. -bei-, referring to region; -gyн,
at; cp. ƭou-bei-bei, at the front]. —— t'н'dliн tou-beigyн dei,
the boy is standing in front of the house.

bei-ƭ-dα (inan. II; bei-dl, dpl; bei-dl- in comp.), external mouth, lip
[unexplained]. Ct. sα'αdl, interior mouth. mнmdei beiƭ-dα,
upper lip; dǫybei beiƭ-dα, lower lip. —— déi-beidl-pн' oudeidα',
I am going to close my mouth, déi-sα'αdl-pн'oudeidα'.

bei-t'ẹi'n-dei, adv., never [bei-, unexplained, w. -t'ẹi'-n- cp. possibly
t'ẹin-dα, to want; -deil]. Cp. 'нn with neg., which is another way
of expressing "never." —— tou bei-t'ẹi'ndei 'αmdeidα', the
house will never be finished. bei-t'ẹi'ndei yнn-'αmdeidα', you
can't do it. bei-t'ẹindei boudldα' (pron. omitted by mistake?),
I don't think I'll get enough to eat.

-bei-yα', postp., from (the region of). —— ƭoudαm-beiyα' 'н̇-tsнn,
I came from the north.

-bei-yα'-tsou, postp., from. —— t'нmtseiyα'-beiyα'tsou 'н̇-tsнn, I
came from the cemetery.

-biн, -biн-m-, bag, in 'н'-biн, paunch; sα'-biн, quiver; biн-m-k'α-e,
bag [Tewa my', bag].

biн-dα, to be foggy [biн-, fog; dα]. —— gyн̇-biн-dα, it is foggy.

biн-gyн (inan. III; biн- in comp.), fog. Cp. biн-dα, to be foggy.
—— biнgyн gyн̇t-bǫy, I saw the fog.

biнm-k'αe (inan. IIª), bag, sack, bladder [biн-m-, bag; k'αe, skin].
Cp. sн'tsoue-biнmk'αe, urinal bladder. —— biнmk'αe gyн̇t-bǫy,
I saw the several bags.

bi̧ꞯ-n (bi̧ꞯ-dɑ, tpl.), large, much [unexplained]. Cp. sɑ-bi̧ꞯn, large; sɑ-p'ꞯn, to be large; 'eidl, large; sɑy-eidl, large; 'ɑe, to be many. —— bi̧ꞯdɑ, tpl. adults, older persons.

bi̧ꞯn-dei, adv., much [bi̧ꞯn; -dei]. —— bi̧ꞯndei bꞯt-pɑtdɑ, you are eating (too) much.

bi̧ꞯ-n-gyꞯ (biꞯndꞯ'dɑ, curs.) to boil intr. Cp. sꞯ̧'-, to boil. —— t'ǫu bi̧ꞯngyꞯ heigɑ, the water has boiled already. t'ǫubi̧ꞯndꞯ' dɑ, the water is boiling.

bou', 1. strong; 2. in Kiowa mythology a little fellow, Bou', who carried a buffalo; so called because he is stout. Cp. bou'-seiseigɑ, flint arrowhead.

bou-, adverbial verb prefix, always, continually. Used with positive only, usually with cursive. Cp. 'ꞯn, always, used with positive and negative. —— 'ꞯ-bou-'ꞯnmꞯ, I am coming all the time. gyꞯ-bo.u-bǫunmɑ, I see him all the time. 'ꞯ-bo.u-dei, I am standing continually. dèi-bou-guɑꞰgoup, I am falling down all the time. dèi-bou-hꞯ'guɑ, I am getting up all the time. gyꞯ-bou-k̇ɑtdɑ, I bite him continually. t'ǫugɑ gyꞯ-bou-bǫunmɑ, a long while ago I saw him all the time (cp. corresponding neg.: hɑ̧n kɑdl hꞯ'gyꞯ gyꞯ-bǫunmɑ, I never used to see him.

bou-'ɑt-ꞯ'-dɑ (inan. IIᵃ; bou-'ɑt-ꞯ', dpl.), tree sp. Described as a small tree which bears red berries [bou-'ɑt-, unexplained; 'ꞯ'dɑ].

-bou in tsei̧n-bou, cow.

-bou- in gyꞯ-bo.u-pǫu-gyꞯ, bullroarer.

-bou- in peigyꞯ-bou-'ǫu, not to think right.

bou-dl (spl.), son, voc. The corresponding nonvocative is covered by 'iꞯ, child, son, daughter —— boudl, 'èim-'ꞯ, son, come here! boudl, bꞯ-'ꞯ, sons (tpl.), come ye here!

bou-dl-, bou-t- in boudl-p'iꞯt-gyꞯ, down in a hole; -bout-dǫu-gyꞯ, under.

-bou-dl-, -bou-t in 'ɑ̧n-bꞯ-boudl-t'ei̧'m, projecting process of ankle; t'ǫu-bout, shin; 'ꞯ'-bou'-gɑ'-t, bough.

bou-dl- in boudl-k'ǫu, to be bay colored.

bou-dl-dɑ, to be sour, spoiled [cp. boudl-kuɑt-gyꞯ, scurf]. —— gyꞯ-boudl-dɑ, it is sour, spoiled.

boudl-kuɑt-gyꞯ (inan. III), scurf, filth on the skin [app. bou-dl-, to be spoiled; kuɑ-t-, unexplained; -gyꞯ].

boudl-k'ǫu to be bay colored [bou-dl-, unexplained; k'ǫu, to be dark]. —— boudlk'ǫu-tsei̧ gyꞯ-bǫu, I saw a bay horse.

bou-k̇ɑe, paper-bread of the Pueblo Indians, acc. to Mr. James Waldo. Mr. Enoch Smoky did not know this word, but considered it intended for bou-k̇ɑ̧-'ei-gɑ, q. v. [unexplained].

bou-k̇ɑ̧-'ei-gɑ (inan. IIᵃ; bou-k̇ɑ̧-'ei, dpl.; bou-k̇ɑ̧-'ei- in comp.), nut of a certain sp. which grew in the former western range of the 'Kiowa [bou-, unexplained; -k̇ɑ̧-, to be greasy].

bou-ƙɑ̨-p'eip (inan. IIᵃ), the tree which bears bou-ƙɑ̨-'eigɑ.

bou-se̜i-n (an. II; bou-se̜i-dɑ, tpl.), buzzard [cp. bo̜ųn-se̜i̜, to stink]. Cp. bou-se̜in-kuɑseit, bird sp.

bouse̜in-kuɑseit (an. II; bouse̜in-kuɑseit̯-dɑ, tpl.), bird sp. [bob-tailed buzzard]. Described as a little larger than a crow, black colored, and bobtailed.

bou'-seisei-gɑ (app. inan. I; bou'-seisei, dpl.), flint arrowhead [bou', strong]. Ct. ƙɑeƙo̜ųgɑ, piece of flint.

bou-t (inan. III), belly [cp. bout̯-da, to be full]. —— bout̯-gyʜ, in the belly. bout̯-to̜ųgyʜ, in the belly; ct. kiʜ-do̜ųgyʜ, in the chest.

bou-t (boudɑ', punct. neg.; bout̯dɑ, curs.; boudlhɑ', curs.; boudldɑ', fut.; boudɑ'dɑ', fut. neg.;' boudl, imp.; pout- in comp.), to eat to fullness [cp. possibly bou-t, belly]. Cp. bout̯-dɑ, to be full; bout̯-houdl, to make eat to fullness. —— dèi-bout, I am full, I have eaten my fill. k'iʜdeidl hɑ̨n dèi-boudɑ', I did not fill up yesterday. miʜn dèi-bout̯dɑ, I am about to get enough. heigɑ dèi-boudlhɑ', I am about to get enough. dèi-boudldɑ', I am going to get enough. bèi-boudl, fill up! béi-boudl, let us eat our fill! poue bèi-boudldɑ', do not eat your fill!.

bou-t, because. —— 'ɑt̯-dou 'ʜgyʜp'ɑ̨e̜gyʜ bout 'ɦ-'iʜ-dei 'ɦ-hei'm-dou, the woman cried all night because her child died. 'ɦ-'ɑdliʜ bout tse̜.ih̜iʜ 'e̜̜i-hei'm-dou, I cried because my dog died. 'ɦ-'ɑdliʜ bout tse̜ih̜i̜ʜ hʜyʜ yɦ̨-'ʜe, I cried because my dog went off somewhere. gyɦ-goup bout 'ɑ̨kɑdl 'ʜdl 'e̜̜i-goup-dou, I hit him because he hit me.

-bou-t in t'o̜ų-bout, shin, see -bou-dl-.

-bou-t in kɑ'-bout, boat, canoe [kɑ'-, referring to swimming or the like].

bout-ɑ̨n, to sound belchingly [to belly sound].—yɦ̨-bout-'ɑ̨'deip, I am gulping up gas.

bout-ʜ'ʜt̯-dɑ (inan. IIᵃ; bout-ʜ'ʜdl, dpl.), growth or lump on abdomen.

bout̯-dɑ, to be full, satiated [bou-t, to eat to fullness; dɑ, to be]. —— 'ɦ-bout̯-dɑ, I am full.

-bout̯-do̜ų-gyʜ, postp., under [bou-t- as in boudl-p'iʜt-gyʜ, down in a hole; -do̜ųgyʜ, under]. —— t'ʜdliʜ tou-bout̯do̜ųgyʜ ʈɑ', the boy is underneath the house.

bout-houdl, to fill up tr., make eat to fullness [to fill kill]. —— gyɦ-bout-houdldɑ', I am going to fill him up. hɑ̨n gyɦ-bout-hougu'ɑdɑ', I am not going to fill him up. k'iʜdeidl hɑ̨n gyɦ-bout-hougu'ɑ, yesterday I did not fill him up. 'ɦ-bout-hou, fill him up, make him eat enough! poue 'ɦ-bout-houdldɑ', do not fill him up!

bout-kyʜe̜-gyʜ, to be bloated [bout, belly; kyʜ-e̜-gyʜ, unexplained]. Cp. p'out-gyʜ, gas in stomach. —— 'ɦ-bout-kyʜe̜-gyʜ, I am flatulent.

bout-k'oup, colic.

\*bout-k'oup (bout-k'oup̣dα, curs.; bout-k'ouyiн, curs.), to have colic [to belly pain]. —— 'н-bout-k'oup̣dα, I have the colic, = 'н-bout-k'ouyiн.

bout-k'oup-'ɑmgyн, to get colic [to get to belly pain]. —— 'н-bout-k'oup-'ɑmgyн, I have the colic, I have gotten the colic.

bout-k'ue-tsǫụn, fish spear [belly puller: k'ue-zǫụn, to pull out, with nominal hardening of z to ts].

bout-poudl (an. II; bout-pout-dα, tpl.), tapeworm [belly worm].

bout-pout-k̃iн [an I; bout-pout-gα, tpl.), glutton [bou-t, belly; pou-t, nominal form of bout, to eat to fullness -k̃iн].

bout-îsǫụ-gα'-t (app. inan. II; bout-îsǫụ-gyн, dpl.), down-feather from belly of bird [belly downfeather]. —— bout-îsǫụ-gyн gyн̀-bǫụ, I saw the featherdown.

bǫụ (bǫụgyн, app. punct.; bǫụmɑ', punct. neg.; bǫụnmɑ̃, curs.; bǫụhн, curs.; bǫụdα', fut.; bǫụmɑ'dα', fut. neg.; bǫụ, imp.; bǫụheidl, infer.; bǫụmɑ'heidl, infer. neg.; as prepound pǫụ-) to see [Tewa mụ̀'ụ̀, to see, pụ̀-wɑ̃̀- as prepound]. Cp. sɑmdα, to look at; sɑm-bǫụ, to see; tɑ'bн, to look at. —— heigα 'ę́i-bǫụgyн gα 'ę́i-tǫụt'нe, as soon as he saw me, he spoke to me. hɑn kɑdl 'ę́im-bǫụmɑ'heidl, they did not see anybody, lit. anybodies. gyн̀-bǫụ, I saw him. hɑn gyн̀-bǫụmɑ', I did not see him. gyн̀-bo.u-bǫụnmɑ, I am seeing him continually. k'yн̥hiн̥gα gyн̀-bǫụnmɑ, I am going to see him tomorrow. k'yн̥hiн̥gα gyн̀-bǫụdα', I shall see him tomorrow. k'yн̥hiн̥gα hɑn gyн̀-bǫụmɑ'dα', I shall not see him tomorrow. poue 'н̀-bǫụdα', don't look at him! 'н̀-bǫụ, see him! 'н̀-bǫụhou', go look at him! heit bн̀-bǫụ, let us see him. heit poue bн̀-bǫụdα', let us not see him. heit poue bн̀-bǫụhoudα', let us not go look at him. k'yн̥hiн̥gα gyн̀-bǫụhoudα', tomorrow I am going to go to see him. 'н̀-pǫụ-bн, I went to see him. tsęi bǫụnmɑ, he is going to look at the horse. hɑ́m-(for hα 'ę́im-)pǫụ-'ɑndα, do you want to see him? 'н̀-pǫụ-'ɑndα, I want to see him. pн'gα gyн̀-bǫụ k̃yн̥hị'н, I saw the one man. t'ǫụgα gyн̀-bǫụnmɑ, I saw him a long time ago. gyн̀-bǫụnmɑ, I am about to see him, I wish to see him.

bǫụ-, referring to light, transparency, in bǫụ-dα, to be light; bǫụ-ę, transparent; bǫụ-gyн, light; bǫụ-'ǫụ-gyн, light; P'iн-bǫụ, prsn. of Mr. Light; etc. [cp. pǫụ-gα't, bead; and possibly bǫụ, to see].

bǫụ- in bǫụ-hǫụ-dα, hat.

-bǫụ' in k̃eidl-bǫụ', knee.

bǫụ-dα, to be light [dα, to be]. —— gyн̀-bǫụ-dα, it is light.

bǫụ-ę, transparent [bǫụ-, referring to transparency; -ei]. Cp. bǫụe-bн-heip̣-gyн, lightning; bǫụe-bн-toubн  bǫụe-bн-toubн-hɑndei-gα, strainer; îsou-bǫụe, rock crystal; etc.

bǫụe-bн-heip̣-gyн (inan. I), lightning [bǫụ-ę, transparent; -bн-, w. -hei-p- cp. bǫụ-hн'beip, to sparkle; -gyн].

bǫүẹ-bн-toubн-hǫndei-gɑ (inan. IIᵃ; bǫүẹ-bн-toubн-hǫndei, dpl.), strainer [bǫүẹ, transparent; -bн-; -toubн- as in toubн-'oup, to strain; hǫndei-gɑ, thing, instrument].

bǫүẹ-'ei-gɑ (inan. IIᵃ; bǫүẹ-'ei, dpl.), plant sp. [transparent fruit]. Described as a daisy-like plant having yellowish flowers and semi-transparent tubers (whence the name of the plant) which were dug and eaten. This plant grows where the topweed does; topweed is a sign for the presence of this plant.

bǫүẹ-ꝁɑ'нꞓ-dɑ (inan. IIᵃ; bǫүẹ-ꝁɑ'нdl, dpl.; bǫүẹ-ꝁɑ'нdl- in comp.), glass tumbler, glass dish [transparent dish].

bǫү-gyн (inan. III), light [bǫү-, referring to light, transparency; -gyн]. Cp. bǫү-'ǫү-gyн, light. —— bǫүgyн gyн̀-'н̨, the light approached.

bǫү-hн'beip, to sparkle [bǫү-, referring to transparency; w. -hн'beip cp. bʼǫүẹ-bн-heiᵽ-gyн, lightning]. —— bǫү-hн'beip, it is sparkling. bǫү-hн'beiᵽ-dei gyн̀-bǫү, I saw the sparkling ones. bǫү-hн'-beip gyн̀ꞓ-bǫү, I saw the tpl. sparkling ones.

bǫү-hẹi'iн (an. II), china doll [bǫү-, referring to transparency; hẹi-'iн, doll].

bǫү-hǫү-dɑ (inan. II; bǫү-hǫү, dpl.; bǫү-hǫү- in comp.), hat [unexplained]. Also ꝁǫn-bǫүhǫүdɑ, hat (ꝁǫn-, stiff).

bǫү'-n (bǫүndɑ', fut.), to bend tr. Cp. bǫү'n-dɑ, to be bent; etc. —— t'ǫүn bǫү'n, he (the scorpion) bent his tail. 'н'dɑ dei-bǫү'n, I bent the stick. 'н'dɑ dei-bǫү'ndɑ', I am going to bend the stick.

bǫү-n-, to be rotten, in bǫүn-gyн, to be rotten; bǫүn-sẹi, to stink [cp. bou-sẹi-n, buzzard].

-bǫү'n, to be bent, in bǫү'n-'ǫ̨'mẹi, to bend; bǫү'n-dɑ, to be bent; bou'n-gyн, to be bent; p'ɑ̨'-bǫү'n, fur crook [Tewa bʉ́-ŋ, to be bent].

bǫү'n-'ǫ̨'mẹi, to bend ['ɑ̨'mẹi, to make].

bǫү'n-dɑ, to be bent [dɑ, to be]. Cp. bǫү'n-gyн, to be bent. —— bǫү'n-dɑ, it is bent (said e. g. of stovepipe with jog in it).

bǫүn-dɑ, to be rotten [dɑ, to be]. Cp. bǫүn-gyн, to be rotten. —— hǫmdei bǫүndɑ'dei gyн̀-bǫү, I saw something rotten. hǫndei gyн̀-bǫүn-dɑ'dei gyн̀ꞓ-bǫү, I saw tpl. rotten things.

bǫү'n-gyн (bǫү'ndeidɑ', fut.), to be bent. Cp. bǫү'n-dɑ, to be bent. —— 'ẹi-bǫү'ngyн, (the stick) is bent or arched. 'н'dɑ 'ẹi-bǫү'n-gyн'-gɑ dei-bǫү, I saw the bent stick. 'н' gyн̀-bǫү'ngyн'-dei gyн̀ꞓ-bǫү, I saw the tpl. bent sticks.

bǫүn-gyн, to be rotten [cp. bǫүn-sẹi, to stink]. Cp. bǫүn-dɑ, to be rotten. —— bǫүngyн, it is rotten.

bǫүn-ꝁɑ, to lie rotten [ꝁɑ, to lie]. —— tsẹihiн̨ bǫүn-ꝁa, the (dead) dog lies rotten.

-bǫүn-mǫẹ, to indicate, in gyн̀-tн'-bǫүnmǫẹ, tendril of watermelon vine, lit. it ripe indicates [w. -bǫү-n- cp. bǫү, to see; -mǫ-ẹ, unexplained].

bǫ ʉn-sęį, to stink [bǫ ʉn-, to be rotten; sęį, to smell intr.].    Cp.
bou-sęį-n, buzzard. —— bǫ ʉn-sęį, it stinks.    'į( н)hɑ gyн̀-bǫ ʉn-
sęį, it stinks here.    kiн 'нn bǫ ʉn-sęį, the meat stinks.
bǫ ʉ-'ǫ ʉ, to be clear, transparent [bǫ ʉ-; 'ǫ ʉ]. —— t'ǫ ʉ 'нn bǫ ʉ'ǫ ʉ,
the water is clear.    t'ǫ ʉ-bǫ ʉ'ǫ ʉ gyн̀-bǫ ʉ, I saw the clear water,
= t'ǫ ʉ 'ɑn bǫ ʉ-'ǫ ʉ-dei gyн̀-bǫ ʉ.
bǫ ʉ'ǫ ʉ-gyн (inan. III), light; said to refer to any artificial or natural
light, also to daylight.    Cp. bǫ ʉ-gyн, light.
-byʉ-'ę, circular, in tou-byʉ'ę, camp circle; 'н'-toubyʉ'ę, circular
opening in forest.

<h2 style="text-align:center">d</h2>

dɑ (dɑ̨'mɑ̨', punct. neg.; dɑ'beip, curs.; dɑ'tɑ', fut.; dɑ'mɑ̨'tɑ', fut.
neg.; dɑ', dɑ'dei, -dɑ'bei, imp.; dɑ'męį', infer.; dɑ̨'mɑ'heidl, infer.
neg.), 1. to be (frequent as verb denoting existence, condition, and
as copula, but position is denoted by ƙɑ, dei, bн, etc.; also frequent
as adj. postpound); 2. to be born. [Tewa ná, to be]. —— 1. nɑ̨
'н̀-dɑ, it is I, I am the one.    nɑ̨ 'èi-dɑ, we are the ones.    'нm tsęį
gyн́-dɑ, it is your horse.    'нm tsęį bá-dɑ̀, it is the horse of ye
tpl.    tou-hęį dɑ, it is not a house.    ƙyн̨hį'н p'нę tou-hęį dɑ, the
man has no house.    p'нę tou-hęį 'н̀-dɑ, I have no house.    yiн
nèį-pн'bi-dɑ, I have two brothers.    But néį-pн'bi-ƙɑ, they are
my two brothers.    ƙyнtнeƙiн dɑ'tɑ, he will be a chief.    hɑn ƙyнtнeƙiн dɑ̨'mɑ', he was not chief.    ƙyнtнeƙiн dɑ̨'męį, he was a
chief (infer.).    'нm ƙyнtнeƙiн 'ęįm-dɑ'dei, you be a chief!    poue
bèi-ƙyнtнeƙiн-'ɑmdɑ', don't you be a chief!    poue 'нm 'èįm-
ƙyнtнeƙiн-dɑ̨'mɑ̨'tɑ', you don't want to be a chief.    hн'deidl dɑ,
who did it?    nɑ̨ 'н̀-dɑ, I did it (ans.).    'ɑt'нtнę-hęį gyн̀-dɑ, there
is no salt.    mɑ̨'tsнę-hęį gyн̀-dɑ, there is no paper.    piн-hęį
gyн̀-dɑ, there is nothing to eat.    piн-hęį yá-dɑ, I haven't anything to eat on the place.    piн-hęį 'н̀-dɑ, I haven't eaten yet.
piн-hęį gyн̀-dɑ̨'męį', there was nothing to eat (infer.).    tɑ'dei hęįgyн
dɑ̨'męį' gɑ hн'ouei sɑt tsнnheidl, I heard that he was away for a
long time and that he came back after a long time just recently.
2. 'н̀-dɑ, I was born.    hн'gyн 'èįm-dɑ, where were you born?
syнn 'н́-dɑ, she gave birth to a baby.    mн'yiн į'н-p̄ɑ'gyн 'н́-dɑ,
the woman gave birth to a child.    k'iнdeidl syнn 'éį-dɑ, my child
was born yesterday.    heidɑ hɑn syнn 'н́-dɑ̨'mɑ̨', the child is not
born yet.    k'yнhįнgɑ syнn 'н́-dɑ'tɑ' the child is going to be
born to-morrow.    k'yнhįнgɑ hɑn syнn 'н́-dɑ̨'mɑ̨'tɑ', the child
will not be born to-morrow.    Teihн̨'nęį-dɑmgyн 'н̀-dɑ, I was born
in Texas.    hɑn 'н̀-dɑ̨'mɑ̨' Teihн̨'nęį-dɑmgyн, I was not born in
Texas.    Teihн̨'nei-gyн 'н̀-dɑ̨'męį', they say that I was born
in Texas.    hɑn Teihн̨'nei-dɑmgyн 'н̀-dɑ̨'mɑ̨'heidl, they say that
I was not born in Texas.    miнn syнn 'н́-dɑ'beip, the child is

about to be born.  heigɑ syн̥ɴ 'н̓-dɑ, the child is already born.
'ę̀įm-k'ou-dɑ, be born now!  'ę̀įm-dɑ, you are born.  hн̥yн'
'ę̀įm-dɑ, what is wrong (with you)?  But hн̥yн' 'ę̀įm-bн, where
are you?  mн̥'yįн̥ 'ǫndɑ' syн̥'dɑ, dɑ, the woman has borne five
children.

dɑ-, dɑ'-, medicine, orenda, in dɑ-e, medicine; Dɑ'-ꝁiн, the Great
  Spirit; dɑ'-k'iн, Sunday; dɑ'-tsнe, to pray; etc. [cp. possibly dɑ-,
  dɑ'-, to sing].

dɑ-, dɑ'-, to sing, in dɑ'-gyн, song; dɑ'-ꝁyн̥hį'н̥, singer; dɑ'-mн̥yįн̥
  singing woman; dɑ'-p̃н'egɑ, to sing; dɑ'-dɑ, to sing [cp. possibly
  dɑ-, dɑ'-, medicine].

dɑ-, dɑ'-, to kill, in 'ɑdl-dɑ'-kuɑngyн, scalp dance; dɑ-'н̥, to come
  to kill; dɑ-'ǫ̃'mę̣i, to make kill; dɑ'-dǫyn, to hunt to kill; dɑ'-ꝁiн,
  killer; sę̣įm-dɑ'ꝁiн, murderer; tsę̣įnbou-dɑ'ꝁiн, killer (in a slaugh-
  terhouse) [Tewa nɑ̨́-ŋ, to strike].

dɑ- in dɑ-'н̓t-dɑ bucket.  Cp. ꝁɑ-'н̓t-dɑ, dish.

-dɑ, noun, adj. and postp. postfix [cp. -dн, noun postfix].  Cp.
  'н̥'-dɑ, wood; -t̃н̓t-dɑ, between.

dɑ-'ǫ̃'mę̣i, to make kill [dɑ-, to kill].  —— 'oueidei gɑ-dɑ-'ǫ̃'dɑ', I
  am going to have him kill them.

dɑ'н̥dl-'н̥'-dɑ (inan. IIª; dɑ'н̥dl-'н̥', dpl.), crook for hanging kettle
  over fire [kettle stick].

dɑ'н̥dl-kuɑ (an. II; dɑ'н̥dl-kuɑ-gɑ, tpl.), bird sp. [bucket hitter,
  since it makes a sound like tapping a bucket].  Described as a
  little larger than a mockingbird.

dɑ-'н̓t-dɑ (inan. IIª; dɑ-'н̥dl, dpl.; dɑ-'н̥dl- in comp.), bucket,
  kettle, pot [dɑ-, unexplained; 'н-dl-, 'н-t-, round; -dɑ; cp.
  ꝁɑ-'н̓t-dɑ, dish].  Cp. tsoue-dɑ'н̓tdɑ, coffee pot.  —— dɑ'н̓tdɑ
  déi-bǫy, I saw the bucket.  hǫndei 'ɑ̓-dɑ'н̥dl-tseidl, somebody
  had a kettle stake (said of the spots on the moon).  déi-dɑ'н̥dl-
  tseidɑ', I am going to set the kettle.

dɑ-'н̥, to come to kill ['н̥, to come].  —— 'н̓-dɑ-'н̥, I have come to
  kill him, ='н-'н̥ gyн̓-houdldɑ'-dou, I have come in order to kill
  him.  hǫn 'н̓-dɑ-'н̥mǫ', I have not come to kill him, =hǫn
  gyн̓-houdldɑ'-dou hǫn 'н̓-'н̥'mǫ'.

dɑ-e (inan. III), medicine, orenda [dɑ- as in Dɑ'-ꝁiн, the Great
  Spirit, lit. orenda man; -ei].  —— dɑe gyн̓t-bǫy, I saw the
  medicine.

dɑe-'ǫm-ꝁiн (an. I), medicine-man, doctor [cure man].

dɑe-'ǫ̃'mę̣i, to cure, doctor [to medicine-fix].  —— gyн̓-dɑe-ǫ̃'mę̣i,
  I cured him.

dɑ-e-gɑ (dɑedeidɑ', fut.), to strip [unexplained].  —— déi-'н̥'p'ɑdl-
  dɑedeidɑ', I am going to pull the blade of the feather from the
  quill.  heigɑ déi-'н̥'p'ɑdl-dɑegɑ, I stripped the feather-blade off.

dɑ'-, medicine, see dɑ-.

dɑ'-, to sing, see dɑ-.

dɑ'dɑ (dɑ'dɑ'gu'ɑ, punct. neg.; dɑ'dɑ, imp.), to sing. Cp. dɑ'-p̄ʜ'egɑ, to sing; etc.; pɑdl-dou', to be singing and drumming. —— k'yꞑhįꞑgɑ dèi-dɑ'dɑ, I was singing yesterday. dèi-dɑ'dɑ, I am singing. 'ęįhɑ dèi-dɑ'dɑ, I am singing here or now (two meanings). heigɑ dèi-dɑ'dɑ, I am singing already. hꞕn dèi-dɑ'dɑ'gu'ɑ, I am not singing. dèi-yɴt̀bʜhei-dɑ'dɑ, I am singing a Warrior Song.

dɑ'-gyʜ (app. inan. III), song [dɑ-, to sing; -kyʜ]. —— hʜ'oudei dɑ'gyʜ 'ʜ-t̂ɑ, I heard several songs.

Dɑ'-k̂iʜ (an. I), the Great Spirit, God [orenda man].

dɑ'-k̂iʜ (an. I; s. better dɑ'-k̂yꞑhį'ʜ; dɑ'-gɑ, tpl.), singer; medicine man who belongs to the singing class [sing man].

dɑ'-k̂iʜ (an. I), killer [kill man].

Dɑ'k̂iʜ-'eidl (an. I), the Great Spirit, God [great orenda man, imitating Eng. "Great Spirit," Ojibway Gi'tci-manitō, etc.].

dɑ'-k'iʜ, Sunday [orenda day, God day]. Cp. dɑ'k'iʜ-tou, church; dɑ'k'iʜ-syꞑngyʜ, Saturday, lit. little Sunday; etc.].

dɑ'k'iʜ-hꞕ'k̂oudlp'ʜ-'gɑ, church-bell [Sunday bell].

dɑ'k'iʜ-k̂įꞑhįꞑ, Monday [after Sunday: -k̂yꞑhįꞑ, after].

dɑ'k'iʜ-syꞑn-gyʜ, Saturday [on little Sunday: syꞑn, small; -gyʜ].

dɑ'k'i(ʜ)-tou (inan. I), church [Sunday house]. Ct. dɑ'-tou, singing hall. —— dɑ'k'iʜ-tou'e, in the church, church interior, church room.

dɑ'-mꞑyįꞑ (an. I), singing woman, medicine woman [mꞑyįꞑ, woman].

dɑ'-p̄ʜ'egɑ (dɑ'-p̄ʜ'egɑ', punct. neg.; dɑ'-p̄ʜ'egoup, curs.; dɑ'-p̄ʜ'e-deidɑ', fut.; dɑ'-p̄ʜ'egɑ'dɑ', fut. neg.), to sing [dɑ'- as in dɑ'dɑ, to sing; p̄ʜ'egɑ]. Cp. dɑ'-p̄ʜ'egyʜ, a song. —— dʜ dèi-dɑ'p̄ʜ'-edeidɑ', I am going to sing. hꞕn dʜ dèi-dɑ'p̄ʜ'egɑ'dɑ', I am not going to sing. bèi-dɑ'p̄ʜ'edei, you sing! poue bèi-dɑ'p̄ʜ'edeidɑ', don't sing! (heit̀) béi-dɑ'p̄ʜ'edei, let us dpl. incl. sing! (heit̀) poue béi-dɑ'p̄ʜ'edeidɑ, let us dpl. incl. not sing! t̂ʜ'gyʜ 'ęįm-dɑ'p̄ʜ'egɑ, that is good singing. 'ęįm-dɑ'p̄ʜ'egɑ'-'ęį 'ʜ-tsʜn, they had commenced to sing when I got there. But 'ęįm-dɑ'dɑ'-'ęį 'ʜ-tsʜn, I came when they were singing. k̂yꞑhį'ʜ heigɑ miʜn 'èįm-dɑ'p̄ʜ'egoup̀-dei gyʜ-bọụ, I saw the the man who was about to sing. k'yꞑhį'ʜgɑ dèi-dʜ'p̄ʜ'egɑ, I sang yesterday. hꞕn k'yꞑhį'ʜgɑ dèi-dɑp̄ʜ'egɑ', I did not sing yesterday. heigɑ miʜn dèi-dɑ'p̄ʜ'egoup, I am about to sing. heigɑ miʜn hꞕn dèi-dɑ'p̄ʜ'-egɑ', I am not about to sing. k̂yꞑhį'ʜ hꞕn 'ꞑn 'èįm-dɑ'p̄ʜ'egɑ-dei gyʜ-bọụ, I saw the man who never sings. déi-tọụbʜ-dɑ'p̄ʜ'edeida', I am going to play the flute, lit. I me flute sing will.

dɑ'-p̄ʜ'e-gyʜ (app. inan. III), a song, a singing.

dɑ'-p'ʜt̀gyʜ (dɑ'-p'ʜtgɑ', punct. neg.; dɑ'-p'ʜ'yʜ, curs.; dɑ'-p'ʜt̀-deit̂ɑ', fut.; dɑ'-p'ʜtgɑt̂ɑ', fut. neg.; dɑ'-p'ʜtdei, imp.), to cease to

sing [p‘ʜɨgyʜ, to cease]. —— ꝁyꞧhiꞧ’ꞧn-dɑ’p‘ʜɨgyʜ, the man
quit singing. miʜn ’ꞧn-dɑ’p‘ʜ’yʜ, he is about to quit singing.
hɑn ’ʜn-dɑ’p‘ʜɨgɑ’dɑ’, he will not quit singing. yꞧn-dɑ’p‘ʜɨdei,
you stop singing! gyʜɨt-dɑ’p‘ʜɨdei, let us quit singing; cp.
gyʜɨt-sɑ’dei-p‘ʜɨdei, let us quit working.

dɑ’-tou (inan. I), singing hall, singing house. Ct. dɑ’k‘iʜ-tou,
dɑ’tǫu-tou, church building.

dɑ’tǫu-kuɑt (app. inan. III) bible [preaching book]. —— dɑ’tǫu-kuat
gyʜ-da, it is the preaching book.

dɑ’tǫu-tou (inan. I), church [preaching house].

dɑ’-t‘ɛindɑ (dɑ’-t‘ɛindɑ’ɨɑ’, fut.), to want to kill [t‘ɛin-dɑ, to desire].
—— ’ɛi-dɑ’-t‘ɛindɑ’ɨɑ’ gɑ heigɑ gyʜ-’oubʜ-houdldɑ’, I could kill
him if I wanted to. ’ɛi-dɑ’-t‘ɛindɑ nɛi hʜ’-tsou ’-houdldɑ’, I could
not kill him if I wanted to.

dɑ’-tsʜe (dɑ’-tsʜyɑ’, punct. neg.; dɑ’-tsʜɨdɑ, curs.; dɑ’-tsʜedɑ’, fut.;
dɑ’-tsʜyɑ’dɑ’, fut. neg.; dɑ’-tsʜe, imp.), to pray [to orenda ask].
—— k‘yꞧhi’ꞧgɑ dèi-dɑ’tsʜedɑ’, tomorrow I am going to pray.
k‘ʜdeidl dèi-dʜ’tsʜe, I prayed yesterday. k‘iʜdeidl hɑn dèi-
dɑ’tsʜyɑ’, yesterday I did not pray. heigɑ dèi-dɑ’tsʜɨdɑ, I am
praying right now. hɑn dèi-dɑ’tsʜyɑ’, I am not praying now.
miʜn dèi-dɑ’tsʜɨdɑ, I am about to pray. hɑn dèi-dɑ’tsʜyɑ’dɑ’, I
am not going to pray. ’ꞧm bèi-dɑ’tsʜe, you pray! poue bèi-
dɑ’tsʜedɑ’, don’t pray! (heit) béi-dɑ’tsʜe, let us dpl. incl. pray!
(heit) poue béi-dɑ’tsʜedɑ’, let us dpl. incl. not pray!

dɑ-m (app. inan. IIᵃ), earth, ground, floor, country, world, place
[Tewa nǫ-ŋ, earth, ground, country]. Also as postpound of loc.
force e. g. in p‘iʜ-dɑm, fireplace; ɨou-dɑm-bei, in the north; etc.
—— dɑmgyʜ ’èi-ɨɑ’, we are living on earth. dɑm-’ɑ’ dèi-ɨsʜndei-
dɑ’, I am going to run a footrace, lit. on the ground.

dɑm-’ɑn-t‘ǫu, ocean [dɑm, earth; -’ɑn-, unexplained; t‘ǫu, water].

dɑm-dǫugyʜ-tou’e (inan. I), cellar [beneath floor room].

dɑm-guɑdl, red clay [red earth]. Also called tsɛin-guɑdl, red mud.

*dɑ-m-gyʜ, to shoot up, implied in dɑmgyʜ-dɑ, to be shot up.

dɑmgyʜ-dɑ, to be shot up [dɑ-m-gyʜ-, unexplained; dɑ, to be].
—— tei k‘oubʜ dɑ-dɑmgyʜ-dɑ, his body is all shot up.

dɑm-ku’ɑ (an. II; dɑm-ku’ɑ-gɑ, tpl.), digging stick; evidently also
spade, shovel, hoe [earth hitter: gou-p, to hit, peck]. Cp. dɑmku’ɑ-
syʜn, hoe; peidei-dɑmku’ɑ, spade, shovel.

dɑmku’ɑ-syʜn, hoe [small digging stick].

dɑm-ꝁɑ’dɑ (inan. II; dɑm-ꝁɑ’-n, dpl.), clod [app. ꝁɑ-n, stiff].

dɑm-poudl (an. II; dɑm-pouɨ-dɑ, tpl.), angleworm, earthworm.

dɑm-sʜ’bɑ (inan. IIᵃ; dɑm-sʜ, dpl.), plow [earth-burster: sʜ . . . , to
burst tr.].

dɑm-t‘ʜdl (an. II; dɑm-t‘ʜɨ-dɑ, tpl.), toad (frog?) sp. [ground bur-
rower: t‘ʜ . . . , to pierce, make hole in].

dǫ-n (inan. II^a), shoulder blade.  Cp. k‘ɑ’-t‘ǫu̯-, shoulder.

dн, emphatic or hortative particle, just. —— heit bн̀t-’ɑe-’ɑm nǫ dн hǫn ’èim-t‘нhouguɑdɑ’ nǫ, do it again and see if I don’t whip you.  heigɑ houdldei dн (’нdl) ’н-bн̂’ĩɑ’, I will go after a while (dн can be omitted, but ’нdl cannot be used except after dн).  dн́ ’н̀-dн̯’m, you must tire him.  dн bн́-dн̯’m, let’s tire him!  dн dèi-dɑ’p̄н’edeidɑ’, I am going to sing.  hǫn dн dèi-dɑ’p̄н’egɑ’dɑ’, I am not going to tire him.  gyн-dн̯’mdɑ’, I am going to tire him; but dн gyн̀-dн̯’mdɑ’, I will make him tired (the emphatic force of dн in this sentence was clearly explained).  k‘yн̥hi̯’н̥gɑ dн ’èim-’н̥, come tomorrow!

-dн, noun and adv. postfix, in k‘iн-dн, day; sн’dн, winter; houdl-dн, shirt; ’нdl-dн-, backward; etc. [cp. -dɑ, noun and adj. postfix].

-dн, intr. verb postfix, in sнdl-dн, to be tanned (with sun); t‘н̥’-dн’-, wet (cp. t‘н̥’-hou-p, moist).

dн-dl-, dн-t-, referring to standing up, in dнdl-ĩн’-dou’, to raise oneself up; possibly in k̄ɑ’dнdl, wheel; p‘iн-dн̀t-gyн, ridged; sн̀t-dнdl-ĩɑ’-dou’, to stand up straight with the heat (ss.); sн̀t-dнdl-t‘ɑ’-dou’, to stand up straight with the heat (tpls.); sei̯n-p‘ɑ’-dнdl, catfish [cp. possibly dei, to stand].

dнdl-ĩн’-dou’, to raise oneself up higher or straighter; to come to the surface of the water (ss.).  Tpls. correspondent dнdl-t‘н’-dou’. [dнdl-, up; ĩн’-, t‘н’-, prepound form of hн’, to stand up; dou’.]  Cp. sн̀t-dнdl-ĩн’-dou’, to stand up straight with the heat.

dнdl-t‘н’-dou’, to raise selves up higher or straighter; to come to the surface of the water. (tpls.).  Ss. correspondent dнdl-ĩн’-dou’ [for etym. see dнdl-ĩн’-dou’].

dн-t, standing up, see dн-dl-.

dн̯’-m (dн̯’mǫ’, punct. neg.; dн̯’mǫ, curs.; dн̯’mdɑ’, fut.; dн̯’mǫ’dɑ’, fut. neg.; dн̯’m, imp.), to tire tr. [cp. dн̥m-gyн, to be tired]. —— gyн̀-dн̯’m, I tired him.  hǫn gyн̀-dн̯’mǫ’, I did not tire him.  gyн̀-dн̯’mdɑ’, I am going to make him tired.  hǫn gyн̀-dн̯’mǫ’dɑ’, I shall not tire him.  poue ’н̀-dн̯’mdɑ’, don’t tire him (out)!  ’н̀-dн̯’m, tire him!  bн́-dн̯’m, let’s tire him.  tsei̯ gyн̀-dн̯’m, I worked my horse down.

dн̥m-gyн (dн̥mgɑ’, punct. neg.; dн̥mdeiĩɑ’, fut.; dн̥mgɑ’ĩɑ’, fut. neg.; dн̥mdei, imp.; dн̥mdeiheidl, infer.), to be tired [cp. dн̯’m, to tire tr.].  Cp. dн̥mgyн-dɑ, to be tired. —— ’н̀-dн̥mgyн, I am tired.  pн̥hi̯н ’н̀-dн̥mgyн, I’m sure I’ll be tired.  ’н̀-koudou-dн̥mgyн, I am very tired.  heigɑ dн̥mdeiheidl, he is about to die, so I heard.  hǫn ’н̀-dн̥mgɑ’ĩɑ’, I shall not be tired.  ’èim-dн̥mdei, be tired!  hǫn ’èim-dн̥mgɑ’ nǫ nǫ ’èim-guɑdɑ’, if you don’t get tired, I’ll hit you.

dн̥mgyн-dɑ, to be tired [dɑ, to be]. —— ’н̀-dн̥mgyн-dɑ, I am tired.  hǫn ’н̀-dн̥mgyн-dǫ’mǫ’, I am not tired.  heigɑ ’н̀-dн̥mgyн-dɑ’-’ei̯

'èi-tsḥn, I was tired already when we arrived. tsḥnɩ̈ɑ' heigɑ
'ḥ-dḥmgyн-dɑ'ɩ̈ɑ', I shall be tired when he arrives. poue 'èịm-
dḥmgyн-dɑ'ɩ̈ɑ', gyḥ-k̄ɑ'dei, don't be tired, it is not good (i. e. is
unpleasant to be tired). tseiguɑn dḥmgyн-dɑ'dei gyḥ-bǫụ, I saw
the tired dog. tseiguɑdɑ 'èi-dḥmgyн-dɑ'gɑ déi-bǫụ, I saw the tpl.
tired dogs.

dei (deigɑ', punct. neg.; deidei, curs.(?); deiyɑ', curs.(?); deidɑ',
fut.; deigɑ'ɩ̈ɑ', fut. neg.; deidei', infer.), to stand (spl.) [cp. possibly dн-dl-, dн-t-, standing up; Tewa dè-gị̈-n-dì-, erect, standing].
—— 'ḥ-dei, I am standing. tou dei, the house is standing. hǫn
'ḥ-deigɑ', I am not standing. 'ḥ-bou-dei, I am standing all the
time. 'ḥ-deidei', they say I was standing. k'yḥhị'ḥgɑ 'ḥ-deidɑ',
I shall be standing tomorrow. hǫn 'ḥ-deigɑ'ɩ̈ɑ', I shall not be
standing. miнn 'ḥ-deidei, I am about to be standing. poue
'èịm-deidɑ', don't be standing! heiɩ̈ nǫ gɑ 'ḥm bḥ-deidei, let
you and I be standing. 'èi-deidei, the cattle (all) are standing.
tsęị dei, the horse is standing. 'ɑ'gɑ tou'e 'ḥ-deiyɑ'-dei-'ịḥ
'ḥ-heibeiɩ̈ɑ', I am going in where the people are standing in the
room. But 'ɑ'gɑ tou'e dei-dei-'ịḥ 'ḥ-heibeiɩ̈ɑ', I am going in
where the man is standing in the room (it was stated that -deiyɑ-
can not be used in the s.). k̄yḥhị'ḥ dei-dei gyḥ-bǫụhoudɑ', I am
going over to see the man who is standing. k̄yḥhyoup 'ḥ-dei-gɑ
dèi-bǫụhoudɑ', I am going over to see the tpl. men who are standing.
nǫ-'ɑk̄oubei mḥ'youp 'ḥ-deiyɑ', the women were standing all
about me. 'ǫ'gɑpịḥgɑ pн'gyнp deiyɑ', the buffaloes are all
over the prairie. 'ǫ'gɑpịḥgɑ pн'gyнp 'èi-deidei', the buffaloes
are all over the prairie (infer.).

-dei, 1. noun postfix; -gɑ, -dou-p, -gou-p, tpl. correspondents; 2.
forming pronouns from dem. stems and from adverbs of place;
-gɑ, tpl. correspondent; 3. derivative postfix, forming proper
names from nouns; -gɑ, tpl. correspondent; 4. postfixed to nouns
and certain pronouns to emphasize possessive case; -gɑ, tpl. correspondent; 5. locative postposition on nouns, at; 6. adverbial
postfix, cp. -gɑ; 7. participial verb postfix; -gɑ, tpl. correspondent;
8. subordinating postfix on verbs, when, since [cp. -dei-dl, pron.
and adv. postfix]. —— 1. ɩ̈ɑ'-dei, ear, fr. ɩ̈ɑ'-, to hear; ɩ̈ɑ'-gɑ,
tpl. 2. 'ouei-dei that one; 'ouei-gɑ, tpl., from 'oue, there.
kɑ'-dei, the other one; kɑ'-gɑ, tpl. 3. 'ɑ'dɑ'-dei, prsn., from
'ɑ'dɑ, island. 4. 'H'deik̄iн-dei Р̈ɑ', "Medicine-bag-man's Creek."
'ǫ'kɑ-dei tsęị (less clearly 'ǫ'gɑ tsęị), his own horse. 'ǫ'gɑ-dei
k̄yḥhyoup gɑ mḥ'youp, his own men and women. 5. р̈ɑ'-dei 'èi-ɩ̈ɑ',
they tpl. (the kingfishers) stay along the river. 'ɑ'pịḥdɑ р̈ɑ'-dei
'èi-ɩ̈ɑ', they tpl. (the fishes) stay in the river. nǫ k'ougyнр̣-dei,
on my body. 6. p'iн-dei (or p'iн) 'ḥ-bḥnmн, I am going downstream. biнn-dei bнɩ̈-pɑɩ̈dɑ, you are eating (too) much (biнn, to

be much). 7. tsei̯hi̯ṇ pei-k̄α-dei gyн̇-bou̯, I saw the dead dog;
tsei̯hi̯ṇ 'è̯i-pei-k̄α-dei nè̯in-bou̯, I saw the d. dead dogs; tsei̯hyoup
è̯i-pei-k̄uαdl-gα déi-bou̯, I saw the tpl. dead dogs. Cp. tsei̯hi̯ṇ
gyн̇-bou̯ nǫ pei-k̄α, I saw the dead dog, another common way of
rendering Eng. relative clause construction. 'oueidei da tsei̯hi̯ṇ
'ṇm k̄yṇhi̯'ṇ hᾱ'gyн-dei, that is the dog that the man got. 'oueigα
'èi-dα tsei̯hyoup 'ṇm k̄yṇhi̯'ṇ 'éi-hᾱ'gyн-gα, those are the tpl. dogs
that the man got. t̂нp̀ pei̯n-dᾱ'-dei gyн̇-bou̯, I saw the butchered
antelope. t̂нp 'è̯i-pei̯n-dᾱ'-dei nè̯in-bou̯, I saw the d. butchered
antelopes. t̂ᾱ'seidl 'èi-pei̯n-dᾱ'-gα déi-bou̯, I saw the tpl. butchered
antelopes. k̄yṇhi̯'ṇ gyн̇-sᾱ'deidᾱ'yiн-dei gyн̇-bou̯, I saw the man
who had been working. 'è̯im-hout̄dα-dei, I saw him who killed
them tpl., I saw the killer; 'é̯in-hout̄dα-dei nè̯in-bou̯, I saw them
d. who killed them tpl., I saw the d. killers. 'é̯im-hout̄dα-gα
dèi-bou̯, I saw them tpl. who killed them tpl., I saw the tpl.
killers. 8. heigα 'è̯i-bou̯-dei heigṇn (for heigα 'ṇn) 'é̯i-tou̯t'нt̄dα,
he spoke to me whenever he saw me. heigα 'é̯i-goup-dei 'oue hǫn
kαdl gyн̇-tou̯t'н'guα, I have not spoken to him since he hit me.
heigα gα 'н̇-goup-dei 'oue hǫn kαdl dèi-tou̯t'н'guα, I have not
spoken to them since they hit me.

-dei in k̄iн-dei, to have a husband; t'н'-dei, to have a wife.

-dei-dl, noun, pronoun and adverb postfix, in t̂нm-deidl, mountain-
lion; hн'-deidl, who? somebody; k̄ǫ'-deidl, badly; k'iн-deidl,
yesterday; etc. [-dei; -dl].

-dei-p, adv. postfix, in p̄iн-dei-p, from waist down [-dei-; -p].

dei-yα', possibly a tpl. correspondent of dei, to stand, q. v.

dei̯-, prepound referring to sleep, in dei̯-houdldн, nightshirt; dei̯-mǫ,
to go to sleep; dei̯-hei̯-hei̯'m, to go to sleep; dei̯-k̄α, to lie asleep;
etc. [cp. possibly t'ei̯-dei-p, to be asleep].

dei̯- in dei̯n-sнdl, to be peppery [cp. possibly dei̯-n, tongue].

-dei̯-gα in 'нe-dei̯-ga, leaf.

dei̯-hei̯'m, to go to sleep, to fall asleep [to sleep die]. —— 'н̇-dei̯-
hei̯'m, I went to sleep. k'yṇhi̯нgα 'н̇-dei̯-he̯.imн, tomorrow I am
going to go to sleep, =k'yṇhi̯нgα 'н̇-dei̯-hi̯'нt̄α'. hǫm-dei̯-hei̯mн,
are you sleepy? (hǫm- for hα 'è̯im-). hǫ'nei̯, hǫn 'н̇-dei̯-hei̯mǫ',
no, I am not sleepy (ans.). 'н̇-dei̯-hei̯'m, I went to sleep. 'н̇-
k'ou-dei̯hi̯нt̄α', I am going to go to sleep. 'н̇-dei̯-hei̯mн I am
getting sleepy now.

dei̯-houdl-dн (inan. III), nightshirt [sleeping shirt].

dei̯-k̄α, to lie asleep [to sleep lie]. Tpl. correspondent: dei̯-k̄uαdl.
—— 'н̇-dei̯-k̄α, I am lying asleep. hǫn 'н̇-dei̯-tsougα', I am not
lying asleep, =hǫn 'н̇dei̯-k̄α'gα'. 'н̇-bou-dei̯-k̄α, I am sleeping all
the time. poue 'è̯im-dei̯-tsout̄α', don't lie asleep (one cannot say:
*poue 'ei̯m-dei̯-k̄α't̄α'). heit̄ bн̇-dei̯-tsoudei, let us dpl. incl. lie
asleep! k'iнdeidl 'н̇-dei̯-k̄α, I lay asleep yesterday (one cannot

say: *k'ından'ı'ı-deị-tsou). k'ından'ı hąn 'ṅ-tsougα', I did not lie asleep yesterday. hąn 'ṅ-deị-tsọųgα'îα, I am not going to be lying asleep. 'è̱ịm-deị-tsoudei, be lying asleep! mṅ-deị-tsoudei, ye d. be lying asleep! deị-k̄α, he is lying asleep, he is sleeping.

deị-k̄oup, to put several to sleep, with refl. to spend night when on journey [k̄ou-p, to lay several]. So. correspondent is deị-t̄seip.
—— déi-deị-k̄oup, I put them tpl. to sleep. hąn déi-deị-k̄uαgu'α, I did not put them tpl. to sleep. mihn déi-deị-k̄uαp̄dα, I am about to put them tpl. to sleep. déi-bou-deị-k̄uαp̄dα, I put them tpl. to sleep all the time. k'yṉhịηgα déi-deị-k̄uαdα', tomorrow I am going to put them tpl. to sleep. k'yṉhịηgα hąn dèi-deị-k̄uαgu'α-dα', I shall not put them to sleep. béi-deị-k̄uα, put them tpl. to sleep!

deị-k̄uαdl, several lie asleep. [k̄uα-dl, several lie]. Ss. correspondent is deị-k̄α. —— 'èi-bou-deị-k̄uαdl, we tpl. excl. are lying asleep all the time. k'ında'ıdl 'èi-deị-k̄uαdl, we tpl. excl. were lying asleep yesterday. k'ındadl hąn 'èi-deị-koup̄gα', yesterday we tpl. excl. were not lying asleep. k'yṉhịηgα 'èi-deị-k̄uαdldα' (or 'èi-deị-koup̄îα'), tomorrow we tpl. excl. will not lie asleep. k'yṉhịηgα hąn 'èi-deị-koup̄gα'îα', tomorrow we tpl. excl. will not be lying asleep. poue bṅ-deị-koup̄îα', don't ye tpl. be asleep! heiŧ bṅ-deị-k̄oup̄dei, let us tpl. be lying asleep! bṅ-deị-koup̄dei, yet pl. be lying asleep!

deị-mą, to go to sleep, app. lit. to lie down and go to sleep [mą, to lie down]. Cp. deị-k̄α, to lie asleep. —— bèi-deị-mą, go to sleep! dèi-deị-mą'dα', I am going to go to sleep.

deịm-guαdl (an. II; deịm-guαŧdα, tpl.), bird sp. [red breast].

deị-m-gyн (inan. III; deị-m- in comp.), chest (anat.). —— deịm-dọųgyн, inside my chest.

deịm-t'ọų (inan. I; deịm-t'ọų in comp.), breastbone [breastbone].
—— 'oueidei deịm-t'ọų gyṅ-bọų, I saw his breastbone.

deị-n (an. II; deị-dα, tpl.), tongue.

deịn-αŧ-îǫ'ŧ'ǫ'nei (an. II; deịn-αŧ-îǫŧ'ǫ'nou-p, tpl.), mussel [deị-n-, tongue; -αŧ-, unexplained; îǫ'ŧ'ąn, spoon; -ei]. Described as a fresh-water bivalve having yellowish shells about 5 inches long. The animal projects at times from the gaping shell like a tongue. The shells were formerly used as spoons.

deịnαŧîǫ'ŧ'ǫ'neị-'eidl (an. II; deịnαŧîǫ'ŧ'ǫ'neị-'eiŧ-dα, tpl.), conch shell. Identified from specimen. Apparently this name is applied to αbαlone also [large mussel].

deị-pн'dlei', to be sleepy [deị-, referring to sleep; -pн'-dl-ei' as in t'ọų-pн'dlei', to be thirsty]. —— 'ṅ-deị-pн'dlei', I am sleepy.

deị-sнdl, 1. to be peppery; 2. to be sour [w. deị- cp. possibly deị-n, tongue]. Cp. -'н-'ǫ'-, sour (?). —— gyṅ-deịsнdl, it is peppery (said e. g. of chile).

dẹịsʜdl-'ʜ'dα (inan. IIᵃ; dẹịsʜdl-'ʜ', dpl.), plant sp. [peppery plant]. Described as a kind of weed which sticks to one's feet when one steps on it barefooted.

dẹịsʜdl-t'ọụ, vinegar [sour water].

dẹị-tou'e (inan. I), sleeping room.

dẹị-t͡seip, to put one to sleep [t͡sei-p, to put one]. Tplo. correspondent is dẹị-k͡oup. —— gyʜ-dẹị-t͡seip, I put him to sleep. hǫn gyʜ-dẹị-t͡sougu'α, I did not put him to sleep. miʜn heigα gyʜ-dẹị-t͡soup̀dα', I am about to put him to sleep. gyʜ-bou-t͡soup̀da, I put him to sleep all the time. poue 'ʜ-dẹị-t͡soudα', don't put him to sleep! 'ʜ-dẹị-t͡sou, put him to sleep! heit bʜ-dẹị-t͡sou, let us put him to sleep! hǫn gyʜ-dẹị-t͡sougu'αdα', I am not going to put him to sleep.

-dl, noun adj. and pron. postfix, often varying with -t.

-dl, intr. verb postfix, in t͡ʜ-t, to sever; t͡ʜ-dl, to be severed; tsei, to put in; tsei-dl, to be in.

dou' (dougα', punct. neg.; dougu'α, dougα', curs.; doudα', fut.; dougα'dα', dougu'αdα', fut. neg.; dou', doudei, imp.; tou'- in comp.), to hold, have, have on. Cp. mǫn-sou-dou', bracelet; 'ou-t'ʜ'-dou', to raise chin; t͡soudl-touhα'-'ǫm-dou', to soar; tọụbʜ-tou'-k͡iʜ, bugle man; pα'-dou', to keep (an animal); etc. —— gyʜ-dou', I am holding it. hǫn gyʜ-douga', I am not holding it. gyʜ-bou-dou', I am continually holding it. gyʜ-doudα', I shall hold it. hǫn gyʜ-dougu'αdα', I shall not hold it. 'ʜ-doudei, hold it! bʜ-doudei, let us dpl. incl. hold it! mǫn-dou gyʜ-dou', I am holding it with my hand. mǫn-gyʜ t͡sou gyʜ-dou', I have a stone in my hand. k͡α' hα 'ʜ-dou', have you a knife? hα, k͡α' gyʜ-dou', yes, I have a knife (ans.). yiʜ k͡α' nẹịn-dou', I have two knives. hʜ'oudei k͡α'gα déi-dou', I have several knives. houdldʜ gyʜt-dou', I have my coat on. houdldʜ hǫn gyʜt-do.ugα', I have no coat on, =houdldʜ-hẹị 'ʜ-dα. míʜn houdldʜ gyʜt-dougu'α, I am just going to put my coat on. houdldʜ gyʜt-doudα', I shall put my coat on. houdldʜ bʜt-dou', put your coat on! poue bʜt-houdldʜ-doudα', do not put your coat on! heit béi-houdldʜ-dou', let us put our coats on. houdldʜ gyʜt-dou'gu'α, I am putting my coat on.

-dou, 1. postp. with, in, by, as; in so and so many places; 2. verb post-fix, because, in order to. —— 1. 'ʜ'-dou gyʜ-gu'αdα', I am going to hit him with a stick. yʜeba-dou 'ʜ-gu'α, hit him with the rope! tsou-dou gyʜ-k͡iʜgyʜ, I threw a stone at him. 'ǫnsou-dou gyʜ-mǫnseip̀gα, I rubbed him with my foot. zeibʜt-dou t'αtgα, he shot him with the arrow. hǫ'-zeibʜt-dou t'αtgα, he shot him with a bullet. hǫndei-dou t'αtgα, what did he shoot him with? hǫ'-zeip̀-dou, with a gun (ans.). k͡αtsẹị-dou, in nine places. 2. 'ẹ̀ịm-hẹịdeidα-dou-dou gyʜ-goup, I hit her (the cow) so that she would go away. t͡sou'eigyʜ mǫn k'oup̀bei-tα'-'ʜ-doup̀-dou, he fell down because maybe he was running. 'ṅ-ŋ gyṅ-houdldɑ-dou, I have come in order to kill him. hɑ̨n gyṅ-houdldɑ-dou hɑ̨n 'ṅ-'ŋmɑ', I have not come here to kill him. mɑ̨n-dou gyṅ-dou', I am holding it with my hand, in my hand. mɑ̨n-dou gyṅ-hʜ'bɑ, I carried it off in my hand. mɑ̨nt̃sǫy-dou gyṅ-hʜ'bɑ, I carried it off in my claws, =gyṅ-mɑ̨nt̃sǫy-hʜ'bɑ. pʜdl-dou, in bed. p'ŋ'ou-dou, in three places, all three. tsęįhįŋ 'ę́į-p̃ɑe-dou 'ṅ-'ɑ'dliʜ, I cried because I lost my dog.

dou-dl-ei-, referring to sliding, in doudlei-'out, to slide down.

doudlei-'out, to slide down ['ou-t, to descend]. —— dèi-doudlei-'out, I slid down (e. g. boys would throw water on bank to make it sleek and would then slide down).

dou-e-, adverbial verb prefix, excessively, too much; also in 'ɑn-gɑ-douy-ei-dei, too much [cp. possibly kou-dou-, very]. —— doue-p'iʜ, it is too heavy. gyṅ-'ɑ'k'ɑ, gyṅ-doue-'ɑ'k'ɑ, they tpl. are light, too light.

-dou-p, noun postfix, tpl. correspondent of -dei, in p'ɑ'-k̃ou-dei, measuring worm, p'ɑ'-k̃ou-dou-p, tpl.; p'ɑ-'ʜt̃-dou-p, ball, p'ɑ-'ʜt̃-dei, dpl.; etc. [-dou, ev. ablaut form of -dei; -p].

dǫy-, prepound form of dǫy'-m, down, under, in, in -dǫy-bʜ, down; dǫy-gyʜ, down; etc.

dǫy-bʜ, adv., under, at the under surface of [dǫy-; -bʜ]. Also used as postp. —— dǫy-bʜ, at (or on) the bottom surface (of the basket).

-dǫy-bʜ, postp., down, under, at the under surface of. Also used as adv. —— k̃ɑ't̃ęįnįʜ-dǫybʜ, underneath the roots. 'ɑn-dǫybʜ, 1. under the foot, on the bottom of the foot, 2. sole of foot, ='ɑn-dǫybʜe. k̃ɑ'nɑsɑp'ouyiʜ pįʜ'ʜ'-dǫybʜ k̃ɑ, the fly is (lit. lies) on the underside of the table. t̃soudl-dǫybʜ, under the arm, armpit.

-dǫy-bʜ-e, under, in 'ɑn-dǫybʜe, sole of foot, ='ɑn-dǫybʜ. dǫy-bei-, under, in dǫybei-beit̃dɑ, lower lip.

-dǫy-bei-hįʜ, way down under [-hįʜ, real]. 'ɑ'pįʜdɑ t'ǫy-dǫybeihįʜ 'èi-ze.imʜ, the fishes are way down at the bottom of the water. p̃ɑ'-tǫybeihįʜ, at the bottom of the river.

dǫy-dei, adv., upside down, face down, inverted [dǫy-, down; -dei]. Cp. t̃sou-yʜp, right side up. —— dǫydei 'èi-tseidl, it (the tumbler) is inverted. dǫydei déi-t̃soudɑ', I am going to invert it.

dǫy-gyʜ, adj. and adv. (dǫy-gɑ'-t, tpl.), underneath, inside; as noun, dǫy-gɑ'-t (inan. IIᵃ; dǫy-gyʜ, dpl.), seed, lit. inside one. Also used as postp. [dǫy-; -gyʜ]. Cp. 'ei-gɑ, fruit, seed; 'ei-k̃uɑ-'ei-gɑ't, seed for planting; 'ei-tɑ̨'-dǫygɑ't, wheat seed; p'įʜdʜt̃gyʜ-dǫygɑ't, muskmelon seed. —— tou dǫygyʜ p̃ɑ'-bʜbʜ' tseidl, the house is way down next to the creek.

-dǫu̯-gyн, postp., down, down in, in, under, at the bottom of, also used
as adv. [dǫu̯-; -gyн]. —— 'oueidei-dǫu̯gyн, under that fellow.
'oueigα-dǫu̯gyн, under them tpl. nǫ̃-dǫu̯gyн, under me, below
me (e. g. the dog lies under my feet). dα̨m-dǫu̯gyн, in the ground,
underground (e. g. where the gopher lives; but dα̨m-gyн, on the
ground, on earth). tou-dǫu̯gyн, on the floor; cp. tou dǫu̯'m, floor,
lit. under house. —— tou-dǫu̯gyн 'н̃-k̃α, I am lying on the floor.
tou-dǫu̯gyн dèi-mǫ̃'dα', I am going to lie down on the floor. k̃αdl-
dǫu̯gyн, in the chewing gum. hǫ̃'p'iн-dǫu̯gyн gyн̃t-sα, I put
them tpl. in the stove. 'α̨nhн̃'dei gyн̃-bǫu̯ 'α'-(dǫu̯)gyн, I saw
the bear in the woods. 'н̃-p̃α'e 'н̃'-dǫu̯gyн (or v. v.), I got lost in
the woods. guαdl-tsę̃i-dǫu̯gyн, in the red horse, = tsę̃i-guαdl-
dǫu̯gyн. guαdl-tsę̃i-bout̃-(dǫu̯)gyн, in the red horse, in the red
horse's belly. 'α'gα'dǫu̯gyн, (down) in the well. p̃α-'dǫu̯gyн, in
the moon.
dǫu̯-m (an. I; dǫu̯-bα, tpl.), 1. father-in-law; 2. son-in-law. Cp.
k̃iн-'eidl, father-in-law; yнt̃-k̃iн, son-in-law. —— nǫ̃ dǫu̯m, my
father-in-law, my son-in-law.
dǫu̯'-m, (dǫu̯'-m-, dǫu̯- in comp.), adv., down, under, in. Also used
as postp. [cp. Tewa nu̯', -nu̯'ų́, down under; -m]. —— dǫu̯'m
gyн̃t-'нedα', I am going to go down (said e. g. by a man in an
airplane); also dǫu̯'m 'н̃-bн̃'k̃α'; also dǫu̯'m dèi-'oudlda'.
-dǫu̯'-m, postp., down, under, in. Also used as adv. —— t'ǫu̯-
-dǫu̯'m t̃sou k̃α, there is a rock at the bottom of the water. t'ǫu̯-
-dǫu̯'m t̃sou gyн̃-k̃uαdl, there are tpl. rocks at the bottom of the
water. poudl t̃sou-dǫu̯'m tsǫu̯-heibн, the bug crawled under the
rock. t̃oudl-dǫu̯'m, under the snow. tę.i̯gyн-dǫu̯'m, under the
ice, in the ice. 'αdl-dǫu̯'m dèi-p̃ǫ'ǫ̃'dα', I am going to wash my
hair, head, scalp, lit. in my hair. tou-dǫu̯'m, floor, lit. under
house; cp.
-dǫu̯'m-dei, down, under, in [-dei]. —— 'н̃'dǫu̯mdei-k̃iн, Gulf
State Indian man, lit. in woods man. tou-dǫu̯'mdei-k'αe, rug
mat, lit. floor cloth.
-dǫu̯'m-guα, postp., down, under, in [-guα]. —— 'н̃'-dǫu̯mguα, in
the woods.
-dǫu̯'m-gyн, postp., down, inder, in [-gyн]. —— tou-dǫu̯'m-gyн,
on the floor.
dǫu̯-n (dǫu̯nα', punct. neg.; dǫu̯nmǫ̃, curs.; dǫu̯ndα', fut.;
dǫu̯nα'dα', fut. neg.; dǫu̯n, imp.; tǫu̯- in comp.), to seek,
hunt for [Tewa nu̯'-wн̃, to seek]. Cp. tǫu̯-bн, to go to hunt for;
peidl-dǫu̯n, to think, lit. to think seek. —— gyн̃-dǫu̯n, I
hunted for it. hα̨n gyн̃-dǫu̯nα', I did not hunt for it. gyн̃-bou-
-dǫu̯nmǫ̃, I am hunting for it continually. miнn gyн̃-dǫu̯nmǫ̃, I
am about to look for it. gyн̃-dǫu̯ndα', I shall hunt for it. hα̨n
gyн̃-dǫu̯nǫ̃'dα', I shall not hunt for it. 'н̃-dǫu̯n, hunt for it! poue

'ꞑ-dọụndɑ', do not hunt for it!  heiꞇ bꞗ-dọụn, let us dpl. incl. look
for it!  heiꞇ bꞗ-dọụnhou, let us dpl. incl. go look for it!  'ꞑ-dọụn-
hou, you go look for it!  gyꞑ-dọụnhoudɑ', I am going to go look
for it.  poue 'ꞑ-dọụnhoudɑ', don't go look for it!  k'yꞑhiꞑgɑ hɑn
gyꞑ-dọụnhougu'ɑdɑ', tomorrow I am not going to go hunt
for it.

dọụ-n-gyн-e (dọụngyнeꞇɑ', fut.), to smell tr. —— bọụngi(н)
'ꞑ-dọụngyнe, I smelled a stink, something rotten. 'ꞑ-dọụngyнeꞇɑ',
I will smell of it.

'ei-, prepound form of 'ei-gɑ, fruit, seed.

### ei

-'ei, -ei, noun, adj. and adv. postfix. Cp. tsou-e, water; 'ɑ-ꞇɑ-ę,
smooth; ꞇн'gyн-e, well, nicely.

-'ei, -ei, postp., in, at. Also postfixed to other postpositions, e. g.
in -bн-e, -mꞑ-ę. —— t'н'dliн 'н-'e 'ꞑ'gyн, the boy is sitting up
in the tree. tou-'e 'ꞑ-ꞇɑ', I was in the house. tou-'e 'ꞑ-bн'ꞇɑ',
I am going to go to the house or camp. tou-'e heibн, he went into
the house (ct. tou-yɑ' t'eip, he came out of the house). 'ou-e,
there. 'ou-ei-dei, that one.

-'ei, my, our, postfixed to 1st person possessive forms of certain
relationship terms, in tɑ'tɑ-'e, my or our father; kɑ'kɑ-'e, my or
our mother; seigyн-'e, my or our maternal uncle; Ct. 'н-, prefixed
to 2nd and 3rd person possessive forms.

-'ei, formative element in pн'gɑ-'e, to be lone; sɑ-'e, to be swift; etc.

-ei, causative verb postfix in sɑ-e, to seat (cp. sɑ'-gyн, to seat oneself); etc.

-'ei-bɑ, fruit, seed, in tọụn-'н'-'ei-bɑ, pecan nut; etc. See 'ei-gɑ.

'ei-dl ('ei-ꞇ-dɑ app. only used as inan. II and inan. IIᵃ s.; an. tpl. is
supplanted by biн-dɑ, from biꞑn, to be large, much; but an. tpl.
-'ei-p in K'i(ꞑ)-'eip, Big Shields; 'ei-dl-, 'ei-t- in comp.), large,
much [unexplained; cp. 'ei-t in k'ou-'ei-t, wide]. Cp. 'eiꞇ-dei,
much; 'eidl-ꞗiн, old man; 'eidl-mꞑ, old woman; ꞗiн-'eidl, father-
in-law; sɑy-eidl, to be large; biꞑn, to be large; sɑ-biꞑn, to be large;
sɑ-p'ꞑn, to be large. —— tseį-'eidl, a large horse; tseį-biꞑdɑ,
tpl. large horses. kн'boudliн-hɑ'ꞇн'dei-'eidl, sheep ranch, lit. big
patch wire-fenced for sheep.

'eidl-ꞗiн (an. I; 'eidl-ꞗyou-p, tpl.), old man [large man]. Ct. ꞗiн-
'eidl, father-in-law. —— 'eidlꞗyoup 'Ḙi-t'н'bн-ꞗuadl, the old
men sit smoking, name of the Northern Crown constellation.

'eidl-mꞑ (an. I; 'eidl-mꞑ-you-p, tpl.), old woman. Cp. tsнdliн-
tsọụhiꞑ, old woman.

'ei-gɑ (s. also -ei-bɑ, -'ei-gɑ'-t; inan. IIᵃ; 'ei, dpl.; 'ei- in comp.),
1. fruit, vegetable, edible seed; 2. loaf of bread, bread. Cp.
dọụgɑ't, seed, lit. inside one; 'ei-kuɑ'n, mush; 'ei-t'нꞇ-dɑ, grain of

corn; t̨o̧un-'ʜ'-'ei-bɑ, pecan nut; 'eiḵuɑ-'ei-gɑ̃'-t, seed (for planting). —— 'eigɑ déi-bo̧u̧, I saw the (s.) fruit, the loaf of bread.
dɑ́-'ei-mn̨'dei, give us our bread!
'ei-goup (inan. IIᵃ), corn plant, corn stalk [seed plant].
'eigou̧p̀-t'ǫ̧u̧, corn stalk juice.
'ei-guɑt̀ḵou-dɑ (inan. IIᵃ; 'ei-guɑt̀ḵou-dɑ̃'-gɑ, tpl.), lemon [yellow
fruit]. Cp. t'o̧u-'ʜ'ɑ̃'-mɑ, lemon.
-'ei-gyʜ in pʜdlk'ou-'eigyʜ, to turn back.
'ei-kuɑ'n, mush [explained as 'ei- fruit, edible seed; kuɑ'-n, to mix].
'ei-ḵoudl-'ɑm-dɑ (inan. IIᵃ; 'ei-ḵoudl-'ɑm-dɑ̃'-gɑ, tpl.), pear [necked
fruit: 'ei-gɑ, fruit; ḵou-dl, neck; 'ɑm- as in 'ɑm-dɑ, to be made;
app. -dɑ, noun postfix].
'ei-ḵoup, to plant ['ei-gɑ, fruit, seed; ḵoup, to lay several]. Cp.
'ei-ḵuɑ, planted field. —— gyʜ̀t-'ei-ḵuɑdɑ', I am going to plant
the field; cp. heigɑ yɑ̃-'ei-ḵuɑdl, my field is already planted.
'ei-t'ʜdl gyʜ̀-'eiḵuɑdɑ', I am going to plant corn. déi-ḵuɑdɑ', I
am going to plant it.
'ei-ḵuɑ, planted field ['ei-ḵuɑdl, to be planted]. —— nɑ̃ 'ei-ḵuɑ, my
planted field.
'ei-ḵuɑ-'ʜ'-dɑ (inan. IIᵃ; 'ei-ḵuɑ-'ʜ', dpl.), fence post (of field)
[planted-field post]. Cp. hɑ̃'sɑ̃'-'ʜ'dɑ, barbed wire fence post.
-'ei-ḵuɑ-bɑ, planting machine, in 'eit'ʜdl-'eiḵuɑbɑ, corn planting
machine; etc.
'eiḵuɑ-do̧u̧'m (inan. III), planted field [-do̧u̧'m, in].
'ei-ḵuɑdl, to be planted (tpls.). Cp, 'ei-ḵoup, to plant. ——
gyʜ̀-'ei-ḵuɑdl, it is already planted. yɑ̃-'ei-ḵuɑdl, it is my crop,
my planting.
'eiḵuɑ-'ei-gɑ̃'-t (inan. IIᵃ; 'eiḵuɑ-'ei, dpl.), seed (for planting)
[planted field seed]. Cp. do̧u̧-gɑ̃'t, seed. —— 'eiḵuɑ-'ei gyʜ̀t-bo̧u̧,
I saw the seed (coll.).
'ei-k'ǫ̧u̧-gɑ̃'-t (inan. II; 'ei-k'ǫu-gyʜ, dpl.), mole (anat.) [black seed].
'ei-mɑkу̧ȩgyʜ-'ʜ'-dɑ (inan. IIᵃ; 'ei-mɑkу̧ȩgyʜ-'ʜ', dpl.), stirring stick
[seed stir stick].
'ei-'ou-kuɑ-'ei-gɑ (inan. IIᵃ; 'ei-'ou-kuɑ-'ei, dpl.), rice [-'ou-kuɑ-,
unexplained]. —— 'ei-'oukuɑ'ei gyʜt-bo̧u̧, I saw the rice (coll.).
'ei-p (inan. Iᵃ; 'ei-p̀-gyʜ, tpl.; 'ei-p̀- in comp.), live coal. To dead
coal, piece of charcoal, also 'eip̀-k'ǫu-gyʜ, lit. black coal, is applied.
-'ei-p in K'i̧(ʜ)-'ei-p, tpl., name of a Kiσwa division, "big shields"
acc. to Mooney, p. 411, and therefore apparently a tpl. form
of 'ei-dl, to be large (cp. loss of t before auslaut p). But
the informants did not know this etymology and Mr. James Waldo
explained -'ei-p in this word as meaning "right up to" [see -'ei-p,
postp.].
-ei-p, postp., in, at, "right up to" [-'ei; -p̣].

'eiᵽ-k'ǫų-gyʜ (inan. I and II), piece of charcoal; also applied to mineral coal [black coal]. —— On separate occasions both 'eiᵽ-k'ǫų̱gyʜ gyʜ̇-bǫų and 'eiᵽ-k'ǫų̱gyʜ déi-bǫų were obtained for "I saw the piece of charcoal."

'eiᵽk'ǫų̱gyʜ-t'ǫų̱n (inan. III), coal mine [t'ǫų-n, pit].

'ei-poudl (an. II; 'ei-pouᵗ-dɑ, tpl.), worm or bug such as gets on or into fruit, seed, etc. Applied even to sow-bug. [fruit bug].

'ei-ᵽɑ̃'-gyʜ (inan. I), roasting ear ['ei-, seed, corn; ᵽɑ̃'-gyʜ, to be newborn, fresh]. Cp. 'iʜ-ᵽɑ̃'gyʜ, (newborn) baby.

'ei-p'ʜe-'ʜdl-t'out (inan. IIᵃ), corn cultivator ['ei-gɑ, fruit, corn; -p'ʜ-e-, unexplained; app. -'ʜdl-, to drive; -t'ou-t].

'ei-sɑhyei-gɑ (inan. IIᵃ; 'ei-sɑhyei, dpl.), watermelon, = tʜ'-hęi-pịʜ [green fruit]. —— 'ei-sɑhyeigɑ déi-bǫų, I saw the watermelon.

'ei-sǫų-bɑ (inan. IIᵃ; 'ei-sǫų, dpl.; 'ei-sǫų- in comp.), metate [seed grinder: sǫų-m, to grind up].

'eit-ɑ-bʜ-dou-p, mortar ['ei-t-'ɑ-, unexplained; app. -bʜ-; -doup].

'ei-tʜ'-poudl (an. II; 'ei-tʜ'-pouᵗ-da, tpl.), cicada [fruit ripe bug, so called from their appearance in the summer season].

'ei-tɑ̨' (inan. III; 'ei-tɑ̃'- in comp.), wheat; wheat flour ['ei-gɑ, seed; -tɑ̨', unexplained].

'eitɑ̨'-'eiꝁuɑ-bɑ, wheat planting machine.

'eitɑ̨'-goup (inan. IIᵃ), wheat plant.

'eitɑ̨'-dǫų-gɑ̃'-t (inan. IIᵃ; 'eitɑ̨'-dǫų-gyʜ, dpl.), wheat seed.

'eit-k'ɑ̨'dei-dou', to be bunched [unexplained; app. dou']. —— 'eit-k'ɑ̨'dei-dou' déi-bǫų, I saw the bunch (of grapes).

'eit-dei, adv., much, many, too much, too many ['ei-dl, to be large; -dei]. —— 'eit-dei tʜ̨' ᵽeitgyʜ, there are lots of stars falling. pʜ 'eit-dei gyʜ̇-tǫų̱zʜ̨nmʜ, some people are talking too much. 'eit-dei gyʜ̇-tǫų̱zʜ̨nmʜ, I am talking too much.

'eitdei-dou, many times [-dou, by, as]. —— 'eitdei-dou 'ɑ̨n-guɑt, I wrote to him many times. koudou-eitdei-dou 'ɑ̨n-guɑt, I wrote to him very many times.

'ei-îʜt-bɑ̃'-t (inan. IIᵃ; 'ei-îʜt-bʜ, dpl.), pie [between bread, i. e. between crusts].

'ęį-, to hunt, in 'ęį-bʜ, to go hunting.

'eit'ʜdl-'eiꝁuɑ-bɑ (inan. IIᵃ; 'eit'ʜdl-'eiꝁuɑ, dpl.), corn planting machine ['ei-t'ʜt-dɑ, grain of corn; -'eiꝁuɑ-bɑ, planting machine].

'eit'ʜdl-goup (inan. IIᵃ), corn plant, corn stalk, = 'ei-goup. Cannot say *'eit'ʜdl-p'eip, for it is not a bush [corn grain plant].

'eit'ʜdl-k'ɑ̨ę (inan. IIᵃ), corn cob, corn husk [corn grain little skin].

'ei-t'ʜt-dɑ (inan. II; 'ei-t'ʜdl, dpl.; 'ei-t'ʜdl- in comp.), given as meaning grain of corn, ear of corn, plant of corn ['ei-, seed, etc.; w. -t'ʜ-dl, -t'ʜ-t- cp. t'ʜdl, liver, kidney, 'ɑ̨n-t'ʜdl, toe].

'eizęįn, agent [fr. Eng.].

'eizęįn-gyʜ, agency [-gyʜ, postp.].

ę̄į

'ę̄į-, dem. stem referring to more definite locality here.  Also used as
postfix, -'ę̄į.  Cp. 'ę̄į-m-; 'įн-.
'ę̄į- in 'ę̄į-bн, to go hunting.
-'ę̄į, 1. postp., at, among; 2. subordinating verb postfix, when, if
['ę̄į-, dem. stem, as postfix].  Cp. -t͡seį, subordinating verb postfix,
when. —— 1. p‘н̣’ou sнe Kунe-’ę̄į ’н̄-k̂iнунt͡ɑ’, I lived three years
with the Comanches.  p‘н̣’ou sнe Kɑe-’ę̄į (or Kɑe-gi(н)) ’н̄-t͡ɑ’, I
lived three years among the Kiowas.  ’н̄-bн’t͡ɑ’ tɑ’tɑ’e ’ɑ’gɑ-’ę̄į
kiнdl-dei-’ę̄į, I am going to where my father lives.  pн’byou’e
tou-gун ’н̄-bн’t͡ɑ’, I am going to go to where my brothers live..
’н̄-bн’t͡ɑ’ ’oueigɑ ’н̄’-hyųę ’ei-t͡seidl-dei-’ę̄į, I am going to go over
where the cottonwood tree is standing.  ’н̄-bн’t͡ɑ’ ’oueigɑ ’н̄’-hįн̣
sɑdl-dei-’ę̄į, I am going to go over where the tpl. cottonwood trees
are standing.  ’ɑ̄’gɑpįн̣ ’éį-kɑdl-guɑnmн̣ę néį-k̂iнgун ’oueihįн̣
tsęįhįн̣ dei-dei-’ę̄į ’н̄-t͡soueigyн, the buffalo hooked and threw me
and I fell way over where the dog was standing. —— 2. ’èįm-
dɑ’dɑ’-’ę̄į ’н̄-tsн̣n, I came when they were singing.  (heiga)
’н̄-dн̣mgyн-dɑ-’ę̄į ’ei-tsн̣n, we dpl. excl. arrived with me already
tired.  tsн̣nt͡ɑ-’ę̄į heigɑ ’н̄-dн̣mgyн-dɑ’t͡ɑ’, I shall be tired when
he arrives.  tseiguɑn tsęįn-dou ’н̄-’ɑ̄’mɑ̄-’ę̄į gyн̄-bǫų, I saw the
dog when they were making it out of mud.  tseiguɑn tsęįn-dou
’н̄-’ɑ̄’mɑ̄-’ę̄į dèi-bǫų, I saw the people when they were making the
dog out of mud.  tseiguɑn tsęįn-dou heigɑ ’ǫmgyн-’ę̄į ’н̄-tsн̣n, I
came when the dog had just been made of mud.
-’ę̄į- in ’н̄-k̂ɑ̄’dei-’ę̄į-dɑ, I feel sad.
’ę̄į-bн, to go hunting [bн, to go]. —— ’н̄-(t͡нp-)’ę̄į-bн̣nmн̣, I am
going (deer) hunting.  k‘yǭhįн̣gɑ ’н̄-’ę̄į-bн, yesterday I went
hunting.
’ę̄į-dei (’ę̄į-gɑ, tpl.), dem. pron. and adv., this, here ['ę̄į-, dem. stem;
-dei].  Cp. ’įн-dei, this one. —— ’ę̄įdei, this (fellow).  ’ę̄įgɑ,
this (e. g. chair or tumbler).  ’ę̄įdei dɑ̄’k̂iн-kuɑt gyн̄-dɑ, this is
God's book.
’ę̄įdei-hɑ̄’-tsou, adv., there ['ę̄įdei, this one; -hɑ̄’tsou, postp., at]. ——
’ę̄įdei-hɑ̄’tsou isн̣n, hǫn ’oueidei-tsou tsн̣’nɑ̄’, he came from there
(gesture), but not from there.
’ę̄įdei-tsou, adv., this way, thus ['ę̄į-dei, this one; -tsou, postp., like].
—— ę̄įdei-tsou béi-p‘н̣’ę, tie it like this!  ’ę̄įdei-tsou bнt-’ɑ̄’m, do
it this way!
’ę̄į-gɑ, 1. dem. pron., tpl. of ’ę̄į-dei, this; 2. adv., here ['ę̄į-, dem.
stem; -gɑ].
’ę̄į-hɑ̄’, adv., 1. right here, ct. ’ę̄į-m-hɑ̄’, hereabouts; 2. now ['ę̄į-,
dem. stem; -hɑ̄’, postp., at]. —— 1. ’ę̄įhɑ̄’ ’н̄-t͡ɑ̄’dei’, I heard that
they are staying here, are they staying here?  poue ’ę̄įhɑ̄’ ’èįm--

îɑ'îɑ', don't stay here! 'ẹihɑ' 'Ɦ-tseidl, I was right in there.
'ẹihɑ' poue béi-k̒uɑdɑ', don't camp here! 'ẹihɑ' hẹi'm, he died
right here.  'ẹihɑ' 'Ɦ-kiꞰdl, I live here.  'ẹihɑ' gyꞪ-bọụ, I saw him
here.  sꞪ'dꞪ îou 'ẹihɑ', it is cold in the winters here (at this very
spot); ct. sꞪ'dꞪ îou 'ẹimhɑ', it is cold in the winters hereabouts
(e. g. here in Oklahoma). —— 2. 'ẹihɑ' dèi-dɑ'dɑ, 1. I am singing
here, 2. I am singing now.

'ẹihɑ'-dei ('ẹihɑ'-gɑ, tpl.), dem. pron. and adv., this, here ['ẹi-hɑ',
here; -dei]. —— 'ẹihɑ'-dei dɑmgyꞪ, here on earth.  'ẹihɑ'-gɑ
k̒yꞰkɑ̯'mbɑ, these people.  tei(p'ɑe) 'ẹihɑ'gɑ, all of us here.

'ẹi-m-, dem. stem referring to more indefinite locality here.  Also
used as postfix, -'ẹim.  ['ẹi-, dem. stem; -m, referring to region].

-'ẹi-m, 1. postp., at, referring to more indefinite locality; 2. subordinating verb postfix, where ['ẹim-, dem. stem, hereabouts, as postfix].
Ct. -'ẹi, postp., at, referring to more exact locality. —— 'ẹimgɑ
yi'ꞰyꞪ-'ẹim 'Ɦ-îɑ', I stay west of here.  'ẹimgɑ bɑ'deip-'ẹim 'Ɦ-îɑ'
(or 'Ɦ-bꞪ'îɑ'), I am staying (or going to go) east.  poue 'ɑþgɑ
gyꞪ-'adlk'ɑe-dɑ'dei-'ẹim dɑ̒-pɑ'hiꞰdɑ', lead us not into evil!  yiꞰ
nɑ̯-'ẹim 'ꞩ-kuɑt, he owes me two dollars.  'Ɦ-bꞪ 'ɑ'gɑ þɑ'-'eidl-
k̒ɑ'dei-'ẹim, I went to where the big river was.  sꞪ'dɑ kuɑtk̒uɑdl-
'ẹim 'Ɦ-bꞩnmꞪ, I am going to go down to where the children are in
school.  'Ɦ-bꞩnmꞪ 'ɑ̯'gɑ tsꞪ'dei kiꞰdl-dei-'ẹim, I am going to go
down to where my friend lives.

'ẹim-dei ('ẹim-gɑ, tpl.), dem. pron. and adv., this one hereabouts,
hereabouts ['ẹi-m-, dem. stem; -dei].

'ẹim-gɑ, 1. dem. pron., tpl. of 'ẹim-dei, this one hereabouts; 2. adv.,
hereabouts ['ẹi-m-, dem. stem; -gɑ].

'ẹimgɑ-t'ɑp, this way [-t'ɑ-p, beyond].  Cp. 'ẹim-tsou, this way.
'ẹimgɑ-t'ɑp bꞪ-bꞪ, let us dpl. incl. go (up) this way! ='ẹim-tsou
bꞪ-bꞪ!

'ẹim-hɑ' hereabouts, here, there ['ẹi-m- dem. stem; -hɑ', postp., at].
Ct. 'ẹi-hɑ', right here, right there.

'Ẹ̀im-hɑ'-'Ɦ', prsn. of Delos Lonewolf, explained as meaning "he
captured them," or "he took them away (from the people)" ['ẹ̀im-,
app. pron., he—them tpl. an maj.; hɑ'- as in hɑ'gyꞪ, to get;
'Ɦ', unexplained].  Mr. Lonewolf's other Indian name is K'ọụ-
'eidl, Great Dark.

'ẹim-hꞪ'-mẹi (an. II; 'ẹim-hꞪ'-mou-p, tpl.), large red ant sp.; also
ant in general [cp. possibly 'ɑdl-hꞩẹmẹi, mosquito.]

'ẹimhꞪ'mẹi-guɑdl-'eidl (an II; 'ẹimhꞪ'mẹi-guɑdl-biꞩ-dɑ, tpl.), ant
sp. [big red ant].

'ẹimhꞪ'mẹi-k'ọụ-'eidl (an. II; 'ẹimhꞪ'mẹi-k'ọụ-biꞩ-dɑ, tpl.), ant sp.
[big black ant].

'ẹimhꞪ'mẹi-k'ọụ-gyꞪ (an. II; 'ẹimhꞪ'mẹi-k'ọụ-gɑ'-t, tpl.), ant sp.
[black ant].

’ęimhą’męi-p‘ʜ’syʜ’n (an. II; ’ęimhą’męi-p‘ʜ’syʜ’-dα, tpl.), ant sp. [tiny ant].

’ęimhą’męi-sįʜn (an. II; ’ęimhą’męi-syʜ’-dα, tpl.), ant sp. [small ant].

’ęimhą’męi-t͡soudl-sα (an. II; ’ęimhą’męi-t͡soudl-sα’-gα, tpl.), winged ant [t͡soudl-, wing; app. sα, to put several in, set several].

’ęim-tsou, adv., this way [’ęi-m-, dem. stem; -tsou, postp., like]. Cp. ’ęimgα-t’αp, this way. —— ’ęim-tsou bʜ-bʜ, let us dpl. incl. go this way. ’ęim-tsou yʜ-k‘oup, it pains me here (with gesture at afflicted part). sαt tsʜn nęi ’ęim-tsou ’ęim-k‘uαt, he came here a while ago but went out this way.

## g

gα, particle, and, and then. Cp. nα, and. Also in heigα, already. Sometimes heard assimilated as gei in gei heigα, and already. —— ky̨ʜhi’ʜ gα mą’yįʜ, the man and the woman. gyʜ-kuαt gα gyʜ-’αe-tsei, I pulled it out and· then I put it back in again. sα’α’dei-dα gα tsʜn, he came angry. ’ʜ-houndldα’ gei heigα m-t‘oup‘ʜtα’, if you kill him, they’ll get you. gei heigα hʜyʜ’ bʜ’gyʜdei gα hαn gyʜ-hʜegα’, and they don’t know where he went to.

-gα, 1. noun postfix, tpl. correspondent of -dei; 2. forming pronouns from dem. stems and from advs. of place, tpl. correspondent of -dei; 3. derivative postfix, forming proper names from nouns, tpl. correspondent of -dei; 4. postfixed to nouns and certain pronouns to emphasize possessive case, tpl. correspondent of -dei; 5. adverbial postfix, cp. -dei; 6. participal verb postfix, tpl. correspondent of -dei [cp. possibly -gyʜ, -gα’-t, noun and adjective postfix]. —— For use as adverbial postfix cp. k‘y̨ʜhįʜ-gα, to-morrow; ’ou-gα, yonder; t‘ou-gα, long ago; mʜm-gα, on high; t‘α’-gα, from afar.

-gα- in ’αn-gα-douy-ei-dei, too much.

-gα-dʜ- in goum-gαdʜ-’ei-ga, cabbage.

-gα’-t, adj. postfix, tpl. of -gyʜ. Cp. k‘ou-gyʜ, dark; k‘ou-gα’-t, tpl.; etc.

gαp-ʜe-goup, to swap [gα-p-ʜ-e-, unexplained; goup, to hit]. —— ’éit-tsęi-gαp-ʜe-goup, we are going to swap horses.

gei-gα, for gα hei-gα. —— pʜ t͡αþp‘ʜdl houdlheidl geigα pęinheidl, he killed a buffalo and butchered it. geigα k‘αe-’α’yʜdlheidl, and then he skinned it.

gįʜ-, prepound form of gįʜ-gyʜ, night.

gįʜ-gα, adv., in the morning [gįʜ-, night; -gα]. —— gįʜgα hęi’m, she died in the morning. k‘iʜdeidl gįʜgα, yesterday morning.

gįн-gyн (gįн- in comp.), night; in the night. —— gyн̥-gįн-sнdl, it is a hot night. gyн̥-sнdl gįн̥gyн, it was hot last night. gįн̥gyн hęį'm, she died in the night.

gįн-poudl (an. II; gįн-pouṫ-dα, tpl.), night insect (of any kind) [night bug].

gou-bα' (goubα', punct. neg.; gouboup, curs.; goubeidα', fut.; goubα'dα', fut. neg.; goubei, imp.), to miss (not to hit). Opp. of guαbн, to hit. —— gyн̥-goubα', I missed it (the bull's-eye). hǫn gyн̥-goubα', I did not miss it. gyн̥-bou-gouboup, I am missing it all the time. hǫn gyн̥-goubα'dα', I am not going to miss it. 'н̥-goubei, you miss it! poue 'н̥-goubeidα', don't miss it!

gou-p (inan. IIᵃ), plant, vine. —— goup déi-bǫụ, I saw the vine (but recorded on another occasion as pн̥'gα goup gyн̥ṫ-bǫụ, I saw one vine). goup gyн̥ṫ-bǫụ, I saw the tpl. vines.

gou-p (guαguα, guαhн, "guαyiнdα'," curs.; guαdα', fut.; gu'α, imp.), to hit (e. g. with stick), whip; to pound; to peck. Cp. gǫp-нe-goup, to swap; -kuα, -ku'α, hitter; t'н̥'hou-goup, to whip; zouṫ-syн̥n-goup, to be a waterfall; zouṫ-bн-t'oue-goup, to eddy. —— gyн̥-goup, I hit him. gyн̥-guαdα', I shall hit him. gyн̥-'н̥'t'ǫụ-goup, I hit him with a stick. 'н̥'-dou gyн̥-guαdα', I am going to hit him with a stick. gyн̥-goup bout 'ǫ̥'kαdl 'нdl 'ę́i-goup-dou, I hit him because he hit me. 'н̥-gu'α, hit him! poue 'н̥-guαhн, don't hit him! =poue 'н̥-guαdα'. gyн̥-guαguα, I am pecking it. heigα '-goup (or gyн̥-goup instead of last word), I pecked it already. gyн̥-guαdα', I am going to peck it. gyн̥-k'ou-guayiнdα', I am going to be pecking it now.

-gou-p, noun postfix, in tαe-gou-p, g-string, tαe-dei, tpl.; ꞇнe-gou-p, cover, ꞇнe-dei, dpl.

gouṗ-t'ǫụ-bα (inan. IIᵃ; gouṗ-t'ǫụ, dpl.), stem (e. g. of apple, ear of corn, etc.) goup, plant; -t'ǫụ, stick; -bα]. —— 'нdlα'-gouṗt'ǫụbα, apple stem. 'eit'нdl-gouṗt'ǫụbα, stem of ear of corn.

gǫụ-m- (does not occur without postposition or postpounded stem in the material obtained), back, in gǫụm-ǫ̥', at the back, on the back; gǫụm-t'ǫụ, backbone; -gǫụm-bн, behind; etc. [cp. gu-e, behind].

gǫụm-ǫ̥', at the back [-ǫ̥', at]. Cp. -gǫụm-ᾱ'-ꞇsou, at the back of. —— gǫụm-ǫ̥' yḁ́-k'oup, my back aches, lit. it pains me in the back. nǫ̥'-gǫụm-ǫ̥' yḁ́-dα, he is on my back.

-gǫụm-ǫ̥'-tsou, postp., at the back of, behind. —— tou-gǫụm-ǫ̥'-tsou tsн̥n, he came from behind the house, =tou-gǫụm-bн-tsou tsн̥n.

-gǫụm-bн, postp., behind. —— p'н̥n-gǫụmbн p̄α' k̄α, the moon is behind a cloud, =p'н̥n-t'ᾱ'gyн p̄α' k̄α, ꞇeidlbǫụ-gǫụmbн, kneepit, lit. back of the knee. t'нdliн tou-gǫụmbн dei, the boy is standing back of the house.

-gǫụm-bн-tsóu, postp., behind. —— tou-gǫụmbн-tsou tsн̥n, he came from behind the house, =tou-gǫụm-ǫ̥'-tsou tsн̥n.

gǫu̯m-d . . . (gǫu̯mdeip, curs.), to blow (of wind). —— gǫu̯mdeip, the wind is blowing now.

gǫu̯m-gα-dн-'ei-gα (inan. II[a]; gǫu̯m-gα-dн-'ei, dpl.), cabbage [explained as wind fruit or vegetable; -gα-dн-, unexplained; 'ei-gα, fruit, vegetable].

gǫu̯-m-gyн (app. an. I; gǫu̯-m- in comp.), wind, air [Tewa wą̀', wind]. —— gǫu̯mgyн gyн̀-bǫu̯, I saw the wind.

gǫu̯m-hą̇'n, to cease to blow (of wind). —— 'è̩m-gǫu̯m-hą̇'n, the wind quit blowing.

gǫu̯m-hą̇'-gyн (app. inan. I), pendant hanging down back; cp. Mooney, p. 403 [back metal].

gǫu̯m-k'iнbα (goum-k'iнboup, curs.), to blow (of wind) [k'iнbα, to walk off, fly away]. —— miнn 'è̩m-gǫu̯mk'iнboup, the wind is going to blow. mą̇'t'oui(н)gyн 'ouei gǫu̯m-k'iнbα, the whirlwind went away from over yonder.

gǫu̯m-î̩нe (gǫu̯m-î̩н̩e-mą̇, tpl.), to be striped on the back [to be back white]. —— tнdl-gǫu̯mî̩н̩e gyн̀-bǫu̯, I saw the striped skunk. tнdl-gǫu̯mî̩н̩emą̇ dé̩i-bǫu̯, I saw tpl. striped skunks.

gǫu̯m-t'н'bei (an. II; gǫu̯m-t'н'bou-p, tpl.), chipmunk [explained as meaning " the wind carries him," but t'н'bei, carrier off, is active e. g. in zǫu̯n-t'н'bei, tree squirrel, lit. nut carrier off; from hн'bα, to carry off].

gǫu̯m-t'ǫu̯ (an. II; gǫu̯m-t'ǫu̯-gα, tpl.), backbone [back bone]. Cp. tн̩'-gǫu̯mt'ǫu̯, milky-way. —— ną̇ gǫu̯m-t'ǫu̯, my backbone.

gǫu̯m-tsн̩'dei, to be blown on wind [tsн̩'dei, to travel, move]. —— gyн̀-gǫu̯m-tsн̩'dei 'нep'iнbei, the pollen is blowing on the wind.

guα (guαgα', punct. neg.), to be wise. Cp. pei-guα, to revive (from fainting). —— 'н̩m kiн-t'α̇'-hi̩н̩ yн̩́n-guα, you are very wise. ną̇ yн̩́-guα, I am very wise. hą̇n yн̩́-guαgα', I am not wise. yн̩́-guα bн̀-'α̇'deip, I think I am wise. hн'gyн yн̩́-guα, I used to be wise. guα-he̩i yн̩́-dα, I am not wise.

guα . . . (guα-dl, imp.), to owe. Cp. kuα-t, to owe. —— kαdl bн̩́-guadl, let us owe him!

-guα, postp., toward, to. —— hн'yн' m-bн̩'î̩α', where are you going to go to? k̂oup̂-guα 'н̀-bн̩'î̩α', I am going to go to the mountain (ans.). Peip̂α'eidl-guα 'н̀-bн̩nmн̩, I am going to go down to Red River, lit. "big sand river." Lawton-guα 'н̀-bн̩nmн̩, I am going to go to Lawton. p̂α'-guα 'н̀-bн̩nmн̩, I am going to go to the river. sн̩'pei-guα 'н̀-bн̩nmн̩, I am going north.

-guα, tpl. noun and adj. postfix, in Kαe-k̂iн, Kiowa man, Kαe-guα, tpl.; sα'e, to be swift, sα'e-guα, tpl.; etc.

-guα- in tei-guα-t'eibei, snail.

guα-'ą̇mgyн, to get wise. —— guα-'α̇'mн̩, I am getting smart. k'iнdeidl yн̩́-guα-'ą̇mgyн, I got smart yesterday. k'yн̩guα-'hi̩нgα yн̩́-guα-ą̇mdeiî̩α', tomorrow I am going to get smart. k'yн̩hi̩н̩gα

hǫn yɧ-guα-'ǫmgα'ȋα, tomorrow I shall not get smart. poue
yɧn-guα-'ǫmdeiȋα', don't be smart! yɧn-guα-'ǫmdei, you be
smart now!

guα-bн (guαbα', punct. neg.; guαbeip, curs.; guαbeiȋα', fut.; guαbα'ȋα',
fut. neg.; guαbei, imp.), to hit (not to miss). Opp. of gou-bα', to
miss. Cp. gou-p, to hit; and possibly guα-p̣-gα, to fall down.
—— gyὰ-guabн, I hit him (when I shot at him). hǫn gyн̀-guαbα',
I did not hit him. gyн̀-bou-guαbeip, I am hitting the mark all
the time. gyн̀-guαbeiȋα', I shall hit it. hǫn gyн̀-guαbα'ȋα', I
shall not hit it. gyɧ-guαbei, hit it! poue gyɧ-guαbeiȋα', don't
hit it! heiȋ dά-guαbei, let us hit it. gyн̀-t'αȋgα nei hǫn 'ę̇i-guαbα',
I took a shot at him but did not hit him.

-guα-bн, postp., behind, beyond [cp. gǫu-m-, back; gu-e, behind].
—— tou-'eidl-guαbн 'н̀-kiнdl, I live beyond the large house.
But tou-'eidl-t'α' 'н̀-tsɧn, I came from beyond the large house.

-guα-bн-tsou, postp., from behind. Cp. gue, behind; -gǫum-bн-
tsou, from behind; etc. —— tou-'eidl-guαbнtsou dèi-'q̦,zǫun, I
started from behind the big house.

guα-dα (inan. II; guα, dpl.), rib, =guα-t'ęi'm, guα-t'ǫubα, rib [cp.
Tewa wǎ, breast]. Cp. k̬uнtне-guαdα, the lowest rib, lit. the
chief's rib.

guα-dl (guα-ȋ-dα, tpl.; guα-dl, guα-t- in comp.), 1. colored; 2. red.
Cp. Span. coloreado and colorado. [Cp. guα-dl-hǫ'n, to burn tr.;
guα-dl-hǫn, to be burnt.] Cp. guαt, to paint, mark; kuα-t, to
be painted. —— hǫndei guαdl, what color? hн'tsoudei guαdl,
what color? gyн̀-guαdl-bα'dн, the red came up (said of the
dawn). gyн̀-guαdl-bα'dн-'ęi heigα 'óit-hн', we dpl. got up when
dawn came. guαdl-tsęigα, red horses.

-guα-dl in tou-guαdl, young man [possibly guα-dl, red].

guαdl-q̦'męi, to redden tr., to paint red. —— gyн̀-guαdl-ǫmdα', I
am going to paint it red, dye it red.

guαdl-biнmk'αe (inan. IIª), paint bag [guαdl- =guαdl-hyṵ'e, Indian
red paint; biнmk'αe, bag].

guαdl-dα, to be red [dα, to be].

guαdl-hǫn (guαdl-hq̦'nq̦', punct. neg.; guαdl-hǫnmн, curs.: guαdl-
hǫnȋα', fut.; guαdl-hq̦'nq̦'dα', fut. neg.), to be burnt, get burnt
(an. subject) [guαdl-, colored, red, here ev. referring to fire; hǫ-n,
to burn intr.]. Cp. guαdl-hǫ'n, to burn tr.] Cp. guαdl-k'ǫn-dα, to
be burnt; tsęin-hǫn, to get burnt. —— tsęi guαdl-hǫn, the horse
got burnt, scorched. tsęi hǫn guαdl-hq̦'nq̦', the horse did not get
burnt. tsęi guαdl-hǫnmн, the horse is going to get burnt. poue
'ę̇im-guαdl-hǫnȋα', don't get burnt! hǫn guαdl-hq̦'nq̦'dα', he
will get burnt.

guαdl-hǫ'n (guαdl-hq̦'nq̦', punct. neg.; guαdl-hǫ'nmα, curs.; guαdl-
hǫnȋα', fut.; guαdl-hq̦'nq̦'dα', fut. neg.; guαdl-hǫ'n, imp.), to

burn tr. (used both of scorching animal body or meat, or of burning an., or inan. object up entirely [guɑ-dl-, colored, red; hɑ̨'-n, to
burn tr.]. Cp. guɑ-dl-hɑ̨-n, to be burnt. —— gyȟ-guɑdl-hɑ̨'n, I
scorched it, burnt it. tou gyȟ-guadlhɑ̨'n, I burnt the house
down. hɑ̨n gyȟ-guɑdl-hɑ̨'nɑ̨', I did not burn it. miȟn gyȟ-
guadl-hɑ̨'nmɑ̨, I am about to burn it. k'yȵhįȵgɑ gyȟ-guɑdl-
hɑ̨nɩ̂ɑ', tomorrow I am going to burn it. k'yȵhįȵgɑ hɑ̨n
gyȟ-guɑdlhɑ̨'nɑ̨'dɑ', tomorrow I am not going to burn it.
'ȟ-guɑdl-hɑ̨'n, burn it! heiɩ̂ nɑ̨ bȟ-guɑdl-hɑ̨'n, let us burn it!
poue 'ȟ-guɑdl-hɑ̨'ndɑ', don't burn it! kiȟ gyȟ-guɑdl-hɑ̨'n, you
are burning your meat. poue 'ȟ-guɑdl-hɑ̨nɩ̂ɑ' kiȟ, don't burn
your meat! kiȟ gyȟ-guɑdl-hɑ̨'n, I burnt the meat; ct. kiȟ 'ę̨i-
guɑdl-hɑ̨n, my meat got burnt.
guɑdl-hɑ̨'-dei (an. II; guɑdl-hɑ̨'-dou-p, tpl.), flicker [said to mean
colored all over; app. the one who has been burnt: guɑdl-hɑ̨n, to
get burnt; -dei.
guɑdl-hyų-'ę (inan. II; guɑdl-hį'ȟ, dpl.), Indian red paint [guɑdl,
to be red; -hį'ȟ, real]. Obtained at bluffs or on prairie by digging.
—— guɑdl-hyų'ę déi-boų, I saw the red paint (the dpl. form
would refer to several pieces but would scarcely be used).
guɑdl-k'ɑ̨'n, to be burnt. Cp. guɑdl-hɑ̨n, to be burnt; guɑdl-k'ɑ̨'n-da,
to be burnt. —— 'ɑ̄'pįȟ guɑdl-k'ɑ̨'n gyȟ-hȟ'n, I ate the burnt
fish. kiȟ 'ei-guɑdl-k'ɑ̨'n gyȟ-hȟ'n, I ate the burnt meat. guɑdl-
k'ɑ̨n-hęi dɑ, it is not burnt.
guɑdl-k'ɑ̨'n-dɑ, to be burnt [dɑ, to be]. Cp. guɑdl-k'ɑ̨'n, to be
burnt. —— kiȟ guɑdl-k'ɑ̨'ndɑ, the meat got burnt, tastes burnt.
kiȟ hɑ̨n guɑdl-k'ɑ̨'ndɑ'mɑ̨', the meat did not get burnt.
guɑdl-k'įȟn, to sneeze [app. to red cough, to burn cough]. ——
'ę̨i-guɑdl-k'iȟn, I sneezed.
guɑdl-p'ou (an. II; guɑdl-p'ou-gɑ, tpl.; guɑdl-p'ou- in comp.), flea
[red head-louse].
-guɑ-dou'e- in 'ɑ̨'-guɑ-dou'e-gyȟ, to taste good [-guɑ-, unexplained;
-dou'e, excessively].
Gu(ɑ)hɑ̄'dei, prsn. [explained as meaning "cut ribs off"; guɑ-, rib;
-hɑ̄'-, unexplained; -dei]. Americans call him Woohaw.
gu(ɑ)-hei-gɑ (inan. IIᵃ; guɑ-hei, dpl.; guɑ-hei- in comp.), mesquite
bean [unexplained].
guɑhei-kuɑ'n, mesquite bean mush. Cp. 'ęi-kuɑ'n, mush; ɩ̂eidei-
'ei-kuɑ'n, grape mush.
guɑhei-p'eip (inan. IIᵃ), mesquite bush.
guɑ-n (inan. I), tipi pole. Also guɑn-hįȟ [-hįȟ, real]; tou-guɑn [tou,
house]. Cp. possibly tsęi-guɑn, dog. —— hȟ'oudei (tou-)guɑn
gyȟ-boų, I saw several tipi-poles.
guɑ-n (guɑnɑ̨', punct. neg.; guɑnmɑ̨, curs.; guɑndɑ', fut.; guɑnɑ̨'dɑ',
fut. neg.; guɑn, imp.), 1. to throw (away); 2. with refl. to throw

oneself in or out; to dance. Cp. kuɑɑn-k̑iн, dancer; kuɑɑn-guн,
dance; kuɑɑn, thrown away thing; k‘yнe-guɑɑn, to jump; ’oubн-
guɑɑn, to dive; p‘oue-t̑eidl-’нdldн-guɑɑn, to turn somersault;
gyнt̑-guɑɑndɑ’, I am going to throw it away. dèi-guɑɑn, 1. I
rushed in; 2. I danced. dèi-bou-guɑɑnmǫ, I dance all the time.
dèi-k̑ɑ’tou-guɑɑnmǫ, I am dancing the sun dance. dèi-’ɑdl-dɑ’-
guɑɑnmǫ, I am dancing the scalp dance.
guɑɑn-dǫm, dance-ground, dancing-place.
guɑɑn-hįн, tipi pole, =guɑɑn [-hįн, real].
-guɑɑn-houdl in pou-guɑɑn-houdl, muskrat.
guɑɑn-mн̨ę, to hook with horns [w. guɑ-n- cp. gǫǫ-dei, horn; -mн̨-ę,
unexplained]. —— ’ǫ’gɑpįн ’ę̑i-kɑdl-guɑɑnmн̨ę, the buffalo hooked
me.
guɑþ-gɑ (guɑþgɑ’, punct. neg.; guɑþgoup, curs.; guɑþdeidɑ’, fut.;
guɑþgɑ’dɑ’, fut. neg.; guɑþdei, imp.), to fall down. Cp. gou-p,
to hit; guɑ-bн, to miss. —— dèi-guɑþgɑ, I stumbled. hǫn dèi-
guɑþgɑ’, I did not fall down. dèi-bou-guɑþgoup, I fall down all
the time. hǫn (’н̨) dèi-guɑþgɑ’, I never fall down. dèi-guɑþ-
deidɑ’, I am going to fall down. hǫn dèi-guɑþgɑ’dɑ’, I am not
going to fall down. bę̑i-guɑþdei, fall down! poue bę̑i-guɑþdeidɑ’,
do not fall down!
guɑþ-gyн (guɑþ-gɑ’-t, tpl.), rough. Cp. k̑ouþ-guɑþgɑ’t, war-club,
lit. rough knob.
guɑþgyн-dɑ, to be rough [dɑ, to be]. —— ’н’dɑ ’èi-guɑþgyн-dɑ,
the stick is rough. ’н’ ’ę̑i-guɑþgyн-dɑ, the two sticks are rough.
’н’dɑ déi-bǫų nǫ ’ę̑i-guɑþgyн-dɑ, I saw the rough stick.
guɑ-t (guɑdɑ’, punct. neg.; guɑt̑dɑ, curs.; guɑdldɑ’, fut.; guɑdɑ’dɑ’,
fut. neg.; guɑdl, imp.), to mark, paint, write. Cp. kuɑt, to be
painted; t̑oue-guɑt, to spot; guɑdl, to be red; etc. —— nǫ
gyн-guɑt, I painted it. heigɑ gyн-guɑt̑dɑ, I am about to paint it.
hǫn gyн-guɑdɑ’, I did not paint it. k‘yн̨hįнgɑ gyн-guɑdldɑ’,
to-morrow I shall paint it. hǫn gyн-guɑdɑ’dɑ’, I did not paint it.
heit̑ nǫ bн̑t̑-guɑdl, let us write it. poue bн̑t̑-guɑdldɑ’, don’t write
it! k̑ɑ’gyн gyн̑t̑-guɑdldɑ’, I am going to draw a picture on your
skin.
guɑt̑-k̑iн (an. I; guɑt̑-dɑ, tpl.), artist (man).
guɑt̑-k̑ou (guɑt̑-k̑ou-bɑ, guɑt̑-k̑ou-gɑ, tpl.; guɑt̑-k̑ou- in comp.)
yellow [guɑ-t-, red; -k̑ou, unexplained]. —— guɑt̑k̑ou-tsę̑i gyн̑-bǫų,
I saw a yellow horse. guɑt̑k̑oubɑ, yellow paint.
guɑt̑k̑ou-dɑe (inan. III), sulphur [yellow medicine].
Guɑt̑-k‘ɑe-dei, persn. of James Waldo [said to mean new buffalo-hide:
guɑt̑-, red; k‘ɑe, skin; -dei]. His recent name is K̑out̑-k̑ɑe-t‘ɑdl,
“lean elk.”
guɑ-t‘ę̑i’m (inan. IIᵃ; guɑ-t‘ǫų, dpl.), rib. Cp. guɑ-dɑ, guɑ-t‘ǫų-bɑ,
rib.

guɑ-t'ǫu-bɑ (inan. IIᵃ; guɑ-t'ǫu, dpl.), rib.   Cp. guɑ-t'ẹi'm, guɑ-dɑ, rib.

guɑt-ḥ'-yɑ' (inan. III), writing table [writing wood place].   Cp. guɑt-ḥ'-dɑ, pen, pencil.

guɑ-yɑ' (inan. III), a writing place.

gụǫ-, prepound form of gụǫ-dei, horn.

gụǫ-dei (an. II; gụǫ-dɑ, tpl.; gụǫ- in comp.), horn.   Cp. ȶḥ᷈-gụǫdei, deer-horn; ȶsou-gụǫ, great horned owl, lit. down-horn.

gụǫ-dei (an. II; gụǫ-gɑ, tpl.), afterbirth, =syḥn-gụǫdei, lit. child-afterbirth [app. connected with -guɑ-bḥ, behind; gue, behind; gǫum-, the back].

-gụǫ-gɑ in tḥn-gụǫ-gɑ, forehead.

gụǫ-seiȶ-dɑ (inan. II; gụɑ-seidl, dpl.), spear [gụǫ-, unexplained; w. -sei-dl cp. sei-bɑ, to stab].

gu-e, adv., behind, outside, outdoors [cp. guɑ-bḥ, behind; gǫu-m-, the back].   —— gue 'ḥ, he is coming behind.   gue t'ouyḥ, he is walking behind (after us).   gue dɑ́-'ḥ, he is coming behind us. gue 'ḥ-bḥȶɑ', I am going to follow behind.   gue ȶɑ', he is outside; ct. 'ɑhɑ' ȶɑ, he is inside.   gue 'ẹihɑ' 'ḥ-'ḥ'gyḥ, I am sitting outside here.   gue 'ḥ-k'iḥȶɑ', I am going to go outside.

Gu-e-gyḥ-ḳiḥ (Gu-e-gyḥ-gɑ, tpl.; Gu-e-gyḥ- in comp.), Pawnee man [gu-e-gyḥ-, unexplained; -ḳiḥ].

guegyḥ-p'eip (inan. IIᵃ), dogwood [Pawnee bush].

gue-tsou, adv., behind, outside.   —— gue-tsou 'ḥ-ȶɑ', I was outside.

-gyḥ, 1. noun postfix; -gɑ'-t, tpl. correspondent; 2. postp., at, on, in; 3. adverb postfix [cp. -gɑ, -gɑ'-t].   —— 1. k'ǫu-gyḥ, dark; k'ǫu-gɑ't, tpl. 2. ḳyḥhị'ḥ 'ḥn tougyḥ bou-ȶɑ', the man stays at home all the time.   dǫm-gyḥ 'èi-ȶɑ', we are on the ground.   ȶoup'ouȶ-gyḥ dèi-sɑ'dɑ', I am going to sit in the shade, =dèi-ȶoup'ouȶ-sɑ'dɑ'. pḥ'gyḥ, prairie.   pḥ'gi 'ḥ-bḥ'ȶɑ', I am going to go out on the prairie.   piḥn t'ḥdl-gyḥ m-guɑn, the gopher went into his hole, =piḥn boudlp'iḥȶ-gyḥ m-guɑn.   Lawton-gyɑ kiḥdl, he is living at Lawton.   t'ḥdl-gyḥ gyḥ-k'uɑt, I got him out of the hole, =boudl-p'iḥȶ-gyḥ gyḥ-zǫun.   tou-gi 'ḥ-tsḥn, I reached home.   pḥ'byou'e tou-gyḥ 'ḥ-bḥ'ȶɑ', I am going to where my brothers live.   t'ḥ'dliḥ t'ǫu-gyḥ 'ḥ'gyḥ, the boy is sitting in the water.   pḥe-gyḥ hẹi'm, he died in the summer; ct. ȶou᷈dei pḥe hẹi'm, he died last summer. sḥe-gyḥ hẹi'm, he died in the winter.   hḥ'-gi 'ḥ-hɑ'gyḥ, where have you got it?   sɑ'ɑdl-gyḥ gyḥ-hɑ'gyḥ, I have it in my mouth (ans.).   hḥ'-bḥ gɑ̀-goup, where did he hit you?   beidl-gyḥ 'ẹi-goup, he hit me in the mouth (ans.).   tḥ'-gyḥ 'ẹi-goup, he hit me in the eye (ans.).   mǫn-gyḥ ȶsou gyḥ-dou', I have a stone in my hand.   'ɑdl-gyḥ dèi-p̱ǫ'ǫ'dɑ', I am going to wash my hair. 'ɑdlt'ǫu-gyḥ 'ẹi-goup, he hit me on the head.   3. ḳiḥ-gyḥ, afterward.

gyн̇-bou-pǫy̨-gyн-gɑ (inan. IIª; gyн̇-bou-pǫy̨-gyн, dpl.), bullroarer [-bou-, unexplained; pǫy̨-, prepound form of pǫy̨ę, to sound intr.; -gyн, noun postfix; -gɑ, noun postfix]. —— gyн̇-bou-pǫy̨gyн gyн̇t-’ɑ’męi, I made several bullroarers.

gyн̇-guɑdl-dɑ’-dei (inan. IIª), beet, =guɑdl-’ei-gɑ [the red fruit]. —— gyн̇-guɑdldɑ’dei gyн̇t-bǫy̨, I saw some beets.

-gyн-e in hн’-gyнe, which one? [-gyн; -ei].

-gyн-p, 1. noun postfix in k̑ɑ’-gyнp, cliff; pн’gyнp, prairie; k‘ou-gyнp, body; etc. 2. postp., at, on, in yiн-gyнp, on both sides; etc. [-gyн; -p].

-gyн’-t‘ɑ’-bɑ, postp., on, beyond, back of [-gyн; -t‘ɑ’; -bɑ]. Cp. -gyнp, on. —— yiн-gyн’t‘ɑ’bɑ k̑yнtнek̑yн toudɑ, the followers of the chiefs on both sides. gei heigɑ hǫn yiн-gyн’t‘н’bɑ gyн̇-hнegɑ’ hнyн’ ’н̇-bн’gyн’dei, and on neither side was it known where they (the other side) went to.

gyн̇-tн’-bǫy̨nmǫę, tendril (e. g. of watermelon vine) [it ripe indicates: gyн̇-, it; tн’-, to be ripe; bǫy̨-n-mǫ-ę, to indicate; bǫy̨, to see; -n-; -mǫ-ę, unexplained]. It was stated that Kiowas tell whether watermelons are ripe by looking to see if the tendrils are curled. Ct. mǫk̑uɑngyн-goup, tendril (of other vines than watermelon).

gyн̇-tн’-sɑdl-gɑ (inan. IIª; ’ęi-tн’-sɑdl-dei, d.; gyн̇-tн’-sɑdl-dei, tpl.), coconut [the one that has eyes].

## h

hɑ, interr. particle [Tewa há, interrogative particle]. — hɑ kɑdl (’нdl) t‘ǫy̨, do you want some water? hǫ’nęi, no (ans.). hɑ bн̇t-sɑ’deidɑ, have you been working? hɑ k̑н’gyн, is it (the watch) a good one?

-hɑ, -hɑ’ possibly in bɑdl-hɑ’, hill; tou-hɑ’, cliff; -k̑ɑ-hɑ (in mǫ-k̑ɑhɑ, to be hook-nosed; k̑ouṗ-k̑ɑhɑ’-sɑdl, range of mountains; t‘ǫy̨-k̑ɑhɑ’-sɑdl, waterfall).

hɑ’ (hiнgu’ɑ, punct. neg.; hiнtdɑ, curs.; hiнdɑ’, fut.; hiнgu’ɑdɑ’, fut. neg.; hiн, imp.), to bring [cp. possibly hɑ’-d . . ., to take; hɑ’-gyн, to get; or Tewa hò’ò, to take along, bring]. Cp. pɑ’-hɑ’, to take along; bɑ’, to bring; kǫ’n, to bring. —— heigɑ gɑ̇t-hiнdɑ’, we will bring it to you, =heigɑ gɑ̇t-bɑ’dɑ’.

-hɑ’, postp., at, in the manner of, in ’iн-hɑ’, ’ęi-hɑ’, here; ’ɑ-hɑ’, ’ɑp-hɑ’, there; tsoudl-hɑ’, thus; etc. After ei, -hɑ’ appears as -hyɑ’, due to retrogression of h; e. g., ’oue-hyɑ’, there. Cp. -ɑ’, at; -yɑ’, at.

-hɑ-e-gɑ, postp., beside, near [-hɑ- as in hɑ’-bн, beside; -ei; -gɑ]. —— t‘нdliн tou-hɑegɑ dei, the boy is standing by the house.

hɑ’, affirmative particle, yes [Tewa hǫ̀’, yes].

-hɑ’- in Gu(ɑ)-hɑ’-dei, prsn., explained as meaning "He Cuts Ribs Off."

-hɑ'- in 'ę̀im-t͡soudl-touhɑ'-'ɑm-dou', he soars; see -tou-hɑ'-.

hɑ'-bʜ, adv., beside, at one side [hɑ'- as in -hɑ-e-gɑ, beside; -bʜ]. Also used as postp. Cp. hɑ'-bʜ-p, on the side of. —— t͡ɑ'-bʜ hɑ'-bʜ 'ęi-tǫudɑ, talk into my ear!

-hɑ'-bʜ, postp., beside, at one side of, close to. Cp. hɑ' bʜ, adv. —— 'ɑdl-hɑ'bʜ, at one side of the head, referring to a style of hairdressing; cp. 'ɑdl-hɑ'bʜ-k̑iʜ.

-hɑ'-bʜ-p, postp., on the side of [cp. -hɑ'bʜ, beside]. —— nǫ k̑oup-hɑ'bʜp, 'ʜ̇-kiʜdl, I live on the side (on the slope) of the mountain, =nǫ 'ʜ̇-kiʜdl k̑oup-hɑ'bʜp.

hɑ'-d . . . (hɑ'deidɑ, fut.), to take [cp. hɑ'-gyʜ, to get, take]. —— k̑ǫn gyʜ̇-hɑ'deida', I am going to pull the scab off.

hɑ'-gyʜ (hɑ'gu'ɑ, punct. neg.; hɑ'dɑ, curs.; hɑ'dɑ', fut.; hɑ'gu'ɑdɑ', fut. neg.; hɑ', hɑ'hou, imp.; hɑ'heidl, infer.; hɑ'gu'ɑheidl, infer. neg.; k'ɑ'- in comp.), to get, take [Tewa xǫ́-ŋ, to get]. Cp. k̑ǫ'dɑ-hɑ'gyʜ, to buy; mǫn-k'ǫn-hɑ'gyʜ, to take a handful; k̑iʜ-hɑ'gyʜ, to marry a man; t'ʜ'-hɑ'gyʜ, to marry a woman. —— mǫn-dou gyʜ̇-hɑ'gyʜ, I took it with my hand. nǫ bʜ́-hɑ', let's get it! nǫ gyʜ̇-hɑ'dɑ', I am going to get it. 'ʜm 'ʜ̇-hɑ', you get it! miʜn déi-hɑ'dɑ', I am about to take or get it. 'ęi-hɑ'heidl, he took them. hǫn 'ęi-hɑ'gu'ɑheidl, he did not take them. poue 'ʜ̇-hɑ'dɑ', don't get them! 'ʜm mèin-hɑ', you get them (the two milk bags)! hʜ'gi(ʜ) 'ʜ̇-hɑ'gyʜ, where have you got it? sɑ'ɑdl-gyʜ gyʜ̇-hɑ'gyʜ, I have it in my mouth (ans.). dei-hɑ'dɑ, I have been taking (or am taking) them all the time (referring to buying cattle). hǫn déi-bou-hɑ'gu'ɑ, I am not buying them all the time. heit poue béit-hɑ'dɑ', let us not take it! gyʜ̇-t'ɑ'-hɑ'gyʜ, I took her for wife. tsęi t'ǫu gyʜ̇-hɑ'gyʜ, I took the water away from the horse. 'ʜ̇-hɑ'hou, take it!

hǫ-n, neg. particle, not [cp. hǫ'-n-ęi, no; hęi, away; -hęi, privative noun and adj. postfix]. Cp. poue, proh. particle. —— hǫn dèi-boudɑ'dɑ', I shall not get enough to eat. hǫn k'iʜdeidl dèi-dɑ'p̑ʜ'egɑ', I did not sing yesterday. hǫn kɑdl 'ęim-bǫumǫ'heidl, they did not see anybody.

hǫ-n, interr. pron., what? [Tewa hǫ́-ŋ, what?]. Cp. hǫn-dei, what? hǫn-dou, why? —— hʜ'deidl nǫ hǫn, who and what?

hǫ'-n (hǫ'nǫ', punct. neg.; hǫnhɑ', hǫnmʜ, curs.; hǫn, imp.), to finish tr., finish eating, eat up [Tewa hǫ́-ŋ, to finish tr., to eat up, -xǫ̀-m-bè, to cease]. Cp. gǫum-hǫ'n, wind ceases to blow (refl.); hʜ'n, to eat; pɑ', to eat. —— heigɑ gyʜ̇-hǫ'n nǫ bʜ-bʜ, when you finish your dinner, let's go! mǫ́-hǫ'n, finish it! bǫ́-hǫ'n, you tpl. finish it! hǫn yʜ́-hǫ'nǫ', I did not finish it. yʜ́-hǫndɑ', I shall finish it. miʜn yʜ́-hǫnmʜ, I am about to finish it.

hǫ'-n (hǫ'nǫ', punct. neg.; hǫndɑ', fut.), to win [possibly the same as hǫ'-n, to finish tr.]. —— 'éit-hǫndɑ', I am going to win the game.

béit-hǫndα', we are going to win the game.    béit-hǫ'n, we won.
hǫn hн'bei 'éit-hǫ'nǫ', we neither of us won.

-hǫ-n (hǫ'- in comp.), to finish intr., cease, be consumed, be satiated,
in k'yнdl-hǫn, to get wet through; tǫų-hǫn, to cease talking;
t'нp-hǫn, to dry up intr.; tsęin-hǫn, to get burnt [Tewa -hǫ́-ŋ, to
finish intr.].

-hǫ-n, to burn intr., in guαdl-hǫn, to get burnt; guαdl-hǫ'dei, flicker
[Tewa hǫ́-ŋ, thing burns].

-hǫ'-n, to burn tr., in guαdl-hǫ'n, to burn tr.  [Tewa hǫ́-ŋ, to burn
(a thing); hǫ́-nǫ́, to make a burn on tr. (flesh)].

hǫn-dei (hǫn-gα, tpl., but -hǫn-dei-gα when forming instrumental
nouns of class inan. II), what? what kind of? something, thing;
also used as a postpound to form nouns of instrument, e. g. bǫųebн-
toubн-hǫndeigα, strainer; p'iнhout-hǫndeigα, flying machine [hǫ-n,
what?; -dei].  Cp. hǫn, what?  hн'-tsoų-dei, what kind of?  ——
hǫndei, what (do you want)?  =hǫn-dei mǫ́n-dα? hǫndei guαdl,
what color?  =hн'tsoudei guαdl, what kind of color?  hǫndei-dou
m-t'αtgα, what did he shoot with?  'нm hǫndei gyн-houdl, I
killed yours.  nǫ hǫndei, it is mine.  hǫndei (hǫ'k̑yнk̑iн tsн̣n,
what kind of a person (tribesman) came?  hǫngα 'ǵi-tsн̣n, who tpl.
came?  hǫngα hǫ'k̑yнgα 'ǵi-tsн̣n ('ǵi-tsн̣n where we should expect
'éi-tsн̣n), what kind of tribesmen came?  K̑yнeguα, Comanches
(ans.).  'oueidei hǫn hǫndei 'ǫ́n-hнeguн-dα, that man does not
know anything.  hǫn yǵi-hнegα' hǫndei 'ǫ'mi'н̣guн', I do not
know what he is doing.  hǫndei 'ǫ'mα, he is doing something.  tei
hǫndei, everything.  sα'dei-hǫndei, a tool, lit. a work thing.

hǫn-dou, adv., why? [hǫn, what? -dou, postp., by].  —— nǫ
hǫn-dou, what (do you want), how now, why?  hǫn-dou hǫn
'н̇-houguα, why didn't you kill him?

hǫ, interj. of pain.

hǫ'-, breath, in sнdl-hǫ'-t'ǫų-gyн, steam, lit. hot breath water;
hǫ'-zǫųn, to breathe [Tewa hǫ́, breath, life].

hǫ'-, prepound form of hǫ'-gyн, metal, iron.

hǫ'-'αdlsǫųm, metal comb [metal hairbrush].

hǫ'-'ǫnk'iн-gα (inan. II; hǫ'-'ǫnk'iн, dpl.), railroad-train [hǫ'-, iron;
'ǫnk'iн-, nominal form of 'ǫnhiн-t, to go along; -gα].  ——
hǫ'-'ǫnk'iн-gα béit-'ǫn, the train whistled.

hǫ'-'нt-gyн (an. II; hǫ'-'нtgα't, tpl.), buffalo fish [hǫ'-, metal; w.
-'нt- cp. p'α-'нt-doup, to be round; -gα't: the name is said to refer
to discs the size of a half dollar on that fish].

hǫ'-'eit-dα (inan. II[a]; hǫ'-'eidl, dpl.), anvil [big iron].  ——hǫ'-'eitdα
déi-bǫų, I saw the anvil.

hǫ'-gα'-t (inan. II[a]; hǫ'-gyн, dpl.; hǫ'- in comp.), piece of metal,
iron, or wire.  Cp. 'αdl-hǫ'-gyн, money, lit. metal with a head

stamped on it; 'ʜ'-t̂ɑsʜ'-hǫ'-gyʜ, wedge. —— hǫ'gɑ't déi-bǫu, I
saw a piece of iron.    hǫ'-gyʜ gyʜ̇t-bǫu, I saw the iron (coll.).

hǫ'-kuɑt (inan. Iᵃ), telegraph, typewriter, =.hǫ'-tǫu-kuɑt [iron
writing-instrument].    Cp. hǫ'gɑ't déi-guɑdɑ', I am going to telegraph, lit. I am going to wire write.

hǫ'kuɑt-ʜ'-dɑ (inan. II; hǫ'kuɑt-ʜ', dpl.; hǫkuɑt-ʜ'- in comp.),
telegraph pole.

hǫ'-k̂ɑ' (an. II; hǫ'-k̂ɑ'-gɑ, tpl.; hǫ'-k̂ɑ'- in comp.), iron knife.

hǫ'-k̂oudl-p'ʜ'-gɑ (inan. II; hǫ-k̂oudl-p'ʜ', dpl.; hǫ'-k̂oudl-p'ʜ'- in
comp.), bell [metal neck tied; said originally of cow or horse bell
tied around the neck of the animal]. —— hǫ'k̂oudlp'ʜ' gyʜ̇-bǫu,
I saw the bells.

hǫ-k̂yʜ-k̂iʜ (an. II; hǫ-k̂yʜ-gɑ, tpl.), alien man, man of some other
tribe—Wichita, Arapaho, Sioux, Oto, or any tribe other than the
Kiowa [unexplained]. —— hǫndei hǫ'k̂yʜk̂iʜ tsʜn, what kind of
tribesman came?

hǫ'-n-ęį, neg. particle, no (in ans. to question) [hǫ-n, not; -ęį, unex-
plained]. —— hɑ kɑdl t'ǫu, do you want some water? hǫ'nęį,
no (ans.).    hǫ'nęį, hǫn t̂ʜt̂gɑt̂ɑ', no, it will not be severed.

hǫ'-p'iʜ-dɑ (inan. II; hǫ'-p'iʜ, dpl.; hǫ'-p'iʜ- in comp.), stove [iron
fire]. —— hǫ'p'iʜ-dǫugyʜ gyʜ̇t-sɑ, I put them in the stove.

hɑ'-p'ou (inan. III; hǫ'-p'ou- in comp.), iron fishhook [p'ou, trap,
snare, fishhook].    Cp. t'ǫusei-p'ou, bone fishhook.

hǫ'-sɑ'-'ʜ'-dɑ (inan. II; hǫ'-sɑ'-'ʜ', dpl.; hǫ'-sɑ'-'ʜ'- in comp.),
barbed wire fence post [iron put-in post].    Cp. 'eik̂uɑ'ʜ'dɑ, fence
post, lit. planted field post.

hǫ'-sei-sei-gɑ (inan. Iᵃ; hǫ'-sei-sei, tpl.; hǫ'-sei-sei- in comp.), iron
arrowhead.

hǫ-tǫu-kuɑt (inan. Iᵃ), telegraph, typewriter, =hǫ'-kuɑt [iron talk
writing-instrument].

hǫ'-t̂ɑ'-kuɑ (inan. Iᵃ; hǫ'-t̂ɑ'-kuɑ- in comp.), iron nail [hǫ'-, iron;
t̂ɑ'-, by a blow; -kuɑ, hitter, fr. gou-p, to hit].

hǫ't̂ɑ'kuɑ-'ɑdlt'ęį'-m (inan. IIᵃ; hǫ't̂ɑ'kuɑ'-ɑdlt'ǫu, dpl.; hǫ't̂ɑ'kuɑ-
-'ɑdlt'ǫu- in comp.), nail head. —— hǫ't̂ɑ'kuɑ 'ɑdlt'ǫu-hęį dɑ,
the nail is headless.

hǫ'-t̂ʜ'-dou-p (inan. IIᵃ; hǫ'-t̂ʜ'-dei, dpl.; hǫ'-t̂ʜ'- in comp.), piece
of barbed wire (fencing) [iron enclosed: hǫ'-, iron; t̂ʜ-dei, shut in].
Cp. kʜ'boudliʜ-hǫ't̂ʜ'dei-'eidl, sheep ranch, lit. big sheep iron
enclosure.

hǫ'-t'ʜt̂-dɑ (inan. II; hǫ'-t'ʜdl, dpl.; hǫ'-t'ʜdl- in comp.), drill for
boring metal [iron borer: hǫ'-, iron; w. t'ʜ-dl-, t'ʜ-t- cp. t'ʜ' . . .,
to pierce; -dɑ].

hǫ-t'ǫu (inan. II; hǫ'-t'ǫu- in comp.), axe, tomahawk [iron club].

hǫ'-tsǫu-n (inan. IIᵃ), windpipe [breather: fr. hǫ'-zǫu-n, to breathe].

hǫ'-tsǫųn-gyн (inan. III), breath [nominal form of hǫ'-zǫų-n, to breathe; -gyн]. —— nǫ hǫ'zǫųngyн, my breath.

hǫ'-ts̄ou-t'н-'e (inan. IIᵃ), hammer (hǫ'-, iron; ts̄ou-t'н'e, pounding stone; ts̄ou, stone; t'н'e, unexplained].

hǫ'ts̄out'н'e-'eit-dɑ (inan. IIᵃ; hǫ'tsout'н'e-'eidl, dpl.), sledge hammer [big hammer].

hǫ'-zei-bɑ'-t (inan. IIᵃ; hǫ'-zei-bн, dpl.), bullet; also piece of lead, pig of lead [metal arrow].

hǫ'-zeip̀-gɑ (inan. II; hǫ'zeip, dpl.; hǫ'-zeip- in comp.), gun, rifle [metal bow]. —— hǫ'zeip̀-dou, with the gun.

hǫ-zǫų-n (hǫ'zǫųnɑ', punct. neg.; hǫ'zǫųnmǫ, curs.; hǫ'zǫųndɑ', fut.; hǫ'zǫųnǫ'dɑ', fut. neg.; hǫ'zǫųn, imp.), to breathe [hǫ'-, breath; zǫųn, to take]. —— dèi-hǫ'zǫųn, I took a breath. dèi-bou-hǫ'zǫųnmǫ, I am breathing all the time. bèi-hǫ'zǫųn, take a breath! dèi-hǫ'zǫųnmǫ, I am breathing.

hн' (hн'gu'ɑ, punct. neg.; hн'guɑ, curs.; hн'dɑ', fut.; hн'gu'ɑdɑ', fut. neg.; hн, imp.; app. îн'-, t'н'- in comp.), to stand up, get up. Cp. *'ǫn-hн', to stand up; pei-seį-hн', to revive intr.; îн'-dou', one is erect; t'н'-dou', tpl. are erect; *zout-bɑdlhɑ'-hн'-guɑ, to have waves. —— dèi-hн', I stood up. hǫn dèi-hн'gu'ɑ, I did not get up. dèi-bou-hн'guɑ, I am getting up all the time. bèi-hн, get up! heit bèi-hн, let's get up! heidɑ poue bèi-hн'dɑ', don't get up!

hн-dl-, to hurry, in hнdl-'н̨, to hurry.

-hн-dl-,-hн-t-in 'н'-t'ɑ-t̄-bн-hн-t̄-dɑ ('н'-t'ɑ-t̄-bн-hн-dl, dpl.), chair, lit. wood one sits on.

-hн-dlin t'ǫų-hнdl, lame [t'ǫų-, leg].

-hн-dl- in -pн'-hнdl-dou', to have confluence [pн'-, together].

hнdl-н̨ (curs.; hнdl-н̨'mǫ, curs. neg.; hнdl-н̨nmн̨, imm.; hнdl-н̨'dɑ', fut.; hнdl-н̨'mǫ'îɑ', fut. neg.; hнdl-н̨, imp.), to hurry [hн-dl-, referring to hurrying; 'н̨, to come]. There is no such form as hнdl-bн (bн, to go). Cp. k̄uɑn-dɑ, to hurry. —— 'н̀-hнdl-н̨, I was in a hurry. 'н̀-bou-hнdl-н̨, I am in a hurry all the time. 'èįm-hнdl-н̨, hurry, run!

hн-e-gyн (stat.; hнegɑ', stat. neg.; hнeyн, imm.; hнedeiîɑ', fut.; hнegɑ'dɑ', fut. neg.), to know [Tewa hą́, hą́-ŋ-gí-, to know]. —— yн́-hнegyн, I know; also I came to from a faint, I recovered consciousness. hǫn yн́-hнegɑ', I do not know. miнn yн́-hнeyн, I am about to know. hǫn miнn yн́-hнegɑ', I am not about to know.

hнegyн-dɑ, to know [-dɑ, to be]. —— hǫndн́n-hнegyн-dɑ (hǫndнn- for hǫndei 'н́n-) he does not know anything.

hнegyн-heį, adv., anywhere, one does not know where [hнegyн, to know; -heį, priv.]. —— 'ɑhyɑ' hнegyн-heį bèi-tsei, just set it (the tumbler) there anywhere!

Hн-e-tsi-k'iн, name of a Kiowa man who was interviewed by Mr. Mooney [unexplained].

-hн-p, excessive usitative postfix, in 'ɑ'-hнp, to be a great gambler; tsнhy-нр̀-ḱiн, asker of many questions [cp. -hн-t, excessive agentive].

-hн-р̀-dɑ (or -hн-t̑-dɑ?) in teigyн ḱɑn-hнр̀dɑ-, icicle, lit. ice hanging.

-hн-t, app. excessive agentive postfix, in sẹim-hнt, thief, mouse [cp. -hн-p, excessive usitative postfix].

-hн-t in t̑ɑ'-hн-t, to listen to [t̑ɑ'-, to hear].

-hн-t̑-gɑin p'oudl-hнt̑gɑ, to tell a lie.

hн'-, interr. stem, in hн'-dei, what kind of? etc. [Tewa hн́', what kind of?].

hн'-b . . . (hн'ba curs. neg.; hн'beidɑ', fut. t'н'bн'- in comp.), to smoke [cp. t'н'bɑ'-t, tobacco]. Cp. t'н'bн'-ḱuɑdl, several sit smoking.

hн'-bɑ (hн'bɑ', punct. neg.; hн'boup, curs.; hн'beidɑ', fut.; hнbɑ'dɑ', fut. neg.; hн'bei, imp.; t'н'bei- in comp.), to lift, carry off [cp. hн'-bн]. Cp. zọun-t'н'bei, tree squirrel, lit. carrier off with his teeth. —— gyн̀-hн'bɑ, I lifted it. hɑ̨n gyн̀-hн'bɑ', I did not lift it. mн̨ẹgyн̀-bou-hн'boup, I am lifting it up all the time. 'н̀-hн'bei, lift it up! heit̑ bн́-hн'bei, let's lift it up! mɑ̨n-dou gyн̀-hн'bɑ, I carried it off in my hand. mн̨ẹ gyн̀-hн'bɑ, I raised it (the window). mɑ̨nt̑sọu-dou gyн̀-hн'ba, I carried it away in my claws. =gyн̀-mɑ̨nt̑sọu-hн'bɑ. peidei déi-hн'bɑ, I stood the pencil on end. k'iнdeidl déi-hн'bɑ, I erected the pole yesterday.

hн'bн, interr. adv., where? [hн'-, interr. stem; -bн, postp., at]. —— hн'-bн gɑ̀-goup, where did he hit you? beidl-gyн 'ẹi-goup, on the mouth (ans.).

hн'-bн (hн'bɑ', punct. neg.; hн'beip, curs.; hн'beit̑ɑ', fut.; hн'bɑ'dɑ', fut. neg.) in k'iнn-hн'bн, to cough up; sɑ-'ọum-hн'bн, to have hemorrhage; zout-hн'bн, to be carried (away) by the current. Also in mн̨ẹgɑ hн'bн-'ẹi, in mid forenoon, explained as high lifted when [cp. hн'-bɑ, to lift].

hн'-bei, interr. and indef. adv., where? somewhere [hн'-, interr. stem; -bei postp., at]. —— hн'-bei hụ'ɑn-t'нe 'ẹim-tsн̨n, on which road did you come? hн'-bei(-tsou) ('èi)m-tsн̨n, where did you come from? ḱoup-yɑ' 'н̀-tsн̨n, from the mountain (ans.). hɑ̨n hн'bei 'éit-hɑ̨'nɑ, we neither of us won, we did not win on either side.

-hн'-bei in 'èim-sнdl-hн'bei, you are making it hotter (possibly from hн'bɑ, to lift).

-hн'-bei-p in bọu-hн'beip, to be sparkling [cp. bọuẹ-bн-hei-р̀-gyн, lightning].

hн'-bei-tsou, interr. and indef. adv., where? somewhere. —— hн'-bei(-tsou) 'èim-tsн̨n, where did you come from?

10559°—28——6

ḣʜ'-dɑ (hʜ'dɑ', punct. neg.; hʜ'doup, curs.; hʜ'deidɑ', fut.; hʜ'dɑ'dɑ',
fut. neg.; hʜ'dei, imp.), to shout. Also in 'ɑt-hʜ'dɑ, to cry;
sɛịm-hʜ'dɑ, to whistle; ꞇɑdl-hʜ'dɑ, to hiccough; tsʜt-hʜ'dɑ, to give
a whoop. —— dèi-hʜ'dɑ, I gave a yell. bèi-hʜ'dei, yell! poue
bèi-hʜdeidɑ', don't yell! 'ę̀ịm-hʜ'deidɑ'-sǫụ, he is going to be
yelling too much. hǫndou bèi-bou-hʜ'doup, what do you keep
yelling all the time for?

hʜ'-dei, interr. and indef. pron., what? what kind of? something,
thing [hʜ'-, interr. stem; -dei]. Cp. hʜ'-dei-dl, who? ꞇʜę-syʜn-
hʜ'dei, dime, lit. white small thing. —— tei hʜ'dei guɑdl, all-
colored. 'ɑp̀gɑ gyʜ̀-ꞣǫ'dei-hʜ'dei-'ęịm, to a bad place.

hʜ'-dei-dl, interr. and indef. pron., who? somebody [hʜ'-, interr.
stem; -dei-dl]. Cp. hʜ'-dei, what? —— hʜ'deidl dɑ, who was it?
nǫ 'ʜ̀-dɑ, it was I (ans.). hʜ'deidl 'ʜ'dɑ 'éi-ꞇɑ'ꞇʜdl, who cut
down this tree? hʜ'deidl tsʜn, who came? hʜ'deidl 'ʜ̀-houdl,
you killed somebody.

hʜ'-gyʜ, interr. and indef. adv., where? somewhere, sometime,
perhaps [hʜ'-, interr. stem; -gyʜ]. Cp. pʜ'-hʜ'gyʜ, sometimes.
—— hʜ'gyʜ hị'ʜgyʜ, 1. where did he die? 2. he died somewhere.
hʜ'gyʜ́ m-kiʜdl (for hʜ'gyʜ 'ęịm-kiʜdl) where do you live? pʜ̣'nyʜ
'ʜn hʜ'gyʜ yʜn-guɑdɑ, I write him just once in a while. pʜ'
hʜ'gyʜ 'ʜn tsʜnmʜ, sometimes he comes. mǫn hʜ'gi 'ʜ̀-ꞇɑ', I
guess somewhere they are staying. hǫn heigɑ hʜ'gyʜ gyʜ̀-
bǫụnmǫ, I am not going to see him at all. hǫn kɑdl hʜ'gyʜ
gyʜ̀-bǫụnmǫ, I never see him. hʜ'gyʜ souꞇɑ', maybe it will
rain.

hʜ'-gyʜ-e, interr. and indef. pron., which one? someone [hʜ'-, interr.
stem; -gyʜ; -ei]. —— hʜ'gyʜe 'ę̀ịm-dɑ, which one of you did it?
'oueidei dɑ, that fellow did it (ans.).

hʜ'-'ou-e, interr. and indef. adv., when? sometime [hʜ'-, interr.
stem; -'ou-e, postp., at]. Cp. hʜ'-'ou-dei, how much, how many?
—— hʜ'oue 'ę̀ịm-bʜnmʜ, when are you going? hʜ'oue béi-
houꞇdɑ', when are you going to kill them? pʜe heigɑ hʜ'oue
yiʜꞇɑ', the sun is going to set sometime. hǫn houdldei tsʜ̣'nǫ'
gɑ sɑt hʜ'oue ꞣiʜgyʜ tsʜn, he did not come back for a long time
and at last way afterward he came back. gɑ hʜ'oue sɑt tsʜnheidl,
and I heard that he came back way after.

hʜ'-'ou-dei (spl.), interr. and indef. pron., how much, how many?
some, several [hʜ'-, interr. stem; -'ou- as in -'ou-e postp., at;
-dei]. Cp. hʜ'-'ou-e, when? —— hʜ'oudei 'ɑdlhǫ̣'gyʜ, how much
money? hʜ'oudei ꞣyʜ̣'hyoup, how many men? hʜ'oudei k'iʜ,
how many days? hʜ'oudei t'ʜdl dɑ, how many holes are there?
hʜ'oudei t'ʜdlgyʜ, in how many holes? hʜ'oudei t'ʜdlgyʜ, in
several holes (ans.; sounds the same as the question). hʜ'oudei
tsęịgɑ 'éi-dɑ, how many horses are there? hʜ'oudei tsęịgɑ 'éi-dɑ,

there are several horses (ans.). hʜ'oudei gɑ́-'iʜ-dɑ, how many
children have you? kɑ'k'iʜ nɑ́-'iʜ-dɑ, I have ten (ans.). hʜ'oudei
tseįgɑ '6i-k̑uɑdl, several horses are lying down.

hʜ'oudei-dou, interr. and indef. adv., how many times? several
times [-dou, postp., by]. —— hʜ' 'oudei-dou (heigɑ) 'ęihɑ'
'ʜ-tsʜn, I came here several times.

hʜ'-tsou, interr. and indef. adv., how? in some way [hʜ'-, interr.
stem; -tsou, postp. like]. —— hʜ'-tsou m-k'ɑ, how is your name?
=hʜ'-tsou 'ʜn bèi-k'ɑ'mɑ, how are you called? hɑn yɑ́-hʜegɑ'
hʜ'-tsou m-k'ɑ'gyʜdei, I don't know what your name is. hʜ'-tsou
gɑ̀-k'ɑ'mdɑ', how are we going to call you? hʜ'-tsou m-tǫųgyʜ,
what did you say? hʜ'-tsou 'ʜ-tǫųę, I said something (ans.).
hɑn hʜyʜ' 'ʜ-tǫųgɑ', I did not say anything (ans.). hʜ'-tsou
gyʜ-tǫųzʜnmʜ, what are they talking about? '6i-dɑ'-t'ęinda nei
hʜ'-tsou houdldɑ', I could not kill him if I wanted to. hʜ'-tsou
k̑sou 'ęidei bʜt-k'ɑ'mɑ, what do you call this stone? hʜ'-tsou
béit-k'ɑ'mɑ 'ʜm, what do you call those tpl. an. min.? hʜ'-tsou
k'ɑ k̑sou, what is "stone" called?

hʜ'tsou-dei, interr. and indef. pron. and adv., of what kind? of
some kind [hʜ'tsou, how? -dei]. —— hʜ'tsoudei guɑdl, what
color? =hɑndei guɑdl?

hʜ-yʜ', interr. and indef. adv., where, in which direction, how? somewhere, somehow. [hʜ'-, interr. stem; -yʜ', postp. at, in the region
of]. Cp. hʜ'-gyʜ, where? —— hʜ-yʜ' m-bʜ, where are you going
to? k̑ouþ-guɑ 'ʜ-bʜ'k̑ɑ', I am going to the hill? hʜ-yʜ' 'ʜ-bʜ'k̑ɑ'
where shall I go? hʜyʜ' bʜ, where did he go? where has he
gone? where is he? hɑn yɑ́-hʜegɑ' hʜyʜ' 'ʜ-bʜ'gyʜ, I don't
know where they went. hʜyʜ' yʜ'e, which way? hʜyʜ' (yʜ'e)
'ʜ-(tsʜe-)bʜ'k̑ɑ', which way am I to go? gei heigɑ hʜy ʜ''-bʜ'-
gyʜ'dei (=hʜyʜ' 'ʜ -) gɑ hɑn gyʜ̀-hʜegɑ', they don't know where
they went to. 'ɑhyɑ'gɑ hʜy ʜ''m-hou'ɑ'zǫųnheidl (=hʜyʜ' '6im-),
they moved off somewhere. hʜyʜ' k'ɑgyʜ k̑sʜdl hɑn yɑ́-hʜegɑ',
I don't know what (lit. where, how) my own name is. hɑn hʜyʜ'
'ʜ-tǫųgɑ', I did not say anything. hʜyʜ' m-dɑ, what is wrong, lit.
where are you?

hʜyʜ'-dou, adv. maybe, if [hʜyʜ', somewhere, somehow; -dou, postp.,
by, as]. —— hʜyʜ'-dou tsʜnk̑ɑ' nɑ hɑn hʜyʜ' yɑ́-tsʜegɑ'dɑ' (or
'ʜ-kiʜt'ʜ'mɑ'k̑ɑ' instead of the last word), if he comes I will not
be afraid. hʜyʜ'-dou 'ʜ-bʜ'k̑ɑ', I may go. hʜyʜ'-dou gyʜ̀t-
sɑ'deidɑ'dɑ' k'yʜhįʜgɑ, I may be working tomorrow.

hʜ-y-ǫų-dei, adv., plainly [hʜ-e-, unexplained; -ǫų, ev. intensive;
-dei]. —— hʜyǫųdei 'ʜ-tǫųk'į'ʜmʜ, you talk just as plain as you
can!

-hʜ-ę- in p'oudl-hʜ-y-įʜ, cottontail rabbit.

hn̄'-n (hn̄'nǫ', punct. neg.; hn̥nmǫ, curs.; hn̥ndɑ', fut.; hn̄'nn̄'dɑ',
fut. neg.; hn̄'n, imp.), to eat [Tewa hú-nyǫ̀, to eat]. Cp. -hn̄'n,
eater; pɑ', to eat; hǫ'n, to eat up. —— gyn̄-hn̄'n, I ate it.   tei
gyn̄-hn̄'n, I ate it all.   mihn gyn̄-hn̥nmǫ, I am about to eat it.
'n̥m 'n̄-hn̄'n, you eat it!   déi-hn̄'n, I ate it (the watermelon).

-hn̄'-n, eater, in sęi-hn̄'n, horned toad, lit. cactus eater [hn̄'n, to eat].

Hn̥ndn̄dlei, prsn. of Andrés Martinez [fr. Span. Andrés].   The
initial h is o. k., despite Mooney and more recent writers who
give it without.

-hn̄'-d . . . in îɑdl-hn̄'-d . . ., to have hiccoughs.

hei, adv., now, already, more commonly occurring as hei-gɑ, of same
mg.   Also said in ans. when one is called to, or in answering the
roll call in school.   —— t'н' 'ę́i-hęi'm hei k̑iнgyн 'н̄-t'ouyн, when
my wife died I went traveling.

hei, interj.   Mr. Smoky has heard that when the Utes start to make
a run (in battle) they cry thus.

hei- in hei-bɑ, to carry in; hei-bн, to enter.

hei- in hei-dǫu'm-tsou, downslope; hei-t'нɒ̀-tsou, upslope.

-hei in sɑ-hy-ei, blue, green.

-hei in p'ɒ'-hei, straight, adv.; p̑ɒ'-hei, in the middle (cp. k'ou-p̑ɒ',
in the middle).

hei-bɑ (heibɑ',·punct. neg.; heiboup, curs.; heibeidɑ', fut.; heibɒ'dɑ',
fut. neg.; heibei, imp.), to take in, carry in [cp. hei-bн, to enter].
—— gyn̄-heibɑ, I˙ carried it in.   gyn̄-bou-heiboup, I carry it in
all the time.   'н̄-heibei, carry it in!   poue 'н̄-heibeidɑ', don't take
it in!

hei-bн (heibɑ', punct. neg.; heibeip, curs.; heibeiîɑ', heibiнîɑ', fut.;
heibɒ'îɑ', fut. neg.; heibei, imp.), to enter [cp. hei-bɑ, to take in].
—— 'ę̀im-heibei, come in!   k̑yн̥hį'н̥ 'н̥'gyн-dei-'įн̥ 'н̄-heibiнîɑ',
I am going to go in to where the man is sitting.   'н̄-heibн, I came in.

hei-dɑ, adv., yet, still [hei, now; app. adverbial -dɑ, but cp. possibly
hei-t, exhortative particle].   —— heidɑ n (for heidɑ hǫn) syn̥n
'н́-dǫ'mǫ', the child is not born yet.   heidɑ hǫn hęimǫ', he is not
dead yet.   heidɑ sнdl, it is still hot; ct. heigɑ sнdl, it is already
hot.

hei-dǫ-n-hn̄'-gyн, adv., never; [app. even not somehow: hei-dǫ-n-
for hei-dɑ hǫ-n, yet not; -hn̄'gyн, somewhere, somehow].   ——
heidǫnhn̄'gyн dèi-boudɑ', I never get enough.

hei-dǫu'm-tsou, adv., downslope (hei- as in hei-t'н-ɒ̀-tsou, upslope;
dǫu'-m, down; -tsou].   —— heidǫu'm-tsou 'н́-bn̄'heidl, they went
downhill.

hei-gɑ, adv., already, now, then, and, and then [hei, now; gɑ, and].
—— heigɑ m-'ɒ̀'zǫun, he (the child or cripple) is already walking.
heigɑ gyn̄-bɑ', I have brought it with me.   heidɑ hǫn pне bɒ'dɑ'
heigɑ dèi-hн', I got up before sunrise.   heigɑ dèi-dɒ'dɑ', I am

singing already, I am singing now. heigɑ miнn hǫn dèi-dɑ̄'p̄н'egɑ',
I am not about to sing. miнn heigɑ gyн̀-dęįťsoup̀dɑ', I am about
to put him to sleep. heigɑ gɑ̀t-hiнdɑ', we'll bring it to you,
= heigɑ gɑ̀t-bɑ̄'dɑ'. heigɑ 'н̀-hęįmǫ, now I am going to die.
heigɑ hęį'm, he already died. heigɑ déi-houtdɑ, I am going to
kill them right now. hǫn déi-houtguɑ heigɑ, I am not killing
them now. heigɑ sнdl, it is already hot; ct. hiedɑ sнdl, it is
still hot.

-hei-p- in bǫųę-bн-hei-p̀-gyн, lightning [cp. bǫų-hн'-bei-p, to be
sparkling].

hei-t, exhort. particle used with fut. and imp.; poue, proh. particle,
follows heit to form the negative [hei, now; -t, unexplained, cp.
possibly heidɑ]. —— heit bн́-'ǫnt̄out'н', let us forgive him!
hèit poue bн́-'ǫnt̄out'н̣'ȋɑ', let us not forgive him! heit bн́-hн̄'bei,
let us lift it up! heit bн́-hou, let us kill it!

hei-t'нp-, upslope, in hų'ǫn heit'нp̀-ꝁɑ, the road runs uphill. See
hei-t'нp̀-tsou.

hei-t'нp̀-tsou, adv., upslope [hei- as in hei-dǫų'-m-tsou, downslope;
t'н-p-, up; cp. t'н-e, on top; -tsou]. —— heit'нp̀-tsou 'н́-'н̣'heidl,
they went uphill.

hęį, adv., away, gone away; well, recovered [cp. -hęį, privative;
hǫ-n, not]. Cp. hęį-gyн, away; hęį-dɑ, to throw away, go away.
—— mǫn heigɑ hęį heigɑ gyн̀-dɑ, bн̀-ꝁyнmdei-bɑ̄'ȋɑ', maybe
they're gone away, we shall be going for nothing; hęį 'ǫmgyн, he
got well; mǫ́n-ꝁɑ̄'yɑ' heigɑ hęį 'н̀-'ǫmgyн, my cut place has
gotten well, lit. at my cut place I have become well.

hęį-, unexplained, in hęį-tei-t, to tell a story or myth.

-hęį, privative, postfixed to nouns and adjectives [hęį, gone away,
used as postfix; cp. hǫn, not]. —— tsęį-hęį ꝁɑ̄'dнdl, automobile,
= tsęį-hęį. k'uep'н [horseless wagon]. tou-hęį dɑ, there is no
house. guɑ-hęį yн̀-dɑ, I am not wise; ct. nꝗ̣ yн̀-guɑ, I am very
wise. seip-hęį gyн̀-dɑ, it is a dry year, lit. rainless it is.

hęį-dɑ (heidɑ', punct. neg.; hęįdoup, curs.; hęįdeidɑ', fut.; hęįdɑ̄'dɑ',
fut. neg.; hęįdei, imp.), to remove tr., depart, separate oneself, go
away, open (door). [Cp. hęį, away.] —— sɑ̄'-p'нn gyн̀-hęįdeidɑ',
I am going to throw away the ashes. dèi-hęįdɑ, I departed, lit.
I awayed myself. hǫn dèi-hęįdɑ', I did not leave. bèi-hęįdei, go
away! poue bèi-hęįdeidɑ', don't go away! heit bèi-hęįdei, let's
leave? ꝁꝗ̣'deidl 'ę́į-'ꝗ̣'męį-dei peidou dèi-hęįdɑ, he treated me
bad and that's why I left. déi-tsнt-hęįdɑ, I opened the door.
tsнt hǫn déi-hęįdɑ', I did not open the door. béi hęįdei, open it!
poue béi-hęįdei, don't open it!

hęį-gyн, adv., away [hęį, away; -gyн]. —— tɑ̄'dei hęįgyн dɑ̄'męį'
gɑ hɑ̄'oue sɑ̀t tsн̣nheidl, I heard that he was away for a long time
and that he came back way after. mǫn hęįgyн dɑ heigɑ, maybe

he's gone now.  hẹịgyʜ '-dɑ-'ẹị mɑ̨n tsʜ̨n, I was away when he came.

hẹị-'iʜ (an. II; hẹị-you-p, tpl.), doll [hẹị- as in Tewa hų''ų`, doll; -'iʜ, child, dim.; the word is equivalent to Tewa hų''ų''ē`, little doll].

hẹị-m (hẹịmgɑ', stat. neg.; hẹịmîɑ', fut.; hẹịmgɑ'îɑ', fut. neg.; hẹịmheidl, infer.), to be short of food, famish [cp. hẹị'-m, to die. —— 'oueigɑ gyʜ̀-hẹịmheidl, those folks in that house were hard up.  'oueidei 'ʜ'n-hẹịm-heidl, he was hard hit for food.  ki'ʜkɑ̨mbɑ gyʜ-hẹịmîɑ', the people are going to be hard up.  k'iʜkɑ̨mbɑ gyʜ̀-hẹị, the people are hard up, =k'iʜkɑ̨mbɑ kouþdei-'ɑ'ʞɑ.  hɑ̨n gyʜ̀-hẹịmgɑ', they are not hard up.

hẹị'-m (also hị'ʜgyʜ, punct.; hẹị'mɑ̨', punct. neg.; hẹị'mʜ̨, curs.; hị'ʜîɑ', fut.; hị'ʜ, imp.; hị'ʜheidl, punct. infer.; hị'ʜyịʜ̨, curs. infer.), to die [cp. hẹị-m, to be short of food; hou-dl, to kill; hou-dl-dɑ, to be sick; Tewa hē`; 1. to kill; 2. to be sick].  —— hʜ'gyʜ hẹị'm, or hʜ'gyʜ hị'ɑ̨gyʜ, 1. Where did he die? 2. he died somewhere.  heigɑ hẹị'm, he already died.  t'ǫụgɑ hei'm, he has been dead a long time.  sat hẹị'm, he died just a little while ago.  hɑ̨n hẹị'mɑ̨', he did not die; cp. pei-hẹị dɑ, he is alive yet.  heidɑ hɑ̨n hẹị'mɑ̨', he is not dead yet.  miʜn 'ʜ̀-hẹị'mʜ̨, I am on the point of dying.  heigɑ houldldei hị'ʜîɑ', he is going to die pretty soon.  bʜ̀-tǫụgyʜ heigɑ, hị'ʜheidl, they say that he died.  bʜ̀-tǫụgyʜ heigɑ hị'ʜyịʜ̨, they say that he is dying.  'ʜ̀-hị'ʜyịʜ̨, they say I was dying.  ʞyʜ̨hị'ʜ 'ẹ̀i-hị'ʜyịʜ̨ nẹ̀in-bǫụhoudɑ', I am going to see the two dying men.  ʞyʜ̨houp 'ʜ̀-hị'ʜyịʜ̨ déi-pǫụhoudɑ', I am going to see the tpl. dying men.  ʞiʜ̨hị'ʜ 'ʜ̀-pǫụbʜ nɑ̨ heigɑ hị'ʜheidl, I went to look at the man who had died.  'ʜ̀-'ɑ'dliʜ bouî tsẹịhịʜ̨ 'ẹ́i-hẹị'm-dou, I cried because my dog died.

hẹịm-'ɑ̨mgyʜ (hẹịm-'ɑ̨'mʜ̨, curs.; hẹịm-'ɑ̨mdeiîɑ', fut.) to get short of food [to famish become].  —— nɑ̨ gyʜ̀t-hẹịm-'ɑ̨mgyʜ, we were hard up for food.  miʜ̨n gyʜ̀-heimɑ̨'mʜ̨, they are on the verge of being short of food.

hẹị-n, adv., maybe [unexplained].  —— mɑ̨ 'ɑ̨nhʜ'dei hẹịn dɑ, maybe it is a bear.

hẹịteiî-gyʜ, story, myth [hẹịteit, to tell a story; -gyʜ].  Cp. p'oudl-hẹịteiîgyʜ, lie, false story.  —— 'ʜ̀-hẹịteiî-îɑ', I heard a myth.  hʜ'oud (for hʜ'oudei) 'ʜ̀-hẹịteiî-îɑ', I heard several myths.

hẹị-tei-t (hẹịteidɑ', punct. neg.; hẹịteiîdɑ, curs.; hẹịteidlldɑ', fut.; hẹịteidɑ'dɑ', fut. neg.; hẹịteidl, imp.; hẹịteidlei', infer.), to tell a story or myth, narrate [hẹị-, unexplained; tei-t, to tell].  Cp. hẹịteiî-dɑ, to be told as a story; hẹịteiîgyʜ, story; hẹịteiî-tǫụk'ɑ̨'m, to mention in a story; p'oudl-hẹịteiîgyʜ, lie.  —— gyʜ̀-hẹịteit, I told a story.  hɑ̨n gyʜ̀-hẹịteidɑ', I did not tell a story.  'ʜ̀-hẹịteidl, tell a story!  poue 'ʜ̀-hẹịteidldɑ', do not tell a story!  'ẹ́i-hẹịteidl, tell me a story!

hẹiteit̂-dɑ, to be told as a story or myth [hẹiteit; dɑ]. —— 'oudeihɑ'
gyн̇-hẹiteit̂-dɑ, that is all there is to the story.

hẹiteit̂-tǫuk‘ɑ'm, to mention in a story [to narrate, mention]. ——
'éit-hẹiteit̂-tǫuk‘ɑ'm-tsẹi 'н̥n 'ɑ̃'zн̃'t̂ǫ'houp ;'éit-k‘ǫ'mɑ, whenever
we mention them in myths we call them Udder-angry Travelers-off.

hiн-dl (inan. I; hiн-dl, also hiн-dl-dн, tpl.), arroyo, draw, gulch
[Tewa hú'ú, hé'é, arroyo].

+hiн-dl- in k̂ɑ'-k‘ɑebiн-hiн̇dl-bн, bank caved out underneath.

hiн-dl-b . . . (hiн̇dlbeidɑ', fut.), to light (fire) [unexplained]. Cp.
t‘н̥'-, app. to light.

hiн-dɑ (hiн̇deidɑ', fut.), to vomit [cp. hiн̇t, to ascend]. Cp. zou-. . .,
to vomit. —— dèi-hiн̇dɑ, I vomited. dèi-hiн̇deidɑ', I am going
to vomit.

hiн-n (hiн̇nǫ', punct. neg.; hiн̇nmɑ, curs.; hiн̇ndɑ', fut.; hiн̇n, imp.),
to dig [cp. k‘iн-n, to dig, cough]. —— 'ɑ̃'gɑ gyн̇-hiн̇ndɑ', I am
going to dig a well. gyн̇-hiн̇n, I dig him up! 'н̇-hiн̇nhou, go and
dig him up!

hiн-t (hiн̇dlt̂ɑ', fut.), to ascend [cp. hiн-dɑ, to vomit]. Cp.t‘ɑᵽ-hiн̇t,
to cross (water); seip, to descend. —— p‘iн-t‘нe 'н̇-hiн̇dlt̂ɑ', I
am going up on top of the hill. 'н̇-hiн̇t, I climbed up. p‘н̥n-mн̥ẹ
hiн̇t, he ascended into the sky. t‘ǫu-gyн p‘ɑ̃hei 'н̇-hiн̇t, I went
right through the water.

-hịн̥, -hị'н̥ (-hyụ-'ẹ, -hyou-p, tpl.; -hịн̥-, -hyụ-'ẹ- in comp.), noun,
adj., verb and adv. postfix, real, right, very, in sн̥'nẹi-hị'н̥, rattlesnake, lit. right snake; 'ɑ-hịн̥, plain; 'ɑ̃'-hị'н̥, to be a good gambler;
mн̥ẹ-hị'н̥, highest (adv.); etc.   Referring to this postfix Gatschet
says: "These Indians [the Kiowa] do not use a special word to
express 'real,' 'principal,' or 'true,' but they append a suffix -hi
(nasalized hiⁿ), for the purpose, according to Mr. Mooney."
(A. S. Gatschet, "Real," "True," or "Genuine" in Indian languages,
American Anthropologist, n. s., I, Jan. 1899, pp. 159–160) [cp.
'ǫm-hyụ'm-dei, right, for *'ǫm-hyụ'ẹ-m-dei]. Cp. 'ǫ'-gɑ, own, real.

hou'-, hou-, to go, travel, in hou'-'ǫ'-zǫun, to travel along; hou'-'н̥, to
travel; p‘iн̇hout-hou'-kǫu'm, to fly around; hou'-sɑm-'ɑ̃'dɑ, sunflower; hou'-t̂н̇t, to travel off apart [cp. hou-t-, to go; -hou, to go;
t‘ou-yн, to go].

-hou (-hougu'ɑ, punct. neg.; -houdɑ', fut.; hougu'ɑdɑ', fut.; -hou',
imp. houheidl, infer.), itive postfix, to go (appears not to harden
the verb) [cp. hou'- to go; t‘ou-yн, to go]. —— 'н̇-dǫun-hou', go
and look for it!   hɑn gyн̇-dǫunhougu'ɑdɑ', I am not going to look
for it.   'н̇-bǫu-hou', go and look at him.

hou'-'ǫ'-zǫu-n (hou'ǫ'zǫunɑ', punct. neg.; hou'ǫ'zǫunmɑ, curs.;
hou'ǫzǫundɑ', fut.; hou'ǫ'zounǫ'dɑ', fut. neg.; hou'ǫ'zǫun, imp.;
hou'ǫ'zǫun-heidl, infer.), to travel, to travel off [to travel foot take
oneself off]. —— dèi-hou'ǫ'zǫun, I traveled (on foot, horseback,

by wagon, etc.). hǫn dèi-hou'ǫ'zǫųnǫ', I did not travel. heit
bèi-hou'ǫ' zǫųn, let's go traveling!

hou'-'ɥ, to come [hou'-, to travel; 'ɥ, to come]. Cp. hou-t-ɥ, to come.
—— 'ɦ-hou'ɥ, I was coming traveling.

hou'-bɥ, to travel [hou-, to travel; bɥ, to go]. —— hɥyɥ' '(ɦ)-
hou'- bɥnmɥ, I am going to go traveling. 'ɦ-houbɥ, I moved.

hou'-dɑ-'ɥ, to travel [hou'-, to travel; -dɑ; unexplained; 'ɥ, to come].
—— hųǫn-t'ʜe 'ɦ-hou'dɑ'ɥ gɑ mį(ɥ) 'ɦ-t'ǫųhęį'm, as I was going
along the road I got pretty thirsty.

hou-dei, to be blind (hou-, unexplained; -dei]. —— yɦ-houdei, I am
blind, = yɦ-touegyʜ-dɑ.

houdei-k̯iʜ (houdei-gɑ, tpl.), a blind man (houdei, to be blind; -k̯iʜ].

hou-dl (hougu'ɑ, houdlgɑ', punct. neg.; hout-da, curs.; houdldɑ',
fut.; hougu'ɑdɑ', fut. neg.; hou, imp.; houdlhʜ, proh.; houdlheidl, infer.). —— to kill [cp. hou-dl-dɑ, to be sick; hęį'm, to die;
hęį-m, to be short of food; Tewa hēʿ; 1. to kill. 2. to be sick].
Cp. bout-houdl, to fill tr. —— hɑ 'ʜm 'ɦ-houdl, did you kill it?
hɑ 'ɥm hǫn 'ɦ-hougu'ɑ, didn't you kill him? hɑ hǫn 'ɦ-hougu'ɑdɑ',
aren't you going to kill him? gyɦ-houdl, I killed him. poue
'ɦ-houdldɑ', don't kill him! =poue 'ɦ-houdlhʜ heit bɦ-hou, don't
let's kill it! 'ę́įm-hou'dɑ-dei gyɦ-bǫų, I saw the killer, =dɑ'k̯iʜ
gyɦ-bǫų. miʜn gyʜ-houtdɑ, I am going to kill him right now.
'ɦ-houdldɑ gɑ heigɑ m-t'ǫųp'ʜ'ĩɑ', if you kill him, they'll get you.
hǫn 'ɦ-hougu'ɑdɑ' nǫ heigɑ hǫn gɑ̀-t'ǫųp'ʜyɑ'dɑ', if you don't
kill him, they won't get you. mį(ɥ) houdl, he pretty near killed
him. nǫ 'éi-houdl, we dpl. excl. killed him.

hou-dl-, referring to sickness, in houdl-dɑ, to be sick; houdl-gyʜ,
houdl-dʜ, etc. [cp. hęį'm, to die].

-hou-dl, intensive, in k'ɑe-k̯ǫn-houdl, dragonfly, lit. rough skin;
k'ɑhy-oudl, lung; k'yʜe-hyoudl, woodrat, lit. jumper; mɥn-p'ɑ-
houdl, lion, lit. upper body furry; pou-guɑn-houdl, muskrat;
tǫų-p'a-houdl, owl sp., lit. leg downy [cp. -p'oudl, intensive].

houdl-dɑ (houdl-dǫ'mɑ', punct. neg.; houdl-dɑ'beip, curs.; houdl-
dɑ'ĩɑ', fut.; houdl-dɑ'mǫ'ĩɑ', fut. neg.; houdl-dɑ'męį', imp.;
houdl-dǫ'męį', infer.), to be sick [houdl as in houdl-gyʜ, sickness;
dɑ, to be]. —— 'ɦ-koudou-houdldɑ, I am very sick. k̯iɥhį'ɥ
houdldɑ̄męį-dei gyɦ-bǫųhoudɑ', I am going to go over to see the
man who is (said to be) sick. k̯yɥhyoup 'ɦ-houdldɑ̄męį-gɑ déi-
bǫųhoudɑ, I am going to go over to see the tpl. men who are said
to be sick.

hou-dl-dʜ (inan. III), shirt, article of clothing, clothes [hou-dl-,
unexplained; -dʜ]. Cp. 'ɑ'yʜ-houdl-dʜ, buckskin dress, lit. fringe
shirt; tǫų-gyʜ, shirt. —— houdldʜ gyɦt-bǫų, I saw the shirt.
houdldʜ-hęį, naked.

-houdl-dʜ, sickness, in t'ęįn- houdldʜ, heart disease; etc.

houdl-dei, adv., soon [hou-dl, unexplained; -dei]. —— heigɑ houdl-
dei hị'ḥîɑ', he is going to die soon.　heigɑ houdl-dei 'ṅ-bḥnmḥ, I
am going soon (e. g. in a few days); but 'ẹihɑ' houdldei heigɑ
'ṅ-bḥnmḥ, I am going soon now (e. g. in a few moments).　hɑ̨n
houdl-dei tsḥ'nɑ̨', he did not come back soon.

houdl-gyḥ (inan. I), sickness [cp. houdl-dɑ, to be sick; -gyḥ].　Cp.-
houdl-dḥ, sickness.

-hou-dl-gyḥ, postp., amidst [hou-dl-, unexplained; -gyḥ]. ——
mḥyịṇ-houdlgyḥ 'ṅ-dei, I was standing in the midst of the women,
'ṅ'-houdlgyḥ, in the midst of the smoke.

hou'-kǫ̣ụ'm (an. I; hou'-kǫ̣ụ'-bɑ, tpl.), coyote, = mɋ̨'t'ọụ̂tsọụhị'ḥ
[traveler about: hou'-, to travel; kǫ̣ụ'm to be about, here used as
a noun stem].　Cp. hou'-k̄iṇ, traveler.

-hou'-kǫ̣ụ'm, to move about, in p'iṇhout-hou'kǫ̣ụ'm, to fly about
[hou-, to travel; -kǫ̣ụ'm, to be about].

hou'-k̄iṇ (an. I, hou-p, tpl.), traveler [hou-, to travel].　Cp. hou'-
kǫ̣ụ'm, coyote, lit. traveler about. —— pḥ'gɑ hou'k̄iṇ gyṅ-bọụ,
I saw a traveler.　hḥ'oudei houp̄ dèi-bọụ, I saw several travelers.

hou-pọụ-ḥ, to go along making a noise [hou-, to travel; pọụ-, to sound;
'ḥ, to come]. —— 'ɑ'bei k'uep'ḥ 'į̣n-hou-pọụ-'ḥ, the wagon
went past making a noise.

hou'-sɑ̨m-'ṅ'-dɑ (inan. II; hou- sɑ̨m-'ṅ', dpl.; hou-sɑ̨m-'ṅ'- in comp.),
a sunflower sp. with flowers only 1½″ diam. [travel look plant,
so called because it turns its gaze: hou'-, to travel; sɑ̨m- to look;
'ṅ'dɑ, stick, plant].　Cp. t'eip̄-sɑe-ṅ'dɑ, sunflower sp. with large
(6″ diam.) flowers.

hou-t-, to go, travel, in hout-ḥ, to come; p'iṇ-hout-, referring to
flying [cp. hou'-, -hou, to go].　Cp. -t'ou-t, which is perhaps the
nominal form of hou-t-.

hou-t-ḥ, to come, in 'ṅ'-hout-ḥ, distant shower comes [hou-t-, to
travel; 'ḥ, to come].　Cp. hou-'ḥ, to come.

hou'-îṇt (hou'-îṅ'dɑ, punct. neg.; hou'îṅ'dɑ, curs.; hou'îṇdldɑ', fut.;
hou'îṇdl, imp.; hou'îṇdlheidl, infer.), to travel off apart [hou'-, to
travel; îṇt, to sever]. —— kɑ'gɑ 'į̣im-hou'îṇt, the others traveled
off apart.　heiî béi-hou'îṇdl, let us separate!

họụ-n-, adverbial verb prefix, last. —— gyṅ-họụn-goup, I hit him
the last time.　k̄yṇhị'ḥ hị'ḥ họụn-dei-dei gyṅ-tsṇe, I asked the
last man (standing).　k̄yṇhyoup 'ṅ-họụn-dei-gɑ dèi-tsṇe, I asked
the last men (standing).

họụn-k̄iṇ (an. I; họụnɋ̨'-gɑ, tpl.), the last man.

hụ'ɑ̨-n (inan. I; hụ'ɑ̨-n- in comp.), trail, road [unexplained]. ——
gyṅ-t'ɑ̨n hụ'ɑ̨n-gyḥ, I found it on the road.

hyḥ, interj. used in calling one's attention.

hyṅ, interj. of scorn.

-hyụ-'ẹ, real, see -hịḥ.

iн

'iн (an. II; 'yue, -you-p, tpl.; 'iн- in comp.), 1. child, offspring, son, daughter (cp. bou-dl, son, voc.) (but 'н-'iн-dei, his or their child); dim. postpound; 2. (for 'iн-t̂н̥ę), egg; semen [Tewa 'ē' child, dim. postpound]. Cp. sун̥n, child, little one; -t'ǫn, dim. —— 'iн gyн̇-bǫy̆, I saw my child. 'yue dèi-bǫy̆ (app. an. I decl. here), I saw my tpl. children. But sун̥n gyн̇-bǫy̆, I saw the child (not my own). sун̥'dα déi-bǫy̆, I saw the children (not my own). t̂ęinęit̂-tseiou 'iн-t̂seip, the hen laid an egg. t̂ęinęit̂-tseioup 'éit̂-'iн-k̂oup, the hens laid eggs. t̂ęineit̂-tseiou-'iн, chicken egg (app. *t̂ęinęit̂-tseiou-sун̥n would be applied to young chicken). t̂sн̥dl-iн, calf. t̂ǫy̆dei-'iн, mouse; hęi-'iн, doll; p'н̥tα-'iн, twin.
'iн-bout̂-dα, to be pregnant [to be child full]. —— 'iн-bout̂dα, she is pregnant. 'ę̀i-'iн-bout̂dα, they d. are pregnant.
'iн-bout̂-mн̥ (an. I; 'iн-bout̂-mн̥ę-mα, tpl.), pregnant woman [cp. 'iн-bout̂dα, to be pregnant].
'iн-k'ǫ' ('iнk'ǫ'nǫ', punct. neg.; 'iнk'ǫnmα, curs.; 'iнk'ǫ'dǫ', fut.; 'iн-k'ǫ'nǫ'dα', fut. neg.; 'iнk'ǫ', imp.; 'iнk'ǫ'heidl, infer.), to fuss over [unexplained]. —— 'ę̀in-'iнk'ǫ', they d. fussed over it (inf. distinguished between quarreling over and fussing over). k'iнdeidl béi-tsęihįн̥-'iнk'ǫnmα, yesterday we were fussing over the dog. k'iнdeidl hǫn béi-tsęihįн̥-iнk'ǫ'nǫ', yesterday we did not fuss over the dog. hǫn bèi-tsęihįн̥-'iнk'ǫ'nǫ'dα', we shall not fuss over the dog. poue bèi-tsęihįн̥-'iнk'ǫ'dα', don't ye (tpl.) fuss over the dog! béi-tsęihįн̥-'iнk'ǫ', ye tpl. fuss over the dog!
'iн-k'ǫę (inan. IIᵃ), womb [child peeling, child bag].
'i(н)-'oup (an. II; 'i(н)-'ouṗ-dα, tpl.; 'i(н)-'oup- in comp.), maggot [possibly 'iн, child 'ou-p, unexplained]. —— mα 'i(н)'oup 'ę́im-zн̥ngoup' (the many people bathing in the reservoir) are moving like maggots (a Kiowa expression).
'iн-p̄α'-gyн (an. I; 'iн-p̄α'-gα't, tpl.; 'iн-p̄α'-gyн- in comp.), (newborn) baby [fresh baby]. Cp. 'ei-p̄α'gyн, roasting-ear of corn.
'iн-tα'-mα (an. I; 'iн-tα'-mн̥ę-mα, tpl.), midwife ['iн, child; -tα'-, unexplained; -mн̥, woman].
'Iн̥tн̥-k̂iн (an. II; 'Iн̥tн̥-gα, tpl.), Ute man.
'iн-t̂н̥ę (an. II; 'iн-t̂н̥ę-mα, tpl.; 'iн-t̂н̥ę- in comp.), egg; (in tpl.) semen [white child]. —— 'iн-t̂н̥ęmα déi-bǫy̆, 1. I saw the tpl. eggs; 2. I saw the semen.
'iнt̂н̥ę-k'ǫę (inan. IIᵃ), eggshell.
'iн-t'н̥' (an. I; 'iн-t'ei, tpl.), daughter [woman child]. Cp. 'iнt'н̥'-t'ǫn, brother's daughter. —— 'н̥-'iнt'н̥'-dei, somebody's daughter. 'oueidei 'iнt'н̥', his daughter. 'oueidei 'iнt'ei, his tpl. daughters.
'iн-t'н̥'-t'ǫn (app. an. I), brother's daughter [little woman child: -t'ǫn, dim.]. Cp. 'iн-t'ǫn, brother's son.

'ɪн-t‘çn (app. an. I), brother's son [little son: -t‘çn, dim.].    Cp.
'ɪн-t‘н'-t‘çn, brother's daughter.
'ɪн-t̄seip, to give birth to a child [t̄sei-p, to lay s. o.]. —— 'ɪн-
t̄souþdɑ', she is going to have a baby.

## ịн

'ịн-, dem. stem, in 'ịн-hɑ', right here, now, etc.; also used as postp.
[cp. 'ẹi-, dem. stem].
-'ịн, postp., at ['ịн-, dem. stem used as postp.]. —— pнdl-t‘нe(-'ịн)
hẹi'm, he died in the bed here. 'н̄-heibн 'ɑ'gɑ 'eidlк̄iн tou'e
t̄ɑ'dei-'ịн, I went in where the old man was staying inside. 'н̄-
heibн 'ɑ'gɑ к̄yнþt‘ɑ'dɑ tou'e t̄ɑ'-dei-'ịн, I went in to where the
old men were staying inside. 'ɑ'gɑ 'нn 'ę́im-kɑ't̄ɑtdɑ-'ịн, a
swimming place. 'ɑ'gɑ tou'e dei-dei-'ịн 'н̄-he.ibeit̄a', I am going
to enter where he is standing inside.
'ị(н)-hɑ', adv., 1. right here; 2. now ['ịн-, dem.; -hɑ']. —— 1. sat
'ị(н)hɑ' sat 'н̄-tsн̨n, this is the first time that I have been up here.
'ị(н)hɑ' 'н̨n 'ę́im-kɑ't̄ɑdɑ, they swim right here; cp. 'ouhyɑ' (or
'ougɑt‘ɑ') 'н̨n 'ę́im-kɑ't̄ɑdɑ, they swim way over there. 'ịн̨hɑ'
'н̨'gyн, he was sitting right here; cp. 'ẹihɑ' 'н̨'gyн, he was sitting
here. 'ẹihɑ'dei pнe 'ịн̨hɑ' 'н̄-t̄ɑ't̄ɑ', I am going to stay right here
this summer.    2. 'ị(н)hɑ gyн̄t-peidldou', I am thinking about it
right now.
'ị(н)hɑ'-dei ('ị(н)hɑ'-gɑ, tpl.), dem. pron. and adv., this one, here
['ị(н)hɑ', here; -dei]. —— 'ị(н)hɑ'dei tou'e 'н̄-kiнdl, I live in this
room.
'ị(н)-dei ('ị(н)-gɑ, tpl.), dem. pron. and adv. this, here ['ị(н)-, dem.
stem; -dei]. —— 'ị(н)dei tou gyн̄-bǫu, I saw this house; stated
by the informant to mean the same as 'ẹidei tou gyн̄-bǫu.    'ị(н)dei
hẹi'm, this part right here (of the tree) is dead.    'ị(н)dei к̄yн̨hị'н̨,
this man right here.    'ị(н)gɑ к̄yн̨hyoup, these tpl. men.    'oueidei
gɑ 'ịн̨dei gɑ 'ẹidei, that one, and this one here, and this one.
'ịн̨dei dɑ, this is the one right here.

## k

kɑ', mother, voc.    Mr. Smoky commented: Young children prolong
the word, older children cut it short.    Cp. tsɑ, mother; kɑ'kɑ'e,
my or our mother; tɑ', father, voc.
kɑ', tpl. others, recorded only with following 'нdl or t̄sнdl: occurring
in kɑ' 'нdl, the others; kɑ' t̄sнdl, the others.    Cp. kɑ'-dei, other.
kɑ-'ɑ (an. II; kɑ-'ɑ'-gɑ, tpl.), a kind of spear having feathers along
the edge.    Cp. Kɑ'ɑ'-piн-t‘çn, prsn.
Kɑ'ɑ'-piн-t‘çn, prsn.; cp. Mooney, p. 408.    [said to mean "he speared
with kɑ'ɑ: -t‘çn, app. dim.].

kɑ-dl (an. II; kɑ-t̄-dɑ, tpl.; kɑ-dl- in comp.); 1. buffalo; 2. cow, cattle
[Tewa kǫ"ǫ'-ŋ, buffalo]. Cp. kɑdl-hįн, buffalo; 'ǫ'gɑpįн, buffalo,
tsẹi-bou, cow, cattle. —— kɑdl gyн̄-bǫʋ, I saw buffalo (app. ꜱ
and also coll.). kɑt̄dɑ déi-bǫʋ, I saw a bunch of cattle. 'ǫ'gɑpįн
'ẹi-kɑdl-guɑnmн̨ę, the buffalo hooked me.

kɑ-dl, hortative or emphatic particle [cp. kǫn-, hortative verb
prefix]. Also in 'ǫ'-kɑdl, particle. —— kɑdl 'ẹi-'ǫ' 'ɑdlhǫ'gyн,
give me some money! kɑdl syǫndei 'ẹi-'ǫ', give me a little! kɑdl
t'н'bɑ't, give me some tobacco! kɑdl t'ǫʋ, I want some water.
hɑ kɑdl 'нdl, do you want some more? hɑ kɑdl 'нdl t'ǫʋ, do you
want some more water? hɑ kɑdl t'ǫʋ, do you want some water?
hǫ'nẹi, no (ans.). kɑdl bн́-guɑdl, let us owe him! kɑdl 'нdl
syн̄'dɑ dɑ't̄ɑ', (the woman has borne five children) and is going
to have some more. hǫn kɑdl 'ę̀im-bǫumǫ'heidl, they did not see
anybody. hǫn kɑdl k̄iнgyн 'ẹim-k̄ɑ'dɑ'heidl, they never afterward met each other. hǫn kɑdl hн'giн gyн̄-bǫʋnmɑ, I never used
to see him.

kɑdl-hįн (an. II; kɑdl-hyʋ-ę, tpl.), buffalo [real buffalo, in contradistinction to cattle: kɑdl, buffalo; -hįн, real].

kɑdl-k'ɑ'-dɑ (kɑdl-k'ɑ', dpl.), buffalo robe (w. -k'ɑ cp. k'ɑe, skin).

kɑdl-sẹim-'н'-k'yн'dlei (an. II; kɑdl-sẹim-'н'-k'yн'dlou-p, tpl.), tadpole [kɑdl-sẹim-'ɑ'-, unexplained; app. k'yн'dlei, to be wet]. Cp.
k'ɑ'dlei-k'yн'dlei, frog sp.

kɑdl-zeip, cow milk [cattle milk]. —— (kɑdl-) zeip gyн̄-t'ǫʋdɑ', I
am going to drink some milk.

-kɑ'e in mǫn-kɑ'e-gɑ, wrist; 'ǫn-k̄ɑ'e, ankle.

Kɑe-k̄ɑt̄dɑ-k̄iн (an. II; Kɑe-k̄ɑt̄dɑ-gɑ, tpl.), Kiowa Arikaree man;
cp. Mooney, p. 410.

Kɑe-k̄iн (an. I; Kɑe-k̄yн̄'hyoup, Kɑe-guɑ, tpl.; Kɑe- in comp.),
Kiowa man (kɑe-, unexplained; -k̄iн, man].

Kɑe-k̄oup, "Kiowa mountains," mountains in Montana region; see
Mooney, p. 153.

Kɑe-mн̨ (an. I; Kɑe-mн̨ę-mɑ, Kɑeguɑ, tpl.), Kiowa woman.

kɑe-sẹi-'н'-dɑ (inan. IIᵃ; kɑe-sẹi-'н', dpl.), box-elder tree [Kiowa
smelling tree].

kɑe-tǫʋzн̄n, to talk Kiowa [tǫʋzн̄n, to talk]. —— yн́-kɑe-tǫʋzн̄nmн̨,
I talk Kiowa.

kɑþk'ǫʋ-'ǫm-dou', to make a shadow. —— gyн̄t̄-kɑþk'ǫʋ-'ǫm-dou',
I am making a shadow.

kɑþ-k'ǫʋ-gyн (inan. III), shadow, shade [kɑ-p-, unexplained; k'ǫʋ-,
to be dark]. —— 'ẹidei kɑþ-k'ǫʋgyн '-t̄oup'out (or gyн̄-t̄oup'out),
it is cool here in the shade. nǭ kɑþ-k'ǫʋgyн, my shadow. kɑþ-
k'ǫʋgyн gyн̄t̄-bǫʋ, I saw the shadow.

kɑ-t (kɑ'dɑ', punct. neg.; kɑt̄dɑ, curs.; kɑdldɑ, fut.; kɑ'dɑ'dɑ', fut.
neg.; kɑdl, imp.), to cross. —— gyн̄-p̄ɑ'-kɑt, I crossed the river,

=p̄ɑ' gyн̄-kɑt. hɑ̨n gyн̄-kɑ̄'dɑ', I did not cross it. miнn gyн̄-kɑtdɑ, I am about to cross it. gyн̄-kɑdldɑ', I shall cross it. hɑ̨n gyн̄-kɑ̄'dɑ̄'dɑ', I shall not cross it. 'н̄-kɑdl, cross it! bн̄-kɑdl, let us cross it!

kɑ-t̄-se̦i, nine (also in an old Kiowa count) [kɑ-t̄-, unexplained, cp. possibly kɑ̄'-k'i̦н, ten; -se̦i as in yнt̄-se̦i, eight]. —— kɑtse̦i k̄yн̄'hyoup, nine men; kɑtse̦i sнe, nine years.

kɑtse̦i-k'i̦н, ninety.

kɑtse̦i-n, nine by nine.

kɑtse̦i-dou, in nine places.

kɑtse̦i-t'н, nineteen.

kɑ-t̂н̂t̂gyн (inan. III), crotch = zнdl-t̂н̂t̂gyн [kɑ-, unexplained; -t̂н̂t̂gyн, between].

kɑ̄'-, referring to swimming, going as boat, in kɑ̄'-'н'dɑ, paddle; kɑ̄'-bout, canoe; kɑ̄'-t̂ɑ'e, to swim; kɑ̄'-zei . . ., to swim [Tewa kō', to bathe, kō'-fé, boat, bridge, footlog].

kɑ̄'-'н'-dɑ (inan. IIᵃ; kɑ̄'-'н', dpl.), paddle, = kɑ̄'bout-'н'-dɑ.

kɑ̄'-bout (inan. IIᵃ), canoe, boat [kɑ̄'- referring to swimming, going as boat; -bou-t, unexplained]. —— kɑ̄'bout 'ɑe, lots of canoes.

kɑ̄'bout-н'-dɑ (inan. IIᵃ; kɑ̄'bout-н', dpl.), paddle, = kɑ̄'-'н'dɑ.

kɑ̄'-dɑ̄'-t̂ɑ̨-m (an. II; kɑ̄'-dɑ̄'-t̂ɑ̨-bɑ, tpl.), red-winged blackbird [unexplained].

kɑ̄'-dei (kɑ̄'-gɑ, tpl.), pron., other [kɑ̄'- occurs without postfix as kɑ', tpl. others (followed by 'нdl or t̂sнdl); -dei]. Cp. kų̄ɑ̨-dei, other. —— kɑ̄'-gɑ, the other fellows.

kɑ̄'-dou-k'i̦н, one hundred [kɑ̄'- as in kɑ̄'-k'i̦н, ten; app. dou, postp.; -k'i̦н, tens]. Cp. kɑ̄'k'i̦н-dou, in ten places]. kɑ̄'douk'i̦н-n was given as meaning "ten by ten." —— kɑ̄'douk'i̦н t'ɑe pн̄'gɑ, one hundred and one, lit. one beyond a hundred.

kɑ̄'douk'i̦н-n, ten by ten, as ten.

-kɑ̄'-gɑ, postp., through [-kɑ̄'- as ın kɑ̄'-gyн, abreast; -gɑ]. —— tsнt̄-kɑ̄'gɑ ɛ̦i-t'ɑt̂gɑ, he shot me through the door.

kɑ̄'-gyн, adv., abreast [kɑ̄'- as in -kɑ̄'-gɑ, postp., through; -gyн]. Cp. ni̦н̄ni̦н, two abreast. k̄yн̄hyoup 'н̄-kɑ̄'gyн-tsн̄'dei, the men are marching two abreast.

kɑ̄'-kɑ-'e, my or our mother. Cp. tsɑ, mother; kɑ', mother, voc.; 'н-kɑ̄'-kɑ, your (spl.) mother; tɑ-dl, father; tɑ̄'-tɑ-'e, my or our father. —— nɑ̨ kɑ̄'kɑ'e 'ɛ̦i-dɑ, it is my mother, = nɑ̨ tsɑ 'ɛ̦i-dɑ. nɑ̨ kɑ̄'kɑ'e dɑ́-dɑ, it is our mother, = nɑ̨ tsɑ dɑ́-dɑ.

kɑ̄'-k'i̦н, ten; so also in an old Kiowa count [kɑ̄'-, unexplained; -k'i̦н, ten, -ty, forming the tens]. Cp. kɑ̄'- dou-k'i̦н, one hundred. —— kɑ̄'k'i̦н k̄yн̄hyoup, ten men. kɑ̄'k'i̦н sнe, ten years.

kɑ̄'k'yн-n-dei, the tenth.

kɑ̄'k'i̦н-dou, in ten places.

kɑ't-eit, wide [kɑ't-, as in kɑ't-syǫn, narrow; w. -'ei-t cp. 'ei-dl, large]. —— p̄ɑ'-kɑ't-eit, a wide river (wide in one place); but p̄ɑ'-k'ou-'eidl, a wide river (wide all the way along, a large river). 'įн̦dei kɑ't-eit, it (the river) is wide right here.

kɑ'ᶦ-syǫn, narrow [kɑ't- as in kɑ't-eit, to be wide; syǫn, a little]. —— p̄ɑ'-kɑ'ᵗsyǫn, a narrow river. 'įн̦dei kɑ'ᶦ-syǫn, it is narrow here.

kɑ'ᶦɑ-'ǫmdɑ, to swim [cp. *kɑ'ᶦɑ-'ǫ'męį, to make swim]. —— gyн̄-kɑ'ᶦɑ-'ǫmdɑ, it is a swimming place.

kɑ'ᶦɑ-'ǫ'męį, to make swim, with refl. to swim [cp. kɑ'-ᶦɑ-'e, to swim.] —— dei-kɑ'ᶦɑ-'ǫmdɑ', I am going to swim. gyн̄-kɑ'ᶦɑ-'ǫ'męį, I made it swim (e. g. plaything on water).

kɑ'-ᶦɑ-'e (kɑ'ᶦɑ'gu'ɑ, punct. neg.; kɑ'ᶦɑtdɑ, curs.; kɑ'ᶦɑ'dɑ', fut.; kɑ'ᶦɑ'gu'ɑdɑ', fut. neg.; kɑ'ᶦɑ, imp.), to make swim, with refl. to swim [app. kɑ'- as in kɑ'-bout, canoe; app. ᶦɑ', to go about; -ei, causative]. Cp. kɑ'ᶦɑ-'ǫmdɑ, to swim; kɑ'ᶦɑ-'ǫ'męį, to make swim; kɑ'-zei . . ., to swim. —— k'iн̦deidl dèi-kɑ'ᶦɑ'e, I swam yesterday. hǫn dèi-kɑ'ᶦɑ'gu'ɑ, I did not swim. dèi-bou-kɑ'ᶦɑtdɑ, I swim all the time. dèi-kɑ'ᶦɑ'dɑ', I shall swim. hǫn dèi-kɑ'ᶦɑ'gu'ɑdɑ', I shall swim. bèi-kɑ'ᶦɑ', swim! poue bèi-kɑ'dɑ', don't swim! béi-kɑ'ᶦɑ', let us swim! 'į(н̦)hɑ' 'н̦n '֥ę́ím-kɑ'-ᶦɑtdɑ, they swim right here. 'ouhyɑ' (or 'ougɑt'ɑ') 'н̦n '֥ę́ím-kɑ'ᶦɑtdɑ, they swim way over there. p̄ɑ'gyн̄ bèi-kɑ'ᶦɑ, take a bath in the creek! 'oueiн̦intoudl-tsou dèi-kɑ'ᶦɑ'dɑ', I am going to swim like a duck.

kɑ'-zei . . . (kɑ'-zeimн̦, curs.), to swim [kɑ'- as in kɑ'-bout, canoe; -zei . . ., unexplained]. Cp. kɑ'-ᶦɑ-'e, to swim; etc. —— 'ɑ'pįн̦dɑ t'ǫu-t'н̦ehįн̦ 'èi-kɑ'zeimн̦, the fishes are swimming at the top of the water.

kǫ (an. II; kǫ'gɑ, tpl.), wild goose sp. [Tewa ką́-gì, Canada goose]. Cp. kǫ'-к̄oudl, squash, lit. "goose" neck; kǫ'-ᶦн̦ę, "white goose."

kǫ' (kǫ'mǫ', punct. neg.; kǫ'mǫ, curs.; kǫ'dɑ', fut.; kǫ'mǫ'dɑ', fut. neg.; kǫ', imp.), to grease, smear. Cp. kǫ'-dɑ, to be greased. Also in к̄ɑdlsei-kǫ', to glue; etc. —— gyн̄-kǫ', I greased it (the wagon). gyн̄-к̄ɑdlsei-kǫ', I glued it, smeared sticking material on it. gyн̄-bou-kǫ'mǫ, I smear it all the time. gyн̄-kǫ'dɑ', I shall smear it. 'н̄-kǫ', you grease it!

*kǫ-m (kǫ'mǫ, curs.), to want. Cp. 'ǫn-dɑ, t'ęin-dɑ, to want. —— 'ǫngɑdouyeidei bн̦ᶦ-kǫ'mǫ, you want too much.

-kǫ-m-, to point, in -kǫm-dou', to point; mǫn-kǫm, index finger.

-kǫm-dou', to point, in mǫn-kǫm-dou', to point; mǫnsɑ-kǫmdou', to point with the thumb; etc. [-kǫ-m-, to point; dou'].

kǫm-yɑ'-gɑ (inan. IIª; kǫm-yɑ', dpl.), notch (in butt of arrow) [unexplained; w. kǫ-m- cp. possibly kǫm-ɑ, to play arrow-throwing game; -gɑ].

kǫ-n, to be many.  Cp. 'ɑe, to be many. —— mǫ'sɑ'gɑ déi-bǫų nǫ
gyн̓-kǫn, I saw ravens and many of them.

kǫ'-n (kǫ'nǫ', punct. neg.; kǫnmǫ, curs.; kǫ'ndɑ', fut.; kǫ'nǫ'dɑ', fut.
neg.), to bring [Tewa kɋ́-ŋ, to bring].  Cp. bɑ', to bring; hɑ', to
bring. —— gyн̓-kǫ'n, I brought it.  hǫn gyн̓-kǫ'nǫ', I did not
bring it.  gyн̓-bou-kǫnmǫ, I bring it all the time.  gyн̓-kǫ'ndɑ', I
shall bring it.  hǫn gyн̓-kǫ'nǫ'dɑ', I shall not bring it.  But 'н̓-bɑ',
bring it here, hand it here! (the imp. of bɑ' is app. substituted for
the imp. of kǫ'n).  t'ǫų gyн̓-kǫ'n, I fetched water.  But t'ǫų
'н̓-bɑ', fetch water!  t͡sou gyн̓-kǫ'n, I brought you a stone.  t͡sou
'ę́i-kǫ'n, he brought me a stone.

kǫ-n-, hortative verb prefix, used with third person in the examples
obtained [cp. possibly kɑdl, particle]. —— kǫn-hęi'm, let him
die!  kǫn-'н̦, let him come.  'ę̇i-kǫn-'н̦, let them d. come!
gyн̓-kǫn-'ǫmgyн, let it happen!

-kǫ-n in sei-kǫn, green scum.

-kǫ'-n, in p'ou-kǫ'n, venter of wind [cp. p'ou- in p'ou-t'ɑ̇gɑ, to vent
wind].

kǫ'dɑ- in kǫ'dɑ-'ǫ, to sell; kǫ'dɑ-hɑ'gyн, to buy [cp. Tewa kú-mн̦,
to buy].

kǫ'dɑ-'ǫ, to sell ·['ǫ, to give]. —— tsęi gyн̓-kǫ'dɑ-'ǫ'dɑ', I am
going to sell the horse.

kǫ'dɑ-hɑ'gyн, to buy [hɑ'gyн, to get]. —— tsęi gyн̓-kǫ'dɑ-hɑ'dɑ',
I am going to buy a horse.

kǫm-ɑ, to play arrow-throwing game [w.kǫ-m- cp. possibly kǫmyɑ'-gɑ
notch (in arrow); 'ɑ, to play]. —— dèi-kǫm-'ɑ'dɑ', I am going to
throw arrows.

kǫm-ɑ'-gyн (inan. III), arrow-throwing game.

kǫ'-t̂н̦ę (an. II; kǫ'-t̂н̦ę-mǫ, tpl.), white goose [kǫ, wild goose sp.].

kiн-dl (kiнgɑ', punct. neg.), to live, dwell.  Cp. -kiнdl, dweller.
—— oueigɑ 'н̓-kiнdl-dei-'ęi 'н̓-yнt-bн'̂t̂ɑ', I am going to live with
those people.

-kiн-dl, dweller, in t'н̓'-kiнdl, prairie-chicken [kiн-dl, to live].

Kiн-guɑdl-dɑ'-dei-k̃iн (an. I; Kiн-guɑdl-dɑ'-gɑ, tpl.), Indian (man)
"red meat man," here referring to skin color: kiн, meat; guɑdl-dɑ,
to be red; -dei; -k̃iн].

kiн (inan. Iᵃ kiн- in comp.), meat, flesh. —— kiн gyн̓-bǫų, I saw
the piece of meat.  nǫ kiн, my flesh.

kiн- (occurring in the material only with postp.), chest (anat.) [cp.
possibly kiн, flesh].  Cp. zeip, female breast; bout-dǫukyн, in
the belly; 'н̓'-kiн-dǫųgɑ't, heart of wood. —— nǫ kiн-dǫųgyн,
in my chest.

kiн- in kyн̦-hįн̦, highest; kiн-t'ɑ'-hį'н̦, very; kyн̦ę-hн̓'dei, highest.

-kiн-dei in t̂eidl-kiн-dei(-tsou), backward, on head [t̂eidl-, rump;
-kiн-, unexplained; -dei].

ki(н)-sǫ'-dɑ, kettle [meat boiler; w. sǫ- cp. sǫn-tsei, to put to boil].

-kiʜ-t- in beidl-kiʜt́-gyʜ, screech-owl.

kiʜ-t'α'-hį'ʜ, adv., very [kiʜ-, app. as in kyʜ'ę-hʜ'-dei, highest; t'α'-hį'ʜ, very far]. —— 'ʜm kiʜt'α'hį'ʜ yᶙn-guα, you are very wise.

*kiʜ-t'ʜ' (*kiʜ-t'ʜ'mα', punct. neg.; kiʜ-t'ʜ'mᶐ'ĭα', fut. neg.), to be afraid [kiʜ-, unexplained; -t'ʜ']. —— hʜyʜ'-dou tsʜnt̂α' nᶐ hᶐn hʜyʜ' yᶙ-tsʜegα'dα' (or 'ʜ-kiʜ-t'ʜ'mᶐ'ĭα'), if he comes, I shall not be afraid.

kiʜ-tsoue (inan. I), broth [meat soup].  Cp. k̂ᶐn-tsoue, tomato soup. —— kiʜtsoue gyʜ-ĭoudlᶐ'bʜ-'ᶐ'nei, I took a taste of broth.

kįʜ-, in kįʜ-hiʜt-, in single file; kįʜ-nįʜ, to be long.

kįʜ-dei- in kįʜ-dei-'ᶐmgyʜ, kįʜ-dei-dα, to menstruate [unexplained].

kįʜ-dei-'ᶐmgyʜ, to menstruate.

kįʜ-dei-dα, to menstruate. —— kįʜdei-dα, she has menstruation.

kįʜ-hiʜ-t-, verb prefix, in single file; one by one, two by two, etc. [cp. -kįʜ-hiʜt in t'αp-kįʜ-hiʜt, to ferry across; and possibly kįʜ-nįʜ, long, tall].  Cp. kα'gyʜ-, abreast. —— k̂yʜhyoup 'ʜ-kįʜhiʜt-tsʜ'dei, the men are marching in single file. k̂yʜhyoup nįʜnyʜ 'ʜ-kįʜhiʜt-tsʜ'dei, the men are marching two abreast. pʜ'nyʜ 'ʜ-kį(ʜ)hiʜt-t'eiþdα, they are coming out one by one.

-kįʜ-hiʜt in t'αþ-kįʜhiʜt, to ferry across. Cp. t'αp-hiʜt, to cross (water); kįʜ-hiʜt-, in single file, etc.

kįʜ-nįʜ (kyų-e, kyų-ę-mᶐ, kįʜ-nyou-p, kįʜ-nou-p, tpl.), long, tall [cp. kįʜ-hiʜt-, in single file].  Cp. 'ᶐntsʜ'-kįʜnįʜ, to be a great walker; etc. —— 'ʜ'-kyųemᶐ déi-bou̯, I saw the long stick. 'ʜ'-kįʜnįʜ nèin-bou̯, I saw d. long sticks. 'ʜ'-kįʜnįʜ gyʜ-bou̯, I saw tpl. long sticks. nᶐ-'αdl-kįʜnįʜ, I have long hair. tseihįʜ-kyųe gyʜ-bou̯, I saw a long dog. tseihįʜ-kįʜnyoup déi-bou̯, I saw long dogs.

kou- in kou-bʜ, app. to enter.

-kou- in ĭα'-kou-dα, to be deaf [cp. possibly kou-t, to be hard].

-kou in bèi-kou, go ahead!

kou-bʜ, app., enter [cp. kou-bei, captive]. —— poudl tʜ'-gyʜ 'ᶒi-koubʜ, a bug has gotten into my eye.

kou-bei (an. I; koubou-p, tpl.), captive [cp. koubʜ, to enter].

kou-dou-, verb prefix, very, very much, very many, pretty [w. kou-cp. possibly kou-t, hard; w. -dou- cp. possibly -dou-e-, too much, or -dou, postp., with, as]. —— koudou-'eitdei-dou yᶙn-guαt, I wrote to him many times. 'ʜ-koudou-houdl-dα, I am pretty sick. 'ʜ-koudou-dʜmgyʜ-dα, I am pretty tired. gyʜ-koudou-zʜdlbei, that is awful. pʜhįʜ yᶙ-koudou-k'oup-'ᶐmgyʜ, I am going to be suffering. k̂iʜkᶐmbα gyʜ-koudou-heim-'αmdeiĭα', the people are going to be hard up.

kou-dl-ou (an. II; kou-dl-ou-gα, tpl.), a small sized dog such as the Kiowa used to have, = tsʜdou.

kou-'e (inan. IIª), pus [unexplained]. ——— kou'e déi-bǫu, I saw the pus. kou'e 'éi-dɑ, there is pus.

kou'e-dɑ, to be mattery [dɑ]. Cp. sou-kou'e-dɑ, to have clap. ——— 'ɑ'p'ḥ 'éi-kou'e-dɑ, my boil is mattery.

kou-kǫu-bɑ (inan. IIª; kou-kǫu'-m, dpl.; kou-kǫu'-m- in comp.), wild gourd fruit [possibly fr. Eng. cucumber]. Cp. t'ǫ'gɑ, gourd rattle.

kou-kǫu'm-goup (inan. IIª), wild gourd plant.

koup̀-gɑ', several do not lie; see k̄uɑdl.

kou-t (kout̀-gɑ, tpl.), hard; strong; expensive [Tewa kē', to be hard, be strong]. ——— t̃sou-kout, a hard rock. t̃sou-kout gyḣ-bǫu, I saw a hard stone. hḥ'oudei t̃sou-kout gyḣt-bǫu, I saw several hard stones. k̄yḥhị'ḥ kout, the man is strong. k̄yḥhyoup 'ḣ-kout, the men are strong. 'èi-kout, it (the wood) is hard. 'ęigɑ 'ḥ'dɑ koutdei déi-ɑmdɑ', I am going to harden this stick. 'ḥ'-kout déi-bǫu, I saw a hard stick. k̄yḥhyoup 'ḣ-koutgɑ dèi-bǫu, I saw strong men. t̃sou gyḣ-kout, they are hard stones. gyḣ-kout, it is (too) expensive.

kout-dei-'ɑ'k̄ɑ, to have hard times [kou-t, hard, expensive; -dei; -'ɑ'-, unexplained; k̄ɑ, to lie]. ——— k̄yḥkɑmbɑ koup̀dei'ɑ'-k̄ɑ, the people are having hard times. k̄yḥkɑmbɑ koup̀dei'ɑ'-tsouyḥ', the people are going to have hard times.

kout-pḥ'egɑ, to wrestle [to strong act, strong fight]. ——— dèi-koutp̃ḥ'egoup, I am going to wrestle.

kout-p̃ḥ'egyḥ-k̄iḥ (an. II; kout-pḥ'egyḥ-gɑ, tpl.), wrestler. ——— koutp̃ḥ'egyḥ-k̄iḥ 'ḣ-dɑ, I am a professional wrestler.

kǫu-m (an. I; kǫu-bɑ, tpl.), friend. Cp. 'ḥ-kǫum, your (spl.) friend; tsḥ'ḥ-dei, friend. ——— kǫum gyḣ-bǫu, I saw a friend. nǫ kǫubɑ, my friends. 'oueidei kǫum, that fellow's friend.

-kǫu'-m, to be about, in 'ɑn-kǫu'm, to buzz; hou'-kǫu'm, coyote, traveler about; p'ǫ'-kǫu'm, to stand; p'iḥhout-hou'kǫu'm, to fly about.

kǫum-'ɑ, to play shinny [kǫum-, unexplained; 'ɑ, to play].

kǫum-'ɑ'-gyḥ (inan. III), shinny game.

kǫum-'ɑ'k̄iḥ (an. I; kǫum-'ɑ'-gɑ, tpl.), shinny player.

kǫum-'ɑ'-t'ǫųę (inan. IIª; kǫum-'ɑ'-t'ǫų, dpl.), shinny stick [t'ǫų-ę, stick].

-kuɑ, -ku'ɑ, hitter, in dɑ'ḥdl-kuɑ, bird sp., lit. bucket hitter; dɑm-ku'ɑ, digging-stick, lit. earth-pecker; hǫ'-k̄ɑ'-kuɑ, iron nail, lit. iron blow hitter [goup, to hit].

kuɑ-n, thrown away thing [cp. guɑ-n, to throw away, dance]. Cp. kuɑn-gyḥ, dance. ——— kuɑn gyḣ-bǫu, I saw the thrown away thing.

kuɑ'-n (kuɑ'ndɑ', fut.), to mix, stir. Cp. 'ei-kuɑ'n, mush. ——— gyḣt-kuɑ'n, I mixed it. gyḣt-kuɑ'ndɑ', I shall mix it.

kuɑn-'eidl, a big dance, fiesta ['eidl, large].

kuɑ-n-gyʜ (inan. III), dance [guɑ-n, to dance].   Cp. kuɑn, thrown
away thing. —— kuɑngyʜ gyʜ̇t-bǫu, I saw the dance.

kuɑn-k̑iʜ (an. II; kuɑn-dɑ, tpl.), dancing man.

kuɑn-mʜ̥ (an. II; kuɑn-mʜ̥ę-mɑ̨, tpl.), dancing woman.

kuɑ-sei-t (kuɑ-sei-t̑-dɑ, tpl.), bob-tailed.  Cp. bousęin-kuɑseit, bird
sp., lit. bob-tailed buzzard. —— kuɑseit, he is bobtailed.

kuɑ-t, 1. marked, painted;  2. as noun (inan. Iᵃ), marking, painting,
picture, writing instrument, pen, pencil, writing table [guɑ-t, to
màrk, paint].   Cp. k̑'ɑ'-kuɑt-ʜ'dɑ, mulberry tree; kuɑt-dɑ, to be
marked;  seit̑-kuɑt, raccoon;  t̑oue-kuɑt, spotted;  tǫu-kuɑt, book;
hɑ̨'-tǫu-kuɑt, telegraph, typewriter. —— 1. t̑sou-kuɑt gyʜ̇-bǫu,
· I saw a painted rock.   2. kuɑt gyʜ̇-bǫu, I saw one picture.   kuɑt̑
gyʜ̇t-bǫu, I saw the tpl. pictures.  'ęidei Dɑ'k̑yʜ kuɑt gyʜ̇-dɑ,
this is God's (preaching) book (words quoted from a Kiowa hymn).

kuɑ-t (kuɑtgɑ, punct. neg.; kuɑdldɑ', fut.; kuɑtgɑ'dɑ', fut. neg.)
to owe.  Cp. k̑'ɑ'-dou', to owe. —— 'oueidei-'ęi 'ęi-kuɑt, I owe
that fellow.  'oueidei-'ęi hɑ̨n 'ęi-kuɑtdɑ, I do not owe that fellow.
'oueidei nɑ̨-'ęim 'ʜ́-kuɑt, that fellow owes me.  'oueidei nɑ̨-'ęim
hɑ̨n kɑdl 'ʜ́-kuɑtdɑ, that fellow does not owe me.  k̑'yʜ̥hįʜgɑ
'oueidei-'ęi 'ęi-kuɑdldɑ', tomorrow that fellow will be owing me.
k̑'yʜ̥hįʜgɑ 'oueidei-'ęi hɑ̨n 'ęi-kuɑtgɑ'dɑ', tomorrow that fellow
will not be owing me.

-kuɑ-t- in boudl-kuɑt-gyʜ, scurf, filth.

kuɑt-ʜ'-dɑ (inan. IIᵃ; kuɑt-ʜ', dpl.), 1. pen, pencil;  2. writing
table [writing wood].   Cp. pįʜ-'ʜ'dɑ, eating table.

kuɑt-dɑ, to be marked, be painted [dɑ]. —— kuɑt-dɑ, it is marked.
kuɑt-hęi dɑ, it is not marked.  gyʜ̇-kuɑt-dɑ't̑ɑ', it is going to be
painted.

kuɑt-hɑ̨'k̑oudlp̑'ʜ̥'-gɑ (inan. II; kuɑt-hɑ̨'k̑oudlp̑'ʜ̥, dpl.), school bell
[marking neck hung metal].

kuɑ-tou (an. II; kuɑ-tou-gɑ, kuɑ-tou-bɑ, tpl.), bird.  Cp. kuɑtou-
hįʜ, eagle;  tsęi-kuɑtou, blackbird sp.;  t̑ęįnęi, bird.

kuɑtou-hįɑ̨ (an. II; kuɑtou-hyu̥-ę, tpl.), eagle [real bird, right bird].

kuɑtouhįʜ-'ʜ'gɑ̄'-t (inan. IIᵃ; kuɑtouhįʜ-'ʜ', dpl.), eagle feather.

kuɑt-outk̑'ɑe (inan. IIᵃ), bookcase, =kuɑt-sɑ̄'-gɑ.  Also tǫukuɑt-
outk̑'ɑe.

kuɑtou-tou (inan. I), bird cage [bird house].  Ct. kuɑtou-tousǫu̥'n,
bird nest.

kuɑtou-tousǫu̥'n (inan. III), bird nest.  Ct. kuɑtou-tou, bird cage.

kuɑt̑-sɑ̄'-gɑ, bookcase, =kuɑt-outk̑'ɑe [sɑ, to put several in].

kuɑt̑-tou (inan. I), schoolhouse [writing house].

kuɑt̑-t̑'ǫu, ink [marking water].

ku-e' (an. II; ku-ei-guɑ, tpl.), wolf [Tewa xu̥'-yó, wolf].  Said to be
the most general term for wolf, including black wolf, gray wolf,

coyote, etc.   Cp. kуʜ-t̑ʜǫ, gray wolf; mǫ̱'t'ǫutsǫu'hi̱'ʜ, hou'kǫu'm, coyote.

kue'-'iʜ (an. II; kue'-'yu-e, tpl.), wolf-cub.

kue'-k'ǫu-gуʜ (an. II; kue'-k'ǫu-gɑ̱'-t, tpl.), black wolf.

Kue'-pʜ'gɑ'e, prsn., Lonewolf; cp. Mooney, p. 404 [kue', wolf; pʜ'gɑ'e, lone: pʜ'gɑ, one; -ei].

kue'syʜn, "little wolf," a descriptive term applied to the coyote by one of the informants.   Cp. mǫ̱'t'ǫutsǫu'hi̱'ʜ, hou'kǫu'm, coyote.

kue'-t̑ʜǫ (an. II; kue-t̑ʜǫ-mǫ, tpl.), white wolf.

kue'-zǫu (an. II; kue'-zǫu-gɑ, tpl.), canine tooth [wolf tooth].

kuǫ̱-dei (kuǫ̱-gɑ, tpl.), pron., other [kuǫ̱-, unexplained; -dei].   Cp. kɑ̱'-dei, other; kɑ', tpl. others. —— kuǫ̱dei tou'e, in the other room.

kуʜ-, wolf, in kуʜ-t̑ʜǫ, gray wolf.

kуʜ-e-, prepound form referring to fighting, enemy, Comanche; scalplock, vertex [cp. kуʜe-dɑ, to fight].

kуʜe-'ɑdlguɑdl (an. II; kуʜe-'ɑdlguɑt-dɑ, tpl.), woodpecker sp. (?) [kуʜ-e-, said to refer to vertex, cp. kуʜe-p̄ǫ̱'-dɑ, scalplock].   Cp. 'ɑdlguɑdl, woodpecker sp., lit. red head.

kуʜe-dɑ (an. I; kуʜe-dɑ̱'-gɑ, tpl.), enemy [cp. kуʜe-k̂iʜ, enemy; etc.]. —— nǫ̱ kуʜedɑ gуn̑-bǫu, I saw my (personal) enemy.

kуʜe-dɑ, to fight [cp. mǫ̱-'iʜ-kуʜ'e, to have cramps, kуʜe-p̄ʜ'egɑ, to fight]. —— 'ęim-kуʜedɑ, they are fighting.

kуʜedɑ̱'-bʜ, to go to fight.   Cp. kуʜe-dɑ̱'-k̂iʜ, warrior. —— 'n̑-kуʜ'edɑ̱'-bʜ't̑ɑ', I am going to go to war.

kуʜedɑ̱'-k̂iʜ (an. I; kуʜe-dɑ̱'-gɑ, tpl.), warrior [kуʜe-dɑ, to fight].

kуʜe-gуʜ (inan. III), war [cp. kуʜe-p̄ʜ'egɑ, to fight; etc.].

kуʜe-k̂iʜ (an. II; kуʜe-guɑ, tpl.), 1. enemy (man); 2. Kуʜe-k̂iʜ, Comanche (man).   In very early times the Comanches were enemies of the Kiowa; hence the name.   Cp. kуʜe-dɑ, enemy; etc. —— Kуʜe-'ęi, among the Comanches.

kуʜe-p̄ʜ'egɑ, to fight, war [cp. kуʜe-gуʜ, war; etc.].   Ct. p̄ʜ'egɑ, to fight (an ordinary fist fight, e. g.). —— heigɑ 'ęim-kуʜe-p̄ʜ'egoup, they are going to fight.

Kуʜe-p̄ǫ̱n-k̂iʜ (an. II; Kуʜe-p̄ǫ̱'dɑ, tpl.), Chinaman, = Tʜn-p̄ǫ̱n-k̂iʜ [scalplock man].   Cp. kуʜe-p̄ǫ̱'dɑ, scalplock.

kуʜe-p̄ǫ̱'dɑ (inan. II; kуʜe-p̄ǫ̱n, dpl.), scalplock [kуʜe-, referring to war; -p̄ǫ̱n, referring to the braid].   Cp. kуʜe-'ɑdlguɑdl, woodpecker sp., in which kуʜe- is said to refer to the vertex.

kуʜe-sɑ̱'-dei (an. II; kуʜe-sɑ̱'dou-p, tpl.), mourning dove [said to sound like "enemy worker"].   Cp. t̑ɑk'ɑe-kуʜesɑ̱'dei, domestic pigeon.

kуʜ'-boudl-iʜ (an. II; kуʜ'-boudl-yu-e, tpl.), domestic sheep.   kуʜ'-boudl-, unexplained; -'iʜ, dim.].

kyꞫ'boudliꞫ-hǫ'tꞫ'dei-'eidl, sheep ranch [sheep wire fenced place large].

kyꞫ'boudliꞫ-p'ɑ'-gyꞫ (inan. III), wool [sheep fur].

kyꞫębꞫ'-p̄Ɜ'egɑ, to take care of [kyꞫębꞫ'- as in kyꞫębꞫ'-dɑ, to take care of; p̄Ɜ'egɑ]. —— gyꞩ-kyꞫębꞫ'-p̄ɑ'egɑ, I cared for him. 'ꞩ-kyꞫę-bꞫ'-p̄Ɜ'edei, take care of him!

kyꞫę-bꞫ'-dɑ (kyꞫębꞫ'dɑ'gu'ɑ, punct. neg.; kyꞫębꞫ'dɑ', imp.), to take care of [cp. kyꞫębꞫ'-p̄Ɜ'egɑ, to take care of]. —— gyꞩ-kyꞫębꞫ'dɑ, I am taking care of him. hǫn gyꞩ-kyꞫębꞫ'dɑ'gu'ɑ, I am not taking care of him. 'ꞩ-kyꞫębꞫ'dɑ', you take good care of him!

kyꞫ'ę-hꞫ'-dei, to be highest [w. kyꞫ-'ę- cp. kiꞫ-t'ɑ'-hiꞫ, very; -hꞫ'- unexplained, cp. possibly hꞫ', to stand up; -dei]. —— k'ǫ'gyꞫ 'ą́n-kyꞫ'ęhꞫ'dei, your name is highest.

-kyꞫ-ę-gyꞫ in bout-kyꞫęgyꞫ, to be bloated.

kyų-ę, see kiꞫ-niꞫ, long.

<h1 style="text-align:center">k̑</h1>

k̑ɑ (defective verb; k̑ɑ'gɑ', tsougɑ', stat. neg.; tsouyꞫ, curs.; tsoutɑ', fut.; k̑ɑ'gɑ'dɑ', tsougɑ'tɑ', fut. neg.; tsoudei, imp.), one lies. Tpls. correspondent is k̑uɑdl. [Cp. k̑uɑ-dl, several lie; k̑ou-p, to lay several; Tewa k̑ó, one lies, k̑ù'ù, to put; and for tsou-gɑ' cp. tsei-p, to lay one]. Cp. dęi-k̑ɑ, to lie asleep; 'ꞩ-'oudl-k̑ɑ, whore; mǫ', to lie down. —— pꞫ'gɑ tsęį k̑ɑ, one horse is lying; yiꞫ tsęį 'ę̀į-k̑ɑ, two horses are lying; but hꞫ'oudei tsęįgɑ 'éi-k̑uɑdl, tpl. horses are lying. pꞫ'gɑ k̑oup 'éi-k̑ɑ, one mountain is lying; yiꞫ k̑oup 'ę̀į-k̑ɑ, two mountains are lying; but hꞫ'oudei k̑oup k̑uɑdl, several mountains are lying. néį-pꞫ'bi-k̑ɑ, they are my d. brothers. 'ę̀įm-tsoudei, lie (there)! poue 'ę̀įm-tsoutɑ', don't lie (there)! heit bꞩ-tsoudei, let us d. lie down! p̄ɑ' k̑ɑ, moon lies, there is a moon. p̄ɑ' k̑ɑ, river lies. pꞪe k̑ɑ, the sun is up.

k̑ɑ' (an. II; k̑ɑ'-gɑ, tpl.; k̑ɑ'- in comp.), knife [cp. k̑ɑ', to cut]. Cp. k̑ɑ'-sǫų, grindstone; k̑ɑe-k̑ǫų-gɑ, flint; hǫ'-k̑ɑ', iron knife. —— k̑ɑ' gyꞩ-dou', I have a knife.

k̑ɑ', to cut [cp. k̑ɑ', knife]. —— pꞫ'gyꞫbei-bꞫ gyꞩ-k̑ɑ', I cut him with the edge. mǫn-k̑ɑ'-yɑ' heigɑ hęį 'ꞩ-'ǫmgyꞫ, my cut place has gotten well, has healed.

k̑ɑ- k̑ɑ'- in k̑ɑ-'Ɦt-dɑ, dish; k̑ɑ'-dꞪdl, wheel.

k̑ɑ-'Ɦt-dɑ (inan. II[a]; k̑ɑ-'Ɦdl, dpl.; k̑ɑ-'Ɦdl-, k̑ɑ-'Ɦt- in comp.), dish (of any kind) [k̑ɑ- as in k̑ɑ'-dꞪdl, wheel; -'Ɜ-dl-, -'Ɜ-t-, round; -dɑ]. Cp. sǫųn-k̑ɑ'Ɦtdɑ, basket, lit. grass dish.

k̑ɑ-dl (inan. I), gum, chewing gum. Cp. k'ǫų-k̑ɑdl, tar, lit. black gum; zǫųn-k̑ɑdl, pitch, lit. pine gum; k̑ɑdl-sei, glue. —— k̑ɑdl-dǫųgyꞫ, in the gum.

-k̑ɑ-dl in pꞫ-k̑ɑdl, clitoris; 'ou-pꞪk̑ɑdl, uvula; 'ou-pǫųm-k̑ɑdl, Adam's apple.

Ḳα-dl-α̃'-k'αy-iн (an. II; Ḳα-dl-α̃'-k'αy-ou-p, tpl.), grasshopper [Ḳα-dl-α̃'-, unexplained; k'αe, app. skin; -iн, dim.].

Ḳαdl-н'-'ei-p'eip (inan. IIª), tree sp. [gum tree fruit bush]. Said to have good-tasting berries of a black color and containing black seeds. Also bark is removed from the tree and gum is scraped from the surface of the wood and used as chewing gum.

Ḳαdl-Ḳiн (an. II; Ḳαⱦ-dα, tpl.), Arikaree man [stated by Mooney, p. 410, to mean "biters"; evidently agentive of Ḳα̃'dlei, to bite]. Cp. Ḳαe-ḲαdlḲiн, Kiowa-Arikaree man.

Ḳαdl-sei (inan. III), glue, paste [Ḳαdl, gum; -sei, unexplained]. Cp. Ḳαdlsei-Ḳǫ', to glue.

Ḳαdlsei-Ḳǫ', to glue [Ḳαdlsei, glue; Ḳǫ', to smear]. —— 'н-Ḳαdlsei-Ḳα you glue it!

Ḳαdlsei-Ḳǫ'-dα, to be glued [dα, to be]. —— heigα Ḳαdlsei-Ḳǫ'dα, it is already glued. ⱦsou Ḳαdlsei-Ḳǫ'dα'-dei gyн-bǫy, I saw the stone with glue smeared on it. heigα k'αdlsei-Ḳǫ'-heį dα, it is not glued yet.

Ḳαe-Ḳǫy-gα (inan. IIª; Ḳαe-Ḳǫy, dpl.), flint [Ḳα', knife; -ei; Ḳǫy, unexplained; -gα].

-Ḳα-t'ou-e- in 'Ǫ́dl-Ḳαt'oue-Ḳiн, Nez Perce Indian.

Ḳα̃'-, referring to cold, in Ḳα̃'-heį'm, to freeze to death; etc. [Tewa Ḳõ'-, referring to cold, in Ḳõ'-sά̨-pò'ò, to feel cold; etc.].

Ḳα̃'- in Ḳα̃'-gα, cliff; Ḳα̃'-gyнp, cliff; Ḳα̃'-dα, to be precipitous [Tewa Ḳǫ'-ŋ, barranco].

Ḳα̃'-dα (Ḳα̃'deidα', Ḳiнdα', fut.), to burst open tr. Cp. sн' . . ., to burst tr.; ⱦα-Ḳα̃'dα, to burst by hitting, zeįm-Ḳα̃'dα, to crack with teeth. —— t'ǫydei gyн-Ḳiнdα', I am going to break open the marrow.

Ḳα̃'-dα, to be precipitous, be a cliff [Ḳα̃'- as in Ḳα̃'-gα, Ḳα̃'-gyнp, cliff; dα, to be]. —— 'èi-Ḳα̃'-dα, it is a cliff, it drops off precipitously.

Ḳα̃'-dн-dl (an. II; Ḳα-dн-ⱦ-dα, tpl.), circular, cylindrical; as noun, circular, cylindrical thing, wheel, wagon (=k'uep'н, wagon) [Ḳα- as in Ḳα-'нⱦdα' dish; -dн-dl-, -dн-ⱦ-, unexplained]. Ct. p'α'нⱦdoup, ball. Cp. ⱦнę-Ḳα̃'dнdl-'eigα, turnip, lit. white cylindrical. —— p̃α' 'α̨n- (Ḳα̃'dнdl)-kuαt, there is a ring around the moon, lit. the moon is ring marked.

Ḳα̃'dнdl-k'uep'н (inan. III), harness [Ḳα̃'dнdl, wheel, wagon; k'uep'н, harness, wagon].

Ḳα̃'dнdl-dα, to be circular, cylindrical, be a wheel, a wagon [dα, to be]. —— gyн-Ḳα̃'dнdl-dα, it is round (said of a tumbler).

Ḳα̃'-dei (Ḳα̃'dα', punct. neg.; Ḳα̃'doup, curs.; Ḳα̃'deidα', fut.; Ḳα̃'dα'dα', fut. neg.; Ḳα̃'dei, imp.; Ḳα̃'dα'heidl. punct. neg. infer.), to meet. —— gyн-Ḳα̃'dei, I met him. hα̨n gyн-Ḳα̃'dα', I did not meet him. miнn gyн-Ḳα̃'doup, I am about to meet him. gyн-bou-Ḳα̃'doup, I meet him all the time. gyн-Ḳα̃'deidα', I shall meet

him.  hǫn gyн̇-k̑ɑ'dɑ'dɑ', I shall not meet him.   poue 'н̇-k̑ɑ'deidɑ',
don't you meet him!  'н̇-k̑ɑ'dei, you meet him!  heiṫ bн́-k̑ɑ'dei,
let us meet him!  heiṫ poue bн́-k̑ɑ'deidɑ', let us not meet him!
k̑ɑ'-dl-ei (k̑ɑ'dɑ', punct. neg.; k̑ɑtdɑ, k̑ɑdlhн, curs.; k̑ɑdldɑ', fut.;
k̑ɑ'dɑ'dɑ', fut. neg.; k̑ɑdl, imp.), to bite [cp. Tewa k̑õ`, to eat].
Cp. K̑ɑdl-k̑iн, Arikaree man, ev. biter.  —— gyн̇-k̑ɑ'dlei, I bit
him.  hǫn gyн̇-k̑ɑ'dɑ', I did not bite him.  gyн̇-bou-k̑ɑtdɑ, I
bite him continually.  gyн̇-k̑ɑdldɑ', I shall bite him.  hǫn gyн̇-
k̑ɑ'dɑ'dɑ', I shall not bite him.  'н̇-k̑ɑdl, bite him!  bн́-k̑ɑdl, let
us bite him!  k̑yн̇hi̧'н̇ 'éi-sн̧'nei̧-k̑ɑ'dlei nǫ heidǫn (for heidɑ hǫn)
tou tsн̧n gɑ heigɑ hei̧'m, the man bitten by a rattlesnake died
before reaching camp.  'éi-k̑ɑ'dlei, he bit me, also he stung me
(e. g. of yellowjacket).  'н̧n 'ȩ̀im-k̑ɑtdɑ tsei̧hi̧н̧, he is a dog who
is always biting people.
k̑ɑ'-dǫu-bei-tsǫu-hi̧н̧ (k̑ɑ'-dǫu-bei-tsǫu-hyou-p, tpl.), a kind of idol
[unexplained: k̑ɑ'-, app. cliff; -dǫu-bei-, app. in, under; app.
tsǫuhi̧н̧, mother-in-law].
k̑ɑ'gɑ (inan. II; k̑ɑ', dpl.; k̑ɑ'- in comp.), cliff, = k̑ɑ'gyнp.  Cp.
k̑ɑ'-dɑ, to be precipitous; touhɑ', cliff; yн̇dldн̇, cliff.
k̑ɑ'-gyн (inan. Iᵃ; ev. k̑ɑ-gɑ'-t, tpl.; k̑ɑ'-gyн-, 'ɑ'- in comp.), 1.
skin; 2. rubber (so called from its resemblance to skin) [cp. 'ɑ'-,
skin, in 'ɑ'-yн-t, to skin; etc.; also possibly -k̑ɑ̧ in tн̇'-k̑ɑ̧, eyelid,
which may be a dim. of k̑ɑ'-].  Cp. 'ɑt-k̑ɑ'-gɑ't, scalp; k'ɑe, skin;
tei-t, skin.  —— k̑ɑ'gyн-dǫy'm, under (my) skin, = teiṫ-dǫy'm.
k̑ɑ'-gyнp (inan. III), cliff, = k̑ɑ'-gɑ.  Cp. k̑ɑ'-dɑ, to be precipitous;
yн̇dldн̇, cliff.
k̑ɑ'gyнp̀-pн̇'dǫn (an. II; k̑ɑ'gyнp̀-pн̇'dɑ̧'-dɑ, tpl.), chickenhawk sp.
[said to sound like cliff-prairie: k̑ɑ'gyнp, cliff; pн̇'-, prairie;
-dɑ̧-n, unexplained].  Cp. k̑yнp̀-pн̇'dǫn, which is evidently another
form of the same name.
k̑ɑ'gyн-t͡sout'н̇'e (inan. Iᵃ), yucca plant [hammer skin: k̑ɑ'gyн,
skin; t͡sout'н̇'e, hammer-stone].
k̑ɑ'-hei̧'m, to feel cold; to die of cold [k̑ɑ'-, referring to cold; hei̧'m,
to die].  —— 'н̇-k̑ɑ'-hei̧'m, I am cold.  k̑ɑ'-hei̧'m, he froze to
death.  miнn 'н̇-k̑ɑ'-hei̧mн̧, I am dying with the cold.  k̑yн̧'hi̧'н̧
mi(н) k̑ɑ'-hi̧н̧heidl, the man almost died from the cold.
k̑ɑ'houdl-sн̇dl-'ɑ̧mgyн, to have chills and fever [app. to be chill sick
feverish; k̑ɑ'-, referring to cold; app. houdl- as in houdl-dɑ, to be
sick; sн̇dl-'ɑ̧mgyн, to have fever].
k̑ɑ'-k'ɑe-bi(н)-hiн̇dl-bн̇ (inan. III), cave (in bank) [k̑ɑ'-, cliff;
-k'ɑe-bi(н)-, unexplained; w. -hiн̇-dl-, cp. possibly hiн̇-dl, arroyo;
-bн̇, postp. and noun postfix].
k̑ɑ'-sǫy (inan. II; k̑ɑ'-sǫy-gɑ, tpl.; k̑ɑ'-sǫy- in comp.), grindstone
[app. k̑ɑ', knife; -sǫy, grinder, cp. sǫy-m, to grind; cp. 'ei-sǫy-bɑ,
metate, lit. seed grinder].

-K̆ɑ-t- in p'ou-K̆ɑt-dɑ, to be syphilitic [cp. -K̆iн in toudl-K̆iн, to have venereal disease].

K̆ɑ'-tou (inan. I), sundance [K̆ɑ'-, unexplained; -tou is said to sound like tou, house].

K̆ɑ'tou-tou (inan. I), sundance house [tou, house].

K̆ɑ'-tнt, to cut in two with a knife [to knife sever]. —— gyн̀-K̆ɑ'tнt, I cut it (the meat) with a knife. déi-K̆ɑ'tнt, I cut it (the bread) with a knife.

K̆ɑ'-tẹi-niн-bɑ (inan. IIª; K̆ɑ'-tẹi-niн, dpl.; K̆ɑ'-tẹi-niн- in comp.), root [unexplained; K̆ɑ'- said to sound like cliff; -bɑ]. —— K̆ɑ'tẹiniн-doубн, underneath the roots.

K̆ɑ'tẹiniн-syн̯'-dɑ (inan. IIª; K̆ɑ'tẹiniн-syн̯n, dpl.), rootlet [syн̯n, to be small].

K̆ọ' (inan. IIª; K̆ɑ'-dɑ, tpl.; K̆ọ-n- in comp.), wild tomato, tomato [cp. K̆ọ'-n, to scowl, be puckered; it was explained that the part of the wild tomato fruit adjacent to the stem is puckered, whence the name]. Cp. K̆ọn-tsoue, tomato soup.

-K̆ọ in tн̄'-K̆ọ, eyelid [cp. possibly K̆ɑ'-gyн, skin].

K̆ọ-n (inan. I), scab [cp. K̆ọn-, stiff; K̆ọn-dɑ, to be stiff, chapped]. —— K̆ọn gyн̀-hɑ'deidɑ', I am going to pull off the scab.

K̆ọ'-n, to scowl (wrinkle forehead), be puckered [cp. K̆ọ', wild tomato fruit]. —— dèi-K̆ọ'n, I scowl.

-K̆ọ-n-, stiff, hard, chapped, rough, in dọm-K̆ọ̃'-dɑ, clod; (K̆ọn-)-boубọу-dɑ, hat; K̆ọn-k'iн, turtle, app. hard shield; k'œe-K̆ọn-houdl, dragonfly, lit. rough skin; sɑt-K̆ọn, hard animal excrement; tẹigyн K̆ọn-hнt-dɑ, icicle, lit. ice hanging down; tsoudl-K̆ọn-bн-tsнt, wing feather.

-K̆ọ-n in 'ọn-K̆ọn, hoof ['ọn-, foot].

-K̆ọ'-n in mọ̃'-K̆ọ'n, nose [mọ̃'-, nose].

K̆ọn-boубọу-dɑ (inan. II; boубọу, dpl.; boубọу- in comp.), hat, = boубọу-dɑ [K̆ọn, stiff].

K̆ọn-dɑ, to be stiff, hard, chapped [dɑ, to be]. —— gyн̀-K̆ọn-dɑ, it is stiff. 'н̀-mọn-K̆ọn-dɑ, my hand is chapped.

kọn-k'iн (an. II; K̆ọn-k'iн-gɑ, tpl.; kọn-k'iн- in comp.), soft-shelled turtle [app. hard shield: K̆ọn-, to be stiff; -k'iн-, shield]. Also called K̆ọnk'iн-p'нtgyн, thin soft-shelled turtle. Cp. t'ọу-K̆ọnk'iн, hard-shelled turtle, lit. water hard shield.

K̆ọnk'iн-p'нt-gyн (an. II; K̆ọnk'iн-p'нt-gɑ'-t, tpl.), soft-shelled turtle [p'нt-gyн, thin]. Also merely K̆ọnk'iн. Cp. t'ọу-K̆ọnk'iн, hard-shelled turtle.

K̆ọn-tsoue, tomato soup [K̆ọ-n-, (wild) tomato; tsou-e, soup].

K̆ọ̃'-, to be greasy, in K̆ọ̃'gyн, grease; K̆ọ̃'-dɑ, to be greasy; *K̆ọ̃'-tọ', to fry; poudl-K̆ọ̃'-tọ'ẹ, pinacate; etc.

K̆ọ̃'-'ọ'mẹi, to grease [Tewa K̆ạ-n-ạ'-ŋ, to grease]. —— k'uep'н̯ gyн̀-K̆ọ̃'-'ọmdɑ', I am going to grease the wagon.

ꝁꝗ'dɑ (inan. III), sweetbread [the greasy one, the one which is fried: *ꝁ'ꝗ-, to be greasy; -dɑ].

ꝁꝗ'-dɑ, to be greasy [dɑ, to be]. Cp. ꝁꝗ'-gyн, grease; etc. ——
'н'dɑ 'èi-kꝗ'dɑ déi-bǫy, I saw a greasy stick. 'н' 'ęį-ꝁꝗ'dɑ nęįn-bǫy, I saw d. greasy sticks. 'н' gyн̇-ꝁꝗ'dɑ gyн̇ṫ-bǫy, I saw tpl. greasy sticks. kꝗ'-hęį dɑ, it is not greasy.

ꝁꝗ'-dei, to be bad, unpleasant. Cp. ꝁꝗ'-dei-dl, badly; 'н'ꝁꝗ'dei, toudl-ꝁꝗ'dei, app. swallow sps. —— tsę.įhįн gyн̇-ꝁꝗ'dei, your dog is no good. gyн̇-ꝁꝗ'dei, it is not good (for me to see you tired). gyн̇-ꝁꝗ'dei, it is no good; also too bad!

ꝁiн-dei (ꝁiнdeigɑ', punct. neg.; ꝁiнdeideip, curs.; ꝁiнdeiîɑ', fut.; kiнdeigɑ'îɑ', fut. neg.; ꝁiнdeidei, imp.), to have a husband [ꝁiн, husband; -dei as in t'н'-dei, to have a wife]. Cp. ꝁiн-hɑ'gyн, to be married, get a husband. —— 'н̇-ꝁiнdei, I have a husband. hǫn 'н̇-ꝁiнdeigɑ', I am not married. miнn 'н̇-ꝁiнdeideip, I am about to be married. 'н̇-ꝁiнdeiîɑ', I shall have a husband. hǫn 'н̇-ꝁiнdeigɑ'îɑ', I shall not have a husband. 'ęįm-ꝁiнdeidei, be married! mн̨'yiн ꝁiнdei-dei gyн̇-bǫy, I saw the married woman, = ꝁiнdei-mн̨yiн-dei gyн̇-bǫy.

ꝁꝗ'-dei-dl, badly [ꝁꝗ'- as in ꝁꝗ'dei, to be bad; -dei-dl]. —— ꝁꝗ'deidl 'ę́į-'ꝗ'męį-dei peidou dèi-hęįdɑ, he did not treat me well and that is why I left.

ꝁꝗ'dei-'ęį-dɑ, to feel bad, sad [ꝁꝗ'dei, to be bad; -'ęį-, unexplained; dɑ, to be]. —— 'н̇-ꝁꝗ'dei-'ęį-dɑ, I feel bad.

ꝁiн-'eidl (an. II; ꝁiн-'eiṫ-dɑ, tpl.), father-in-law [ꝁiн-, man; 'eidl, big, here in the sense of old; ct. 'eidl-ꝁiн, old man, which has the same stems in reversed order]. Cp. dǫym, father-in-law, son-in-law; yнṫ-ꝁiн, son-in-law.

ꝁꝗ'-gyн (inan. III; ꝁꝗ- in comp.), grease, greasy place [ꝁꝗ'-, to be greasy; Tewa ꝁɑ́, grease; -gyн]. Cp. ꝁꝗ'-pǫye, to sizzle; *ꝁꝗ'-tɑ', to fry; tн̨'-gyн, grease. —— ꝁꝗ'gyн gyнṫ-bǫy, I saw some grease.

ꝁꝗ'-mǫ-n (inan. Iᵃ), testicles.

ꝁꝗ'mǫn-biнmk'ɑe (inan. IIᵃ), scrotum [testicles bag].

ꝁꝗ'nǫṫ-sɑp'ouy-iн (an. II; ꝁꝗ'nǫṫ-sɑp'ouy-ou-p, tpl.; ꝁꝗ'nǫṫ-sɑp'ouy-iн-, in comp.), fly [app. ꝁꝗ'nǫṫ- as in ꝁꝗ'nꝗ'-t'ꝗ', spider; sɑ, unexplained; -p'oue-iн: p'ou, trap, web; -ei; -'iн, dim.].

ꝁꝗ'nǫṫsɑp'ouyiн-'eidl, blue fly [large fly].

ꝁꝗ'-nꝗ'-t'ꝗ' (an. II; ꝁꝗ'-nꝗ'-t'ꝗ'-gɑ, tpl.; ꝁꝗ'-nꝗ'-t'ꝗ'-, in comp.), spider (said to refer to any kind) [cp. ꝁꝗ'nǫṫ-sɑp'ouy-iн, fly].

ꝁꝗ'nꝗ't'ꝗ'-k'ǫy-'eidl (an. II; ꝁꝗ'nꝗ't'ꝗ'-k'ǫy-bįн-dɑ, tpl.), tarantula [large black spider].

ꝁꝗ'nꝗ't'ꝗ'-k'ǫy-gyн (an. II; ꝁꝗ'nꝗ't'ꝗ'-k'ǫy-gɑ'-t, tpl.), black spider.

ꝁꝗ'nꝗ't'ꝗ'-p'ou (inan. III), spider web [spider trap].

ꝁꝗ'-pǫye, to sizzle [to grease sound: ꝁꝗ'-, grease; pǫye, to sound]. —— kiн 'н̨n ꝁꝗ'-pǫygyн, the beef is sizzling.

Ꝁꬵ'-p'oudl (an. II; Ꝁꬵ'-p'out-dα, tpl.; Ꝁꬵ'-p'oudl- in comp.), wart
[unexplained]. Cp. 'н'-Ꝁꬵ'p'oudl, excrescence on a tree.
Ꝁꬵ'-p'oup (an. II; Ꝁꬵ'-p'oup-gα'-t, tpl.; Ꝁꬵ'-p'oup- in comp.), bobcat
[Ꝁꬵ'-, unexplained; app. p'ou-p, to be spotted].
*kꬵ'-tꬵ' (Ꝁꬵ'-tꬵ'dα', fut.), to fry [Ꝁꬵ'-, grease; *tꬵ', to roast]. ——
gyн̇-Ꝁꬵ'tꬵ'dα', I am going to fry it.
Ꝁiн (an. I; Ꝁyн-e-guα, tpl.; Ꝁiн- in comp.), husband. Cp. Ꝁyн̯hi̯'н̯,
man; Ꝁiн-'eidl, father-in-law; -Ꝁiн, man; Ꝁiн-dei, to have a husband; Ꝁiн-hα'gyн, to marry a man; t'н', wife. —— nꬵ Ꝁiн, my
husband. nꬵ Ꝁyнeguα, my husbands.
-Ꝁiн (an. I and an. II, usually the latter; in tribe names, adjective
forms and agentives usually replaced by a noun postfix in tpl.,
although -Ꝁyн̯hi̯'н̯ can be substituted in sd. and -Ꝁyн̯hyoup in tpl.;
but in animal names indicating the male, -Ꝁyн̯hi̯'н̯ is not substituted
in sd., and the tpl. is -Ꝁiнgα, -Ꝁiнbα), man, male: postpounded to
the stems of nouns, especially to tribe names and animal names,
and to adjective stems to indicate masculine gender, and to verb
stems to indicate masculine agentive -Ꝁiн- in comp. The corresponding feminine postpound is -mн̯. Cp. Ꝁiн, husband;
Ꝁyн̯-hi̯'н̯, man. The chance -gee, -kee of Eng. Muskogee, Cherokee was felt to be -Ꝁiн, these names being taken over as Mαskou-
Ꝁiн (Mαskou-gα, tpl.), Tseirou-Ꝁiн (Tseirou-gα, tpl.) respectively.
—— Kαe-Ꝁiн, Kiowa man; Kαe-guα, tpl. tseįhiн̯-Ꝁiн, male dog;
tseįhiн̯-Ꝁiн-gα, tpl. pei-Ꝁiн, dead man; pei-gα, tpl.; guαn-Ꝁiн
(male) dancer; guαn-mн̯, (female) dancer; guꬵdα, tpl. of common
gender; but also guαn-Ꝁyн̯hi̯'н̯, masc. s.; guαn-Ꝁyн̯hyoup, masc.
tpl.; guαn-mн̯yiн, fem. s.; guαn-mн̯emα, guαn-mн̯youp, fem. tpl.
Ꝁiн- in Ꝁiн-'нtdα'-dei, tonsil.
Ꝁiн- in Ꝁiн-tн̯'-dн, to be frosty.
Ꝁiн-, to get firewood, in Ꝁiн-'н̯, to come for firewood; Ꝁiн-bн, to go
for firewood. [cp. Ꝁiн-bα, firewood]. Cp. Ꝁiн-t'eįm-bн, to go to
get firewood.
-Ꝁiн, -Ꝁyн in toudl-Ꝁiн, to have venereal disease [cp. -Ꝁα-t- in p'ou-
Ꝁαt-dα, to be syphilitic].
-Ꝁiн-'н in Seit-'eįm-Ꝁiн-'н, prsn., lit. "bear knocking them over."
-Ꝁiн-'н in Seit-'eįm-Ꝁiн'н, prsn., Bear Knocking Them Over.
Ꝁiн-'нt-dα'-dei (inan. III), tonsil [Ꝁiн-, unexplained; -'н-dl-, -'н-t-,
round; app. dα, to be; -dei].
Ꝁiн-'н̯, to come to get firewood. —— 'н̇-Ꝁiн-'н̯, I am on my way
to get firewood.
Ꝁiн-bα (inan. II; Ꝁiн, dpl.; Ꝁiн- in comp.), 1. stick of firewood,
firewood; 2. fire, in 'èi-Ꝁiн-k'uαt, there is a fire (over there) (-k'uαt
with sbje, series unexplained, app. distinct from k'uαt, to pull
out) [cp. Ꝁiн-, to get firewood]. Cp. 'н'-dα, stick of wood; p'iн,
fire. —— Ꝁiнbα déi-bꭓu, I saw a stick of firewood. Ꝁiн nèin-bꭓu,

I saw two sticks of firewood. ꞣiʜ gyꞧ-bǫꭗ, I saw some firewood, a bunch of firewood.

ꞣiʜ-bʜ, to go to get firewood. —— 'ꞧ-ꞣiʜbʜ'tɑ', I am going to go after wood.

ꞣiʜ-dei (ꞣiʜdeideip, curs.), to have a husband [ꞣiʜ, husband; -dei as is t'ʜ'-dei, to marry a woman]. Cp. ꞣiʜ-hɑ'gyʜ, to marry a man. —— 'ꞧ-ꞣiʜdei, I have a husband.

ꞣiʜ-gɑ'-m (also ꞣiʜgɑ'mei, stat.; ꞣiʜgɑ'mɑ', punct. neg.; ꞣiʜgɑ'mɑ, curs.; ꞣiʜgɑmdɑ', fut.; ꞣiʜgɑ'mɑ'dɑ', fut. neg.; ꞣiʜgɑ'm, ꞣiʜgɑ'miʜ, imp.), to rule [w. ꞣiʜ- cp. ꞣyʜʜeꞣiʜ, chief; -gɑ'm, unexplained]. Cp. ꞣiʜgɑ'm-gyʜ, ꞣiʜgɑ'm-dʜ, rule kingdom. —— nɑ gyꞧ-ꞣiʜgɑ'mɑ, I am ruling (said e. g. by chief). gyꞧ-ꞣiʜgɑmdɑ, I am going to rule. hɑn gyꞧ-ꞣiʜgɑ'mɑ'dɑ', I am not going to rule. 'ꭗm bꞧ-ꞣiʜgɑ'-miʜ, you rule! 'ꭗm mɑ́n-ꞣiʜgɑ'miʜ, ye d. rule! poue bꞧ-ꞣiʜgɑmdɑ', don't rule! nɑ bꞧ-ꞣiʜgɑm, let us rule! heit poue bꞧ-ꞣiʜgɑmdɑ', let us not rule! gyꞧ-ꞣiʜgɑ'mei, I ruled. hɑ́n gyꞧ-ꞣiʜgɑ'mɑ, I did not rule. nɑ gyꞧ-ꞣiʜgɑ'm, I am the ruler. 'ꭗm bꞧ-ꞣiʜgɑ'm, you are the ruler.

ꞣiʜgɑ'm-dʜ (inan. Iᵃ), rule, kingdom. —— 'ꭗm ꞣiʜgɑ'mdʜ gyꞧ-bǫꭗ, I saw thy kingdom. 'ꭗm ꞣiʜgɑ'mdʜ gyꞧt-bǫꭗ, I saw thy kingdoms.

ꞣiʜgɑ'm-gyʜ (inan. III), rule, kingdom. —— ꞣiʜgɑ'mgyʜ gyꞧt-bǫꭗ, I saw the kingdom.

ꞣiʜgɑ'm-tou (inan. I), courthouse [ꞣiʜgɑ'm, to rule; tou, house].

ꞣiʜ-gyʜ (ꞣiʜgu'ɑ, punct. neg.; ꞣiʜdɑ, curs.; ꞣiʜdɑ', fut.; ꞣiʜgu'ɑdɑ', fut. neg.; ꞣiʜ, imp.), to throw [Tewa kē'-, to toss]. Cp. mꭗedei-ꞣiʜ, plaited sinew used in game, lit. thing thrown up; tsou-ꞣiʜ-k'ɑe, sling; p'ou-ꞣiʜgyʜ, to lasso; etc. —— t'ǫꭗgyʜ nɛ́i-ꞣiʜgyʜ, he threw me into the water. tsou-dou gyꞧ-ꞣiʜgyʜ, I threw a stone at him. 'ɑ'gɑpiꞧ 'ɛ́i-kɑdl-guɑnmꭗe nɛ̀i-ꞣiʜgyʜ 'oueihiꞧ, the buffalo hooked me and threw me way over. nɛ́i-ꞣiʜ, push me (said when sitting on swing)! tsou neịn-ꞣiʜgyʜ, I threw a stone. hɑn neịn-ꞣiɑgu'ɑ, I did not throw it. miʜn nɛ́ịn-ꞣiʜdɑ, I am about to throw it. tsou nɛ̀ịn-ꞣiʜdɑ, I shall throw the stone. hɑn tsou nɛ̀ịn-ꞣiʜgu'ɑdɑ', I shall not throw the stone. tsou 'ɛ́ịm-ꞣiʜ, throw the stone! 'ꞧ-ꞣiʜ, you throw at him! 'ɛ́ị-tsou-ꞣiʜgyʜ, he threw at me with a stone. tsou neịn-ꞣiʜdɑ', I am going to throw stones.

ꞣiʜ-gyʜ, adv., afterward [ꞣiʜ-, unexplained; -gyʜ]. Cp. ꞣiʜgyʜ-e-, next; ꞣiʜgyʜ-tsou, afterward; -ꞣiʜ-hiꞧ, after. —— nɑ ꞣiʜgyʜ kɑ'dei ꞣyʜʜeꞣiʜ tsꭗnheidl, and later the other chief came up. hɑn kɑdl ꞣiʜgyʜ 'ɛ́ịm-ꞣɑ'dɑ heidl, they never met again. hɑn houdldei tsꭗ'nɑ gɑ sɑt hʜ'oue ꞣiʜgyʜ tsꭗn, he did not come back for a long time, and he came way afterwards.

ꞣiʜ-gyʜ-e (ꞣiʜgɑ', punct. neg.; ꞣiʜdeip, curs.; ꞣiʜgyʜetɑ', fut.; ꞣiʜgɑ'tɑ, fut. neg.; ꞣiʜdei, imp.), to be stuck in. —— 'ꞧ-ꞣiʜgyʜe,

I am stuck (e. g. in a hole which I was crawling through). mαn
'ẹi-k̑iнgyнe, my finger is stuck. hαn 'н̇-k̑iнgα', I was not stuck.
miнn 'н̇-k̑iнdeip, I am about to be stuck. 'н̇-k̑iнgyнet͡α', I shall
be stuck. hαn 'н̇-k̑iнgα't͡α', I shall not be stuck. 'ẹim-k̑iнdei, be
stuck! (ct. 'ẹim-k̑iнdei, you are married, said to woman).

k̑iнgyн-e, next [k̑iнgyн, afterward; -ei]. —— k̑iнgyнe-p̑α 'heigα 'αe
tsн̯nmн̯, he is going to come back next month. k̑iнgyнe pнe, next
summer. k̑iнgyнe-sнe-, next winter.

k̑iнgyн-tsou, adv., afterward [-tsou, like]. —— 'ẹihα' hαn tseiguαn
gyн̇-p̑α'hiнguαdα' nei k̑iнgyн-tsou heigα gyн̇-p̑α'hiнdα', I am not
going to take the dog this time, but will take him later.

-k̑iн-hн', -k̑iн-hн̯'-, in 'αdl-k'αe-k̑iнhн', 1. crest, 2. kingfisher;
'αdl-t'ọụ-(k'αe-)k̑iнhн̯'-k̑iн, Flathead man; k̑iнhн̯'-bн̑p̑-gα, occiput;
k'αe-k̑iнhн', sun-perch, lit. crested (referring to the dorsal fin).

k̑iнhн̯'-bн̑p̑-gα (inan. IIª; k̑iнhн̯'-bн̑p̑-dei, k̑i̯нhн̯'-bн̑p, dpl.), occiput,
back of head [-k̑iнhн̯'- as in 'αdl-k'αe-k̑iнhн', crest; -bн-p, postp.,
at; -gα].

k̑iн-hα̑'gyα, to marry a man [hα̑'gyн, to take, get]. Cp. k̑iн-dei, to
have a husband. —— gyн̇-k̑iнhα̑'gyн, I married him, I took him
as husband.

k̑iн-k̑oup, to make a fire [k̑oup, to lay several]. —— déi-k̑iн-k̑oup, I
made a fire. hαn déi-k̑iнk̑u'α, I did not make a fire. béi-k̑iнk̑uα
light the fire!

k̑iн-syн̯-dα (inan. II; k̑iн-syн̯n, tpl.), piece of kindling wood, kindlings
[small firewood]. —— k'yн̯hi̯н-k̑iн-syн̯n, morning kindlings.

k̑iн-t̂н̯'-dα, to be frosty [k̑iн-, said to refer to freezing solid; -t̂н̯', -t̂н̯'-,
white; dα].

k̑iн-t'ẹim-bн, to go to get firewood [k̑iн-, here app. noun; -t'ẹi-m-,
unexplained; bн, to go]. Cp. k̑iн-bн, to go to get firewood. ——
'н̇-k̑iн-t'ẹimbн̯'t͡α', I am going to go for firewood.

k̑iн-tsei-bα (inan. IIª; k̑iн-tsei, dpl.), stick hidden in hand in hand-
game [w. k̑iн- cp. possibly k̑iн-yн, opponent in game; tsei-, unexplained; -bα]. Cp. tou-'α, to play hand game.

k̑iн-yн (an. I; k̑iнyн̇'gα, tpl.; k̑iн-yн- in comp.), opponent (in
game).

k̑iн-yн-, verb prefix, beside, among. —— néi-k̑iнyн-sα, you sit
down beside me! mн̯'yiн 'ẹi-k̑iнyн-'н̯'gyн, the woman was
sitting beside me. mн̯'yiн gyн̇-k̑iнyн-'н̯'gyн, I was sitting beside
the lady. p'н'ou sнe Кунe-'ẹị 'н̇-k̑iнyн-t͡α', I lived three years
among the Comanches.

k̑iн-yнe-bα (inan. Iª), wood-gathering rope.

-k̑i̯н-hi̯н, postp., after, in dα'k'iн-k̑i̯нhi̯н, Monday, lit. after Sunday
[-k̑i̯н- as in k̑iн-gyн, afterward; -hi̯н].

k̑ou- in k̑ou-gαe, elk.

k̑ou- in k̑ou-k̑iн, spy; k̑ou-bн, to go spying.

-k̑ou in guɑt-k̑ou, yellow [guɑdl-, guɑt-, red].

k̑ou-bʜ, to go spying.  Cp. k̑ou-k̑iʜ, spy.

-k̑ou-dei in pʻɑʼk̑ou-dei, measuring-worm.

k̑ou-dl (an. II; k̑out-dɑ, tpl.; k̑oudl- in comp.), neck [Tewa k̑è, neck]
[cp. ʼou-sei, throat; ʼou-, throat, neck in comp.].  Cp. k̑o̜ʼ-k̑oudl,
squash, lit. goose neck; ho̜ʼk̑oudl-pʻn̥ʼ-gɑ, bell, lit. metal tied at
the neck.

k̑oudl-dei-pʻn̥ʼ-gɑ (inan. IIa; k̑oudl-dei-pʻn̥, dpl.; k̑oudl-dei-pʻn̥ʼ- in
comp.), necktie [k̑oudl, neck; -dei; -pʻn̥ as in k̑oudl-pʻn̥, necklace].
Cp. k̑oudl-pʻn̥, necklace.

k̑oudl-guɑdl, a red-neck, red-necked person.  Cp. k̑oudl-t̑n̥e̜, bald
eagle.

k̑oudl-guɑdl-dɑ, to be red-necked. —— ʼn̥-k̑oudl-guɑdl-dɑ, I am
red-necked.

k̑oudl-pʻn̥ (inan. III), necklace [k̑oudl-, neck; pʻn̥, to be tied].  Cp.
k̑oudl-dei-pʻn̥ʼ-gɑ, necktie; tʻo̜u̥sei-k̑oudlpʻn̥, necklace of long beads,
= k̑oudlpʻn̥-hyu̥ʼe̜.

k̑oudlpʻn̥ʼ-hyu̥-e̜ (inan. II; k̑oudlpʻn̥ʼ-hin̥, dpl.; k̑oudlpʻn̥ʼ-hin̥- in
comp.), necklace of long bone beads, = tʻo̜u̥sei-k̑oudlpʻn̥ [real
necklace].

k̑oudl-t̑n̥e̜ (an. II; k̑oudl-t̑n̥e̜-mɑ, tpl.; k̑oudl-t̑n̥e̜- in comp.), bald
eagle [white neck].  Cp. k̑oudl-guɑdl, red-necked person.

k̑oudl-tʻʜp-ei-gɑ (inan. IIa; k̑oudl-tʻʜp-ei, dpl.), fall-grape.  The
grapes are small where fastened to the stem and that portion is
called the neck [dry neck fruit].  Cp. k̑eidei-ʼei-gɑ, wild grape.

K̑oue-tse̜i-k̑iʜ (an. I; K̑oue-tse̜i-gɑ, tpl.), member of a Kiowa order;
cp. Mooney, p. 230 [k̑ou-e, unexplained; app. -tse̜i-, horse; -k̑iʜ].

k̑ou-gɑ-e (an. II; k̑ou-gɑ-e-guɑ, tpl.; k̑ou-gɑ-e- in comp.), elk [unex-
plained; k̑ou- was thought by Mr. Waldo to mean big].

K̑ougɑe-k̑iʜ, member of a Kiowa division, lit. elk man; cp. Mooney,
p. 228.

K̑ougɑe-tʻɑdl, "lean elk," recent prsn. of Mr. James Waldo.

k̑ou-k̑iʜ (an. I; k̑ou-gɑ, tpl.), spy.  Cp. k̑ou-bʜ, to go spying.

k̑ou-p, k̑you-p (inan. II), 1. knob (e. g. at end of war club); 2. mountain [Tewa k̑ūʻ, stone].  Cp. k̑oup-guɑþgɑʼt, war club; bɑdlhɑʼ, hill;
pʻiʜgɑ, hill. —— pʜʼgɑ k̑oup ʼéi-k̑ɑ, one mountain is lying.  yiʜ
k̑oup ʼè̜i-k̑ɑʼ, two mountains are lying.  hʜʼoudei k̑oup k̑uɑdl,
several mountains are lying.

k̑ou-p (k̑uɑgu'ɑ, punct. neg.; k̑uɑþdɑ, curs.; k̑uɑdɑʼ, fut.; k̑uɑgu'ɑdɑʼ,
fut. neg.; k̑uɑ, imp.), to lay several.  So. correspondent is t̑seip.
[cp. k̑ɑ, one lies; k̑uɑdl, several lie].  Cp. *ʼɑʼ-k̑oup, to put away
several. —— déi-k̑oup, I laid them.  hɑ̜n déi-k̑uɑgu'ɑ, I did not
lay them.  déi-bou-k̑uɑþdɑ, I am laying them all the time.  miʜn
déi-k̑uɑþdɑ, I am about to lay them.  déi-k̑uɑdɑʼ, I shall lay them.
hɑ̜n déi-k̑uɑgu'ɑdɑ, I shall not lay them.  béi-k̑uɑ, lay them!

bèi-k̄uα, you camp! heit béi-k̄uα, let us put them.  hèit bèi-k̄uα, let us camp.  poue béi-k̄uαdα', don't lay them!  'ẹihα' poue bèi-k̄uαdα', don't you camp here!  sọụn pн'н'gα gyн̀t-k̄uαdα', I am going to stack the hay, lit. I am going to put the hay in one place.

-k̄ouþ-dei in p'iн-k̄ouþ-dei, crane.

K̄oup-'eit-dα, Mount Scott [big mountain].

k̄oup-guαþ-gα'-t (inan. II; k̄oup-guαþ-gyн, dpl.), war club [rough knob: k̄oup, knob; guαþ-gyн, rough].

K̄oup-ou-t'н'-bα, plcn. [mountain that is raising its chin: cp. 'ou-t'н'-dou', to raise chin, throw head back; -bα].

k̄oup-t̂αhᾱ'-sαdl, range of mountains [-t̂αhᾱ'- as in mᾳ'-t̂αhα, to be hook-nosed; t'ọụ-t̂αhᾱ'-sαdl, waterfall; sαdl, several stand].

K̄ouþ-t̂α'k'αe-k̄iн (an. II; K̄oup-t̂α'k'αe, tpl.; K̄oup-t̂α'k'αe- in comp.), Mexican man [mountain Whiteman].

k̄ouþt̂α'k'αe-sн̄'nẹị (an. II; k̄ouþt̂α'k'αe-sн̄'nou-p, tpl.), campamocha [Mexican snake].

k̄ouþ-t̄sou (inan. Iᵃ), mountain rock.

-k̄ou-t in 'н'-k̄out, to smoke tr.

-k̄ọụ in k̄αe-k̄ọụ-gα, flint.

-k̄ọụ-m, said to mean old, in tsн-k̄ọụm-zн̄'dlei, ground squirrel [cp. possibly k̄ọụm-sα, jackrabbit].

k̄ọụm-sα (an. II; k̄ọụm-sᾱ'-gα, tpl.; k̄ọụm-sᾱ'- in comp.), jack-rabbit [w. k̄ọụ-m- cp. tsн-k̄ọụm-zн̄'dlei, ground squirrel; Tewa kwᾴ-ŋ, jackrabbit; app. -sα, augmentative].

-k̄uα- in 'ᾱ'-k̄uα-tou'e, storeroom; 'ᾱ'k̄uα-soudei, hook for hanging things away [k̄ou-p, to lay several].

k̄uα-dl (defective verb), 1. (kouþgα', punct. neg.; kouþt̂α', fut.; kouþgᾱ't̂α', fut. neg.; kouþdei, imp.), several lie: ss. correspon-dent is k̄α; 2. (k̄uαdl, kuαyα', stat. positive; all other forms sup-plied from 'н̄'gyн, to sit), several sit: ss. correspondent is 'н̄'gyн [cp. k̄α, one lies; k̄ou-p, to lay several]. —— 1. pн'gα tsẹị k̄α, one horse is lying.  yiн tsẹị 'èị-k̄α, two horses are lying.  hн'oudei tsẹịgα 'èi-k̄uαdl, several horses are lying.  hᾳn 'èi-kouþgα', they are not lying down.  tн̄' k̄uαdl p'н̄m-bei, the stars are in the sky. —— 2. 'н̀-'н̄'gyн, I am sitting.  'èi-'н̄'gyн, we d. are sitting. 'èi-k̄uαdl, 1. we tpl. are sitting; 2. we tpl. are lying.  hᾳn 'èi-н̄'gα', we dpl. are not sitting.  hᾳn 'èi-kouþgα', we tpl. are not lying.

k̄uα-n-dα, to be in a hurry (dα, to be). Cp. hн̄dl-н̄, to be in a hurry. —— 'н̀-k̄uαn-dα, I am in a hurry.  hᾳn 'н̀-k̄uαn-dᾳ'mᾳ', I am not in a hurry.

k̄u-e-gyн, to fall. Cp. 'outgyн, one fall, þeitgyн, several fall. —— t̄sou gyн̀-k̄uegyн, the rocks are falling down.

k̄yн-k̄ọụ-m-, k̄iн-k̄ọụ-m-, alive, in k̄yнk̄ọụm-dн, k̄yнk̄ọụm-gyн, life; kyнk̄ọụm-t̂α', to be alive; etc. [unexplained].

ƙyнkǫ̞ᶙm-dн, life, = ƙyнkǫ̞ᶙm-gyн. —— nǫ̞ ƙyнkǫ̞ᶙm-dн, my life.

ƙyнkǫ̞ᶙm-gyн (app. inan. III), life, = ƙyнkǫ̞ᶙm-dн.

ƙyнkǫ̞ᶙm-ƙiн (an. I; ƙyнkǫ̞ᶙm-gɑ, tpl.), person (masc.), people.

ƙyнkǫ̞ᶙm-mн (an. I; ƙyнkǫ̞ᶙm-gɑ, ƙyнkǫ̞ᶙm-mн̞e̞-mɑ, tpl.), person (fem.), people.

ƙyнkǫ̞ᶙm-t̂ɑ', to be alive [t̂ɑ', to be around]. —— heidɑ 'н̇-ƙyн-
kǫ̞ᶙm-t̂ɑ', I am still alive. Cp. heidɑ pei-he̞i 'н̇-dɑ, I am alive,
lit. I am not dead.

ƙyнɓ-pн'dǫ̞n (an. II; ƙyнɓ-pн'dǫ̞'-dɑ, tpl.), chicken hawk sp. Evidently another form of ƙɑ'gyнɓ-pн'dǫ̞n, q. v.

ƙyн-ɓ-t̓ɑ (an. I; ƙyн-ɓ‧t̓ɑ'-dɑ, tpl.), old man [unexplained]. Cp.
T̂sн̞n-ƙyнɓt̓ɑ, "cheating old man," a name of Se̞i̞ndei; 'eidl-ƙiн,
old man.

ƙyн-t (ƙyнdldɑ', fut.; ƙyнdl, imp.), to open. Cp. t̂sнt-ǫ̞'me̞i̞, to
close. —— de̞i-sɑ'ɑdl-ƙyнt, I opened my mouth. be̞i-sɑ'ɑdl-
ƙyнdl, open your mouth! de̞i-sɑ'ɑdl-ƙyнdldɑ', I shall open my
mouth.

ƙyнtнe-guɑ-dɑ (inan. II; ƙyнtнe-guɑ, dpl.), the lowest rib [chief
rib].

ƙyн-tн-e-ƙiн (an. I; ƙyн-tн-'e, tpl.), chief [w. ƙyн- cp. ƙiн-gǫ̞'m, to
rule; -tн-e-, -tн-'e-, unexplained; -ƙiн].

ƙyн'-dl-ei (ƙyн'dɑ', punct. neg.; ƙyнt̂dɑ, curs.; ƙyнdldɑ', fut.;
ƙyн'dɑ'dɑ', fut. neg.; ƙyн'dl, imp.), to call, summon, invite [cp.
Tewa tǫ̇-ƙɑ́-mɑ́, to call, summon]. —— de̞i-ƙyн'dlei, I summoned
them. hǫ̞n de̞i-ƙyн'dɑ', I did not summon them. miнn de̞i-
ƙyнt̂dɑ, I am about to summon them. hǫ̞n miнn de̞i-ƙyн'dɑ', I
am not about to summon them. de̞i-ƙyнdldɑ', I shall summon
them. hǫ̞n de̞i-ƙyн'dɑ'dɑ', I shall not summon them. poue be̞i-
ƙyнdldɑ', do not summon them! be̞i-ƙyнdl, summon them! he̞it̂
be̞i-ƙyнdl, let us summon them! he̞it̂ poue be̞i-ƙyнdldɑ', let us
not summon them. gyн̇-bou-kyнt̂dɑ, I call him over all the time.
'н̇-ƙyн'dl, call him over!

ƙyн'-gou-p, (inan. IIᵃ), brain [unexplained].

ƙyн̞-m-dei-, adverbial verb prepound, in vain [unexplained; -dei].
—— mǫ̞n heigɑ he̞i ne̞i̞gɑ gyн̇-dɑ, bн̇-ƙyн̞mdei-bн't̂ɑ', maybe he
is gone, we d. will be going there for nothing.

ƙyн̞-hi̞'н̞, (an. I; ƙyн̞-hyou-p, tpl.; ƙyн̞-hi̞'н̞- in comp.), man [ƙiн-
as -ƙiн, man; ƙiн, husband; -hi̞'н̞, real]. Cp. mн̞y-i̞н̞, woman;
'eidl-ƙiн, old man.

k̓

-k̓ɑ in t̂ɑ'-bн-k̓ɑ, earwax.

-k̓ɑ in pɑdl-k̓ɑ'-gɑ, drum [cp. possibly k̓ɑ-e, skin].

k̓ɑ-deidl, used in the expression k̓ɑdeidl 'e̞i̞m-dɑ, = sɑp̓oudl 'e̞i̞m-dɑ.
See sɑp̓oudl.

k'α-dl-hei-, adverbial verb prepound, together. —— 'ʜ' k'αdlhei-sαdl, the trees are standing together, are in a grove.

k'α-e (an. II; k'α-e-guα, tpl.; k'α-e- in comp.; k'αę, dim.), skin, hide, tegument, membrane, cloth, mat [Tewa xò-wᾱ, skin]. Cp. k̂ᾱ'gyʜ, skin; k'αę, little skin, rind; k'ᾱ'-dα, blanket; tou-dǫumdei k'αe, mat; t̂oubʜ'-k'αe, cradle hood, lit. face-cloth; k'αhy-oudl, lung; biʜm-k'αe, bag; poudl-α-k'αe, connective tissue, membrane of meat; p'eip̂oup̀-k'αe, navel cord; t̂sou-k̂yʜ-k'αe, sting; etc.

k'αe-bʜ-toudlei (an. II; k'αebʜ-toudlou-p, tpl.; k'αebʜ-toudlei- in comp.), butterfly [explained as meaning skin flapper, referring to its flapping skinlike wings: k'αe, membrane; -bʜ-; w. -tou-dl-ei cp. tou-t̂-goup, to flap, flutter]. Cp. k'αebʜtoudlei-'αt̂αę, bat, lit. smooth skin flapper; k'αe-k̂ᾳnhoudl, dragonfly, lit. rough skin.

k'αebʜtoudlei-'αt̂αę (an. II; k'αebʜtoudlei-'αt̂αę-mα, tpl.; k'αebʜtou-dlei-'αt̂αę- in comp.), bat [smooth skin flapper].

-k'αe-bi(ʜ)- in k̂ᾱ'-k'αebi(ʜ)-hiʜdl-bʜ, bank caved out underneath.

k'αe-k̂ᾳnhoudl (an. II; k'αe-k̂ᾳnhout̂-dα, tpl.; k'αe-k̂ᾳnhoudl- in comp.), dragonfly [rough skin: k̂ᾳn, stiff, rough; -hou-dl, intensive]. Cp. k'αebʜtoudlei-'αt̂αę, bat.

k'αe-k̂i(ʜ)hʜ' (an. II; k'αe-k̂i(ʜ)hʜ'-gα, tpl.; k'αe-k̂i(ʜ)hʜ'- in comp.), sun-perch [skin crest, so called from arched dorsal fin: k'αe, skin; -k̂iʜhʜ', crest]. Cp. 'Ὰdlt'ǫu-(k'αe)k̂i(ʜ)hʜ'-k̂iʜ, Flathead man, lit. head-crested man.

k'αek̂i(ʜ)hʜ'-'ei-p'eip (inan. IIª), a bush which bears bluish edible berries, flattish or arched in shape [skin crest berry bush].

k'αe-p'ʜę, to tie cloth (around head) [to cloth tie]. —— 'αdlt'ęi'm déi-k'αe-p'ʜędα', I am going to tie a cloth around my head.

k'αhy-oudl (inan. III), lung [ev. k'αe, skin; -houdl, intensive].

k'αhyoudl-k'oup̀-dʜ, pneumonia [lung pain].

k'α-t̂-gyʜ, bunch, knob. Cp. t̂αę-k'αt̂-gyʜ, knob, lit. smooth knob; k'ᾱ'-dei-dou', to be in a bunch.

k'αt̂gyʜ-dα, to be in a bunch [dα, to be]. Cp. k'ᾱ'dei-dou', to be in a bunch. —— p'ʜn k'αt̂gyʜ-dα, the clouds are in a bunch.

k'ᾱ'-, prepound form of hᾱ'-gyʜ, to get, in k'ᾱ'-'ʜ, to come to get; k'ᾱ'-bʜ, to go to get; k'ᾱ'-toudα, to send to get. k'ᾱ'-t̂α', to want to get; k'ᾱ'-t'ęindα, to want to get; etc. [Tewa xǫ́-ŋ-, to get].

k'ᾱ'-ʜ, to come to get [Tewa xǫ́-ŋ-'ᾲ, to come to get]. —— 'ᾱ̀-k'ᾱ'-'ʜ, I have come after it.

k'ᾱ'-bʜ, to go to get [Tewa xǫ́-m-mᾲ, to go to get]. —— 'ᾱ̀-k'ᾱ'-bʜ, I went after it.

k'ᾱ'-dα (inan. II; k'ᾱ', dpl.; k'ᾱ'- in comp.), blanket [cp. k'α-e, hide, cloth]. Cp. kαdl-k'ᾱ'dα, k'ᾱ'-hi̭'ʜ, buffalo robe.

k'ᾱ'-dei (inan. III), pants [k'ᾱ'-, blanket; -dei].

k‘ɑ’-dei-dou’, to be in a bunch [cp. k‘ɑt-gyн, bunch, knob]. Cp.
k‘ɑtgyн-dɑ, to be in a bunch. ——— ’èit-k‘ɑ’dei-dou’ déi-bǫṵ, I
saw a bunch (e. g. of grapes).

k‘ɑ’dlei-k‘yн’dlei (an. I; kɑ’dlei-k‘yн’dlou-p, tpl.; k‘ɑ’dlei-k‘yн’dlei-
in comp.), frog sp. [k‘ɑ’dlei, unexplained; w. k‘yн’dlei cp. k‘yн-dl-,
wet]. Cp. k‘ɑdleik‘yн’dlei-’eidl, bullfrog; kɑdl-sęim-’ɑ’-k‘yн’dlei,
tadpole.

k‘ɑ’dleik‘yн’dlei-’eidl (an. II; k‘ɑ’dleik‘yн’dlei-bį̄н-dɑ, tpl.), bullfrog
[large frog].

k‘ɑ’-dou’, to owe [app. k‘ɑ’-, to get; dou’]. Cp. kuɑt, to owe. ———
’ɑdlhǫ’gyн ’ęi-k‘ɑ’-dou’, he owes me money.

k‘ɑ’-toudɑ, to send to get. ——— gyн̀-k‘ɑ’toudldɑ’, I am going to
send after it.

k‘ɑ’-ku’ɑ (an. II; k‘ɑ’ku’ɑ-gɑ, tpl.; k‘ɑ’ku’ɑ- in comp.), badger
[unexplained, hardly -ku’ɑ, hitter].

k‘ɑ-kuɑt-н’dɑ (inan. IIᵃ; k‘ɑ’-kuɑt-н’, dpl.; k‘ɑ’-kuɑt-н’- in comp.),
mulberry tree [painted blanket tree].

k‘ɑ’-p‘eidl (k‘ɑ’p‘eit-dɑ, tpl.), flat, broad, wide [w. k‘ɑ’- cp. possibly
k‘ou- in k‘ou-’eit, broad; w. -p‘ei-dl cp. Tewa fɑ́-gì, fí’-gì, to be
flat, broad]. Cp. k‘ɑ’p‘eidl-syн̨n, to be narrow; k‘ou-’eit, to be
wide; Mǫ-k‘ɑ’p‘eidl, prsn., “flat nose.” ’н’-k‘ɑ’p‘eitdɑ déi-bǫṵ,
I saw a broad board. ’н’-k‘ɑ’p‘eidl gyн̀t-bǫṵ, I saw tpl. broad
boards.

k‘ɑ’p‘eidl-syн̨n (k‘ɑ’p‘eidl-syн̨’-dɑ, tpl.), narrow [broad-small].
’н’-k‘ɑ’p‘eidl-syн̨’dɑ, a narrow board.

k‘ɑ’-îɑ’, to want to get [app. îɑ’, to be around]. Cp. k‘ɑ’-t‘ęindɑ, to
want to get. ——— ’ɑ’zнe ’н̀-k‘ɑ’-îɑ’, I wanted the udder. hɑn
’н̀-k‘ɑ’-îɑ’gɑ’, I did not want it. k‘yн̨hįngɑ-tsou ’ɑ’zнe ’н̀-k‘ɑîɑ’-
îɑ’, I shall want the udder tomorrow. poue ’ę̀im-k‘ɑ’-îɑ’îɑ’,
don’t you be wanting to get it!

k‘ɑ’-îн̨ę (an. II; k‘ɑ’-îн̨ę-mɑ, tpl.; k‘ɑ’-îн̨ę- in comp.), bumblebee
[k‘ɑ’-, unexplained; app. îн̨ę, to be white, referring to the whitish
stripe on the bumblebee].

k‘ɑ’-t‘ęindɑ, to want to get. Cp. k‘ɑ’-îɑ’, to want to get. ——— hɑ
gyн̀-k‘ɑ’-t‘ęindɑ, do you want to get it? ’ɑ’zнe hɑn ’ę́i-k‘ɑ’-
t‘ęindǫ’mɑ̨’, I did not want to get the udder (yesterday).

k‘ɑ’-t‘ǫṵ, shoulder, in k‘ɑ’t‘ǫṵ-guɑdl, red-winged blackbird; k‘ɑ’t‘ǫṵ-
’ei-gɑ, “shoulder bread” [k‘ɑ’-, unexplained; t‘ǫṵ-, bone]. Cp.
dǫn, shoulder blade.

k‘ɑ’t‘ǫṵ-’ei-gɑ (inan. IIᵃ; k‘ɑ’t‘ǫṵ-’ei, dpl.), “shoulder bread.” It
was stated that Mexicans make this, and Kiowas used to trade a
horse for a sack of it.

k‘ɑ’t‘ǫṵ-guɑdl (an. II; k‘ɑ’t‘ǫṵ-guɑt-dɑ, tpl.), red-winged blackbird
[red shoulder].

k'ǫ (stat. also k'ǫ'gyн; k'ǫ'gα', stat. neg.; k'ǫ'îα', fut.; k'ǫ'gα'îα', fut. neg.), to be called, named [Tewa xǫ̀-wн̩̀, 1. to be called, 2. name]. Cp. k'ǫ'-m, to call; k'ǫ'-gyн, name. —— P'α'dl 'н̩-k'ǫ, Paul is my name. hǫn P'α'dl 'н̩-k'ǫ'gα', I am not called Paul. P'α'dl 'н̩-k'ǫ'îα', I shall be called Paul. P'α'dl hǫn 'н̩-k'ǫ'gα'îα', I shall not be called Paul. hнyн' 'н̩-k'ǫ'gyн t͡sнdl hǫn yн̩́-hнegα', I do not know what my own name is. hǫn yн̩́-hнegα' hн'-tsou m-k'ǫ'gyн'-dei, I do not know what your name is. hн'-tsou m-k'ǫ, what is your name? tseihịн T'eidei 'ę̀i-k'ǫ, I call my dog Teddy.

k'ǫ-ę (inan. IIª; k'ǫ-ę- in comp.), little skin, rind, pod, bark [dim. of k'α-e, skin]. Cp. 'αhịн-k'ǫę, cedar bark;gu (α)hei-k'ǫę, mesquite pod; k̃ǫnk'įн-k'ǫę, turtle shell; k'ǫę-k'uαt, to remove skin whole; sαdl-k'ǫę, leaf tripe. —— k'ǫę dèi-bǫu̩, I saw an (orange) peel.

k'ǫę-k'uαt, to remove skin whole [k'uα-t, to pull off]. —— hou'kǫu̩'m gyн̩-k'ǫę-k'uαt, I pulled the skin off the coyote.

k'ǫ-hou-dl- in mн̩mdei k'ǫ-houdl-dǫu̩bα, (at) the roof of the mouth.

k'ǫ'-m (k'ǫ'mǫ', punct. neg.; k'ǫ'mǫ, curs.; k'ǫ'mdα', fut.; k'ǫ'mǫ'dα', punct. neg.; k'ǫ'mǫ, curs.; k'ǫ'mdα', fut.; k'ǫ'mǫ'dα', fut. neg.; k'ǫ'm, imp.), to call, name [k'ǫ, to be called; -m, causative]. Cp. tǫu̩-k'ǫ'm, to speak of. —— gyн̩-k'ǫ'm, I called him. gyн̩-k'ǫ'mǫ, I am calling him. hǫn gyн̩-k'ǫ'mα', I did not call him. gyн̩-k'ǫ'mdα', I shall call him. hǫn gyн̩-k'ǫ'mǫ'dα', I shall not call him. 'н̩-k'ǫ'm, call him! bн̩́-k'ǫ'm, let us call him! poue 'н̩-k'ǫ'mdα', do not call him! hα 'è̩i-k'ǫ'm, did you call me? tsoudlhα dǫ́-k'ǫ'mǫ, that is just the way they call us. hн'-tsou gǫ̀-k'ǫ'mǫ, what do they call you? hн'-tsou tseihịн 'н̩-k'ǫ'mdα', what are you going to call your dog? tseihịн T'eidei gyн̩-k'ǫmdα', I am going to call my dog Teddy (ans.). poue T'eidei 'н̩-k'ǫmdα', don't you call him Teddy! T'eidei 'н̩-k'ǫ'm, call him Teddy! T'eidei heì̃ bн̩́-k'ǫ'm, let us call him Teddy! T'eidei poue bн̩́-k'ǫ'mdα', let us not call him Teddy! kα'gα 'н̩n 'Œ'zн'îǫ'houp 'ę̀im-k'ǫ'mǫ, those others they call 'Œ'zн'îǫ'houp.

k'ǫmeisei, commissioner (fr. Eng.).

-k'ǫ-n-, referring to end, fullness, in 'αǫ̀-k'ǫn-, referring to end; mǫn-k'ǫn-hα'gyн, to get a handful [cp. Tewa xǫ́-ŋ-gè, at the end].

k'ǫ'-, referring to being pitiable, in k'ǫ'-'ǫn, to be pitiable; k'ǫ'-t'н̩', to pity.

k'ǫ'-'ǫn (inan. Iª), moccasin [w. k'ǫ'- cp. Tewa xó, legging; -'ǫ-n, unexplained]. Cp. tou-dei, tou-hịн, moccasin.

k'ǫ'-'ǫn, to be pitiable [k'ǫ'- as in k'ǫ'-t'н̩', to pity; -'ǫ-n, unexplained]. —— k'ǫ'-'ǫn, poor fellow! k̃yн̩hị̩'н̩ k'ǫ'ǫn, poor man! k̃yн̩hyoup 'н̩-k'ǫ'ǫn, poor men!

k‘ǫ’ǫn-k̄iн (an. I; k‘ǫ’ǫ’-dα, tpl.), poor man (in sense of either pitiable or not rich).  Ct. ’ǫy̨dei-k̄iн, rich man.

k‘ǫ’-gyн (inan. III), name [k‘ǫ, to be called; -gyн].  —— nǫ k‘ǫ’gyн, my name.

k‘ǫ’-hi̧’н̨ (inan. I), buffalo robe, =kαdl-k‘ᾱ’dα [real blanket].

k‘ǫ’-t‘н̨’ (k‘ǫ’t‘н̨’mǫ’, punct. neg.; k‘ǫ’t‘н̨’mǫ, curs.; k‘ǫ’t‘н̨’ῑα’, fut.; k‘ǫ’t‘н̨’mǫ’ῑα’, fut. neg.; k‘ǫ’t‘н̨, imp.), to pity [k‘ᾱ’- as in k‘ᾱ’-’ǫn, to be pitiable; -t‘н̨’].  —— gyн̇-k‘ǫ’t‘н̨, I pitied him. hǫn gyн̇-k‘ǫ’t‘н̨’mǫ’, I did not pity him.  gyн̇-bou-k‘ǫ’t‘н̨’mǫ, I pity him.  gyн̇-k‘ǫ’t‘н̨’ῑα, I shall pity him.  hǫn gyн̇-k‘ǫ’t‘н̨’mǫ’ῑα’, I shall not pity him.  ’н̇-k‘ǫ’t‘н̨, pity him!

k‘iн, day [cp. Tewa kí-pò’ò, to dawn; kí-nä́, to be daylight, be visible].  Cp. k‘iнdн, day; k‘iн-bн’, daytime; k‘iн-sα, noon; k‘iн-deidl, yesterday; k‘yн̨-hi̧н̨-gα, tomorrow; etc.  —— tei k‘iн, every day.  k‘iнdeidl nǫ-’ei̧m ’н̇-kuαt, ’ei̧hᾱ’dei k‘iн ’ȩ̈i̧-’ǫ, he owed me yesterday but payed me today.  ῑoup̄dei k‘iн, day before yesterday.

k‘iн- in k‘iн-bǫy̨-m, to save.

-k‘iн, in poudl-k‘iнdei, worm sp. which bores holes in wood.

k‘i’н-bα (k‘i’нbα’, punct. neg.; k‘i’нboup, curs.; k‘i’нbeidα’, fut.; k‘i’нbᾱ’dα’, fut. neg.; k‘i’нbei, imp.), to walk off, fly away.  Cp. p‘iнhouῑ-k‘i’нbα, to fly away.  —— dèi-k‘i’нbα, I walked off, flew away.  hǫn dèi-k‘i’нbα’, I did not walk off.  dèi-k‘i’нboup, I walk off all the time.  dèi-k‘i’нbeidα’, I shall walk off.  bèi-k‘i’нbei, walk off!

k‘iн-bǫy̨-dα, to be saved.  Cp. k‘iн-bǫy̨m, to save.  —— ’ȩ̈i̧m-k‘iнbǫy̨-dα, you are saved.  k̄yн̨hi̧’н̨ k‘iнbǫy̨dα’dei ’-bǫy̨houdα’, I am going to go to see the saved man.

k‘iн-dн (inan. I), day, daytime.  Cp. k‘iн.  —— k‘iнdн sнdl, the day is hot.

-k‘iн-dei in poudl-k‘iнdei, worm sp.

k‘iн-deidl, adv., yesterday [k‘iн, day; -dei-dl].  —— k‘iнdeidl hei̧’m, she died yesterday.  k‘iнdeidl gi̧н̨gα hei̧’m, she died yesterday morning.

k‘iн-bǫy̨-m (k‘iн-bǫy̨mǫ’, punct. neg.; k‘iнbǫy̨nmǫ, curs; k‘iн-bǫy̨dα’, fut.; k’iн-bǫy̨mǫ’dα, fut. neg.), to save.  [cp. k‘iн-bǫy̨-dα, to be saved; -m, causative].  —— gyн̇-k‘iнbǫy̨m, I saved him (e. g. from drowning).  hǫn gyн̇-k‘iнbǫy̨mǫ’, I did not save him. miнн gyн̇-k‘iнbǫy̨nmǫ, I am about to save him.  hǫn miнн gyн̇-k‘iнbǫy̨mǫ’, I am not saving him.  gyн̇-k‘iнbǫy̨dα’, I shall save him.  k‘yн̨hi̧н̨gα hǫn gyн̇-k‘iнbǫy̨mǫ’, tomorrow I shall not save him.

k‘iн-gu’α, not to take out.  See t‘eip.

k‘iн-n (inan. I), phlegm [cp. k‘iн-n, to cough].

k'iн-n (k'iнnɑ̨', punct. neg.; k'iнnmɑ̨, curs.; k'iнndɑ', fut; k'iнnɑ̨'dɑ', fut. neg.; k'iнn, imp.), 1. to dig; 2. to cough [cp. hiн-n, to dig; k'iн-n, phlegm; Tewa xǫ́-ŋ, to dig]. Cp. guɑdl-k'iнn, to sneeze; k'iнn-'ɑ̨mgyн, to catch cold; k'iнn-hн̄'bн, to cough; etc. —— 1. gyн̀-k'iнn, I dug a hole. hɑ̨n gyн̀-k'iнnɑ̨', I did not dig. gyн̀-bou-k'iнnmɑ̨, I am digging. gyн̀-k'iнndɑ', I shall dig. hɑ̨n gyн̀-k'iнnɑ̨'dɑ', I shall not dig. bн̀-k'iнn, you dig a hole! heit bн́-k'iнn, let us dig a hole! dɑ̨m-gyн gyн̀-k'iнn, I dug in the ground. 'ɑdlhɑ̨'gyн gyн̀-k'iнn, I dug up some money. —— 2. gyн̀-k'iнn, I coughed. gyн̀-bou-k'iнnmɑ̨, I am coughing all the time.

k'iнn-'ɑ̨mgyн, to catch cold [to cough get]. —— k'iнdeidl 'ɛ̨i-k'iнn-'ɑ̨mgyн, yesterday I caught cold.

k'iнn-hн̄'bн (k'iнn-hн̄'bɑ', punct. neg.; k'iнn-hн̄'beip, curs.; k'iнn-hн̄'beiⁱɑ', fut.; k'iнn-hн̄'bɑ̄'dɑ', fut. neg.), to cough [k'iнn, to cough; -hн̄'bн as in sɑ-'ǫm-hн̄'bн, to have a hemorrhage]. —— hɑ̨n 'ɛ̨i-k'iнnhн̄'bɑ', I was not coughing. 'ɛ̨i-k'iнnhн̄'bн, I coughed. 'ɛ̨i-bou-k'iнnhн̄'beip, I am coughing all the time. 'ɛ̨i-k'iнnhн̄'beiⁱɑ', I shall cough. hɑ̨n 'ɛ̨i-k'iнnhɑ̄'bɑ̄'dɑ', I shall not cough. But 'н̀-k'iнn, cough!; can not form *k'iнnhн̄'bei, imp.

k'iн-pн' (inan. III), daylight, daytime [k'iн, day; -pн', light, shine]. Cp. k'iнpн̄'-tou'e, sitting room.

k'iнpн̄'-tou'e (inan. I), sitting room [daytime room]. Ct. dęi-tou'e, sleeping room.

k'iн-sɑ, noon [k'iн, day; app. -sɑ, augmentative]. Cp. k'iнsɑ-t'ɑ', afternoon. —— k'iнsɑ hęi'm, she died at noon.

k'iнsɑ-pįн̄ (inan. III), dinner [noon food].

k'iнsɑ-t'ɑ', adv., in mid-afternoon [k'iнsɑ, noon; -t'ɑ', beyond]. —— k'iнsɑ-t'ɑ' hęi'm, she died in the middle of the afternoon.

k'iн-ⁱн̄'-gyн, at dawn [k'iн, day; -ⁱн̄'-, white; -gyн]. —— k'iн-ⁱн̄'gyн hęim, she died at dawn.

k'į'н̄ (k'į'н̄dɑ, k'į'н̄mн̄, curs.), to blossom. k'į'н-guɑdl-'н̄'dɑ, tree sp. —— gyн̀-k'į'н̄dɑ, it is blossoming. heigɑ '-k'į'н̄mн̄, it is about to blossom. gyн̀-k'į'н̄, it blossomed.

k'iн̄-, prepound form of k'yų-'ę, shield.

-k'įн, -ty, in p'н̄'ou-k'įн, thirty; kɑtsęi-k'įн, ninety; etc. Cp. -t'н̄, -teen.

k'įн̄-bįн̄mk'ɑe (inan. IIᵃ), shield bag.

K'įн̄-'eip (tpl.; s. not obtained), name of a Kiowa division [explained by Mooney, p. 411, as "big shields," -'ei-p being therefore evidently connected with 'eidl, to be large; but Mr. James Waldo denied this and explained -'ei-p as the postposition meaning "right up to"].

k'į'н̄-guɑdl-'н̄'dɑ (inan. IIᵃ; k'į'н̄-guɑdl-'н', dpl.), tree sp. [red blossoming tree].

k‘ịḥ-t‘ʜdl (an. II; k‘ịḥ-t‘ʜt̓-dα, tpl.), moth [unexplained].  Said also to be prsn. of Mr. James Waldo’s sister.

k‘ou-, verb prepound, now [cp. perhaps ’ʜ-k‘ou, hello; ’ʜ-hou, thanks]. —— gyȧ̇-k‘ou-gu’αyiʜdα’, I am going to peck it now. ’ḕịm-k‘ou-dα’, be born now! ’ȧ̇-k‘ou-t‘ʜ’dl, break it in two now! ’ḕịm-k‘ou-’ʜ, you would better come now. ’ḕịm-k‘ou-bʜ, you would better go now.  ’ȧ̇-k‘ou-dẹịhị’ʜt̂α’, I am going to go to sleep now.

k‘ou-, prepound form of k‘ou-gyʜp, body, in k‘ou-pei-dα, to be paralyzed; k‘ou-’ʜ’ʜt̓dα, lump on body; etc.

k‘ou- in k‘ou-’eit, wide [cp. possibly k‘α’- in k‘α’-p‘eidl, to be wide].

k‘ou-’ʜ’ʜt̓dα (inan. IIᵃ; k‘ou-’ʜ’ʜdl, dpl.), lump on body [body lump].

k‘ou-bei, to be too bad [unexplained].  Cp. k‘oubei-peidlp̄ʜ’egα, to get angry at. —— gyȧ̇-k‘oubei, too bad!

k‘ou-bei, adv., everywhere [k‘ou- as in k‘ou-gyʜ, everywhere; -bei] [cp. k‘ou-gyʜ-e, everywhere]. —— tei k‘oubei bȧ̇-kiʜdl, we live all over.

k‘oubei-peidlp̄ʜ’egα, to get angry at [k‘oubei, to be too bad; peidlp̄ʜ’egα, to think].  Cp. sọ̆’ọ̆’dei, to be angry. —— gyȧ̇-k‘oubei-peidlp̄ʜ’egα, I got mad at him.

k‘ou-’ei-t, wide [w. k‘ou- cp. possibly k‘α’- in k‘α’-p‘eidl, to be wide; w. ’ei-t cp. ’ei-dl, large]. —— p̄α’-k‘ou-’eit, a wide river.

k‘ou-gyʜ-e, adv., everywhere [k‘ou- as in k‘ou-bei everywhere; -gyʜ-e, postp.]. —— tei k‘ougyʜe guαdl tsẹị gyȧ̇-bọụ, I saw a many-colored horse (k‘ougyʜe refers to various places).

k‘ou-gyʜ-p (an. I; k‘ou- in comp.), body; on body [-gyʜ-p, noun postfix and postp.]. —— nọ̆ k‘ougyʜp, my body.  k‘ougyʜ̀-dei, on the body.  k‘ougyʜ̀gyȧ̇-dou’, I had it right up next to my body.  poudl k‘ougyʜp ’ḕị-tsọụ-’ʜ, there is a bug on my body.

k‘ou-hʜ-e, particle, own [k‘ou- as in k‘ọụ-hịḥ, own; -hʜ-e, unexplained].  Cp. ’ọ̆’gα, own. —— ’ʜm tsẹị gyȧ́-dα, that is your horse.  ’ʜm k‘ouhʜe tsẹị gyȧ́-dα, that is your own horse.

k‘ou-p (k‘ouþdα, k‘ouyiʜ, curs.), to pain, hurt, ache, be sore.  Cp. k‘ouþdʜ, pain, ailment; bout-k‘oup, to have colic; t‘ʜdl-k‘oup, to have smallpox; k‘oup-t‘ʜ’, to suffer; etc. —— t̂α’-dọụgyʜ yȧ́-k‘oup, I have the earache.  gyȧ̇-k‘oup, it hurts.  ’αdlt‘ẹị’m nọ̆-k‘oup, my head aches.  tʜ’-dei nḗị-k‘oup, my eyes ache.  mọ̆n ’ḕịk‘oup, my fingers ache.

-k‘ou-p in tọ̆ẹ-k‘oup, firefly [explained as meaning “something like sparkling”].

k‘ouþ-’ọ̆mgyʜ, to get to paining. —— pʜ’hịḥ yȧ́-koudou-k‘oup-ọ̆mgyʜ, I am going to be suffering.

k‘ou-þ-bei-, referring to running, in k‘ouþbei-’ʜe, to run; etc.

k'oupbei-'нe (k'oupbei-'нуɑ', punct. neg.; k'oupbei-'нeguɑ, curs.;
k'oupbei-'нedɑ', fut.; k'oupbei-'нуɑ'dɑ', fut. neg.; k'oupbeı-'нe,
imp.), to run [k'oupbei-, as in k'oupbei-tɑ'-'н, to run; 'нe, to run].
Cp. t̂ǫɥm-'нe, to run away; t̂sн̥ndei, to run. —— gyн̂t-k'oupbei-
'нe, I ran. hǫn gyн̂t-k'oupbei-'нуɑ', I did not run. gyн̂t-bou-
k'oupbei-'нeguɑ, I run all the time. gyн̂t-k'oupbei-'нedɑ', I shall
run. hǫn gyн̂t-k'oupbei-'нуɑ'dɑ', I shall not run. bн̂t-k'oupbei-
'нe, run! 'ǫ'kɑdl hǫn gyн̂t-k'oupbei-'нуɑ'-'ęi, heigɑ 'ęi-tęi'dɑ', if
I had not run he would surely have caught me.
k'oupbei-tɑ'-'н, to run [k'oupbei- as in k'oupbei-'нe, to run; tɑ'-'н,
to chase]. —— k'oupbei-tɑ'-'н gɑ mǫn t̂sou'eigyн, he was running and maybe he fell down. t̂sou'eigyн mǫn k'oup'bei-tɑ'н̥'-
doup-dou, he fell down because he was running.
k'oup-dн, pain, ailment. Cp. k'ɑhyoudl-k'oupdн, pneumonia.
k'oup-dei, adv., very much [cp. possibly k'oup, to pain -dei]. ——
k'oupdei 'éi-'ǫ'męi, they (the Mexicans) injured me much (by
stealing my land).
k'oup-gɑ'-t, adv., on side [k'ou-p- as in k'oup-sнt, on side; -gɑ'-t].
—— k'oupgɑ't déi-mǫ'dɑ', I am going to lie on my side. k'oupgɑ't
béi-mɑ, let us lie on our sides (not on back or stomach). k'oupgɑ't
'н̂-k̄ɑ, I am lying on my side. k'oupgɑ't 'èi-k̄ɑ, it (the tumbler)
is lying on its side.
k'ou-pei-dɑ, to be paralyzed [to be body dead]. —— 'н̂-k'ou-pei-dɑ,
I am paralyzed.
k'ou-pei-k̄iн (k'ou-pei-dɑ, tpl.), paralyzed man.
k'oup-sнt, adv., on side [k'ou-p- as in k'oup-gɑ'-t, on side; -sн-t,
unexplained]. Also used as postp. —— k'oupsнt 'èi-k̄ɑ, it (the
stove) is lying on its side. k'oupsнt yн̂-k'oup, I have a pain in
my side.
-k'oup-sнt, postp., at side of. Also used as adv. —— t'н̥'dliн
tou-k'oupsнt dei, the boy is standing beside the house.
k'oup-t'н̥', to suffer [k'ou-p, to pain; -t'н̥' as in k'ǫ'-t'н̥', to pity,
etc.]. —— 'н̂-k'oupt'н̥', I suffered (e. g. when the Mexicans were
stealing my land); ct. yн̂-k'oup, I suffered (e. g. when sick).
k'ou-p̄ǫ', adv. in the middle, halfway, half [k'ou-, unexplained; w.
-p̄ǫ' cp. p̄ǫ'-hį'н-dei, half dollar]. Also used as postp. ——
k'oup̄ǫ' 'ęi-t̂нdl, cut it for me right in the center! k'oup̄ǫ' 'ęi-'ǫ',
give me half!
-k'ou-p̄ǫ', postp., in the middle of, halfway on. Also used as adv.
—— hu'ɑn-k'oup̄ɑ', halfway on the road.
-k'ou-p̄ǫ-'ę-guɑ, postp., through the middle of [-k'ou-p̄ǫ', in the
middle of; -'ei; -guɑ]. —— t'ǫu-k'oup̄ɑ̨eguɑ 'н̂-hiнt, I went right
through the water, = t'ǫugyн p̄ǫ'hei 'н̂-hiнt.
-k'ou-p̄ǫ-'ę-gyн, postp., in the middle of. —— tou'н̥'-k'oup̄ǫ'ęgyн
'н̂-dei, I was standing in the middle of the corral. giн-k'oup̄ǫ'ęgyн

hẹị'm, he died in the middle of the night. 'Ɦ'-k'ouβɑ̨'ẹgyꞪ, in the middle of the woods. 'Ɦesẹị-k'ouβɑ̨'ẹgyꞪ, in the smoke.

-k'ou-βɑ̨-'ẹ-yɑ', postp., from the middle of. —— 'Ɦ'-k'ouβɑ̨'ẹyɑ' 'Ꞩ-tsꞪn, I came from the middle of the woods.

k'ou-p'ɑ̀t-dɑ (inan. II[a]; k'ou-p'ɑdl, dpl.; k'ou-p'ɑdl- in comp.), body hair [body hair]. —— 'oueidei k'ou-p'ɑdl-sɑdl, he is hairy on his body.

K'ou-tsẹịn-ꞰiꞪ (an. II; K'ou-tsẹịn-dɑ, tpl.; K'ou-tsẹịn- in comp.), Navaho man = NꞪbꞪhou-ꞰiꞪ [mud body man]. The Navaho used to have their bodies all painted up, hence this nickname; they never had mud on their bodies; it does not refer to mud on their bodies, but to paint.

k'ǫ̣u, dark, black; as noun, night [Tewa xꞁ', to be dark, night]. Cp. k'ǫ̣u-gyꞪ, dark, black; k'ǫ̣u-dɑ, to be dark, black; k'ǫ̣u-gyꞪ, darkness, night; kɑþ-k'ǫ̣ugyꞪ, shadow, etc. —— t͡sou-k'ǫ̣u gyꞩ-bǫ̣u, I saw a dark or black stone, = t͡sou-k'ǫ̣ugyꞪ gyꞩ-bǫ̣u. t͡sou-k'ǫ̣u gyꞩt-bǫ̣u, I saw tpl. dark or black stones, = t͡sou-k'ǫ̣ugyꞪ gyꞩt-bǫ̣u. —— hꞪ'oudei k'ǫ̣u, how many nights (ago)? p'Ɜ'ou k'ǫ̣u, three nights (ans.), = p'Ɜ'ou k'ǫ̣ugyꞪ.

k'ǫ̣u-dɑ, to be dark, be black [dɑ, to be]. —— gyꞩ-βɑ-e-k'ǫ̣u-dɑ, the moon is dark, app. lit. it is dark in the moon. hꞪ'oudei heigɑ '-k'ǫ̣u-dɑ, how many nights ago? yiꞪ gyꞩ-k'ǫ̣u-dɑ, two nights ago (ans.).

k'ǫ̣u-dei, grandfather, see k'ǫ̣u-gyꞪ.

K'ǫ̣u-'eidl, a prsn. of Mr. Delos Lonewolf [great dark]. Mr. Lonewolf's other Indian name is 'Ɜ̨ịm-hɑ'-'Ɜ', He Captured Them.

-k'ǫ̣u-ẹ in sei-k'ǫ̣u-ẹ, large intestine [app. dark gut; notice that the ending is dropped in sei-k'ǫ̣u, dpl.]

k'ǫ̣u-hịꞪ, particle, own [k'ǫ̣u- as in k'ou-hꞪ-e, own; -hịꞪ, real]. Cp. 'ꞁ'-gɑ, own. —— nꞁ 'iꞪ k'ǫ̣uhịꞪ, my own child.

k'ǫ̣u-gyꞪ (s. also k'ǫ̣u-dei; an. I; k'ǫ̣u-gyou-p), grandfather (paternal or maternal); man's grandson. —— nꞁ k'ǫ̣ugyꞪ, my grandfather.

k'ǫ̣u-gyꞪ (k'ǫ̣u-gɑ'-t, tpl.; k'ǫ̣u- in comp.), dark, black; as noun (inan. III), darkness, night, blackness, black paint [k'ǫ̣u, dark; -gyꞪ]. Cp. k'ǫ̣u, dark, night; gịꞪ, night. —— tꞪdl-k'ǫ̣ugyꞪ gyꞩ-bǫ̣u, I saw a black skunk. tꞪdl-k'ǫ̣ugɑ't déi-bǫ̣u, I saw tpl. black skunks. touꞰɑt-Ɜ'-k'ǫ̣ugɑ't, a black oak. pꞪ'gɑ k'ǫ̣ugyꞪ, one night; p'Ɜ'ou k'ǫ̣ugyꞪ, three nights. k'ǫ̣ugyꞪ gyꞩt-bǫ̣u, I saw the black paint.

k'ǫ̣ugyꞪ-dɑ, to be dark, black. —— tsẹịgɑ 'èi-k'ǫ̣ugyꞪ-dɑ, the horses are black.

k'ǫ̣ugyꞪ-'ǫ̣u, very black.

K'ǫ̣ugyꞪ-'ǫ̣u-ꞰiꞪ (an. II; K'ǫ̣ugyꞪ-'ǫ̣u-gɑ, tpl.; K'ǫ̣ugyꞪ-'ǫ̣u- in comp.), Negro [very black man].

k'ǫ̣u-Ʇɑdl (inan. I), tar, = k'ǫ̣u-Ʇɑdlsei [black gum].

k'ǫu̜-k̑ɑdlsei (inan. III), tar, = k'ǫu̜-k̑ɑdl [black gum].

-k'ǫu̜'-m in tḥę-k'ǫu̜'m, firefly [unexplained].

k'ǫu̜m-pɑ̄'-gɑ (inan. IIᵃ; k'ǫu̜m-pɑ, dpl.; k'ǫu̜m-pɑ̄'- in comp.), windshield of smokehole; chimney [unexplained; -gɑ]. Cp. k'ǫu̜mpɑ̄'gyH, smokehole; etc.

k'ǫu̜mpɑ̄'-gyH (inan. III), place of the windshield, smokehole.

k'ǫu̜mpɑ̄'-bi̜ḥn (inan. IIᵃ), large windshield. —— k'ǫu̜mpɑ̄'-bi̜ḥn gyn̄t-bǫu̜, I saw tpl. windshields.

K'ǫu̜mpɑ̄'-bi̜ḥn-k̑iH (an. I; K'ǫu̜mpɑ̄'-bi̜ḥ-dɑ, tpl.), Kiowa man, = Kɑe-k̑iH; cp. Mooney, p. 412 [large windshield man].

k'ǫu̜mpɑ̄'-tou (inan. I), house having a chimney (in contradistinction to a tipi) [chimney house].

k'ǫu̜m-sei (inan. III), old canvas, rags [k'ǫu̜-m-, unexplained; app. -sei, noun formative].

k'ǫu̜msei-'ɑ̄'pi̜ḥ (an. II; k'ǫu̜msei-'ɑ̄'pi̜ḥ-dɑ, tpl.), fish sp. [old canvas fish]. Described as spotted; called trout by one informant.

k'ǫu̜mtou-dɑ̜m-gyH, happy hunting grounds, = k'ǫu̜mtou-gyH [spirit country].

k'ǫu̜mtou-gyH (inan. III), happy hunting grounds, = k'ǫu̜mtou-dɑ̜mgyH [spirit place].

k'ǫu̜mtou-k̑iH (an. I; k'ǫu̜mtou-gɑ, tpl.; k'ǫu̜mtou- in comp.), spirit man, ghost [k'ǫu̜-m-tou-, unexplained, cp. possibly kɑꝑ-k'ǫu̜gyH, shadow; -k̑iH].

k'ǫu̜mtou-mḥ (an. I; k'ǫu̜mtou-gɑ, tpl.), spirit woman.

k'ǫu̜-îɑ', to spend night on road [k'ǫu̜, night; îɑ', to be around]. —— pHdl yiH yn̄-k'ǫu̜-îɑ', I am going to sleep two nights on the road.

k'ǫu̜-t'Hdl, buckeye [black pierce]. The seeds were pierced and strung as necklace; hence the name.

k'ǫu̜-t'H'dliH (an. I; k'ǫu̜-t'H'dlou-p, k'ǫu̜-t'H'dlyu-e, tpl.), name of a Kiowa division [black boy].

k'ǫu̜-yi̜H, night passes, comes [-yi̜H, unexplained]. —— pHdl yiH yn̄-k'ǫu̜yi̜H, I was two nights on the road. pHdl yiH gyn̄t-k'ǫu̜yi̜H, we were two nights on the road. sɑ̄'deidɑ heigɑ 'i̜n-k'ǫu̜yi̜H, he worked all day, lit. he worked and it got dark on him.

k'uɑ-t (k'uɑdɑ', punct. neg.; k'uɑtdɑ, curs.; k'uɑdldɑ', fut.; k'uɑdɑ̄'dɑ', fut. neg.; k'uɑdl, imp.), to pull out, pull off; w. refl. to go out [Tewɑ xwɑ̄', to drag]. Cp. tęim, to pull [cp. k'u-e-, to drag, pull]. —— gyn̄-k'uɑt, I pulled it out. hɑ̜n gyn̄-k'uɑdɑ', I did not pull it out. gyn̄-bou-k'uɑtdɑ, I am pulling it out continually. gyn̄-k'uɑdldɑ', I shall pull it out. hɑ̜n gyn̄-k'uɑdɑ̄'dɑ', I shall not pull it out. 'n̄-k'uɑdl, pull it out! gyn̄-k'uɑt gɑ gyn̄-'ɑe-tsei, I pulled it out and then I put it back in again. sɑ̂t tsḥn nei 'ęim-tsou 'ęim-k'uɑt, he came here a while ago but he went out this way.

-k'uɑ-t in 'èi-k̑iH-k'uɑt, there is a fire (over there) (with sbj. series).

K‘uȧt-k̇iн (an. I; K‘uȧt-dα, tpl.), an extinct Kiowa division; cp. Mooney, p. 413 [puller].

k‘u-e-, to drag, pull, in k‘ue-bα, k‘ue-hн’bα, k‘uehy-α’, to drag; k‘ue-zǫ̣un, to pull out; etc.

k‘ue-bα, to drag [bα, to bring]. —— gyн̇-k‘uebα, I am dragging it.

k‘ue-hн’bα, to drag [hн’bα, to lift, carry]. —— déi-k‘ue-hн’beidα’, I am going to drag it.

k‘uehy-α’ (k‘uehyiнgu’α, punct. neg.; k‘uehyiнtdα, curs.; k‘ue-hyiнdα’, fut.; k‘uehyiнgu’αdα’, fut. neg.; k‘uehyiн, imp.), to drag [hα’, to bring]. —— gyн̇-k‘uehyα’, I dragged it. hǫ̣n gyн̇-k‘uehyiнgu’α, I did not drag it. miнn gyн̇-k‘uehyiнtdα, I am about to drag it. gyн̇-k‘uehyiнdα’, I shall drag it. hǫ̣n gyн̇-k‘uehyiнgu’α, I shall not drag it! ’н̇-k‘uehyiн, you drag it! poue ’н̇-k‘uehyiнdα’, don’t drag it! heiȧ nǫ̣ bн̇-k‘uehyiн, let us drag it! heiȧ poue nǫ̣ bн̇-k‘uehyiнdα’, let us not drag it. dèi-k‘uehyα’, I crawl (as snake does); ct. tsǫ̣u-bн, to crawl on all fours.

k‘ue-kǫ’n, to drag [kǫ’n, to bring]. —— ’Ȧdltʿei̯’m ’Éiȧ-k‘ue-kǫ’n-dei P̊α’, plcn., “head dragging creek.”

k‘ue-p‘н̣ (inan. III), harness, wagon [drag tied]. Cp. k̇α’dн̣dl, wheel, wagon; k̇α’tн̣dl-k‘uep‘н̣, wagon harness; tseį-k‘uep‘н̣, horse harness.

-k‘ue-tsǫ̣un, puller, in bouȧ-k‘uetsǫ̣un, fish spear.

k‘ue-zǫ̣un, to pull out [zǫ̣un, to take out]. —— y᷄н̣n-k‘uezǫ̣undα’, I am going to pull it out.

k‘yн, to stretch tr. —— gyн̇-k‘yн, I stretched it (e. g. a rubber).

k‘yн-dl- in k‘yн̣dl-dα, to be wet; k‘yн̣dl-hǫ̣n, to get wet through; k̇oudl-k‘yн̣dl-н’dα, sagebush; k̇ouȧ-k‘yн̣dl, spittle. Cp. -k‘yн’-dl-ei in kαdlseįm’α’-k‘yн’dlei, tadpole; k‘α’dlei-k‘yн’dlei, frog sp.

k‘yн̣dl-dα, to be wet [dα, to be]. Cp. t‘н̣’-dн’-dα, to be wet. —— gyн̇-k‘yн̣dl-dα, it is wet.

k‘yн̣dl-hǫ̣n, to get wet through [k‘yн-dl-, wet; -hǫ̣-n, to be finished, be satisfied]. —— ’н̇-k‘yн̣dl-hǫ̣n, I got wet through (in the rain).

-k‘yн-e- in ’oubн-k‘yнe, to swallow; k‘yнe-guαn, to jump.

k‘yнe-guαn (an. II; k‘yнe-gųǫ̣-dα, tpl.), deer; the name k̇нp is also applied to this sp. of deer and also to the antelope [jumper].

k‘yнe-guαn, to jump [guαn, to throw oneself, dance]. —— dèi-k‘yнe-guαn, I jumped. dèi-k‘yнe-guαndα’, I am going to jump. hǫ̣n dèi-k‘yнe-guαnα’, I did not jump. bèi-k‘yнe-guαn, jump!

k‘yнehy-oudl (an. II; k‘yнehy-ouȧ-dα, tpl.), mouse or rat sp. [said to mean jumper: k‘yнe- as in k‘yнe-guαn, to jump; -hou-dl, inten-sive]. Cp. k‘yнe-guαn, deer, lit. jumper.

-k‘yн-ȧ-dα in mǫ̣’-k‘yн̣tdα, septum of nose.

-k‘yн’-dl-ei in kαdlseįm’α’-k‘yн’dlei, tadpole; k‘α’dlei-k‘yн’dlei, frog sp. Cp. k‘yн̣dl-, wet.

-k‘yн̣- in tou-k‘yн̣-hi̯’н̣-dα, to be homesick.

k'yน̥-hį'н̥-gα, adv., tomorrow, tomorrow morning, the next day, the next morning [k'iн, day; -hį'н̥, real; -gα, adverbial]. Cp. k'yน̥hį'-н̥gα-tsou, tomorrow; k'yน̥hį'н̥-'oue, tomorrow morning; etc. —— k'yน̥hi'н̥gα hįн̥tα', he will die tomorrow, in the morning.

k'yน̥hį'н̥gα-t'α'-dei k'iн, day after tomorrow. —— k'yน̥hį'н̥gα-t'α'dei k'iн hįн̥tα', he will die day after tomorrow.

k'yน̥hį'н̥gα-tsou, adv., tomorrow [-tsou, postp., like]. —— k'yน̥hį'-αgα-tsou 'α'zн'e 'н̥-k'α'îα'îα', I shall want the udder tomorrow.

k'yน̥hį'н̥-'oue, adv., tomorrow morning [-'ou-e, postp., on, at].

k'yน̥hį'н̥-pįн̥ (inan. III), breakfast [morning food].

k'yน̥-'ę (inan. II; k'įн̥, dpl.; k'įн̥- in comp.), shield [unexplained]. Cp. k'įн̥-biнmk'œe, shield-bag; k̄αn-k'įн̥, turtle, app. stiff shield; etc.

### m

-m, postfix added to postps. referring to more indefinite locality, in 'ęi-m, at the region of (cp. -'ęi, right at); etc.

-m, intr. verb postfix, in hęį'-m, to die; etc.

-m, tr. verb postfix, in k'α'-m, to call (cp. k'α, to be called); etc.

mα-'αdą̄'-mą' (punct. neg.), to be unable to do [app. mą-, hand; -'α-dα'- as in 'α-'α'-dα', to be unable; -mą, unexplained]. —— hαn hαndei gyн̥-mα'αdą̄'mα', there is nothing too great for you to do.

Maskou-k̄iн (an. II; Maskou-gα, tpl.), Creek man [fr. Eng. Muskogee].

mą (*mą̄'mą', punct. neg.; mą̄'mą, curs.; mą̄'dα', fut.; mą' imp.), to move (from one place to another), change camp, travel, go. —— bн̥-mą̄'mą, we are going to move camp. 'н̥-mą', you move (to another house or out)! poue 'н̥-mą̄'dα', don't move!

mą' (mą̄'mą', punct. neg.; mą̄'mą, curs.; mą̄'dα', fut.; mą̄'mą̄'dα', fut. neg.; mą', imp.), to lie down (to assume lying position). Cp. k̄α, k̄uαdl, to lie (to be in lying position). —— dèi-mą', I lay down. hαn dèi-mą̄'mą', I did not lie down. miнn dèi-mą̄'mą, I am about to lie down. dèi-bou-mą̄'mą, I keep lying down all the time. dèi-mą̄'dα', I am going to lie down. hαn dèi-mą̄'mą̄'dα', I am not going to lie down. bèi-mą', lie down! poue bèi-mą̄'dα', don't lie down! béi-mą-'ye tpl. lie down! heit tei béi-mą', let us tpl. lie down! k'oupゝgα't déi-mą̄'dα', I am going to lie on one side.

mą-, mą̄'-, mą-n-, verb prefix, with the hand, in mą-kyę, to stir; mąn-'αn-'α, to play arrow throwing game; mąn-seiゝgα, to rub; mą-tsнę, to wrap; mą̄'-guα, to let loose; mą̄'-k̄uαngα, to twist; mą̄'-'oudα, to cover; mą̄'-tα'dei, to turn over; etc. [Tewa mə̀-, verb prefix, with the hand]. Cp. mą-n-, prepound form of mą̄'-dα, hand.

-mą, noun and adj. postfix, in Tsęi-t'н̥-ę-n-mą, Horse Headdresses; -mн̥-ę-mą, women; etc.

-mɑ̨-e̜ in -bǫ̨n-mɑ̨e̜, to indicate [cp. possibly mɑ̨'-dɑ, hand].

mɑ̨-'iн-kyн'e, to have cramps [mɑ̨-'iн-, unexplained; -kyн-'e, app.
as in kyнe-dɑ, to fight].    —— 'н-(t'ǫ̨dei)-mɑ̨'iнkyн'e, I have
cramps (in my leg).

mɑ̨-kųe̜ (mɑ̨-kųe̜deidɑ', fut.), to stir [mɑ̨-, hand; w. kų-e̜ cp. perhaps
kuɑ'-n, to mix].    —— gyн̇t-mɑ̨gųe̜deidɑ', I am going to stir it
(the mush).

mɑ̨-n, particle of uncertainty, perhaps, maybe, like [cp. mɑ̨', like].
    —— k'oup̌bei-tɑ'-'н̨ gɑ mɑ̨n t͡sou'eigyн, he was running and
maybe he fell down.   t͡sou'eigyн mɑ̨n k'oup̌beitɑ'-'н-doup̌-dou, he
fell down maybe because he was running.   mɑ̨n heigɑ he̜i heigɑ
gyн̇-dɑ, maybe he has gone.   mɑ̨n hн'gi 'н̨-t͡ɑ', I guess they are
staying somewhere.   mɑ̨n he̜i gyн̇-dɑ heigɑ, maybe he is gone
now.

mɑ̨-n-, prepound form of mɑ̨'-dɑ, hand.

mɑ̨-n-, verb prefix, with the hand, see mɑ̨-.

mɑ̨n-'ɑ̨n-'ɑ (mɑ̨n'ɑ̨n'ɑ̃'dɑ', fut.), to play arrow throwing game [mɑ̨n-,
unexplained, possibly mɑ̨n-, hand; -'ɑ̨n-, unexplained; 'ɑ, to
play].

mɑ̨n-'ɑ̨n-'ɑ̃'-gyн (inan. III), arrow throwing game, a game played
by throwing four arrows with the hand.   He who throws the arrow
closest wins one point.   Four counter-sticks (toudl) are used [cp.
mɑ̨n-'ɑ̨n-'ɑ, to play the game].

mɑ̨n-'н'н̇t-dɑ (inan. IIª; mɑ̨n-'н'нdl, dpl.), lump or excrescence on
hand [hand lump].

mɑ̨n-goup, to hit with the hand [to hand hit].    —— mɑ̨n-dou 'н̇-guɑ,
hit him with your hand! = 'н̇-mɑ̨n-guɑ.

mɑ̨n-kɑ'e-gɑ (inan. IIª; mɑ̨n-kɑ'e-dei, dpl.), wrist ⸴ [mɑ̨n-, hand;
-kɑ'e-dei, app. ptc. of a verb *kɑ-'e . . .].

mɑ̨n-kɑ̨m, index finger [pointer finger].

mɑ̨n-kɑ̨m . . . (mɑ̨n-kɑ̨mdɑ', fut.), to point [mɑ̨n-, hand].   Cp.
mɑ̨n-kɑ̨m-dou', to point; mɑ̨n-kɑ̨m, index finger.    —— gyн̇t-mɑ̨n-
kɑ̨mdɑ', I am going to point.

mɑ̨n-kɑ̨m-dou', to point [app. dou'].    —— gyн̇t-mɑ̨n-kɑ̨m-dou',
I point (with hand).   gyн̇t-mɑ̨nsɑ-kɑ̨m-dou', I point with thumb.
gyн̇t-beidl-mɑ̨n-kɑm-dou', I point with lips.

mɑ̨n-k'ɑ-'iн (also recorded as mɑ̨n-k'ɑ-y-iн, inan. I), cyclone [cp.
mɑ̨'-t'ou-i(н)-gyн, whirlwind].    —— mɑ̨nk'ɑyiн dɑ̨́-'н̨, a cyclone
is coming our way.

mɑ̨n-k'ɑ̨n-hɑ̃'gyн, to take a handful [mɑ̨n-, hand; -k'ɑ̨-n-, referring
to end, fullness; hɑ̃'gyн, to get, take].    —— 'oudeihįн gyн̇t-mɑ̨n-
k'ɑ̨n-hɑ̃'gyн, I have taken a handful.

mɑ̨n-poudl-t'ɑtgɑ (mɑ̨n-poudl-t'ɑtdeidɑ', fut.), to snap fingers [mɑ̨n-,
hand; -pou-dl-, unexplained, hardly related to pǫ̨ų-e̜, to sound;
t'ɑtgɑ, to shoot].    —— dèi-mɑ̨n-poudl-t'ɑtgɑ, I snapped my fin-

gers. dèi-mǫn-poudl-t'ɑ̀tdeidɑ', I shall snap my fingers. poue
bèi-mǫn-poudl-t'ɑtdeidɑ', don't snap your fingers!

mḥn-p'ɑ-houdl (an. II; mḥn-p'ɑ-hout̂-dɑ, tpl.), given as a name of
the mountain lion equivalent to 'ḥ'-kу̨ę', but the meaning would
suggest that perhaps the old world lion is intended [upper or fore
part of body very hairy: mḥ-n-, up; p'ɑ'-, fur, body-hair;
-houdl, intensive].

mǫn-p'ɑ̀t-dɑ (inan. IIᵃ; mǫn-p'ɑdl, dpl.), hair of hand. ——
mǫnp'ɑdl-dǫу̨'m, under the hair of (my) hand.

mǫn-sɑ (an. II; mǫn-sɑ'-gɑ, tpl.), thumb, lit. big-finger [mǫn-,
hand, finger; -sɑ, big, as in 'ou-sɑ, crop (of bird, lit. big-throat,
etc.]. —— mǫn-sɑ '-bǫу̨, I saw the thumb.

mǫnsɑ-t̂ęįnęį (an. II; mǫnsɑ-t̂ęįnou-p, tpl.), humming bird [thumb
bird, so called because it is the size of one's thumb].

mǫn-seiþ-gɑ (mǫn-seiþgɑ', punct. neg.; mǫn-seiþgoup, curs.; mǫn-
seiþdeidɑ', fut.; mǫn-seiþgɑ'dɑ', fut. neg.; mǫn-seiþdei, imp.), to
rub, stroke [mǫn-, hand; whether -seiþgɑ can be used independ-
ently was not ascertained]. —— gyн̇-mǫn-seiþgɑ, I stroked or
rubbed him (with my hand). 'ǫnsou-dou gyн̇-mǫn-seiþgɑ, I
rubbed him with my foot. hǫn gyн̇-mǫn-seiþgɑ', I did not rub
him. gyн̇-mǫn-seiþgoup, I am rubbing him. gyн̇-mǫn-seiþdeidɑ',
I shall rub him. hǫn gyн̇-mǫn-seiþgɑ'dɑ', I shall not rub him.
'н̇-mǫn-seiþdei, rub him! bн̇-mǫn-seiþdei, let us rub him!

mǫn-sou-dei (app. inan. I), fingering; also sou-dei; [mǫn-, hand; sou-
as in sou . . . , to insert; -dei]. Cp. mǫn-sou-dou', bracelet. ——
(mǫn)soudei 'ę́į-soudei-dɑ, I have a ring on my finger.

mǫn-sou-dou' (inan. II; mǫn-sou-dei, dpl.), bracelet [mǫn-, hand,
arm; -sou- as in mǫn-sou-dei, with which the present word is
perhaps identical; dou'].

mǫn-tɑ'-gyн (inan. III), palm of hand [-tɑ'-gyн, flat].

mǫn-t̂ou-gu'ɑ (an. II; mǫn-t̂ou-gu'ɑ-dɑ, tpl.), salamander sp. which
lives in moist places on the prairie [app. mǫn-, hand; -t̂ou-, explained as equivalent to t̂ou-e, spotted (the sp. is spotted); gu'ɑ,
app. connected with kuɑ-t, painted].

mǫn-t'ęį'm (inan. II; mǫn-t'ǫу̨, dpl.), elbow, elbow-bone, funny-bone
[arm bone].

mǫn-t̂sǫу̨ (an. II; mǫn-t̂sǫу̨-gɑ, tpl.), fingernail, claw of hand [-t̂sǫу̨
as in 'ǫn-t̂sǫу̨, toenail, claw of foot]. —— mǫn-t̂sǫу̨-dou hн̇'ba,
he carried it off in his claws.

mǫnt̂sǫу̨-'н̇'p'eip (inan. IIᵃ), a sp. of bush [claw wood bush].

mǫnt̂sǫу̨-tęį', to grab hold of [to claw catch].

mǫnt̂sou-t'н̇'bei (an. II; mǫnt̂sou-t'н̇'bou-p, tpl.), hawk sp. [carrier-off
with claws: -t'н̇'bei, carrier-off, hardened form connected with
hн̇'bɑ, to carry off]. Cp. gǫу̨m-t'н̇'bei, chipmunk.

mɑ̨-sɑ', six; so also in an old Kiowa count obtained [app. mɑ̨-, hand; -sɑ' equivalent to Tewa sí, six]. —— mɑ̨sɑ' ky̨ɐ̨'hyoup, six men. mɑ̨sɑ', sнe, six years.

mɑ̨sɑ̄'-k'įн, sixty.

mɑ̨sɑ̄'-t, six by six.

mɑ̨sɑ̄'-dei, mɑ̨sɑt-dei, the sixth.

mɑ̨sɑ̄'-dou, in six places.

mɑ̨sɑ̄'-t'н, sixteen.

mɑ̨-tɑ̄'-dei (mɑ̨-tɑ̄'deidɑ', fut.), to turn over tr. [mɑ̨-, hand; -tɑ̄'-dei, unexplained]. —— gyн̀-mɑ̨tɑ̄'dei, I turned it (e. g. a stone) over. gyн̀-mɑ̨tɑ̄'deidɑ', I am going to turn it over.

mɑ̨-t͡sн̨ę-mɑ̨ (inan. IIᵃ; mɑ̨-t͡sн̨ę, dpl.; mɑ̨-t͡sн̨ę- in comp.), sheet of paper, paper [wrapping: fr. mɑ̨t͡sн̨ę, to wrap; -mɑ̨]. Cp. mɑ̨t͡sн̨ę-t'н'bɑ, cigarette.

mɑ̨-t͡sн̨-ę (mɑ̨-t͡sн̨ędɑ', fut.), to wrap [mɑ̨-, hand; -t͡sн̨-, unexplained; -ei, causative]. Cp. mɑ̨-t͡sн̨ę, sheet of paper. —— déi-mɑ̨t͡sн̨ę, I wrapped it up.

mɑ̨t͡sн̨ę-t'н'-bɑ (app. inan. II; *mɑ̨t͡sн̨ę-t'н'-bн, dpl.), cigarette [paper cigar]. Cp. t̃ɑ̃'k'ɑe-t'н'bɑ, white man cigar.

mɑ̨', particle or adv., like [cp. mɑ̨-n, perhaps]. Cp. -tsou, like. —— mɑ̨' 'н̀-houdl-dɑ, I feel sickish, like sick. mɑ̨' pęinhн̃'-dɑ, it is sweetish. mɑ̨' 'ę̇i-pęinhн̃'-dɑ, they d. are sweet. t͡sou mɑ̨' guɑdl-dɑ, the stone looks like red, reddish. mɑ̨' tндl (dɑ), just like a skunk. mɑ̨' tsęihį̇н dɑ, he is like a dog, = tsęihį̇н-tsou dɑ. mɑ̨' Tsн̃neikiн 'н̀-dɑ, I look like a Chinaman. mɑ̨' sy̨н̨n 'н̀-dɑ, I am just like a child.

mɑ̨'-, verb prefix, with the hand, see mɑ̨-.

mɑ̨'-, prepound form referring to nose, in Mɑ̨'-seiþ̇-kiн, Caddo man; mɑ̨'-'н'нtdɑ, lump on the nose; etc. Cp. mɑ̨'-kɑ̨'n, nose; p'ǫ̨ɥ-, nose. —— mɑ̨-bн-tsнt-ɑ', at the end of the nose, at the point.

mɑ̨'-'н'нtdɑ (inan. IIᵃ; mɑ̨'-'н'нdl, dpl.), lump on nose [nose lump].

mɑ̨'-dɑ (inan, II; mɑ̨n, dpl.; mɑ̨-n-, in comp.), hand, arm [Tewa mɑ̨̀-ŋ, hand, arm]. —— mɑ̨'dɑ déi-bǫ̨ɥ, I saw the hand. 'ɑ̨nt̃ɑ' mɑ̨n 'ę̇i-dɑ, I have five fingers. mɑ̨'dɑ nɑ̨̇-goup, he hit my arm, he hit me on the arm. gyн̀-mɑ̨n-goup, I hit him with my hand (or arm). mɑ̨n 'ę̇i-kiнgyнe, my fingers are stuck (e. g. in a crack). mɑ̨n-t̃ouþ̇t'нe, on top of the hand.

mɑ̨'-dɑ-, referring to widower, widow, in mɑ̨'dɑ-kiн, widower; mɑ̨'dɑ-mн̨, widow [unexplained].

mɑ̨'dɑ-kiн (an. I; mɑ̨'dɑ-gɑ, tpl.), widower.

mɑ̨'dɑ-mн̨ (an. I; mɑ̨'dɑ-gɑ, tpl.), widow.

mɑ̨'-guɑ (mɑ̨'-guɑgu'ɑ, punct. neg.; mɑ̨'-guɑdɑ, curs.; mɑ̨'-guɑdɑ', fut.; mɑ̨'-guɑgu'ɑdɑ', fut. neg.; mɑ̨'-guɑ, imp.), to let loose [mɑ̨'-, hand; -guɑ, unexplained]. —— gyн̀-mɑ̨'guɑ, I let him loose. hɑ̨n gyн̀-mɑ̨'guɑgu'ɑ, I did not let him loose. miнn gyн̀-mɑ̨'guɑdɑ,

I am about to let him loose.  gyн̇-mǫ'guɑdɑ', I shall let him loose.
'н̇-mǫ'guɑ, let him loose!  hǫn gyн̇-mǫ'guɑgu'ɑdɑ', I shall not let
him loose.  hǫn 'ę́i-mǫ'guɑ-t'ęindǫ'mǫ', I do not feel like turning
him loose.  tsęihįн̨ 'н̇-mǫ'guɑ, let the dog loose!

mǫ'-hǫn (mǫ'-hǫn, imp.), to finish [mǫ'-, hand; hǫn, to finish]. ——
bн̇t-mǫ'hɑn, finish!

mǫ'-hįн̨ (an. II; mǫ'-hįн̨-gɑ, tpl.; mǫ'-hįн̨- in comp.), horned owl
sp., also called t͡sǫuguɑ and t͡sǫuguɑ-mǫ'hįн̨. [Tewa mɑ́hú, horned
owl].  Cp. mǫ'hįн̨-t͡нę, horned owl sp.

mǫ'hįн̨-t͡нę (an. II; mǫhįн̨-t͡нę-mɑ, tpl.), horned owl sp. [white
horned owl].

Mǫ-k'ɑ'-p'eidl, prsn., "flat nose;" see Mooney, p. 414 [mǫ'-, nose;
k'ɑ'-p'eidl, flat].

mǫ'k̄ǫ'n (inan. II; mǫ'-k̄ǫ'n-, mǫ'-k̄ǫ'- in comp.), nose [mǫ'-, nose;
-k̄ǫ'n unexplained]. —— 'н̨m mǫ'k̄ǫ'n, your nose, noses of ye d.
('н̨m) mǫ'k̄ǫ'n mɑ́-bǫu, I saw the noses of ye d.  ('н̨m) mǫ'k̄ǫ'n
bɑ́-bǫu, I saw the noses of ye tpl.  kuɑtou-mǫ'k̄ǫ'n, bird's nose.

mǫ'k̄ǫn-'eidl-k̄iн̨ (an. I; mǫ'k̄ǫn-bįн̨-dɑ, tpl.), large-nosed man.
Some of the Kiowa had large noses. —— mǫ'k̄ǫn-bįн̨dɑ dèi-bǫu,
I saw some big-nosed fellows.

mǫ'k̄ǫ'n-goup, to bump into with the nose [goup, to hit].

mǫ'k̄ǫn-t͡нę (an. II; mǫ'k̄ǫn-t͡нę-mɑ, tpl.), mud hen [white nose,
said to be so called because the tip of the nose is white].

mǫ'k̄ǫ'-kyų'ę (an. II; mǫ'k̄ǫ'-kyu'e-mɑ, mǫ'k̄ǫ'-kyu'e-guɑ, tpl.;
both s. and tpl. forms were given by another informant with
mǫ'k̄ǫ'n- as prepound), garfish [long nose].

mǫ'-k̄uɑn-gɑ (mǫ'-k̄uɑngɑ', punct. neg.; .mǫ'-k̄uɑndoup, curs.;
mǫ'-k̄uɑndeidɑ', fut.; mǫ'-k̄uɑngɑ'dɑ', fut. neg.; mǫ'-k̄uɑndei,
imp.), to twist; to turn crank [mǫ'-, hand; w. k̄uɑ-n-gɑ cp. possibly
k̄uɑ'-n, to mix, stir].  Cp. mǫ'k̄uɑn-gɑ't, grinder, lit. cranker. ——
gyн̇-mǫ'k̄uɑngɑ, I twisted it, I cranked it.  hǫn gyн̇-mǫ'k̄uɑngɑ',
I did not twist it.  miнn gyн̇-mǫ'k̄uɑndoup, I am about to twist
it.  gyн̇-mǫ'k̄uɑndeidɑ', I shall twist it.  hǫn gyн̇-mǫ'k̄uɑngɑ'dɑ',
I shall not twist it.  'н̇-mǫ'k̄uɑndei, twist it!

mǫ'k̄uɑn-gɑ'-t, grinder, lit. cranker, in tsoue-mǫ'k̄uɑngɑ't, coffee
grinder.

mǫ'-k'ɑ-'iн̨ (an. II; mǫ'-k'ɑ-'yu-'e, tpl.; mǫ'-k'ɑ-'iн̨- in comp.),
minnow [unexplained; -'iн̨, dim.].

mǫ'-k'yн̨t-dɑ (inan. IIª; mǫ'-k'yн̨dl, dpl.; mǫ'-k'yн̨dl- in comp.),
septum of nose [mǫ'-, nose; k'yн̨dl, unexplained].

mǫ'-'ou-dɑ (mǫ'-'oudɑ', punct. neg.; mǫ'-'oudoup, curs.; mǫ'-'oudeidɑ', fut.; mǫ'-'oudɑ'dɑ', fut.; mǫ'-'oudei, imp.), to cover [mǫ'-,
hand; w. -'oudɑ cp. possibly 'out, to descend]. —— gyн̇-mǫ'oudɑ,
I covered him up.  hǫn gyн̇-mǫ'oudɑ', I did not cover him.
gyн̇-mǫ'oudeidɑ', I shall cover him.  miнn gyн̇-mǫ'oudoup, I am

about to cover him.  hǫn gyн̥-mǫ̃'oudɑ̃'dɑ', I shall not cover him
'н̥-'mǫ̃'oudei, cover him!

mǫ̃'-p̃нdl (inan. III), rubbish pile [unexplained]. —— hн̥'oudei
mǫ̃'-p̃нdl gyн̥t-bǫu, I saw several rubbish piles.

mǫ̃'-p'ɑt-dɑ (inan. IIᵃ; mǫ̃'-p'ɑdl, dpl.), nostril hair [nose hair].

mǫ̃'-sɑ (an. II; mǫ̃'sɑ̃'-gɑ, tpl.), raven [unexplained].  mǫ̃'sɑ̃'t̂н̥ę,
white raven; sɑkɑhɑ, crow. —— mǫ̃'sɑ̃'gɑ déi-bǫu nɑ gyн̥-kǫn,
I saw ravens and lots of them.  mɑsɑ' mǫ̃'sǫ̃'gɑ, six ravens.

mǫ̃'sɑ-t̂н̥ę (an. II; mǫ̃'sɑ-t̂н̥ę-mɑ, tpl.), white raven.

Mǫ̃'seip̀-k̃iн (an. II; Mǫ̃-seip̀-gɑ, tpl.), Caddo man [pierced nose
man: mǫ̃'-, nose; sei-p-, related to sei-bɑ, to stab, pierce; -k̃iн].
Cp. Mooney, p. 414.

Mǫ̃'sou-dɑ-e, prsn. of Adam Smoky, said to mean "to pass each
other" [unexplained].

mǫ̃'-t̂ɑ-hɑ, to be hook-nosed [mǫ̃'-, nose; t̂ɑ-hɑ, as in k̃oup̀-t̂ɑhɑ'-
sɑdl, mountain range].  Cp. mǫ̃'t̂ɑhɑ-k̃iн, hook-nosed man. ——
'н̥m 'ę̇im-mǫ̃'t̂ɑhɑ, you are hook-nosed.

mǫ̃'t̂ɑhɑ-k̃iн (an. I; mǫ̃'t̂ɑhɑ-gɑ, tpl.), hook-nosed man [mǫ̃'-t̂ɑhɑ,
to be hook-nosed].

mǫ̃'-t̂ɑ-ku'ɑ (an. II; mǫ̃'-t̂ɑ-kuɑ-gɑ, tpl.), woodpecker sp., said to
be another name for 'ɑdl-guɑdl [app. hook-nosed pecker: mǫ̃'-t̂ɑ-
possibly as in mǫ̃'-t̂ɑhɑ, to be hook-nosed; -ku'ɑ, hitter].

mǫ̃'-t'нdl (inan. III), nostril [nose hole].

mǫ̃'-t'ęi'm (inan. II; mǫn-t'ǫu, dpl.), nose bone.

mǫ̃'-t'ou-'i(н)-gyн, whirlwind [cp. mǫn-k'ɑ-'iн, cyclone; -gyн].
—— mǫ̃'t'ou'iнgyн 'ouei gǫum-k'iнbɑ, a whirlwind went on
away from over yonder.

mǫ̃'-t'ǫu, watery mucus [nose water].

mǫ̃'-t'ǫu-tsǫu-hį'н (an. II; mǫ̃'-t'ǫu-tsǫu-hyou-p, tpl.; mǫ̃'-t'ǫu-
tsǫu-hį'ɑ- in comp.), coyote [explained as sharp nose; app. nose
bone awl: mǫ̃'-, nose; t'ǫu-, bone; tsǫu-hį'н, awl].  Cp. hou'-
kǫu'm, kue'-syн̥m, coyote.

mǫ̃'-tsнt (an. II; mǫ̃'-tsнt-dɑ, tpl.; mǫ̃'-tsнt- in comp.), point [mǫ̃'-,
nose; -tsн-t, point, as in mǫ̃'-bн-tsнt-ɑ', at end of nose].  Cp.
zeip-mǫ̃'tsнt, point of breast, nipple; etc. —— k̃ɑ'-mǫ̃tsнt
gyн̥-bǫu, I saw the point of the knife.  gyн̥-mǫ̃'tsнt-se.ibɑ, I
stabbed him with the point of the knife, =mǫ̃'tsнt-dou gyн̥-seibɑ.
k̃oup̀-mǫ̃'tsнt-ɑ', at the peak of the mountain; cp. k̃oup̀-t'нe, on
top of the mountain.  p'iн-mǫ̃'tsнt-ɑ' 'н̥-bн't̂ɑ', I am going to
go up to the top of the hill.  p'iн-yɑ' 'н̥-bн't̂ɑ', I am going to go
up on the hill.

mн̥, adv., up, above [Tewa mǫ̇-kówá, up, above].  Also used as
postp.  Cp. mн̥-, mн̥'-, verb prefix, up; mн̥-ę, adv., up; mн̥-m,
adv., up; mн̥-n, adv., up; etc. —— mн̥ 'н̥-bн̥nmн̥, I am going
to go up, =mн̥n 'н̥-bн̥nmн̥, I am going to go upstream.

mʜ-, mʜ̱'-, verb prefix, up, in mʜ̱'-hɑ', to carry on the back; mʜ̱'-dou', to carry on the back [cp. mʜ, adv., up].

mʜ-, assertive verb prefix, indeed. —— 'ʜm 'ʜ-houdlgɑ', didn't you kill him? But 'ʜm 'ʜ-mʜ-houdlgɑ', didn't you kill him (said when I am certain that you killed him)?

-mʜ (an. II; -mʜ-ę-mɑ, -mʜ̱'-gɑ tpl.; in tribe names, adjective forms and agentives -mʜ̱yiʜ can be substituted in sd. and mʜ̱youp in tpl.; in animal names indicating the female, -mʜ̱yiʜ, -mʜ̱youp cannot be substituted; -mʜ̱'- in comp.), woman, female. This is the feminine postpound corresponding to -kiʜ, man, male. Cp. mʜ̱yiʜ, woman. —— Kɑe-mʜ, Kiowa woman; Kɑe-mʜęmɑ, tpl. tsęihiʜ-mʜ, tsęihiʜ-mʜęmɑ, tpl. tsęi-mʜ, mare; tsęi-mʜ̱'gɑ, tpl. pei-mʜ, dead woman; pei-mʜęmɑ, tpl. guɑn-mʜ, dance-woman (feminine correspondent to guɑn-kiʜ, dancer, dance-man), =guɑn-mʜ̱yiʜ; guɑn-mʜęmɑ, tpl., =guɑn-mʜ̱youp.

-mʜ, postp., up, above, over. Also used as adv. —— p̄ɑ'-mʜ 'ʜ-bʜnmʜ, I am going to go way up river. p'ʜn-mʜ îɑ', he is in heaven, lit. above the sky, on top of the clouds, =p'ʜn-mʜę îɑ'.

mʜ-'ʜ-dei, the upper part of the body from waist up; also said of the fore part of the body of horizontal-bodied animals. [mʜ, up; -'ʜ-, unexplained; -dei]. Cp. p̄iʜ-dei-p, the part of the body from waist down.

mʜ-ę, adv., up, above [mʜ, adv., up; -ei]. Also used as postp.

-mʜ-ę, postp., up, above. Also used as adv. —— p'ʜn-mʜę îɑ', he is in heaven, lit. above the sky, =p'ʜn-mʜ îɑ'.

mʜę-dei, up, in mʜędei-kiʜ-'ɑ, to play the sinew game [mʜ-ę, up; -dei]. Cp. mʜę-gɑ, up.

mʜędei-kiʜ (inan. III), plaited sinew used in game [thing thrown up].

mʜędei-kiʜ-'ɑ, to play a game in which a braid of sinew eight inches long is shot at with a bow ['ɑ, to play].

mʜę-gɑ, adv., up, high [mʜ-ę, up; -gɑ]. —— mɑ mʜęgɑ hʜ'bʜ-'ęi hęi'm, he died in the mid-forenoon (mʜęgɑ hʜ'bʜ-'ęi explained as meaning when high; see hʜ'bʜ).

mʜę-hį'ʜ, adv., very high [-hį'ʜ, real]. —— 'ʜm k'ɑ̱'gyʜ mʜęhį'ʜ, your name is highest, real high.

mʜ-m, adv., up, above [mʜ, up; -m]. Also used as postp.

-mʜ-m, postp., up, above. Also used as adv. —— kuɑtoubɑ t'ǫu-mʜm (or t'ǫu-t'ʜe) 'éi-p'iʜhout-houkǫu'm, the tpl. birds are flying above the water (t'ǫu-mʜm means only above the water; t'ǫu-t'ʜe means either above or on the surface of the water). p'ʜn-mʜm, in heaven, above the sky or clouds, =p'ʜn-mʜ.

mʜm-dei, up, upper, roof. —— mʜm-dei beitdɑ, upper lip. mʜm-dei, roof, =tou-t'ʜe-dei.

mн̥m-gα, adv., up, high. —— mн̥m-gα gyн̀t-'нedα', I am going to
swing high. 'н̥m k'ǫ̀'gyн mн̥mgα, your name is highest.

mн̥-n (mн̥-n- in comp.), adv., up, above [mн̥, adv., up; -n]. Also
used as postp. —— mн̥n 'н̀-bн̥nmн̥, I am going to go up. mн̥n-
p'ǫ̀'houdl, (Old World?) lion, lit. above hairy.

-mн̥-n, postp., up, above. Also used as adv. —— p̃ǫ̀'-mн̥n
'н̀-bн̥nmн̥, I am going to go up river.

mн̥nн̥̀'nн̥ (inan. IIᵃ), banana [fr. Eng.].

mн̥n-tsou, up. —— mн̥n-tsou t'ǫu-dα, his legs are in the air (said
of a man standing on his head).

-mн̥'-dei-tsou, up. —— p̃α-mн̥'-dei-tsou 'н̀-tsн̥n, I came from up
river.

mн̥'-dou', to carry on back [app. mн̥-, up; dou', to have]. Cp.
*mн̥'-hα', to carry on back. ——. gyн̀-mн̥'-dou', I am carrying
it on my back.

mн̥'-gα (mн̥'gα', punct. neg.; mн̥'goup, curs.; mн̥'dα', fut.; mн̥'gǫ̀'dα',
fut. neg.; mн̥'dei, imp.), to give, hand [Tewa mн̥́-gì, to give].
Cp. *mн̥'-hα', to give; 'ǫ̀, to give. —— gyн̀-mн̥'gα, I gave it.
hǫn gyн̀-mн̥'gα', I did not give it. miнn gyн̀-mн̥'goup, I am about
to give it. gyн̀-mн̥'dα', I shall give it. 'н̀-mн̥'dei, give it!
heit bн́-mн̥'dei, let us give it!

*mн̥'-hα' (mн̥'-hi'н, imp.), to give [mн̥'- as in mн̥'-gα, to give; app.
hα', to bring, carry]. —— tei k'iн piнgyн 'ḗi-hα'dei k'iн dα-
mн̥'hi'н, give us today our daily bread!

*mн̥'-hα' (mн̥'-hiнdα', fut.), to carry on back [app. mн̥, up; hα', to
bring, carry]. ¦

mн̥'-t'ǫn (an. I; mн̥'-t'ǫ̀'-dα, tpl.), little girl [mн̥'- as in mн̥̀-yiн,
woman; -t'ǫn, dim.].

mн̥-y-iн (an. I; mн̥-y-ou-p, tpl.), woman [app. for mн̥-ę-hiн; mн̥-ę-
as in -mн̥-ę-mα, tpl. women; -hiн, real; cp. k̃yн̥hi̦'н, -k̃iн, man].
Cp. -mн̥, woman, female.

miн-n, adv., soon, about to; maybe [cp. mi̦(н), almost, qui̅te]. App.
used with curs. positive and fut. positive only. —— miн̥n gyн̀-
bǫnmα, I was thinking about bringing it. miн̥n 'н̀-pi̦н-bн̥nmн̥,
I am about to go to eat. miн̥n heigα gyн̀-dęi-t̃souр̀dα', I am
about to put him to sleep. miнn 'н̀-k̃iн-deideip, maybe I am going to get married.

mi̦(н), adv., almost, nearly, pretty, quite [cp. miн-n, pretty soon].
—— k'yн̥hi̦'нgα mi̦(н) 'н̀-sнdl-hęi'm, yesterday I pretty nearly
died from the heat. mi̦(н) houdl, he pretty nearly killed him.
mi̦(н) 'н̀-'outgyн, I came pretty near to falling down. hų'ǫn-t'нe
'н̀-houdα-'н̥ gα mi̦(н) 'н̀-t'ǫu-hęi'm, when I was going along the
road I got pretty thirsty.

mi̦ni̦t, minute [fr. Eng.]. —— 'ǫnt̃α mi̦ni̦t, five minutes.

## n

-n, postfix forming distributive numerals, in kɑtsei̯-n, nine by nine; etc. Certain numeral stems take -t instead of -n.

nǫ, particle, and, and then, that (conj.). Cp. nei̯gɑ (fr. nǫ heigɑ), and already; nei̯ (fr. nǫ hei), but; gɑ, and. —— nǫ dèi-dɑ'dɑ nǫ 'oueidei 'èi̯m-'ɑ'guɑ, I was singing and he was gambling. pʜ'bʜ tǫu̯gyʜ nǫ hi̯'ʜheidl, some said that he died. nei̯n-'ʜ'nei̯ nǫ sǫ'ǫ'dei, I waked him up and he got mad. hǫn 'ʜ-houguɑdɑ' nǫ heigɑ hǫn gɑ̀-t'ǫu̯p'ʜyɑ'dɑ', if you don't kill him they won't arrest you. heigɑ gyʜ̀-hǫn nǫ bʜ̀-bʜ, when you finish eating, let us go. nǫ nǫ 'ʜ̀-tǫu̯tɑ', and I am going to say it. k̑yʜ̑hi̯'ʜ tʜt nǫ (nǫ) gyʜ̀-bǫu̯, I saw the man break it. 'ʜ̀-tɑ' nǫ yʜebɑ 'ʜn tʜtgyʜ-pǫu̯e, I heard the rope break. hǫn 'èi̯-bǫu̯mǫ'dɑ' nǫ hǫn gyʜ̀-tǫu̯-t'ʜ'guɑdɑ', I shall not speak to him unless he sees me. k̑yʜ̑hi̯'ʜ 'ǫ́i̯-goup nǫ gyʜ̀-t'ɑtgɑ, when the man hit me, I shot him. nǫ hǫndou (or nǫndou), what do you want?

nǫ, independent personal pronoun, I, my, we, our, spl. [Tewa nɑ̄`, I]. —— yiʜdei nǫ, we d. tei nǫ, all of us. nǫ 'iʜ, my son, our son.

Nʜbʜhou-k̑iʜ (an. II; Nʜbʜhou-gɑ, tpl.), Navaho man = K'ou-tsei̯n-k̑iʜ, lit. mud body man [fr. Sp. or Eng.].

nei̯, fr. nǫ hei, and now, and, but. —— nei̯ t'ʜǫn-gyʜ 'ʜ̀-tɑ', but I was in town. nei̯ hǫn tsʜ'nǫ', but he did not come. 'ǫ́i̯-dɑ'-t'ei̯ndɑ nei̯ hʜ'-tsou houdldɑ', I could not kill him if I wanted to. gyʜ̀-t'ɑtgɑ nei̯ hǫn 'ei̯-guɑbɑ', I shot at him but did not hit him.

nei̯-gɑ, fr. nǫ hei-gɑ, and already.

niʜ-nyʜ, two by two, two abreast [cp. yiʜ, two; yiʜ-nyʜ, alternately]. —— k̑yʜ̑hyoup niʜnyʜ 'ʜ̀-k̑iʜhi̯ʜt-tsʜ'dei, the men are marching two abreast.

-nyʜ, adverbial, in pʜ'nyʜ, one by one; niʜ-nyʜ, two by two; yi(ʜ)-nyʜ, alternately.

niʜnyʜt-dei, the second.

## ou

ou, adv., there [this is the bare dem. stem used as an adverb; the other dem. stems cannot be used without postfixes; cp. Tewa 'ò'ò, 'ō`-, 'ò-, there]. Cp. 'ou-e, there; etc. —— tsei̯ 'ou bʜ, the horse is going over there. sɑt 'ou 'ʜ̀-tsʜn, I just came from over there.

'ou, interj. of surprise. Cp. 'uh.

'ou-, prepound form of 'ou-sei, throat, referring to throat, neck [cp. k̑ou-dl, neck]. —— 'ou-dǫu̯gyʜ k̑iʜ-'ʜtdɑ'dei, tonsil, lit. lump in the throat.

10559°—28——9

'ou-'н'нᶖ-dɑ (inan. IIᵃ; 'ou-'н'нdl, dpl.), lump in the throat, said to
be applied not to the tonsils but to small nodules which one can
feel by laying the fingers on the throat [throat lump].

'ou-bɑ-e, adv., surely, really [unexplained].  Also used as verb
prefix. —— 'ǫ'kɑdl 'ɑdlhǫ'gyн 'ę̣i-'ɑe-tsęi, ('oubɑe) tsęi (kɑdl)
gyн̀-hɑ'dɑ' (if oubɑe is added, kɑdl must be inserted also), if I
had a lot of money I would buy me a horse.

'ou-bɑ-e-, adverbial verb prefix, surely, really [unexplained].  Also
used as free adverb. —— 'н̀-'oubɑe-houdldɑ' nɑ heigɑ gɑ̀-
houdldɑ', if you (really) killed him, they will kill you. 'ę̣i-dɑ'-
t'ęindɑ'îɑ' gɑ heigɑ gyн̀-'oubɑe-houdldɑ', I could kill him if
I wanted to.  tsн̀nîɑ' gɑ heigɑ 'ę̣i-'oubɑe-bǫudɑ', if he comes
he will surely see me. 'ǫ'kɑdl tsн̣nîɑ' nɑ heigɑ '-'oubɑhy-
-oudldɑ', if that man had come, I would have killed him.

'ou-bн- in 'oubн-k'yнe, to swallow; -'oubн-dɑ, to taste intr.

'oubн-dɑ, to taste intr. [dɑ, to be]. —— pęinhн-'oubн-dɑ, it tastes
sweet.

'oubн-k'yнe (inan. III), gullet [swallower].

'oubн-k'yнe ('oubн-k'yнedɑ', fut.), to swallow ['oubн-; -k'yнe, as in
k'yнe-guɑn, to jump].

'ou-bн-hɑ', adv., enough ['ou, dem. stem.; -bн, postp., at; -hɑ',
postp., at].  Cp. 'ou-dei-hɑ', that is all, enough. —— 'oubнhɑ',
translated "that's enough."

'ou-dнᶖ-gyн- in 'oudнᶖgyн-guɑn, to jump out of [unexplained].

'oudнᶖgyн-guɑn, to jump out of [guɑn, to jump, dance]. ——
'ɑ'pįн t'ǫu-gyн 'ę̀im-'oudнᶖgyн-guɑn, a fish jumped out of the
water.

*'ou-dei, dem. pron. and adv., that, there, implied in 'oudei-hɑ',
that's enough ['ou, dem. stem; -dei].

'ou-dei-hɑ', enough, that is all [*'ou-dei, that; -hɑ', postp., at].  Cp.
'ou-bн-hɑ', enough; 'oudei-hɑ'-tsou, there; 'oudei-hįн, there,
enough; 'ouei-gɑ, there, only so far. —— 'oudei-hɑ' gyн̀-hęidei-dɑ,
that is all the story (said at the end of a story).

'oudei-hɑ'-tsou, there. —— 'oudei-hɑ'-tsou tsн̣n, he came from
over there.

'oudei-hįн, there, enough. —— 'oudeihįн gyн̀ᶖ-mǫn-k'ǫn-hɑ'gyн,
I have taken a handful.

'ou-dl (inan. II; 'ou-dl-, 'ou-t- in comp.), load; clothes, property,
provisions.  Cp. 'oudl-k̄oup, to load; 'oudl-poudl, clothes moth;
etc. —— pн̄'gɑ 'oudl k̄iн, one load of wood.

'ou-dl-, 'ou-t-, prepound form of 'out, to descend.

'oudl-dou', to overhang ['oudl-, compl. form of 'out, to descend;
dou']. —— 'éi-beidlk'ɑe-'oudl-dou', the lip is hanging over (said
of overhanging lower lip).

'oudl-guɑdlhǫ'n, to cremate property. —— gyн̀t-'oudl-guɑdlhǫndɑ',
I am going to burn the things up.   pe.iк̄iн yɑ̨n-'oudl-guɑdlhǫndɑ',
I am going to burn the dead man's things up.

'oudl-к̄oup, to load [к̄ou-p, to lay several]. —— gyн̀t-'oudl-к̄oup,
I put the load (on my back).

'oudl-poudl (an. II; 'oudl-pout-dɑ, tpl.), clothes moth (applied both
to larva and adult) [clothes bug].

'oudl-p‘н, to be loaded [p‘н, to be tied]. —— tsęi 'ɑ̨n-'oudl-p‘н, the
horse is loaded.

'oudl-p‘н'ę, to tie load on [p‘н-'ę, to tie]. —— yɑ̨n 'oudl-p‘н'ędɑ',
I am going to load (the pack horse).

'oudl-p‘н̄'-gɑ in t‘ǫų-'oudlp‘н̄'gɑ, water jug made of internal organ of
buffalo [app. load tied?].

'oudl-tsн̄'-dɑ (inan. II[a]; 'oudl-tsн̨n, dpl.), rawhide box for storing
clothes or provisions [-tsн̄'-dɑ, unexplained].

'ou-e, adv., there, look there!  Also used as postp. ['ou-, dem. stem;
-ei, postp., at].   Cp. 'ou, 'ouehy-ɑ', 'ouhy-ɑ', 'ouei-gɑ, all meaning
there. —— 'oue kiн̄dl, he lives there.   'oue 'н̄'gyн, he is sitting
there.   'oue 'н̄-ı̄ɑ'dei, they are staying over there.

'oue, look there! used in calling attention (cp. 'oueigɑ, 'ɑ'gɑ, look
there!).

-'ou-e, 1. postp., at, when; 2. subordinating verb postfix, **when
since.**  Also used as adv. —— 1. h'н̄'-'oue, when?   k‘yн̨hi̧'н-oue,
tomorrow morning.   2. heigɑ 'ęi-goup̀-dei-'oue, hǫn kɑdl gyн̀-tǫų-
t‘н̄'guɑ, I have not spoken to him since he hit me.   heigɑ gɑ
'н̄-goup-dei-'oue, hǫn kɑdl dèi-tǫų-t‘н̄'guɑ, I have not spoken to
them since they hit me.   k‘yн̨hi̧'н-'oue, tomorrow morning.

'ouehy-ɑ, adv., there ['ou-e, there; -hɑ', postp., at].  Cp. 'ouhy-ɑ',
there. —— 'ouehyɑ' kiн̄dl, there he lives.

'ouei-dei ('ouei-gɑ, tpl.), dem. pron. and adv., that, there ['ouei, there;
-dei]. —— 'oueidei yiн̄dei, they d. 'oueigɑ, those people.   'oueidei
tsɑ, his mother.   'oueidei tɑdl, his father.

'ouei-gɑ, 1. dem. pron., tpl. of 'oueidei, that; 2. adv., there, look
there!; only so far, somewhat, slightly ['ouei, there; -gɑ]. ——
'oueigɑ dei, he is standing over there.   'oueigɑ t‘ɑe, way over
there.   'oueigɑ guɑdl, to be somewhat red, a little red (opp. of
guɑdl-'ǫų, to be very red).   'oueigɑ guɑdl-dɑ, it (the stone) is a
little red.   'oueigɑ ı̄ou, it is somewhat cold, a little cold.   'oueigɑ,
look there! (cp. 'ɑ'gɑ, look there!).

'ouei-hi̧н, adv., way over there ['oue, there; -hi̧н, real].  Cp. 'ouhi̧н,
way over there.

'ou-ei-к̄yн-toudl, 'oueiк̄iн-toudl (an. II; 'ou-ei-к̄yн-tout-dɑ, tpl.),
duck [unexplained].

'ou-gɑ, 1. dem. pron., tpl. of 'ou-dei, that one; 2. adv., there ['ou, there; -gɑ]. —— 'ougɑ 'н̥-tsн̥'dei, they tpl. are traveling over yonder. 'ougɑ-t'ɑ', way over there.

'ou-guɑtkou (an. II; 'ou-guɑtkougɑ, tpl.), a blackbird sp. with yellow stripe around the neck ['ou-, throat; guɑtkou, yellow].

'ou-hi̥ɪ, adv., way over there ['ou, there; -hi̥ɪ, real]. Cp. 'oueihi̥ɪ, way over there. —— 'ouhi̥ɪ 'н̥-tsн̥n, I came from way off there.

'ou-ho̥ʊ-mɑ̥-kuɑn, war dance ['ou-ho̥ʊ-mɑ̥-, unexplained; kuɑn, dance].

'ou-hyɑ', adv., there ['ou-, dem. stem; -hɑ', postp., at; for possible etymology see 'ɑhyɑ', there, and cp. 'ou-ehy-ɑ', there]. —— 'ouhyɑ' ĩɑ', he is staying there.

'ou'-gɑt-н' (inan. III), pole mattress, made of poles of 'нeƀiн (willow sp.) woven side by side ['ou'-gɑt-, unexplained; -'н', wood, poles].

'ou-p ('oudɑ', fut.), to dip up. Cp. to.ubн-'oup, to strain; t'o̥ʊ-'oup, dipper; t'o̥ʊ-'oudl-p'н̥'-gɑ, water jug. —— heigɑ gyн̥-'oup, I dipped it up.

'ou-p-, dem. stem, in 'oup-hɑ', there, etc. ['ou, there; -p-].

-'oup, dipper, in t'o̥ʊ-'oup, dipper ['oup, to dip up].

'ou-pн̥t-kɑdl (an. II; 'ou-pн̥t-kɑt-dɑ, tpl.), uvula [throat clitoris]. Cp. 'ou-po̥ʊm-kɑdl, Adam's apple.

*'ouꝑ-dei, dem. pron. and adv., that one, there; implied in 'ouphɑ'tsou, there ['oup-, dem. stem; -dei].

*'ouꝑ-gɑ, 1. dem. pron., tpl. of 'ouꝑdei, that one; 2. adv., there; implied in 'ouphɑ'tsou, there ['oup-, dem. stem; -gɑ].

*'oup-hɑ', adv., there, implied in 'ouphɑ'tsou, there ['oup-, dem. stem; -hɑ', postp., at].

'oup-hɑ'-tsou, adv., there, in that direction ['oup-, dem. stem; -hɑ'-tsou, postp., at]. —— zнedei kyн̥hyoup 'ouphɑ'tsou 'н̥-bн̥'-heidl, half of the men went in that direction.

'ou-po̥ʊm-kɑdl (inan. Iᵃ), Adam's apple ['ou-, throat; po̥ʊm-kɑdl is said to be applied to "soft joints of boiled up calf-meat," whether it may be a general term for gristle is uncertain; kɑdl as in 'ou-pн̥t-kɑdl, uvula]. Cp. 'ou-pн̥t-kɑdl, uvula.

'ou-p'н̥-'ei-gɑ (inan. IIᵃ; 'ou-p'н̥-'ei, dpl.), chokecherry fruit [tied at neck fruit].

'ou-p'н̥-yнe-bɑ (inan. Iᵃ), a kind of band, split at one end, worn diagonally across the chest [neck tie rope].

'ou-sɑ (inan. III), crop (of bird) [app. big-throat: 'ou-, throat; -sɑ, big, as in mɑn-sɑ, thumb, lit. big finger, etc.].

'ou-sei (an. II; 'ou-seigɑ, tpl.; 'ou-, 'ou-sei- in comp.), throat, often also translated neck ['ou-, throat; -sei as in t'o̥ʊ-sei, bone; etc.].

'ousei-ĩн̥'ę-hęi'm, to be choked to death [-ĩн̥-'ę, unexplained]. —— 'ousei-ĩн̥'ę-hęi'm, he was choked to death.

'ousei-îн'ǫhy-oudl, to choke to death tr. [-îн'ǫ-, unexplained]. ——
gyн̊-'ousei-îн'ǫ-hyoudl, I choked him to death.  hǫn gyн̊-'ousei-
îн'ǫ-houtgu'α, I did not choke him to death.  miнn gyн̊-'ousei-
îн'ǫ-hyóutdα, I am about to choke him to death.  gyн̊-'ousei-
îн'ǫ-hyoudldα', I shall choke him to death.
'ou-t ('oudldα', fut. 'oudl-, 'out- in comp.), to descend; to slide down.
Cp. 'oudl-dou', to overhang; doudlei-'out to slide down; 'out-
'out-bн-tsнy-iн-'нe, to swing in swing. —— dǫu'm dèi-'oudldα', I
am going to descend (e. g. in airplane), I am going to slide down
(e. g. a bank).
'out-bн-tsнy-iн-'нe, to swing in swing ['out-bн-tsнy-iн, swing; 'нe, to
run, go]. —— gyн́t-'outbнtsнyiн-'нedα', I am going to swing;
cp. mн̥mgα gyн̊t-'нedα', I am going to swing high.
'out-bн-tsнe-you-p (inan. II; 'out-bн-tsнy-iн, dpl.; 'out-bн-tsнy-iн-
in comp.), swing [app. 'ou-t, to descend; -bн-; -tsн-e-, to go; 'iн,
dim.].
'ou-t̂-gyн ('outgα', punct. neg.; 'oudliн, curs.; 'outdeidα', fut.;
'outgα'îα', fut. neg.; 'outdei, imp.), one falls (from elevated position). Tpl. correspondent p̄eit̂-gyн [cp. 'ou-t, to descend]. Cp.
îsoueigyн, to fall. —— 'н̊-'outgyн, I fell.  hǫn 'н̊-'outgα', I did
not fall. 'н̊-bou-'oudliн, I fall constantly.  miнn 'н̊-'outgyн, I
came pretty near to falling.  miнn 'н̊-oudliн, I am about to fall.
k'yн̥hį'н̥gα 'н̊-'outdeidα', tomorrow I shall fall.  k'yн̥hį'н̥gα hǫn
'н̊-'outgα'îα', tomorrow I shall not fall.  'ę̀im-'outdei, fall off!
heit̂ bн̊-'outdei, let us fall off!  t'ǫu-gyн 'н̊-'outgyн, I fell into the
water.  tн̥' 'outgyн, a star fell (said of a shooting star); cp. 'eit-dei
tн̥' p̄eit̂gyн, there are lots of stars falling.
-'out-k'αe- in kuαt̂-'outk'αe, bookcase; 'out-k'αe-sα, to put several in.
'outk'αe-sα, to put several in [sα, to put several in]. —— gyн̊t-
'outk'αe-sᾱ'dα', I am going to put it in (into the sacks).
'ou-toudl-t'ęį'm (app. inan. IIª; 'ou-toudl-t'ǫų, dpl.), collar bone
['ou-, neck; -toudl-, unexplained]. —— yiнkyнp 'ou-toudl-t'ǫų,
both collar bones, lit. the collar bones on both sides.
'out-t'н (inan. Iª), carrying strap (of quiver, cradle, etc.) ['out-, load;
t'н, unexplained].
'ou-îαt-bн-t'н, to mock [unexplained]. —— gyн̊-'outαt̂bнt'н pęi-
syн̥n, I mocked the quail.
'ou-îᾱ-, referring to edge or corner, in 'outᾱ'-bн, in corner; 'outα'-yα',
on the edge of.
'outᾱ'-bн, in the corner (e. g. of the room).
'outᾱ'-yα', on the edge of. —— k̄ǫ'nαtsαp'ouyiн 'outᾱ'-yα' (or
'αp̀k'ᾱ'n-ǫ') 'н̥'gyн, the fly is standing on the edge (of the table).
'ou-îн-dн, to be choked ['ou-, throat; w. îн'-dн cp. îн'-dei, to be
shut in].

'ou-t‘α̅’-gα, to push [’ou-t‘α̅’-, unexplained; -gα]. Cp. tẹịm, to pull.
—— gyн̇-’out‘α̅’gα, I pushed it.
’ou-t‘н̅’-dou’, to have the chin raised [’ou-, throat; t‘н̅’-, tpls. prepound form of hн̅’, to stand; dou’]. —— dèi-’out‘н̅’dou’, I have
my chin raised.
’ouyαdl-t̂н̨ę (an. II; ’ouyαdl-t̂н̨ę-mą̇, dpl.), yellow horse [white
mane].
’ou-y-α̅’-dα (inan. II; ’ouy-αdl, dpl.), mane.   ’ouyα̅’dα was explained
as meaning mane, and not single hair of mane; ’ouy-αdl as
meaning dpl. manes; this is prob. due to Eng. influence [’ou-,
neck; -ei; ’αt̂-dα, hair].

## ǫu̧

’ǫu̧, quotative particle. —— k̄ун̅нєk̄iн̅-dei t‘н̅’ ’ǫu̧ hн̅ун̅’ bн̅’heidl,
the chief’s wife went off somewhere.
’ǫu̧-, to like, in ’ǫu̧-dα, ’ǫu̧-dei, ’ǫu̧-peidl-dou’, to like; ’ǫu̧-t̂α, to be
dissatisfied; ’ǫu̧-t‘н̅ . . ., to be happy; ’ǫu̧-t‘н̅’-dα, to be happy.
-ǫu̧, intensive noun, adjective and verb [postfix, denoting intensity,
abundance, in ’at‘н̨t̂н̨ę-’ǫu̧, to be (too) salty; t̂sou-’ǫu̧, to be
rocky; guαdl-’ǫu̧, to be very red; sαhyei-’ǫu̧, to be very blue;
-sęị-’ǫu̧-, to be sweet smelling; ’αdlk‘αe-’ǫu̧, to be crazy. [cp.
’ǫu̧-dei, much; ’ǫu̧-dα, ’ǫu̧-dei, to like; and possibly -sǫu̧, intensive verb postfix].
’ǫu̧-’α̅’t̂н̨m-poudl (an. II; ’ǫu̧-’α̅’t̂н̨m-pout̂-dα, tpl.), leech [blood
suck bug: ’ǫu̧-, blood; ’α̅’t̂н̨m-, to suck; poudl, bug].
’ǫu̧-bн̅’-, referring to diving, drowning, in ’ǫu̧bн̅’-guαn, to dive;
’ǫu̧bн̅’-hęị’m, to be drowned; etc.
’ǫu̧bн̅’-guαn, to dive. —— dèi-’ǫu̧bн̅’-guαn, I dived.
’ǫu̧bн̅’-hęị’m, to be drowned. —— ’ǫu̧bн̅’-hęị’m, he was drowned.
’ǫu̧bн̅’-houdl, to drown tr. —— gyн̇-’ǫu̧bн̅’-houdl, I drowned him.
’ǫu̧-dα (’ǫu̧-dα̅’mą̇’, punct. neg.; ’ǫu̧-dα̅’bei, imp.), to like [’ǫu̧- as in
’ǫu̧-dei, to like; dα]. —— hąn ’н̇-’ǫu̧-dα̅’mą̇’, I don’t like him.
’ǫu̧-dα, to be bloody. —— ’ǫu̧-dα, it is bloody.   mą̇’k̄ą̇’n gα̇-’ǫu̧-dα,
your nose is bloody.
’ǫu̧-dei (’ǫu̧gα’, punct. neg.; ’ǫu̧deip, curs.], to like [cp. ’ǫu̧-dα, to
like]. —— yн̋-’ǫu̧deip, I like it.  k̄iн̅ yн̋-’ǫu̧deip, I like beef.
hąn yн̋-’ǫu̧dα’, I do not like it.  déi-’ǫu̧dei, I am glad.
’ǫu̧-dei, adv., much [cp. -’ǫu̧, intensive noun, adj. and verb postfix].
Cp. ’ǫu̧dei-k̄iн̅, rich man. —— hąn ’ǫu̧-dei yн̋n-guαdα’, I do not
write to him very much.
’ǫu̧-dei-k̄iн̅ (an. I; ’ǫu̧-goup, tpl.), rich man [’ǫu̧dei, much; -k̄iн̅].
’ǫu̧’-m (inan. IIᵇ; ’ǫu̧- in comp.), blood [Tewa ǫ̇’-ŋ, blood]. sα-’ǫu̧m-
hн̅’beip, to have hemorrhage, etc. —— ’ǫu̧’m déi-bǫu̧’, I saw
blood, particle of blood, spot of blood. ’ǫu̧-dǫu̧gyн̅, in the blood.

'ǫu-peidl-dou', to like ['ǫu-, to like; peidl-dou', to think]. ——
'èim-'ǫupeidldou', I like you.  hɑ̄, gyн̀t-'ǫupeidldou' dèi-'ɑdɑ'-dei,
yes, I like to gamble.
'ǫu-p̄eiṫgyн, to bleed intr., in p'ǫu-'ǫup̄eiṫgyн, to bleed at the nose
[blood falls].
'ǫu-t̂ɑ', to be wanting something better, be dissatisfied ['ǫu-, to like;
t̂ɑ', to stay]. —— 'н̀-'ǫut̂ɑ', I want something better (said when
I am dissatisfied with what I have and keep wanting something
better).
'ǫu-t'н . . . ('ǫu-t'н't̂ɑ', fut.; 'ǫu-t'н'- in comp.), to be happy ['ǫu-,
to like; -t'н- . . . , unexplained].  Cp. 'ǫu-t'н'-dɑ, to be happy.
—— poue 'èim-'ǫutəн't̂ɑ', don't be happy!
'ǫu-t'н'-dɑ, to be happy ['ǫut'н'-, to be happy; dɑ, to be]. ——
'н̀-'ǫut'н'-dɑ, I am happy.  bн̀-'ǫut'н'-dн̄'bei, let us be happy!
heit̂ poue bн̀-'ǫut'н'-dɑ't̂ɑ, let us not be happy!  'èim-'ǫut'н'-
dɑ'bei, you be happy, = 'èim-'ǫudɑ'bei.  'èim-'ǫut'н'-dɑ't̂ɑ', don't
be happy!  hɑ̨n 'н̀-'ǫut'н'dн̨'mɑ̨', I was not happy.
*'ǫu-zeip ('ǫu-zoudliн, curs.), to bleed intr. [to blood flow]. ——
'ǫu-zoudliн, he is bleeding.

## p

-p, 1. noun postfix in -you-p, tpl. of 'iн, child; k'ou-gyн-p, body;
etc.; 2. postp. postfix in -bн-p, at (cp. -bн, at); -tɑ-p, beyond
(cp. -t'ɑ', beyond).
-p, intr. verb postfix, in 'ɑ'-hн-p, to be a great gambler; etc.
-p, tr. verb postfix, in k̂ou-p, to lay several (cp. k̂uɑ-dl, several lie).
pɑ' (also pɑ'gyн, punct.; pɑ'dɑ', punct. neg.; pɑtdɑ, curs.; pɑdldɑ',
fut.; pɑ'dɑ'dɑ', fut. neg.; pɑ, imp.), to eat.  Cp. piн̨, food; pei-dн,
to have plenty to eat; hн̨'n, to eat; hɑ̨'n, to eat up. —— gyн̀t-
pɑ'gyн, I ate.  hɑ̨n gyн̀t-pɑ'dɑ', I did not eat.  gyн̀t-bou-pɑtdɑ,
I am eating all the time.  gyн̀t-pɑdldɑ', I shall eat.  hɑ̨n gyн̀t-
pɑ'dɑ'dɑ', I shall not eat.  bн̀t-pɑ, eat!  heit̂ bн̀t-pɑ, let us eat!
poue bн̀t-pɑdldɑ', let us not eat!  k̂yн̨hį'н̨ hɑ̨n gyн̀-pɑ'dɑ', the
man is fasting, not eating.
pɑ-dl-, to sing, in pɑdl-dei, singer; pɑdl-dou', to sing; pɑdl-k'ɑ'-gɑ,
drum.
pɑdl-dei (pɑdl-gɑ, tpl.), singer;  also Pɑ-dl-dei, persn. of Mr. Light,
his other name being P'iн-bǫu, Light [pɑ-dl-, to sing; -dei].
pɑdl-dou', to sing [pɑ-dl-, to sing; -dou'].  Cp. dɑ'p̄н'egɑ, dɑ'dɑ, to
sing.
pɑdldou'-k̂iн (an. I; pɑdldou'gɑ, tpl.), singer (man).
padl-k'ɑ'-gɑ (inan. II; pɑdl-k'ɑ, tpl.; pɑdl-k'ɑ'- in comp.), drum
[pɑdl-, explained as in pɑdl-tou', to sing; w. -k'ɑ cp. possibly k'ɑ-e,
hide; k'ɑ'-dɑ, blanket].

pɑdlk‘ɑ’-t‘ǫų̧ę (inan. II[a]; pɑdlk‘ɑ’-t‘ǫų̧, dpl.; pɑdlk‘ɑ’-t‘ǫų̧- in comp.), drumstick.

pɑ-’ei-dou’, to resemble [pɑ-’ei-, unexplained; -dou’].      —— tsęįhyoup ’èi-pɑ’eidou’, they tpl. look like dogs.

pɑ̄’-, prepound form, thigh, in pɑ̄’-t‘ǫų̧dei, thigh; pɑ̄’-kiʜ, flesh of thigh; pɑ̄’-p‘ɑtdɑ, hair of thigh; etc. [Tewa pó, thigh].

pɑ̄’-, app. prepound form of bɑ̄’-dʜ, to rise, in t‘ǫų̧-pɑ̄’-t‘out, pump, windmill.

pɑ̄’-, adverbial verb prefix denoting accompaniment, in pɑ̄’-bɑ’, to bring along; pɑ’-hɑ’, to take along; pɑ̄’-heibɑ, to take into; pɑ̄’-hęįdɑ, to remove tr.; pɑ̄’-dou’, to keep (an animal); pɑ̄’-t‘ŋ̧’mǫ’, not to be able.

pɑ̄’-bɑ’, to bring along [bɑ’, to bring].      —— gyn̄-pɑ̄’bɑ’, I brought him along. gyn̄-pɑ̄’bɑ’dɑ’, I shall bring him along.

pɑ̄’-dou’, to keep (animal), treat [dou’, to have].      —— tsęįhįŋ gyn̄-pɑ̄’dou’, I kept a dog. tsęįhyoup déi-pɑ̄’dou’, I kept tpl. dogs. tsęįhyoup hǫn déi-pɑ̄’tougɑ’, I did not keep dogs. tsęįhyoup déi-pɑ̄’toudɑ’, I am going to keep dogs. ’ŋ̧m tsęįhįŋ ’n̄-pɑ̄’-dou’, you keep a dog! hǫn déi-pɑ̄’dougɑ’dɑ’, I am not going to keep dogs. tsęįhįŋ bn̄-pɑ̄’dou’, let us keep a dog! ’n̄-tsęįhįŋ-pɑ̄’dou’, they treat him as a dog, as a slave.

pɑ̄’-dǫų̧bʜ (inan. III), underside or backside of thigh.      —— pɑ̄’-tǫų̧bʜ gyn̄t-bǫų̧, I looked at his thigh. pɑ̄’-tǫų̧bʜ ’èįm-se.ibɑ, he cut himself in the thigh.

pɑ̄’-hɑ’, to take along [hɑ’, to bring, take].      —— dɑ́-pɑ̄’hiʜdɑ’, take us! miʜn gyn̄-pɑ̄’hiʜtdɑ’, I am going to take him away. gyn̄-pɑ̄’hɑ’, I took him along with me. hǫn gyn̄-pɑ̄’hiʜguɑ, I did not take him along. gyn̄-pɑ̄’hiʜdɑ’, I shall take him along. hǫn gyn̄-pɑ̄’hiʜguɑ, I shall not take him along. ’n̄-pɑ̄’hiʜ, take him along! poue ’n̄-pɑ̄’hiʜdɑ’, don’t take him along! heit nǫ̧ bń-pɑ̄’hiʜ, let us take him along! heit nǫ̧ poue bń-pɑ̄’hiʜdɑ’, let us not take him along!

pɑ̄’-heibɑ, to take inside [heibɑ, to take inside].      —— gyn̄-pɑ̄’heibɑ, I took him in (e. g. I led him into a room). hǫn gyn̄-pɑ̄’heibɑ’, I did not take him in. miʜn gyn̄-pɑ̄’heiboup, I am about to take him in. gyn̄-pɑ̄’heibeidɑ’, I shall take him inside. hǫn gyn̄-pɑ̄’hei-bɑ̄’dɑ’, I shall not take him inside. ’n̄-pɑ̄’heibei, take him inside!

pɑ̄’-hęįdɑ, to remove tr. [hęįdɑ, to remove tr.].      —— dɑ́-pɑ̄’hęįdei, keep us away from (evil)! gyn̄-pɑ̄’hęįdeidɑ, I am going to take him away. ’n̄-pɑ̄’hęįdei, remove him! heit nǫ̧ bn̄-pɑ̄’heidei, let us remove him! heit nǫ̧ poue bn̄-pɑ̄’hęįdeidɑ’, let us not remove him!

pɑ̄’-kǫ’n, to bring [kǫ’n, to bring].      —— tsęį gyn̄-pɑ̄’kǫ’ndɑ’, I am going to bring the horse. tsęį gyn̄-pɑ̄’kǫ’n, I brought the horse.

pɑ̄'-kiн (inan. Iᵃ), flesh of the thigh [kiн, flesh].

pɑ̄'-p'iн (inan. I), thigh vein [p'iн, vein].     Applied to large veins visible on thigh.

pɑ̄'-t'ņ'mɑ̨' (punct. neg.; corresponding positive not obtained; pɑ̄'-t'ņ'îɑ', fut.; pɑ̄'-t'ņ'mɑ̨'îɑ', fut. neg.), not to be able [unexplained].   Cp. 'ɑ'ɑ'dɑ', not to be able. —— hɑ̨n 'н̄-pǫų-pɑ̄'-t'ņ'mɑ̨', I could not see him.   beit'ęindei 'н̄-pǫų-pɑ̄'t'ņ'îɑ', I never can see him.

pɑ̄'-t'ǫų-dei (an. II; pɑ̄'-t'ǫų-gɑ, tpl.), thigh [thigh leg, i. e. upper leg].

pɑ̨' . . . (pɑ̨'dɑ', fut.), to extinguish. —— déi-pɑ̨'dɑ' p'iнdɑ, I am going to put out the fire.

pн', one (enumerative series).   Also used as tpl. indef. pron., somebodies.   Cp. pн̄'-gɑ, one (predicative series); pн-'н̄'-gɑ, in one place; etc.

pн', indef. pron. used in tpl. only, 1. somebodies, some (tpl.), = pн̄'-bн. 2. some kinds of [pн', one, used as pron.].   Cp. pн̄'-hɑ̨ndei, somebody; pн̄'-hн̄'gyн, sometimes; hн̄'deidl, somebody. —— 1. hн̄'deidl gyн̄-houdl, I killed somebody; but pн' dèi-houdl, I killed some people.   ƙyņhyoup pн' dèi-houdl, I killed some men. sņnoup pн' déi-houdl, I killed some snakes.   pн' 'нdlɑ̄'gɑ déi-seit, I picked some plums, apples.   pн' (or pн̄'bн) tǫųnęi nɑ̨ hi'нheidl, some said that he was dead; cp. tei(bн) tǫųnęi nɑ̨ hi'нheidl, all said that he was dead.   pн' 'н̄-bņnmн̨ nɑ̨ nɑ̨ hɑ̨n 'н̄-bņnmн̨, some folks are going but I am not going.   pн' 'eiɫdei gyн̄-tǫųzн̨nmн̨, some people are talking too much; cp. 'eiɫdei gyн̄-tǫųzн̨nmн̨, I am talking too much. —— 2. pн' 'нdlɑ̄'gɑ, some kinds of plums.

-pн', pн̄-, light, shine, in k'iн-pн', daylight; pн̄-'н̄'-dɑ, to be mirage; pн̄'-sнɫ-gyн, hot sunshine [cp. pн-e, sun, summer; etc.].

pн-'н̄'-gɑ, adv., in one place [pн', one; -'н̄'-, unexplained; -gɑ].   Cp. pн̄'nyнɫ-dou, in one place. —— sǫųn pн'н̄'gɑ gyн̄ɫ-ƙuɑdɑ', I am going to stack the hay, lit. I am going to put the hay in one place.

pн-dl (inan. III pн-dl- in comp.), bed, bedding, quilt [cp. Tewa pɑ̨'ɑ̨, bed].   Cp. pнdl-'н̄'-syņ'dɑ, stretcher; pнdl-p'ɑɫdɑ, filament of cotton. —— pнdl-dǫų'm, in bed.

pн-dl- in pнdl-gǫųm-bн, knee pit.

pн-dl- in pнdl-н̄'-gɑ, bow. .

pн-dl- in pнdl-k'ou-'ei-gyн, to turn back [cp. Tewa pó-wɑ̨́, to return].

pн-dl- in pнdl-gyн, on this side of.

pнdl-н̄'-gɑ (inan. II; pн-dl-н', dpl.; pн-dl-н̄'- in comp.), bow.   Cp. zeibgɑ, bow.

pнdl-'н̄'-syņ'-dɑ (inan. IIᵃ; pнdl-'н̄'-syн̨n, dpl.), stretcher [small bed pole].

pнdl-gǫųm-bн (inan. III), knee-pit [pн-dl-, unexplained; -gǫųm-bн, behind].

-pн-dl-gyн, postp., on this side of -pн-dl-, unexplained; -gyн].
—— p̃ɑ'-pнdlgyн 'н̓-kiнdl, I live this side of the river.

pнdl-k'ɑe (inan. IIᵃ), quilt [bed cloth]. Cp. 'ɑnbн-pнdlk'ɑe, rug,
lit. foot quilt.

pнdl-k'ou-'ei-gyн, to turn back [pн-dl-, to return; k'ou-ei-, unexplained; -gyн]. —— k̃yн̣i'н̣ p̃ɑ'-beiguɑ bн, nẹi hɑ̣n p̃ɑ'gyн
tsн̣'nɑ̣', pнdlk'ou'eigyн, the man was going toward the river, but
he did not reach the river, he turned back. mн̣'yiн̣ boụgyн gɑ
heigɑ pнdlk'ou'eigyн, he saw a woman and turned back.

pнdl-poudl (an. II; pнdl-pouƚ-dɑ, tpl.; pнdl-poudl- in comp.), bedbug, =pнdl-p'ou, lit. bed louse. Both terms are in use.

pнdl-p'ɑƚ-dɑ (inan. IIᵃ; pнdl-p'ɑdl, dpl.; pнdl-p'ɑdl- in comp.),
filament of cotton, cotton [quilt-fuzz].

pнdl-p'ɑdl-goup (inan. IIᵃ), cotton plant.

pнdl-p'ou (an. II; p'ou-e, tpl.; p'oṷ- in comp.), bedbug [bed louse],
=pнdl-poudl.

pн-e, 1. (an. II; pн-e-guɑ, tpl.), sun, clock, watch; 2. (app. inan. I),
summer, in summer [w. pн- cp. -pн', pн̃'-, light, shine; -ei; cp.
Tewa pá'á-rí, pá'á-gè, sunny place, sunshine, pɑ̃'-yó, summer].
Cp. pнe-dн, summer; pнe-bei-, south. —— 1. pнhy-ẹi'm (for pнe
hẹi'm), the sun is dead (said of eclipse). Pн, dɑ́-boụ, Sun, look
at us! (said in praying to the sun). pнe gyн̓-t'ɑn, I found a
watch. 2. k̃iнgyнe pнe heigɑ hiн̣t̃ɑ', he will die next summer.
ƚouptei pнe hẹi'm, he died last summer. 'ẹihɑ'dei pнe 'iн̣hɑ'
'н̓-t̃ɑ'-t̃ɑ', I am going to stay right here this summer. pнe-gyн,
in the summer, =pн̃y-ɑ'.

pнe-bɑ'deip-, east [pнe-, sun; bɑ'deip, curs. of bɑ'dн, to rise]. ——
'ẹimgɑ pнe-bɑ'deip-'ẹi 'н̓-t̃ɑ', I am staying in the east. pнe-
bɑ'deip-'ẹim 'н̓-bн̣nmн̣, I am going to go east.

pнe-bɑ'deip̀-dei, east. —— pнe bɑ'deip̀dei-beiguɑ 'н̓-bн̃'t̃ɑ', I am
going to go east.

pнe-bei-, south [pн-e-, summer; -bei, at, referring to region]. Cp.
sнdl-dɑ̣m-, south, lit. hot country; sн̃'-bei-, north, lit. at the
region of winter; ƚou-dɑ̣m-, north, lit. cold country.

pнe-bei-bн, in the south. —— pнe-beibн 'н̓-t̃ɑ', I am staying in
the south.

pнe-bei-guɑ, to the south. —— pнe-beiguɑ 'н̓-bн̣nmн̣, I am going
to go south.

pнe-dн, summer [pнe, sun, summer; -dн].

-pн-e-dl in toụ-pнedl, talkative person.

pнe-hụ'ɑn (inan. I), sun-trail, path of the sun through the sky.

pнesẹi'n, five cents (app. with unaspirated p) [fr. Eng.].

pнe-yiнyн-, west [pнe, sun; yiнyн, curs. of yн'e, to set]. ——
'ẹimgɑ (pнe-)yiнyн-'ẹim 'н̓-t̃ɑ', I am staying in the west. pнe-
yiнyн-'ẹim 'н̓-bн̣nmн̣, I am going to go west.

pн-'ou . . . (pн'oudeidα', fut.; pн'oudei, imp.), to close tr. ——
bèi-beidl-pн'oudei, close your mouth! dèi-beidl-pн'oudeidα', I
shall close my mouth.

pн-t- in pн-t̂-kα-dl, clitoris.

pнt̂-k̂αdl (an. II; pнt̂-k̂αt̂-dα, tpl.), clitoris [pн-t̂-, unexplained;
-k̂α-dl as in 'ou-pǫųm-k̂αdl, Adam's apple]. Cp. 'ou-pнt̂kαdl,
uvula.

pн'-, prairie, in k̂α'gyнþ-pн'-dǫn, hawk sp.; pн'-gyн, pн'-gyнp,
prairie; pн'-yα', on the prairie.

pн'-, together, in pн'-gue-gα, in a bunch; pн'-hнdl-dou', to have
confluence; pн'-yα', together [cp. possibly pн', one; or p'н- in
p'н-dα-'iн, twin].

pн'- . . . (pн'deidα', fut.), to sharpen. —— k̂α' gyн̀-pн'deidα', I
am going to sharpen my knife.

pн-'н'-dα, to be mirage [app. pн'-, light, shine; 'н'-dα, to be dewy].
—— gyн̀-pн-'н'-dα, it is mirage.

pн'-bн, indef. pron., somebodies, see pн' [pн', somebodies; -bн].
Cp. tei-bн, all, tpl.

pн'-biн (an. I; pн'-byou-p, tpl.; pн'-biн- in comp.), 1. man's
brother (older or younger); 2. man's great grandson [Tewa pὰ'-ré,
older brother]. Cp. pн'byou-'e, my or our brother. —— nǫ
pн'byoup, my tpl. brothers. 'нm pн'biн, your brother. yiн
nèi-pн'biн-dα, I have two brothers.

pн'-byou-'e, my or our brother.

-pн'-dǫ-n in k̂α'gyнp-pн'dǫn, hawk sp., said to sound like cliff-
prairie.

-pн'-dl-ei in dei-pн'dlei, to be sleepy; t'ǫų-pн'dlei, to be thirsty.

pн'-gα, one. —— pн'gα k̂yн̪hi'н̪, one man. pн'gα sнe, one year.
pн'gα tou-gyн 'н̀-k̂α', I lived in the same house.

pн'gα-'e, lone, in Kue'-pн'gα'e, prsn. Lonewolf [pн'gα- one; -'ei].

pн'gα-dou, one time, once.

pн'gα-yα', at one. —— pн'gα-yα', one hour; at one o'clock.
pн'gα-yα'-t'α' zн'-yα', at half past one.

pн'-gue-gα, adv., together, in a bunch [pн'- as in pн'-ḥнdl-dou', to
have confluence; w. -gu-e- cp. gu-e, behind; -gα]. —— Kyн.eguα
pн'gueguα tsн̪'dei, the Comanches are traveling in one bunch or
company.

pн'-gyн (inan. III), plain, prairie, =pн'-gyнp. [pн'-, prairie; -gyн].
Cp. pн'-yα', on the prairie. —— pн'gyн kiнdl, he lives on the
prairie. hǫn tou'e-'αe-gyн 'н̀-kiнgα', pн'gyн 'н̀-'eik̂uα-kiнdl, I
do not live in town, I live outside of the town on a farm. pн'gi(н)
'н̀-bн'k̂α', I am going to the prairie.

pн'gyн-beibн (inan. Iᵃ), edge [app. pн'gyн, plain; -bei-bн, postp.].
—— k̂α'-pн'gyнbeibн, the edge of the knife. pн'gyн-beibн
gyн̀-k̂α', I cut him with the edge, =pн'gyн-beibнe-dou gyн̀-k̂α'.

pɐ'gyɴ-beibɴ-e in pɐ'gyɴ-beibɴedou, with the edge. Cp. pɐ'gyɴ-beibɴ, edge.

pɐ'-gyɴ-p, plain, prairie, = pɐ'gyɴ. —— pɐ'gyɴp 'ɴ-bɐ'ĩɑ', I am going to go to the prairie. Kyɴ.eguɑ tei pɐ'gyɴp dɑ'mẹi', the Comanches were all over the prairie.

-pɐ'-hɴdl-dou', to have confluence, in p'ɑ'-pɐ'hɴdldou', creeks join [-pɐ'- as in pɐ'-gue-gɑ, in a bunch; -hɴ-dl-, unexplained; -dou'].

pɐ'-hɑndei, indef. pron., somebody [pɐ', one; hɑndei, something]. —— pɐ'hɑndei 'ẹim-teidlei' nɑ hi'ɴheidl, somebody has been telling that he died. pɐ'hɑndei tọunẹi' nɑ hi'ɴheidl, somebody said that he died.

pɐ'-hɐ'gyɴ, adv., sometimes [pʜ', some; hɐ'gyɴ, where? somewhere]. Cp. pɐ'nyɴ 'ɴn hɐ'gyɴ, sometimes. —— pɐ'hɐ'gyɴ 'ɴn tsɴnmɴ, sometimes he comes.

pɐ'-nyɴ, one by one [pɐ'-, one; -nyɴ, adverbial]. —— pɐ'nyɴ 'ɴn hɐ'gyɴ yɴn-guɑdɑ, I write to him just once in a while (cp. pɐ'-hɐ'gyɴ, sometimes).

pɐ'nyɴĩ-dei, the first.

pɐ'nyɴĩ-dou, in one place. Cp. pɴ-'ʜ'-gɑ, in one place.

pɐ'-pɑ'-dɴ (app. inan. I) shine (of sun, moon) [pɐ'- as in pɐ'-sɴĩ-gyɴ, hot sunshine; pɐ-e, sun; k'iɴ-pʜ', daylight; -pɑ'-, unexplained; -dɴ, noun postfix]. —— pɐ'pɑ'dɴ-gyɴ dèi-sɑ'dɑ', I am going to sit in the sunshine, = dèi-pɐ'-sɴĩ-sɑ'dɑ'. pɑ'-pɐ'pɑ'dɴ-kyɴ dèi-sɑ'dɑ', I am going to sit in the moonshine. pɐ'pɑ'dɴ gyɴ-bọu, I saw the sunshine.

pɐ'-sɴĩ-gyɴ (inan. III), warm sunshine [pɐ'- as in pɐ'-pɑ'-dɴ, sunshine; -sɴ-t-, prepound form of sɴ-dl, to be hot]. —— dèi-pɐ'sɴĩ-sɑ'dɑ', I am going to sit in the hot sun; = pɐ'sɴĩgyɴ 'ɴ-sɑ'dɑ'.

pɐ'-t'ʜ, eleven.

pɐ't'ʜ-n, eleven by eleven.

pɐ't'ʜn-dei, the eleventh.

pɐ't'ʜn-dou, in eleven places.

pɐy-ɑ', in summer [pɴe, summer; -ɑ'] Cp. sɐy-ɑ', in winter. —— pɐyɑ' hẹi'ɱ, he died in the summer.

pɐ'-yɑ', on the prairie. —— pɐ'-yɑ' 'ɴ-tsɴn, I came from the prairie.

pɐ'-yɑ', adv., together, at the same place [pɐ'-, together; yɑ']. —— pɐ'-yɑ' bɴ-kiɴdl, we (all) live in the same place.

pɐ'-dɑ, to be sore [pɐ'-, unexplained; dɑ]. —— mɑ'ƙɑ'n nɴ́-pɐ'-dɑ, my nose is sore.

pɐ-hiɴ, adv., indeed, surely [pɐ'-, unexplained; -hiɴ, real]. —— pɐ'hiɴ yɴ́-koudou-k'oup-'ɑmgyɴ, I am going to be suffering. pɐ'hiɴ 'ɴ-dɴmgyɴ, I surely am going to get tired.

pei, dead [cp. Tewa pè-ní, dead person]. —— Tsẹihiɴ-pei gyɴ-bọu, I saw a dead dog. pei-hẹi tsẹihiɴ gyɴ-bọu, I saw a live **dog,**

= tsę̨ihı̨ᴎ-pei-hę̨i gyᴎ̀-bǫu̧. tsę̨ihı̨ᴎ pei-hę̨igɑ déi-bǫu̧, I saw tpl. live dogs.

pei (peigu'ɑ, punct. neg.; peitdɑ, curs.; peidɑ', fut.; peiguɑdɑ', fut. neg.; pei, imp.), to fear tr., be afraid of. —— gyᴎ̀-pei, I was afraid of him. gyᴎ̀-peitdɑ, I am afraid of him. hɑ̨n gyᴎ̀-peigu'ɑ, I was not afraid of him. gyᴎ̀-peidɑ', I shall be afraid of him. hɑ̨n gyᴎ̀-peiguɑdɑ', I shall not be afraid of him. 'ᴎ̀-pei, be afraid of him!

pei- in pei-dei, to be straight; pei-'ǫu̧, to be very straight.

pei-, to think, in pei-gyᴎ, thought; pei-dl-, referring to thought.

pei- d . . . (peidei, imp.), to run one's best. —— bèi-peidei, run your best (in the race)! = tę̨im 'ę̀im-bɑ'dei! (See bɑ'dᴎ, to rise.)

pei-dɑ, to be dead [dɑ, to be]. —— pei-dɑ, he is dead. pei-hę̨i dɑ, he is alive, he is not dead.

pei-dᴎ, to have plenty to eat [cp. possibly pɑ', to eat]. —— gyᴎ̀-peitᴎ,. there is plenty to eat; opp. of pı̨ᴎ-hę̨i dɑ, to be without food.

pei-dei (pei-dou-p, tpl.), to be straight, stiff. Cp. pei-'ǫu̧, to be very straight; peidei-dɑ̨mku'ɑ, spade; peidei-t'ǫu̧ƙiᴎ, stiff-legged man. —— peidei déi-hᴎ'bɑ, I stood it (the stick) up straight. t'ǫu̧-peidei gyᴎ̀-bǫu̧, I saw a stiff leg. t'ǫu̧-peidoup déi-bǫu̧, I saw tpl. stiff legs.

peidei-dɑ̨mku'ɑ (an. II), spade, shovel [straight digging stick].

peidei-t'ǫu̧-ƙiᴎ, a stiff-legged man.

peidei-t'ǫu̧-dei (an. II; peidei-t'ǫu̧-gɑ, tpl.; peidei-t'ǫu̧- in comp.), stiff leg. —— peidei-t'oudei 'ę́i-dɑ, I have a stiff leg.

peidei-dɑ, to be straight, stiff [dɑ, to be]. —— peidei-dɑ, he is straight.

pei-dl-, prepound referring to thinking, in peidl-p̃ᴎ'egɑ, peidl-dou', to think about; peidl-dǫu̧n, to think [pei- as in pei-gyᴎ, thought; -dl-].

-pei-dl-, in tǫu̧-peidl-ƙiᴎ, talkative man.

peidl-dou', to think about. —— 'ı̨(ᴎ)hɑ gyᴎ̀t-peidldou', I am thinking about it right now. gyᴎ̀t-peidl-doudɑ', I shall think about it. hɑ̨n gyᴎ̀t-peidldougɑ', I am not thinking about it. poue bᴎ̀t-peidldou', don't think about it! ƙyᴎhi̧'ᴎ gyᴎ̀t-peidldou', I am thinking about the man. heigɑ hɑ̨n ƙyᴎhi̧'ᴎ gyᴎ̀t-peidldougɑ', I am not going to think about the man any more.

peidl-dǫu̧n, to think [dǫu̧-n, to seek]. —— gyᴎ̀t-peidl-tǫu̧nmɑ, I am thinking (seeking in my mind).

peidl-p̃ᴎ'egɑ, to think about. —— heit bᴎ̀t-peidl-p̃ᴎ'edɑ', let us think about it.

pei-dou, adv., therefore [pei-, unexplained; -dou]. Also used as postp. —— nɑ̨ 'ɑhyɑ'-dei pei-dou m-t̨ǫ'hou'ǫ̧'zǫu̧nheidl, and for that

reason they traveled off angry. k̄ɑ̱'deidl 'ę̆į-'ɑ̱'mei-dei peidou
dę̀i-hę̆įdɑ, he did not treat me right and that is why I left.  tsę̆į
houdl-dei peidou tsę̆į-hę̆į dɑ, he killed his horse and that is why
he has no horse now.  tsę̆įgɑ 'éi-houtdɑ-dei peidou 'ɑ̆-soudei, he
is killing his horses and that is the reason that he has only a few.

-pei-dou, postp., for [=pei-dou, adv.]. —— 'ɴ-tsꜧn nɑ̱ k̄yꜧhį'ꜧ
nɑ̱-peidou t'eip, I arrived and a man came out for me.

pei-gɑ̱'-t (inan. II[a]; pei-gyꜧ, dpl.; pei- in comp.), grain of sand, sand.
Cp. pei-sꜧdl-'ɑt, bird sp. —— peigyꜧ gyɴt-bǫy, I saw the sand.

pei-guɑ (peiguɑyɑ', punct. neg.; peiguɑyꜧ, curs.; peiguɑtɑ', fut.;
peiguɑyɑ̱'tɑ', fut. neg.; peiguɑ, imp.), to revive intr. [app. pei-
=pei, dead, cp. pei-sę̆į-hꜧ', to revive intr.; w. -guɑ cp. possibly
guɑ, to be wise]. —— 'ɴ-peiguɑ, I revived (from a faint).  hɑ̱n
'ɴ-peiguɑyɑ', I did not revive.  miꜧn 'ɴ-peiguɑyꜧ, I am about to
revive.  'ɴ-peiguɑdɑ', I shall revive.  hɑ̱n 'ɴ-peiguɑyɑ̱'tɑ', I shall
not revive.  'ę̀įm-peiguɑ, revive!

pei-gyꜧ (inan. III; pei-gyꜧ- in comp.), thought [cp. pei-dl-, compl.
referring to thinking]. Cp. peigyꜧ-bǫy'ǫy, not to think right;
peigyꜧ-dꜧmgyꜧ, to be thought-tired; etc.

peigyꜧ-bǫy'ǫy, not to think right [w. bǫy- cp. bǫyn-dɑ, to be bent;
-'ǫy, very]. —— peigyꜧ-bǫy'ǫy, he does not think anything
right.

peigyꜧ-dꜧmgyꜧ, to be thought-tired [dꜧmgyꜧ, to be tired], =peigyꜧ-
dꜧmgyꜧ-dɑ.

peigyꜧ-dꜧmgyꜧ-dɑ, to be thought-tired. —— 'ɴ-peigyꜧ-dꜧmgyꜧ-dɑ,
I am thought-tired, worried.

peigyꜧ-sɑ'-'ǫy (peigyꜧ-sɑ' 'ǫy-gɑ, tpl.), to be wise, smart [-sɑ'-, unexplained; -'ǫy, intensive]. —— peikyꜧsɑ'ǫy gyɴ-bǫy, I saw a wise
person.  peikyꜧsɑ'ouka dèi-bǫy, I saw wise people.

pei-k̄ɑ, to lie dead [k̄ɑ, to lie]. —— pei-k̄ɑ, he is dead.  tsę̆įhįꜧ
gyɴ-bǫy peik̄ɑ, I saw a dead dog.

pei-k̄iꜧ (an. I; pei-gɑ, tpl.), dead man.

pei-mꜧ (an. I; pei-mꜧę-mɑ, tpl.), dead woman.

pei-'ǫy, to be very straight [pei- as in pei-dei, to be straight -'ǫy,
intensive]. —— k̄yꜧhį'ꜧ pei'ǫy, the man is straight.

Pei-p̄ɑ'-'eidl, plcn., Red River [big sand river].

pei-sɑegyꜧ, to be benumbed, limb goes to sleep [app. pei, dead, or pei-
to be straight, stiff; -sɑ-e-gyꜧ, unexplained]. —— t'ǫydei 'ę̆į-pei-
sɑegyꜧ, my leg has gone to sleep.

pei-sꜧdl-ɑt (an. II; pei-sꜧdl-ɑt-dɑ, tpl.), bird sp. [explained as
stayer in the hot sand: pei-, sand; sꜧdl, to be hot; -'ɑt, unex-
plained]. The bird is said to live in the desert.

pei-sꜧ'nę̆į (an. II; pei-sꜧ'nou-p, tpl.), snake sp. [sand snake].
Described as being not more than a foot long and having body
striped like a rattlesnake.

pei-sęi-hʜ' (peisęihʜ'gu'α, punct. neg.; peisęihʜ'guα, curs.; peisęihʜ'dα', fut.; peisęihʜ'gu'αdα', fut. neg.; peisęihʜ, imp.), to revive
intr. [pei- evidently as in pei-guα, to revive intr.; -sęi-, unexplained;
app. -hʜ', to stand up]. —— dèi-peisęihʜ', I revived (e. g. from
a faint). hǫn dèi-peisęihʜ'gu'α, I did not revive him. miʜn
dèi-peisęihʜ'guα, I am about to revive. dèi-peisęihʜ'dα, I shall
revive. hǫn dèi-peisęihʜ'gu'αdα', I shall not revive. bèi-pei-
sęihʜ', revive!

pei-t͡sou (inan. Iᵃ), sandstone.

pei-t͡soudl (an. II; pei-t͡soudl-gα, tpl.), "top of thigh" [unexplained;
cp. possibly t͡sout-dα wing].

pęi' (an. II; pęi'-gα, tpl.; pęi'- in comp.), (wild) turkey. Cp.
pęi-syʜn, quail.

pęi-n (pęinǫ', punct. neg.; pęinmα, curs.; pęindα', fut.; pęinǫ'dα',
fut. neg.; pęi'n, imp.; pęinęi, infer.), to butcher [cp. possibly pei,
dead]. Cp.pęin-gyʜ, pęin-dα, to be butchered. —— gyʜ-pęin, I
butchered him. hǫn gyʜ-pęinǫ', I did not butcher him. heigα
gyʜ-pęinmǫ, I am butchering him now. hǫn gyʜ-pęinǫ', I am
not butchering him. miʜn gyʜ-pęinmǫ, I am about to butcher
him. gyʜ-pęindα', I shall butcher him. hǫn gyʜ-pęinǫ' k'yꬻhi'ʜgα,
I shall not butcher him tomorrow.

pęin-dα, to be butchered, =pęin-gyʜ [dα, to be]. —— heigα pęin-dα,
he is already butchered. t͡ʜp pęindα'-dei gyʜ-bǫy, I saw a
butchered antelope. t͡α'seidl 'ei-pęindα'gα déi-bǫy, I saw the
butchered antelope herd.

pęin-gyʜ (pęingα', punct. neg.; pęindeit͡α', fut.), to be butchered,
=pęin-dα [pęin, to butcher; dα, to be]. —— heigα pęindeit͡α', it
will be butchered. heigα pęingyʜ, he is already butchered. hǫn
pęingα', he is not butchered.

pęi-n-hʜ', panocha, honey, sugar, anything sweet. Cp. pęinhʜ'-dα,
to be sweet; etc.

pęinhʜ'-'ʜ'-dα (inan. IIᵃ; pęinhʜ'-'ʜ', dpl.), sugar cane [sugar stick].

pęinhʜ'-dα, to be sweet [dα, to be]. —— yiʜdei mꬻ 'èi-p'ęinhʜ'-dα,
they are both sweet.

pęinhʜ'-k'ǫy-gyʜ, chocolate [black panocha]. —— pęinhʜ'-k'ǫygyʜ
gyʜ-bǫy, I saw the chocolate.˙

pęinhʜ'-poudl (an. II; pęinhʜ'-pout-dα, tpl.), honey bee [honey bug].

pęi-sǫy-dα (inan. IIᵃ; pęi-sǫyn, dpl.), foxtail plant [turkey grass].

pęi-syʜn (an. II; pęi-syʜ'-dα, tpl.), quail [little turkey].

-piʜ- in Kα'α̃'-piʜ-t'ǫn, prsn.

piʜ-t'eidl (an. II; piʜ-t'eit-dα, tpl.), hip [unexplained].

piʜ, food, meal, =piʜ-gyʜ [cp. pα', to eat]. Cp. k'yꬻhi'ʜ-piʜ,
breakfast; k'iʜsα-piʜ, dinner; tei-piʜ, supper; 'ꬻ'gα-piʜ, buffalo;
etc. —— piʜ-hęi 'ʜ-dα, I have nothing to eat. piʜ-hęi gyʜ-

dɑ'mẹị', they had nothing to eat.    miʜn 'ʜ-pịʜ-bʜnmʜ, I am
going to go to eat (app. to meal-go).

-pịʜ, app. fish, in 'ɑ'-pịʜ, fish, q. v.

pịʜ-'ɑm-tou'e, kitchen [food make room].

pịʜ-n (an. II; pịʜ-dɑ, tpl.), gopher.    Cp. piʜn tʜ'hẹị dɑ'dei, mole.

pịʜn tʜ'hẹị dɑ'dei (an. II; piʜn tʜ'hẹị 'ẹị-dɑ'dei, d.; pịʜdɑ tʜ'hẹị
'éi-dɑ'gɑ, tpl.), mole [blind gopher].

pịʜ-tou'e (inan. I), dining room [meal room].

*pịʜ-'ɑ'mẹị, to prepare food, implied in pịʜ-'ɑm-tou'e, kitchen.

pịʜ-'ʜ'-dɑ (inan. IIª; pịʜ-'ʜ', dpl.), eating table.    Ct. kuɑt-'ʜ'dɑ,
writing table.

pịʜ-gyʜ (inan. III), food, = pịʜ.  —— tei k'iæpịʜgyʜ 'ẹihɑ'dei k'iʜ
dɑ́-mʜ'hi'ʜ, give us today our daily bread (lit. food)!

pịʜ-k̄oup, to lay food, feed [k̄oup, to lay tplo.].  —— tsẹị sọụn
yɑ́n-pị(ʜ)-k̄oup, I gave hay to the horse.    Cp. tsẹị sọụn yɑ́n-'ɑ, I
handed or gave the horse some hay.    tsẹị sọụn yɑ́n-k̄oup, I gave
the horse some hay.

pou (an. II; pou-gɑ, tpl.; pou- in comp.), beaver, = t'ọụ-dọụ'mdei
[Tewa 'ò-yò, beaver].    Cp. pou-guɑnhoudl, muskrat.

Pou-boudl-ʜ'-k̄iʜ (an. II; Pou-boudl-'ʜ'-gɑ, tpl.), Pueblo man [unex-
plained; -k̄iʜ].    Cp. Teiguɑ-k̄iʜ, also given as meaning Pueblo
man.

pou-dɑ, to be pit marked [dɑ, to be].    Cp. pou-'eigɑ, strawberry, lit.
pit-marked fruit; t'ʜdl-k'ouᵽ-dɑ, to have smallpox.

pou-dl (an. II; pou-t-dɑ, tpl., pou-dl- in comp.), bug, worm, vermin
[pou- as in Tewa pú-vɑ́, worm, bug].

-pou-dl- in mɑn-poudl-t'ɑtgɑ, to snap fingers [t'ɑtgɑ, to shoot].

poudl-ɑ'-k'ɑe (inan. IIª), membrane of meat, connective tissue
[poudl-ɑ'-, unexplained; -k'ɑe, skin].

poudl-k̄ɑ'-t̂ɑ'ẹ (an. II; poudl-k̄ɑ't̂ɑ'-dɑ, tpl.), pinacate [greasy sleek
bug: -k̄ɑ'- as in k̄ɑ'-gyʜ, grease; -t̂ɑ'ẹ =t̂ɑẹ, to be smooth].    Cp.
p'oue-t̂ɑ'ẹ, nit.

poudl-k'iʜ-dei (poudl-k'iʜ-dou-p), worm that bores holes in wood
[k'iʜ-dei, unexplained].

poudl-p'iʜt, bug hole [-p'iʜ-t, hole].

poudl-syʜn (an. II; poudl-syɑ'dɑ, tpl.), small bug.

pou-e, 1. prohibitive particle used with fut. and rarely with curs.;
2. additional particle, then, again, also [cp. Tewa -pí, neg.].  ——
poue 'ʜ-houdldɑ', don't kill him, = poue 'ʜ-houdlhʜ!    poue
'ʜ-guɑdɑ', don't hit him! = poue 'ʜ-guɑhʜ!  —— 2. gyʜ-goup
gɑ gyʜ-'ɑe-goup, gɑ poue gyʜ-'ɑe-goup, I hit him and hit him
again and then again.

pou-'ei-gɑ (inan. IIª; pou-'ei, tpl.), strawberry [pit-marked fruit:
pou- as in pou-dɑ, to be pit marked].

pou-guɑn-houdl (an. II; pou-guɑn-hout-dɑ, tpl.), muskrat [app. pou, beaver; -guɑ-n- as in tsei-guɑn, dog; -houdl, intensive].

-pou-t̂-gyʜ, round, in t̂ɑ̨ę-pout-gyʜ, spherical; t̂ɑdl-(t‘ɑ̨n)-t̂ɑ̨ępou-t̂gyʜ, kidney, lit. sleek-round liver(let).

pǫ̨ų-, prepound form of pǫ̨ų-gɑ̄’t, bead.,

pǫ̨ų-, prepound form of bǫ̨ų, to see, in pǫ̨ų-’ʜ, to come to see; pǫ̨ų-bʜ, to go to see; pǫ̨ų-k̃iʜ, inspector; etc. [Tewa pų’-w̨ꜝ, prepound form of m̨ų’ų̨, to see].

pǫ̨ų-, prepound form of pǫ̨ų-ę, to sound, in hou-pǫ̨ų-’ʜ, to sound as it travels past; etc.

pǫ̨ų-’ɑ̨ndɑ, to want to see. —— hɑ m-pǫ̨ų’ɑ̨ndɑ, do you want to see him? k‘iʜdeidl ’ꜝ-pǫ̨ų’ɑ̨ndɑ, I wanted to see him yesterday.

pǫ̨ų-’ʜ’-dɑ (inan. IIª; pǫ̨ų-’ʜ’, dpl.), tree sp. [bead tree]. The tree is said to be of medium size, and has bunches of yellow berries containing black seeds which hang down like bunches of grapes.

pǫ̨ų-’ʜ, to come to see [Tewa pų’-w̨ꜝ-’ꜝ, to come to see]. —— ’ꜝ-pǫ̨ų-’ʜ, I came to see him.

pǫ̨ų-bʜ, to go to see [Tewa pų’-w̨ꜝ-mꜝ, to go to see]. —— ’ꜝ-pǫ̨ųbʜ, I went to see him.

pǫ̨ų-t‘ę̨indɑ, to want to see. —— ’ę̨i-pǫ̨ų-t‘ę̨indɑ, I want to see him. hɑ̨n ’ę̨i-pǫ̨ų-t‘ę̨indɑ̄’mɑ’, I do not want to see him.

pǫ̨ų-ę (also recorded pǫ̨ų’ę; pǫ̨ųgyʜ, stat.; pǫ̨ųt̂ɑ’, fut.), to sound, ring [Tewa pų’-ŋ, to sound, ring; bell]. Cp. ’ɑ̨n, to sound. —— kiʜ s ’ɑ̨n-pǫ̨uę, the meat gave a sizzling sound. kiʜ ’ɑ̨n-k̃ɑ̨’-pǫ̨ųgyʜ, the meat is sizzling. heigɑ beit̂-pǫ̨uę, the bell rang just now. heigɑ beit̂-pǫ̨ųt̂ɑ, the bell is going to ring. ’ꜝ-t̂ɑ’ nɑ̨ yʜebɑ ’ɑ̨n-t̂ʜt̂gyʜ-pǫ̨uę, I heard the rope break.

pǫ̨ų-gɑ̄’-t (inan. IIª; pǫ̨ų, dpl.; pǫ̨ų- in comp.), bead [cp. possibly bǫ̨ų-, referring to light, transparency]. Cp. pǫ̨ų-’ʜ’dɑ, tree sp.; etc. —— pǫ̨ų gyʜt-bǫ̨ų, I saw the beads.

-pǫ̨ų-m- in ’ou-pǫ̨ųm-k̃ɑdl, Adam's apple.

pǫ̨ų-k̃iʜ (an. I; pǫ̨ų-gɑ, tpl.), inspector, umpire [pǫ̨ų-, referring to seeing]. p‘ɑ’ʜt̂dei-pǫ̨uk̃iʜ, ball umpire.

## p̃

p̃ɑ’ (inan. I), river; also name of a game [cp. ’ɑ’-, referring to water in several compounds; Tewa p̃ō‘, water, river, ’ɑ‘-, water. —— p̃ɑ’syʜn, a small river.

p̃ɑ’ (an. I ?), moon; month [cp. p̃ɑ-e, moon; Tewa p̃ō‘, moon, month]. —— p̃ɑ’ ’ɑ̨n(-k̃ɑ’dʜdl-)kuɑt, there is a ring around the moon. pʜ’gɑ p̃ɑ’, one month. p‘ʜ’ou p̃ɑ’ heigɑ ’ę̨ihɑ’ kiʜdl, he has lived here three months.

p̃ɑ-e (an. I ?), moon [p̃ɑ, moon; -’ei]. —— gyꜝ-p̃ɑe-k‘ǫ̨ų-dɑ, the moon is dark.

ꞕα-e (ꞕαeĩα’, fut.), to get lost. —— ’ꞑ-ꞕα’e ’ꞑ’-toụgyꞑ, I got lost
in the woods. ’ę̣i-ꞕαe, I lost it. ’ę̣i-ꞕαeĩα’, I shall lose it. mꞑ’yịꞑ
tsę̣ihị̣ꞑ ’ꞑ-ꞕαe, the woman lost her dog.

ꞕα’-’eidl, Rio Grande [big river].

ꞕα’-’eidl-syꞑn, Pecos river [little Rio Grande].

ꞕα’gyꞑ, fresh, newborn. —— ’ei-ꞕα’gyꞑ, roasting ears of corn, lit.
fresh ears. ’iꞑ-ꞕα’gyꞑ, baby, lit. fresh child.

ꞕα’-pꞑ’hꞑdl-, confluence. —— ’ꞑ-bꞑnmꞑ ꞕα’-pꞑ’hꞑdl-α’, I am going to go to the confluence.

ꞕα’-pꞑ’hꞑdl-dou’, to flow together, form a confluence. —— ’ę̣im-
ꞕα’-pꞑhꞑdl-dou’, the two creeks join each other.

ꞕα’-pꞑ’pα’-dꞑ (app. inan. I), moonshine [pꞑpα’-dꞑ, shine of sun or
moon].

ꞕα’-sou-t (an. II; ꞕα’-sou-t-gα, tpl.; ꞕα’-sou-t- in comp.), thunder
[unexplained]. —— ’ꞑn-ꞕα’sout-toụ’ǫ’deip, it is thundering.

ꞕα’sout-sα’-gyꞑ (inan. III), toadstool [thunder's excrement].

-ꞕǫ’, ꞕǫ’-, referring to middle, in kʻou-ꞕǫ’, in the middle; -kʻou-ꞕǫ-
’ę̣-guα, through the middle of; -ꞕǫ-’ę̣-gyꞑ, in the middle of; ꞕǫ’-
hị̣’ꞑ-dei, half dollar [Tewa pị̣-ŋ, heart, middle; pị̣-ŋ-gè, in the
middle].

-ꞕǫ-’ǫ in ’αdl-ꞕǫ’ǫ, yucca(-root), soap, lit. head washer.

ꞕǫ-’ǫ-ę̣ (ꞕǫ’ǫ’dα’, fut.; ꞕǫ’ǫ, imp.), to wash [ꞕα-, app. water; -’ǫ-,
unexplained; -ei, causative]. Cp. ꞕǫ’ǫ-mꞑ, washwoman; ’adl-
ꞕǫ’ǫ, yucca, soap. —— dèi-ꞕǫ’ǫ’dα’, I am going to wash myself. tsę̣ihị̣ꞑ gyꞑ-ꞕǫ’ǫ’dα’, I am going to wash my dog. tsę̣ihị̣ꞑ
gyꞑ-ꞕǫ’ǫę̣, I washed my dog. tsę̣ihị̣ꞑ ’ꞑ-ꞕǫ’ǫ, wash your dog!
’αdl-gyꞑ dèi-ꞕǫ’ǫ’dα’, I am going to wash my head or hair.

ꞕǫ’ǫ-mꞑ (an. I; ꞕǫ’ǫ-mꞑę̣-mǫ, tpl.), washwoman, = ’αdl-ꞕǫ’ǫ-mꞑ.

-ꞕǫ-’ę̣-gyꞑ, in the middle of, in tꞑn-ꞕǫ’ę̣gyꞑ, vertex; ĩou-ꞕǫ’ę̣guꞑ,
cheek [-ꞕǫ’, referring to middle; -’ei; -gyꞑ].

ꞕǫ-n . . . (ꞕǫndα’, fut.), to braid (e. g. hair). Cp. -ꞕǫ’dα, braid.
—— ’α’dα déi-ꞕǫndα’, I am going to braid my hair [Tewa pǫ́ ŋ,
to braid].

ꞕǫ’-hị̣’ꞑ-dei, half-dollar [ꞕǫ’- as in kʻou-ꞕǫ’, in the middle, half;
-hị̣’ꞑ, real; dei].

-ꞕǫ’-dα (inan. II; -ꞕǫ-n, dpl.; -ꞕα-n- in comp.), braid (of hair), in
Кyꞑe-ꞕǫn-ƙiꞑ, Tꞑn-ꞕǫn-ƙiꞑ, Chinaman; ’αdl-ꞕǫ’dα, braid of
hair [ꞕǫ-n . . ., to braid].

ꞕǫ-hei, adv., in the middle [ꞕǫ,- as in kʻou-ꞕǫ’, in the middle; -hei].
—— tʻoụgyꞑ ꞕǫ’hei ’ꞑ-hiꞑt, I went right through the water.

-ꞕꞑ-dl in mǫ’-ꞕꞑdl, rubbish pile.

ꞕꞑ-’e-gα (ꞕꞑ’egα’, punct. neg.; ꞕꞑ’egoup, curs.; ꞕꞑ’edeidα’, fut.;
ꞕꞑ’edei, imp.), 1. to fight; 2. in comp. to act. Cp. dα’-ꞕꞑ’egα, to
sing; kouĩ-ꞕꞑ’egα, to wrestle, lit. to strong-fight; kouĩ-ꞕꞑ’egyꞑ-ƙiꞑ,
wrestler; kyꞑebꞑ -ꞕꞑ’egα, to take care of; kʻoupeidl-ꞕꞑ’egα, to get

angry at; t'oudl-p̃ʜ'egα, to cohabit with; sα̃'dei-p̃ʜ'egα, to work;
etc. —— dèi-p̃ʜ'egα, I fought. dèi-p̃ʜ'edeidα', I am going to
fight.

p̃ei-t̃-gyʜ, several fall. Ss. correspondent 'out-gyʜ. Cp. p'ǫу-'ǫу-
p̃eit̃gyʜ, to bleed at nose. —— gyʜ̃-p̃eit̃gyʜ, they tpl. fell (e. g.
from roof to ground).

p̃ei-t'ʜ̨' (p̃eit'ʜ̨'t̃α', fut.), to laugh [p̃ei-, unexplained; -t'ʜ̨'].  ——
'ʜ̃-p̃eit'ʜ̨', I laughed. 'ʜ̃-p̃eit'ʜ̨'t̃α', I shall laugh.

p̃iʜ (an. I; p̃iʜ-p, tpl.), sister (woman speaking). Cp. t̨α̃', sister
(man speaking).

p̃iʜ, adv., down, downstream. Cp. p̃iʜ-dei, down. —— p̃iα
'ʜ̃-bʜ̨nmʜ̨, I am going to go downstream, = p̃iʜdei 'ʜ̃-bʜ̨nmʜ̨.

p̃iʜ-dei, adv., down, downstream. Also used as postp. [p̃iʜ, down;
-dei]. —— 'ʜe-p̃iʜgα, weeping willow, lit. downward (turned)
willow; p̃iʜdei 'ʜ̃-bʜ̨nmʜ̨, I am going down, downstream.

-p̃iʜ-dei, postp., down, downstream. Also used as adv. ——
p̃α̃'-p̃iʜdei 'ʜ̃-bʜ̨nmʜ̨, I am going down river.

p̃iʜ-dei-p, adv., from waist down [p̃iʜ-dei, down; -p]. Cp. mʜ̨-'ʜ̨-dei,
from waist up.

-p̃iʜdei-tsou, postp., down. —— p̃α̃'-p̃iʜdeitsou 'ʜ̃-tsʜ̨n, I came
from down river.

## p'

p'α-'ʜ' (inan. II), temple (anat.), lit. ball, p'α-'ʜt̃-bʜ, p'α-'ʜt̃-bʜ-e
[p'α-'ʜ', p'α-'ʜt̃- as in p'α'ʜt̃-dou-p, ball; p'α- unexplained; -'ʜ-dl-,
'ʜ-t-, -'ʜ', round]. Cp. p'α-'ʜt̃-doup, ball.

p'α-'ʜt̃-bʜ (inan. II), temple [-bʜ].

p'α-'ʜt̃-bʜ-e (inan. II), temple [-bʜ; -ei].

p'α-'ʜt̃-dou-p (inan. II; p'α-'ʜt̃-dei, dpl.; p'α-'ʜt̃-dei- in comp.), ball
(of shinny, baseball, etc.) [p'α-'ʜt̃-, ball, p'α-'ʜ', p'α-'ʜt̃-, temple;
-dou-p].

p'α'ʜt̃dei-pǫу-k̃iʜ (an. I; p'α'ʜt̃dei-pǫу-gα, tpl.), ball umpire [ball
inspector].

-p'α-e in tei-p'αe, all.

-p'α-houdl, hairy, in t'ǫу-p'αhoudl, to be hairy-legged; mʜ̨n-p'αhoudl,
lion, lit. hairy above [p'α̃'-, body hair; -hou-dl, intensive].

p'α-t̃-dα (inan. IIᵃ; p'α-dl, dpl.; p'α̃'- in comp.), body-hair, fur,
fuzz; also including beard-hair as in seịn-p'α̃'gα, beard-hair;
t̃soudl-p'αt̃dα, armpit hair; but never applied to t̃sǫуkα̃'t, feather
down, or to 'α'dα, head hair [Tewa fó, hair]. Cp. p'α̃'gyʜ, body
hairs; beidl-p'α̃'-, pubic hair. —— p'αt̃dα déi-bǫу, I saw one
body hair. p'αdl gyʜ̃t̃-bǫу, I saw the fur.

p'α̃'-, prepound form of p'α-t̃-dα, body häir.

-p'α̃'- in 'α̨n-p'α̃'-gα, heel.

p'ɑ'·bǫʊ'n (an. II; p'ɑ'-bǫʊ-dɑ, tpl.), fur-crook; see Mooney, pp. 415–416 [-bǫʊ'n as in bǫʊ'n-dɑ, to be bent, bǫʊ'n-gyʜ, to be bent].

p'ɑ'-gyʜ (inan. III; p'ɑ'-gyʜ- in comp.), body hair, fur, wool, fuzz, velvet [cp. p'ɑ-t̂-dɑ, body hair]. Cp. 'ʜ'k'įʜ-p'ɑ'gyʜ, stamens, lit. flower fuzz. —— tseįhįʜ-p'ɑ'gyʜ, dog fur.

p'ɑ'gyʜ-'ʜdlɑ'-gɑ (inan. II; p'ɑ'gyʜ-'ʜdlɑ', dpl.), peach; apricot [fuzz plum].

p'ɑ'-k̂ou-dei (an. II; p'ɑ'-k̂ou-dou-p, tpl.), measuring worm [p'ɑ'-, body-hair; k̂ou-dei, said to refer to going like a measuring worm].

p'ɑ'-t̂ǫʊ-dɑ, scraper (for hides) [fur scraper: p'ɑ'-, fur; t̂ǫʊ-dɑ, scraper]. Cp. t̂ʜb̦-t̂ǫʊ-dɑ, skin scraper.

p'ǫ (p'ǫ'mǫ', punct. neg.; p'ǫ'mʜ, curs.; p'ǫ't̂ɑ', fut.; p'ǫ'mǫ't̂ɑ', fut. neg.; p'ǫ, imp.), to stand up. Cp. p'ǫe, to erect; p'ǫ'-kǫʊ'm, dei, to stand. —— 'ʜ-p'ǫ'mʜ, I am about to stand up. hǫn 'ʜ-p'ǫ'mǫ't̂ɑ', I am not going to stand up. 'ʜ-bǫʊ-p'ǫ'mʜ, I keep standing up all the time. k'iʜdeidl 'ʜ-p'ǫ, I stood up yesterday. k'iʜdeidl hǫn 'ʜ-p'ǫmǫ', I did not stand up yesterday. 'ęim-p'ǫ, stand up! poue 'ęim-p'ǫ't̂ɑ', do not stand! heit bʜ̦-p'ǫ, let us stand up!

p'ǫ-ę (p'ǫędɑ', fut.; p'ǫe, imp.), to erect [p'ǫ, to stand; -ei, causative]. —— gyʜ̦-p'ǫędɑ', I am going to stand him up. gyʜ̦-p'ǫe, I stood him up. 'ʜ-p'ǫe peidei, stand him up! k̂yʜ̦hį'ʜ tsęį pɑ'kǫndɑ' nǫ tsęį-tou'ʜ'-tou'e gyʜ̦-p'ʜędɑ', if the man brings his horse, I am going to put him in the barn for him.

-p'ǫ'- in 'ʜ-sɑ'-p'ǫ'-tsʜn, I have returned from defecating.

p'ǫ'-hei, adv., app. straight. —— t'ǫʊ-gyʜ p'ǫ'hei 'ʜ-hiʜt, I went straight through the water, = t'ǫʊ-k'oup̂ǫę-gu(ɑ) 'ʜ-hiʜt.

p'ǫ'-kǫʊ'm, to stand, = dei [p'ǫ', to stand up; -kǫʊ'm, to be about]. —— 'ʜ-p'ǫ'kǫʊ'm, I am standing, = 'ʜ-dei.

p'ʜ-dɑ-'iʜ, twin [p'ʜ-dɑ-, explained as meaning right together, e. g. like two forefingers held together; w. p'ʜ- cp. possibly pʜ'-, together;· 'iʜ, dim.]. mʜ'yįʜ 'oueidei p'ʜdɑ'iʜ 'ęin-dɑ, that woman has twins.

-p'ʜ-dl in t̂ɑb̦-p'ʜdl, buffalo bull.

-p'ʜ-e- in 'ei-p'ʜe-'ʜdlt'out, corn cultivator.

p'ʜ-t̂-gyʜ (p'ʜt̂gɑ', punct. neg.; p'ʜ'yʜ, curs.; p'ʜt̂deit̂ɑ', fut.; p'ʜt̂gɑ't̂ɑ', fut. neg.; p'ʜt̂dei, imp.), to cease, back out; also as cessative verbal postpound]. —— 'ʜ-bʜnmʜ Teihʜ'nęi-guɑ nęi heigɑ yʜ̂-p'ʜt̂gyʜ, I was intending to go to Texas, but I backed out. k̂yʜ̦hį'ʜ 'ʜn-dɑ'-p'ʜt̂gyʜ, the man quit singing.

p'ʜ-t̂-gyʜ (p'ʜ-t̂-gɑ'-t, tpl.), fine, thin [cp. possibly -p'ʜ-n in t̂ęin-p'ʜn, unidentified internal organ of buffalo]. Cp. p'ʜ-'ǫ'męi, to grind fine; p'ʜ'-syʜn, small; tęin-p'ʜt̂gɑ't, sleet, lit. fine ice. —— tǫʊkuɑt gyʜ̦-p'ʜt̂gyʜ, it is a thin book. p'ʜt̂gyʜ gyʜ̦t-bǫʊ, I saw the drygoods, lit. the thin stuff.

p'ʜ-'ꝗ'mẹi, to grind up fine [p'ʜ'- as in p'ʜt̄-gyʜ, fine; 'ꝗ'mẹi, to make]. Cp. *ꞇαꝥ-p'ʜt̄dα, to grind fine. —— gyʜt̄-p'ʜ'ꝗ'mẹi, I ground it up fine. gyʜt̄-p'ʜ'ꝗmdα', I shall grind it fine. bʜt̄-p'ʜ'ꝗm, grind it up!

p'ʜ'-syʜn (p'ʜ'-syʜ'-dα, tpl.), small [p'ʜ'- as in p'αt̄-gyʜ, fine]. Cp. 'ẹimhʜ'mẹi-p'ʜ'syʜn, piss ant, lit. tiny ant.

p'ʜ, to be tied [cp. Tewa pᶁ-ŋ, prisoner]. Cp. k̄oudldei p'ʜ'gα, necktie; k̄oudl-p'ʜ, necktie; k'ue-p'ʜ, harness, wagon; 'ou-p'ʜ-'eigα, chokecherry; p'ʜ-ẹ, to tie; p'ʜ'-toup, cradle; p'ʜ'-ꞇseip, to lock up; p'ou-p'ʜ, to be tied in a bundle; tꝗn-p'ʜ'gα, belt; t'ọu-p'ʜ . . ., to lock up. —— nꝗn-dou (for nꝗ hꝗn-dou) 'αdlt'ẹi'm gα-(k'αe-)p'ʜ, why do you have your head tied up (with a rag)? tsẹi 'ḫn-'oudl-p'ʜ, the horse is loaded, lit. is load-tied.

-p'ʜ in 'α'-p'ʜ, boil.

p'ʜ-ẹ (inan. III), dust, dirt [cp. p'ʜ'- in p'ʜ'-gyʜ, bloom; and possibly p'ʜ-n, cloud]. Cp. p'ʜẹ-'ꝗ'mẹi, to rile. p'ʜẹ-dα, to be riled. *p'ʜẹ-p'iʜt, to dust. p'ʜẹ-tou, adobe house, lit. dirt house. —— p'ʜẹ gyʜt̄-bọu, I saw the dust. p'ʜẹ 'ʜ'gyʜ, the dust is blowing, it is dust-windy.

*p'ʜ-ẹ (p'ʜẹdα', fut.; p'ʜẹ, imp.), to tie [p'ʜ, to be tied; -ei, causative]. —— gyʜ-p'ʜẹdα', I am going to tie it. gyʜ-p'ʜmsα-p'ʜẹdα', I am going to tie it in a hard knot. 'ẹidei-tsou béi-p'ʜẹ, tie it like this! yḫn-'oudl-p'ʜẹdα', I am going to load him (the pack horse). sọun gyʜt̄-p'ʜẹdα', I am going to bale the hay. 'αdlt'ẹi'm déi-k'αe-p'ʜẹdα', I am going to tie a cloth around my head.

p'ʜẹ-'ꝗ'mẹi, to rile, make muddy [p'ʜẹ- as in p'ʜẹ-dα, to be riled, muddy; 'ꝗ'mẹi, to make]. —— gyʜ-p'ʜẹ-'ꝗ'mẹi, I riled it (the water).

p'ʜẹ-dα, to be riled [w. p'ʜẹ- cp. p'ʜẹ, dust, dirt; dα, to be]. Cp. p'ʜẹ-'ꝗ'mẹi, to rile. —— p'ʜẹ-dα, it (the water) is riled, dirty. t'ọu p̄'ʜẹ-dα'dei gyʜ-bọu, I saw the riled water.

p'ʜẹ-p'iʜdl-ʜ'-dα (inan. IIª; p'ʜẹ-p'iʜdl-ʜ'; dpl.), whisk broom, =p'ʜẹ-p'iʜt̄-dα [dust sweep stick].

*p'ʜẹ-p'iʜt, to dust, implied in p'ʜẹ-p'iʜdl-ʜ'dα, p'ʜẹ-p'iʜtdα, whisk broom.

p'ʜẹ-p'iʜt̄-dα (inan. IIª; p'ʜẹ-p'iʜdl, dpl.; p'ʜẹ-p'iʜdl- in comp.), whisk broom, =p'ʜẹ-p'iʜd-ʜ'dα.

p'ʜẹ-tou (inan. I), adobe house [dirt house]. —— nꝗ p'ʜẹ-tou 'ẹi-dα, that is my adobe house.

p'ʜ-m-sα-, verbal prepound referring to tying a hard knot, in p'ʜmsα-p'ʜẹ, to tie in a hard knot.

p'ʜmsα-p'ʜẹ, to tie in a hard knot. —— gyʜ-p'ʜmsα-p'ʜẹdα', I am going to tie it in a hard knot.

p'ʜ-n (app. inan. II), 1. cloud; 2. sky [cp. possibly p'ʜẹ, dust]. Cp. p̄α'sout̄-p'ʜn, thundercloud. p'ʜn-'ꝗmgyʜ, to cloud up. p'ʜn-dα, to be cloudy. seiᵽ-pʻн̩n, rain cloud. —— pʻн̩n-t̑н̩е̨, a white cloud; but pʻн̩n-sɑʻhyei, the blue sky (not a blue cloud). pʻн̩n-bн, pʻн̩n-bei, in the sky; but pʻн̩n-mн̩, pʻн̩n-mн̩е̨, pʻн̩n-mн̩m, in heaven, above the sky. tн̩ʻ k̑uɑdl pʻн̩n-bei, the stars are in (or along) the sky. pʻн̩n-mн̩е̨ t̑ɑʼ, he is in heaven. pʻн̩n gyн̀-bǫu̯, 1. I saw the cloud; 2. I saw the sky.

-pʻн̩-n, stated to mean thin in t̑е̨in-pʻн̩n, unidentified internal organ [cp. possibly pʻн̩tgyн, fine, thin].

pʻн̩n-ʼǫmgyн, to cloud up [pʻн̩n as in pʻн̩n-dɑ, to be cloudy]. —— miн̩n pʻн̩n-ʼǫ̨ʼmн̩, it is about to cloud up.

pʻн̩n-dɑ, to be cloudy [pʻн̩n- as in pʻн̩n-ʼǫmgyн, to cloud up; dɑ, to be]. —— pʻн̩n-dɑʼt̑ɑʼ, it is going to be cloudy.

pʻн̩ʼ-gyн (inan. III), 1. bloom (on fruit); 2. =t̑ou-tʻeitdɑ, face-powder [cp. pʻн̩-е̨, dust; etc.]. —— pʻн̩gyн gyн̀t-bǫu̯, I saw the bloom. ʼèi-pʻн̩ʼ-k̑uɑdl, they have bloom on them (said of a bunch of grapes).

pʻн̩n-k̑iʼн-t, to be puckery [unexplained]. —— gyн̀-pʻн̩nk̑iʼн̩t, it is puckery-tasting.

pʻн̩-n-sе̨i, seven. —— pʻн̩nsе̨i k̑yн̩ʼhyoup, seven men. pʻн̩nsе̨i sн̩e, seven years.

pʻн̩nsе̨i-dou, in seven places.

pʻн̩nsе̨i-kʻin̩н, seventy.

pʻн̩nsе̨i-n, seven by seven.

pʻн̩nsе̨i-n-dei, the seventh.

pʻн̩nsе̨i-tʻн̩, seventeen.

pʻн̩ʼ-ʼou, three [Tewa pó-yè, three]. —— pʻн̩ʼou k̑yн̩ʼhyoup, three men. pʻн̩ʼou sн̩e, three years.

pʻн̩ʼou-dl, seven (in an old Kiowa count).

pʻн̩ʼou-k̑ou, three (in an old Kiowa count).

pʻн̩ʼou-kʻin̩н, thirty.

pʻн̩ʼoukʻin̩н pн̩ʼtʻн̩, thirty-one.

pʻн̩ʼou-t, three by three.

pʻн̩ʼout-dei, the third.

pʻн̩ʼou-t̑-dou, in three places. —— pʻн̩ʼout-dou ʼн̩-dei, they stand in three places. pʻн̩ʼout-dou dèi-bǫu̯, I saw all three of them. pʻн̩ʼout-dou kiн̩dl, he lives in three places.

pʻн̩ʼou-tʻн̩, thirteen.

pʻн̩ʼou-yɑʼ-dei, the third. —— pʻн̩ʼouyɑʼ-dei t̑sou gyн̀-bǫu̯, I saw the third stone, =t̑sou pʻн̩ʼou-yɑʼdei gyн̀-bǫu̯.

pʻн̩ʼ-tou-p (inan. II; pʻн̩ʼ-toudl, dpl.), cradle [app. pʻн̩, pʻн̩ʼ-, to be tied; w. -toup cp. tou-p, handle, or tou-p, dpl. toudl, counting stick]. Cp. tʻǫu̯k̑ɑe-pʻн̩ʼtoup, old-time cradle.

pʻн̩ʼ-t̑seip, to lock up [t̑sei-p, to lay one]. —— ʼн̩-pʻн̩ʼt̑sou, lock him up! gyн̀-pʻн̩ʼt̑seip, I locked him up. gyн̀-pʻн̩ʼt̑soudɑʼ, I shall lock him up.

p'ei (inan. III), vulva [cp. possibly p'ei-p'out, navel]. p'ei-beit̯-dɑ (inan. II; p'ei-beidl, dpl.; p'ei-beidl- in comp.), labium. —— p'eibeidl-'ɑ'k̄oubei, at pubic region of woman.

p'ei-p (inan. IIª), bush [Tewa fé, stick, plant]. Cp. 'Ɑdl-p'eip-dei, persn., "bush head."

p'ei-p- in p'eip-t̯ʜę̨, to be gray.

p'eiþ̯-t̯ʜę̨, to be gray [p'ei-p-, unexplained; t̯ʜę̨, to be white].

p'eiþ̯t̯ʜę̨-sɑhyei, to be grayish blue [sɑhyei, to be blue].

p'eiþ̯-t̯ę̨inę̨i-guɑdl (an. II; p'eiþ̯-t̯ę̨inę̨i-guɑt̯-dɑ, tpl.), bird sp. [red bush bird].

p'ei-p'ɑt̯-dɑ (inan. IIª; p'ei-p'ɑdl, dpl.; p'ei-p'ɑdl- in comp.), pubic hair of woman.

P'ei-p'ɑt̯-k̄iʜ, white man, opprobrious term based on Beidl-p'ɑt̯-k̄iʜ, white man [pubic hair man].

p'ei-p'ou-t (inan. II), navel [w. p'ei- cp. possibly p'ei, vulva -p'ou-t, unexplained]. Cp. p'eip'out̯-k'ɑe, navel cord.

p'eip'out̯-k'ɑe (inan. II), navel cord [navel skin].

-p'ei-dl in k'ɑ'-p'eidl, flat [Tewa fá-gì, fī'-gi, flat].

p'iʜ (an. II; p'iʜ-dɑ, p'iʜ-gɑ, tpl.; p'iʜ- in comp.), porcupine [explained by an old Kiowa as referring to the arched shape of the porcupine; cp. p'iʜ-gɑ, hill]. Cp. p'iʜ-t'ǫuɳ, porcupine quill.

p'iʜ (inan. III; p'iʜ- in comp.), fire [Tewa fɑ`, fire]. Cp. p'iʜ-dɑ, fire. —— p'iʜ gyʜt̯-'ʜesę̨i, the fire is smoky.

p'iʜ (inan. I; p'iʜ- in comp.), vein. Cp. t'ę̨in-p'iʜ, heart vein; pɑ'-p'iʜ, thigh vein. —— p'iʜ-biʜn, p'iʜ-'eidl, a large vein.

p'iʜ (p'iʜ-dɑ', stat. neg.; p'iʜ- in comp.), to be heavy. Cp. p'iʜ-'ǫmgyʜ, to become heavy. —— 'è̯im-p'iʜ, you are too heavy. hɑ̨n 'è̯im-p'iʜgɑ', you are not too heavy. doue p'iʜ, it is too heavy. 'ę̨idei t̄sou 'eidl p'iʜ, this big stone is heavy. p'iʜ, it is heavy. k̄yʜ'hi̯'ʜ-p'iʜ-dei gyʜ̀-bǫu, I saw a heavy man. k̄yʜ'hi̯'ʜ-p'iʜgɑ dèi-bǫu, I saw heavy men.

p'iʜ-, prepound form of p'iʜ, p'iʜ-dɑ, fire.

p'iʜ-, prepound form of p'iʜ, vein.

p'iʜ-, prepound form of p'iʜ-gɑ, hill.

p'iʜ-, prepound form of p'iʜ, to be heavy.

p'iʜ- in p'iʜ-hout-, referring to flying.

p'iʜ-'ʜmgyʜ, to become heavy. —— 'ʜ̀-p'iʜ-ɑ̨'mʜ̨, I am going to be too heavy. hɑ̨n 'ʜ̀-p'iʜ-'ǫmkɑ'tɑ', I am not going to be too heavy.

P'iʜ-bǫu, prsn. of Mr. "Light," said to mean light, bright [app. p'iʜ, fire; -bǫu, referring to light]. Mr. Light's other name is Pɑdldei, singer.

p'iʜ-dɑ (inan. II; p'iʜ, dpl.; p'iʜ- in comp.), fire [p'iʜ, fire; -dɑ]. Cp. hɑ̨'-p'iʜdɑ, stove. k̄iʜbɑ, firewood, fire. P'iʜ-bǫu, prsn.

p'iн-guɑdl, p'н-seidl, brown.  —— p'iнdɑ déi-bǫu, I saw a fire.
p'iн-gyн, in the fire.

p'iн-dɑm (inan. III), fireplace [p'iн-, fire; dɑm, earth, ground].

p'iн-dнŧ-gyн (p'iн-dнŧ-gɑ'-t, tpl.), ridged [p'iн-, hill; -dн-dl-, dн-t-,
referring to standing up; -gyн].  As noun p'iнdнŧgɑ't (inan. IIª;
p'iнdнŧgyн, dpl.), muskmelon, lit. ridged one.

p'iн-gɑ (inan. II; p'iн, dpl.; p'iн- in comp.), hill [Tewa p̓į-ŋ, moun-
tain].  Cp. p'iн-tнŧgyн, ridged.  k̓oup, mountain.  bɑdlhɑ', hill.
—— p'íн-yɑ' tou tseidl, the house stands on top of the hill.
p'íн-t'нe 'н̓-hiнdlŧɑ', I am going to go up to the top of the hill.
p'iн-yɑ' 'н̓-tsн̨n, I have been up on the hill.

p'iн-guɑdl (p'iн-guɑt-dɑ, tpl.), brown [app. p'iн-, fire; guɑdl, red].
Cp. p'iн-seidl, brown.

p'iн-hou-t-, referring to flying, in p'iнhout-hɑndeigɑ, flying machine;
p'iнhout-hou'kǫu'm, to fly about; p'iнhouŧ-k'iнbɑ, to fly away; etc.
[p'iн-, unexplained; w. -hou-t- cp. possibly -hout-н̨], (distant shower)
comes.

p'iнhout-hɑndei-gɑ (inan. II; p'iнhout-hɑndei, dpl.), flying machine
[hɑndei, something, thing; -gɑ].

p'iнhout-houkǫu'm, to fly about [p'iнhout-, referring to flying; hou-,
to travel; -kǫu'm. to be about].  —— kuɑtoubɑ t'ǫu-t'нe 'èi-
p'iнhout-hou'kǫu'm, the birds are flying above the water.

p'iнhouŧ-k'i'нbɑ, to fly away [p'iнhout-, referring to flying; k'iнbɑ,
to walk off, fly away].  —— 'ę̀im-p'iнhouŧ-k'iнbɑ, he (the bird)
flew away.

p'iнhouŧ-dɑ, to project [p'iнhout-, referring to flying; dɑ, to be].  ——
'èi-dɑm-p'iнhouŧ-dɑ, there is a point of land (projecting into the
lake).

p'iн-k̓ou-p (an. II; p'iн-k̓oup̓-gɑ'-t, tpl.), crane sp. [app. p'iн-,
heavy; -k̓ou-p, unexplained].

p'iн-sei-dl, brown [app. p'iн-, fire; -seidl, unexplained].  Cp. p'iн-
guɑdl, brown.

p'iн-t (p'iнdldɑ', fut.; p'iнdl, imp.), to wipe, brush.  Cp. ŧɑ̨e-p'iнt,
to sweep; sęin-p'iнŧ-dɑ, handkerchief; p'н̨e-p'iнŧ-dɑ, whisk broom.
—— déi-p'iнt, I wiped it off.  déi-p'iнdldɑ', I shall wipe it off.

-p'iн-t, hole, in poudl-p'iнt, bug hole; boudl-p'iнŧgyн, down in a
hole [Tewa fõ`, hole].  Cp. possibly tн'-p'iнt, to be one-eyed, app.
to be eye-holed.

p'iнŧ-dɑ, to foam [dɑ, to be].  —— t'ǫu p'iнŧ-dɑ, the water is
foaming.

p'iн-ŧ-gyн (inan. III; p'iн-t- in comp.), foam.  Cp. p'iнŧ-dɑ, p'iнŧ-
k̓uɑdl, to foam.  —— p'iнŧgyн gyн̓ŧ-bǫu, I saw the foam.

p'iнŧ-k̓uɑdl, to foam [k̓uɑ-dl, several lie].  —— t'ǫu p'iнŧ-k̓uɑdl,
the water is foaming.

p'iнŧ-t'ǫu (app. inan. I), beer [foam water].

p'iн-t'ǫųn (an. II; p'iн-t'ǫų-dɑ, tpl.), porcupine quill(?). The form
given means lit. porcupine tail [t'ǫųn, tail].

p'ң-ę, app. intensive particle. —— k̄yң'hį'ң p'ңę tou-hęį dɑ, the man
has no house. p'ңę tou-hęį 'н̄-dɑ, I am without house.

p'ou (an. II; p'ou-e, tpl.; p'ou-e- in comp.), head-louse [Tewa fē`,
head-louse]. Cp̀. p'oue-t̄ɑ̨'ę, nit.

p'ou (inan. III; p'ou- in comp.), trap, snare, fishhook [cp. p'ou-,
to catch, trap]. Cp. hɑ̨'-p'ou, iron fishhook; t'ǫųsei-p'ou, bone
fishhook.

p'ou-, to catch, trap, in 'ɑ̄'pįн-p'ou-bн, to go fishing; p'ou-k̄iнgyн,
to lasso; p'ou-tęį', to trap [cp. p'ou, trap].

p'ou-, referring to venting wind, in p'ou-t'ɑt̀gɑ, to vent wind;
p'ou-k̄ɑ̨'n, venter of wind [cp. Tewa fę́-ŋ, to vent wind; cp. also
p'ou-dl-ei, to blow].

p'ou- in p'ou-sou . . . to weave.

p'ou- in p'ou-p'ң, to be tied in a bundle.

p'ou-'ɑ̨'męį, to make a loop in [p'ou, snare]. Cp. p'ou-k̄iнgyн,
lasso. —— gyн̄-p'ou-'ɑ̨mdɑ', I am going to put a loop on it,
i. e. make a loop at the end of the rope.

-p'ou-bн, to go to catch, in 'ɑ̄'pįн-p'oubн, to go fishing.

p'ou-dl (inan. II), branch, limb (of tree) [cp. k̄ɑ̨'-p'oudl, wart]. ——
'éi-p'oudl-'ɑe, it (the tree) has many branches.

p'ou-dl- in p'oudl-'ң̄'-hįн, cottontail rabbit.

p'ou-dl-, prepound form of p'oudl-gyн, lie.

-p'ou-dl, intensive, in 'ɑt̀-p'oudl-t'н̄dliн, crybaby boy [cp. possibly
-hou-dl, intensive].

-p'ou-dl in t'ǫųn-k̄ɑ'-p'oudl, fish, lit. split tail.

-p'ou-dl in sɑ-p'oudl, owl sp., mountain ghost.

p'oudl-ң̄'-hįн (an. II; p'oudl-ң̄'-hyoup, tpl.; p'oudl-ң̄'-hįн- in
comp.), cottontail rabbit, = tsң̄'-hįн.

p'ou-dl-ei (p'oudldɑ', fut.), to blow [cp. Tewa fé-rè, to blow tr.; cp.
also p'ou-, referring to venting wind; p'ou-t̀-gyн, to be bloated.
—— nɑ̨ dèi-p'oudlei, I blew. dèi-p'oudldɑ', I am going to blow.
tǫųbɑ̄'t déi-p'oudldɑ', I am going to blow the bugle.

p'oudl-hн̄t-gɑ (p'oudl-hн̄t̀gɑ', punct. neg.; p'oudl-hн̄t̀goup, curs.;
p'oudl-hн̄t̀teidɑ', fut.; p'oudl-hн̄t̀kɑ̄'dɑ', fut.; p'oudl-hн̄t̀dei,
imp.), to lie [p'oudl- as in p'oudl-gyн, lie; p'oudl-k̄iн, liar; hн̄t̀gɑ,
unexplained]. —— dèi-p'oudlhн̄t̀gɑ, I told a lie. hɑ̨n dèi-
p'oudlhн̄t̀gɑ', I did not tell a lie. dèi-bou-p'oudlhн̄t̀goup, I tell
lies all the time. dèi-p'oudlhн̄t̀deidɑ', I am going to tell a lie.
hɑ̨n dèi-p'oudlhн̄t̀gɑ̄'dɑ', I shall not tell a lie. béi-p'oudlhн̄t̀dei,
tell a lie! heit béi-p'oudlhн̄t̀dei, let us tell a lie!

p'ou-dl-gyн (inan. III), lie. —— p'oudlgyн 'н̄-k̄ɑ', I heard a lie.

p'oudl-hęįteit̀-gyн, lie, false story [p'oudl- as in p'oudl-gyн, lie;
heiteit̀-gyн, story].

p‘oudl-ƙiн (an. I; p‘oudl-gα, tpl.), liar (male).

p‘ou-e- in p‘oue-ƭeidl-’нdldн’-guαn, to turn somersault.

p‘oue-ƭα̨’ę (an. I; p‘oue-ƭα̨’dα, tpl.), nit [app. smooth louse].

p‘oue-ƭeidl-нdldн’-guαn, to turn somersault [p‘ou-e-, unexplained; ƭei-dl, buttocks; ’н-dl-dн-, ’нdl-dн’-, backward; guα-n, to jump]. —— dèi-p‘oue-ƭeidl-’нdldн’-guαn, I turned a somersault.

p‘ou-kα̨’n, to be venter of wind [p‘ou- as in p‘ou-t‘αtgα, to break wind; -kα̨’n, app. excessive usitative].

p‘ou-ƙαƭ-dα, to be syphilitic [p‘ou-, unexplained; w. -ƙα-t- cp. -ƙiн in toudl-ƙiн, to have venereal disease; dα]. —— ’н̇-p‘ouƙαƭ-dα, I have syphilis.

p‘ou-ƙiнgyн, to lasso [p‘ou, trap, snare; ƙiнgyн, to throw]. —— nę́in-p‘o.u-ƙiнdα’, I am going to lasso him.  yiнdei mę́in-p‘ou-ƙiнdα, I am going to lasso both.  béiƭ-p‘ou-ƙiнdα’, I am going to lasso them (tpl. cattle).

p‘ou-ƙiн-yнe-bα (inan. I), lasso [p‘ouƙiн-, prepound form of p‘ouƙi-нgyн, to lasso; yнe-bα, rope].

p‘ou-p, (finely) spotted.  Cp. p‘oup̀-dα, to be spotted; ƙα̨’-p‘oup, bobcat; ƭou’e-kuαt, (coarsely) spotted. —— tsęihįн-p‘oup gyн̇-bǫu, I saw a spotted dog.

p‘oup̀-dα, to be spotted [dα, to be]. —— ’н̇-p‘oup̀-dα, I am spotted.

p‘ou-p‘н̨, to be tied in a bundle [p‘ou-, referring to being in a bundle; p‘н̨, to be tied]. —— gyн̇-p‘ou-p‘н̨’-dei gyн̇ƭ-bǫu, I saw the bundle.

p‘ou-sou . . . (p‘ou-soudeidα’, fut.), to weave [p‘ou-, unexplained; app. sou . . ., to sew]. —— k‘α’dα déi-p‘ou-soudeidα’, I am going to weave a blanket.

-p‘ou-t in ƭou-p‘out, shade.

-p‘ou-t in p‘ei-p‘out, navel.

p‘ou-tęi’, to trap [to trap catch: p‘ou, trap; tęi’, to catch]. —— gyн̇-p‘ou-tęi’, I trapped him.  gyн̇-p‘ou-tęidα’, I shall trap him. ’н̇-p‘ou-tęi’hou, go and trap him!

p‘ou-ƭ-gyн, to be bloated; as n. (inan. III), gas on stomach [w. p‘ou-ƭ- cp. p‘ou-dl-ei, to blow; -gyн].

p‘ou-t‘αtgα, to vent wind [p‘ou- as in p‘ou-kα̨’n; t‘αtgα, to shoot]. —— dèi-p‘ou-t‘αtgα, I vented wind.

p‘ouƭ-t‘нdl-нe, to knot (at end) [unexplained; app. ’нe, to go]. —— tęigα̇’t déi-p‘ouƭt‘нdlнe, I knotted the thread at the end.

-p‘ouyiнy-iн in t‘ǫun-p‘ouyiнy-iн, to be swallow-tailed [unexplained; -iн, dim.].

p‘ou-, nose, in p‘ǫu-’ǫu-, referring to blood from nose.

p‘ǫu-hǫun-’н’-dα (inan. IIª; p‘ǫu-hǫun-’н’, dpl.), (wild) walnut tree [p‘ǫu-hǫu-n-, unexplained].

p‘ǫuhǫun-’ei-gα (inan. IIª; p‘ǫuhǫun-’ei, dpl.), (wild) walnut nut.

p'ǫ̣-n, pay.  Cp. p'ǫ̣n-ǫ̆, to pay. —— p'ǫ̣n y̆ǫ̆-dɑ, that is my pay.

p'ǫ̣n-ǫ̆, to pay [p'ǫ̣n, pay; 'ǫ̆, to give]. —— gyн̇-p'ǫ̣n-ǫ̆'dɑ', I am going to pay him.  gyн̇-p'ǫ̣n-ǫ̆, I paid him (also merely gyн̇-'ǫ̆).

p'ǫ̣-'ǫ̣-, referring to blood from nose [p'ǫ̣-, nose; 'ǫ̣-, blood], in p'ǫ̣'ǫ̣-zeip, to bleed at nose; p'ǫ̣'ǫ̣-p̄eitgyн, to have blood fall from nose.

p'ǫ̣'ǫ̣-p̄eitgyн, to have blood fall from nose [p̄eitgyн, several fall]. ——'ɑ-p'ǫ̣'ǫ̣-p̄eitgyн, blood falling from his nose.

p'ǫ̣'ǫ̣-zeip, to bleed at nose [zeip, to flow].

## s

sɑ (sɑ̄'gu'ɑ, punct. neg.; sɑtdɑ, curs.; sɑ̄'dɑ', fut.; sɑ̄'gu'ɑdɑ', fut. neg.; sɑ, imp.), 1. to put several in; 2. to set, erect several.  So. correspondent is tsei. [Cp. sɑ-dl, several are in; several stand; Tewa sɑ', several are (in position), sɑ''ɑ', to put several]. —— gyн̇t-sɑ, I put them in.  hǫn gyн̇t-sɑ̄'gu'ɑ, I did not put them in. gyн̇t-bou-sɑtdɑ, I put them in all the time.  gyн̇t-sɑ̄'dɑ', I shall put them in.  hǫn gyн̇t-sɑ̄'ku'ɑdɑ', I shall not put them in. bн̇t-sɑ, put them in!  poue bн̇t-sɑ̄'dɑ', don't put them in!  heit bн̇t-sɑ, let us put them in.  tou'e-tsou gyн̇t-sɑ, I put them in the house.  hǭ'p'iн-dǫ̣gyн gyн̇t-sɑ, I put them into the stove.  t'ǫ̣ tн̣nguɑ gyн̇-sɑ̄'dɑ', I am going to put water on top of my head. déi-sɑ̄'dɑ', I am going to put it (the tobacco) in (the pipe); béi-sɑ, put it in (ans.).

sɑ-, sɑ̄'-, in sɑ-dl, food in the bowels; sɑ-t, animal excrement; sɑ̄'-bн, ire cacandum; sɑ̄'-gyн, excrement; sɑ̄'-bɑ, to defecate; etc. [Tewa sɑ́, excrement, sɑ́-ŋ, to defecate].

sɑ-, sɑ̄'-, to seat, in sɑ-e, to seat; sɑ̄'-gyн, to seat oneself [cp. Tewa só-gè, to seat].

-sɑ-, sɑ̄'-, large, augmentative prepound and postpound, in sɑ-bн̣n, large; sɑ-p'н̣n, large; mǫn-sɑ, thumb, lit. big finger; 'ou-sɑ, crop of bird, lit. big throat; etc. [Tewa sō'-, to be large].

-sɑ in k'iн-sɑ, midday [possibly -sɑ-, large, augmentative].

-sɑ- in 'ęimhн̄'męi-t̄soudl-sɑ, winged ant; peigyн-sɑ-'ǫ̣, to be wise; t̄soudl-sɑ-mн, angel [possibly sɑ, to put several in, set several].

sɑ-'ɑ-dl (inan. III), mouth (referring to the cavity or interior of the mouth whereas beit-dɑ refers to the lips) [cp. Tewa só, mouth]. Cp. sɑ'ɑdl-kyн, mouth; and possibly sɑ-'ǫ̣'m, hemorrhage. —— sɑ'ɑdl gyн̇t-bǫ̣, I saw a mouth.

sɑ-'ɑdl-gyн (app. an. I), mouth (internal, ct. beidl-gyн, lips) [sɑ'ɑdl; -gyн]. —— sɑ'ɑdl-gyн 'ę̀im-bǫ̣dɑ', let me look at your mouth!

sɑ-bн̣n (sɑ-bн̣н-dɑ, tpl.), large [-sɑ-, large; bн̣n, large].  Cp. sɑy-eidl, large; the an. tpl. of sɑy-eidl is app. supplanted by sɑ-bịн̣-dɑ, cp. 'eidl; cp. also sɑ-p'н̣n, large. ⸻ tou-sɑ-bịн̣n gyн̀-bọụ, I saw a big house.

sɑ-dl (inan. III), food in the bowels [cp. sɑ-t, animal excrement; sɑ̄'-gyн excrement; etc.]. Cp. sɑdl-k'ɑe, leaf tripe; Sɑdlk'ɑe-k̄oup, the Black Hills.

sɑ-dl (sɑ̄'gɑ', punct. neg.; sɑ̄'t̂ɑ', fut.; sɑ̄'gɑ̄'t̂ɑ', fut. neg.), several are in; to stand several [cp. sɑ, to put several in; to set several]. Ss. correspondent is tseidl. ⸻ 'н̄-sɑdl, they are inside. hɑ̣n 'н̄-sɑdlgɑ', they are not inside. 'н̄-bou-sɑdl, they are inside all the time. 'н̄-sɑ̄'t̂ɑ', they will be inside. hɑ̣n 'н̄-sɑ̄'gɑ̄'t̂ɑ', they will not be inside. poue bн̀-sɑ̄'t̂ɑ' 'ɑe, don't ye be in the ditch! poue bн̀-sɑ̄'t̂ɑ', don't ye be in that hole! hн'oudei gyн̀-'н̂ɑhɑ'e-sɑdl, they tpl. have war bonnets on. yiнgyнt 'н̄-t'ọụ-sɑdlgɑ, four-legged creatures.

sɑdl-k'ɑẹ (inan. IIᵃ), leaf tripe, many plies. Described as an internal organ of cattle which has lobes like the leaves of a book [undigested food membrane].

Sɑdlk'ɑẹ-k̄oup, Leaf-tripe Mountains, Kiowa name of the Black Hills of South Dakota. The Black Hills were the home of the Kiowa in an early period of the migrations of the tribe. The name is given because of the peculiar appearance of the Black Hills, resembling the leaf tripe of the buffalo (see Mooney, p. 156) [food in bowels membrane mountains].

sɑ-e-, blue, green, in t'eip-sɑe-'н'dɑ, sunflower sp. [sɑ- as in Tewa tsɑ́-ẉɑ́, to be blue, green; -ei]. Cp. sɑ-hy-ei, blue, green.

sɑ-e (sɑedɑ', fut.; sɑe, imp.), to seat [sɑ-, to seat; -ei, verb formative]. Cp. sɑ̄'-gyн, to seat; t'ɑ'dɑb . . ., to seat. ⸻ heigɑ '-sɑedɑ', I am going to seat him. 'н̀-sɑe, seat him! = 'н̀-t'ɑ'dɑ'bei!

-sɑ-e- in pei-sɑ-e-gyн, (limb) is asleep.

sɑ-'e (sɑ-'e-guɑ, tpl.), to be swift [sɑ- = Tewa cɑ́, to be swift; -'ei]. Cp. 'ɑn-tsн̣'-sɑ'e, to be a fast walker; etc. ⸻ 'н̀-sɑ'e, I am swift, I am a swift runner. tsẹi-sɑ'e gyн̀-bọụ, I saw a swift horse. tsẹi-sɑ'eguɑ déi bọụ, I saw tpl. swift horses.

sɑ-hy-ei (sɑ-hy-ei-gɑ, tpl.), blue, green [sɑ-e-, blue, green; -hei, unexplained].

sɑhyei-'ei-goup (inan. IIᵃ), 1. lettuce; 2. cucumber [green fruit plant].

sɑhyei-t̂ẹịnẹị (an. II; sɑhyei-t̂ẹịnou-p, tpl.), bluebird [blue bird].

sɑ-kɑ-hɑ (an. II; sɑ-kɑ-hɑ-e-guɑ, tpl.), crow [unexplained]. Cp. mɑ̄'sɑ, raven.

sɑ-'ọụ'm, hemorrhage [app. big bleeding: -sɑ-, large, augmentative; 'ọụ'm, blood; although sɑ- as possibly a prepound form of sɑ'ɑdl, mouth, is also to be thought of].

sɑ'ọụ'm-hн'bн, to have a hemorrhage [hн'bн as in k'iнn-hн'bн, to cough]. ⸻ 'н̀-sɑ'ọụm-hн'beip, I have a hemorrhage.

sɑ-p'н̣n, large [-sɑ-, large; -p'н̣-n, unexplained]. Cp. sɑ-bịн̣n, large.

sɑ-pʻoudl (an. II; sɑ-pʻou-t̑-dɑ, tpl.), 1. a large-sized owl sp.; 2. = Ƙoub̞-sɑpʻoudl, lit. mountain owl sp., one of a kind of mythological beings called by the Kiowa in English "mountain ghosts." Mr. Lonewolf expressed the theory that they must be gorillas. sɑpʻoudl is also used as an oath, e. g. sɑpʻoudl 'ȩim-dɑ, you devil!, lit. you are a mountain ghost [sɑ-, unexplained; -pʻoudl, probably -pʻoudl, intensive].

sɑ-t (inan. III), animal excrement, = sɑt-ƙɑn [cp. sɑ-dl, food in the bowels; sɑ-gyʜ, excrement; etc.]. Cp. tsȩi-sɑt, horse manure.

sɑ-t, adv., just now, now, then, recently, at last [cp. sɑt-dei, to be new]. —— sɑt hȩi'm, he just now died (ct. tɑ'tɑ'e tʻougɑ hį'ʜheidl, my father died long ago); hɑn houldei tsʜ'nɑ' gɑ sɑt hʜ'oue ƙiʜgyʜ tsʜn, he did not come back for a long time, he came back way afterward; gyh̞-pʻʜ'ou-goup nɑ 'ɑhyɑ' sɑt 'ȩim-'ɑthʜ'dɑ, but when I hit him the third time, he cried; ƙoup-yɑ' sɑt̑ tsʜn, he just came from the mountain; sɑt 'į(ʜ)hɑ sɑt̑ 'h̞-tsʜn, this is the first time that I have been here.

sɑt-ƙɑn (inan. III), (dry) animal excrement, = sɑt [ƙɑn, stiff, hard]. Dry horse manure (spoken of as sɑt̑-ƙɑn) is used as kindling material when making fire with firesticks.

sɑt-dei (*sɑt̑-gɑ, tpl.), to be new [sɑ-t, just now; -dei]. —— sɑt̑-dei sʜ'dʜ, new year. sɑt̑-dei tsȩi, a new horse. sɑt̑-dei tsȩi 'ȩi-dɑ, it is my new horse. 'ȩigɑ sɑt̑dei-tsȩ.igɑ nɑ̑-dɑ, these are my tpl. new horses. sɑt̑-dei p̄ɑ', it is new moon.

sɑy-eidl (sɑy-eit̑-dɑ app. only used as inan. II and inan. IIᵃ s.; an. tpl. is supplanted by sɑ-bįʜ-dɑ; see sɑ-bįʜn; sɑy-eidl- in comp.), large [for sɑ-e-'ei-dl; -sɑ-, large; -ei, formative; 'eidl, large]. Cp. 'eidl, large; sɑ-bįʜn, large; sɑ-pʻʜn, large.

sɑ̄'-, excrement, see sɑ-.

sɑ̄'-, to seat, see sɑ-.

sɑ̄'-, large, see sɑ-.

sɑ̄'- in sɑ̄'-pʻʜn, ashes.

sɑ̄'-bɑ (sɑ̄'beidɑ', fut.; sɑ̄'bei, imp.), to defecate. —— dèi-sɑ̄'bɑ', I already defecated. dèi-sɑ̄'beihoudɑ', I am going to go to defecate. bèi-sɑ̄'hou, go and defecate!

sɑ̄'-bįʜ (inan. Iᵃ), quiver [sɑ, to put several in; bįʜ as in 'ɑ̄'-bįʜ, paunch; cp. biʜm-kʻɑe, bag]. —— sɑ̄'-bįʜ gyh̞-boų, I saw the quiver.

sɑ̄'-dei, work. —— ƙyʜ'hį'ʜ sɑ̄'dei-'eidl gyh̞-'ɑ̄'mȩi-dei gyh̞-boų, I saw the man who did the great work.

sɑ̄'-dei-, prepound form of sɑ̄'deidɑ, to work.

sɑ̄'dei-bʜ, to go to work. —— 'h̞-sɑ̄'dei-bʜ'tɑ', I am going to go over to work.

sɑ̄'dei-hɑndei (inan. III), tool [work thing]. —— sɑ̄'dei-hɑndei gyh̞t̑-boų, I saw the tool(s).

sɑ'dei-ḱiн (an. I; sɑ'dei-gɑ, tpl.), workman.

sɑ'dei-p̄н'egyн (sɑ'dei-p̄н'edeidɑ', fut.), to work [p̄н'egyн, to act].

sɑ'dei-p'нt̓gyн, to stop working. —— gyн̓t-sɑ'dei-p'нt̓dei, let us stop working!

sɑ'-dei-dɑ (sɑ'deidɑ'dɑ', fut.; sɑ'deidɑ'yiн, infer.), to work [unexplained]. Cp. sɑ'dei-bн, to go to work; sɑ'dei-ḱiн, workman; sɑ'dei, work; etc. —— ḱyн̓'hi̓'н̣ gyн̀-bo̜u gyн̀-sɑ'deidɑ'dei, I saw the man who was working. ḱyн̓'hi̓'н̣ gyн̀-sɑ'deidɑ'yiн-dei gyн̀-bo̜u, I saw the man who had been working. ḱyн̓'hyoup 'ćit̓-sɑ'deidɑ'yiн-gɑ déi-bo̜u, I saw the tpl. men who had been working. hɑ bн̀t̓-sɑ'deidɑ, have you been working?

sɑ'-tou (inan. I), privy.

sɑ'-gyн (inan. III), excrement [sɑ'-, as in sɑ'-bɑ, to defecate; -gyн]. Cp. p̄ɑsout̓-sɑ'gyн, toadstool, lit. Thunder's excrement; sɑ-dl, food in bowels; sɑ-t, animal excrement; sɑt̓-ḱɑn, hard manure; sɑ'-bɑ, to defecate; t̓eit̓, soft manure; etc.

sɑ'-gyн (sɑ'dɑ, fut.; sɑ, imp.), to seat oneself, sit down [sɑ-, sɑ'-, to seat; -gyн]. —— bèi-sɑ, sit down! dèi-sɑ'dɑ', I am going to sit down. dèi-'н̓'t'ɑt̓bнhнdl-sɑ'dɑ', I am going to sit on the chair. hɑ dèi-sɑ'gyн, did I sit down?

sɑ'-p'ǫ'-tsн̣n, to return from defecating [-p'ǫ', unexplained]. —— 'н̀-sɑ'-p'ǫ'-tsн̣n, I have already returned from defecating.

sɑ'-p'н̣n (inan. I), ashes [unexplained; w. -p'н̣-n cp. possibly p'н̣-n, cloud, sky, p'н̣-e̜, dust]. —— sɑp'н̣n gyн̀-he̜ideidɑ', I am going to throw away the ashes.

sɑ'toudl-t̓sou (inan. Iᵃ), pipestone [pipe stone].

sɑ'-tou-p (inan. II; sɑ'toudl, dpl.), pipe [sɑ'-, explained as sɑ, to put several in, as in sɑ'-bi̜н, quiver, but cp. possibly Tewa sɑ', tobacco; -toup, unexplained].

sǫ-, unexplained verb prefix in sǫ-'ǫ'dei, to be angry; cp. 'ǫ'dei, to be mean.

sǫ-'ǫ'-dei (sǫ'ǫ'dɑ', punct. neg.; sǫ'ǫ'deip, sǫ'ǫ'deihн, curs.; sǫ'ǫ-'deit̓ɑ', fut.; sɑ'ǫ'dɑ't̓ɑ', fut. neg.; sǫ'ǫ'dei, imp.; sǫ'ǫ'deiheidl, infer.), to be angry [sǫ-, unexplained verb prefix; 'ǫ'dei, to be mean]. Cp. sǫ'ǫ'dei-dɑ, to be angry. —— 'н̀-sǫ'ǫ'dei, I am mad. k'iнdeidl 'н̀-sǫ'ǫ'dei, yesterday I got mad. k'yн̓'hi̜нgɑ 'н̀-sǫ'ǫ'deit̓ɑ', tomorrow I shall be mad. k'yн̓'hi̜нgɑ hǫn 'н̀-sǫ'ǫ'dɑ't̓ɑ', tomorrow I shall not be angry. hǫn 'н̀-sǫ'ǫ'dɑ', I am not angry. míнn 'н̀-sǫ'ǫ'deip, I'll be angry pretty soon. heit̓ bн̀-sǫ'ǫ'dei, let us get angry! heit̓ poue bн̀-sǫ'ǫ'deit̓ɑ', let us not be angry. poue 'è̜im-sǫ'ǫ'deihн, don't you get angry!

sǫ'ǫ'dei-'ǫ'me̜i, to make angry. —— 'é̜i-sǫ'ǫ'dei-'ǫ'me̜i, he made me angry. 'é̜i-sǫ'ǫ'dei-'ǫ'mɑ, he is trying to make me angry, he is making me angry.

sǫ'ǫ'dei-dα, to be angry [dα, to be]. —— hǫn 'ʜ-sǫ'ǫ'dei-dǫ'mǫ', I was not angry. nǫ 'ʜ-sǫ'ǫ'dei-dα, I am mad. 'ʜ-sǫ'ǫ'dei-dα'tα', I shall be angry. sǫ'ǫ'dei-dα gα tsʜn, he came mad.

-sǫ-m-, prepound form of sǫmdα, to look (at), in sǫm-bǫu, to look at; 'α'gα-sǫm, window; hou-sǫm-'ʜ'dα, sunflower sp.; etc.

sǫm-bǫu, to look at. —— k̑yn̑hį'ʜ 'ę̀im-guαnmǫ'-dei gyʜ-sǫmbǫ-u̯dα', I am going to look at the man dance. k̑yn̑'hyoup 'ę̀im-guαnmǫ'-gα dèi-sǫm-bǫu̯dα', I am going to watch the men dance. 'ę̀i-sǫm-bǫu̯nmα, he is going to look at me.

sǫ-m-dα (sǫm- in comp.) to look at. —— 'ę̀i-sǫmdα, he is looking at me. gyʜ-bǫu̯ nǫ 'ę̀i-sǫmdα neigα hɑ̑yʜ'-tsou gyʜ̑t-bǫu̯, seeing that he was looking at me, I looked away.

sǫ-n-, prepound form of verb, to boil, in sǫn-tsei, to set to boil [cp. -sǫ'-, to boil; Tewa sá-yè, to boil intr.]. Cp. biʜngyʜ, to boil intr.

sǫn-tsei, to set to boil [sǫ-n-, prepound form of verb, to boil, as in kiʜ-sǫ'-dα, kettle; tsei, to set (so.)]. —— gyʜ-sǫntseidα', I am going to boil it.

-sǫ'-, to boil, in ki(ʜ)-sǫ'dα, kettle, lit. meat boiler [cp. sǫ-n- in sǫn-tsei, to set to boil].

sʜ-dl (sʜ-dl-, sʜ-t- in comp.), to be hot [cp. Tewa tsá-w̑ʜ̑, to be hot]. Cp. dęi-sʜdl, to be peppery; pei-sʜdl-'αt, bird sp.; sʜdl-hęi'm, to feel hot; etc. —— 'ęihα'dei k'iʜ gyʜ-sʜdl, it is pretty hot today. t̑sou sʜdl, the rock is hot. t̑sou 'ę̀i-sʜdl, the d. rocks are hot. t̑sou gyʜ-sʜdl, the tpl. rocks are hot. k'iʜdʜ sʜdl, the day is hot. gyʜ-gįʜ-sʜdl, it is a hot night. t̑sou-sʜdl gyʜ-bǫu̯, I saw a hot stone. t̑sou-sʜdl gyʜ̑t-bǫu̯, I saw the tpl. hot stones.

sʜdl-'ǫmgyʜ, to have fever, in 'ʜ-k̑α'houdl-sʜdl-'ǫmgyʜ, I have chills and fever [to become hot].

sʜdl-dαe (inan. III), quinine [fever medicine].

sʜdl-dǫm-, south [hot country]. Cp. pʜe-bei-, south, lit. in the region of summer; t̑ou-dǫm-, north; sʜ'-bei-, north.

sʜdl-dǫm-guα, to the south.

sʜdl-dǫm-gyʜ, in the south.

sʜdl-hɑ̑'b . . ., in the expression 'ę̀im-sʜdl-hɑ̑'bei, you are making it hotter (said to one who is making a noise, e. g. singing, in hot weather) [-hɑ̑'bei, app. identical with hɑ̑'bei, imp. of hɑ̑'bα, to lift].

sʜdl-hǫ̑'-t'ǫu̯-gyʜ, steam [hot breath water].

sʜdl-hęi'm, to feel hot; die with heat. —— 'ʜ-sʜdl-hęimʜ, I am awfully hot. sʜdl-hęi'm, he died with heat, got a sunstroke. k'yʜ̑'hįʜgα mį(ʜ) 'ʜ-sʜdl-hęi'm, yesterday I pretty nearly died with the heat.

sʜdl-kyu̯'ę, typhoid fever [long fever].

sʜdl-tʜ', to be tanned (with the sun) [app. tʜ', to be ripe, cooked]. —— 'ʜ-sʜdltʜ', I am tanned. mǫdα nǫ́-sʜdltʜ', my arm is

tanned.    koudl 'ꞕ-sꜱdltꜱ', I am sunburnt on my neck, also koudl
nꝗ-sꜱdltꜱ'.

Sꜱdl-ตa'k'œkiꜱ, Southerner [southern white man].    Cp. T'ou-ตa꞉-
k'œkiꜱ, Northerner.

sꜱdl-t'eip, to sweat [sꜱdl-, referring to heat; t'ei-p, to come out].
Cp. sꜱdl-t'ọu, sweat.  —— heigα sꜱdl-t'eip, he is sweating now.
'ꞕ-sꜱdl-t'eip̣dα, I am sweating.

sꜱdl-t'ọu, sweat [sꜱdl-, referring to heat; t'ọu, water].    Cp. sꜱdl-t'eip,
to sweat.

sꜱ-e (app. inan. I), winter, year [cp. sꜱ'-dꜱ, winter, year].  ——
p'ꞕ'ou sꜱe, three years.  kiꜱgyꜱe sꜱe, next year.  sꜱ'y-α', in
winter.  sꜱ-t-, to be hot, see sꜱ-dl-.

sꜱt-αt'ọ'n, to melt intr. [sꜱt-, prepound form of sꜱdl, to be hot;
'αt'ọ'n, to clear away].  —— koudl sꜱt-αt'ọn, the snow melted
away.  heigα 'èi-sꜱt-αt'ọn, it (the lead) melted away.  But
'èi-zeip, it (the lead) melted.

sꜱต-dꜱdl-ตꜱ'-dou', to stand straight up with the heat (ss.).  Tpls.
correspondent sꜱต-dꜱdl-t'ꜱ'-dou'.  [sαt-, prepound form of sꜱdl,
to be hot; dꜱdl-, referring to standing up; ตꜱ'-, t'ꜱ'-, prepound
forms of hꜱ', to stand up; dou'].

sꜱต-dꜱdl-t'ꜱ'-dou', several stand straight up with the heat.  Ss.
correspondent sꜱต-dꜱdl-ตa'-dou'.  [For etym. see sꜱต-dꜱdl-ตꜱ'-
dou'].  —— 'éiต-sꜱตdꜱdlt'a'dou', they (the prairie dogs) are
sitting up straight with the heat (old expression said of a hot day).

sꜱ-ต-gyꜱ, to be burst open [cp. sꜱ'-dα, to have a hole; sꜱ'- . . .,
to burst; dọm-sꜱ'bα, plow; etc.].  —— 'èi-sꜱตgyꜱ, it (the wood,
e. g.) is burst open.

sꜱ' . . ., to burst tr., in ตα-sꜱ' . . ., to split with wedge dọm-sꜱ'bα,
plow; sꜱ'-dα, to have a hole in; sꜱต-gyꜱ, to be burst open; etc.
Cp. ka'dα, to burst tr.

sꜱ'-bei-, north [sꜱ'- as in the sꜱ'-dꜱ, winter, year; -bei- referring
to side, region].    Cp. ตou-dọm-, north.

sꜱ'bei-bꜱ, on the north side [-bꜱ, postp.].  —— sꜱ'bei-bꜱ 'ꞕ-ตa',
I am staying on the north side, e. g. on the north side of a street;
also I am staying in the north.

sꜱ'bei-guα, to the north.  —— sꜱ'bei-guα 'ꞕ-bꞕnmꞕ, I am going
north.

sꜱ'-dα, to have a hole in, be burst open [dα, to be].  —— houdldꜱ
yꞕ-sꜱ'-dα, my shirt has a hole in it.  'èi-dọm-sꜱ'-dα, the ground
has been plowed up, is loose; cp. dọm-sꜱ'bα, plow.  ka'bout
'éi-sꜱ'-dα, the boat is leaking.

sꜱ'-dꜱ (inan. I), winter; year.  Cp. sꜱ'-bei, north; sꜱe, winter, year.
  —— sαตdei sꜱ'dꜱ, new year.  sꜱ'dꜱ ตou, it is a cold winter.
sꜱ'dꜱ ตou 'ẹihα', it is cold in the winter here.

sн'-dl-ei (an. II; sн'-dl-ou-p, sн'-dl-ei-gα, tpl.), dog.   Cp. tsęį'hįн, dog.

sн'-t̯ęįnęį, bird sp. [winter bird].

sн'-tsoue (inan. I), urine [sн'- as in Tewa sò'-yǫ'-ŋ, to urinate; tsoue, water].

sн'tsoue-bįнmk'αe (inan. II), urine bladder [urine bag].

sн'tsoue-tou, urinal [urine house].

sнy-α', in winter [sнe, winter; -α'].   Cp. pнy-α', in summer.

-sн-n- in t'ǫų 'ę̀įm-zouȶ-sн̥n-goup, there is a waterfall.

sн̯'-nęį (an. II; sн̯'-nou-p, tpl.), snake.   Cp. sн̯'nęį-'α'pįн, eel; 'н'-sн̯'nęį, bullsnake; sн̯'nęį-hį'н̥, rattlesnake; ƙoup̀tα'k'αe-sн̯'nęį, campamocha.

sн̯'nęį-'α'pįн (an. II; sн̯'nęį-'α'pįн'-dα, tp.), eel [snake fish].

sн̯'nęį-ȶαę (an. II; sн̯'nęį-ȶн̥ę-mαę, tpl.), whipsnake [sleek snake].

sн̯'nęį-'ei-gα (inan. IIª; sн̯'nęį-'ei, tpl.), (wild) blackberry fruit [snake fruit].

sн̯'nęį-'ei-p'eip (inan. IIª), (wild) blackberry vine.

sн̯'nęį-hį'н̥ (an. II; sн̯'nęį-hyų-'ę, tpl.), rattlesnake [real snake].

sн̯'nęį-k'ǫų-gyн (an. II; *sн̯'nęį-k'ǫų-gα'-t, tpl.), blacksnake [black snake].

sei- in sei-k'ǫų'e, large intestine; sei-ȶн̥ę, small intestine [Tewa sĩ', belly].

sei- in sei-tsou, lake; sei-kαn, green scum; perhaps also in 'α'-sei, little creek.

-sei in ƙαdl-sei, glue; k'ǫųm-sei, old canvas; 'ou-sei, throat; t'ǫų-sei, bonė.

sei-bα, to stab.   Cp. gųαę-sei-dα, fish spear; mǫ'-seip̀-ƙiн, Caddo man; and possibly sαi-sei-gα, arrowhead.   —— mǫ'tsнȶ-dou gyн̀-se.ibα, I stabbed him with the point (of the knife).

-sei-dl- in sei-dl-dα, to be tangled, bushy (of hair); ȶα'-sei-dl, herd of antelopes.

-sei-dl in p'iн-seidl, brown.

sei-dl-dα, to be matted, tangled [dα, to be].   —— nǫ́-'αdl-seidl-dα, my hair is tangled, bushy.

sei-gyн (an. I; sei-gyн-p̀-dα, tpl.), 1. maternal uncle; 2. sister's child. Used with 2nd and 3rd person possessive [unexplained].   Cp. seigyн-'e, my or our paternal uncle; tαdl, 1. father, 2. paternal uncle.   —— 'oueidei seigyн, his maternal uncle. 'oueidei sei-gyн̀p̀dα, his maternal uncles.

sei-gyн-'e, my or our maternal uncle.

sei-kαn (inan. III), 1. green scum; 2. (as prepound) green [sei- possibly as in 'α'-sei, little creek, sei-tsou, lake; or to be compared with sα-e-, blue, green; -kαę-n, unexplained].   —— sei-kαn gyн̀ȶ-bǫų, I saw the green scum. seikαn-t̄sou, a green stone.

sei-k'ǫu̧-ę (inan. I; sei-k'ǫu̧, dpl.), large intestine [app. dark gut: sei- as in sei-t̂ᴴ-ę, small intestine, app. white gut; k'ǫu̧, dark; -ei]. Cp. zнdl-seik'ǫu̧ę, rectum.

sei-p, rain. —— seip̧-hęį gyн̇-dα, it is a dry time, a rainless season.

sei-p (sougu'α, punct. neg.; seip̧dα, souyiн, curs.; sout̂α, fut.; sougu-'αdα', fut. neg.), 1. to fall (as rain), to rain; 2. to descend. Cp. seip, rain. —— 1. t̂oudl seip, snow fell, it snowed. seip, it rained. hǫn sougu'α, it did not rain. bou-seip̧dα, it is raining all the time. miнn so.uyiн, it is about to rain. bou-souy(i)н, it has rained a good many times. hн'gyн sout̂α', maybe it will rain. hǫn sougu'αdα', it will not rain. dἀ-bou-so.uyн, we have been having a good deal of rain. hα sout̂α', is it going to rain? hн'oue sout̂α', when is it going to rain? miнn t̂oudl so.uyiн, it is going to snow. miнn souyiн, it is going to rain. k'iнdeidl seip̧dα, it rained yesterday. —— 2. 'н̇-seip, I descended (e. g. mountain or tree). 'н̇-sout̂α', I am going to descend.

-sei-p- in t̂eidl-seip, yellowjacket, lit. tail-stinger; Mǫ'-seip̧-k̂iн, Caddo man, lit. pierced-nosed man. Cp. sei-bα, to stab.

-sei-p- in mǫn-seip̧-goup, to rub with the hand.

Seip-yнdl-dα, plcn., "Rainy Mountain;" cp. Mooney, p. 421 [rain cliff].

seip̧-mǫn-tęį (an. II; seip-mǫn-tou-p, tpl.), crayfish [said to sound like rain hand-catch].

seip̧-p'н̇n, rain-cloud.

seip̧-t'ǫu̧, rainwater.

sei-sei-gα (inan. Iᵃ; sei-sei, tpl.; sei-sei- in comp.), arrowhead [app. reduplicated form of sei- in sei-bα, to stab, gu̧ǫ-sei-dα, fish-spear; cp. possibly zei-bǎ'-t, arrow].

sei-t (an. II; sei-t̂-dα, tpl.), bear. Cp. 'ǫnhн'dei, bear); seit̂-kuαt, raccoon.

sei-t, to pick. —— pн 'нdlǎ'gα déi-seit, I picked some plums, or apples.

Soit-'ęįm-k̂iн'н, prsn., "Bear Knocking Them (people) Over;" cp. Mooney, p. 421 [k̂iн-'н, unexplained].

seit̂-kuαt (an. II; seit̂-kuαt-dα, tpl.), raccoon [seit, bear; app. kuαt, painted].

seit̂-t̂нdlt'ǫn-'н'-dα (inan. IIᵃ; seit̂-t̂нdlt'ǫn-'н', dpl.), tree sp. [app. bear bean tree]. Described as a medium sized tree bearing large pods containing black beans.

Seit̂-t̂н̧ę-dei, prsn., "Satanta;" cp. Mooney, p. 422. The name was also given as Seit̂-t̂н̧ę [white bear].

seit̂-tseiou (an. II; seit̂-tseiou-p, tpl.), pig [bear young one].

sci-t̂н-ę (app. inan. I), small intestine [app. white gut: sei- as in sei-k'ǫu̧-ę, large intestine, app. dark gut; t̂н̧ę, white]. —— seit̂н̧ę-gyн, in the bowels.

sei-t̯ɥ̥ę, eight (in an old Kiowa count).

sei-tsou (inan. I), lake [sei- as in 'ɑ̄'-sei, little creek; sei-kɑ̨-n, scum on stagnant water; -tsou as in tsou-e, water].

sęį, to smell intr., stink.   Cp. bǫʉn-sęį, to stink; 'ʜe-sęį, to be smoky; kɑ.e-sęį-'ʜ'dɑ, box-elder tree; sęį-mɥ̥ę, to smell tr. [Tewa -sʉ̨`, to smell intr.].  —— gyǹ-sęį, it stinks.

sęį-, prepound form of sęį-gɑ, peyote, cactus; sęį-gɑ̄'-t, thorn; in sęį-'ʜdlɑ̄'gɑ, prickly pear; t'ɑgue-sęį, sand bur, lit. Apache bur; etc.

-sęį- in pei-sęįhʜ', to revive intr.

sęį-'ʜdlɑ̄'-gɑ (inan. II; sęį-ʜdlɑ̄', dpl.), prickly-pear fruit.

sęį-'ʜ'-dɑ (inan. IIª; sęį-'ʜ', dpl.), willow sp. [sęį-, unexplained; 'ʜ'dɑ, wood].

sęį-'ʜ'-toudl-'ei-gɑ (inan. IIª; sęį-'ʜ'-toudl-'ei, dpl.), topweed fruit; any top [app. thorn stick stake fruit].

sęį-'ʜ'-toudl-'ei-goup (inan. IIª), topweed plant.   A stick is inserted in the marble-sized fruit and the top thus made is spun.

sęį-'ei-gɑ (inan. IIª; sęį-'ei, dpl.), sweet potato [app. thorny fruit].

sęį-gɑ (inan. II; sęį, dpl. sęį- in comp.), cactus, peyote, bur [Tewa sɥ̨́, opuntia cactus].   Cp. sǫʉn-sęįgɑ, bur, lit. sand bur; sęį-gɑ̄'t, thorn; etc.

sęį-gɑ̄'-t (inan. I; sęį, dpl.; sęį- in comp.), thorn.   Cp. sęį-gɑ, peyote, cactus.   —— sęįgɑ̄'t déi-bǫʉ, I saw one thorn.

sęį-goup (inan. IIª), cactus plant.

sęį-hɥ̨'n (an. II; sęį-hɥ̨'-dɑ, tpl.), horned toad [cactus eater].

sęį-m-, referring to secret action, in sęįm-dɑ̄'-k̯iʜ, murderer; sęįm-hʉt, thief, Kiowa Apache; sęįm-hʜ'dɑ, to whistle; sęįm-houdl, to murder.

-sęįm-'ɑ- in kɑdl-sęįm-'ɑ-k'yʜ'dlei, tadpole.

sęįm-'ɑ̄'-dɑ (inan. II; sęįm-'ɑ̨-n, dpl.), cocklebur [said to mean " sticker weed "; -dɑ].

sęį-mɥ̨-ę (sęį-mɥ̥ędɑ', fut.; sęį-mɥ̥ę, imp.), to smell tr.   Cp. sęį-yįʜ, to smell tr.   [sęį, to smell intr.; -mɥ̨-ę unexplained.]

sęįm-dɑ̄'-k̯iʜ (an. I; sęįm-dɑ̄'gɑ, tpl.), murderer.   [dɑ-, to kill.]   Cp. dɑ̄'-k̯iʜ, murderer; sęįm-houdl, to murder.

sęįm-hʉt (an. II; sęįm-hʉt-dɑ, tpl.), 1. thief; 2. mouse; 3. Sęįm-hʉt, Kiowa Apache, =T'ɑ̄'gu'e; also Sęįm-hʉt-k̯iʜ.   For "thief" the common word is sęįm-k̯iʜ, q. v. [sęį-m-, referring to secret action; -hʉ-t, excessive agentive or usitative, cp. -hʜ-p].

sęįm-hʜ'dɑ (sęįm-hʜ'deidɑ', fut.), to whistle [sęįm-, secretly, softly; hʜ'dɑ, to shout].   —— dèi-sęįmhʜ'deidɑ', I am going to whistle.

sęįm-houdl, to murder.   —— gyǹ-sęįm-houdl, I murdered him.

sęįm-k̯iʜ (s. also sęįm-k̯yɥ̨'hį'ɥ̨; sęįm-k̯yɥ̨'hyou-p, tpl.), thief.   Cp. sęįm-hʉt, also used in the sense of thief.

sęį-n (inan. I), mucus of the nose [Tewa cʉ̨, nose; cʉ̨-wɥ̨̀, mucus].

Sẹi-n-dei, name of the culture hero [sẹi-n-, unexplained; app. -dei]. Cp. Tsḥnꞧyḥþt‘α, another name for Sẹindei.

Sẹindei-’iн (an. I; Seindei-’yu-e, tpl.), member of a certain band of the Kiowa camp circle, lit. Sẹindei’s child; cp. Mooney, p. 228.

-sẹin-hн’- in t‘ọu-sẹinhн’yiн, scorpion, said to mean the one that bends his tail back.

sẹin-p‘ᾱ’-gα (s. app. also sẹin-p‘α; sẹin-p‘α, dpl.; sẹin-p‘ᾱ’- in comp.), beard-hair, coll. beard, whiskers; also applied to corn silk. —— sẹin-p‘ᾱ’gα déi-zọundα’, I am going to pull out my beard hairs.

sẹinp‘ᾱ’-dнdl (an. II; sẹinp‘ᾱ’-dнt-dα, dpl.), catfish [explained as meaning whiskers coming to surface of water: -dн-dl as in dнdl-în’dou’, to sit up straighter].

sẹin-p‘iнt-dα (inan. IIᵃ; sẹin-p‘iнdl, dpl.; sẹin-p‘iнdl- in comp.), handkerchief [mucus wiper]. —— sẹinp‘iнdα nǫ́-tн’bн-t‘ꞥ’dн’-dα, my handkerchief is wet with tears.

-sẹi-’ọu- in ’н’-sẹi-’ọu-gᾱ’t, plant sp., lit. sweet smelling plant; tsoue-sẹi-’ọu-gyн, pepper, lit. coffee-smelling [sẹi, to smell intr.; -’ọu, intensive].

sẹi-îçę-t‘нdl (inan. IIᵇ; sẹi-îçę-t‘нt-dα, tpl.), 1. pineapple; 2. fig [explained as cactus (or thorn) sleek hole]. When questioned as to why "hole" is applied, it was pointed out that canned pineapple has a hole in the center.

sẹi-yiн, to smell tr. Cp. sẹi-mнę, to smell tr. —— ’н̇-sẹiyiн, I smelt of it.

sou . . . (soudα, -soudeidα’, fut.), to sew, mend. Also in p‘ou-sou . . ., to weave (blanket). —— houdldн gyн̇t-soudα’, I am going to sew my shirt. houdldн yǫ́-sн’-dα, gyн̇t-soudα’, my shirt has a hole in it, I am going to mend it.

sou- in (mǫn-)sou-dei, finger ring; sou-dei-dα, to be on (said of ring on finger).

-sou- in ’ᾱ’-ꞧuα-sou-dei, hook on which to hang things, lit. store-away hook.

sou-dei (app. inan. I), finger ring, =mǫn-soudei, q. v.

sou-dei, to be few [sou-, unexplained; -dei]. —— tsẹigα ’éi-houtdα-dei pe.i-dou ’ǫ́-sou-dei, he is killing his horses and that is why he has only a few left.

sou-dei-dα, to be on (of ring on finger). Cp. mǫn-soudei, finger ring; sou-doup, to string. Also app. in înę-soudei-dα, to be cross-eyed.

sou-dou-p (soudeit, curs.), to string. Cp. soudei-dα, to be on (of ring on finger). —— pọugyн gyн̇t-soudeit, I am going to string the beads, =gyн̇t-pọu-soudeit. k‘iнdeidl gyн̇t-pọu-soudoup, yesterday I strung the beads.

soudlei-ꞧiн (an. I; soudlei-gα, tpl.), soldier [fr. Eng.].

-sou-e in ’ǫn-soue, foot.

sou-kou'e-dɑ, to have clap [sou-, penis; -kou-'e-, pus; dɑ]. ——
soukou'e-dɑ, he has clap.

sou-p (inan. II; sou, dpl. sou- in comp.), penis.

sou-k‘ɑe (inan. IIᵃ), foreskin.

sou-p‘ɑt̓-dɑ (inan. IIᵃ; sou-p‘ɑdl, dpl.), man's pubic hair.

sou-t̓-dɑ (inan. IIᵃ; sou-dl, dpl.), 1. wild onion sp.; 2. onion [w. sou-t-
cp. Tewa sī‘, onion; -dɑ].

-sǫu̧ in k̓ɑ'-sǫu̧, grindstone; 'ei-sǫu̧bɑ, metate. Cp. sǫu̧, to grind.

-sǫu̧, intensive adj. and verb postfix in 'ɑ'-sǫu̧, roan; 'ęi̧m-hₙ'deidɑ'-
sǫu̧, he is going to be yelling too much [cp. -'ǫu̧, intensive noun
postfix].

sǫu̧-dɑ (inan. IIᵃ; sǫu̧-n, dpl.; sǫu̧-n- in comp.), plant or tuft of grass,
coll. grass; hay.

sǫu̧-m (sǫu̧dɑ', fut.), 1. to grind; 2. to brush (hair). Cp. 'ɑdl-sǫu̧m,
hair brush, comb; 'ei-sǫu̧-bɑ, metate; k̓ɑ'-sǫu̧, grindstone; p‘ₙ-'ɑ'-
męi̧, to grind up fine. —— gyₙ-sǫu̧m, I ground it up. gyₙ-sǫu̧dɑ',
I am going to grind it. déi-sǫu̧dɑ', I am going to brush my hair,
=déi-'ɑdl-sǫu̧dɑ', = 'ɑ'dɑ dèi-sǫu̧dɑ'.

-sǫu̧-m in 'ɑdl-sǫu̧m, hair brush, comb [sǫu̧-m, to brush].

sǫu̧-n-, prepound form of sǫu̧-dɑ, grass.

sǫu̧n-'ei-gɑ (inan. IIᵃ; sǫu̧n-'ei, dpl.), single grain of oats, oats [grass
seed]. Probably also applied more generically.

sǫu̧n-guɑdl (an. II; sǫu̧n-guɑt̓-dɑ, tpl.), illegitimate child [red grass].

sǫu̧n-k̓ɑ'ₙt̓-dɑ (inan. IIᵃ; sǫu̧n-k̓ɑ'ₙdl, dpl.), basket [grass dish].
Baskets were made of the 'ₙepiₙ willow sp., it was stated.

sǫu̧n-mɑ̨'hi̧ₙ (an. II; sǫu̧n-mɑ̨'hi̧ₙ-gɑ, tpl.), owl sp. [grass owl].
Lives in the prairie grass; hence the name.

sǫu̧n-sęi-gɑ (inan. II; sǫu̧n-sęi, dpl.), grass bur [sęi-gɑ, peyote,
cactus, bur].

Sǫu̧n-tou-k̓iₙ (an. II; Sǫu̧n-tou-gɑ, tpl.), Shoshone man [grass house
man].

sǫu̧n-t̂ₙ (inan. III), buffalo grass [-t̂ₙ, unexplained, but reminding
the informant of t̂ₙ-ę, to be white].

syɑ̨-n, adv., a little. syɑ̨n-dei is the commonly used form and was
given in the examples of use, but it was stated that syɑ̨n is also
a word [cp. syₙ-n, small]. Cp. kɑ't̓-syɑ̨n, narrow; syɑ̨n-'ɑ̨mgyₙ,
to grow small; syɑ̨n-dei, a little.

syɑ̨n-'ɑ̨mgyₙ, to grow small, wane. —— p̄ɑ' syɑ̨n-'ɑ̨mdeihɑ, the
moon is growing smaller, is waning. p̄ɑ' syɑ̨n-'ɑ̨mdeit̂ɑ', the
moon is going to wane.

syɑ̨n-dei, a little [syɑ̨n; -dei]. —— kɑdl syɑ̨ndei, give me a little!
=kɑdl syɑ̨ndei 'ęi̧-'ɑ̨'! syɑ̨ndei yɑ̨́n-guɑt, I just wrote to him a
few times. syɑ̨ndei 'ęi̧-bɑ', bring me a little! syɑ̨ndei gyₙ́-t'ǫu̧dɑ',
I am going to give you a little drink.

syₙ-n (s. also si̧ₙ-n; an. II; syₙ'-dɑ, tpl.), small; child (of someone)

[Tewa tcᶇ-, to be small, child, sweetheart]. Cp. syǫn, a little; p'ᶇ'-syᶇn, to be small; 'iн, child. —— ʦou-siᶇn, a little stone. mᶇ't'ǫn-syᶇn, a little girl. mᶇ't'ǫn-syᶇdα, tpl. little girls. nǫ syᶇn, my child. syᶇ'dα déi-bǫu, I saw the children; ct. biᶇdα dèi-bǫu, I saw the adults, elders. t'ᶇ'dloup syᶇ'dα, the male children. poudl-syᶇn gyн̀-bǫu, I saw a little bug. tsęi-syᶇn, a small-sized horse.

syᶇn-guǫ-dei, afterbirth, = guǫdei, q. v.

t

-t, noun, pronoun and adj. postfix, often varying with -dl.

-t, postfix forming distributive numerals, in p'ᶇ'ou-t, three by three; etc.　Certain numeral stems take -n instead of -t.

tα', father, voc.　Cp. tαdl, father; tα'tα'e, my or our father; kα', mother, voc. —— tα', hн'tsou m-k'ǫ', father, what is your name?

tα-dl (an. I; tα-t̀-dα, tpl.), 1. father, 2. paternal uncle.　Used with 1st, 2nd and 3rd person possessive; cp. tα'tα'e, my or our father; tα', father, voc.; seigiн, maternal uncle.　No forms were recorded corresponding to 'нkα'kα, your (spl.) mother, or 'нtsα'dei, his or their mother [Tewa tᵈ, tᵈ-rᵈ, father]. —— nǫ tαdl, my or our father, = tα'tα'e. 'ǫ'gα tαdl, my or our (own) father. t'н'dliн tαdl gyн̀-bǫu, I saw the boy's father. t'н'dliн 'ęidei tαdl gyн̀-bǫu, I saw this boy's father. 'oueigα tαtdα, their fathers.

tα-e- in tαe-zout-ᶇ, to float.

tα-e-gou-p (inan. I; tα-e-dei, tpl.), g-string [w. tα-e- cp. possibly tα'-, groin; -gou-p].

tαe-zout-ᶇ, to float [tαe-, unexplained; zout-, referring to current; 'ᶇ, to come]. —— 'èi-tαe-zout-ᶇ t'ǫu-t'нe, it (the log) is floating on top of the water.

tαtα, interj., = 'αtα, q. v.

-tα̃'- in 'iн-tα̃'-mᶇ, midwife.

tα'-, groin, in tα'-'н'нt̀dα, lump on groin.

tα'-'н'нt̀dα (inan. IIᵃ; tα'-'н'нdl, dpl.), lump on groin [tα'-, evidently referring to groin].　Cp. possibly tα-e- in tαe-goup, g-string.

*tα'-'ᶇ, to chase (so.) [tα'-, unexplained; app. 'ᶇ, to come].　Tplo. correspondent 'нdlei.　Also in k'ouᵽbei-tα'ᶇ, to run. —— kαdl tα'ᶇ, he is chasing the buffalo; but 'éi-kαdl-'нdlei, he is chasing buffaloes.

tα'-bн (tα'bei, infer.), to look at.　Cp. bǫu, to see. —— dǫm déi-tα'bн, I am looking at the land. ʦou'-tα'bн, I am looking at the stone. tǫugyн 'ęi-tα'bei, he said that he saw me. tsęi tα'bн, he is looking at the horse.

-tα'-bн in kyнe-tα'bн, to go to fight.

tɑ̄'-dei adv. for a long time [tɑ̄'-, unexplained].  —— tɑ̄'dei hei̱gyн
dɑ'mei̱', I heard that he was away for a long time.

-tɑ̄-gyн, flat, mɑ̨n-tɑ̄'gyн, palm of hand [cp. Tewa θɑ́-gì, flat and
round].

tɑ̄'-tɑ-'e, my or our father. Cp. tɑ-dl, father; tɑ, father, voc.; tsɑ,
mother; kɑ̄'-kɑ-'e, my or our mother.  —— nɑ̨ tɑ̄'tɑ'e 'ę́i-dɑ, it
is my father, =nɑ̨ tɑdl 'ę́i-dɑ. nɑ̨ tɑ̄'tɑ'e dɑ́-dɑ, it is our father,
=nɑ̨ tɑdl dɑ́-dɑ.

tɑ̄'-tseidl (inan. I), goal [unexplained].

-tɑ̨' in 'ei-tɑ̨', wheat, wheat flour [Tewa tɑ̨́, seed, tɑ̨́tɑ̨́, wheat].

tɑ̨-n (inan. III), gap, mountain pass; evidently also narrowness at
waist. Cp. tɑ̨n-p'н̨'gɑ, belt.  —— tɑ̨n gyн̀t-bo̧u̧, I saw the gap.

tɑ̨n-p'н̨'-gɑ (inan. II; tɑ̨n-p'н̨, dpl.; tɑ̨n-p'н̨- in comp.), belt [gap tie;
p'н̨, to be tied; -gɑ].  —— tɑ̨n-p'н̨'gɑ déi-bo̧u̧, I saw the belt.

tɑ̨' (an. I; tɑ̨'-dɑ, tpl.), brother (woman speaking); sister (man
speaking). Cp. tsɑ̄'-tɑ̨', mother's brother.  —— hн'deidl tɑ̨'
gyн̀-bo̧u̧, I saw somebody's brother (or sister).

tɑ̨' . . . (tɑ̨'dɑ', fut.), to roast, cook. Cp. k̄ɑ̨'-tɑ̨' . . ., to fry,
lit. to grease cook. Ct. tн', to be ripe, cooked.  —— gyн̀-tɑ̨'dɑ',
I am going to roast the meat.

tн, interj. of surprise.

tн' (an. II; tн'-gɑ̄, tpl.; tн'- in comp.), eye [Tewa tsï', eye].  —— nɑ̨
tн', my eye. nɑ̨ tн'dei, my d. eyes. 'н̨m tн'dei nę́in-bo̧u̧, I saw
your eyes. 'oueidei tн'dei 'ę́i-goup, he hit me in the eyes.
k̄yн̨hi̧'н̨ pн̄'gɑ tн̨' 'н́-dɑ, the man has (only) one eye. tн'dei
nę́i-k'oup, my eyes ache.

tн', to be ripe, be cooked [Tewa tsï`, to be cooked]. Cp. 'ei-tн'-poudl,
cicada, lit. ripe fruit bug; gyн̀-tн'-bo̧u̧nmн̨e, tendril (of watermelon
vine), lit. ripe indicator, sн̄dl-tн', to be tanned with the sun;
tн'-t͡seip, to put on the fire; and possibly tɑ̨' . . ., to roast, cook.
—— heigɑ gyн̀-tн', it is already ripe. tн'-hei̱ 'ei̱-dɑ, they d. are
raw, uncooked.

tн-dl (an. II; tн-t̀-dɑ, tpl.), skunk.

tн̄dl-iн, young skunk [-'iн, dim.].

tн̄dl-tou'ekuɑt, skunk sp., evidently small striped skunk [coarsely
spotted skunk: tou'ekuɑt, coarsely spotted, blotched].

tн-e (tн'ı̃ɑ', fut.; tне, imp.), to wake intr. Cp. 'н̨'nei̱, to wake tr.
—— yн́-tне, I woke up.

tн'- in tн'-t͡seip, to put on the fire [cp. possibly tн', to be cooked].

-tн̄'- in 'н̄'-tн̄'-bɑ, drawknife.

tн'-'ɑt̀-dɑ (inan. II; tн'-'ɑdl, dpl.), eyelash [eye head-hair].

tн'-'н̄н̄t̀-dɑ (inan. IIᵃ; tн'-'н̄'нdl, dpl.), lump on eye [eye lump].

tн'-bн (inan. I), tear [tн'-, eye; -bн, unexplained].

tн'hei̱-pi̧н-gɑ (inan. IIᵃ; tн'hei̱-pi̧н, dpl.), watermelon, =sɑhyeigɑ
[raw food].

tɐ'-k̄ɋ (an. II; tɐ'-k̄ɋ'-gɑ, tpl.; tɐ'-k̄ɋ'- in comp.), eyelid [tɐ'-, eye; -k̄ɋ is perhaps dim. of k̄ɑ'- in k̄ɑ'-gyɐ, skin; cp. 'ɑ'-, prepound form of k̄ɑ'-gyɐ, skin].

tɐ'-k'ɋu-gyɐ (an. II; tɐ'-k'ɋu-gɑ'-t, tpl.), pupil of eye [black eye].

tɐ'-p'iɐt, to be one-eyed [app. to be eye holed: tɐ'-, eye; -p'iɐ-t, hole].
——— nɋ 'ę́i-tɐ'-p'iɐt, I am one-eyed. 'ɐm 'ɐdl gyɐ́-tɐ'-p'iɐt, you are one-eyed.

tɐ'-p'iɐt-k̄iɐ (tɐ'-p'iɐt-gɑ, tpl.), one-eyed man [app. eye-holed man].

tɐ'-tɑ'-guɑdl (an. II; tɐ'-tɑ'-guɑt-dɑ, tpl.), meadow lark [unexplained; app. -guɑdl, red].

tɐ'-t̄ɐę (an. II; tɐ'-t̄ɐę-mɋ, tpl.), white of eye [white eye]. ———
tɐ'-tɐę-bei gyɐ̀-bɋu, I saw the white of one eye.

tɐ'-t̄seip, to put on the fire [w. tɐ'- cp. possibly tɐ', to be cooked; t̄sei-p, to lay (so.)]. ——— k̄iɐ gyɐ̀-tɐ'-t̄seip gɑ 'ɐ̀-tsęįnhɋn, I burnt me when I put the meat on the fire.

tɐ̨' (an. II; tɐ̨'-gɑ, tpl.; tɐ̨'- in comp.), star. Cp. tɐ̨'-'eidl, morning star; tɐ̨'-goumt'ɋu, milky way, lit. star backbone; tɐ̨'-hęi'm, to be dizzy and see stars, lit. to star-die. ——— tɐ̨' k̄uɑdl p'ɐn-bei, the stars are in the sky.

tɐ̨-ę- in tɐ̨ę-k'ɋu'm, firefly.

tɐ̨-ę- in tɐ̨ę-sɑ, cross.

-tɐ̨-ę- in 'ɑ'piɐ̨-tɐ̨ę-gɑ, fish net.

tɐ̨-ę-bei-'ei-gɑ (inan. IIª; tɐ̨-ę-bei-'ei, dpl.), skunkberry [unexplained].

tɐ̨ę-bei-'ei-p'eip (inan. IIª), skunkberry bush.

Tɐ̨ębei-k̄iɐ (an. I; Tɐ̨ępei-gɑ, tpl.), name of a Kiowa order; see Mooney, p. 228 [skunkberry man].

tɐ̨-ę-k'ɋu'-m (an. II; tɐ̨ę-k'ɋu'-m-gɑ, tɐ̨ę-k'ɋu'-m-bɑ, tpl.), firefly, locally called lightning bug [unexplained].

tɐ̨-ę-sɑ (an. I; tɐ̨-ę-sɑ'-gɑ, tpl.), cross [unexplained].

tɐ̨-n-, vertex, top of head, in tɐ̨n-t̄ɋę, bald; tɐ̨n-gɋɋ-gɑ, forehead; tɐ̨n-p̄ɋę-gyɐ, vertex; etc. [unexplained]. Cp. t̄ɑp̄gɑ't, vertex.

tɐ̨n-gɋɋ-gɑ (inan. IIª; tɐ̨n-gɋ'ɋ, dpl.; tɐ̨n-gɋ'ɋ- in comp.), forehead [app. tɐ̨n- vertex, top of head; w. -gɋɋ-gɑ cp. perhaps gɋɋ-dei, horn].

tɐ̨n-p̄ɋ'ę-gyɐ (inan. III), vertex, top of head [tɐ̨n-, vertex; -p̄ɋ'ęgyɐ, in the middle of]. Cp. t̄ou-p̄ɋ'ęgyɐ, cheek.

Tɐ̨np̄ɋ'ęgyɐ-kyɐep̄ɋn-k̄iɐ (an. I; Tɐ̨np̄ɋ'ęgyɐ-kyɐep̄ɋ'dɑ, tpl.), Chinaman, = Кyɐep̄ɋn-k̄iɐ [vertex scalplock man].

tɐ̨n-t̄ɋę, bald [vertex sleek].

tɐ̨n-t̄ɋę-dɑ, to be bald [dɑ, to be].

tɐ̨n-t̄ɋę-k̄iɐ (tɐ̨n-t̄ɋę-gɑ, tpl.), bald man [-k̄iɐ, man].

tɐ̨'-'eidl, the morning star [big star].

tɐ̨'-gɋumt'ɋu, milky way [star backbone].

tꞐ'-gyн (inan. III), lard, grease [cp. possibly toꞅ-n, fat]. Cp.
kꞯ'-gyн, grease.

tꞐ'gyн-dɑ'нt̓-dɑ (inan. IIᵃ; tꞐ'gyн-dɑ'нdl, dpl.), lard bucket.

tꞐ'-heị'm, to be dizzy and see stars [to star-die].

TꞐ'-mꞐ't'ɑn (an. I; TꞐ'-mꞐ't'Ꞑ'-dɑ, tpl.    TꞐ'-m̓Ꞑt'ɑn- in comp.),
Pleiad, tpl. the Pleiades [star girl].

TꞐ'mꞐ't'ɑn-'Ꞑ'-p̄ɑ', Salt Fork of Red River; see Mooney, p. 341
[Pleiades wood river].

TꞐ'mꞐ't'ɑn-'Ꞑ'-p̄ɑ'-kꞯ'tou, Salt Fork of Red River sun dance; see
Mooney, p. 341.

tei (tei, tei-bн, tpl.), all, whole.    Cp. tei-p'ɑe, all; for -bн, tpl., cp.
pꞐ'-bн, somebodies. —— tei kꞯ'dei tou gyн̓-boꞅ, I saw all the
other houses.    'oueidei tei tsẹị'gɑ 'ẹịn-houdl, they d. killed the
tpl. horses of them tpl.    tei k'oubei bн̓-kiнdl, we live all over,
everywhere.    teibн toꞅnẹị nɑ hịнheidl, all say that he died.    tei
dɑ, or tei p̄ɑ' dɑ, it is full moon.

Teiguɑ-kiн (an. II; Teiguɑ-gɑ, tpl.), Pueblo man [fr. Span. Tegua,
Tigua].    Cp. Pouboudlн̓'-kiн, Pueblo man.

teiguɑ-t'eibei (an. II; teiguɑ-t'eibou-p, tpl.), snail [teiguɑ-, unexplained; -t'eibei as in t'eibei-dou', to adhere (to a thing)].

TeihꞐ'nẹị-kiн, Texan man [fr. Span. Tejano; -kiн].

TeihꞐ'nẹị-dɑm, Texas [dɑm, land]. —— TeihꞐ'nẹị-dɑmgyн 'н̓-dɑ,
I was down in Texas.

tei-hịн, adv., in the evening [tei- as in tei-pịн, supper, Tewa θé'-ì-,
evening; -hịн, real, cp. k'yꞐ'hịнgɑ, tomorrow, etc.]. —— teihịн
heị'm, he died in the evening.

tei-pịн, supper [evening meal: tei- as in tei-hịн, in the evening].

teip̀-dei (an. I; teip̀-gou-p, tpl.; teip̀-dei- in comp.), relative [w.
tei-p- cp. tou- in tou-dɑ, relatives; -dei].

teip̀dei-kiн (an. I; teip̀-gou-p, tpl.), man relative.

teip̀dei-mꞍ (an. I; teip̀-gou-p, tpl.), woman relative.

tei-p'ɑ-e (tpl. in the examples obtained), all [tei, all; -p'ɑ-e, unex-
plained]. —— 'oueidei tsẹ.igɑ teip'ɑe mẹ́in-houdl, we killed all
of the horses of them d.    teip'ɑe (or tei) 'н' yꞍ́-'ꞯ', give me all
the sticks!

tei-t (teidɑ', punct. neg.; teit̓dɑ, curs.; teidldɑ', fut.; teidꞯ'dɑ', fut.
neg.; teidl, imp.; teidlei', teidlheidl, infer.), to tell.    Cp. heị-teit,
to tell a story or myth, narrate. —— pꞐ'hɑndei 'ẹịm-teidlei nɑ
hị'нheidl, someone has been telling that he died.    toꞅgyн 'oueigɑ
kyꞐ'hyoup 'ẹịm-teidlheidl, he says that he told them.

tei-t̓-, ev. skin, in teit̓-doꞅ'm, under my skin, = kꞯ'gyн-doꞅ'm.

tẹị' (tẹịmɑ', punct. neg.; tẹịmɑ, curs.; tẹịdɑ', fut.; tẹịmꞯ'dɑ', fut.
neg.; tẹị', imp.), to catch.    Cp. p'ou-tẹị', to trap; zoꞅn-tẹị', to
bite; seip̀-mɑn-tẹị, crawfish. —— gyн̓-tẹị', I caught him.    mɑn-
dou gyн̓-tẹị', I caught hold of him with my hand.    zoꞅ-bн nẹ́ị-

tȩimɑ, it sticks to my teeth.   'ᴎ-tȩi-hou, go and catch him!
gyᴎ-tȩidɑ', I will catch him.

tȩi-, prepound form of tȩi-gɑ't, tȩi-hyu̧-ȩ, sinew.

tȩi-bei (an. II; tȩi-bou-p, tpl.), mountain sheep.

tȩi-gɑ'-t (inan. II; tȩi, dpl.; tȩi- in comp.), sinew, thread, cord.   Cp.
tȩi-hyu̧ȩ, sinew.

tȩi-gyᴎ (app. inan. II; tȩi-n-, tȩi-gyᴎ- in comp.), piece of ice, ice.
Cp. tȩin-p'ᴎ'gɑ't, sleet; tȩigyᴎ-k̑ɑn-hᴎtdɑ, icicle. —— tȩigyᴎ-
do̧u'm, in the ice.

tȩigyᴎ-k̑ɑn-hᴎt-dɑ, icicle [tȩigyᴎ, ice; k̑ɑn-, stiff; -hᴎ-t-dɑ, said to
refer to hanging down].

tȩi-hyu̧-ȩ (inan. II; tȩi-hi̧ᴎ, dpl.), sinew [real sinew].   Cp. tsȩibou-
tȩihyu̧ȩ, beef sinew.

tȩi-m, to pull.   Cp. k'uɑt, to pull out; 'out'ɑ'gɑ, to push. ——
gyᴎ-tȩim, I pulled it.

tȩi-m, adv., strongly. —— tȩim 'ȩim-bɑ'dei, do your best in the
race, lit. rise strongly!   = bèi-peidei!

tȩin-p'ᴎ'-gɑ'-t, sleet [fine ice].

tou (inan. I), house, tipi [Tewa tē`, house].   Cp. tou'e, room; tou-'ᴎ,
corral; etc. —— tou 'ɑe, many houses, a town.

tou-, prepound form of tou-dei, moccasin.

tou-, prepound form of tou-dɑ, relatives.

tou-'ɑ, to play the hand-game [to house play]. —— dèi-tou-'ɑ'dɑ',
I am going to play peon.

tou-'ɑtdɑ (tou-'ɑ'dliᴎ, curs.), to cry for a relative [tou- as in tou-dɑ,
relatives; 'ɑtdɑ, to cry]. —— 'ᴎ-tou-'ɑ'dliᴎ, they tpl. are having
a cry.   'ᴎ-tou-'ɑtdɑ, I am in mourning.

tou-'ɑ'-dɑ'-gyᴎ (inan. I), hand-game song.

tou-'ɑ'-gyᴎ (inan. III), hand-game [house game].

tou-'ɑ'-k̑iᴎ (an. I; tou-'ɑ'-gɑ, tpl.), hand-game player.

tou-'ᴎ (inan. I), corral [app. tou, house; -'ᴎ, unexplained].   Cp.
tsȩi-tou'ᴎ, horse corral; tsȩibou-tou'ᴎ, cow corral.

tou-b . . . (toubei, imp.), to be quiet. —— bèi-toubei, be quiet (said
to one fidgeting about)!

tou-bᴎ-, referring to straining, in toubᴎ-'oup, to strain; bo̧u̧ȩbᴎ-
toubᴎ-hɑndeigɑ, strainer.

toubᴎ-'ou-p (toubᴎ-'oudɑ', fut.), to strain [toubᴎ- as in bo̧u̧ȩbᴎ-
toubᴎ-hɑndeigɑ, strainer; 'oup, to dip up]. —— gyᴎ-toubᴎ-'oudɑ',
I am going to strain it.

tou-byu̧'ȩ (inan. III), camp circle [house circle: byu̧-'ȩ, circular].
Cp. 'ᴎ'-toubyu̧'ȩ, circular opening in the forest.

tou-dɑ (obtained in tpl. only), relatives, followers [w. tou- cp. tei-p-
in tei-b̧-dei, relative, or tou-dɑ, to pick up; -dɑ].   Cp. tou-'ɑtdɑ,
to cry for a relative. —— nɑ̧ toudɑ, my relatives.   k̑yᴎtᴎek̑iᴎ
toudɑ, the chief's followers.

tou-dα (toudeip, curs.; toudeidα', fut.; toutα'dα', fut. neg.; toudei, imp.), to pick up, gather, convene.  Cp. 'нdl-toudα, to round up (e. g. cattle). —— gyȟt-toudeidα', I am going to pick them (e. g. marbles) up. 'ę̀im-toudα, he gathered (his kinsfolk). кунтне k'yn̥'hį'нgα 'н́-toudeip gα 'н́-toųmk'į'нmн, the chiefs are going to have a meeting tomorrow to talk about certain things.

tou-dei (inan. Iᵃ; tou- in comp.), moccasin, shoe.  Cp. tou-hį'н, k'ǫ̧'ǫn, moccasin. —— toudei gyȟ-dα, they are tpl. shoes. tou-dǫųgyн, in my shoe. 'нm toudei, your shoes.  tou-hęi dα,[he is barefooted, = k'ǫ̧'ǫn-hęi dα.

tou-dl, to be soft [Tewa tɨ́-vì, to be soft].  Cp. toudl-k̂iн, to have venereal disease. —— 'éi-toudl, it (the wood) is soft.

tou-dl-, prepound form of tou-p, stick, stake.

-tou-dl in 'ouei k̂yн-toudl, duck sp.; toudl-k̂ǫ̧'dei, swallow sp.

-tou-dl-ei in k'αebн-toudlei, butterfly; k'αebн-toudlei-'ǫ̧'t̂ǫ̧e, bat.

toudl-kout-н'-dα (inan. IIᵃ; toudl-kout-н', dpl.), tree sp. [hard tipi-stake tree].

toudl-k̂ǫ̧'-dei (an. II; toudl-k̂ǫ̧'-dou-p, tpl.), swallow [tou-dl- possibly as in 'ouei k̂yн-toudl, duck sp.; k̂ǫ̧'-dei, bad].

toudl-k̂iн, to have venereal disease [app. tou-dl, to be soft; w. -k̂iн cp. -k̂α-t- in p'ou-k̂αt-dα, to be syphilitic]. —— 'н́-toudlk̂yн, I have venereal disease (of any kind).  tei k'ou-toudlk̂yн 'ɨ́n-'н'pα̃'dн, he is all crippled up (k'ou-, body).

tou-dǫų'mdei-'н'-dα (inan. IIᵃ; tou-dǫų'mdei-'н', dpl.), house post, tipi pole; woodwork inside a house [inside house stick].

tou-dǫų'mdei-k'αe (inan. IIᵃ), rug, mat [inside house cloth].

tou-'e (inan. I), room [tou, house; -'ei, postp.]. —— tou'e 'н̀-dα, I am in the room.

tou-e-gyн (tou-e-gα̃'-t, tpl.), tⁿ be blind.  Cp. touegyн-dα, to be blind; touegyн-k̂iн, blind man; touegyн-'н'dα, cattail.

touegyн-'н'-dα (inan. IIᵃ; touegyн-'н', dpl.), cattail [blind stick].  ●

touegyн-k̂iн (touegyн-gα, tpl.), blind man. —— touegyнgα, blind people, = touegα̃'t.

touegyн-dα, to be blind [dα, to be]. —— yɨ́-touegyн-dα, I am blind.

tou-'e-kuαt (tou-'e-kuαt-dα, tpl.), (coarsely) spotted, blotched.  Cp. p'ou-p, (finely) spotted. —— tнdl-tou'ekuαt gyȟ-bǫų, I saw a spotted skunk.

tou-guαdl (an. I; tou-guαt-dα, tpl.; tou-guαdl- in comp.), young man, youth [unexplained, app. guα-dl, red].  Cp. touguαdl-t̂н'dei, lizard sp.

touguαdl-t̂н'-dei (an. II; touguαdl-t̂н'-dou-p, tpl.), lizard sp. described as greenish and about 6 inches long [said to sound like young man shut in: touguαdl, young man; t̂н'-dei, shut in].

tou-hɑ' (inan. III), cliff, precipice [cp. possibly -t̂ɑ-hɑ]. Cp. k̓ɑ'gɑ, k̓ɑ'gyнp, cliff; yнdldн, cliff.

tou-hɑ̄'-'ɑ̨'mei̯, to slant tr., in tsoudl-touhɑ̄' 'ɑ̨m-dou', to soar, lit. to hold wings slanted [cp. possibly tou-hɑ' cliff].

Touhɑ̄'-syн̨n, prsn., Little cliff. See Mooney, p. 399.

tou-hi̯'н̨ (inan. Iᵃ), moccasin [tou- as in tou-dei, moccasin; hi̯'н̨, real]. Cp. tou-dei, moccasin, shoe; k'ɑ̨'ɑ̨n, moccasin.

touk̓ɑt-н̓'-dɑ (inan. II; touk̓ɑt-н̓', dpl.), oak tree [tou-k̓ɑ-t-, oak, unexplained].

touk̓ɑt-н̓'-k'ǫy̨-gɑ̄'-t (inan. II; touk̓ɑt-н̓'-k'ǫy̨-gyн, dpl.), black oak tree.

touk̓ɑt-ei-gɑ (inan. IIᵃ; touk̓ɑt-ei, dpl.), acorn [oak fruit].

tou-k'y̨н̨hi̯'н̨-dɑ, to be homesick [tou, house; k'y̨н̨'hi̯'н̨-, unexplained, cp. possibly k'y̨н̨'hi̯'н̨, tomorrow; dɑ, to be].

tou-p (inan. II; tou-dl, dpl.; tou-dl- in comp.), stick, counting-stick for keeping the count in any game, stake, tipi-stake [unexplained; cp. tou-p, handle]. Cp. 'ou-toudl-t'ei̯'m, collarbone; sɑ̄'-toup, tobacco pipe; sei̯-'н̓'-toudl-'ei-gɑ, top (to spin); t̂ɑ̨m-toup, tipi-stake; t'н̓'-toup, match.

tou-p (inan. II), handle (e. g. of a knife) [app. the same word as tou-p, stick: cp. t̂ɑ̨m-t'ǫy̨-tɑ, handle, -t'ǫy̨, stick].

tou-sǫy̨'n (inan. III), nest [grass house: tou, house; w. -sǫy̨'n cp. sǫy̨n-, grass]. Cp. guɑtou-tousǫy̨'n, bird nest. —— nɑ̨ tousǫy̨'n y̨н́-dɑ, it is my nest(s).

tou-t (toudldɑ', fut.), to send. —— heigɑ '-tout, I already sent him. gyн̀-toudldɑ', I am going to send him.

tout-goup, to flap, flutter [tou-t- as in k'ɑebн-tou-dl-ei, butterfly; goup, to hit]. —— dèi-toutgoup, I flap. dèi-t̄soudl-toutgoup, I flap my wings.

tǫy̨-, prepound form of tǫy̨-e̯, to say, talk.

tǫy̨-'ɑ̨n, to sound (of thunder) [to talk-sound]. —— 'y̨n-p̄ɑ'sout-tǫy̨'ɑ̨'deip, it is thundering. k'iнdeidl 'н̨n-p̄ɑ̄sout-tǫy̨'ɑ̨n, it thundered yesterday. y̨n-tǫy̨'ɑ̨'n, thunder!

tǫy̨-bɑ̄'-t (inan. II; tǫy̨-bн, dpl.; tǫy̨-bн- in comp.), flute, wind instrument [cp. Tewa té-ŋ, tube, flute]. Cp. 'н̓-tǫy̨-bɑ̄'t, wooden flute. t̄soudlt'ei̯'m-tǫy̨bɑ̄'t, wingbone whistle; tǫy̨bн-'н̓'dɑ, reed.

tǫy̨-bн, to go to hunt for [tǫy̨-, prepound form of dǫy̨-n, to hunt for; bн, to go]. —— k'iнdeidl 'н̀-tǫy̨bн, I went to hunt for it yesterday.

tǫy̨bн-'н̓'-dɑ (inan. IIᵃ; tǫy̨bн-'н̓', dpl.), reed [flute plant].

tǫy̨bн-dɑ'p̄н'egɑ, to play the flute [to flute sing]. —— dèi-tǫy̨bн-dɑ'p̄н'edeidɑ', I am going to play the flute.

tǫy̨bн-tou'-k̓iн (an. I; tǫy̨bн-tou'-gɑ, tpl.), bugle man [-tou'-, prepound form of dou', to have].

tǫu-ę (tǫugɑ', punct. neg.; tǫugyн, app. curs.; tǫuîɑ', fut.; tǫugɑ'îɑ', fut. neg.; tǫunęi', infer.; tǫu- in comp.), to say, talk [Tewa tü, to say]. Cp. tǫu-hǫn, to become silent; tǫu-guɑt, to write; tǫu-hęi-ḱiн, silent person; tǫu-gyн, word, language; tǫu-k'ǫ'm, to talk about; tǫu-m-k'į'н, to talk about; tǫu-pнedl, talkative person; *tǫu-zн̥n, to talk about; etc. ―― 'ę̀im-tǫuę, you say! nǫ nǫ 'н̀-tǫuîɑ', and I am going to say. 'н̀-tǫuę, I said. hǫn 'н̀-tǫugɑ', I did not say. heigɑ 'н̀-tǫuę, I already said. míнn 'н̀-tǫugyн, I am about to say. hǫn 'н̀-tǫugɑ'îɑ', I am not going to say. poue 'ę̀im-tǫuîɑ', do not say! bн̀-k'ou-tǫuę, let us say it. heiê poue bн̀-k'ou-tǫuîɑ', let us not say it. hн̄'-tsou m-tǫugyн, what did you say? hǫn hн̄yн' 'н̀-tǫugɑ', I did not say anything. hн̄'-tsou 'н̀-tǫuę, I said something. pн 'н́-tǫugyн hęi'm, some people say that he died. pн̄'-hǫndei tǫunęi' nǫ hį'н̥heidl, somebody said that he died. îɑ'-bн hɑ̄'bɑ 'ę́i-tǫuîɑ', talk into my ear, lit. close at my ear! 'н̀-houdl-dɑ tǫunęi', he said he was sick, lit. I am sick.

tǫu-guɑt, to write [to talk mark].

tǫu-guɑt-ḱiн, writer (man), author.

tǫu-gyн (inan. III; tǫu- in comp.), word, language, talk [tǫu-, to say, talk; -gyн]. ―― pн̄'gɑ tǫugyн 'н̀-îɑ', I heard one word. tǫugyн gyн̀-'œe, there are many languages. hн̄'oudei tǫugyн gyн̀-dɑ, there are several words.

tǫu-hǫn (tǫu-hɑ̄'nǫ', punct. neg.; tǫu-hǫndɑ', fut.; tǫu-hǫ'n, imp.), to become silent [to talk cease]. ―― dèi-tǫuhǫn, I shut up. hǫn déi-tǫuhɑ̄'nǫ', I did not shut up. 'ǫ'gɑ bèi-tǫuhǫ'n, you yourself shut up!

tǫu-hęi-ḱiн (an. I; tǫu-hęi-gɑ, tpl.), silent man, dumb man [tǫu-, talk; -hęi, privative; -ḱiн].

tǫu-kuɑt (inan. III), book [talk marked]. Cp. dɑ̄'-tǫukuɑt, preaching book, bible.

tǫu-kuɑtou (an. II; tǫu-kuɑtou-gɑ, tpl.), parrot [talk bird].

tǫu-ḱiн (an. I; tǫu-gɑ, tpl.), councilman (such as Mr. Delos Lonewolf is) [talk man].

tǫu-k'ǫ'm, to speak of [to talk call]. ―― nǫ dèi-tǫuk'ǫ'm-tsęi 'ɑ̄'zнîǫ'houp dèi-k'ǫ'mǫ, whenever I speak of them I call them 'ɑ̄'zнîǫ'houp.

tǫum-k'į'н (tǫum-k'į'н̥mн̥, curs.; tǫum-k'į'н̥îɑ', fut.; tǫum-k'į'н̥, imp.), to talk about, talk plain [w. tǫu-m-, cp. tǫu-, to say, talk; -k'į'н̥-, unexplained]. ―― 'н́-tǫumk'į'н̥mн̥, they are going to talk about certain things. mǫ bн̀-tǫumk'į'н̥, let us say something (and not sit silent). hн̄yǫudei 'н́-tǫumk'į'н̥mн̥, you talk just as plain as you can! k'iнdeidl 'н̀-tǫumk'į'н̥, I was talking yesterday.

tǫu-n (tǫu-dɑ, tpl.), adj., fat; as. n. (inan. III), fat [Tewa tú, meat, flesh; tú-mǫ', to be fat; cp. possibly also tн̄'-gyн, lard, grease]. Cp. tǫun-'н̄'-'eibɑ, pecan nut. ―― ḱyн̄'hį'н̥-tǫun gyн̀-bǫu, I saw

the fat man, =tǫ̨ṇ-k̓yн̩'hi̩'н̩ gyн̀-bǫ̨. k̓yн̩'hi̩'н̩-tǫ̨udα dèi-bǫ̨,
I saw the tpl. fat men.  tǫ̨ṇ gyн̀t-bǫ̨, I saw the fat.

tǫ̨ṇ-'н̩'-'н̩'-dα (inan. IIᵃ; tǫ̨ṇ-'н̩'-'н̩', dpl.), pecan tree [fat wood
tree].

tǫ̨ṇ-'н̩'-'ei-bα (inan. IIᵃ; tǫ̨ṇ-'н̩'-'ei, dpl.), pecan nut [fat wood
nut].

tǫ̨-pнedl (an. I; tǫ̨-pнet̓-dα, tpl.; tǫ̨-pнedl- in comp.), talkative
person [tǫ̨-, to say, talk; -pн-e-dl, unexplained].  Cp. tǫ̨upнedl-
t̓einei̩, mockingbird.

tǫ̨upнedl-k̓iн (an. I; tǫ̨upнet̓-dα, tpl.), talkative man.

tǫ̨upнedl-t̓einei̩ (an. II; tǫ̨upнedl-t̓einou-p, tpl.), mockingbird [talk-
ative bird].

tǫ̨-tou (inan. I), office [talk house].

tǫ̨-t‘нe (tǫ̨-t‘н̩'guα, punct. neg.; tǫ̨-t‘н̩'dα, curs.), to speak to
[tǫ̨-, to say, talk; -t‘н-e, unexplained]. —— heigα 'é̩i-bǫ̨-dei
heigα 'н̩n 'é̩i-tout‘н̩'dα, he spoke to me whenever he saw me.
'oueidei gα nн̩ hⱥn 'н̩n 'é̩it̓-tǫ̨-t‘н̩'guα yiнgyнt‘ⱥe, that man and
I do not speak together mutually.

tǫ̨-zн̩nmн̩ (curs.), to talk about, talk [tó̩-, to say, talk; -zн̩nmн̩,
unexplained]. —— hн̩'-tsou gyн̀-tǫ̨-zн̩nmн̩, what are they talking about?  yⱥ́-kα.e-tǫ̨uzн̩nmн̩, I talk Kiowa.

## t̓

t̓α, (an. I; t̓α'-dα, tpl.; t̓α'- in comp.), daughter-in-law.  Cp. yнt̓mн̩,
daughter-in-law.

t̓α' (t̓α'-t̓α', fut.; t̓α'-dei, imp.; t̓α'dei', infer.), to stay, live, be about,
go about; sometimes assuming ambulative or desiderative mg. as
postpound [Tewa θα`, to live, stay].  Cp. k‘α'-t̓α', to want to get;
t̓ⱥ'-t̓α', to be angry. —— hн̩'gi(н) 'н̀-t̓α'dei' Kα.eguα, somewhere there are Kiowas.  Tα'tα'e mн̩' t̓α'-dei, our Father (staying) in heaven.  poue 'ei̩hα' 'è̩im-t̓α'dei, don't you stay here!
'ei̩hα' bн̀-t̓α'dei, let us stay here!  'ei̩hα' 'н̀-t̓α', I am staying
right here.

t̓α' (t̓α'yα', punct. neg.; t̓α'yα, curs.; t̓α'ı̓α', fut.; t̓α'yα't̓α', fut. neg.;
t̓α', imp.), to hear [Tewa t̓õ`, to hear].  Cp. t̓α'-hнt, t̓α'-t‘нdl-dou',
to listen to; t̓α'dei, ear. —— 'н̀-t̓α', I heard it.  hⱥn 'н̀-t̓α'yα', I
did not hear it.  heigα miнn 'н̀-t̓α'yα', I am about to hear it.
'н̀-t̓α't̓α', I shall hear it.  hⱥn 'н̀-t̓α'yα't̓α', I shall not hear it.
hα 'è̩im-t̓α', did you hear it?  'è̩im-t̓α', hear it!  poue 'è̩im-t̓α't̓α',
don't hear it!  heit̓ bн̀-t̓α', let us hear it!  poue bн̀-t̓α't̓α', let us
not hear it!  hн̩'-tsou m-tǫ̨ue nⱥ hⱥn 'н̀-t̓α-t̓α'yα', I did not hear
what you said.

t̓α- t̓α'-, verb prefix, by a blow, by hitting, in hⱥ'-t̓α'-guα, iron nail;
t̓α'-gyнe, to burst forth; t̓α'-kн̩'dα, to burst by hitting; t̓α'-p‘н̩'t

. . ., to pound up; t͡ɑ'-sн't . . ., to split with wedge; t͡ɑ'-t͡нt, to chop one in two; t͡ɑ'-t'н', to chop several in two; etc. [Tewa t͡ɑ́-, by a blow].

-t͡ɑ- in kɑ'-t͡ɑ-'ǫ'mẹi, to make swim; kɑ-t͡ɑ-'e, to swim.

t͡ɑ-'ɑ-dl, five (in an old Kiowa count).

t͡ɑ-dl (an. II; t͡ɑ-t̥-dɑ, tpl.; t͡ɑ-dl- in comp.), liver, kidney. Cp. t͡ɑdl-'eidl, liver; t͡ɑdlt'ǫn, t͡ɑdl-syн̥n, kidney.

t͡ɑ-dl- in t͡ɑdl-hн̥'dɑ, to hiccough.

t͡ɑ-dl- in t͡ɑdl-kǫu̥-t͡ɑ'dlei, hawk sp.

t͡ɑdl-eidl (an. II; t͡ɑdl-biн̥-dɑ, tpl.), liver [t͡ɑdl, liver, kidney; 'eidl, to be large].

t͡ɑdl-hн̥'dɑ (t͡ɑdl-hн'doup, curs.), to hiccough [t͡ɑ-dl-, unexplained; hн'dɑ, to shout]. —— dèi-t͡ɑdl-hн̥'doup, I have hiccoughs.

t͡ɑdl-kǫu̥-t͡ɑ'dlei (an. II; t͡ɑdl-k̥ǫu̥-t͡ɑ'dlou-p, tpl.), hawk sp. [unexplained].

t͡ɑdl-syн̥n (an. II; t͡ɑdl-syн̥'-dɑ, tpl.), kidney [t͡ɑdl, liver, kidney; syн̥n, small].

t͡ɑdl-t͡ǫępout̥-gyн (app. an. II; *t͡ɑdl-t͡ǫępout̥-gɑ'-t, tpl.), kidney, =t͡ɑdlt'ǫn-pout̥-gyн, =t͡ɑdlt'ǫn-t͡ǫępout̥-gyн [t͡ɑdl, liver, kidney; t͡ǫę-pout̥-gyн, sleek and round].

t͡ɑdl-t'ǫn (an. II; t͡ɑdl-t'ǫ'-dɑ, tpl.), 1. kidney; 2. (inan. II ᵃ; also t͡ɑdl-t'ǫ'-dɑ, s.; t͡ɑdl-t'ǫn, dpl.), bean, pea (so called from its kidney-like shape) [t͡ɑdl, liver, kidney; -t'ǫn, dim.]. Cp. seit̥-t͡ɑdlt'ǫn-'н'-dɑ, tree sp.

t͡ɑdlt'ǫn-pout̥-gyн, kidney, =t͡ɑdl-t͡ɑepout̥-gyн, q. v. [round kidney].

t͡ɑdlt'ǫn-sɑhyei-gɑ (inan. II ᵃ; t͡ɑdlt'ǫn-sɑhyei, dpl.), green pea [green bean].

t͡ɑdlt'ǫn-t͡ǫępout̥-gyн, kidney, =t͡ɑdl-t͡ǫępout̥-gyн, q. v. [sleek round kidney].

-t͡ɑ-hɑ in mǫ'-t͡ɑhɑ, to be hook-nosed; k̥oup̥-t͡ɑhɑ'-sɑdl, range of mountains; t'ǫu̥-t͡ɑhɑ'-sɑdl, waterfall (sɑdl, several stand) [-t͡ɑ-, unexplained; for -hɑ see -hɑ, -hɑ'].

t͡ɑ-k̥ɑ'dɑ, to burst by hitting [t͡ɑ-, by hitting; k̥ɑ'dɑ, to burst open tr.]. Cp. t͡ɑ-k̥ɑ'dei, stallion. —— gyн̥-t͡ɑ-k̥ɑ'dɑ, I burst it open by hitting it. gyн̥-t͡ɑ-k̥ɑ'deidɑ', I shall crack it open by hitting it.

t͡ɑ-k̥ɑ'-dei (an. II; t͡ɑ-k̥ɑ'-dou-p, tpl.), stallion [cp. t͡ɑ-k̥ɑ'-dɑ, to burst by hitting].

t͡ɑ-p-, t͡ɑ'-, deer, antelope, in t͡ɑp̥-k'ɑe, buckskin; t͡ɑp̥-p'нdl, buffalo bull; t͡ɑ'-'iн, fawn; t͡ɑ'-seidl, herd of antelope [cp. t͡н-p-, deer, antelope].

t͡ɑp̥-gɑ'-t, vertex, top of head [t͡ɑ-p-, unexplained; -gɑ'-t]. Cp. tн̥n-, vertex. —— t͡ɑp̥gɑ't gyн̥-goup, I hit him on the top of the head. t͡ɑp̥gɑ't 'ẹi-goup, he hit me on the top of the head.

t͡ɑp̥-k'ɑe, buckskin [t͡ɑ-p-, t͡ɑ'-, deer, antelope; k'ɑe, skin]. Cp. t͡нp̥-t͡ou-dɑ, skin scraper, in which t͡н-p- refers to "buckskin."

t̂αɒ̀k'αe-houdl-dʜ (inan. III), buckskin shirt.  Cp. 'α̇'yʜ-houdl-dʜ, buckskin dress, lit. fringe shirt.

t̂αɒ̀k'αe-yʜe-bα (inan. Iᵃ), buckskin thong.

t̂αɒ̀-p'ʜdl (an. II; t̂αɒ̀-p'ʜt̂-dα, tpl.; t̂αɒ̀-p'ʜdl- in comp.), buffalo bull [t̂α-p-, t̂α'-, deer, antelope; -p'ʜ-dl, unexplained].  For t̂α-p-, t̂α'- of such wide reference cp. t̂α'-t̂seiou, colt.

t̂α-p̃ęi̯n-k̃oup, to part (hair) [app. t̂α-, by hitting; p̃ęi̯-n, unexplained; k̃ou-p, to lay several].  —— dèi-t̂αp̃ęi̯n-k̃uαdα', I am going to part my hair.

t̂α-p'ʜ'-d . . . (t̂α-p'ʜ'deidα', fut.), to pound up [app. t̂α-, by a blow, w. p'ʜ'-d . . . cp. p'ʜ-t̂-gyʜ, fine thin, p'ʜ'-syʜn, small].

-t̂α-p'oudl in t'ǫu̯-t̂α-p'oudl, fish, lit. split tail [t̂α-, by a blow; -p'ou-dl unexplained].

t̂α-sʜ'- (prepound form; t̂α-sʜ'dα', fut.), to split tr. (e. g. with wedge) [t̂α-, by a blow; -sʜ'- as in dα̨m-sʜ'-bα, plow; etc.].  Cp. 'ʜ'-t̂α-sʜ'-hʜ̨'-gyʜ, wedge.

-t̂αsʜ'-hǫ̨'gyʜ in 'ʜ'-t̂αsʜ'-hʜ̨'gyʜ, wedge.

-t̂αt̂-bʜ-t'ʜ in 'ou-t̂αt̂-bʜ-t'ʜ, to mock.

t̂α'-, deer, antelope; see t̂α-p-.

t̂α'-, prepound form of t̂α'-dei, ear, [cp. t̂α'-, to hear].

t̂α'-, prepound form of t̂α', to hear, in t̂α'-hʜt, t̂α'-t'ʜdl-dou', to listen to [cp. t̂α'-, ear; Tewa t̂ō', to hear].

t̂α'-, verb prefix, by a blow, by hitting, see t̂α-.

t̂α'-'ʜ (inan. III), earring [t̂α'-, ear; -'ʜ, unexplained].

t̂α'-bʜ-k'α (inan. III), earwax [t̂α'-, ear; -bʜ-; -k'α, unexplained].

t̂α'-boudl-p'iʜt (inan. III), ear hole, = t̂α̨'-t'ʜdl [w. -boudl-p'iʜt cp. boudl-p'iʜt̂-gyʜ, down in a hole].

t̂α'-d . . . (t̂α'deip, curs.), to be kind [unexplained].  —— yʜ̨-t̂α'-deip, I am kind.

t̂α'-dei (an. II; t̂α'-gα, tpl.; t̂α'- in comp.), ear [cp. t̂α', to hear].  —— nǫ̨ t̂α'dei, my ear(s).  nǫ̨ t̂α'-dǫu̯gyʜ poudl néi̯-guαn, the bug went into my ear.

t̂α'-gα, adv., away from [t̂α'-, unexplained; -gα].  —— 'iʜhα' t̂α'gα m-ǫ̨'zǫu̯n, he went away from (right) here.  p̃α'-gyʜ t̂α'gα sαt̂ tsʜn, he just came from the river.

t̂α'-gyʜ-e (t̂α'dei, curs.; t̂α'gyʜe, imp.), to burst forth [t̂α'-, by hitting; -gyʜ-e, unexplained].  —— heigα miʜn t'ǫu̯ t̂α'dei, the water is about to burst forth.  heigα t̂α'gyʜe, it (the water) already burst forth.  'ęi̯m-t̂α'gyʜe, burst forth! (said to water).

t̂α'-hʜ-t (t̂α'hʜ'dα', punct. neg.; t̂α'hʜt̂dα, curs.; t̂α'hʜdldα', fut.; t̂α'hʜ'dα'dα', fut. neg.; t̂α'hʜdl, imp.), to listen to [cp. t̂α'-t'ʜdl-dou', to listen to; t̂α', to hear; -hʜdl-, -t'ʜdl-, unexplained].  —— dèi-t̂α'hʜt, I listened.  hα̨n dèi-t̂α'hʜ'dα', I did not listen.  miʜn dèi-t̂α'hʜt̂dα, I am about to listen.  dèi-t̂α'hʜdldα', I shall listen.  hα̨n dèi-t̂α'hʜ'dα'dα', I shall not listen.  bèi-t̂α'hʜdl, listen!  poue

bėi-ꞇɑ'hнdldɑ', don't listen!   heiꞇ bėi-ꞇɑ'hнdl, let us listen!   heiꞇ
poue bėi-ꞇɑ'hнdldɑ', let us not listen!   nę́i-ꞇɑ'hнdl, listen to me.
nę́in-ꞇɑ'hнt, I listened to you.   bėiꞇei-ꞇɑ'hнdl, let us listen to him!

ꞇɑ'-'iн (an. II; ꞇɑ'-'yu-e, ꞇɑ'-'iн-gɑ, tpl.), fawn [ꞇɑ-p-, ꞇɑ'-, deer,
antelope; 'iн, dim.].   Cp. ꞇɑ'-'i(н)-yнꞇmн̨, bird sp.

ꞇɑ'-'i(н)-yнꞇmн̨ (an. II; ꞇɑ'-'i(н)-yнꞇmн̨'-gɑ, ꞇɑ̨'-'i(н)yнꞇmн̨ę-mɑ,
tpl.), bird sp., possibly the bluejay [app. fawn daughter-in-law].

ꞇɑ'-kou (ꞇɑ'-kou-gɑ, tpl.), deaf [-kou, unexplained; cp. possibly kou-t,
hard].

ꞇɑ'-kou-k̃iн (ꞇɑ'-kou-gɑ, tpl.), deaf man.

ꞇɑ'-kou-dɑ, to be deaf [dɑ, to be].  —— 'н̓-ꞇɑ'-kou-dɑ, I am deaf.

ꞇɑ'k'ɑe (an. II; ꞇɑ'k'ɑe-guɑ, tpl.), mule [said to sound like ear skin:
ꞇɑ'-, ear; k'ɑe, hide; but cp. possibly ꞇɑ-p-, ꞇɑ'-, deer, antelope,
ꞇɑᵽ-k'ɑe, buckskin].   Cp. ꞇɑ'k'ɑe-k̃iн, white man, app. mule man.

ꞇɑ'k'ɑe-, prepound form of ꞇɑ'k'ɑe-k̃iн, white man.

ꞇɑ'k'ɑe-'нdl-ɑ, to play white man cards ['нdl-ɑ, to play cards].

ꞇɑ'k'ɑe-kyнesɑ'-dei, domestic pigeon [white man dove].

ꞇɑ'k'ɑe-k̃iн (an. II; ꞇɑk'ɑe, tpl.; ꞇɑk'ɑe- in comp.), white man [app.
mule man: ꞇɑ'k'ɑe, mule; -k̃iн, man].

ꞇɑ'k'ɑe-mн̨, white woman.

ꞇɑ'k'ɑe-t'н'-bɑ, cigar [American cigar].

ꞇɑ'-poudl (an. II; ꞇɑ'-pouꞇ-dɑ, tpl.), cricket [ear bug].

ꞇɑ'-p'ɑꞇ-dɑ (inan. IIᵃ; ꞇɑ'-p'ɑdl, dpl.), hair of ears [ear body hair].

ꞇɑ'-seidl (app. an. II coll. s. used as tpl. to ꞇнp in its mg. of antelope),
herd of antelopes [ꞇɑ-p-, ꞇɑ'-, deer, antelope; possibly -sei-dl as in
seidl-dɑ, to be tangled, bushy].   —— ꞇɑ'-seidl gyн̓-boц, I saw a
herd of antelopes.

ꞇɑ'-ꞇнt, to chop one down or off [ꞇɑ'-, by hitting; ꞇн-t, to sever one].
Tplo. correspondent ꞇɑ'-t'н'.   Cp. ꞇɑ'ꞇнꞇdɑ, cut off stump.  ——
hн'teidl 'н'dɑ 'éi-ꞇɑ'ꞇнt, who cut down this tree?   déi-ꞇɑ'ꞇнt, I
cut it off (ans.).

ꞇɑ'-ꞇнt-dɑ, ꞇɑ'-ꞇн'-dɑ (inan. II; ꞇɑ'-ꞇнdl, dpl.; ꞇɑ'-ꞇнdl- in comp.),
cut-off stump [fr. ꞇɑ'-ꞇнt, to chop down].

ꞇɑ'-t'н', to chop several down or off [ꞇɑ', by hitting; t'н', to sever
several].   —— 'н' nɑ̨ gyн̓ꞇ-ꞇɑ'-t'н', I cut the tpl. trees down.

ꞇɑ'-t'нdl (inan. III), ear hole, = ꞇɑ'-boudl-p'iнt [t'н-dl, hole].  ——
ꞇɑ'-t'нdl-gyн, inside the ear hole.

ꞇɑ'-t'нdl-dou' (ꞇɑ'-t'нdl-tougɑ', punct. neg.) to listen [cp. ꞇɑ'-hн-t, to
listen to: -t'н-dl- app. hard form of -hн-dl-, -hн-t-; -dou'].  ——
dėi-ꞇɑ'-t'нdl-dou', I am listening.   hɑ̨n nę̇in-ꞇɑ'-t'нdl-dougɑ', I am
not listening to you.

ꞇɑ'-tseiou (an. II; ꞇɑ'-tseiou-p, ꞇɑ'-tseiou-gɑ, tpl.; ꞇɑ'-tseiou- in
comp.), colt, = tseiou [app. ꞇɑ-p-, ꞇɑ'-, deer, antelope; tseiou, colt,

also in bн'ou-tseiou, cat]. Cp. t͡ɑ'-'iн, fawn; t͡ɑb-p'нdl, buffalo bull.

t͡ɑ (an. II; t͡ǫ'gɑ, tpl.; t͡ǫ'- in comp.), spoon. Cp. t͡ǫ'-hịн, t͡ɑ'-t'ǫn, spoon.

t͡ɑ-, t͡ǫ'-, mean, angry, in t͡ɑ-'ǫ'zǫụn, to go off angry; t͡ɑ-'н, to feel angry; t͡ǫ'-bн, to go off angry; t͡ǫ'-hout͡нt, to go off angry; t͡ǫ'-t͡ɑ', to be angry [cp. t͡ɑ-n, to be mean; 'ǫ'-dei, to be mean; Tewa t͡ē', to be angry].

t͡ɑ-'ǫ'zoun, to go off angry ['ǫ'-zǫụn, to walk, go]. —— dèi-t͡ɑ-'ǫ'zǫụn, I went away mad.

t͡ɑ-'н, to feel angry ['н, to come]. —— nǫ 'н̇-t͡ɑ-'н, I feel angry.

t͡ɑ-ę (t͡ɑ-ę-mɑ, tpl.), smooth, sleek [Tewa 'ǫ́-nyǫ́, to be smooth]. Cp. -'ɑ'-t͡ɑ-ę, smooth; poudl-k͡ɑ'-t͡ɑę, pinacate; poue-t͡ɑę, nit; tн̇n-t͡ɑę, to be bald; t͡ɑę-k'ɑtgɑ't, knob; -t͡ɑę-poutgyн, sleek and round; t͡ɑę-p'iнt, to sweep; etc. —— 'н'-t͡ɑęmɑ, a smooth stick.

-t͡ɑę-ǫ'-bɑ (inan. IIᵃ; -t͡ɑę-'ǫm. dpl.) in 'н'-t͡ɑę-'ǫ'-bɑ, plane.

t͡ɑę-'ǫ'męi, to make smooth ['ǫ'męi, to make]. Cp. 'н'-t͡ɑę-'ǫ'-bɑ, plane. —— déi-t͡ɑę-'ǫmdɑ', I am going to make it smooth.

t͡ɑę-k'ɑt͡-gɑ'-t (inan. IIᵃ; t͡ɑę-k'ɑt͡-gyн, dpl.; t͡ɑę-k'ɑt͡-gyн- in comp.), knob [-k'ɑ-t-, unexplained; -gɑ't] tsн̇t-t͡ɑęk'ɑtgɑ't, door knob. —— t͡ɑęk'ɑtgyн-syн̇'dɑ déi-bǫụ, I saw the little knob (at end of stamen).

t͡ɑę-pout͡-gyн (t͡ɑę-pout͡-gɑ'-t, tpl.), round, lit. sleek round, in t͡ɑdl(t'ǫn)-t͡ɑępoutgyн, kidney, lit. sleek round liver(let); t͡ɑępoutgyн-ei-gɑ, cherry; t͡eidlbǫụ-t͡ɑępoutgyн, kneecap [t͡ɑę-, smooth; -pou-t-, unexplained, ev. meaning round; -gyн].

t͡ɑępoutgyн-'ei-gɑ (inan. IIᵃ; t͡н̇ępoutgyн-'ei, dpl.; t͡ɑępoutgyн-'ei- in comp.), cherry [round fruit]. —— k'ǫụ-t͡н̇ępout͡gyн-'ei-gɑ, black cherry.

t͡ɑę-p'iнdl-'н'-dɑ (inan. IIᵃ; t͡ɑę-p'iнdl-'н', dpl.), broom, =t͡ɑę-p'iнt-dɑ [smooth wipe stick].

t͡ɑę-p'iнt, to sweep [to smooth wipe]. Cp. t͡ɑęp'iнdl-'н'-dɑ, t͡ɑę-p'iнt͡-dɑ, broom. —— gyн̇t-t͡ɑęp'iнdldɑ', I am going to sweep.

t͡ɑę-p'iн̇t-dɑ (app. inan. II; t͡ɑę-p'iн-dl, dpl.) broom, =t͡ɑę-p'iнdl-'н'dɑ [smooth wiper].

-t͡ɑę-t'eidl in 'н'-t͡ɑę-t'eidl, a clearing [app. smooth cut, see -t'ei-dl].

t͡ɑ-m-, adv. prefix, first, in t͡ɑm-dɑ, to be foremost; t͡ɑm-dou', to place foremost; t͡ɑm-hyụ'ę-gɑ-, verb prepound, first; t͡ɑm-k͡ɑ, to be the first (lying); t͡ɑm-tseidl, to be the first (standing); t͡ɑm-dei, to be the first (standing); t͡ɑm-goup, to hit the first time; etc.

t͡ɑ-m- in t͡ɑm-toup, tipi pin; t͡ɑm-t'ǫụdɑ, handle.

t͡ɑ-m- in *t͡ɑm-'н̇'nęi, to measure.

t͡ɑm-'ǫn (inan. III), measure [cp. *t͡ɑm-'ǫ'nęi, to measure].

t͡ɑm'ǫn-'н'-dɑ (inan. IIᵃ; t͡ɑm'ǫn-'н', dpl.; t͡ɑm'ǫn-'н'- in comp.), measuring stick, ruler [measure stick].

\*t̑ɑm-'ɥ'neị (t̑ɑm-'ɑ̣ndɑ', fut.; t̑ɑm-'ɑ̣n- in comp.), to measure [app.
t̑ɑm-, first; -'ɑ̣'-n-eị as in t̑oudlɑ̣'-bɥ-'ɑ̣'neị, to taste of]. Cp.
t̑ɑm-'ɑ̣n, measure; t̑ɑm'ɑ̣n-'ɥ'dɑ, measuring stick.

t̑ɑm-dɑ, to be foremost [dɑ, to be]. —— 'ɥm k'ɑ̣'gyɥ gyɥ̀-t̑ɑm-dɑ,
your name is foremost.

t̑ɑm-dou', to place foremost; to be ahead; to put on (e. g. shirt)
first [dou', to hold]. —— k̑yɥ'hị'ɥ 'ei-t̑ɑm-dou', the man is at
the head (of those marching). nɑ̣ déi-t̑ɑm-dou', I am at the head
of the column. gyɥ̀t-t̑ɑm-dou'dɑ', I am going to put it (the shirt)
on first.

t̑ɑm-hyụ'ẹ-gɑ-, verb prepound, first, to begin [t̑ɑm-, first; -hyụ'ẹ-,
intensive; -gɑ]. —— 'ẹihɑ'dei 'ẹihɑ' 'ɥ̀-t̑ɑmhyụ'ẹgɑ-tsɥn, this is
the first time that I came here. heigɑ m-t̑ɑmhyụ'ẹgɑ-dɑ'p̑ɥ'egɑ,
he began to sing. heigɑ dèi-t̑ɑmhyụ'ẹgɑ-guɑn, I began to dance.
heigɑ gyɥ̀t-t̑ɑmhyụ'ẹgɑ-sɑ'deipɥ'egɑ, I began to work. k'yɥ'hị'-
ɥgɑ heigɑ gyɥ̀t-t̑ɑmhyụ'ẹgɑ-sɑ'deip̑ɥedeidɑ', tomorrow I shall
begin to work.

t̑ɑm-tou-p (inan. II; t̑ɑm-toudl, dpl.), tipi pin (used for staking
base of tipi to the ground) [possibly t̑ɑ-m-, as in t̑ɑm-t'ọudɑ,
handle; tou-p, stick].

t̑ɑm-t'ọu-dɑ (inan. IIᵃ; t̑ɑm-t'ọu, dpl.; t̑ɑm-t'ọu- in comp.), handle
(e. g. of frying pan) [t̑ɑm-, possibly as in t̑ɑm-toup, tipi pin; app.
-t'ọu, stick (cp. tou-p, stick, tou-p, handle); -dɑ]. Cp. tou-p,
handle.

t̑ɑ-n (t̑ɑ-n-gɑ, tpl.), to be mean, cross [cp. t̑ɑ-, t̑ɑ̱-, mean, angry;
'ɑ̣'-dei, to be mean]. —— tseịhị̈ɥ 'ḱn-t̑ɑn-dei '-bọụ, I saw a
cross dog. hɥ'oudei tseịhyoup béit-t̑ɑngɑ déi-bọụ, I saw several
cross dogs. 'ḱn-t̑ɑn, he is cross. 'ɥm tseịhị̈ɥ 'ḱn-t̑ɑn, your
dog is cross.

t̑ɑ̣'-, prepound referring to being angry; see t̑ɑ-.

-t̑ɑ̣'- in tsɥ'-t̑ɑ̣'-dei, weasel [said to mean resembling a prairie dog:
tsɥ, prairie dog; -dei].

t̑ɑ̣'-bɥ, to go off angry [bɥ, to go]. —— 'ɥ̀-t̑ɑ̣'-bɥ, I went (off) mad.

t̑ɑ̣'-hị̈ɥ, buffalo horn spoon [real spoon: t̑ɑ, spoon; -hị̈ɥ, real].

t̑ɑ̣'-hou-t̑ɥt, to separate and travel off angry [t̑ɑ̣'-, referring to being
angry; hou-, to travel; t̑ɥt, to sever one]. —— 'ẹịm-t̑ɑ hout̑ɥdl-
heidl, they separated and went off aggrieved.

t̑ɑ̣'-dei (an. II; t̑ɑ̣'-dou-p, tpl.), gall. —— hɥ'oudei t̑ɑ̣'doup déi-bọụ,
I saw several galls.

t̑ɑ̣'dei-sɑhyei (t̑ɑ̣'dei-sɑ'hyei-bɑ, tpl.), green [gall blue].

t̑ɑ̣'-t̑ɑ', to be angry, aggrieved, hurt in feeling, disappointed [t̑ɑ', to
be around]. —— 'ɥ̀-t̑ɑ̣'-t̑ɑ', I was aggrieved.

t̑ɑ̣'-t'ɑn (an. II; t̑ɑ̣'-t'ɑ̣'-dɑ, tpl.), spoon [t̑ɑ, spoon; -t'ɑn, dim.].

t̑ɥ-dl, to be severed, =t̑ɥt-gyɥ [cp. t̑ɥ-t, to sever; Tewa tsɑ́, to sever,
tsɑ́-ŋ, to be severed]. —— t̑ɥdl, it (a string) is broken. t̑ɥdl-heị

dα, it is not broken.  yнebα în̂dl gyн̂-bǫ̧ų, I saw the broken rope,
=yнebα t‘нîgyн gyн̂-bǫ̧ų; but yнebα t‘нîgyн gyн̂t-bǫ̧ų, I saw the
broken pieces of rope.

în̂e-gou-p (inan. IIᵃ; în̂e-dei, dpl.), cover, lid [w. în̂-e- cp. possibly
în̂’-dα, to shut; -gou-p].

în̂-p (an. II; în̂-p, tpl., deers or antelopes; but îα’-seidl, app. an. II
coll. s. used as tpl., mg. antelopes în̂-p-, îα-p-, îα’- in comp.), deer,
antelope [cp. îα-p-, îα’-, deer, antelope; Tewa îǫ‘, antelope].  ——
în̂p bн, the deer (or antelope) went.  în̂p ’éi-bн, the tpl. deer (or
antelopes) went; but îα’seidl ’éi-bн, the tpl. antelopes went.
îα’-seidl gyн̂-bǫ̧ų, I saw the herd of antelopes.

în̂p-’нdlα’-p‘eip (inan. IIᵃ), a bush sp. [deer or antelope plum bush].

în̂p-ęîbн, to go deer hunting [’ęîbн, to go hunting].

în̂p̀-gųα-dei (an. II; în̂p̀-gųα-dα, tpl.), deer antler.

în̂p̀-k‘ǫų-gyн (în̂p̀-k‘ǫų-gα’-t, tpl.), deer sp. [black deer].

în̂p̀-p‘αdl-dα, to be deer-colored [-p‘αdl-, unexplained].  ——
în̂p̀-p‘αdl-dα, he (a horse) is deer-colored.

în̂p̀-îǫų-dα, skin scraper [în̂-p-, deer, antelope, here referring to
buckskin, cp. îα’-k‘αe, buckskin; îǫų-dα, scrape].  Cp. p‘α-tǫų-dα,
fur scraper.

în̂-t (în̂’ dα’, punct. neg.; în̂tdα, curs.; în̂dldα’, fut.; în̂’dl, imp.;
în̂dlheidl, inf.), to sever one, cut one, to break a string in one
place.  Tplo. correspondent t‘н’, to sever several [cp. în̂-dl, one
is severed; t‘н’, to sever several; t‘н-î-gyн, several are severed;
Tewa tsɑ̃́, to sever, tsɑ̃́-ŋ, to be severed].  Cp. zǫų-în̂t, to bite in
two (e. g. a rope); hou-în̂t, to sever oneself from others and travel
off.  —— k‘iнdeidl yнebн gyн̂-în̂t, yesterday I broke the rope in
two.  gyн̂-în̂dldα’, I shall break it in two.  miнn gyн̂-în̂tdα, I am
about to break it in two.  hα̧n gyн̂-în̂’dα’, I did not break it in
two.  hα̧n miнn gyн̂-în̂’dα’, I am not about to break it in two.
poue ’н̂-în̂dldα’, do not break it in two!  ’н̂-în̂’dl, break it in two!
’н̂-k‘ou-în̂’dl, break it now!  heiî nα̧ bн̂t-în̂dl, let us break it in
two!  heiî poue bн̂t-în̂dldα’, let us not break it in two!  k̂yн̂’hį’н̂
în̂t nα̧ (nα̧) gyн̂-bǫ̧ų, I saw the man break it in two.  dèi-p‘iн̂-
în̂dldα’, I am going to cut across the hill, lit. I am going to cut the
hill.  k‘o.up̄α̧’ ’ę́i-în̂’dl, cut it for me right in the center!  kαdl
tęįgyн ’ę́i-în̂’dl, cut me a piece of ice!

-în̂-t-, between, in -în̂t-bн, în̂t-dα, -în̂t-gyн, between.

-în̂t-bн, postp. (-în̂t-bα’-t, tpl.), between [-în̂-t-, between; -bн,
postp., at].  —— îsou-în̂tbн, between the stones.  ’ei-în̂tbα’t,
pie, lit. between bread.

-în̂t-dα, postp., between [-în̂-t-, between; -dα].  —— k̂oup̀-în̂tdα
’н̂-tsн̧n, I came from between the two mountains.  k̂oup̀-în̂tdα
’н̂-bн̂’îα’, I am going to go between the two mountains.

t̂ht̂-gyн (t̂ht̂gα’, punct. neg.; t̂н’dlyн, curs.; t̂αt̂deit̂α’, fut.; t̂ht̂gα’t̂α’, fut. neg.); to be severed (ss.). Tpls. correspondent is t‘нt̂gyн [passive of t̂нt, to sever]. Cp. t̂нdl, to be severed. —— t̂ht̂gyн, it is broken in two. miнn t̂нdlyн, it (the rope) is about to break in two. t̂ht̂deit̂α’, it will break in two. hαn t̂ht̂gα’t̂α’, it will not be broken. k‘iнdeidl hαn t̂ht̂gα’, it did not break in two, it is not broken in two. ’н̂-t̂α’ nα yнebα ’n̂n-t̂ht̂gyн-pọụẹ, I heard the rope break. yнebα t̂ht̂gyн, the rope broke.

-t̂ht̂-gyн, postp., between [-t̂н-t-, between; -gyн]. —— mn̂’yi(н)-t̂ht̂gyн ’н̂-dei, I was standing between two women. yiн k̂oup-t̂ht̂gyн ’н̂-liнdl, I live between the two mountains. kα-t̂ht̂gyн, depression between buttocks, = zнdl-t̂ht̂gyн.

t̂н’-dα (t̂н’deidα’, fut.; t̂н’dei, imp.), to shut, shut in. Cp. *t̂н’dei, shut in. —— gyн̂t-t̂н’dα, I closed it. yn̂n-t̂н’deidα’, I am going to shut him up.

t̂α’-dou’, to be erect (ss.), in dнdl-t̂н’-dou’, to raise oneself up higher; sнt̂-dнdl-t̂н’-dou’, to stand up straight with the heat. Tpls. correspondent t‘н’-dou’ [t̂н’-, t‘н’-, app. prepound forms of hн’, to stand up; dou’].

t̂н’-gyн (t̂н’-gα’-t, tpl.), to be good. Cp. k̂α’dei, to be bad. —— tseịhịн t̂н’gyн ’ệi-dα, I have a good dog. tseịhịн ’ệi-t̂н’gyн, my dog is good. k‘iнtн t̂н’gyн, it is a nice dog. k̂yн̂’hị’н̂-t̂н’gyн, a good man. k̂yн̂’hị’н̂-t̂н’gα’t tpl. good men. gyн̂-t̂н’gyн, it is good, thanks, = ’н̂-hou, thanks. hαn gyн̂-t̂н’gyн, no good. t̂н’gyн ’èịm-dα̂’pн̂’egα, that is good singing. hα t̂н’gyн, is it a good one? hα ’н̂-t̂н’gyн, are they tpl. good fellows? ’н̂’-t̂н’gα̂’t déi-bọụ, I saw a good stick. ’н̂’-t̂н’gyн gyн̂t-bọụ, I saw tpl. good sticks.

t̂н’gyн-e, adv., well, nicely [t̂н’gyн, to be good; -ei]. —— t̂н’gyнe ’н̂-p‘oụp̂-dα, I am prettily spotted.

t̂н’-dei, shut in (t̂н’-dou-p, tpl.) [cp. t̂н’-dα, to shut in]. Cp. hα̂’-t̂н’-dou-p, piece of barbed wire (fencing); kyн̂’boudl’iн-hα̂’t̂н’dei-’eidl, sheep ranch; touguαdl-t̂н’dei, lizard sp.; t‘ọụ-t̂н’dei, dam.

t̂н’dei-dα, to be shut in.

t̂н̣ . . . (t̂н̣’mα, curs.; t̂н̣mdα’, fut.), to suck [cp. t̂н̣’meị, to suckle]. Cp. ’α̂’-t̂н̣ . . ., to suck; ’ọụ-’α̂’t̂н̣’-poudl, leech. —— ’iн-p̂α̂’gyн t̂н̣’mα, the baby is sucking. ’iн’p̂α̂’gyн t̂нmdα’, the baby is going to suck.

-t̂н̣, -t̂н̣’-, white, in k‘iн-t̂н̣’-gyн, at dawn; k̂iн-t̂н̣’-dα, to be frosty; sọụn-t̂н̣, buffalo grass [cp. t̂н̣-ẹ, to be white; Tewa t̂sн̣, to be white].

t̂н̣-ẹ (t̂н̣-ẹ-mα, t̂н̣-ẹ-guα, tpl.), to be white [-t̂н̣, white; -ei]. Cp. ’αt‘н̣-t̂н̣ẹ-mα, grain of salt; ’iн-t̂н̣ẹ, egg; goum-t̂н̣ẹ, to be striped; kyн̂’-t̂н̣ẹ, gray wolf; t̂н̣ẹ-soudei-dα, to be cross-eyed; etc.

-t̂н̣-’ẹ- in ’ousei-t̂н̣’ẹ-hyoudl, to choke to death.

t̂ḥẹ-k̂ɑ'dʜdlei, turnip [white cylindrical: w. -k̂ɑ'-dʜdl-ei cp. k̂ɑdʜdl-dɑ, to be cylindrical].

t̂ḥẹ-k'ɑ'-tẹi-gɑ'-t (inan. II; t̂ḥẹ-k'ɑ'-tẹi̡, dpl.), cotton thread [cotton cloth thread].

t̂ḥẹ-k'ɑ'-dɑ (inan. II*; t̂ḥẹ-k'ɑ', dpl.), cotton cloth [white blanket]. —— t̂ḥẹ-k'ɑ'dɑ déi-bọu̡, I saw a piece of cotton cloth. t̂ḥẹ-k'ɑ' gyʜt̂-bọu̡, I saw some cotton cloth.

t̂ḥẹ-sou-dei-dɑ, to be cross-eyed [app. t̂ḥẹ, to be white; -sou-, unexplained; -dei; -dɑ].

t̂ḥẹ-sou-dei-k̂iʜ (an. I; t̂ḥẹ-soudei-gɑ, tpl.), cross-eyed man.

t̂ḥẹ-syʜn-hʜ'-dei (inan. I; t̂ḥẹ-syʜn-dei, dpl.), dime [white small one: hʜ'-dei, thing; but for dpl. simply -dei was volunteered].

t̂ḥẹ-tou (inan. I), canvas tent [white house].

t̂ḥm-deidl (an. II; t̂ḥm-deit̂-dɑ, tpl.; t̂ḥm-deidl- in comp.), mountain lion [unexplained]. Cp. t̂ḥ'-, white, see -t̂ḥ.

t̂ḥ'-houdl, to cheat [t̂ḥ'-, unexplained; hou-dl, to kill].

t̂ḥ'-mẹi, to suckle [cp. t̂ḥ . . ., to suck]. —— gyʜ̀-t̂ḥ'mẹi, I suckled him.

tei-dʜ-tsei, to splice [tei-dʜ-, unexplained; tsei, to put one in, insert one]. —— gyʜ̀-t̂eidʜtseidɑ', I am going to splice it (e. g. a rope).

t̂eidei-'ei-gɑ (also t̂eidei-'ei-bɑ; inan. II*; t̂eidei-'ei, dpl.), (wild) grape fruit [t̂ei-dei-, unexplained; 'ei-gɑ]. Cp. k̂oudl-t'ʜp-ei-gɑ, fall grape.

t̂eidei-'ei-kuɑ'n, wild grape mush.

t̂eidei-'ei-p'eip (inan. II*), grape vine.

t̂ei-dl (an. II; t̂ei-t̂-dɑ, tpl.), buttocks, rump. Cp. p'oue-t̂eidl-'ʜdl-dʜ'-guɑn, to turn somersault; t̂eidl-kiʜdei-tsou, backward; t̂eidl-seip, yellowjacket, lit. tail stabber; t'ou-dl-, zʜ-dl, rump.

t̂eidl-'ʜ'ʜt̂-dɑ (inan. II*; t̂eidl-'ʜ'ʜdl, dpl.), lump on buttocks.

t̂eidl-bọu̡' (an. II; t̂eidl-bọ.u̡-gɑ, tpl.; t̂eidl-bọu̡'- in comp.), [w. t̂ei-dl- cp. t̂ei-p, calf of leg, possibly for t̂ei-dl-, t̂ei-t̂-, plus -p, cp. tou-p, stick, for tou-t̂-p; or possibly t̂ei-dl, buttocks; -bọu̡', unexplained].

t̂eidlbọu̡'-t̂ɑ̨ẹpout̂-gyʜ (an. II; t̂eidlbọu̡ -t̂ḥẹpout̂-gɑ'-t, tpl.), kneecap [t̂ḥẹ-pout̂-gyʜ, round].

t̂eidl-kiʜ-dei, adv., backward, on head [t̂ei-dl-, buttocks; -kiʜ-, unexplained -dei]. Cp. t̂eidl-kiʜdei-tsou, backward. —— t̂eidl-kiʜdei dei, he is standing on his head.

t̂eidl-kiʜdei-tsou, adv., backward, on head [-tsou]. —— t̂eidl-kiʜdei-tsou 'ʜ̀-'ʜ, I am walking (lit. coming) backward, = t̂eidl-kiʜdei-tsou 'ʜ̀-'ɑ̨ntsʜ'ʜ.

t̂eidl-poudl (an. II; t̂eidl-pout̂-dɑ, tpl.), pinworm.

t̂eidl-seip (an. II; t̂eidl-seip̂-dɑ, tpl.), yellow jacket [tail (or rump) stinger: -seip as in mʜ'-seip̂-k̂iʜ, Caddo man, lit. pierced-nose man; cp. seibɑ, to stab].

t̓eidlsei᷂-k‘ǫu̧-gyн (an. II; t̓eidlseip-k‘ǫu̧-gɑ’t, tpl., black hornet
[black yellow jacket].

t̓eidlsei᷂-pȩịnhн’, yellow-jacket honey.

t̓eidlsei᷂-tou (inan. I), honey comb [yellow-jacket house].

t̓ei-p (an. II; t̓ei-᷂-dɑ, tpl.), calf of leg [cp. possibly t̓ei-dl-, buttocks,
t̓ei-dl-bǫu̧’, knee].

t̓ei-t (inan. I), soft excrement. Cp. sɑ’gyн, excrement.

t̓ȩị-n (inan. IIª), hailstone. Cp. t̓ȩịn-p‘нt̓gɑ’t, sleet particle. ——
t̓ȩịn gyн̓-bǫu̧, I saw a hailstone. t̓ȩịn seip, it hailed.

t̓ȩị-nȩị (an. II; t̓ȩị-nou-p, tpl.; t̓ȩị-nȩị-t̓- in comp.), bird [cp. Tewa
tsí-ré, bird]. Cp. kuɑtou, bird; t̓ȩịnȩịt̓-tseiou, chicken; mɑnsɑ-
t̓ȩịnȩị, hummingbird, lit. thumb bird p‘eip-t̓ȩịnȩị-guɑdl, sɑ’hyei-
t̓ȩịnȩị, sн’-t̓ȩịnȩị, bird sps.; t̓ǫu̧-t̓ȩịnȩị, killdee, lit. water bird.

t̓ȩịnȩịt̓-tseiou (an. II; t̓ȩịnȩịt̓-tseiou-p, tpl.; t̓ȩịnȩịt̓-tseiou- in comp.),
chicken [domestic bird]. —— t̓ȩịnȩịttseiou᷂ nǫ̧-’ɑe, I have a lot
of chickens.

t̓ȩịn-p‘нt̓-gɑ’-t (inan. II; t̓ȩịn-p‘нt̓-gyн, dpl.; t̓ȩịn-p‘нt̓-gyн- in comp.),
sleet particle [fine hailstone]. —— t̓ȩịnp‘нt̓gyн seip, it sleeted.

t̓ȩịn-p‘н̧n (an. II; t̓ȩịn-p‘н̧’-dɑ, tpl.), name of an unidentified internal
organ [t̓ȩịn-, unexplained; -p‘н̧-ṅ, said to mean thin, cp. possibly
p‘нt̓-gyн, fine, thin].

t̓ȩịn-seip, hail [hailstone rain].

t̓ou, to be cold [cp. t̓ou-dl, snow; Tewa t̓ɪ’, to be cold]. Cp. t̓ou-p‘out,
shade; t̓ou-dɑm-, north, lit. cold country. —— gyн̓-koudou-t̓ou,
it is very cold (of weather). gyн̓-t̓ou ’ȩịhɑ’dei k‘iн, it is cold
today, = ’ȩịhɑ’dei k‘iн gyн̓-t̓ou. t̓ou, it is cold.

t̓ou-, prepound form of t̓ou-bн, face [Tewa t̓sé, face].

t̓ou-, spotted, in mɑn-t̓ou-ku‘ɑ, salamander sp. [cp. t̓ou-e-, spotted;
Tewa θu̧’-ŋ, spotted].

t̓ou-’н’нt̓-dɑ (inan. IIª; t̓ou-’н’нdl, dpl.), lump on the face.

t̓ou-bн (inan. III; t̓ou- in comp.), face [cp. t̓ou-p-; face, front, former].
Cp. t̓oubн’e, face. —— nǫ t̓oubн, my face.

t̓ou-bн-’e (inan. III), face [-’ei].

t̓oubн’-k‘ɑe (inan. IIª), cradle hood [face skin].

t̓ou-bei-bei, at the front [t̓ou-, prepound form of t̓oubн, face; -bei-bei,
postp.]. —— t̓oubeibei-zǫu̧, front tooth.

t̓ou-bei-guɑ, forward, toward the way one is facing; from now on
[t̓ou-, face; -bei, at; -guɑ, toward]. —— heit̓ béi-k‘ou-’ɑ̧’zǫu̧n
t̓oubeiguɑ, let us march forward! t̓oubeiguɑ poue ’ȩịhɑ’ hɑ̧ndei
bн̓-’ɑdlk‘ɑe-’ɑ̧mdɑ’, from now on don’t ye tpl. do anything wrong!

t̓ou-dɑm-, north [t̓ou, to be cold; dɑm, country]. Cp. sнdl-dɑm-,
south. —— t̓ou-dɑm-bei ’н̓-t̓ɑ’, I was up north. t̓ou-dɑm-gyн
’н̓-t̓ɑ’, I was up north.

t̂ou-dl (inan. I), snow [cp. t̂ou, to be cold]. —— t̂oudl-dǫu'm,
down in the snow, under the snow. t̂oudl seip, it snowed, lit.
snow-rained.

t̂ou-dl- in t̂oudl-k'yнdl-'н'dɑ, bush sp. [cp. t̂out-k'yнdl, spittle].

t̂ou-dl- in t̂oudl-ǫ', to taste good.

t̂oudl-ǫ' (t̂oudl-ǫ̧'gɑ', punct. neg.), to taste good, be sweet [t̂ou-dl-,
unexplained; -'ǫ' as in 'ǫ̧'-guɑdou'egyн, to taste good]. Cp.
t̂oudl-ǫ-'ǫ̧'mẹi, to sweeten. —— hн'-tsou, hɑ t̂oudlǫ', how (does
it taste)? does it taste good? t̂oudlɑ, it tastes good (ans.);
also it tastes sweet; ct. k̂ǫ̧'dei, it tastes bad. 'н'dlɑ' t̂oudlǫ̧'dei
'-bǫu, I saw the sweet apples. hɑn t̂oudlǫ̧'gɑ', it does not taste
good, = t̂oudlǫ̧'-hẹi dɑ.

t̂oudl-ǫ-'ǫ̧'mẹi, to sweeten [caus. of t̂oudl-ǫ', to be sweet]. ——
gyн-t̂oudlǫ̧'-'ǫ̧'mẹi, I am going to sweeten it.

t̂oudlǫ̧'-bн-'ǫ̧'nẹi, to taste of [-bн-; -'ǫ̧'nẹi as in t̂ɑm-'ǫ̧'nẹi, to
measure]. —— kiн-tsoue gyн-t̂oudlǫ̧'-bн-'ǫ̧'nẹi, I took a taste
of the soup. 'нm 'н̂-t̂oudlǫ̧'bн-'ǫ'n, taste of it! hɑn gyн-t̂oudlǫ̧'-
bн-'ǫ̧'nɑ', I did not taste of it. gyǫ̧-bou-t̂oudlǫ̧'-bн-'ɑnmɑ, I
taste of it all the time. gyн-t̂oudlǫ̧'-bн-'ɑndɑ', I shall taste
of it. gyн-t̂oudlǫ̧'-bн-'ǫ̧'nǫ̧'dɑ', I shall not taste of it. heit̂ nǫ̧
bн̂-t̂oudlǫ̧'-bн-'ǫ'n, let us taste of it.

t̂oudl-k'yнdl-'н'-dɑ (inan. IIª; t̂oudl-k'yнdl-'н', dpl.), bush sp. It
grows on the prairie and resembles sagebrush. If you break a
stem there oozes out a gum resembling spittle [cp. t̂out-k'yнdl,
spittle].

t̂oudl-t'ǫu, snow water.

t̂ou-e-, spotted, in t̂oue-guɑt, to spot; t̂oue-kuɑt, spotted [t̂ou-,
spotted, as in Tewa θụ'-ŋ, to be spotted; -ei].

t̂oue-guɑt, to spot [guɑ-t, to mark]. —— gyн-t̂oue-guɑdldɑ', I am
going to spot it.

t̂ou-kuɑt, spotted . [kuɑ-t, marked]. —— gyн-t̂oue-kuɑt, it is
spotted. tsẹi-t̂oue-kuɑt̂gɑ déi-bǫu, I saw the tpl. spotted horses.

t̂ou-p-, face, front, former, in t̂oup̂-dei, front, former; t̂oup̂-gɑ,
before; -t̂ou-p̂-t'нe, on top of; t̂oup̂-t'ei-dɑ, face powder particle
[cp. t̂ou-bн, face].        .

t̂oup̂-dei, front, former, in t̂oup̂dei-'н'-dɑ, wagon tongue; t̂oup̂dei-
k'iн, day before yesterday; t̂oup̂dei-pнe, last summer [t̂ou-p-,
face, front, former; -dei].

t̂oup̂dei-'н'-dɑ (inan. IIª; t̂oup̂dei-'н', dpl.), wagon tongue [front
pole].

t̂oup̂dei-k'iн, day before yesterday, = 'ǫ̧'kɑdl-t̂oup̂dei-k'iн [former
day].

t̂oup̂-gɑ, adv., before [t̂ou-p-, face; -gɑ]. —— t̂oup̂gɑ gyн-tǫut'нe
nǫ̧ sɑt̂ (k̂iнgyн) 'ẹi-bǫu, I spoke to him before he saw me.

-t̓ouр̀-t‘не, postp., on the surface of [t̓ou-p-, face; -t‘не, on]. ——
’ɑ̨n-t̓ouр̀t‘не, on top of the foot, = ’ɑ̨n-t‘не, mɑ̨n-t̓ouр̀t‘не, on top
of the hand. ’ɑ̨n-t̓ouр̀t‘не gyн̇t-bǫy̨, I saw the top of the foot.

t̓ouр̀-t‘eit̀-dɑ (inan. II^a; t̓ouр̀-t‘eidl, dpl.), particle of face powder,
face powder [t̓ou-p-, face; t‘eit̀-dɑ, particle of white clay]. ——
t̓ouр̀-t‘eit̀dɑ déi-bǫy̨, I saw a particle of face powder. t̓ouр̀-t‘eidl
gyн̇t-bǫy̨, I saw the face powder.

t̓ou-p̄ɑ̨’ǫgyн (inan. III), cheek, = t̓ou-p̄ɑ̨’ǫgyн-e [t̓ou-, face; -p̄ɑ̨ǫgyн,
in the middle of]. Cp. t̓ou-t‘ęi’m, cheek bone; tн̨n-p̄ɑ̨’ǫgyн, vertex,
top of head.

t̓ou-p̄ɑ̨’ę-gyн-e (inan. III), cheek, = t̓ou-p̄ɑ̨ę-gyн [-’ei].

t̓ou-p‘ou-t (inan. III), shade, shadiness [t̓ou, to be cold; -p‘ou-t,
unexplained]. Cp. kɑр̀-k‘ǫy̨gyн, shadow. —— t̓ou-p‘out gyн̇t-
bǫy̨, I saw the shade. t̓ou-p‘out̀gyн, in the shade. t̓ou-p‘ou̯t̀gyн
dèi-sɑ̄’dɑ’, I am going to sit in the shade. ’ęidei (’ǫy̨dei) t̓ou-
p‘out-hęi gyн̇-dɑ, it is not (very) shady here.

t̓ou-p‘out-dɑ, to be shady [dɑ, to be]. —— t̓ou-p‘ou̯t-dɑ, it is shady.

t̓ou-t- in t̓ou̯t-k‘yнdl, spittle.

t̓ou̯t-k‘yн-dl, spittle. Cp. t̓oudl-k‘yнdl-н̇’dɑ, bush sp. which has
gum like spittle.

Tou-t̓ɑ̄’k‘ɑe-к̃iн (an. I; t̓ou-t̓ɑ̄’k‘ɑe, tpl.), Northerner [cold or north
white man]. Ct. Sнdl-t̓ɑ̄’k‘ɑeк̃iн, Southerner.

t̓ou-t‘ęi’m, cheek bone [t̓ou-, face; cp. t̓ou-p̄ɑ̨ęgyн, cheek; t‘ęi’m,
bone.

t̓ǫy̨ . . . (t̓ǫy̨nmɑ̨, curs.; t̓oundɑ’, fut.; t̓oum, imp.), to scrape.
Cp. t̓ǫy̨-dɑ, scraper for skins. —— gyн̇-t̓ǫy̨ndɑ’, I am going to
scrape it. t̓ǫy̨nmɑ̨, he is scraping it. ’н̇-t̓ǫy̨m, scrape it!

t̓ǫy̨-dɑ (inan. II^a; t̓ǫy̨, dpl.), scraper (for hides) [t̓ǫy̨ . . ., to
scrape; -dɑ]. Cp. guɑ-t‘ǫy̨-bɑ, rib (used as a scraper); p‘ɑ̄’-
t̓ǫy̨-dɑ, fur scraper; t̓н̨р̀-t̓ǫy̨-dɑ, buckskin scraper.

t̓ǫy̨-dei-’iн (an. II; t̓ǫy̨dei-’yu-e, t̓ǫy̨dei-you-p, tpl.), mouse [unex-
plained; -’iн, dim.]. It was stated that the mouse is also sometimes spoken of as sęimhнt, thief. —— t̓ǫy̨dei-’iн ’ɑ’gɑ̄’gyн
tseidl, the mouse (“rat”) is in the well.

t̓ǫy̨dei’iн-p‘ɑdl, mouse-colored [-p‘ɑ-dl, unexplained].

t̓ǫy̨dei’iн-p‘ɑdl-dɑ, to be mouse-colored [dɑ, to be]. —— t̓ǫy̨dei’iн-
p‘ɑdldɑ̄’dei gyн̇-bǫy̨, I saw a mouse-colored one (e. g. horse).

t̓ǫy̨-gyн (inan. III; t̓ǫy̨- in comp.), shirt, article of clothing [cp. possibly Tewa tō‘, shirt]. Cp. houdl-dн, shirt, article of clothing.
—— nɑ̨ t̓ǫy̨gyн, my shirt. p‘н̨t̀gyн-t̓ǫy̨gyн, thin shirt. t‘нedei-
t̓ǫy̨gyн, coat, lit. overshirt.

t̓ǫy̨gyн̄’-poudl (an. II; t̓ǫy̨gyн̄’-pou̯t-dɑ, tpl.), body louse [shirt bug].

t̓ǫy̨-m- in t̓ǫy̨m-’не, to run away; t̓ǫy̨m-tsн̨n, to come as a fugitive.

t̓ǫy̨m-’не, to run away [-’не, to run]. —— к̃yн̄’hi̯’н̨ gyн̇-houdl
geigɑ gyн̇t-t̓ǫy̨m-’не, after I killed the man I ran away. к̃yн̄’hi̯’н̨

gyн̇-houdl-tsẹį heigα gyн̇t-ꞇǫųm-'нe, when I killed the man I ran
away. bн̇t-ꞇǫųm-'нe, let you and me run away! bн̇t-ꞇǫųm-'нe,
run away! gyн̇-ꞇǫųm-'нe, he ran away.
ꞇǫųm-tsн̨n, to come as a fugitive [tsн̨-n, to arrive]. —— ꞇǫųm-tsн̨n,
he came home as a truant or fugitive.

## t‘

-t‘α', postp., beyond, across.  Also in t‘α-e, -t‘α-e, -t‘α-p, beyond.
—— tou-'éidl-t‘α' 'н̇-tsн̨n, I came from the other side of the big
house.  p'α'-t‘α' 'н̇-kiн̇dl, I live across the river.  p'α'-t‘α' 'н̇-tsн̨n,
I came from across the river.  k‘yн̨hị'н̨gα-t‘α'-dei k‘iн tsн̨nꞇα', she
will come day after tomorrow.  k‘iнsα-t‘α', in mid afternoon, afternoon.  'ougα-t‘α', way over there.
t‘α-dl (t‘α-ꞇ-dα, tpl.), lean.  —— k‘yн̨hị'н̨-t‘αdl gyн̇-bǫų, I saw the
lean man.  k‘yн̨hị'н̨-t‘αꞇgα dèi-bǫų, I saw the lean man.  Ꝁoup̀-
k‘αe-t‘αdl, "lean elk," recent persn. of Mr. James Waldo.
t‘α-e, adv., beyond.  Also used as postp. [-t‘α', beyond; -ei].  ——
t‘αe-dei-ꞇǫųgyн, overcoat.
-t‘α-e, postp., beyond; also postfixed to the word for one hundred
in forming numerals beyond one hundred.  Also used as adv.
Cp. -t‘αe-gα, apart from.  —— 'oueigα-t‘αe hẹį'm, he died over
there.  kα'douk‘įн̨-t‘αe pн'gα, one hundred and one.
-t‘α-e-gα, postp., apart from [-t‘α-e, beyond; -gα].  —— p̄α'-t‘αegα
'н̇-kiн̇dl, I live way off from the river.
-t‘α-p, postp., beyond [-t‘α' beyond; -p].  —— p'α'-t‘αp 'н̇-bн̨nmн̨, I
am going to cross the river.  p'α'-t‘αp hiнt, he crossed to the other
side of the river.  'ẹįmgα-ꞇ‘αp bн̇-bн, let us go (up) this way!
-t‘α-ꞇ-bн- in 'н'-t‘αꞇbн-hнꞇdα, chair, said to mean "wood one sits
on" [w.  -t‘α-ꞇ- cp. t‘α'-dα . . ., t‘α-'iн . . ., to seat, t‘α'-gyн, saddle;
-bн-].  Cp. t‘α'-'н'-dα, elm tree, lit. saddle or sit tree.
t‘α-ꞇ-gα (t‘αꞇdeidα', fut.; t‘αꞇdei, imp.), to shoot [Tewa θǫ'-ŋ, to
shoot].  Cp. p'ou-t‘αꞇgα, to vent wind; mα̨n-poudl-t‘αꞇgα, to snap
the fingers.  —— zeibнꞇ-dou t‘αꞇgα, he shot him with the arrow.
'ẹį-t‘αꞇgα, he shot at me.  'н̇-t‘αꞇdei, shoot him!
t‘α'-, prepound form of t‘α'-gyн, saddle.
t‘α'-, in t‘α-'hị'н̨, very far; t‘α'-gα, far.
t‘α'-'н'-dα (inan. IIᵃ; t‘α'-'н', dpl.), elm tree [saddle tree, so called
because the wood is good for making saddles].
-t‘α'-bα, beyond, back of, in yiн-gyн'-t‘α'-bα, on both sides.  [-t‘α',
beyond; -bα', postp., at].
t‘α'-dα . . . (t‘α'dα'beidα', fut.; t‘α'dα'bei, imp.), to seat [cp. t‘α-
'iн . . ., to seat; t‘α'-gyн, saddle].  Cp. sαe, to seat.  —— heig∢
'-t‘α'dα'beidα', I am going to seat him.  'н̇-t‘α'dα'bei, seat him!

t‘ɑ’-gɑ, far [cp. t‘ɑ’-hịн, very far]. ―― t‘ɑ’gɑ ’н̓-tsн̣n, I came from way off.

T‘ɑ’-gue-k̓iн (an. II; T‘ɑ’gu’e, T‘ɑ’-gue-dɑ, tpl.), Apache man, gen. name for Apache, including Kiowa Apache [unexplained; -gu-e- app. distinct from Gu-e-gyн-k̓iн, Pawnee man; -k̓iн]. Cp. Sẹimhн̣t, Kiowa Apache.

t‘ɑ’gue-sẹi-gɑ (inan. II; t‘ɑ’gue-sẹi, dpl.), sand bur. A kind of weed that extends five feet or more along the ground, flat on the ground [Apache cactus].

t‘ɑ’-gyн (inan. III; t‘ɑ’- in comp.), saddle [cp. t‘ɑ’-dɑ . . . t‘ɑ-’н . . ., to seat].

-t‘ɑ’-gyн, postp., beyond, behind, =-gọụm-bн, q. v. [-t‘ɑ’; -gyн].

T‘ɑ’-k̓oup, Saddle Mountain, cp. Mooney, p. 424, [saddle mountain].

t‘ɑ’-hịн, farthest, very far [t‘ɑ’- as in t‘ɑ’-gɑ, far; -hịн, real, very]. Cp. k̓iн-t‘ɑ’hịн, very. ―― t‘ɑ’hịн ’oueiga ’н’dɑ, that is the farthest tree.

t‘ɑ’-hẹi’m, to be hungry, starve [w. t‘ɑ’- cp. t‘ɑ-dl, lean; hẹi’m, to die]. ―― ’н̓-t‘ɑ’-heịmн̣, I am hungry, I am starving to death. heigɑ ’н̓-t‘ɑ’-hẹi’m, I starved to death. heigɑ ’н̓-t‘ɑ’-hị’н̣t̂ɑ’, I shall starve. heigɑ ’н̓-t‘ɑ’-hị’н̣yịн, they say I was starving. nɑ̨ ’н̓-t‘ɑ’-hị’н̣heidl, I starved to death. ’ę̀im-t‘ɑ’-hị’н̣, starve! poue ’ę̀im-t‘ɑ’-hị’н̣t̂’ɑ’, do not starve! heit̂ bн̓-t‘ɑ’-hị’н̣, let us starve to death! hɑ̨n ’н̓-t‘ɑ’-heịmɑ̨, I am not hungry.

t‘ɑ’-’iн . . . (t‘ɑ’iнdɑ’, fut.), to seat [cp. t‘ɑ’-dɑ . . ., to seat]. ―― nę̀in-t‘ɑ’iнdɑ’, I am going to seat them d.

-t‘ɑ̨’ in k̓ɑ̨’nɑ̨’-t‘ɑ̨’, spider [cp. k̓ɑ̨’nɑ̨t̂-sɑp‘ouy-iн, fly].

t‘ɑ̨-n (t‘ɑ̨’dɑ’, fut.), to find. Cp. p̄ɑ’e, to lose. ―― gyн̓-t‘ɑ̨n hụ’ɑ̨n-gyн, I found it on the road. pнe gyн̓-t‘ɑ̨n, I found a watch.

-t‘ɑ̨-n (t‘ɑ̨’- in comp.) dim., in mн̣’-t‘ɑ̨n, little girl; t̂ɑdl-t‘ɑ̨n, kidney; t̂ɑdl-t‘ɑ̨’dɑ, bean; t̂ɑ̨’-t‘ɑ̨n, spoon; tsɑ̄-t‘ɑ̨’-dɑ, maternal aunt. Cp. -’н, dim.

-t‘ɑ̨’-, dim., see -t‘ɑ̨n.

t‘ɑ̨’-gɑ (inan. II; t‘ɑ̨’, dpl.; t‘ɑ̨’- in comp.) cultivated gourd fruit. Cp. koukọụ-bɑ, wild gourd fruit.

t‘ɑ̨’-goup, gourd vine.

t‘н’ (an. I; t‘ei, t‘н-gɑ, tpl.; t‘н’- in comp.), wife, woman. Cp. ’iн-t‘н’, daughter, ’iн-t‘н’-t‘ɑ̨n, brother’s daughter; t‘н’-dei, to have a wife; t‘н’-dl-iн, paternal grandmother; t‘н̣’-, app. dim., little wife, in t‘н̣’-dei, maternal grandmother; t‘н̣’-giн, paternal grandmother. ―― ’ɑ́-t‘н’-’ɑe, he had a lot of wives. nɑ̨ t‘н̣’, my wife. ’oueidei t‘ei dèi-bọụ, I saw his wives, =’oueidei t‘н’gɑ dèi-bọụ.

t‘н’ (t‘н’gu’ɑ, punct. neg.; t‘н’guɑ, curs.; t‘н’dɑ’, fut.; t‘н’gu’ɑdɑ, fut. neg.; t‘н’, imp.), to sever several, cut several. So. correspondent t̂н-t [cp. t̂н-t, to sever one; ’ɑ-t‘ɑ̨’-n, to make a clearing;

’ʜ’-îɑ̨-ę-t‘ei-dl, a clearing; and possibly -pɑ̄’-t‘ʜ̨-mɑ̨’, to be unable].
Cp. t‘ʜ̂gyʜ, several are severed. ’ɑdl-t‘ʜ’, to cut hair. ’ɑt-t‘ʜt̂-dɑ,
scalp. ’ʜ’-t‘ʜ’-bɑ, saw. îɑ̄’-t‘ʜ’, to chop several down or off.
—— gyʜ̀-t‘ʜ’, I cut them. hɑ̨n gyʜ̀-t‘ʜ’gu’ɑdɑ, I shall not cut
them. ’ʜ̀-t‘ʜ’, cut them! ’ʜ̀-t‘ʜ’-hou, go and cut them!

t‘ʜ . . ., to pierce, in dɑ̨m-t‘ʜdl, toad sp., lit. makes a hole in the
ground; k‘ǫu-t‘ʜdl, buckeye, lit. black pierce; t‘ʜdl, hole; -tʜt̂-gɑ,
borer; etc.

t‘ʜ- in t‘ʜ-e, -tʜ-e, on top.

-t‘ʜ in ’out-t‘ʜ, carrying strap of quiver, cradle, etc.

-t‘ʜ . . . in ’ǫu-t‘ʜ- . . ., to be happy.

t‘ʜɑn-gyʜ, adv., in town [t‘ʜan, fr. Eng. town; -gyʜ].   —— t‘ʜɑngyʜ
’ʜ̀-t‘ɑ’, I was in town.

t‘ʜ-dl, hole [cp. t‘ʜ- . . ., to pierce]. Cp. mɑ̨’-t‘ʜdl, nostril; îɑ̄’-
t‘ʜdl, earhole; t‘ʜdl-k‘ouᵽ-gyʜ, smallpox; -t‘ʜt̂-gɑ, borer.   ——
pįʜn ’ḱn-t‘ʜdl-dɑ, the gopher has a hole. hʜ’oudei t‘ʜdl dɑ, how
many holes are there? hʜ’oudei t‘ʜdl-gyʜ, in how many holes?

t‘ʜdl-k‘oup-, prepound form referring to smallpox [t‘ʜdl, hole, pock;
k‘oup, to pain, be sore]. Cp. pou-dɑ, to be pit marked.

t‘ʜdl-k‘ouᵽ-dɑ, to have smallpox [dɑ, to have].   —— ’ʜ̀-t‘ʜdl-
k‘ouᵽ-dɑ, I have smallpox.

t‘ʜdl-k‘oup-hęi’m, to die of smallpox [hole sore die].   —— t‘ʜdl-
k‘oup-hęi’m, he died of smallpox.

t‘ʜdl-k‘ouᵽ-gyʜ (inan. I), smallpox.

t‘ʜ-e, adv., 1. on top; 2. above. Also used as postp. [w. t‘ʜ- cp.
possibly -t‘ʜ̨, app. above, forming numerals between the tens;
-ei]. Cp. t‘ʜe-hįʜ̨, on the very top.   —— t‘ʜe ’ę́i-’ʜ’gyʜ, he was
sitting on top of me. t‘ʜe kiʜsɑ̨’dɑ déi-tseidɑ’, I am going to put
the kettle on top (of the rock rests).

t‘ʜ-e-, verb prepound, denoting accompaniment, with, after, along,
in t‘ʜe-bɑ’ to come along; t‘ʜe-dɑ, to be with; tʜhy-ɑ’, to go
along.

-t‘ʜ-e (-t‘ʜ’guɑ, punct. neg.; -tʜ’dɑ, curs.) in tǫu-t‘ʜe, to speak to
[tǫu-, to say, talk].

-t‘ʜ-e, postp., 1. on, on top of, of the surface of; 2. above. Also
used as adv. Cp. -îouᵽ-t‘ʜe, on the surface of; -mʜ̨’m, above.
—— kuɑtoubɑ t‘ǫu-t‘ʜe (or tou-mʜ̨’m) ’èi-p‘iʜhout-houkǫu’m,
the birds are flying above the water. hʜ’beí hu̧’ɑn-t‘ʜe ’ę̀im-tsʜ̨n,
on which road did you come? Cp. hʜ’bei m-tsʜ̨n, where did you
arrive? ’ɑnîouᵽ-t‘ʜe, on top of the foot. t‘ǫun-t‘ʜe yʜ̨́-k‘oup,
the small of my back aches, lit. above the tail. pʜdl-t‘ʜe (’įʜ)
hęi’m, he died (right here) on this bed. ’ʜ’ ’éi-tɑe-zout-ʜ̨ t‘ǫu-t‘ʜ̨e,
the log is floating on top of the water. tei dɑ̨m-t‘ʜe, in all the
world, lit. on top of all the ground. dɑ̨m-t‘ʜe bʜ̀-î‘ɑ, we incl.
are living on earth; cp. dɑ̨m-gyʜ bʜ̀-îɑ, we are on the ground.

'ɑdl-t'ʜe gyʜ̀-hiʜdɑ', I am going to carry it on my head.  t'ʜdliʜ
t͡sou-t'ʜe 'ʜ̩'gyʜ, the boy was sitting on the rock.  mɑ̨n-t'ʜe or
mɑ̨n-t͡oup-t'ʜe, on top of the hand.  bout͡-t'ʜe, on the belly.
t'ʜdliʜ tou-t'ʜe t͡ɑ, the boy is on top of the house.  p'iʜ-t'ʜe
'ʜ̀-hiʜdlt͡ɑ', I am going to go up to the top of the hill.  hu̩'ɑ̨n-t'ʜe,
in the trail.  t'ʜe-dei t͡ou̩gyʜ, coat, lit. top shirt.  hu̩'ɑ̨n-t'ʜe̩
zʜ'yɑ' 'ʜ̀-t͡ɑ, I live midway on the road.

-t'ʜ-'e in t͡sou-t'ʜ'e, pounding stone, hammer; hɑ̨'t͡sou-t'ʜ'e iron
hammer; k͡ɑ'gyʜ-t͡sout'ʜ'e, yucca [unexplained].

t'ʜe-bɑ', to come with, accompany [bɑ', to bring].  —— dɑ̀-t'ʜebɑ',
he came along with us.  'e̩im-t'ʜebɑ', I went with you.  gɑ̀-t'ʜebɑ',
they d. are coming along with you.  bʜ́-t'ʜebɑ', we follow him
(the chief).

t'ʜe-dei, adj. and adv., over [t'ʜe; -dei].  —— t'ʜedei t͡ou̩gyʜ, coat,
lit. overshirt.

t'ʜe-dou', to be with [dou', to hold].  —— kyʜ̩hi̩'ʜ 'oueidei 'e̩i-t'ʜe-
dou', that man is living with me.

t'ʜe-hi̩ʜ, postp., on the very top [-hi̩ʜ intensive].  —— 'ɑ̄'pi̩ʜdɑ
t'ou̩-t'ʜehi̩ʜ 'èi-kɑ̄'zeimʜ, the fishes are swimming at the very
surface of the water.

t'ʜhy-ɑ' (t'ʜhyi'ʜdɑ', fut.), to go with, accompany [hɑ', to bring].
—— 'e̩im-t'ʜhyi'ʜdɑ', I am going to accompany you.  tɑ̄'tɑ'e
ghʜ̀-t'ʜhyɑ', I went with my father.  tse̩ihi̩ʜ 'e̩i-t'ʜhyɑ', the
dog went along with me.

-t'ʜe-tsou, postp., on top [-t'ʜe; -tsou].  —— p'iʜ-t'ʜetsou 'ʜ̀-tsʜn,
I have come from the top of the hill.

-t'ʜ-'ou-t'ʜ in tse̩i-t'ʜ'out'ʜ, fox [tse̩i-, dog].

t'ʜ-p, dry [Tewa t͡ɑ', to be dry].  —— kiʜ-t'ʜp gyʜ̀-bou̩, I saw a
piece of dried meat.  kiʜ-t'ʜp gyʜ̀t-bou̩, I saw dried meat.

t'ʜ-p-, up, in hei-t'ʜp̀-tsou, upslope [t'ʜ- as in t'ʜ-e, on top; -p].

t'ʜp-ɑ̨'mei̩, to make dry [t'ʜp, dry; 'ɑ̨'mei̩, to make].  —— gyʜ̀t-
-t'ʜp-'ɑ̨'mei̩, I made it dry.  sou̩n gyʜ̀t-t'ʜp-'ɑmdɑ', I am going
to dry the hay.

t'ʜp̀-dɑ, to be dry [dɑ, to be].  —— t'ʜp̀-dɑ, it is dry.  gyʜ̀-t'ʜp̀-dɑ,
they tpl. are dry.

t'ʜp-hɑ̨n (t'ʜp-hɑ̨nhɑ', curs.; t'ʜp-hɑ̨nt͡ɑ', fut.), to dry up intr. [t'ʜp,
dry; hɑ̨n, to finish].  —— t'ou̩ t'ʜp-hɑ̨n, the water dried up.
t'ʜphɑ̨nhɑ', the water is drying up right now.  t'ou̩ t'ʜphɑ̨nt͡ɑ',
the water is going to dry up.

t'ʜp-houdl-dɑ, to be consumptive [to be dry sick].  —— 'ʜ̀-t'ʜp-
houdl-dɑ, I have the consumption.

t'ʜp-houdl-dʜ, consumption [dry sickness].

-t'ʜt͡-dɑ, borer in 'ʜ'-t'ʜt͡gɑ, auger for wood; hɑ̨'-t'ʜt͡dɑ, drill for iron;
[t'ʜ- . . ., to pierce].

-t'ʜ-t̂-dα in 'αt̂-t'ʜt̂-dα, scalp [-t'ʜt- as in t'ʜ-t̂-gyʜ, several are cut; -dα].

t'ɴ'-dou', several are erect, in dʜdl-t'ɴ'-dou', to raise selves up higher; 'ou-t'ɴ'-dou', to have the chin raised; sʜt̂-dʜdl-t'ɴ'-dou', several stand erect with the heat. Ss. correspondent t̂ɴ'-dou' [t̂ɴ'-, prepound form of hʜ', to stand up; dou'].

t'ʜt̂-gyʜ (t'ʜt̂gα', stat. neg.; prepound form app. t'ɴ'- in t'ɴ'-dα, to be cut), several are severed. Ss. correspondent is t̂ædl, t̂ʜt̂-gyʜ. The last form presupposes perhaps an unrecorded form *t'ʜdl.

t'ɴ'-, prepound form of t'ʜ', wife.

t'ɴ'-, prepound form of t'ɴ'-gα'-t, sagebrush.

t'ɴ'- in t'ʜt̂-gyʜ, several are severed; t'ɴ'-dα, several are severed.

t'ɴ'-, app. to light, in t'ɴ'-toup, match [cp. Tewa fα̃-t̂é-gì, to light fire. Cp. hiʜ-dl-b . . ., to light fire.

-t'ɴ'-bα, cigar, in mα̃'tsʜe-t'ɴ'bα, cigarette, lit. paper cigar; t̂α̃'k'αe-t'ɴ'bα, cigar, lit. white man cigar. Cp. t'ɴ'-bα̃'t, tobacco particle.

-t'ɴ'-bα, cutter, in 'ɴ'-t'ɴ'-bα, saw [t'ʜ', to cut several].

t'ɴ'-bα̃'-t (inan. II; t'ɴ'-bʜ, dpl.; t'ɴbʜ'- in comp.), particle or piece of tobacco [cp. hʜ'-b . . ., to smoke]. Cp. -t'ɴ'-bα, cigar. —— t'ɴ'bα̃'t déi-boụ, I saw a piece of tobacco. t'ɴ'bʜ gyʌ̀-boụ, I saw tobacco.

t'ɴ'bʜ'-goup, tobacco plant.

-t'ɴ'bʜ'-k̂uαdl, several sit smoking, in 'eidlk̂youp 'ei-t'ɴ-bʜ-k̂uαdl, old men sit smoking a pipe, name of the Northern Crown constellation [t'ɴ'-bʜ'-, prepound form of hʜ'-b . . ., to smoke; k̂uαdl, several sit].

-t'ɴ'-bei, carrier off, in goụm-t'ɴ'bei, chipmunk, lit. wind carries him; mα̃ntsoụ-t'ɴ'bei, hawk sp., lit. carrier off with claws; zoụn-t'ɴ'bei, tree squirrel, lit. carrier off (e. g. pecan nuts) with teeth [hʜ'bα, to lift, carry off].

t'ɴ'-dα, several are severed [t'ɴ'-, app. prepound of t'ʜt̂-gyʜ, several are severed; dα]. —— 'ʌ̀-t'ɴ'-dα, I was all cut up.

t'ɴ'-dei (t'ɴ'deideip, curs.), to have a wife [t'ʜ', wife; -dei as in k̂iʜ-dei, to have a husband. —— 'ʌ̀-t'ɴ'dei, I am married. 'ʌ̀-t'ɴ-deideip, I am going to be married.

t'ɴ-dl- in t'ɴ-dl-iʜ, boy.

t'ɴ-dl-iʜ (an. I; t'ɴ-dl-you-p, t'ɴ-dl-yu-'e, tpl. t'ɴ-dl-iʜ in comp.), youth, boy [t'ɴ-dl-, unexplained; 'iʜ, child, dim.].

t'ɴ'-dl-iʜ (an. I; t'ɴ'dl-you-p, t'ɴ'-dl-you-p̀-gα, t'ɴ'-dl-yu-'e, tpl.), paternal grandmother [cp. t'ɴ̣'-giʜ, maternal grandmother; t'ʜ', wife, woman, and possibly t'ɴ-dl-iʜ, boy]. nα̃ t'ɴ'dliʜ, my paternal grandmother. 'oueigα t'ɴ'dlyoup, their tpl. grandmothers.

t'ɴdliʜ-dαe, boy medicine; see Mooney, p. 390.

t'ꜧ'-dou', several are erect.  Ss. correspondent îꜧ'-dou' [îꜧ'-, t'ꜧ'-, app. prepound forms of hꜧ', to stand up; -dou'].

t'ꜧ'-gɑ̄'-t (inan. IIᵃ; t'ꜧ'-gyꜧ. dpl., t'ꜧ'- in comp.), sagebrush [unexplained].  Cp. t'ꜧ'-kiꜧdl, prairie chicken.  —— t'ꜧ'gɑ̄'t déi-bǫu, I saw one sagebrush plant.  t'ꜧ'gyꜧ gyꜧ̀t-bǫu, I saw sagebrush.

t'ꜧ'-kiꜧdl (an. II; t'ꜧ'-kiꜧt-dɑ, dpl.), prairie chicken [app. t'ꜧ'-, sagebrush; -kiꜧdl, dweller].

t'ꜧ'-tou-p, match [t'ꜧ'-, app. to light, cp. possibly t'ǫu, to burn intr. tou-p, stick].

-t'ꜧ, app. postp., above, forming numerals between the tens, e. g., yiꜧ-k'iꜧ pꜧ'-t'ꜧ, twenty-one, lit. two-ten one-above; yꜧ̀tsęi-k'iꜧ yꜧ̀sęi-t'ꜧ, eighty-eight, lit. eight-ten eight-above.  But the word for ten is omitted, e. g. pꜧ'-t'ꜧ, eleven (with a preceding kɑ̄'-k'iꜧ, ten, suppressed).  In the numerals beyond one hundred, -t'ɑe, beyond, is suffixed to kɑ̄'douk'iꜧ, hundred, and in one hundred-one to one hundred-nine, inclusive, -t'ꜧ is of course not added to the unit: e. g. kɑ̄'dou-k'iꜧ-t'ɑe pꜧ'gɑ, one hundred and one; but kɑ̄'dou-k'iꜧ-t'ɑe pꜧ'-t'ꜧ, one hundred and eleven [cp. possibly t'ꜧ- in t'ꜧ-e, -t'ꜧ-e, on top, above].

-t'ꜧ' in 'ꞓn-îou-t'ꜧ', to forgive; kiꜧ-t'ꜧ', to be afraid; k'ɑ̄'-t'ꜧ', to pity; k'ou▷-t'ꜧ', to suffer; p̄ei-t'ꜧ', to laugh.

t'ꜧ-ę-męi (app. an. I), a sacred fetish; see Mooney, p. 242.  The word is spelled "tɑi'me" by Mr. Mooney.  [Cp. t'ꜧęmęi, to be desolate].

t'ꜧ-ę-męi, to be desolate [unexplained; cp. t'ꜧemęi, name of a sacred fetish].  —— gyꜧ̀-t'ꜧęmęi, it is solitude, said of a lonesome place; but 'ꜧ̀-tou-k'yꜧ̄hi'ꜧdɑ, I am lonesome, homesick.

t'ꜧ-m in t'ꜧm-tsei, to bury; t'ꜧm-tseidl, to be buried; etc.

t'ꜧm-t'oun (inan. III) grave [t'ꜧ-m-, referring to burying; t'ǫu-n as in 'ɑdlhɑ̄'-t'ǫun, mine].  —— t'ꜧm-t'ǫun gyꜧ̀t-bǫu, I saw the grave.

t'ꜧm-tsei (t'ꜧm-tseidɑ', fut.), to bury [t'ꜧ-m-, referring to burying; tsei, to put in].  —— gyꜧ̀-t'ꜧm-tsei, I buried him.  gyꜧ̀-t'ꜧm-tseidɑ', I am going to bury him.  'ɑ̀-t'ꜧm-tseihou, go and bury him!

t'ꜧm-tseidl, to be buried [t'ꜧ-m-, referring to burying; tsei-dl, to be in].

t'ꜧm-tsei-dɑꞓm, (inan. II), graveyard.  —— t'ꜧmtseidɑꞓm déi-bǫu, I saw the graveyard.  t'ꜧmtseidɑꞓm gyꜧ̀-bǫu, I saw the tpl. graveyards.

t'ꜧm-tsei-k̄iꜧ (an. I; t'ꜧm-tsei-gɑ, tpl.), burier (man), undertaker [t'ꜧm-tsei, to bury; -k̄iꜧ].

t'ꜧm-tsei-yɑ', graveyard [t'ꜧm-tsei, to bury; -yɑ', at].  —— t'ꜧmtsei-yɑ' 'ꜧ̀-bꜧ'îɑ', I am going to go to the graveyard.  t'ꜧmtsei-yɑ̄'-bei-yɑ̄'-tsou 'ꜧ̀-tsꜧn, I came from the cemetery.

-t‘ʜ-n in ’ʜ’t‘ʜn, tassel (of corn).

t‘ʛ’-, app. dim. of t‘ʜ’, wife, woman, in t‘ʛ’-dei, my or our maternal grandmother; t‘ʛ’-giʜ, maternal grandmother.

t‘ʛ’- in t‘ʛ’-dʜ’-, wet; t‘ʛ’-houp, moist [cp. t‘ǫy, water].

t‘ʛ’-dʜ’-, wet, in t‘ʛ’-dʜ’-dα, to be wet; t‘ʛ’- as in t‘ʛ’-hou-p, moist; -dʜ, app. intr. verb postfix.   Cp. k‘yʜdl-, wet.

t‘ʛ’-dʜ’-dα, to be wet [dα, to be].   Cp. k‘yʜdl-dα, to be wet. ——— sęinp‘iʜdα nǫ t‘ʜ’bʜ t‘ʛ’dʜ’-dα, my handkerchief is wet with tears.

t‘ʛ’-dei, my or our maternal grandmother; cp. t‘ʛ’-giʜ, your, his, their maternal grandmother [t‘ʛ’-, app. dim. of t‘ʜ’, wife; -dei].

t‘ʛ’-gyʜ (an. I; t‘ʛ’-gyou-p, t‘ʜ’-gyou-ᵽ-gα, tpl.), maternal grand-mother, used non-possessively or with 2nd and 3rd pers. possessive; cp. t‘ʛ’-dei, my or our maternal grandmother [t‘ʛ’-, app. dim. of t‘ʜ’, wife; -giʜ, unexplained; cp. t‘ʜ’-dl-iʜ, paternal grandmother]. ——— ’oueidei t‘ʛ’giʜ, his maternal grandmother.   t‘ʛ’giʜ dǽ-dα, we d. have a maternal grandmother.

t‘ʛ’-hou-goup (t‘ʛ’hou-guαdα’, fut.), to whip [t‘ʛ’-hou-, unexplained; goup, to hit]. ——— heit bʜt-’αe-’ǫm nǫ dʜ hǫn ’ęim-t‘ʛ’hou-guαdα’, do it again and see if I don’t hit you.

t‘ʛ’-hou-p, moist [t‘ʛ’- as in t‘ʛ’-dʜ’-, wet; cp. t‘ǫy, water; -hou-p, unexplained].   Cp. t‘ʛ’-dʜ’-dα, k‘yʜdl-dα, to be wet.

t‘ʛhouᵽ-dα, to be moist [dα, to be]. ——— gyʜ-t‘ʛhouᵽdα it is moist.

-t‘ei-bei- in teiguα-t‘eibei, snail; t‘ei-bei-dou’, to adhere to [unex-plained].

t‘eibei-dou’, to adhere to [dou’]. ——— dèi-t‘eibei-dou’, I adhere, I stick to.

-t‘ei-dl in piʜ-t‘ei-dl, hip [piʜ-, unexplained; w. -t‘ei-dl cp. possibly t‘ou-dl-, rump].

-t‘ei-dl in ’ʜ’-ϯα-ę-t‘ei-dl, a clearing [cp. t‘ʜ’, to cut several].

t‘ei-p (k‘i’ʜgu’α, punct. neg.; t‘eiᵽdα, k‘i’ʜguα, k‘i’ʜboup, curs.; k‘i’ʜdα’, fut.; ki’ʜgu’αdα’, fut. neg.; k‘i’ʜ, imp.; t‘eipheidl, k‘i’ʜheidl, inf.], defective verb, 1. to go out; 2. to take out, carry out.   Cp. ’ʜdl-t‘eip, to drive out; gǫym-k‘i’ʜboup, wind is about to blow; ki(ʜ)hiʜ-t‘eip, to come out in groups; t‘ǫy-t‘eip, spring of water. ——— 1. heiga ’ʜ-t‘eip, I went out already.   hǫn ’ʜ-k‘i’ʜgu’α, I did not go out.   ’ʜ-k‘i’ʜϯα’, I am going to go out. ’ęim-k‘i’ʜ, get out!   Cp. bèi-heidei, go away from here!   2. gyʜ-t‘eip, I carried it out.   hǫn gyʜ-k‘i’ʜgu’α, I did not carry it out. gyʜ-bou-t‘eiᵽdα, I carry it out all the time, =gyʜ-bou-k‘i’ʜgu’α. gyʜ-k‘i’ʜdα’, I am going to carry it out.   ’ʜ-k‘i’ʜϯα, I am going to go outdoors.   poue ’ʜ-k‘i’ʜdα’, don’t carry him out!   heit bʜ-k‘i’ʜ, let’s carry him out!   heigα gyʜ-t‘eipheidl, I must have carried him out, =heigα gyʜ-k‘i’ʜheidl.

t‘ei-p- in t‘eip-sαe-’ʜ’dα, sunflower sp.

-t‘ei-p in t‘ǫy-t‘eip, spring of water [t‘ei-p, to go out, issue].

t‘eiꝑ-sɑe-ɦ’-dɑ (inan. IIª; t‘eiꝑ-sɑe-ɦ’, dpl.; t‘eiꝑ-sɑe-ɦ’- in comp.), sunflower sp. with flowers 6″ diam.; cp. hou-sɑm-’ɦ’dɑ, sunflower sp. with flowers 1½″ diam. [t‘ei-p-, unexplained; sɑe, green; ’ɦ’dɑ, stick, plant].

t‘ei-ṭ-dɑ (inan. IIª; t‘ei-dl, dpl.; t‘ei-dl- in comp.), particle of white earth, kaolin; one of the sites where this substance was obtained was at a little bluff at Red Stone, 6 m. n. of Anadarko. [Tewa θú’ú, white earth]. Cp. ṭou-t‘eiṭ-dɑ, face powder. —— t‘eiṭdɑ déi-bǫy, I saw a piece or particle of white earth.   t‘eidl gyɦṭ-bǫy, I saw some white earth.

t‘ęi’-m (inan. IIª; t‘ǫy-sei, dpl., but guɑ-t‘ǫy, dpl. of guɑ-t‘ęi’m, guɑ-t‘ǫy-bɑ, rib; gǫym-t‘ǫy-gɑ, tpl. of gǫym-t‘ǫy, backbone; t‘ou- in comp.), bone [cp. t‘ǫy-dei, leg, marrow].  —— Cp. t‘ǫy-sei-bɑ, bone, which likewise has its dpl. t‘ǫy-sei.

t‘ęi’-m (t‘ęi’m- in comp.), to break (off) tr. Cp. t‘ęi’m-bɦ, to go to break; t‘eimgyɦ, to be broken.  —— déi-t‘ęi’m, I broke it (the stick).

t‘ęi’m-bɦ, to go to break off tr.  —— ’ɦ-ꝁiɦ-t‘ęi’m-bɦ’îɑ’, I am going to go to get (lit. break off) firewood.

t‘ęi’m-gyɦ, to be broken (off) [t‘ęi’m, to break tr.; -gyɦ].  —— ’èi-t‘ęi’mgyɦ, it (the wood) is broken in two.

t‘ęi-n (an. II; t‘ęi-dɑ, tpl.; t‘ęi-n- in comp.), heart [cp. t‘ęin-, referring to desire]. Cp. t‘ęin-t‘ǫy, stomach; etc.  —— t‘ęin-gyɦ, in the heart.

t‘ęi-n-, referring to desire, in t‘ęin-’ɑmgyɦ, to desire; t‘ęin-dɑ, to desire [cp. t‘ęi-n, heart].

-t‘ęi’-n- in bei-t‘ęi’n-dei, never.

t‘ęin-’ɑmgyɦ (t‘ęin-’ɑ’mɦ, curs.; t‘ein-’ɑmdei, imp.), to desire intr.; to get a desire for [t‘ęin-; ’ɑmgyɦ].  —— miɦn ’ę́i-t‘ęin-’ɑ’mɦ, I am beginning to want to. heiṭ dǽ-t‘ęin-’ɑmdei, let’s want to do it!

t‘ęin-dɑ (t‘ęin-dɑ̨’mɑ’, punct. neg.; t‘ęin-dɑ’îɑ’, fut.; t‘ęindɑ’mɑ̨’îɑ’, fut. neg.), to desire intr. [t‘ęin-; dɑ].  —— ’ę́i-t‘ęin-dɑ, I want to. hɑn ’éi-t‘ęin-dɑ, I don’t want to. dǽ-t‘ęin-dɑ, we want to. hɑn ’ęi-piɦ-t‘ęindɑ̨’mɑ’, I don’t want to eat. ’ę́i-dɑ’-t‘ęindɑ, I would like to kill him. hɑn ’ę́i-dɑ’-t‘ęindɑ̨’mɑ’, I don’t want to kill him. ’ę́i-pǫy-t‘ęindɑ, I want to see.

t‘ęi-dei-p, to be asleep [cp. possibly dęi-, referring to sleep].  —— heigɑ t‘ęideip, he is asleep. heigɑ m-t‘ęideip, you’re asleep!

t‘ęin-houdl-dɦ, heart disease.

t‘ęin-p‘iɦ (inan. I; t‘ęin-p‘iɦ- in comp.), heart vein.

t‘ęin-t‘ǫy (inan. I; t‘ęin-t‘ǫy in comp.), stomach [water heart, said to be so called "because it is the place that the vomit comes from"].  ——nɑ̨ t‘ęin-t‘ǫy-gyɦ, in my stomach.

t'oubeitsei, two bits [fr. Eng.].

t'ou-dl-, rump, in t'oudl-dɑ, to cohabit with; t'ou-dl-p̄ʜ'egɑ, to cohabit with. Cp. ᵗei-dl, zʜ-dl, rump.

t'oudl-dɑ (curs.), to cohabit with. —— gyꜣ̇-t'oudl-dɑ, I am cohabiting.

t'oudl-p̄ʜ'egɑ (t'oudl-p̄ʜ'egɑ', punct. neg.), to cohabit with. —— hɑ̨n gyꜣ̇-t'oudl-p̄ʜ'egɑ', I did not cohabit.

-t'ou-e- in 'ɑdl-k̄ɑ'-t'oue-k̄iʜ, Nez Perce man; zouᵗ-bʜ-t'oue-ḡoup, to eddy.

t'ou-gyʜ-e, to go past, through. —— k̄y p̄hį'ʜ t'o̧ugyʜe 'ęim, a man passed by there. ᵗʜp 'ęi-t'ougyʜe zeibʜ-dou, the deer was pierced through by me with an arrow.

-t'ou-t, possibly the hardened form of hou-t-, to go, travel, in 'ɑ̨n-t'out-'ʜ'dɑ, ladder; 'ei-p'ʜe-'ʜdl-t'out, corn cultivator; t'o̧u-pɑ̄'-t'out, pump.

t'ou-yʜ (t'ouyiʜᵗɑ', fut.), to go, travel [cp. hou-, -hou, to go]. —— gue t'ouyʜ, he is traveling behind (us). 'ꜣ̇-t'ouyʜ, I am walking around. t'ʜ' 'ęi-hęi'm hei k̄iʜgyʜ 'ꜣ̇-t'ouyʜ, when my wife died, I went traveling. heigɑ 'ꜣ̇-t'ouyiʜᵗɑ', I am going to go traveling.

t'o̧u (inan. I; t'o̧u- in comp.), water [the informants did not assent to Kiowa-Apache origin for this word; cp. t'o̧u-m, to drink; t'ʜ'-dʜ'-, wet; t'ʜ'-houp, moist; and possibly tsoue, water]. Cp. p̄ɑ', river; 'ɑ-, 'ɑ'-, water; dɑ̨m-'ɑ̨n-t'o̧u, ocean. —— mɑ̨ t'o̧u dɑ, it looks like water.

t'o̧u, to burn intr. —— p'iʜ t'o̧u, the fire was burning.

t'o̧u- . . ., to cause to drink [cp. t'o̧u-m, to drink]. —— syɑ̨ndei gyꜣ̇-t'o̧udɑ', I am going to give you a little drink.

t'o̧u- in t'o̧u-p'ʜ- . . . to arrest.

-t'o̧u, stick, club, in 'ʜ'-t'o̧u, wooden club; hɑ̨'-t'o̧u, axe. Cp. -t'o̧u-bɑ, stem; t'o̧u-ę, stick; ᵗɑ̨m-t'o̧u-dɑ, handle.

-t'o̧u in k'ɑ'-t'o̧u, shoulder.

t'o̧u-'ɑdlk'ɑe, whisky [crazy water].

t'o̧u-'ɑdlk'ɑe-goup, mescal plant [whisky plant].

t'o̧u-'ɑdlso̧u-m (an. II; t'o̧u-'ɑdlso̧u-gɑ, tpl.), bone comb.

t'o̧u'ɑ'-k̄ou- (inan. III), shore, in t'o̧u-'ɑ'k̄ou-bʜ, t'o̧u-'ɑ'k̄ou-bei, at the shore. —— t'o̧u-'ɑ'k̄ou-bʜ gyꜣ̇ᵗ-bo̧u, I saw the shore.

t'o̧u-'ɑe-poudl, (an. II; t'o̧u-'ɑe-p'ouᵗ-dɑ, tpl.), centipede [leg many bug].

t'o̧u-'ʜ-'ɑ̨'-mɑ̨ (inan. II; t'o̧u-'ʜ-'ɑ̨'-mɑ̨'-gɑ, tpl.), lemon [sour juice (?): to̧u, water, juice; -'ʜ-'ɑ̨'-, app. sour, -'ʜ-, unexplained, -'ɑ̨'-, to be sweet; -mɑ̨]. Cp. 'ei-guɑᵗ-k̄ou-dɑ, lemon, lit. yellow fruit; t'o̧u-ᵗoudlɑ̨'-bɑ, orange, lit. sweet juice.

-t'o̧u-bɑ, stem, in goup̄-t'o̧u-bɑ, stem [t'o̧u, stick].

t'ǫụ-bout (inan. II; t'ou-bouṫ-dα, tpl.), shin [t'ǫụ-, leg; w. -bou-t
cp. -bou-dl- in 'ǫn-bн-boudl-t'ẹim, ankle process].  —— t'ǫụ
bouṫdα déi-bǫụ, I saw the shins.

-t'ǫụ-dα in ṫǫm-t'ǫụdα, handle [cp. -t'ǫụ, stick].

t'ǫụ-dei (an. II; t'ǫụ-gα, tpl.; t'ǫụ- in comp.), 1. leg (from hip to
foot); 2. marrow [cp. t'ẹi-m, t'ǫụ-sei, bone]. Cp. pα̇'-t'ǫụdei,
thigh; t'ǫụ-p'αṫdα, leg hair; etc.  —— t'ǫụ-dǫụ'm,̣ in the leg.
t'ǫụdei gyн̇-pαdldα', I am going to eat the marrow.  t'ǫụdei gyн̇-
к̃iнdα', I am going to break open the marrow.

t'ǫụ-dǫụ'm-dei (an. II; t'ǫụ-dǫụ'm-gα, tpl.); beaver, lit. the one
under the water, = pou. [t'ǫụ; -dǫụ'm; -dei].

t'ǫụ-e (inan. IIª; -t'ǫụ, dpl.; t'ǫụ- in comp.), stick, club [cp. -t'ǫụ,
club, stick].  Cp. kǫụm-'α̇'-t'ǫụe, shinney stick; pαdl-k'α-t'ǫụe,
drumstick.

t'ǫụ-'ei (app. inan. IIª, obtained in dpl. only), water cress [water
fruit].

t'ǫụ-gα, adv., long ago [t'ǫụ-, unexplained; -gα].  Cp. t'ǫụ-gα-e-,
old time.  —— tα̇tα'e t'ǫụgα hị'н̇heidl, my father died long ago.
t'ǫụgα gyн̇-bǫụnmα̣, I saw him long ago.  heigα gyн̇-к̃αdlsei-kα̣
t'ǫụgα, I glued it some time ago.

t'ǫụ-gα-e-, early, old time, in t'ǫụgαe-p'н̇'toup, old time cradle
[t'ǫụgα,; -ei].

t'ǫụgαe-p'н̇'tou-p, old fashioned cradle.

-t'ǫụ-goup, hitter with a stick, in zeiꝑ-t'ǫụ-goup, prsn., lit. hitter
with a bow as a club.

t'ǫụ-hнdl, having one leg short, lame.  Also T'ǫụhнdl, prsn. of Mrs.
Laura D. Pedrick, [t'ǫụ-, leg; -hн-dl, unexplained].

t'ǫụ-hнdl-dα, to have one leg short, be lame.  —— 'н̇-t'ǫụhнdl-dα,
I am lame thus.

t'ǫụhнdl-к̃iн (an. I; t'ǫụhнṫ-dα, tpl.), lame man.

t'ǫụ-hẹi'm, to be thirsty [app. to drink die; w. t'ǫụ- cp. t'ǫụm, to
drink; hẹi'm, to die].  Cp. t'ǫụ-pн̇'dlei, to be thirsty.  ——
'н̇-t'ǫụ-hẹi'm, I got thirsty.

t'ǫụ-к̃ǫnk'iн̇ (an. II; t'ǫụ-к̃ǫnk'iн̇-gα, tpl.; t'ǫụ-к̃ǫnk'iн̇- in comp.),
hard-shelled turtle [water hard shield].  Cp. к̃ǫnk'iн̇, soft-shelled
turtle.

T'ǫụ-k'ǫụgyн-к̃iн (T'ǫụ-k'ǫụgyн-gα̇'-t, tpl.), Black Leg man, member of a certain Kiowa order; see Mooney, p. 230 [t'ǫụ-, leg;  .
k'ǫụgyн, black; -gα̇'t].

t'ǫụ-m (t'ǫụdα', fut.; t'ǫụm, imp.; t'ǫụ- in comp.), to drink [cp.
t'ǫụ- water].  Cp. t'ǫụ- . . ., to cause to drink; t'ǫụ-hẹi'm, to be
thirsty, lit. to drink die; t'ǫụ-pн̇'dlei, to be thirsty.

t'ǫụ-n (an. II; t'ǫụ-dα, tpl.; t'ǫụ-n- in comp.), tail.  —— t'ǫụ-t'нe
yн̣-k'oup, the small of my back aches, lit. above tail.

-t'ǫu-n, in p'iн-t'ǫu-n, porcupine quill [p'iн-, porcupine; -t'ǫu-n app. the same as t'ǫu-n, tail].

-t'ǫu-n (inan. III), pit, in 'ɑdlhǫ̨'-t'ǫun, mine; t'нm-t'ǫun, grave.

t'ǫun-'ɑt̂ǫę (an. II; t'ǫun-'ɑt̂ǫę-mɑ, t'ǫun-'ɑt̂ǫ̨'-dɑ, tpl.; t'ǫun-'ɑt̂ǫę- ·in comp.), opossum [smooth tail].

-t'ǫun-guɑdl (an. II; t'ǫun-guɑt-dɑ, tpl.), red-tailed hawk [red tail].

t'ǫun-kįнnįн (an. II; t'ǫun-kįнnyou-p, t'ǫun-kiнnou-p, tpl.), tail feather [long tail].

t'ǫun-p'ouyiнy-iн (an. II; t'ǫun-p'ouyiн-you-p, dpl.), hawk sp., described as blackish with a swallow tail; the name is said to mean swallow tail [t'ǫun, tail; p'ou-yiн-y-, unexplained. -'iн, dim.].

t'ǫun-sęinhн'y-iн (an. II; t'ǫun-sęinhн'-you-p, t'ǫun-sęinhн'-gɑ, tpl.), scorpion, said to mean the one that bends its tail back [t'ǫun, tail; sęin-hн'-y-, sęinhн'- unexplained -'iн, dim.].

t'ǫun-t̂ɑ-p'oudl, 1. fish, = 'ɑ'pįн; 2. swallowtail coat [split tail, t'ǫu-n, tail; t̂ɑ-, by a blow; -p'oudl, unexplained].

t'ǫu-'oudl-p'н̨'-gɑ (inan. IIᵃ; t'ǫu-'oudl-p'н̨, dpl.), water jug, made of clay; they also had them made of tsoudlpн̨-k'ɑe, an interior organ of the buffalo [t'ǫu, water; w. -'oudl- cp. ev. 'oudl, load, 'oudl-k̂oup, to put load ·on back; -p'н̨'-, unexplained; -gɑ.].

t'ǫu-'ou-p (inan. IIᵃ), dipper [t'ǫu, water; 'ou-p to dip up].

t'ǫu-pɑ̨'t'out (inan. IIᵃ), pump, windmill, said to mean water raiser [t'ǫu, water; w. pɑ̨'t'out cp. possibly bɑ̨'dн, to rise].

t'ǫu-pн̨'dlei, to be thirsty [t'ǫu-; to drink; pн̨'dlei as in dęi-pн̨'dlei, to be sleepy].    Cp. t'ǫu-hęi'm, to be thirsty. —— 'н̨-t'ǫu-pн̨'dlei, I am thirsty.

t'ǫu-poudl (an. II; t'ǫu-pout-dɑ, tpl.; t'ǫu-poudl- in comp.), water bug, any water insect [water bug].

t'ǫu-p'ɑt-dɑ (inan. IIᵃ; t'ǫu-p'ɑdl, dpl.; t'ǫu-p'ɑ̨'- in comp.), leg hair.

t'ǫu-p'ɑ̨'-houdl (an. II; t'ǫu-p'ɑ̨'-hout-dɑ, tpl.), 1. a large owl sp. (has no horns); 2. chicken of one of the several varieties that have feathered legs; 3. Norman horse [leg-downy, leg-hairy].

t'ǫu-p'н̨ . . . (t'ǫu-p'н̨t̂ɑ', t'ǫu-p'н̨edɑ', fut.; t'ǫu-p'н̨yɑ̨'dɑ', fut. neg.), to lock up [t'ǫu-, unexplained; -p'н̨ . . . as in p'н̨'-tseip, to lock up]. —— gɑ̀-t'ǫup'н̨yɑ̨'-dɑ', they'll lock you up.

t'ǫu-sн̨'nęį (an. II; t'ǫu-sн̨'n-oup, tpl.), water moccasin snake [water snake].

t'ǫu-sei-bɑ (inan. IIᵃ; t'ǫu-sei, dpl.; t'ǫu-sei- in comp.), bone [t'ǫu-, prepound form of t'ęi'-m, bone; -sei; -bɑ]. Cp. t'ęi'm, bone, which likewise has its dpl. t'ǫu-sei.

t'ǫu-sei-k̂oudl-p'н̨ (inan. III), necklace of long beads; the beads are 3'' in length, cp. Mooney, p. 222, = k̂oudlp'н̨-hyu'ę [bone necklace].

t'ǫusei-p'ou (inan. III), bone fishhook.  But the informant never heard of these, only of hǫ̨'-p'ou, iron fishhooks.

t‘ǫu-t̂н’-dei (inan. I), dam [t‘ǫu, water; t̂н’dei, to be shut in].

t‘ǫu-t̂ęinęi (an. II; t‘ǫu-t̂ęinou-p, tpl.), killdeer [water bird].

t‘ǫu-t̂oudlǫ̃’-bɑ (inan. II; t‘ǫu-t̂oudlǫ̃’, dpl.), orange [sweet juice.
    tǫu, water; t̂oudlǫ̃’, to taste good, be sweet; -bɑ]. Cp. t‘ǫu-
    ’н’ǫ̃’-mɑ, lemon, app. sour juice.

t‘ǫu-t‘eip (inan. I), spring of water [t‘ǫu, water; t‘ei-p, to issue].

t‘ǫu-zǫunyị’н̣ (inan. I), meadow [shallow water].

ts

tsɑ (an. I; tsɑ̃’-gɑ, tpl.), 1. mother; 2. maternal aunt.  Used with 1st
    and 3rd person possessive; cp. kɑ̃’kɑ’e, my or our mother; ’нkɑ̃’kɑ,
    your (spl.) mother; ’нtsɑ̃’dei, his or their mother; kɑ’, mother,
    voc.; tsн̣’-yiн, paternal or maternal aunt; tsɑ̃’tǫ̃’-dɑ, maternal
    aunt [Tewa yíн, mother]. ⸺ nǫ̃ tsɑ, my or our mother,
    =kɑ̃’kɑ’e.  hн̣’deidl tsɑ gyн̀-bǫu, I saw somebody’s mother.
    hн̣’deidl tsɑ, whose mother?  ’oueidei tsɑ, his mother (ans.).
    ’oueigɑ tsɑ̃’gɑ béit̂-dɑ, they are those fellows’ mothers.  ’ǫ̃’gɑ
    tsɑ, my or our (own) mother.  But cannot say *’н̣m tsɑ, your
    mother.

tsɑ̃’-bн-, unexplained, in poue tsɑ̃’bн-’ǫmdɑ, don’t you do it!

tsɑ̃’-t‘ǫ̃’-dɑ (an. I), maternal aunt [little mother; tsɑ, mother; -t‘ǫn,
    dim.; -dɑ]. ⸺ tsɑ̃’t‘ǫ̃’dɑ ’ęi-dɑ, it is my mother’s sister,
    =kɑ̃’kɑ’e p̂iн ’н̣-dɑ.

tsн (an. II; tsн̣-gɑ, tpl.; tsн̣’- in comp.), prairie dog.  Cp. tsн-
    yiнt̂k̂iн, ground owl, sp., lit. prairie-dog accompanier.

tsн-’н-dei, (an. I; tsн-’н-gɑ, tpl.), friend.  Used with 1st and 3rd
    person possessive.  Cp. ’н-kǫum, your (spl.) friend.  [tsн-’н-,
    unexplained; -dei]. ⸺ tsн’нdei gyн̀-bǫu, I saw my friend.
    But ’нkǫum gyн̀-bǫu, I saw your (spl.) friend.  tsн’нgɑ dèi-bǫu,
    I saw my friends.  ’oueidei tsн’нdei gyн̀-bǫu, I saw that fellow’s
    friend.  ’oueidei tsн’нdei nęin bǫu, I saw that fellow’s d. friends.

tsн-dou (an. II; tsн-dou-gɑ, tpl.), a small sized, long haired dog
    such as the Kiowa used to have, before their conquest by the
    whites made the native dog become extinct, =kou-dl-ou.

tsн-e (tsнyɑ’, punct. neg.; tsн̣’dɑ, curs.; tsнedɑ’, fut.; Tsнeyɑ̃’dɑ’,
    fut. neg.; tsнe, imp.), to ask [cp. Tewa tsì-ká-nyị-ŋ, to ask].  Cp.
    tsнhy-нp̀-k̂iн, asker of questions; dɑ̃’-tsнe, to pray; etc. ⸺
    gyн̀-tsнe, I asked him.

tsн-e-, to go, walk, in tsнe-bн, to go, walk; ’out̂-bн-tsнe-youp,
    swing; etc. [cp. tsн̣’-, to go, walk; tsн̣’-dei, to travel; Tewa yí-é,
    to walk].

tsнe-bн (tsнe-bн’t̂ɑ’, fut.), to go, walk.  [tsнe-; bн]. ⸺ hн̃yн’
    ’н̀-tsнebн’t̂ɑ’, which way am I to go?

tsнhy-нp̀-k̂iн (an. I; tsнhy-нp, tpl.), asker of questions [tsнe, to
    ask; -нp, excessive usitative postfix; -k̂iн].

tsн-t (inan. II; tsн-t- in comp.), door [cp. tsн-t-, by closing]. ——
tsнȼ-yɑ' 'ȩ̨i-t'ɑȼgɑ, he shot me through the door.    tsнȼ béi-ȼsou!
close the door, = béi-tsнt-'ɑ'm!  heigɑ déi-tsнt-'ꭓ'mȩ̨i, I closed
the door already.   déi-tsнt-'ɑmdɑ', I am going to close the door.
tsнȼ déi-boʋ̥, I saw the door.   tsнȼ gyн̇-boʋ̥, I saw the doors.

tsн-t-, by closing in tsнt-ꭓ'mȩ̨i, to close door; tsнȼ-ȋн'dei, to be
shut in; tsнȼ-ȋн'dɑ, to shut in; tsнȼ-ȋseip, to shut out.

tsн-t- in tsнt-hн'dɑ, to yell, give whoop.

-tsн-t, point, in mꭓ'-tsнt, point; mꭓ-bн-tsнt-ɑ', at the end of the
nose, at the tip; ȼsoudl-ꝁɑn-bн-tsнt, wing feather; zeiꝑ-mꭓ'tsнt,
point of the breast, nipple.

tsнt-'ꭓ'mei, to close door [tsнt-; 'ꭓ'mȩ̨i]. —— ꝟéi-tsнt-'ɑ'm, close
the door! = tsнȼ béi-ȼsou!

tsнt-gyн (app. inan. III), doorway [tsн-t, door; -gyн].

tsнt-hн'dɑ' (tsнt-hн'deidɑ', fut.), to give a whoop. —— [tsнt-,
unexplained; hн'dɑ, to shout]. —— dèi-tsнt- hн'deidɑ', I am
going to give a whoop.

tsнȼ-ȋꭤȩ̨-k'ɑȼ-gꭤ'-t (inan. IIª; tsнȼ-ȋн̨e-k'ɑȼgyн, tpl.), door knob
[tsнȼ, door; ȋꭤȩ̨-k'ɑȼ-gꭤ't, knob].

tsнt-ȋн'dɑ (tsнȼ-ȋнdeidɑ', fut.), to shut in with a door [tsнt-;
ȋн'dɑ]. —— yн̨n-tsнȼ-ȋн'dɑ, I shut him in the room.

tsнt-ȋн'dei-dɑ, to be shut in [tsнt-; ȋн'dei; dɑ].

tsнt-ȋseip (tsнȼ-ȋsoudɑ', fut.; tsнȼ-ȋsou, imp.), to shut out [tsнt-;
ȋseip, to put one]. —— gyн̇-tsнȼ-ȋseip, I shut him out.  'н̇-tsнȼ-
ȋsou, shut him out!

tsн'-ꝁoʋ̥m-zн'-dl-ei (an. II; tsн'-ꝁou-m-zн'dloup, tpl.), ground
squirrel [tsн'-, prairie-dog; -ꝁoʋ̥m, explained as meaning old;
zꭤ'-dl-ei, unexplained].

tsн'-ȋꭓ-dei (an. II; tsн'-ȋꭓ'-dou-p, tpl.), weasel [said to mean resembling a prairie dog: tsн, prairie dog; ȋꭓ-, unexplained; -dei].

tsн-yнȼ-ꝁiн (an. II; tsн-yнȼꝁyн-ba, tpl.), ground owl sp., lit. prairie-
dog accompanier.   Rattlesnakes, rabbits, owls and prairie dogs
live together in peace in the holes [tsн, prairie dog; yн-t-, referring
to accompaniment; -ꝁiн].

tsн'-y-iн (an. I; tsн'-y-ou-ꝑ-gɑ, tpl.) —— paternal aunt.  Used
with 1st and 3rd person possessive, cp. 'нtsн'yiн, your aunt [tsн-e-,
unexplained; -iн, dim.].

tsн̨-ȩ̨ (tsн̨ȩ̨gɑ', punct. neg.; tsн̨ȩ̨gɑ'dɑ', fut. neg.), to be afraid. ——
hнyн'-dou tsн̨nȋɑ nꭤ hꭤn hнyн' yн̨-tsн̨ȩ̨gɑ'dɑ' (or 'н̇-ꝁiнt'н'
mꭓ'ȋɑ' instead of last word), if he comes I will not be afraid.

Tsн̨ȩ̨nȩ̨i-ꝁiн, Chinaman [tsн̨ȩ̨nȩ̨i fr. Eng. Chinee or China-man; -ꝁiн].

tsн̨-n (tsн̨nɑ', punct. neg.; tsн̨nmн̥, curs.; tsн̨nȋɑ, fut.; tsнndou,
imp.; tsн̨nheidl, inf.), to come, arrive [cp. possibly tsн'-dei, to
travel; etc.].   Cp. ȋoʋ̥m-tsн̨n, to come as a fugitive. —— 'н̇-tsн̨n,
I arrived.   pн' hн'gyн 'нn tsн̨nmн̥, sometimes he comes.  ꝁiнgyн

p̄α' heigα 'αe tsʜnmʜ, he is going to come back next month.
-tsʜ'-, to go, walk, 'αn-tsʜ-, going on foot [cp. tsʜ'-dei, to travel,
tsʜ-e-, to go, walk].
-tsʜ'-dα (-tsʜ-n, dpl.) in 'oudl-tsʜ'-dα, rawhide box.
tsʜ'-dei (curs.), to travel, move, march [cp. tsʜ'-, to go; tsʜe, to go;
and possibly tsʜ-n, to arrive]. Cp. gᴏʏm-tsʜ'dei, to be blown on
wind. —— 'ougα 'ʜ-tsʜ'dei, they tpl. are traveling over yonder.
t̃αseidl tsʜ'dei, a herd of antelopes is moving along. gyʜ-gᴏʏm-
tsʜ'dei 'ʜep'ɪʜbei, the pollen is blowing on the wind.
tsei (tseigu'α, punct. neg.; tseit̃dα, curs.; tseidα', fut.; tseigu'αdα',
fut. neg.; tsei, imp.; tsei-dei', hort.), 1. to put one in; 2. to set,
erect one. Tpl. correspondent is sa [cp. possibly t̃sei-p, to lay
one]. Cp. tsei-dl, one is in, one stands; t̃eidʜ-tsei, to splice;
t'ʜm-tsei, to bury. —— 1. gyʜ-tsei, I put it in. hᴏn gyʜ-
tseigu'α, I did not put it in. gyʜ-bou-tseit̃dα, I put it in all the
time. miʜn gyʜ-tseit̃dα, I am about to put it in. heigα gyʜ-tsei,
I already put it in. gyʜ-tseidα', I shall put it in. hᴏn gyʜ-
tseigu'αdα', I shall not put it in. 'ʜ-tsei, put him in! poue
'ʜ-tseidα', don't put him in! heit̃ bʜ-tsei, let's put him in. heit̃
bʜ-tseidei', let's put him in! 2. pʜ'gα tou gyʜ-tseidα', I am going
to erect one house. yiʜ tou nèin-tseidα', I am going to erect two
houses. hʜ'oudei tou gyʜ-sα'dα', I am going to erect several
houses.
tsei-, dog, pet, in tsei-guαn, dog; tsei-'ou, young of animal, pet; tseị,
horse; tseị-hịʜ, dog [Tewa tsé, dog].
tsei-dl (stat.; tseigα, stat. neg.; tseit̃α', fut.; tseigα't̃α', fut. neg.)
1. one is in; 2. one stands (but dei, 1. animal stands). Tpl. correspondent is sα-dl [cp. tsei-p, to put one in; to erect one]. ——
'ʜ-tseidl, I was inside. hᴏn 'ʜ-tseigα', I was not in (the ditch).
'ʜ-bou-tseidl, I am inside all the time. 'ʜ-tseit̃α', fut. 'αhyα'
'èim-tseidl, you are in there. poue 'αhyα' 'èim-tseit̃α', don't be in
there! 'eịhα 'ʜ-tseidl, I was right in there. t̃sou 'éị-tseidl tou-
dᴏʏgyʜ, I have a stone in my shoe. poudl peigyʜ gyʜ-tseidl, the
bug is inside the sand. 2. k̄oup 'èi-tseidl, the mountain stands.
yiʜ k̄oup 'èị-tseidl, two mountains stand. tou tseidl, the house
stands. hʜ'oudei k̄oup sαdl, tpl. mountains stand. 'ʜ'dα 'èị-tseidl,
the tree stands. But tseị dei, the horse stands. hᴏndei 'ʜ́-dα'ʜdl-
tseidl, somebody has a spit (?) said of the spots on the moon.
heigα t̃ᴏʏgyʜ tseidl, I already have my coat on.
-tsei-dl in tα'-tseidl, goal [ev. tseidl, one stands].
tseidlei (inan. III; tseidlei- in comp.), chile [fr. Eng.].
tsei-guα-n (an. II; tsei-gᴏ̈α-dα, tpl.), dog, = tseịhịʜ, dog. [tsei-,
dog; -guα-n unexplained]. —— tseiguαn dʜmgyʜ-dα'-dei gyʜ-
bᴏʏ, I saw the tired dog. tseịgᴏ̈αdα 'èi-dʜmgyʜ-dα'-gα déi-bᴏʏ,
I saw the tpl. tired dogs.

tsei-ou (an. II; tsei-ou-p, -tsei-ou-gɑ, tpl; tsei-ou- in comp.), young
(male) animal, pet; colt, in bʜ'ou-tseiou, cat; seit-tseiou, pig, lit.
bear young; tɑ'-tseiou, colt; teineit-tseiou, chicken; t͡sou-t'eineit-
tseiou, roadrunner [tsei-, dog, pet; -ou, unexplained].   Cp. t͡sʜdliʜ,
young female animal.

tsei-p- in tsei-p̀-dɑ, to be high water.

tsei-p̀-dɑ (tseip̀-dɑ'-t͡ɑ', fut.), to be high water [tsei-p, unexplained;
dɑ, to be].

Tseirou-k̂iʜ (an. II; Tseirou-gɑ, tpl.), Cherokee man.   Doubtless the
pronunciation Tseidlou-k̂iʜ is also heard [fr. Eng., the last syl.
assimilated to -k̂iʜ, man].

tsei̯ (an. II; tsei̯-gɑ, tpl.; tsei̯- in comp.), horse [app. dim. of tsei-,
dog, pet].   Cp. tsei̯-bou, cow; tsei̯-t'ʜ'out'ʜ, fox.

-tsei̯, subordinating verb postfix, when, if, whenever.  —— Cp. -ei̯,
subordinating verb postfix, when.  —— 'éit-hei̯dei-toʋk'ɑm-tsei̯
'ʜn 'ɑ'zʜt͡ɑ'houp 'éit-k'ɑ'mɑ, whenever we speak of them in a
myth we call them the Udder-angry Travelers-off.   nɑ gyʜ̀-boʋ-tsei̯
'ʜ̀-sɑ'ɑ'dei, whenever I see it I get mad.   'ɑ'kɑdl 'ɑdlhɑ'gyʜ
'éi̯-'ɑe-tsei̯, ('oubɑe) tsei̯ (kɑdl) gyʜ̀-hɑ'dɑ, if I had lots of money
I would buy me a horse (the words in parenthesis may be omitted,
but if 'oubɑe is added kɑdl must also be inserted).   'ɑ'kɑdl
gyʜ̀t-k'oup̀bei'ʜe-tsei̯, if I had run.   'ɑ'kɑdl hɑn gyʜ̀t-k'oup̀bei-
'ʜyɑ'-tsei̯ (or -ei̯ instead of -tsei̯), if I had not run.

Tsei̯-'ɑdlk'ɑe, prsn., Crazy Horse; see Mooney, p. 228.

tsei̯-bou (an. II; tsei̯-bou-gɑ, tpl.; tsei̯-bou- in comp.), cow, cattle,
= kɑ-dl [app. tsei̯-, horse; bou, unexplained].   tsei̯bougɑ déi-boʋ,
I saw the cattle.   kɑtdɑ' déi-boʋ.

tsei̯bou-tei̯hyʋ-'e (inan. II; s. also tsei̯bou-tei̯-gɑ'-t; tsei̯bou-tei̯hiʜ,
dpl.), beef sinew.

tsei̯bou-tei̯-gɑ'-t, see tsei̯nbou-tei̯hyʋ-'e.

tsei̯-hiʜ (an. II; tsei̯-hyou-p, tsei̯-hyʋe, tpl.; tsei̯-hiʜ- in comp.)
dog, = tsei-guɑn. [tsei-, dog, pet; -hiʜ, real].

tsei̯hiʜ-'iʜ puppy, = tsei̯hiʜ-syʜn.

tsei̯hiʜ-k̂iʜ (an. II; tsei̯hiʜ-k̂iʜ-gɑ, tpl.), male dog.

tsei̯hiʜ-mʜ (an. II; tsei̯hiʜ-mʜe-mɑ, tpl.), female dog.

tsei̯hiʜ-syʜn (an. II; tsei̯hiʜ-syʜ'-dɑ, tpl.), puppy, = tsei̯hiʜ-'iʜ.

tsei̯-kuɑtou (an. II; tsei̯-kuɑtou-gɑ, tsei̯kuɑtou-bɑ, tpl.), blackbird
sp. [horse bird].

tsei̯-k'uep'ʜ (inan. III), horse harness.

tsei̯-mʜ (an. II; tsei̯-mʜ'-gɑ, tpl.; tsei̯-mʜ'- in comp.), mare.

tsei̯-n (inan. III), mud.   [Tewa p̄ō'-tsí, mud].  —— tsei̯n-gyʜ, in
the mud.   tsei̯n gyʜ̀t-boʋ, I saw some mud.

tsei̯-n- in tsei̯n-hɑn, to get burnt; tsei̯n-kiʜ roast beef.

tsei̯n-dɑ'ʜt-dɑ (inan. II, tsei̯n-dɑ'ʜdl, dpl.; tsei̯n-dɑ-'ʜdl-, tsei̯n-dɑ'ʜt-
in comp.), pottery vessel.

tsẹịn-guɑdl (inan. III), red clay [red mud].   Also called dɑm-guɑdl,
   red earth.

tsẹịn-hɑn (tsẹịnhɑnî̠ɑ', fut.), to get burnt [tsẹịn-, app. as in tsẹịn-k̑iн,
   roast beef; hɑn, to finish intr., be consumed].   Cp. guɑdl-hɑn, to
   get burnt. ——— 'н̑tsẹịn-hɑn, I got burnt.   mǫ'dɑ nǫ̑-tsẹịn-hɑn,
   I burnt my hand.  'н̑-tsẹịnhɑnî̠ɑ', I am going to get burnt.
   k̑iн gyн̑-tн̑'tseip gɑ 'н̑-tsẹịnhɑn, I burnt me when I put the meat
   on the fire.

tsẹịn-hẹị'iн (an. II; tsẹịn-hẹịyoup, tpl.), mud doll.

tsẹịn-k̑iн (inan. Iᵃ), roast beef [tsẹịn-, app. as in tsẹịn-hɑn to get
   burnt; k̑iн, meat].

tsẹịn-k'ǫy-gyн (inan. III), black mud.

tsẹịn-tou (inan. I; adobe house [mud house].

tsẹịn-t'ǫy (inan. I), muddy water [mud water].

tsẹị-poudl (an. II; tsẹị-pouî-dɑ, tpl.; tsẹị-pou-dl- in comp.), horse fly.

tsẹị-sɑt (inan. III), horse manure.

tsẹị-t'н-'ou-t'н (an. II; tsẹịt'н'ou-t'н'-gɑ, tpl.; tsẹị-t'н'outʼн'- in
   comp., fox [w. tsẹị- cp. tsẹị, horse; t'н-'ou-t'н unexplained].

Tsẹị-t'н̜ę-n-mɑ (tpl., s. unrecorded), "Horse Headdresses," Mooney,
   p. 230.  [tsẹị-. horse; t'н̜-ę-, ev. for -t'н-e, on; -n, unexplained;
   -mɑ].

-tsou in sei-tsou, lake [cp. tsou-e, water].

-tsou, postp., like [cp. tsou-dl-hɑ', thus] like.   Cp. mǫ', adv., like.
   ——— 'нm-tsou, just like you.   'oueidei-tsou bн̑t-'ɑm, make it like
   that!  'oueidei-tsou mn̜̑n-'ɑm, you d. make it like that!  'ouei-
   k̑iнtoudl-tsou dèi-kɑî̠ɑ'dɑ', I am going to swim like a duck.
   gue-tsou, outside.   tou'e-tsou, gyн̑t-sɑ, I put them in the house.

tsou-'н-dɑ (stat.), to believe in [dɑ, to be].   ——— 'н̑-tsou-'н-dɑ
   dɑ'k̑iн, I believe in manito.

tsoudl-ɑdl-bei (an. II; tsoudl-ɑdl-bou-p, tpl.), a bird sp. described as
   having feathers of several colors [w. tsoudl- cp. tsou-e in tsou-e-
   kuɑ-t, rainbow; -ɑ-dl- unexplained; -bei].   ——— mǫ' tsoudlɑdlbei
   dɑ, he is like a tsoudlɑdlbei, said of a gayly dressed man.

tsou-dl-hɑ', adv. thus, so, that way [w. tsou-dl- cp. -tsou, like; -hɑ'].
   Cp. tsou-hɑ', surely.   ——— tsoudlhɑ' dǫ̑-k'ǫ̜'mɑ, that's the way
   they call us.

tsoudl-pн̜-k'ɑe (an. II; tsoudl-pн̜-k'ɑe-guɑ, tpl.; tsoudl-pн̜-k'ɑe- in
   comp.), an interior organ of the buffalo used for making water jugs
   t'ǫy'oudl-p'ǫ̜'-gɑ, water jugs).  [tsoudl-pн̜-, unexplained; k'ɑe,
   skin.]

tsou-e (inan. I; tsou-e- in comp.), 1. water, liquid, soup, coffee, tea.
   But juice is called t'ǫy [w. tsou- cp. -tsou in sei-tsou, lake; -e].
   Cp. tsoue-k'ǫygyн, coffee, lit. black liquid; tsoue-guɑtdɑ, tea, lit.
   red liquid; k̑iн-tsoue, soup; sн̑'-tsoue, urine.

tsoue-dɑ'н̑t-dɑ, coffee pot [liquid bucket].

tsoue-guɑdl (inan. I), tea [red liquid].   Cp. tsoue-guɑtdɑ, tea particle.
tsoue-guɑt-dɑ (inan. IIᵃ; tsoue-guɑdl, dpl.), tea particle, tea leaf.
—— tsoue-guɑtdɑ déi-bǫų, I saw a particle of tea.   tsoue-guɑdl
nę̌in-bǫų, I saw d. particles of tea.   tsoue-guɑdl gyȟt-bǫų, I saw
dpl. particles of tea.   tsoue-guɑdl gyȟ-bǫų, I saw the tea (the
liquid).
tsou-e-kuɑt (inan. II.), rainbow, lit. many-colored [w. tsou-e- cp.
tsou-dl-ɑdl-bei, bird sp.; kuɑt, painted].   —— béi-bǫų tsoue-kuɑt,
look at the rainbow!
tsoue-k‘ǫų-gɑ’-t (inan. IIᵃ; tsoue-k‘ǫų-gyʜ, dpl.) coffee bean.   Cp.
tsoue-k‘ǫų-gyʜ, coffee.   —— tsoue k‘ǫųgɑ’t déi-bǫų, I saw a
coffee bean.   tsoue-k‘ǫųgyʜ nę̌in-bǫų, I saw d. coffee beans.
tsouei k‘ǫųgyʜ gyȟt-bǫų, I saw tpl. coffee beans.   But tsoue-·
k‘ǫųgyʜ gyȟ-bǫų I saw the coffee (the liquid).   tsoue-k‘ǫųgyʜ
bȟt-mǫk̯uɑndei, grind the coffee!
tsoue-k‘ǫų-gyʜ (inan. I, tsoue-k‘ǫų-gyʜ- in comp.), coffee [black
liquid].   Cp. tsoue-sę̌i’ǫų-gyʜ, pepper, lit. coffee-swelling.   But
the word has inan. IIᵃ gender when applied to a coffee bean; see
tsoue-k‘ǫų-gɑ’t.
tsoue-mǫ̌k̯uɑn-gɑ’-t, (inan. IIᵃ; tsoue- mǫk̯uɑn-gyʜ, dpl.), coffee
grinder [tsouė; liquid, coffee; mǫ̌’-k̯ųǫn-, to twist, turn crank;
-gɑ’t].
tsoue-sę̌i-’ǫų-gyʜ (app. tpl. of an unrecorded s. *tsoue-sę̌i’ǫų-gɑ’t,
inan. IIᵃ), pepper [said to mean coffee-smelling; tsoue, coffee;
-sę̌i-’ou-, to smell intr., fr. sę̌i, to smell intr., -’ǫų-, intensive].
tsou-gɑ’, one does not lie, see defective verb k̯ɑ, one lies [cp. t̄sei-p,
to lay one].   Cp. tsou-yʜ-p̣, adv., rightside up, on back.
tsou-hɑ’, adv., surely [tsou as in -tsou, postp., like; -hɑ’].   Cp.
tsoudl-hɑ’, thus.   —— hɑ̄, tsou-hɑ’, yes surely.
tsou-yʜ-p, adv., rightside up, on back [tsou as in tsou-gɑ’, does not
lie; -yʜ; -p].   Cp. dǫų-dei, upside down.   —— tsouyʜp̣ gyȟ-
t̄soudɑ’, I am going to lay it upside down.   tsouyʜp̣ gyȟ-tseidɑ’,
I am going to set it rightside up.   tsouyʜp ’ėi-tseidl, it (the
tumbler) is standing rightside up.   tsouyʜp déi-tsei, I set it rightside up.   tsouyʜp ’ȟ-k̄ɑ, I am lying on my back.
tsǫų (an. II; tsǫų-gɑ, tpl.; tsǫų- in comp.), needle, pin.   Cp. tsǫų-
hį’ʜ, owl [Tewa yų̀-ŋ, to pierce].
tsǫų-, by crawling, in tsǫų-’ʜ, to come crawling; tsǫų-bʜ, to crawl;
tsǫų-heibʜ, to crawl in [Tewa tsí-gì-, by crawling].
tsǫų-’ɑ (tsǫų-’ɑ’dɑ’, fut.), to play the women's awl game.   The
game employs a skin with a p̣ɑ’, river, painted on it.   [To awl
gamble.]
tsǫų-’ɑ’-gyʜ (inan. III), awl game.

tsǫu̜-'ʜ, to come crawling [tsǫu̜-, to crawl; 'ʜ, to come Tewa tsí-gì-'ꞑ', to come crawling]. —— poudl k'ougyʜp 'ę̂i̜- tsǫu̜-'ʜ, there is a bug crawling on my body.

tsǫu̜-bʜ, to crawl, go crawling [tsǫu̜-, to crawl; bʜ, to go]. Cp. k'uɑ-hy-ɑ', to crawl as a snake does. —— 'ꞣ-tsǫu̜-bʜ, I crawled.

tsǫu̜-heibʜ, to crawl in —— poudl ͡tsou-doų̜m tsǫu̜heibʜ, the bug crawled under the rock.

tsǫu̜-hi̜ʜ (an. II; tsǫu̜-hyoup, tpl.; tsǫu̜-hi̜ʜ- in comp.), mother-in-law [unexplained]. Cp. ͡tsʜdliʜ-tsǫu̜hi̜ʜ, old woman; tsǫu̜-hi̜'ʜ, awl. tsǫu̜-hi̜'ʜ (an. II; tsǫu̜-hi̜'ʜ-gɑ, tpl.), bone awl, awl [real awl or needle]. Cp. mꞯ̜'t'ǫu̜-tsǫu̜-hi̜'ʜ, coyote.

-tsǫu̜-n in hꞯ̜'-tsǫu̜n, windpipe, from hꞯ̜'zǫu̜n, to breathe; bout-k'ue-tsǫu̜-n, fish spear, from *bout-k'ue-zǫu̜n, to pull by the belly.

## ͡ts

͡ts, quite audibly clicked, interj. of surprise or disgust said e. g. when one makes a mistake.

͡tsʜ-dl, additional or adversative particle, more, moreover, also, either [cp. possibly 'ʜ-dl, adversative particle; yʜ-dl, optative particle. —— kɑ' ͡tsʜdl, the tpl. other ones, = kɑ' 'ʜdl kɑ'dei 'ʜdl, that other one. hꞥuyʜ' k'ꞯ̜'gyʜ ͡tsʜdl hꞯ̜n yꞣ-bʜegɑ', I don't know what my own (Indian) name is.

͡tsʜ-dl-iʜ (an. II; ͡tsʜ-dl-you-p, tpl.), young female animal, calf [͡tsʜ-dl- unexplained; iʜ, dim.]. Cp. ͡tsʜdliʜ-tsǫu̜hi̜ʜ, old woman; tseiou, young of animal.

͡tsʜdliʜ-tsǫu̜hi̜ʜ (an. II; ͡tsʜdliʜ-tsǫu̜hyou-p, tpl.), old woman [said to sound like mother-in-law calf]. Cp. 'eidl-mʜ, old woman.

͡tsʜ-n-dei (͡tsʜndeidɑ', fut., ͡tsʜndei, imp.; ͡tsʜn- in comp.), to run, race. Cp. ͡tsʜ-n-gyʜ, a race; 'ʜe, to run, k'oub̜bei-'ʜe, to run. —— gyꞣ-͡tsʜndei, he ran. 'ę̂i̜n-͡tsʜndei, they d. ran. gyꞣ-͡tsʜndei, they tpl. ran. béi-͡tsʜndei, let's run a race! bꞣ́t-͡tsʜndei, you run! dèi-͡tsʜndeidɑ', I am going to run a race. dꞯ̜'m-ɑ', dèi-͡tsʜndeidɑ', I am going to run a footrace, lit. on the ground.

͡tsʜ-n-gyʜ (inan. III), race [͡tsʜ-n-, as in ͡tsʜ-n-dei, to run; -gyʜ].

͡tsʜngyʜ-tsęi̜ (an. II; ͡tsʜngyʜ-tsęi̜-gɑ, tpl.; ͡tsʜngyʜ-tsęi̜- in comp.), race horse.

͡tsꞑ'-hi̜ʜ (an. II; ͡tsꞑ'-hyou-p, tpl. ͡tsꞑ'-hi̜ʜ- in comp.), cottontail rabbit, = p'oudlꞥ'hi̜ʜ. This is an old word for cottontail rabbit, never used in common speech, see Mooney, p. 228. [͡tsꞑ'-, unexplained; -hi̜ʜ, real.]

͡tsꞑ'-hou-dl (͡tsꞑ'houdldɑ', fut.), to cheat [͡tsꞑ'- as in ͡tsʜn-ꞣ̃yʜb̜-t'ɑ, the cheater, a by-name of Sęi̜ndei; hou-dl, to kill].

Tsʜ-n-ꞣ̃yʜ-b̜-t'ɑ, the cheater, by-name of Sęi̜ndei [͡tsʜn- as in ͡tsꞑ'-houdl, to cheat; -ꞣ̃yʜ-b̜-t'ɑ, unexplained].

t̄sei (t̄sei-gɑ, tpl.) thick. app. through Eng. influence applied e. g. both
to thick foliage and a thick object. —— p‘eip gyн̓t-t̄sei, the
bushes are thick. ’н̓’-t̄sei, forest, dense foliage. ’н̓’-t̄sei gyн̓-bǫu̦,
I saw the thick woods. ’ǫnhн̓’dei gyн̓-bǫu̦ ’н̓’-t̄sei-gyн, I saw the
bear in the thick woods. k‘ǫnk‘įн̓-t̄sei gyн̓-bǫu̦, I saw a thick
turtle. k̄ǫnk‘įн̓-t̄seigɑ déi-bǫu̦, I saw thick turtles.

t̄sei-p (t̄sougu’ɑ, punct. neg., t̄soup̓dɑ, curs.; t̄soudɑ’, fut.; t̄sougu’ɑdɑ’,
fut. neg.; t̄sou, imp.), to lay one. Tplo. correspondent is k̄oup.
[Cp. tsou-gɑ’,ˮdoes not lie.] Cp. dęi-t̄seip, to put to sleep; p‘н̓’-t̄seip,
to lock up; tsн̓t-t̄seip, to shut in; etc. —— k‘ɑ’dɑ t‘нe gɑ́-t̄seip, I
put a blanket over him. mįн̓n gyн̓-t̄soup̓dɑ, I am going to set the
cat down. gyн̓-bou-t̄soup̓dɑ, I put it all the time. hǫn gyн̓-
t̄sougu’ɑ, I did not put it. gyн̓-t̄soudɑ’, I am going to put it.
’н̓-t̄sou, put it! heit bн̓-t̄sou, let us put it! poue ’н̓-t̄soudɑ’, don’t
put it! k̄yн̓hį’н̓ gyн̓-t̄soudɑ’, I am going to lay the man down.
tsouyнp gyн̓-t̄soudɑ’, I am going to lay it rightside up. dǫu̦dei
’н̓-t̄sou, lay him on face down! ’iн t̄seip, she (the hen) laid an egg.
’éit-iн-k̄oup, they (the hens) laid eggs.

t̄sou (inan. Iᵃ; t̄sou- in comp.), stone. Cp. pei-t̄sou, sandstone;
t̄sou-’ǫu̦, to be rocky; etc. —— t̄sou dɑ, that is a rock. t̄sou
’ę̓i-dɑ, those are d. rocks. t̄sou gyн̓-dɑ, those are tpl. rocks.
t̄sou gyн̓t-bǫu̦, I saw the tpl. rocks. I saw rock patch.

t̄sou-bǫu̦ę (inan. Iᵃ; t̄sou-bǫu̦ę- in comp.), rock crystal [transparent
stone].

t̄sou-dl-, prepound form of t̄sou-t̄-dɑ, wing.

-t̄sou-dl in pei-t̄soudl, “top of thigh.”

t̄soudl-ɑt̄ǫę (an. II; t̄soudl-ɑt̄ǫ’-dɑ, tpl.), (white man’s) devil [smooth
wing].

t̄soudl-dǫu̦bн (inan. III), armpit [under arm].

t̄soudl-k̄ǫn-bн-tsн̓t, wing feather [wing stiff tip: t̄soudl, wing; k̄ǫn-,
stiff; -bн-; -tsн-t, point]].

t̄soudl-p‘ɑt̄-dɑ (inan. Iᵃ; t̄soudl-p‘ɑdl, dpl.; t̄soudl-p‘ɑt̄- in comp.),
armpit hair.

t̄soudl-sɑ-mн̓ (an. II; t̄soudl-sɑ-mн̓ę-mɑ̨, tpl.; t̄soudl-sɑ-mн̓’- in
comp.), angel [winged woman: t̄soudl-, wing; -sɑ-, as in ’ę̓imhн̓’męi-
t̄soudl-sɑ, winged ant].

t̄soudl-touhɑ̃’-’ǫm-dou’, to soar [to have wings slanted: t̄soudl, wing;
tou-hɑ̃’-’ǫm-, to slant tr.; dou’, to hold]. —— ’ę̓im-t̄soudl-
touhɑ̃’ǫmdou’, he soars.

t̄soudl-t‘ę̓i’m-tǫu̦-bɑ̃’-t (inan. II; t̄soudl-t‘ę̓i’m-tǫu̦bн, dpl.; t̄soudl-
t‘ę̓i’m-tǫu̦bн̓’- in comp.), wing bone flute, made of the wing bone
of the eagle.

t̄sou-ei-gyн (t̄soueideit̄ɑ’, fut.), to fall (down). Cp. ’outgyн, one
falls; p̄eitgyн, several fall. —— ’н̓-t̄soueigyн, I fell down (while

walking along). 'n̄-t̄soueideit̄ɑ', I am going to fall down. tsẹihįn-
dei-dei'ẹį 'n̄-t̄soueigyn, I fell where the dog was (standing).
t̄sou-k̄in-k'ɑe (inan. IIᵃ), sling. The Kiowas had slings anciently.
[t̄sou, stone; k̄in-, to throw; k'ɑe, skin]. —— t̄souk̄ink'ɑe-dou
nẹ̀in-k̄in̄dɑ', I am going to throw it with a sling.
T̄sou-k̄oup (an. II), the Rocky Mountains (modeled on the Eng.
name).
t̄sou-'ǫų, to be rocky [t̄sou, stone; -'ǫų]. —— gyn̄-t̄sou'ǫų, it is
rocky.
t̄sou-sɑhyei (inan. Iᵃ), turquoise [blue stones]. —— t̄sousɑhyei-
dóųgyn, inside the turquoise.
t̄sou-sɑ̃'tou-p (inan. II; t̄sou-sɑ̃'toudl, dpl.), stone pipe.
t̄sou-t̄-dɑ, (inan. II; t̄sou-dl, dpl., t̄sou-dl- in comp.), wing. Cp.
t̄soudl-'ɑ̃t̄ɑ̨ę, devil; t̄soudl-dǫųbn, armpit; t̄soudl-p'ɑt̄dɑ, armpit
hair.
t̄sou-tou (inan. I; t̄sou-tou- in comp.), stone house.
t̄sou-touguɑdlt̄n̄'-dei, a lizard sp. described as a foot long, greenish,
with a black neck [rock lizard sp.].
t̄sou-t̄ẹįnẹįt-tseiou (an. II; t̄sou-t̄ẹįnẹįt-tseiou-p, t̄sou-t̄ẹįnẹįt-tsei-
ouga, tpl.), roadrunner [rock chicken].
t̄sou-t'n-'e (inan. Iᵃ), pounding stone, hammer [t'n-'e unexplained].
Cp. k̄ɑ'gyn-t̄sout'n'e, yucca, lit. hammer skin; hɑ̃'-t̄sout'n'e, iron
hammer.
t̄sǫų, fair, light-colored. —— t̄sǫų dɑ, it is light-colored. nɑ̃ 'ɑ'dɑ
nɑ̨̃-t̄sǫų-dɑ, my hair is light-colored.
-t̄sǫų, nail, claw, in 'ɑ̨n-t̄sǫų, toenail mɑn-t̄sǫų, fingernail.
-t̄sǫų in 'n̄'-t̄sǫų, bulb sp. [Mr. Smoky suggested comparison with
t̄sǫų-gɑ̃'-t, down feather].
t̄sǫų-dɑ, to be fair.
t̄sǫų-gɑ̃'-t (inan. IIᵃ; t̄sǫų-gyn, dpl.), down feather, down.
t̄sǫų-gųɑ̨ (an. II; tsǫų-gųɑ̨-gɑ, tpl.), great horned owl [down feather
· horn]. Also called tsǫųgųɑ̨-mɑ̃'hįn.
T̄sǫų-t'n̄dlin, prsn. of Enoch Smoky [fair boy]. Mr. Smoky's new
name is 'Ɑ̃pįn-guɑdl, red fish.

u

'uh, interj. of surprise. Cp. 'ou, interj.

y

-yɑ', postp., at, in, on, out of, through, from [cp. -yn, postp., at].
Cp. -ɑ', at; -hɑ', at; -hyɑ', at. —— p'in-yɑ', on the hill. p'in-yɑ'
tou tseidl, the house is on the hill. tou'n̄-yɑ' he.ibn, he went
into the corral (but tou'n̄'-guɑ bn, he went to the corral. tou'n̄'-yɑ'
t'eip, he came out of the corral. sn̄'-yɑ', in the wintertime.

pн'gα-yα' 'èim-'q̓'zoun, he left here at one o'clock. yiн-yα' hęi'm, he died at two o'clock. p'n̩'ou-yα' tsн̩n, he arrived at three o'clock. t'н̩m-tsei-yα' 'н̀-bн'tɑ', I am going to go to the cemetery. tsн̩t-yα' t'eip, he came out through the door. tou-yα' t'eip, he came out of the house. tsн̩t-yα' 'ęi-t'αtgα, he shot at me through the door. k̄oup-yα' 'н̀-tsн̩n, I came from the mountains (ans. to hн'bei-tsou èim-tsн̩n, where did you come from?). k̄oup-yα' sαt tsн̩n, he has just come from the mountain. pн'-yα' 'н̀-tsн̩n, I came from the prairie.

yα-gα-e (an. I; yα-gα-e-guα, tpl.; yα-gα-e- in comp.), young woman.
yα-guα-t-, a second time [w. yα- cp. yiн, two; guα-t, unexplained, cp. possibly -guα, toward]. —— gyн̀-yαguαt-goup, I hit him a second time, again (cp. gyн̀-tɑ̨m-goup, I hit him the first time). 'oueidei yαguαt-k̄oup, way over yonder is the second camp.
-yα'-t'α', postp., beyond, after [-yα'; -t'α']. —— pн'gα-yα't'α' zн'-yα', at half past one.
yɑ̨-m-gα (yαmgα', punct. neg.; yɑ̨mgoup, curs.; yɑ̨mdeidα', fut.; yɑ̨mgα'dα', fut. neg.; yɑ̨mdei, imp.), to tremble, shiver. —— dèi-yɑ̨mgoup, I am trembling. dèi-bou-yɑ̨mgoup, I am trembling continually. hɑ̨n dèi-yɑ̨mgα', I am not trembling. k'iнdeidl dèi-yɑ̨mgα, I was shaking yesterday. dèi-yɑ̨mdeidα', I shall be trembling. hɑ̨n dèi-yɑ̨mgα'dα', I shall not be trembling. poue bèi-yɑ̨mdeidα', don't be trembling! bèi-yɑ̨mdei, tremble! heit béi-yɑ̨mdei, let us tremble! dèi-k̄α'-yɑ̨mgoup, I am shivering with cold.
-yн', postp., at, in the region of, in hн-yн', in which direction? [occurs also as independent adv. in yн-'e, in a direction; cp. possibly -yα', at].
yн-dl, optative particle [cp. possibly 'н-dl, additional particle; tsн-dl, additional particle]. —— yнdl 'èim-tα', I wish that he were here. yнdl 'oueidei mн̀-tα', I wish that they d. were here. yнdl 'oueigα p'n̩'ou bн̀-tα', I wish that they tpl. were here.
yн-dl-dн (inan. III), cliff, bluff. Cp. k̄α'gα, k̄α'gyнp, cliff; Seip-yнdldн, plcn., Rainy Mountain; touhα', cliff.
yн-e . . ., to play, implied by yнe-'q̓'mei, to play; yнe-bн, to go to play; etc.
yн-'e (yiнyα', punct. neg.; yiнyн', yiнhα', curs.; yiнtα', fut.; yiнyα'tα', fut. neg.), to set (said of luminaries in the material obtained). —— pнe yн'e, the sun went down. pнe hɑ̨n yiнyα', the sun did not set. pнe bou-yiнyн', the sun sets all the time. pнe miнn yiнyн, the sun is about to set. k'yn̩'hiнgα pнe yiнtα', tomorrow the sun will set. hɑ̨n yiнyα'tα', it will not set. pнe yiнhα', the sun is setting. pнe heigα hн'ouei yiнtα', the sun is going to set sometime.
yн-'e, adv., in a direction [w. yн- cp, -yн', postp., in region of; -'ei]. —— hн-yн' yн'e, which way?

ᴜнe-'ǫ'mẹi̯, to play [app. ᴜн-e . . ., to play; 'ǫ'mẹi̯, to make].　——
sʏꞑ'dɑ 'èi-ᴜнe-ǫ'mɑ, the children are playing.

ᴜн-e-bɑ (inan. Iᵃ), string, rope, cord [cp. possibly -'iн- in 'нdl-iн-dɑ,
bowstring].　—— ᴜнepɑ-dou 'н̇-gu'ɑ, hit him with the rope!

ᴜнe-bн, to go to play [bн, to go].　—— sʏꞑ'dɑ 'èi-ᴜнe-bн̨nmн̨, the
children are going to play.

ᴜнe-dou', to play with [app. ᴜнe . . ., to play; dou'].　—— gyн̇-
ᴜнedou', I am playing with it (e. g. with the doll).

-ᴜн-p in tsou-ᴜн-p, rightside up.

*ᴜн-t (ᴜнdldɑ', fut.), to untie.　—— gyн̇-ᴜнdldɑ', I am going to
untie it.

ᴜн-t-, yiн-t-, referring to accompaniment, in ᴜнᵗ-k̑iн, son-in-law;
ᴜнᵗ-mн̨, daughter-in-law; ᴜнᵗ-bнhei-k̑iн, warrior, soldier; t̑ɑ-'i(н)-
ᴜнᵗmн̨, bird sp. tsꞑ-ᴜнᵗ-k̑iн, ground owl, lit. with the prairie dogs;
ᴜнᵗ-bн, to go to live with; etc.

ᴜн-t-, referring to two, see yiн-t-.

ᴜнᵗ-bн, to go to live with [bн, to go].　—— 'н̇-ᴜнᵗ-bн, I went to
live with that family. 'н̇-ᴜнᵗ-bꞑ't̑ɑ', I am going to live together
with (person or persons). 'oueigɑ 'н̇-k̑iнdl-dei-'ẹi̯ 'н̇-ᴜнᵗ-bꞑ't̑ɑ', I
am going to go to live with those tpl. people.

ᴜнᵗ-bн-dou' (app. an. I; ᴜнᵗ-bн-dou'-gɑ, tpl.), domestic animal [app.
what one has living with him: ᴜнᵗ-bн-, to go to live with; dou'].

ᴜнᵗ-bн-hei (an. I; ᴜнᵗ-bн-hei-gɑ, tpl.; ᴜнᵗ-bн-hei- in comp.), 1. warrior, soldier; 2. member of a society, =ᴜнᵗbнhei-k̑iн [ᴜн-t-, app.
as in ᴜнᵗ-bн, to go to live with; bн-hei, unexplained].

ᴜнᵗbнhei-k̑iн (an. I; ᴜнᵗbнhei-gɑ, tpl.), =ᴜнᵗbнhei [-k̑iн, man].

ᴜнᵗgyн-k'i̯н̨, forty.

ᴜнᵗgyн-t'н̨, fourteen.　—— yiнᵗgiнt'н̨ sнe, fourteen years.

ᴜнᵗ-k̑iн (an. I; ᴜнᵗ-k̑yꞑhyoup, tpl.), son-in-law [accompanier, liver
with: ᴜнᵗ- as in ᴜнᵗ-bн, to go to live with; -k̑iн, man]. Cp.
tsꞑ'-ᴜнᵗk̑iн, ground owl, lit. "stayer with the prairie dogs;"
ᴜнᵗ-mн̨, daughter-in-law; dǫu̯m, father-in-law, son-in-law; k̑iн-
'eidl, father-in-law.

ᴜнᵗ-mн̨ (an. I; ᴜнᵗ-mꞑ'-gɑ, ᴜнᵗ-mн̨ẹ-mɑ tpl.), daughter-in-law [ᴜнᵗ-
as in ᴜнᵗ-k̑iн, son-in-law; -mн̨, woman]. Cp. t̑ɑ'-'iн-ᴜнᵗmн̨, bird
sp.; t̑ɑ', daughter-in-law.

ᴜнᵗ-sẹi̯, eight [yiн, two; -t, adverbial; -sẹi̯, as in kɑt-sẹi̯, nine].　——
ᴜнᵗsẹi̯ k̑yꞑhoup, eight men. ᴜнᵗsẹi̯ sнe, eight years.

ᴜнᵗsẹi̯-k'i̯н, eighty.

ᴜнᵗsẹi̯-n, eight by eight.

ᴜнᵗsẹin-dei, the eighth.

ᴜнᵗsẹi̯-dou', in eight places.

ᴜнᵗsẹi̯-t'н̨, eighteen.

yiʜ, twò.  Cp. yiʜ-gyʜ, four; yʜ-t̓-sẹi̯, eight; niʜ-nyʜ, two by two; yiʜ-nyʜ, alternately; etc. —— yiʜ k̓yn̥hyoup, two men; yiʜ sʜe, two years.

yiʜ-dei, both [yiʜ, two; -dei]. —— 'oueidei yiʜdei déit̓-'n̥'nẹi̯, those d. waked you up.  yiʜdei, both of them.

yiʜ-dou, in two places, two times. —— yiʜdou kiʜdl, he lives in two places.  yiʜdou dei, he stands in two places.

yiʜ-gyʜ, four [cp. yiʜ, two; Tewa yó-nù̯, four]. —— yiʜgyʜ k̓yn̥hyoup, four men.  yiʜgyʜ sʜe, four years.

yiʜgyʜ-dou, in four places.

yiʜ-gyʜ-p, on both sides.  Cp. yiʜ-gyʜ-t̓'ɑ̓'-bɑ̓', on both sides. —— yiʜgyʜp 'ou-toudl-t̓'ọụ, both collar bones, the collar bone on both sides.

yiʜgyʜ-t, four by four. —— yiʜgyʜt 'n̥-t̓'ọụ-sɑdlgɑ, four-legged creatures.

yiʜgyʜt̓-dei, the fourth.

yiʜ-gyʜ-t̓'ɑe, on both sides, mutually [-t̓'ɑe, beyond]. —— 'oueidei gɑ nọ̣ hɑ̨n 'ʜn 'éit̓-tọụ-t̓'ʜ'guɑ yiʜgyʜt̓'ɑe, that man and I do not speak mutually.

yiʜ-gyʜ-t̓'ɑ̓'-bɑ, on both sides [-t̓'ɑ̓'-bɑ, beyond]. —— gei heigɑ hɑ̨n yiʜ-gyʜ-t̓'ɑ̓'-bɑ gyʜ-ʜnegɑ' hʜyʜ' 'n̥-bʜ'gyʜ'dei, and neither side knew where they went to.  yiʜ-gyʜ-t̓'ɑ̓'-bɑ̓' k̓yʜtʜek̓iʜ toudɑ, the followers of the chiefs of both sides.

yi(ʜ)gyʜ-t̓'ọụn, four (in an old Kiowa count) [-t̓'ọụn, unexplained].

yi(ʜ)-kɑdl-t̓ʜẹ, two (in an old Kiowa count) [-kɑdl-t̓ʜẹ, unexplained].

yi(ʜ)-kɑ̓'dou-k̓'i̯ʜ, two hundred.

yiʜ-k̓'i̯ʜ, twenty. —— yiʜk̓'i̯ʜ k̓yn̥hyoup, twenty men.  yiʜk̓'i̯ʜ sʜe, twenty years.

yiʜk̓'i̯ʜ pʜ't̓'ʜ, twenty-one. —— yiʜk̓'i̯ʜ pʜ't̓'ʜ k̓yn̥hyoup, twenty-one men.  yiʜk̓'i̯ʜ pʜ't̓'ʜ sʜe, twenty-one years.

yiʜk̓'i̯ʜ-dou, in twenty places.

yi(ʜ)-nyʜ, adv., every other, alternately [yix, two; nyʜ; cp. niʜ-nyʜ, two by two]. —— tei yi(ʜ)nyʜ k̓'iʜ-yɑ' (or k̓'ọụ-yɑ') 'ʜn tsʜnmʜ, he comes every other day (or night).

yiʜ-bʜ'- in yiʜbʜ'-k̓ɑ, to lean against.

yiʜbʜ'-k̓ɑ, to lean against. —— 'n̥-yiʜbʜ'-k̓ɑ tou-bʜ, I am leaning against the house.

yiʜ-t-, yʜ-t- in yiʜ-t̓-gyʜ, the fourth time; yʜ-t̓-sẹi̯, eight [yiʜ, two; -t, adverbial].

yiʜt̓-gyʜ, the fourth time. —— 'oueidei yiʜt̓gyʜ-k̓oup, there is the fourth camp.

yiʜ-t̓'ʜ, twelve. —— yiʜt̓'ʜ k̓yn̥hyoup, twelve men.  yiʜt̓'ʜ sʜe, twelve years.

yūh, interj. of fright or surprise.

Z

zα-'ę . . . (zα-'ę-dα', fut.), to knead. —— gyн̀t-'ei-zα'ędα', I am going to knead the bread.

zн-dl (an. II; zн-t̀-dα, tpl.; zн-dl- in comp.), region about anus, buttocks, rump. Also used as an interjection: zнdl! Cp. t̂eidl, t'ou-dl-, rump.

zнdl-seik'ǫụę (inan. II; zнdl-seik'ǫụ, dpl.), rectum [sei-kǫụę, large intestine].

zнdl-t̂н̀t̀-gyн, crotch, =kα-t̂н̀t̀gyн.

zн-, zн̄'-, in zн-e-dei, half; zн̄'-yα', halfway.

zн-e-dei, half [zн- as in zн̄'-yα', halfway; -'ei; -dei]. Cp. k'ou-pα', half; 'α'-deip̀-dei, the other half. —— zнedei k̂yн̄hyoup 'ouphα'-tsou 'н́-bн̄'heidl, half the men went in that direction. zнedei 'ę́i-'α', give me half! tsęi zнedei gyн̀-bǫụ, I saw one side of the horse. 'н̄'dα zнedei déi-bǫụ, I saw half of the stick.

zнedei-pн̄'biн, half brother.

-zн̄'-dl-ei in tsн̄'-k̂ǫụm-zн̄'dlei, ground squirrel.

zн̄'-, see zн-.

zн̄'-yα', adv., halfway, midway [zн̄'- as in zн-e-dei, half; -yα', at]. —— hụ'αn-t'н̄ę zн̄'-yα' 'н̀-t̂α', I live midway on the road. pн̄'gα--yᾱ'-t't̂α' zн̄'-yα', at half past one.

zн̄-n-gα (zн̄ngα', punct. neg.; zн̄ngoup, curs.; zн̄ndeidα', fut.; zн̄nkᾱ'dα', fut. neg.; zн̄ndei, imp.), to shake tr. —— gyн̀-zн̄ngα, I shook it (e. g. a sheet). hαn gyн̀-zн̄ngα' I did not shake it. gyн̀-bou-zн̄ngoup, I am shaking it all the time. gyн̀-zн̄ndeidα', I shall shake it. hαn gyн̀-zн̄ngᾱ'dα', I shall not shake it. 'н̀-zн̄ndei shake it! poue 'н̀-zн̄ndeidα', don't shake it! heit̀ bн́-zн̄ndei, let us shake it! mᾱ' 'i(н)'oup 'ę́im-zн̄ngoup, (the many people bathing in the reservoir) are moving like maggots. heigα déi-zн̄ngα, I rang (the suspended bell). béi-zн̄ndei hᾱ'k̂oudlp'н̄gα, ring the bell! hᾱ'k̂oudlp'н̄'gα déi-zн̄ndeidα', I am going to ring the bell. k'iн̄deidl dαm 'eit̀-zн̄ngα, there was an earthquake yesterday.

-zн̄-n-mн̄ (curs.) in tǫụ-zн̄nmн̄, to talk about [unexplained].

zei . . . (cp. kα-zei . . .). —— 'ᾱ'pį̈ndα t'ǫụ-dǫụbeihį̈н̄ 'èi-ze.imн̄, the fishes are way down at the bottom of the water.

zei-bᾱ'-t (inan. IIᵃ; zei-bн̄, dpl.; zei-bн̄- in comp.), arrow [cp. possibly sei-sei-gα, arrowhead]. Cp. hᾱ'-zeibᾱ't, piece of lead, bullet; zei-p̀-gα, bow.

zei-dl-bei, to be frightful [unexplained]. —— gyн̀-zeidlbei, it is frightful. gyн̀-koudou-zeidlbei, it is very frightful, awful.

zei-p (an. II; zei-p̀-dα, tpl.; zei-p- in comp.), female breast; milk. Cp. kαdl-zeip, cow's milk. —— zeip biн̄н̄ 'ę́in-dα, she has large breasts.

zei-p (zoudliʜ, curs.; app. zout- in comp.), to flow, melt.  Cp. -zout
in ’ʜ’-zout, driftwood; *’ǫu-zeip, to bleed intr.; tɑe-zout-’ʜ, to
float; etc. —— seịn ’èị-zo.udliʜ, his nose is running.  tʻǫu
zoundliʜ, the water is gushing out.  tei dɑm-tʻʜ tʻǫu zeip, there
was a world flood.  heigɑ ’èi-zeip, it melted (of lead), =heigɑ
’èi-sʜt ’ɑ’tʻɑn (can use this latter verb of snow melting, but can
not use zeip of snow melting).
zei-p-, prepound form of zei-p, breast.
zei-p-, prepound form of zei-p̀-gɑ, bow.
zeip-ʜ’-dɑ (inan. IIª; zeip-ʜ’, dpl.), milkweed [milk plant].
zeip̀-guɑtk̄ou-’ʜ’-dɑ (inan. IIª), Osage orange tree, =zeip̀-guɑtk̄ou-bɑ
[yellow bow tree].
zeip̀-guɑtk̄ou-bɑ (inan. IIª?), Osage orange tree, =zeip̀-guɑtk̄ou-
’ʜ’-dɑ, lit. yellow bow.  The wood was prized for making bows.
zei-p̀-gɑ (inan. II; zei-p, dpl.; zei-p- in comp.), bow.  Cp. hǫ’-
zeip̀ga, gun; pʜdlʜ’gɑ, bow; zei-bɑ’-t, arrow.
zeip̀-mǫ’tsʜt (an. II; zeip-mǫ’tsʜt-gɑ, tpl.), nipple [breast point.]
Zeip̀-tʻǫugoup, “hits with a bow as a club,” prsn. of “Duke Wellington” Jones.  [zeip-, bow; tʻǫu-goup, to hit with a club].
zeịm-k̄ɑ’dɑ (zeịm-k̄ɑ’deidɑ’, fut.), to crack with teeth [zeịm-, tooth;
k̄ɑ’dɑ, to crack].  Cp. zeịm-k̄ɑ’dei, nut. —— déi-zeịm-k̄ɑ’dɑ, I
cracked it with my teeth.  déi-zeịm-k̄ɑ’deidɑ’, I am going to
crack it with my teeth.
zeịm-k̄ɑ’-dei (inan. IIª), nut [teeth-cracked].
zou . . ., to vomit.  Cp. zoudl-gyʜ, vomit; zoudl-tʻǫu, vomit water;
hiʜdɑ, to vomit.
zou-dl-, vomit, in zoudl-gyʜ, vomit, etc. [cp. zou . . ., to vomit].
zou-dl-gyʜ (inan. III), vomit.  From zou- . . ., to vomit.
zoudl-tʻǫu, 1. vomit water, thin vomit; also said of bad drinking-
water; 2. Zoudl-tʻǫu, plcn., see Mooney, p. 430.
zou-t (an. II; zou-t̀-dɑ, tpl.; zou-t- in comp.), shell (of mollusk).
—— zout-’eidl, a large seashell.
-zou-t-, referring to current, in zout-hʜ’bɑ, current carries away;
’ʜ’-zout, driftwood; etc. [cp. zeip, to flow].
*zout̀-bɑdlhɑ’-hʜ’ (zout̀-bɑdlhɑ’-hʜ’guɑ, curs.), to have waves [to
current hill rise]. —— dɑm’ɑntʻǫu ’èịm-zout̀-bɑdlhɑ’-hʜ’guɑ, the
ocean has waves.
zout̀-bʜ-tʻoue-goup, to eddy [zou-t-, referring to current; -bʜ-;
-tʻou-e-, app. as in ’Ɑdl-k̄ɑ’-tʻoue-k̄iʜ, Nez Percé man; goup, to
hit].
zout-hʜ’bʜ, to be carried by current [zout-, referring to current;
-hʜ’bʜ as in k’iʜn-hʜ’bʜ, to cough up; sɑ-’ǫum-hʜ’bʜ, to have
hemorrhage]. —— ’ʜ-zout-hʜ’bʜ, I was carried down by the
water.  p̄ɑ’gyʜ ’ʜ-zout-hʜ’bʜ, I was carried down by the river.
zout̀-kout, current is strong [kou-t, strong].

zouṫ-syḥn-goup, to be a waterfall [zou-t-, referring to current; -syḥ-n-, app. small; gou-p, to hit]. —— t'ǫu 'ę̇im-zouṫsyḥngoup, there is a waterfall.

zǫu (an. II; zǫu-gɑ, tpl.; zǫu-, zǫu-n-, zęi-m- in comp.), tooth. Cp. *zǫu-'eidl, molar tooth; ṫoubeibei-zǫu, front tooth; zǫu-'eigɑ, grain of corn of certain sp.; zęim-k̄ɑ'dɑ, to crack with teeth; zǫun-tęi', to catch with the teeth; etc. —— zǫu-bʜ nę̇i-tęimɑ, it sticks to my teeth.

zǫu-dɑ (inan. II; zǫu-n, dpl.; zǫu-n- in comp.), pine tree sp., =zǫun-'ʜ'-dɑ.

*zǫu-'eidl (an. II; zǫu-biḥ-dɑ, tpl.), molar tooth [big tooth].

zǫu-'ei-gɑ (s. also zǫu-'ei-bɑ; inan. IIᵃ; zǫu-'ei, dpl.), grain or plant of a certain variety of corn [tooth seed].

*zǫu-'ei-guɑṫkou-bɑ (an. IIᵃ; zǫu-'ei-guɑṫkou, dpl.), grain or plant of a corn variety [yellow tooth seed].

zǫu-ę̇, to be deep. Cp. zǫun-yi'ʜ, shallow. —— t'ǫu-zǫuę̇, the water is deep. gyʜ̇-tsęin-zǫuę̇, the mud is deep.

zǫu-n (zǫunɑ', punct. neg.; zǫunmɑ, curs.; zǫundɑ', fut.; zǫunɑ'dɑ', fut. neg.; zǫu'n, imp.), to take out, pull out, take off. Cp. k'ue-zǫun, to pull out; hɑ̇'-zǫun, to breathe; 'ǭ'-zǫun, to go; etc. —— sęin-p'ɑ̄'gɑ déi-zǫundɑ', I am going to pull out my beard hairs. houdldʜ gyʜ̇ṫ-zǫundɑ', I am going to take off my coat.   poue béi-zǫundɑ', don't take it out!   gyʜ̇-zǫun, I took him out.   hɑn gyʜ̇-zǫunɑ', I did not take him out.   gyʜ̇-bou-zǫunmɑ, I take him out all the time.   'ʜ̇-zǫu'n, take him out!   heiṫ bʜ̇-zǫu'n, let us take him out!   tsou 'ę̇i-tseidl tou-dǫugyʜ, gyʜ̇-zǫundɑ', I have a stone in my shoe; I am going to take it out.   déi-tou-zǫundɑ', I am going to take it out of my shoe(s).

zǫu-n-, prepound form of zǫu, tooth.

zǫu-n-, prepound form of zǫu-dɑ, pine tree sp.

zǫun-'ʜ'-dɑ (inan. IIᵃ; zǫun-'ʜ', dpl.), pine tree, =zǫu-dɑ [zǫu-n-, pine; 'ʜ'-dɑ, tree].

zǫun-k̄ɑdl (inan. I), pitch [pine gum].

zǫun-tęi', to bite [to tooth catch]. —— gyʜ̇-zǫuntęi', I bit him. hɑn gyʜ̇-zǫuntęimɑ', I did not bite him.   gyʜ̇-bou-zǫuntęimɑ, I bite him all the time.   gyʜ̇-zǫuntęidɑ', I shall bite him.   hɑn gyʜ̇-zǫutęimǭ'dɑ', I shall not bite him.   'ʜ̇-zǫuntęi', you bite him!

zǫun-îʜdl, bite [fr. zǫu-îʜt, to bite in two]. —— pʜ'gɑ zǫun-îʜdl nǫ̇-'ǭ', give me a bite (of the apple, e. g.)!

zǫun-îʜt, to bite in two [to tooth sever]. —— gyʜ̇-zǫun-tʜdldɑ', I am going to cut (the string) with my teeth.

zǫun-t'ʜ'bei (an. II; zǫun-t'ʜ'bou-p, tpl.), tree squirrel [carrier off with teeth: -t'ʜ'bei, carrier off fr. hʜ'bɑ, to lift, carry off].

zǫun-yi'ʜ, shallow, knee-deep, waist-deep [zǫun- as in zǫuę̇, to be deep; -yi'ʜ, unexplained]. —— t'ǫu-zǫun-yi'ʜ, meadow, lit. shallow water.

a

abreast, kɑ'-gyн.
acorn, touk̄ɑt-ei-gɑ.
accompaniment (referring to), yн-t-.
Adams (Charles E.), former Kiowa agent, 'H'dǫyn.
Adam's apple, 'ǫy-pǫym-k̄ɑdl.
to adhere to, t'eibei-dou'.
adobe house, p'нę-tou, tsęin-tou.
afraid (to be), *kiн-t'н̨', tsн̨-ę.
afterbirth, gyǫ-dei, syн̨m-gyǫ-dei.
afterward, k̄iн-gyн, k̄iнgyн-tsou.
again, 'ɑ-e-.
agency, 'eizęin-gyн.
agent, 'eizęin.
alfalfa plant, 'н'-sɑhyei-gɑ.
alien man, man of some other tribe, hǫ-k̄yн-k̄iн.
alive (to be), k̄yнkǫym-ɩ̄ɑ'.
all, whole, tei, tei-p'ɑ-e.
almost, quite, mį(н̨).
along with, pɑ'-.
already, now, hei-gɑ.
alternately, yi(н)-nyн.
always, continually, 'н̨-n, bou-.
amidst, -hou-dl-gyн.
and, and then, nǫ.
and, and then, gɑ.
and already, nęigɑ.
and now, nęi.
angel, ɩ̄soudl-sɑ-mн̨.
angleworm, earthworm, dǫmpoudl.
angry (to be), sǫ-'н̨'dei, sǫ'н̨'dei-dɑ.
animal (domestic), yнɩ̄-bн-dou'.
animal excrement, sɑ-t.

animal excrement (dry), sɑɩ̄-k̄ǫn.
angry, aggrieved (to be), ɩ̄ǫ'-ɩ̄ɑ'.
ankle, 'ǫn-kɑ'e.
ankle process, 'ǫn-bн-boudl-t'ęi'm.
ant sp. (black), 'ęimhн̨'męi-k'ǫygyн,
ant sp. (large, black), 'ęimhн̨'męi-k'ǫy-'eidl.
ant sp. (large, red), 'ęim-hн̨'-męi.
ant sp. (large, red), 'ęimhн̨'męiguɑdl-'eidl.
ant sp. (small), 'ęimhн̨'męip'н's yн̨n.
ant sp. (small), 'ęimhн̨'męi-sįн̨n.
antelope, deer, ɩ̄н-p, ɩ̄ɑ-p-, ɩ̄ɑ'-.
anvil, hǫ-'eiɩ̄-dɑ.
anywhere, one does not know where, hнegyн-hęi.
Apache man, T'ɑ'-gue-k̄iн.
apart from, -t'ɑ-e-gɑ.
apple juice, cider, 'нdlɑ'-t'ǫy.
Arapaho man, *'Hhy-нdl-k̄iн.
armpit hair, ɩ̄soudl-p'ɑɩ̄-dɑ.
around, at the edge of, -'ɑ'-k̄oubн, 'ɑ'-k̄ou-bei.
arrowhead, sei-sei-gɑ.
Arikaree man, k̄ɑdl-k̄iн.
arrow-throwing game, kǫm-ɑ'gyн.
arrow-throwing game, mǫn-'ǫn-'ɑ'-gyн.
arrow-throwing game, to play, mǫn-'ǫn-'ɑ.
armpit, ɩ̄soudl-dǫybн.
arrow, zei-bɑ'-t.
arroyo, draw, gulch, hiн-dl.
artist (man), guɑɩ̄-k̄iн.
to ascend, hiн-t.

206

ashes, sɑ̄'-p'n̥n.

to ask, tsн-e.

asker of questions, tsнhy-нp̀-k̄iн.

asleep (to be), t'ẹi-dei-p.

at, in, on, -ɑ', -bɑ, -bн-hɑ', -bн-p, -bei, -bei-bei, -'ei, -'ei-p, -'ẹi, -gyн, -hɑ', -'ịн, -yɑ', -yн'.

at, when, -'ou-e.

at, where, -'ẹi-m.

at dawn, k'ін-t̄н̥'-gyн.

at one, pн'gɑ-yɑ'.

at the back, gọụm-ɑ'.

at the back of, behind, -gọụm-ɑ̄'-tsou.

at the end of, 'ɑp̀k̄'ɑ̄'n-ɑ'.

at the end of, -ɑp̀k'ɑn-bн, -'ɑp̀-k'ɑn-gyн.

at the front, t̄ou-bei-bei.

at the side of, -k̄'oup̀-sнt.

auger for boring wood, 'н-t'нt-dɑ.

aunt (maternal), tsɑ̄'-t'ɑ̄'-dɑ.

aunt (paternal), tsн̄'-y-iн.

automobile, 'ɑdlɑmoubi(н)dl.

away, hẹi-gyн.

away, gone away, well, recovered, hẹi.

away from, t̄ɑ'-gɑ.

awl, tsọụ-hị'н̥.

awl game, tsọụ-'ɑ̄'-gyн.

axe, tomahawk, hɑ̄'-t'ọụ.

**b**

baby (newborn), 'iн-p̄ɑ̄'-gyн.

back, gọụ-m-.

backbone, gọụm-t'ọụ.

backward, repeated, again, 'нdl-dн-.

backward, on head, t̄eidl-k̄iн-dei t̄eidl-k̄iн-dei-tsou.

bad, unpleasant (to be), k̄ɑ̄'-dei.

bad, too bad (to be), k'ou-bei.

badger, k'ɑ̄'-ku'ɑ.

badly, k̄ɑ̄'-deidl.

bag, sack, bladder, bịн̥m-k'ɑe.

bald, tн̥n-t̄ɑ̥ẹ.

bald (to be), tн̥n-t̄ɑ̥ẹ-dɑ.

bald eagle, k̄oudl-t̄н̥ẹ.

bald man, tн̥n-t̄ɑ̥ẹ-k̄iн.

ball, p'ɑ-'нt-dou-p.

ball umpire, p'ɑ'нtdei-pọụ-k̄iн.

banana, mн̥nн̥'nн̥.

band (worn diagonally across chest), 'ou-p'н̥-yнe-bɑ.

barbed wire (fencing, piece of), hɑ̄-t̄н'-dou-p.

barbed wire fence post, hɑ̄'-sɑ̄'-'н'-dɑ.

bark, 'æ'-k'ɑ̥ẹ.

basket, sọụn-k̄ɑ'нt-dɑ.

bat, k'ɑebнtoudlei-'ɑt̄ɑ̥ẹ.

bay colored (to be), boudl-k'ọụ.

to be, be born, dɑ.

to be about, -kọụ'-m.

to be in, stand (ss.), tsei-dl.

to be in, stand (tpls.), sɑ-dl.

to be in, kou-bн.

to be on (of ring on finger), sou-dei-dɑ.

to be with, t'нe-dou'.

bead, pọụ-gɑ̄'-t.

bear, 'ɑn-hн̄'-dei, sei-t.

bear cub, 'ɑnhн̄'dei-'iн.

beard hair, coll. beard, sẹin-p'ɑ̄'-gɑ.

beaver, pou, t'ọụ-dọụ'm-dei.

because, bou-t.

because, in order to, by, -dou.

to become heavy, p'iн-'н̥mgyн.

to become silent, tọụ-hɑn.

bed, bedding, pн-dl.

bedbug, pнdl-poudl, pнdl-p'ou.

beef sinew, tsẹibou-tẹihyụ-'ẹ.

beer, p'iнt-t'ọụ.

beet, gyн̀-guɑdl-dɑ̄'-dei.

before, t̄oup̀-gɑ.

behind, -gọụm-bн, -gọụm-bн-tsou.

behind, **outside**, outdoors, gue.

to believe in, tsou-'н-dɑ.

bell, hɑ̄'-k̄oudl-p'н̄'-gɑ.

belly, bou-t.

belly down feather, bout-t̂squ-gɑ̃'-t.

belt, tɑn-p'n̥'-gɑ.

to bend tr., bọụ'-n.

bent (to be), -bọụ'-n, bọụ'n-dɑ, bọụ'n-gyн.

benumbed (to be), pei-sɑegyн.

beside, among, k̂iн-yн-.

beside, at one side, hɑ̃'-bн.

beside, at one side of, -hɑ̃'-bн.

beside, near, -bн-bн.

beside, near, -hɑ-e-gɑ.

beside, on, against, at, -bн.

between, -t̂нt̂-bн, -t̂нt̂-dɑ, -t̂нt̂-gyн.

beyond, t'ɑ-e.

beyond, across, -t'ɑ', -t'ɑ-e, -t'ɑ-p.

beyond, -guɑ-bн.

beyond, after, -yɑ̃'-t'ɑ'.

beyond, behind, -t'ɑ̃'-bɑ, -t'ɑ̃'-gyн.

bible, dɑ̃'tọụ-kuɑt.

biceps, 'ɑ̃'-dou.

Big Head (prsn.), 'Ɑ̃dlt'ọụ-'eidl.

"Big Shields" (name of a Kiowa division), K'į(н)-'eip.

bird, kuɑ-tou, t̂ẹį-nẹį.

bird sp., 'н'-k̂ǫ̃'dei.

bird sp. resembling buzzard, bou-sẹįn-kuɑseit.

bird sp., dɑ̃'нdl-kuɑ.

bird sp., dẹį-m-guɑdl.

bird sp., pei-sнdl-ɑt.

bird sp., p'eip̂-t̂ẹįnẹį-guɑdl.

bird sp., sн'-t̂ẹįnẹį.

bird sp., t̂ɑ̃'-'i(н)-yнt̂mн̥.

bird sp., described as having feathers of several colors, tsoudl-ɑdl-bei.

bird cage, kuɑtou-tou.

bite, zǫụn-t̂нdl.

to bite, k̂ɑ̃'-dl-ei, zǫụn-tẹį'.

to bite in two, zǫụ-t̂нt.

blackberry fruit (wild), sн̥'nẹį-'ei-gɑ.

blackberry vine (wild), sн̥'nẹį-'ei-p'eip.

blackbird sp., 'нp̂-t'ou.

blackbird (red-winged), kɑ̃'-dɑ̃'-t̂ǫ̃-m.

blackbird (red-winged), k'ɑ̃'t̂'ọụ-guɑdl.

blackbird sp., 'ou-guɑt̂kou.

blackbird sp., tsẹį-kuɑtou.

Black Boy (member of Kiowa order), k'ọụ-t'н̥'dliн.

Black Hills (of South Dakota), Sɑdlk'ǫ̃ẹ-k̂oup.

black hornet, t̂eidlseip̂-k'ọụ-gyн.

Black Leg man (member of Kiowa order), t'ọụ-k'ọụgyн-k̂iн.

black mud, tsẹįn-k'ọụ-gyн.

black oak tree, touk̂ɑt-н'-k'ọụ-gɑ̃'-t.

blacksnake, sн̥'nẹį-k'ọụ-gyн.

black spider, k̂ǫ̃'nǫ̃'t'ǫ̃'-k'ọụ-gyн.

black wolf, kue'-k'ọụ-gyн.

blanket, k'ɑ̃'-dɑ.

to bleed intr., 'ọụ-p̂eit̂gyн, *ọụ-zeip.

to bleed at nose, p'ọụ-'ọụ-p̂eit̂gyн, p'ọụ-'ọụ-zeip.

blind (to be), hou-dei, tou-e-gyн, touegyн-dɑ.

blind man, houdei-k̂iн, touegyн-k̂iн.

bloated (to be), bout-kyн̥ẹ-gyн, p'ou-t̂-gyн.

blood, 'ọụ'-m.

bloody (to be), 'ọụ-dɑ.

bloom, face powder, p'н̥'-gyн.

to blossom, k'į'н̥.

to blow (of wind), gọụm-d . . ., gọụm-k'iнbɑ.

to blow, p'ou-dl-ei.

blown on wind (to be), gọụm-tsн̥'dei.

bluebird, sɑhyei-t̂ẹįnẹį.

blue fly, k̂ǫ̃'nɑt̂sɑp'ouyiн-'eidl.

blue, green, sɑ-e-, sɑ-hy-ei.

boat, canoe, kɑ̄'-bout.

bobcat, k̯ɑ'-p'oup.

bobtailed, kuɑ-sei-t.

body, on body, k'ou-gyнp.

body from waist down, p̄iн-teip.

body from waist up, mн-'н-dei.

body hair, p'ɑ-t̷-dɑ.

body hair, fur, wool, fuzz, velvet, p'ɑ̄'-gyн.

body louse, t̯oygyн'-poudl.

boil, 'ɑ̄'-p'н.

to boil tr., sɑ̯-n-, -sɑ̯'-.

to boil intr., bịн̯n-gyн.

book, toy-kuɑt.

bookcase, kuɑt-'outk'ɑe, kuɑt-sɑ̄'-gɑ.

bone, t'ẹị'-m, t'oy-sei-bɑ.

bone awl, awl, tsoy-hị'н.

bone comb, t'oy-'ɑdlsoym.

bone fishhook, t'oysei-p'ou.

borer, -t'нt̷-dɑ.

both, yiн-dei.

bough or limb of tree, 'н'-bou-gɑ̄'t.

bow, pнdl-н'-gɑ, zei-p̯-gɑ.

bowstring, 'нdl-iн-dɑ.

box of rawhide, -tsн'-dɑ.

box-elder tree, kɑe-sẹi-'н'-dɑ.

boy, t'н-dl-iн.

boy medicine, t'нdliн-dɑe.

braid of hair, 'ɑdl-p̄ɑ̯'-dɑ.

to braid, p̄ɑ̯-n . . .

bracelet, mɑ̯n-sou-dou'.

brain, k̯yн'-gou-p.

branch, limb (of tree), p'ou-dl.

to break (off) tr., t'ẹị'-m.

breakfast, k'yн̯hị'н-piн̯.

breast, milk, zei-p.

breastbone, dẹim-t'oy.

breath, hɑ̯'-, hɑ̯'-tsoyn-gyн.

to breathe, hɑ̯-zoy-n.

to bring, bɑ', hɑ', kɑ̯'-n.

to bring along, pɑ̄'-bɑ', pɑ̄'-kɑ̯'n.

to bring and give, *'ɑ̯'-hɑ'.

broom, t̯ɑ̯ẹ-p'iнdl-'н'-dɑ, t̯ɑ̯ẹ-p'iнt̷-dɑ.

broken (to be), t'ẹị'm-gyн.

broth, kiн-tsoue.

brother, pн'-biн; brother (my or our), pн'-byou-'e.

brother, sister, tɑ̯'.

brother's daughter, 'iн-t'н'-t'ɑ̯n.

brother's son, 'iн-t'ɑ̯n.

brown, p'iн-guɑdl, p'iн-seidl.

to brush or comb hair, *'ɑdl-soym.

bucket, kettle, pot, dɑ-'нt̷-dɑ.

buckeye, k'oy-t'нdl.

buckskin, t̯ɑp-k'ɑe.

buckskin shirt, buckskin dress, 'ɑ̄'yн-houdl-dн, t̯ɑp̄k'ɑe-houdl-dн.

buckskin thong, 'ɑ̄'-yнe-bɑ, t̯ɑp̄k'ɑe-yнe-bɑ.

buffalo, kɑdl-hịн, 'ɑ̯'gɑ-piн̯.

buffalo, cattle, kɑ-dl.

buffalo bull, t̯ɑp̄-p'нdl.

buffalo grass, soyn-t̯н.

buffalo horn spoon, t̯ɑ̯'-hịн̯.

buffalo robe, kɑdl-k'ɑ̄'-dɑ, k'ɑ̯'-hị'н.

bug, worm, pou-dl.

bug hole, poudl-p'iнt.

bugle man, toybн-tou-k̯iн.

bulb sp., 'н'-t̯soy.

bullet, piece of lead, pig of lead, hɑ̯'-zei-bɑ̄'-t.

bullfrog, k'ɑ̄'dlei-k'yн'dlei-'eidl.

bullroarer, gyн̄-bou-poy-gyн-gɑ.

bullsnake, 'н'-sн̯'nẹi.

bumble bee, k'ɑ̄'-t̯нẹ.

to bump into with the nose, mɑ̯'kɑ̯'n-goup.

bunch, knob, k'ɑ-t̷-gyн.

bunched (to be), k'ɑt̷gyн-dɑ, k'ɑ̄'dei-dou'.

burier, undertaker, t'нm-tsei-k̯iн.

buried (to be), t'нm-tseidl.

to burn intr., t'oy.

to burn tr. -hɑ̯'n, guɑdl-hɑ̯'n.

burnt (to be), guɑdl-hɑ̯n, guɑdl-k'ɑ̯'n, guɑdl-k'ɑ̯'n-dɑ.

ᵗᵒ burst tr., k̇α'dα, sɴ' . . .

ᵗᵒ burst by hitting, t̂α-k̇α'dα.

ᵗᵒ burst forth, t̂α'-gyɴ-e.

burst open (to be), sɴ-ṫ-gyɴ, sɴ'-dα.

ᵗᵒ bury, t'ʜm-tsei.

bush, p'ei-p.

bush sp., t̂ʜp-ɴdlα'-p'eip.

bush sp., t̂oudl-k'yɴdl-'ɴ'-dα.

ᵗᵒ butcher, pei-n.

butchered (to be), pein-dα, pein-gyɴ.

butter, bα'dlα'.

butterfly, k'αe-bɴ-toudlei.

buttocks, rump, t̂ei-dl, zɴ-dl.

ᵗᵒ buy, kα'dα-hα'gyɴ.

buzzard, bou-sei-n.

c

cabbage, ·gọụm-gα-dʜ-'ei-gα.

cactus plant, sei̯-goup.

Caddo man, 'H̄'-dọụm-dei-k̇iʜ, Mα'-seip̀-k̇iʜ.

ᵗᵒ call, name, k'α'-m.

ᵗᵒ call, summon, k̇yα'-dl-ei.

called (to be), k'α.

calf, young female animal, t̂sʜ-dl-iʜ.

calf of leg, t̂ei-p.

campamocha, k̇oup̀t̂α'k'αe-sɴ'nei̯.

camp circle, tou-byụ'e.

canine tooth, kue'-zọụ.

canoe, boat, kα'-bout.

canvas tent, t̂ʜe-tou.

captive, kou-bei.

carried by current (to be), zout-hɴ'bʜ.

carrier off, -t'ɴ'bei.

carrying strap, 'out̂-t'ɴ.

ᵗᵒ carry on back, mɴ'-dou', *mɴ'-hα'.

ᵗᵒ cast a shadow, kαp̀k'ọụ-'αm-dou'.

cat (domestic), p̀ʜ'ou-tseiou.

ᵗᵒ catch, tei̯'.

ᵗᵒ catch, trap, p'ou-.

ᵗᵒ catch cold, k'iʜn-'αmgyɴ.

catfish, sei̯np'α'-dʜ-dl.

cat-tail, touegyɴ-'ɴ'-dα.

cattle, cow, tsei-bou, kα-dl.

causative verb postfix, -ei.

caved out underneath, k̇α'-k'αe-bi(ɴ)-hiɴdl-bɴ.

ᵗᵒ cease, back out, p'ɴ-ṫ-gyɴ.

ᵗᵒ cease to blow, gọụm-hα'n.

ᵗᵒ cease to sing, dα'-p'ɴt̂gyɴ.

cedar tree, 'α-hi̯ɴ-bα.

cellar, dọm-dọụgyɴ-tou'e.

cent, 'ʜm-guαdl-dα'-dei, 'ɴn-'ɴ't̂αhαe-sαdl-dei.

centipede, t'ọụ-'αe-poudl.

chair, 'ɴ'-t'αt-bɴ-hɴt̂-dα.

charcoal (piece of), 'eip̀-k'ọụ-gyɴ.

ᵗᵒ chase, *tα'-'ʜ.

ᵗᵒ chase several, 'ɴ'-dl-ei.

ᵗᵒ cheat, t̂sɴ'-hou-dl.

Cheater (by-name of Seindei), T̂sʜn-k̇yɴp̀-t'α.

cheek, t̂ou-p̄α'e-gyɴ, t̂ou-p̄α'e-gyɴ-e.

cheek bone, t̂ou-t'ei'm.

Cherokee man, Tseirou-k̇iʜ.

cherry, t̂αepout̂gyɴ-'ei-gα.

chest (anat.), dei-m-gyɴ.

chief, k̇yɴ-tʜ-e-k̇iʜ.

chicken, t̂ei̯neit̂-tseiou.

child, diminutive postpound, egg, semen, 'iʜ.

child, little one, syɴ-n.

chile, tseidlei.

chills and fevers (to have), k̇α'-houdl-sʜdl-'αmgyɴ.

Chinaman, Kyɴe-p̄αn-k̇iʜ, Tɴn-p̄α'egyɴ-kyɴep̄αn-k̇iʜ, Tsɴeṇei̯-k̇iʜ.

china doll, bọụ-hei'iʜ.

chin, beidl-t'ei'm.

chin raised (to have), 'ou-t'ɴ'-dou'.

chipmunk, gọụm-t'ɴ'bei.

chocolate, pȩinhʜ'-k'ǫu̯-gyʜ.
chokecherry fruit, 'ou-p'ʜ-'ei-gɑ.
ᵗᵒ choke to death, 'ousei-îʜ'ȩ-
    hyoudl.
choked (to be), 'ou-îʜ'-dʜ.
choked to death (to be), 'ousei-
    îʜ'ȩ-hȩi'm.
ᵗᵒ chop one down or off, îɑ'-îʜt.
ᵗᵒ chop several down or off,
    îɑ'-t'ʜ'.
church, dɑ'k'i(ʜ)-tou, dɑ'tǫu̯-tou.
church bell, dɑ'k'iʜ-hǫ̈'ɣoudlp'ʜ'-
    gɑ.
cicada, 'ei-tʜ'-poudl.
cigar, -t'ʜ'-bɑ, îɑ'k'ɑe-t'ʜ'-bɑ.
cigarette, mǫ̈tsʜȩ-t'ʜ'-bɑ.
circular, -byu̯-'ȩ.
circular, cylindrical (to be), ɣɑ'-
    dʜdl-dɑ.
circular opening in the timber;
    plcn., 'ʜ'-toubyu̯'ȩ.
circular thing, wheel, ɣɑ'-dʜ-dl.
clap (to have), sou-kou'e-dɑ.
clear, transparent (to be), bǫu̯-
    'ǫu̯.
ᵗᵒ clear away, 'ɑ-t'ǫ̈'n.
clearing, 'ʜ'-îǫ̈ȩ-t'eidl.
cliff, ɣɑ'-gɑ, ɣɑ'-gyʜ-p, tou-hɑ',
    yʜdl-dʜ.
ᵗᵒ climb steps, *'ǫn-t'ou-t-.
clitoris, pʜt-ɣɑdl.
clod, dǫm-ɣǫ̈'-dɑ.
ᵗᵒ close tr., pʜ-'ou . . .
ᵗᵒ close door, tsʜt-'ǫ̈'mei.
closing (by), tsʜ-t-.
clothes moth, 'oudl-poudl.
cloud, sky, p'ʜ-n.
ᵗᵒ cloud up, p'ʜn-'ǫmgyʜ.
cloudy (to be), p'ʜn-dɑ.
club, stick, -t'ǫu̯.
coal (live), 'ei-p.
coal mine, 'eiƀk'ǫu̯gyʜ-t'ǫu̯n.
coconut, gyʜ̀-tʜ'-sɑdl-gɑ.
cocklebur, sȩim-'ǫ̈'-dɑ.
coffee, tsoue-k'ǫu̯-gyʜ.

coffee bean, tsoue-k'ǫu̯-gɑ'-t.
coffee grinder, tsoue-mǫ̈'ɣuɑn-
    gɑ'-t.
coffee pot, tsoue-dɑ'ʜî-dɑ.
ᵗᵒ cohabit with, t'ou-dl-dɑ, t'oudl-
    ƀʜ'egɑ.
coin, dollar, money, 'ɑdl-hǫ̈'-gyʜ.
cold (to be), îou.
cold (referring to), ɣɑ'-.
colic, bouî-k'oup.
colic (to have), *bouî-k'oup.
colored, red, guɑ-dl.
collar bone, 'ou-toudl-t'ȩi'm.
colt, îɑ'-tseiou.
ᵗᵒ come, 'ʜ.
ᵗᵒ come, hou-'ʜ, hou-t-ʜ.
ᵗᵒ come, arrive, tsʜ-n.
ᵗᵒ come as a fugitive, îǫu̯m-tsʜn.
ᵗᵒ come crawling, tsǫu̯-'ʜ.
ᵗᵒ come on foot, 'ǫn-tsʜ'-'ʜ.
ᵗᵒ come to get, k'ɑ'-'ʜ.
ᵗᵒ come to get firewood, ɣiʜ-'ʜ.
ᵗᵒ come to kill, dɑ-'ʜ.
ᵗᵒ come to see, pǫu̯-'ʜ.
ᵗᵒ come up (e. g. of sun), bɑ'dei-'ʜ.
ᵗᵒ come with, accompany, t'ʜe-bɑ'.
commissioner, k'ǫmeisei.
conch shell, dȩinɑîǫ̈t'ǫ̈'nȩi-'eidl.
confluence, ƀɑ'-pʜ-'ʜʜdl-.
confluence (to have), -pʜ'-hʜdl-
    dou'.
consumption, t'ʜp-houdl-dʜ.
consumptive (to be), t'ʜp-houdl-
    dɑ.
corn (grain of), 'ei-t'ʜî-dɑ.
corn plant, cornstalk, 'ei-goup,
    'ei-t'ʜdl-goup.
corncob, corn husk, 'ei-t'ʜdl-
    k'ǫȩ.
corn cultivator, 'ei-p'ʜe-'ʜdl-
    t'out.
corn planting machine, 'eit'ʜdl-
    'eiɣuɑ-bɑ.
cornstalk juice, 'eigouƀ-t'ǫu̯.
corn variety (grain of), zǫu̯-'ei-gɑ.

corn variety (grain of) *zǫu-'ei-guɑt̃k̃ou-bɑ.

corral, tou-'ʜ.

cotton (filament of), pʜdl-p'at̃-dɑ.

cotton cloth (white), t̃ʜę-k'ɑ'-dɑ.

cotton plant, pʜdl-p'ɑdl-goup.

cotton thread, t̃ʜę-k'ɑ'-tęi-gɑ'-t.

cottontail rabbit, p'oudl-ɳ̃'-hįʜ, t̃sɳ̃'-hįʜ.

cottonwood treǝ, 'ʜ'-hyu-ę.

to cough, k'iʜn-hʜ'bʜ.

to cough, dig, k'iʜ-n.

councilman, tǫu-k̃iʜ.

courthouse, k̃iʜgɑm-tou.

cover, t̃ʜe-goup.

to cover, mǫ̃-'oudɑ.

cow, cattle, kɑ-dl, tsęi-bou.

coyote, hou'-kǫu'm, kue'-syʜn, mǫ̃'-t'ǫu-tsǫu-hį'ʜ.

to crack with teeth, zęim-k̃ɑ'dɑ.

cradle, p'ɳ̃'-tou-p.

cradle (old fashioned), t'ǫugɑe-p'ʜ'toup.

cradle hood, t̃ǫubʜ'-k'ɑe.

crane sp., p'iʜ-k̃ou-p.

cramps (to have), mǫ̃-'iʜ-kyʜ'e.

crawling (by), tsǫu-.

crayfish, seiꝑ-mǫn-tęi.

crazy, foolish, 'adl-k'ɑe.

crazy, foolish, an outlaw, evil (to be), 'ɑdlk'ɑe-dɑ, 'ɑdlk'ɑe-'ǫu.

crazy man, outlaw, sinner, 'ɑdlk-'ɑe-k̃iʜ.

craziness, crazy act, sin, 'ɑdlk'ɑe-gyʜ.

Crazy Bluff, plcn., 'Ọ̃dlk'ɑe-touhɑ'.

Crazy Horse, prsn., Tsęi-'ɑdlk'ae.

to crawl, go crawling, tsǫu-bʜ.

to crawl in, tsǫu-heibʜ.

creek, 'ɑ'-sei.

Creek man, Mɑskou-k̃iʜ.

to cremate property, 'oudl-guɑdl-ꝇǫ̃'n.

crest, kingfisher, 'ɑdl-k'ɑe-k̃i(ʜ)-hʜ'.

cricket, t̃ɑ'-poudl.

crippled (to be), 'ʜ'-pɑ̃'-dʜ.

crook for hanging kettle over fire, dɑ'ʜdl-'ʜ'-dɑ.

crop (of bird), 'ou-sɑ.

cross, tʜ-ę-sɑ.

to cross tr., kɑ-t.

cross-eyed (to be), t̃ʜę-sou-dei-dɑ.

cross-eyed man, t̃ʜw̃-sou-dei-k̃iʜ.

crotch, kɑ-t̃ʜt̃gyʜ.

crow, sɑ-kɑ-hɑ.

to cry, weep, 'ɑt̃-dɑ, 'ɑt̃-hʜ'dɑ.

to cry for a relative, tou-'ɑt̃dɑ.

crybaby boy, 'ɑt̃-p'oudl-t'ʜdliʜ.

to cure, doctor, dɑe-'ǫ̃'męi.

current (referring to), -zou-t-.

current is strong, zout̃-kout.

to cut, k̃ɑ'.

to cut in two with a knife, k̃ɑ'-t̃ʜt.

to cut the ḫair, 'ɑdl-t'ʜ'.

cut-off stump, t̃ɑ'-t̃ʜt̃-dɑ.

cyclone, mɑn-k'ɑ-'iʜ.

## d

dam, t'ǫu-t̃ʜ'-dei.

dance, kuɑn-gyʜ.

to dance, throw (away), guɑ-n.

to dance the scalp dance, 'ɑdl-dɑ̃'-guɑn.

dance ground, dancing place, guɑn-dɑm.

dancing man, kuɑn-k̃iʜ.

dancing woman, kuɑn-mʜ.

dark, black, k'ǫu, k'ǫu-gyʜ.

dark, black (to be), k'ǫu-dɑ, k'ǫugyʜ-dɑ.

dark, black (very, to be), k'ǫugyʜ-'ǫu.

darkness, blackness, black paint, k'ǫu-gyʜ.

daughter, 'iʜ-t'ʜ'.

daughter-in-law, t̃ɑ', yʜt̃-mʜ.

day, daytime, k'iʜ, k'iʜ-dʜ.

day after tomorrow, k'yn'hi'ngɑ-t'ɑ'-dei k'iн.

day before yesterday, 'ǫ'kɑdl-t̂oup̂dei-k'iн, t̂oup̂dei-k'iн.

daylight, daytime, k'iн-pн'.

dead, pei.

dead (to be), pei-dɑ.

dead man, pei-k̂iн.

dead woman, pei-mн.

deaf, t̂ɑ'-kou.

deaf (to be), t̂ɑ'-kou-dɑ.

deaf man, t̂ɑ'-kou-k̂iн.

deep (to be), zǫu-ę.

deer, k'yнe-guɑn.

deer, antelope, t̂н-p, t̂ɑ-p-, t̂ɑ'-.

deer sp., t̂нp̂-k'ǫu-gyн.

deer antler, t̂нp̂-guǫ-dei.

deer-colored (to be), t̂нp̂-p'ɑdl-da.

to defecate, sɑ'-bɑ.

to descend (e. g., hill), to fall (as rain), sei-p.

to descend, slide down, 'ou-t.

to desire intr., t'ęi-n-, t'ęin-dɑ, t'ęin-'ǫmgyн.

desolate (to be), t'н-ę-męi.

devil, t̂soudl-'ɑt̂ǫę.

dewy (to be), 'н'-dɑ.

to die, hęi'-m.

to die of smallpox, t'нdl-k'ouphęi'm.

to dig, hiн-n.

to dig, cough, k'iн-n.

digging stick, dǫm-ku'ɑ.

dime, t̂нę-syнn-нн'-dei.

diminutive, -'iн, -t'ǫ-n.

dining room, piн-tou'e.

dinner, k'iнsɑ-piн.

to dig up, 'ou-p.

dipper, t'ǫu-'ou-p.

direction (in a), yн-'e.

dish, k̂ɑ-'нt̂-dɑ.

dissatisfied (to be), 'ǫu-t̂ɑ'.

to dive, 'ǫubн'-guɑn.

diving, drowning (referring to), 'ǫu-bн'-.

dizzy (to be), *'ɑ'-k'oup.

dog, tsęi-hiн, tsei-guɑ-n, sн'-dl-ei.

dog (female), tsęihiн-mн.

dog (male), tsęihiн-k̂iн.

dog, pet, tsęi-.

dog (small, long haired, native), kou-dl-ou, tsн-dou.

dogwood, guegyн-p'eip.

doll, hęi-'iн.

donkey, 'н'-t̂ɑ'k'ɑe.

door, tsн-t.

door knob, tsнt̂-t̂ǫę-k'ɑt̂-gɑ'-t.

doorway, tsн-t̂-gyн.

down, under, dǫu'-m, dǫu-bн, dǫu-gyн.

down, under, -dǫu'-m, -dǫu-bн, -dǫu-gyн.

down, downstream, p̂iн, p̂iн-dei, piн-dei-t̂sou.

down feather, down, t̂sǫu-gɑ'-t.

down slope, hei-dǫu'm-tsou.

to drag, pull, k'u-e-.

to drag, k'ue-bɑ, k'ue-нн'bɑ, k'uehy-ɑ', k'ue-kǫ'n.

dragon fly, k'ɑe-k̂ɑn-houdl.

drawknife, 'н'-tн'-bɑ.

dream, 'н'-yiн.

dreaming (referring to), 'н'-.

driftwood, 'н'-zout.

drill for boring metal, hǫ'-t'н-t̂-dɑ.

to drink, t'ǫu-m.

to drive, 'н-dl-, 'нdl-bɑ', 'нdl-hɑ'.

to drive in, 'нdl-heibɑ.

to drown tr., 'ǫubн'-houdl.

drowned (to be), 'ǫubн'-hęi'm.

drum, pɑdl-k'ɑ'-gɑ.

drumstick, pɑdlk'ɑ'-t'ǫuę.

dry, t'н-p.

dry (to be), t'нp̂-dɑ.

to dry up intr., t'нp-hǫn.

duck, 'ou-ei-k̂yн-toudl.

Duke Wellington Jones, prsn., Zeip̂-t'ǫugoup.

dumb man, touhẹi-k̑iн.
dust, dirt, p'н̣-ẹ.
ᵗᵒ dust, *p'н̣ẹ-p'iнt.
dust-windy (to be), 'н'gyн.
dweller, -k̑iн-dl.

e

eagle, kuαtou-hị̆н̣.
eagle feather, kuαtouhị̆н̣-'н'-gα̃'-t.
early, old time, t'ọu-gα-e-.
earring, îα'-'н.
earth, country, place, dçm.
ear, îα'-dei.
ear hole, îα'-poudl-p'iнt, îα'-
    t'нdl.
earwax, îα'-bн-k'α.
east, pнe-bα'deip-, pнe-bα'deiþ-
    dei.
ᵗᵒ eat, pα', hн̣'-n.
eater, -hн̣'-n.
ᵗᵒ eat to fullness, bou-t.
eating table, pị̆н̣-'н'-dα.
ᵗᵒ eddy, zouî-bн-t'oue-goup.
edge, pн'gyн-beibн.
edge, corner, 'ou-îα'-.
eel, sн̣'nẹi-'α̃'pị̆н̣.
egg, semen, 'iн, 'iн-îн̣ẹ.
eggshell, 'iнîн̣ẹ-k'ᾳẹ.
eight, yн̣î-sẹi.
eight (in an old Kiowa count),
    sei-îн̣ẹ.
eight by eight, yнîsẹi-n.
eight places (in), yнîsẹi-dou.
eighteen, yнîsẹi-t'н̣.
eighth (ordinal), yнîsẹin-dei.
eighty, yнîsẹi-k'ị̆н̣.
elbow bone, mᾳn-t'ẹi'm.
eleven, pн'-t'н̣.
eleven by eleven, pн't'н̣-n.
eleven places (in), pн't'н̣n-dou.
eleventh (ordinal), pн't̑н̣n-dei.
elk, k̑ou-gα-e.
elk order (member of), K̑ougαe-
    k̑iн.
elm tree, lit., saddle tree, t'α̃'-
    'н'dα.

end, fullness (referring to), -k'ᾳ-n-,
    'αþ-k'ᾳn-.
enemy, kyнe-dα.
enemy (man), Comanche (man),
    kyнe-k̑iн.
enough, 'ou-bн'-hα', 'ou-dei-hα'.
ᵗᵒ enter, hei-bн.
ᵗᵒ erect, p'ᾳ-ẹ.
ᵗᵒ erect one, put one in, tsei.
erect several, to put several in, sα.
erect (to be, ss.), îн'-dou'.
erect (to be, tpls.), t'н'-dou'.
evening (in the), tei-hị̆н̣.
everywhere, k'oubei, k'ou-gyн-e.
excrement, sα̃'-gyн.
excrescence on tree, 'н'-k̑ᾳ'-
    p'oudl.
ᵗᵒ extinguish, pᾳ . . .
eye, tн'.
eyelash, tн'-'αî-dα.
eyelid, tн'-k̑ᾳ.

f

face, îou-bн, îou-bн-'e.
face down, inverted, upside down,
    dọu-dei.
face powder (particle of), îouþ-
    t'eiî-dα.
fair, light-colored, îsọu.
fair (to be), îsọu-dα.
ᵗᵒ fall, k̑u-e-gyн, þei-î-gyн.
ᵗᵒ fall (ss.), 'ou-î-gyн.
ᵗᵒ fall (as rain), rain, descend
    (e. g. hill), sei-p.
ᵗᵒ fall (down), guα-þ-gα, îsou-ei-
    gyн.
fall grape, k̑oudl-t'нp-ei-gα.
far, t'α̃'-gα.
farthest, very far, t'α̃'-hị̆н̣.
fast walker (to be), 'ᾳn-tsн'-sα'e.
fat, tọu-n.
father, paternal uncle, tα-dl; my
    or our father, tα̃'tα-'e; father,
    voc., tα'.
father-in-law, k̑iн-'eidl.

father-in-law, son-in-law, dǫu-m.

fawn, t̄ɑ'-'iн.

ᵗᵒ fear tr., pei.

feather, 'н'-gɑ'-t.

feather (fiber of) *'ɑ'-p'ɑt̄-dɑ.

ᵗᵒ feed, pįн-k̄oup.

ᵗᵒ feel angry, t̄ǫ-'н.

ᵗᵒ feel bad, sad, k̄ɑ'dei-'ęi-dɑ.

ᵗᵒ feel cold, die of cold, k̄ɑ'-hęi'm.

ᵗᵒ feel hot, die with heat, sнdl-hęi'm.

fence post, 'ei-k̄uɑ-'н'-dɑ.

fever (to have), sнdl-'ǫmgyн.

few (to be), sou-dei.

fiesta, big dance, kuɑn-'eidl.

fifteen, 'ǫnt̄ɑ'-t'н.

fifth (ordinal), 'ǫnt̄ɑt̄-dei.

fifty, 'ǫnt̄ɑ'-k'įн.

ᵗᵒ fight, kyнe-dɑ.

ᵗᵒ fight, act, p̄н-'e-gɑ.

ᵗᵒ fight, war, kyнe-p̄н'egɑ.

ᵗᵒ fill up tr., bout-houdl.

fin (dorsal of fish), 'ɑ'pįн-'нt̄ɑhɑ'e.

finally, at last, 'ǫn-k̄iн-gɑ.

ᵗᵒ find, t'ǫ-n.

finger nail, mǫn-t̄sǫų.

finger ring, mǫn-sou-dei, sou-dei.

ᵗᵒ finish intr., mǫ'-hǫn.

ᵗᵒ finish intr., cease, be consumed, -hǫ-n.

ᵗᵒ finish tr., finish eating, eat up, hǫ'-n.

fire, p'iн, p'iн-dɑ.

firefly (locally called lightning bug), tне-k'ǫų'm.

fireplace, p'iн-dǫm.

firewood, k̄iн-bɑ.

firewood (to get), k̄iн-.

first, t̄ǫ-m-.

first, to begin, t̄ǫm-hyų'ę-gɑ-.

first (ordinal), p̄н'nyнt̄-dei.

fish, 'ɑ'-pįн, t'ǫun-t̄ɑ-p'oudl.

fish sp., k'ǫųmsei-'ɑ'pįн.

fish bait, 'ɑ'pįн-p'ou-kiн.

fish line, 'ɑ'pįн-p'oue.

fish net, 'ɑ'pįн-tне-gɑ.

fish skin, 'ɑ'pįн-k'ɑe.

fish spear, bout-k'ue-tsǫųn.

five, 'ǫn-t̄ɑ'.

five (in an old Kiowa count), t̄ɑ-'ɑ-dl.

five by five, 'ǫnt̄ɑ-t.

five cents, pнesęi'n.

five places (in), 'ǫnt̄ɑ'-dou.

ᵗᵒ flap, flutter, tout̄-gou-p.

flat, -t̄ɑ-gyн.

flat, broad, wide (to be), k'ɑ'-p'eidl.

Flathead man, 'Ɑdlt'ǫų-(k'ɑe)-k̄i(н)hн'-k̄iн.

flea, guɑdl-p'ou.

flicker, guɑdl-hǫ'-dei.

flint, k̄ɑe-k̄ǫų-gɑ.

flint arrowhead, bou'-seisei-gɑ.

ᵗᵒ float, t̄ɑe-zout-н.

ᵗᵒ flow, melt, zei-p.

ᵗᵒ flow together, p̄ɑ'-pнhнdl-dou'.

flower, 'н'-k'į'н-gɑ.

flute, wind instrument, tǫų-bɑ'-t.

flute (of wing bone), t̄soudl-t'ęi'm-tǫų-bɑ'-t.

fly, k̄ǫ'nǫt̄-sɑp'ouy-iн.

ᵗᵒ fly about, p'iнhout-houkǫų'm.

ᵗᵒ fly away, p'iнhout̄-k'i'нbɑ.

flying (referring to), p'iн-hou-t-.

flying machine, p'iнhout-hǫndei-gɑ.

foam, p'iн-t̄-gyн.

ᵗᵒ foam, p'iнt̄-dɑ, p'iнt̄-k̄uɑdl.

fog, bįн-gyн.

foggy (to be), bįн-dɑ.

food, meal, pįн, pįн-gyн.

food in the bowels, sɑ-dl.

foot, 'ǫn-sou-'e.

foot (with the), 'ǫ-, 'ǫ'-, 'ǫn-.

foottrack, 'ǫn-gyн.

for, postp., -pei-dou.

forehead, tнn-guǫ-gɑ.

foremost (to be), t̄ǫm-dɑ.

foreskin, beidl-k'ǫę, sou-k'ɑe.
to forgive, 'ǫn-t̂ou-t'ɥ'.
forty, ɥнt̂gyн-k'įɥ.
forward, from now on, t̂ou-bei-guɑ.
four, yiн-gyн.
four (in an old Kiowa count), yi(н)gyн-t'ǫụn.
four by four, yiн-gyн-t.
four places (in), yiнgyн-dou.
fourteen, ɥнt̂gyн-t'ɥ.
fourth (ordinal), yiнgyнt̂-dei.
fourth time, yiнt̂gyн.
fox, tsęį-t'н-'ou-t'н.
foxtail plant, pęį-sǫụ-dɑ.
fresh, newborn (to be), p̄ɑ'-gyн.
friend, kǫụ-m, tsн-'н-dei.
frightful (to be), zei-dl-bei.
fringe (pendule of), 'ɑ'-gн'bɑ.
to fringe, 'ɑ'yн-sɑ.
Frizzlehead (prsn., 'ɑdl-p'eip̀-dei.
frog sp. k'ɑ'dlei-k'yн'dlei.
from, see at.
from waist down, p̄iн-dei-p.
front, former, t̂oup̀-dei.
frosty (to be), k̄iн-t̂ɥ'-dɑ.
fruit, seed, bread, 'ei-gɑ, -'ei-bɑ, -'ei-gɑ'-t.
fruit bug, 'ei-poudl.
to fry, *k̄ǫ'-tǫ'.
full, satiated (to be), bout̂-dɑ.
fur crook, p'ɑ'-bǫụ'n.
to fuss over, 'iн-k'ǫ'.

## g

gall, t̂ǫ'-dei.
game, 'ɑ'-gyн.
to gamble much, 'ɑ'-нɑp.
to gamble well, be a good gambler, 'ɑ'-hị'ɥ.
gambler, 'ɑ'-k̄iн, 'ɑ'-нɑp̀-k̄iн.
gap, mountain pass, tǫ-n.
garfish, mǫ'k̄ǫ'-kyụ-'ę.
to get, take, hɑ'-gyн.

to get angry at, k'oubei-peidl-p̄н'egɑ.
to get burnt, tsęįn-hǫn.
to get colic, bout-k'oup-'ǫmgyн.
to get lost, p̄ɑ-e.
to get short of food, hęįm-'ǫmgyн.
to get smoky, 'не-sęį-'ǫmgyн.
to get to paining, k'oup̀-'ǫmgyн.
to get wise, guɑ-'ǫmgyн.
to give, hand, 'ǫ, mɥ'-gɑ, *mɥ'-hɑ'.
to give a whoop, tsнt-hн'dɑ'.
to give birth to a child, 'iн-t̂seip.
glass tumbler, glass dish, bǫụe-k̄ɑ'нt̂-dɑ.
glue, paste, k̄ɑdl-sei.
to glue, k̄ɑdlsei-k̄ǫ'.
glued (to be), k̄ɑdlsei-k̄ǫ'-dɑ.
glutton, bout̂-pout-k̄iн.
to go, bн, 'ǫn-hiнt.
to go (itive), -hou.
to go, travel, hou'-, hou-, t'ou-yн.
to go, walk, tsн-e-, tsне-bн, -tsɥ'-.
to go along making a noise, hou-pǫụ-ɥ.
to go crazy, 'ɑdlk'ɑe-'ǫmgyн.
to go deer hunting, t̂нp-ęįbн.
to go fishing, 'ɑ'pįн-p'oubн.
to go hunting, 'ęį-bн.
to go off angry, t̂ǫ'-bн, t̂ǫ-'ǫ'zǫụn.
to go on foot, 'ǫn-tsɥ'-bн.
to go out, take out, t'ei-p.
to go over to gamble, *'ɑ'-'не.
to go past, through, t'ou-gyн-e.
to go spying, k̄ou-bн.
to go to break off tr., t'ęį'm-bн.
to go to catch, -p'ou-bн.
to go to fight, kyнedɑ'-bн.
to go to get, k'ɑ'-bн.
to go to get firewood, k̄iн-bн, k̄iн-t'ęįm-bн.
to go to hunt for, tǫụ-bн.
to go to live with, ɥнt̂-bн.
to go to play, yне-bн.
to go to see, pǫụ-bн.

ᵗᵒ go to sleep, dẹi-hẹi'm, dẹi-mǫ.

ᵗᵒ go to work, sɑ̃'dei-bн.

ᵗᵒ go with, accompany, t'нhy-ɑ'.

goal, tɑ̃'-tseidl.

going on foot, 'ǫn-tsн̣'-.

good (to be), îн̣'-gyн.

gooseberry bush, 'ɑdlk'oup-'ei-p'eip.

gooseberry fruit, 'ɑdlk'oup-'ei-gɑ.

gourd (wild) fruit, kou-kǫy-bɑ.

gourd (wild) plant, kou-kǫy'm-goup.

gopher, pịн-n.

gourd (fruit of cultivated gourd), t'ǫ̃'-gɑ.

gourd vine, t'ǫ̃'-goup.

ᵗᵒ grab hold of, mǫntsǫy-tẹi'.

grandfather, k'ǫy-gyн.

grandmother (maternal), t'н̣'-giн; grandmother (maternal, my or our), t'н̣'-dei.

grandmother (paternal), t'н̣'-dl-iн.

ᵗᵒ grant, 'ǫ, 'нdl-ǫmgyн.

grape fruit (wild), îeidei-'ei-gɑ.

grapevine, îeidei-'ei-p'eip.

grass (plant or tuft of), sǫy-dɑ.

grass bur, sǫyn-sẹi-gɑ.

grasshopper, kɑ-dl-ɑ̃'-k'ɑy-iн.

grave, t'н̣m-t'oun.

graveyard, t'н̣m-tsei-dǫm, t'н̣m-tsei-yɑ'.

gray (to be), p'eiᵽ-îн̣ę.

grayish blue (to be), p'eiᵽ̃îн̣ę-sɑhyei.

grease, greasy place, kǫ̃'-gyн.

grease, lard, tн̣'-gyн.

ᵗᵒ grease, smear, kɑ', kǫ̃'-ǫ̃'mẹi.

greasy (to be), *kǫ̃'-, kǫ̃'-dɑ.

Great Spirit, Dɑ̃'-kiн, Dɑ̃'kiн-'eidl.

great walker (to be), 'ǫn-tsн̣'-kịн̣nịн.

green, îǫ̃'dei-sɑhyei.

green pea, îɑdlt'ǫn-sɑhyei-gɑ.

ᵗᵒ grind, brush (hair), sǫy-m.

ᵗᵒ grind up fine, p'н̣'-ǫ̃'mẹi.

grindstone, kɑ̃'-sǫy.

groin, tɑ̃'-.

ground owl sp., tsн̣-yнî-kiн.

ground squirrel, tsн̣'-kǫym-zн̣'-dl-ei.

ᵗᵒ grow small, wane, syǫn-'ǫmgyн.

g-string, tɑ-e-gou-p.

gullet, 'oubн-k'yнe.

gum, chewing gum, kɑ-dl.

gun, rifle, hǫ̃'-zeiᵽ-gɑ.

## h

hackberry fruit, 'н-'ei-gɑ.

hackberry tree, 'н-'ei-p'eip.

hail, îein-seip.

hailstone, îẹi-n.

hair of ears, îɑ̃'-p'ɑî-dɑ.

hair of hand, mǫn-p'ɑî-dɑ.

hair of head, 'ɑ̃'-dɑ.

hairbrush, comb, 'ɑdl-sǫym.

hair dressed to one side, 'ɑdl-hɑ̃'bн.

hair dressed to one side (man having), 'ɑdl-hɑ̃'bн̣'-kiн.

hairy, -p'ɑ-houdl.

half, k'ou-ᵽǫ̃', zн-e-dei.

half brother, zнedei-pн̣'biн.

half dollar, ᵽǫ̃'-hị'н̣-dei.

halfway, midway, zн̣'-yɑ'.

hammer, hǫ̃'-îsou-t'н-'e.

hammerstone, îsou-t'н-'e.

hand, arm, mǫ̃'-dɑ.

hand (with the), mǫ-, mǫ̃'-, mǫn-.

hand game, tou-' 'ɑ̃'-gyн.

hand-game player, tou-'ɑ̃'-kiн.

hand-game song, tou-'ɑ̃'-dɑ̃'-gyн.

handkerchief, sẹin-p'iнî-dɑ.

handle, tou-p, îǫm-t'ǫy-dɑ.

happy (to be), 'ǫy-t'н̣'-dɑ.

hard, strong, kou-t.

hard knot (referring to), p'н̣-m-sɑ-.

hard times (to have), kouî-dei-'ɑ̃'kɑ.

harness, wagon, k'ue-p'ꜧ, k̄ɑ'-dꜧdl-k'uep'ꜧ.

hat, bǫų-hǫų-dɑ, k̄ɑn-bǫųhǫų-dɑ.

hawk sp., 'ꜧ-kɑ-e.

hawk sp., 'ꜧkɑe-t̄ꜧę.

hawk sp., 'ꜧkɑe-k'ǫų-gyꜧ.

hawk sp., k̄ɑgyꜧꝑ-pꜧ'-dǫn, k̄yꜧꝑ-pꜧ'-dǫn.

hawk sp., mǫnt̄sou-t'ꜧ'bei.

hawk sp., t̄ɑdl-kǫų-t̄ɑ'dlei.

hawk sp., t'ǫųn-p'ouyiꜧy-iꜧ.

hawk (red-tailed), t'ǫųn-guɑdl.

head, 'ɑdl-t'ęį'm.

head, hair, 'ɑ-dl-, 'ɑ-t-.

headache, 'ɑdlt'ǫų-k'oup.

headache fruit, 'ɑdl-k'oup-'ei-gɑ.

Head Dragging Creek (plcn.), 'Ɑdlt'ęį'm.

head louse, p'ou.

to hear, t̄ɑ'.

heart, t'ęį-n.

heart disease, t'ęįn-houdl-dꜧ.

heart of tree, 'ꜧ'-gyꜧ-dǫų-gɑ'-t.

heart vein, t'ęįn-p'iꜧ.

heel, 'ǫn-p'ɑ'-gɑ.

hello, 'ꜧ'-k'ou.

hemorrhage, sɑ-'ǫų'm.

hemorrhage (to have), sɑ-'ǫųm-hꜧ'bꜧ.

herd of antelopes, t̄ɑ'-seidl.

to herd, 'ꜧdl-dou'.

here, 'ęį-hɑ', 'ęįm-hɑ'; 'į(ꜧ)-hɑ'; also 'ęįdei-hɑ', 'ęįmdei-hɑ', etc.

here, now, 'į(ꜧ)-hǫ'.

heavy (to be), p'iꜧ.

hiccoughs (to have), t̄ɑdl-hꜧ'-dɑ.

high (very, to be), kyꜧ'ę-hꜧ'-dei, mꜧę-hį'ꜧ.

high water (to be), tsei-ꝑ-dɑ.

hill, bɑ-dl-hɑ', p'iꜧ-gɑ.

hip, piꜧ-t'eidl.

his, their, your, prefixed to certain relationship terms, 'ꜧ-.

to hit, gou-p.

to hit (not to miss), guɑ-bꜧ.

to hit with the hand, mǫn-goup.

hitter with a stick, -t'ǫų-goup.

hitting (by), t̄ɑ-, t̄ɑ'-.

hoe, dǫmku'ɑ-syꜧn.

to hold, have, have on, dou'.

hole, t'ꜧ-dl, -p'iꜧ-t.

homesick (to be), tou-k'yꜧhį'ꜧ-dɑ.

honey, panocha, pęį-n-hꜧ'.

honeybee, pęįnhꜧ'-poudl.

honeycomb, t̄eidlseiꝑ-tou.

hoof, 'ǫn-k̄ǫn.

hook for hanging things away, 'ɑ'-k̄uɑ-sou-dei.

to hook with horns, gųǫn-mꜧę.

hook-nosed (to be), mǫ'-t̄ɑ-hɑ.

hook-nosed man, mǫ't̄ɑhɑ-kiꜧ.

horn, antler, gųǫ-dei.

horned owl sp., mǫ'-hiꜧ.

horned owl sp., mǫ'hiꜧ-t̄ꜧe.

horned owl sp., t̄sǫų-gųǫ.

horned toad, sęį-hꜧ'n.

horse, tsęį.

horsefly, tsęį-poudl.

horse harness, tsęį-k'uep'ꜧ.

"Horse Headdresses" (Kiowa order), Tsęį-t'ꜧ-ę-n-mǫ.

horse manure, tsęį-sɑt.

hortative or emphatic particle, kɑ-dl.

hortative, particle used with fut., hei-t.

hortative verb prefix, kǫ-n-.

hot (to be), sꜧ-dl.

hot sunshine, dꜧ'-sꜧt̄-gyꜧ.

house, tipi, tou.

house having a chimney, kǫųmpɑ'-tou.

house post, tipi pole, tou-dǫųm-dei-'ꜧ'-dɑ.

how? in some way, hꜧ'-tsou.

how many times? several times, hꜧ'oudei-dou.

how much, how many? some, several, hꜧ'-'ou-dei.

hungry (to be), t'ɑ'-hęį'm.

husband, k̑iн.
husband (to get), k̑iн-hɑ̈'gyн.
husband (to have), k̑iн-dei.
humming bird, mɑnsɑ-ťęinęi.
ᵗᵒ hurry, нн-dl-н̦, k̑uɑ-n-dɑ.

### i

I, my, we, our, nɑ̈.
ice (piece of), tęi-gyн.
icicle, tęigyн-k̑ɑn-hнť-dɑ.
idol (a kind of), k̑ɑ̈'-dọu-bei-tsọu-hi̦н.
illegitimate child, sọun-guɑdl.
in, at, see at.
in front of, -bei-gyн.
in the middle, halfway, k'ou-p̑ɑ̈', p̑ɑ̈'-hei.
in the middle of, -p̑ɑ̈-'ę-gyн, -k'ou-p̑ɑ̈', -k'ou-p̑ɑ̈-'ę-gyн.
in vain, k̑yн̦-m-dei-.
indeed, mн̦-, mн̦'-.
indeed, surely, pн̦'-hi̦н.
index finger, mɑn-kɑm.
Indian (man), Kiн-guadltɑ̈'dei-k̑iн.
Indian red paint, guɑdl-hyụ-'ę.
indicator, -bọun-mɑę.
ink, kuɑť-t'ọu.
inspector, umpire, pọu-k̑iн.
intensive, -hou-dl, -p'ou-dl, -'ọụ, -sọụ.
intensive particle, p'н̦-ę.
interj. of admiration or surprise, 'ɑtɑ.
interj. of pain, hɑ̈.
interj. used by Utes in battle, hei.
interj. used in calling one's attention, hyн.
interj. of scorn, hyн̦.
interj. 'ou.
interj. of surprise, tн.
interj. of surprise or disgust, ťs.
interj. of surprise, 'uh.
interj. of fright or surprise, yuh.

10559°—28——15

interr. particle, hɑ.
interr. stem, hн̦'-.
intestine, sei-.
intestine (small), sei-ťн̦-ę.
intestine (large), sei-k'ọụ-ę.
iron, metal wire (piece of), nɑ̈-gɑ̈'t.
iron arrowhead, hɑ̈'-sei-sei-gɑ.
iron fishhook, hɑ̈'-p'ou.
iron knife, hɑ̈'-k̑ɑ'.
iron nail, hɑ̈'-ťɑ̈'-kuɑ.
island, 'ɑ̈-dɑ.
Island, prsn., 'ɑ̈'dɑ̈'dei.

### j

jackrabbit, k̑ọụm-sɑ.
ᵗᵒ jump, k'yнe-guɑn.
ᵗᵒ jump out of, 'oudнťgyн-guɑn.
just, emphatic or hortative particle, dн.
just now, then, recently, at last, sɑ-t.

### k

ᵗᵒ keep (animal), treat, pɑ̈'-dou'.
kettle, ki(н)-sɑ̈'-dɑ.
ᵗᵒ kick, 'ɑn-goup.
kidney, ťɑdl-syн̦n, ťɑdl-ťɑępouť-gyн, ťɑdlt'ɑn-pouť-gyн, ťɑdl-t'ɑn-ťɑępouť-gyн.
kidney, bean, pea, ťɑdl-t'ɑn.
ᵗᵒ kill, dɑ-, dɑ̈'-, hou-dl.
killdeer, t'ọu-ťęinęi.
killer, dɑ̈'-k̑iн.
kind (to be), ťɑ'-d . . .
kindling wood (piece of), k̑iн-syн̦-dɑ.
kingfisher, crest, 'ɑdl-k'ɑe-k̑i(н)-hн̦'.
Kiowa man, Kɑe-k̑iн, K'ọụmpɑ̈'-bi̦н̦n-k̑iн.
Kiowa Arikaree man, Kɑe-k̑ɑťdɑ-kiн.
"Kiowa mountains" (mountains in Montana region), Kɑe-k̑oup.

Kiowa order (member of), 'Hdl-dou'-'iн.

Kiowa order (member of), Кoue-tseįкiн.

Kiowa order (member of), K'uαt-кiн.

Kiowa order (member of), Seįn-dei-'iн.

Kiowa order (member of) Тн̨e-bei-кiн.

Kiowa woman, Кαe-mн̨.

kitchen, pįн̨-'αm-tou'e.

to knead, zα̨-'e̩. . . .

knee, ̃teidl-bǫų'.

kneecap, ̃teidlbǫų'-̃tн̨epouι-gyн.

knee pit, pн̨dl-gǫų̨m-bн.

knife, к̃α'.

knob, ̃tα̨e-k'αt-gα'̃t.

knob, mountain, кou-p.

to knot (at end of string), p'out-t'н̨dl-нe.

to know, нн-e-gyн, ннegyн-dα.

l

labium, p'ei-beit-dα.

ladder, 'α̨n-t'out-'н̨'dα.

lake, sei-tsou.

lamb's quarter, beidl-seį-'н̨'-dα.

lame (by having one leg short), t'ǫų-нн̨dl.

lame (to be), t'ǫų-нн̨dl-dα.

lame man, t'ǫųhн̨dl-кiн.

lard, grease, tн̨'-gyн.

lard bucket, tн̨'gyн-dα'н̨t-dα.

large, much, 'ei-dl, say-eidl, bįн̨-n, sα-bįн̨n, sα-p'н̨n, -sα-, -sα̨'-.

large-nosed man, mα̨'к̨α̨n-'eidl-кiн.

large windshield, k'ǫųmpα̨'-bįн̨n.

lasso, p'ou-кiн-yнe-bα.

to lasso, p'ou-кiнgyн.

last, hǫų-n-.

last man, hǫųn-кiн.

to laugh, р̃ei-t'н̨'.

to lay one, ̃tsei-p.

to lay several, кou-p.

leaf, 'нe-deį'-gα.

leaf tripe, many plies, sαdl-k'α̨e̩.

lean, t'α-dl.

to lean against, yiн-bн̨'-к̃α.

leech, 'ǫų-'α̨'̃tн̨m-poudl.

left, 'α̨m-t'н̨m-dei.

leg, marrow, t'ǫų-dei.

leg hair, t'ǫų-p'α-̃t-dα.

lemon, 'ei-guαt̃кou-dα, t'ǫų-'н̨-'α̨'-mα̨.

to lend, 'α̃-'α̨.

-less, privative, postfixed to nouns and adjectives, -heį.

to let loose, mα̨'-guα.

lettuce, cucumber, sαhyei-'ei-goup.

liar, p'oudl-кiн.

lie, p'ou-dl-gyн.

to lie, p'oudl-hн̨tgα.

to lie (in position, ss.), к̃α; does not lie, tsou-gα'.

to lie (in position, tpls.), к̃uα-dl.

to lie asleep (ss.), deį-к̃α.

to lie asleep (tpls.), deį-к̃uαdl.

to lie dead (ss.), pei-к̃α.

to lie down, mα̨'.

to lie rotten (ss.), bǫųn-к̃α.

life, к̃yнkǫųm-dн, к̃yнkǫųm-gyн.

to lift, hн̨'bн.

to lift, carry off, hн̨'-bα.

light, bǫų-gyн.

Light, prsn., P'iн-bǫų.

light, shine, -pн'.

light, bright (to be), bǫų-dα.

light (in weight, to be), 'α̃'-k'α̨.

to light (fire), hiн-dl-b . . .

lightning, bǫų̨e-bн-heip̃-gyн.

like, mα̨', -tsou.

to like, 'ǫų-dα, 'ǫų-dei, 'ǫų-peidl-dou'.

lion, 'н̨'-kų̨e', mн̨n-p'α-houdl.

lion (mountain lion), ̃tн̨m-deidl.

lip, beidl-k'αe.

to listen, ̃tα̃'-t'н̨dl-dou'.

to listen to, ĩɑ'-hн-t.
little (a small quantity), syɑ̨-n, syɑ̨n-dei.
Little Cliff, prsn., Touhɑ'-syн̨n.
little girl, mɑ̨'-t'ɑ̨n.
to live, dwell, k̃iн-dl.
liver, kidney, ĩɑ-dl.
liver, ĩɑdl-eidl.
lizard sp., touguɑdl-ĩн'-dei.
lizard sp., t̃sou-touguɑdlĩн'dei.
load, clothes, property, provisions, 'ou-dl.
to load, 'oudl-k̃oup.
loaded (to be), 'oudl-p'н̨.
to lock up, p'н̨'-t̃seip, t'ǫu-p'н̨ . . .
lone, pн̨'gɑ-'e.
Lonewolf, prsn., Kue'-pн̨'gɑ'e.
Lonewolf, Delos, prsns. of, K'ǫu-'eidl, 'Ę'im-hɑ'-'н̨.
long, tall, k̨iн-niн̨.
long (for a long time), tɑ'-dei.
long ago, t'ǫu-gɑ.
to look at, sɑ̨-m-dɑ, sɑ̨m-bǫu, tɑ'-bн.
lump, excrescence, 'н-'н-ĩ-dɑ.
lump in the throat, 'ou-'н'нĩ-dɑ.
lump on abdomen, bout-н'нĩ-dɑ.
lump on body, k'ou-'н'нĩ-dɑ.
lump on eye, tн'-'н'нĩ-dɑ.
lump on groin, tɑ'-'н'нĩ-dɑ.
lump on face, ĩou-'н'нĩ-dɑ.
lump on hand, mɑ̨n-'н'нĩ-dɑ.
lump on nose, mǫ'-'н'нĩ-dɑ.
lung, k'ɑhy-oudl.

m

maggot, 'i(н)-'oup.
magpie, 'ɑ̨-'ɑ'-dei.
made (to be), 'ɑ̨m-dɑ.
made (to be), happen, become, 'ɑ̨-m-gyн.
to make, 'ǫ'-mei, 'ɑ̨m-dou'.
to make a fire, k̃iн-k̃oup.
to make a loop in, p'ou-'ǫ'mei.
to make angry, sɑ̨'ǫ'dei-'ǫ'mei.

to make crazy, to do wrong, 'ɑdlk'ɑe-'ǫ'mei.
to make to drink, t'ǫu- . . .
to make dry, t'нp-'ǫ'mei.
to make hotter, sнdl-hн'b . . .
to make kill, dɑ-'ǫ'mei.
to make run, 'нe-'ǫ'mei.
to make smooth, ĩɑ̨e-'ɑ'mei.
to make swim, kɑ'ĩɑ-'ǫ'mei.
man, k̃yн̨-hi'н̨.
man, male, -k̃iн.
mane, 'ou-y-ɑ'-dɑ.
many (to be), 'ɑ-e, kɑ̨-n.
many times, 'eiĩdei-dou.
mare, tsei-mн̨.
to mark, paint, write, guɑ-t.
marked, painted, kuɑ-t.
marked (to be), kuɑĩ-dɑ.
marrow, leg, t'ǫu-dei.
Martinez, Andres, prsn., Hн̨ndн̃dlei.
match, t'н̃'-tou-p.
matted (to be), tangled, sei-dl-dɑ.
maybe, hн̃yн̃'-dou, hei-n, mɑ̨-n.
meadow, t'ǫu-zǫunyi'н̨.
meadow lark, tн̃'-tɑ'-guɑdl.
mean (to be), 'ǫ'-dei, ĩɑ-n.
measure, ĩɑ̨m-'ɑ̨n.
to measure, *ĩɑ̨m-'ǫ'nei.
measuring stick, ĩɑ̨m'ɑ̨n-'н̃'-dɑ.
measuring worm, p'ɑ'-k̃ou-dei.
meat, flesh, k̃iн.
meat, membrane of, poudl-ɑ'-k'ɑe.
medicine, dɑ-e.
medicine, orenda, dɑ-, dɑ'-.
medicine bag (a kind of), 'н̃'dei-k̃iн.
Medicine-bag Man, prsn.,'H'dei-k̃iн.
Medicine-bag Man creek, 'H'dei-k̃iн-dei P̃ɑ'.
medicine man, doctor, dɑe-'ɑ̨m-k̃iн.
to meet, k̃ɑ'-dei.

<sup>to</sup> melt intr., sʜt-ɑt'ɑ̧'n.

<sup>to</sup> menstruate, ḳi̧ɴdei-'ɑ̧mgyʜ, ḳi̧ɴdei-dɑ.

<sup>to</sup> mention in a story, hei̧dei-tǫuk'ɑ̧'m.

mescal plant, t'ǫu-'ɑdlk'ɑe-goup.

mesquite bean, gu(ɑ)-hei-gɑ.

mesquite bean mush, guɑhei-kuɑ'n.

mesquite bush, guɑhei-p'eip.

metal comb, hɑ̧'-'ɑdlsǫum.

metate, 'ei-sǫu-bɑ.

Mexican man, Ḳoup̣-t̑ɑ'k'ɑeḳiʜ.

mid-afternoon (in), k'iʜsɑ-t'ɑ'.

midwife, 'iʜ-tɑ'-mʜ̧

milk, breast, zei-p.

milk (of cow), kɑdl-zeip.

milky way, tɑ̧'-gǫumt'ǫu.

milkweed, zeip-ʜ̧'-dɑ.

mine, 'ɑdlhɑ̧'-t'ǫun.

minnow, mɑ̧'-k'ɑ-'iʜ.

minute, mi̧ni̧t.

mirage (to be), pʜ-'ʜ̧-dɑ.

<sup>to</sup> miss (not to hit), gou-bɑ'.

<sup>to</sup> mix, kuɑ'-n.

moccasin, k'ɑ̧-'ɑ̧n, tou-hi̧'ʜ̧.

moccasin, shoe, tou-dei.

<sup>to</sup> mock, 'ou-t̑ɑt̑-bʜ-t'ʜ.

mockingbird, tǫupʜedl-t̑ei̧nei̧.

moist, t'ʜ̧'-hou-p.

moist (to be), t'ʜ̧-houp̣-dɑ.

molar tooth, *zǫu-'eidl.

mole, 'ei-k'ǫu-gɑ̧'-t, pi̧ʜ̧n tʜ'hei̧.

Monday (on), dɑ'k'iʜ-ḳi̧ʜ̧hi̧ʜ̧.

money, coin, dollar, 'ɑdl-hɑ̧'-gyʜ.

moon, month, p̱ɑ'.

moon, p̱ɑ-e.

moonshine, p̱ɑ'-pʜ̧'pɑ'-dʜ.

more, moreover, also, either, 'ʜ-dl, t̑sʜ-dl.

morning (in the), gi̧ʜ̧-gɑ.

morning star, tʜ̧'-'eidl.

mortar, 'eit-ɑ-bʜ-dou-p.

mosquito, 'ɑdl-hʜ̧ǫmei̧.

moth, k'i̧ʜ̧-t'ʜdl.

mother, maternal aunt, tsɑ; my or our mother, kɑ'kɑ'e; mother, voc., kɑ'.

mother-in-law, tsǫu-hi̧ʜ̧.

Mount Scott, Ḳoup-'eit̑-dɑ.

mountain, knob, ḳou-p.

mountain ghost; owl sp., sɑ-p'oudl.

mountain lion, t̑ʜ̧m-deidl.

mountain range, ḳoup-t̑ɑhɑ̧'-sɑdl.

mountain rock, Ḳoup̣-t̑sou.

mountain sheep, tei̧-bei.

mourning dove, kyʜe-sɑ'dei.

mouse, t̑ǫu-dei-'iʜ.

mouse or rat sp., k'uʜehy-oudl.

mouse-colored, t̑ǫudei-'iʜ-p'ɑdl.

mouse-colored (to be), t̑ǫudei'iʜ-p'ɑdl-dɑ.

mouth, sɑ-'ɑ-dl, sɑ'ɑdl-gyʜ.

mouth (external), lip, bei-t̑-dɑ, beidl-gyʜ.

<sup>to</sup> move, mɑ̧.

<sup>to</sup> move about, -hou-kǫu'm.

much, many, 'eit̑-dei, bi̧ʜ̧m-dei.

much (very), k'oup̣dei.

much, adv., 'ǫu-dei.

much, too much, excessively, 'ɑ̧n-gɑ-douy-ei-dei, dou-e-.

mucus of the nose, sei̧-n.

mucus (watery), mɑ̧'-t'ǫu.

mud, tsei̧-n.

mud doll, tsei̧n-hei̧'iʜ.

mud hen, mɑ̧'ḳɑ̧n-t̑ʜ̧ǫ.

muddy water, tsei̧n-t'ǫu.

mulberry tree, k'ɑ̧-kuɑt-ʜ̧'dɑ.

mule, t̑ɑ'k'ɑe.

<sup>to</sup> murder, sei̧m-houdl.

murderer, sei̧m-dɑ'-ḳiʜ.

mush, 'ei-kuɑ'n.

muskrat, pou-guɑn-houdl.

mussel, dei̧n-ɑt-t̑ɑ̧'t'ɑ̧'nei.

my, our, nɑ̧; postfixed to 1st person possessive forms of certain relationship terms, -'ei.

n

nail, claw, -t͡sǫu̧.
nail (of iron), hǫ̃'-t͡ɑ'kuɑ.
nail head, hǫ̃'t͡ɑ'kuɑ-'ɑdlt'ęi̧'m.
name, k'ǫ̃'-gyн.
narrow, kɑ't-syǫ̧n.
narrow (to be), k'ɑ'p'eidl-syн̧n.
Navaho man, K'ou-tsęin-k̃iн, Nн-
    bнhou-k̃iн.
navel, p'ei-p'ou-t.
navel cord, p'eip'out-k'ɑe.
neck, k̃ou-dl.
neck, throat, 'ou-.
necklace, k̃oudl-p'н̧.
necklace of long bone beads,
    k̃oudlp'н̧'-hyu̧-ę, t'ǫu̧sei-koudl-
    p'н̧.
necktie, k̃oudldei-p'н̧'-gɑ.
needle, pin, tsǫu̧.
Negro, K'ǫu̧gyн-'ǫu̧-k̃iн.
nest, kuɑtou-tousǫu̧'n, tou-sǫu̧'n.
never, bei-t'ęi̧'n-dei,  hei-dǫ̧-n-
    hн̃'-gyн.
new (to be), sɑt-dei.
next, k̃iнgyн-e-.
Nez Percé man, 'ɑ̃dl-k̃ɑ'-t'oue-
    k̃iн.
night, k'ǫu̧.
night, in the night, gi̧н-gyн.
night (through the),  'н̃'-k'yн-
    p'ɑ̧-e-gyн.
night passes, k'ǫu̧-yi̧н.
night insect, gi̧н-poudl.
nightshirt, dęi̧-houdl-dн.
nine, kɑt͡sęi̧.
nine by nine, kɑt͡sęi̧-n.
nine places (in), kɑt͡sęi̧-dou.
nineteen, kɑt͡sęi̧-t'н̧.
ninety, kɑt͡sęi̧-k'i̧н.
nipple, zeip̧-mǫ̃'tsнt.
nit, p'oue-t͡ɑ̧'ę.
no, hǫ̃'-n-ęi̧.
noon, k'i̧н-sɑ.
north, sн̃'-bei-, k̃ou-dǫ̧m-.
north (to the), sн̃'-bei-guɑ.

Northerner, T͡ou-t͡ɑ'k'ɑe-k̃iн.
nose, mǫ̃'-k̃ǫ̧'n, mǫ̃'-, p'ou-.
nose bone, mǫ̃'-t'ęi̧'m.
nostril, mǫ̃'-t'нdl.
nostril hair, mǫ̃'-p'ɑt-dɑ.
not, hǫ̧-n.
not to be able, pɑ̃'-t'н̧'mǫ̃'.
not to carry outside, k'iн-gu'ɑ.
not to lie, koup̧gɑ'.
not to think right, peigyн-bǫu̧'ǫu̧.
notch, kǫ̧m-yɑ̃'-gɑ.
now, already, hei.
now, k'ou-.
nut, zęim-k̃ɑ̃'-dei.
nut (of unidentified sp.), bou-
    k̃ɑ̧-ei-gɑ.

o

oak tree, touk̃ɑt-н̃'-dɑ.
oats (grain of), sǫu̧n-'ei-gɑ.
occiput, back of head,  k̃iнhн̃'-
    bнp̧-gɑ.
ocean, dǫ̧m-'ǫ̧n-t'ǫu̧.
of what kind? of some kind,
    hн̃'tsou-dei.
office, tǫu̧-tou.
old man, 'eidl-k̃iн, k̃yнp̧-t'ɑ.
old woman, 'eidl-mн̧,  t͡sнdliн-
    tsǫu̧hi̧н̧.
old canvas, rags, k'ǫu̧m-sei.
on top, above, t'н-e.
on, above, over, -t'н-e, -t'нe-tsou.
on, beyond, back of, -gyн̃'-t'ɑ̃'-bɑ.
on both sides, yiн-gyн-p, yiн-
    gyн-t'ɑe, yiн-gyн-t'ɑ̃'-bɑ.
on side, k'ou-p̧-gɑ'-t, k'oup̧-sнt.
on the edge, 'out͡ɑ̃'-yɑ'.
on the surface of -t͡oup̧-t'нe.
on the side of, -hɑ̃'-bн-p.
on the very top, t'нe-hi̧н̧.
on this side of, -pн-dl-gyн.
one (enumerative series), pн̃'.
one, pн̃'-gɑ.
one (in an old Kiowa count),
    'ɑ-gɑ-k̃ou.

one by one, pн'-nyн.
one by one, in single file, kiн-
    hiн-t-.
one place (in), pн'nyнt-dou, pн-
    'н'-gα.
one time, once, pн'gα-dou.
one-eyed (to be), tн'-p'iн-t.
one-eyed man, tн'-p'iнt-ƙiн.
one hundred, kα'dou-k'iн.
ᵗᵒ open, ƙyн-t.
opossum, t'oun-'αtαę.
opponent, ƙiн-yн.
optative particle, yн-dl.
organ of buffalo used for making
    water jugs, tsoudl-pн-k'αe.
organ (of body, unidentified),
    tein-p'нn.
orange, t'ou-toudlα'-bα.
Osage orange tree, zeip-guαtƙou-
    'н'-dα, zeiþ-guαtƙou-bα.    ·
other, kα'-dei, kuα-dei; others
    (tpl.), kα'.
other half, 'α'-deiþ-dei.
otter, 'α'-pα-ę.
outside, gue-tsou.
ᵗᵒ overhang, 'oudl-dou'.
own, 'α'-gα.
ᵗᵒ owe, gua . . ., kuα-t, k'α'-
    dou'.
owl sp. (screech owl), beidl-kiнt-
    gyн.
owl sp.; mountain ghost, sα-
    p'oudl.
owl sp., soun-mα'hiн.
owl sp., t'ou-p'α'-houdl.
own, k'ou-hн-e, k'ou-hiн.

### p

paddle, kα'-'н'-dα, kα'-bout-н'-
    dα.
pain, ailment, k'ouþ-dн.
ᵗᵒ pain, ache, k'ou-p.
paint bag, guαdl-biнmk'αe.
palm, mαn-tα'-gyн.
panocha, honey, sugar, pei-n-hн'.

pants, k'α'-dei.
paper (sheet of), mα-tsнę-mα.
paper bread of the Pueblo In-
    dians, bou-ƙαe.
paralyzed (to be), k'ou-pei-dα.
paralyzed man, k'ou-pei-ƙiн.
parrot, tou-kuαtou.
ᵗᵒ part (hair), tα-þein-ƙoup.
past, there, 'α'-bei.
paunch, gizzard, 'α'-biн.
Pawnee man, Gu-e-gyн-ƙiн.
pay, p'ou-n.
ᵗᵒ pay, p'oun-α.
peach, apricot, p'α'gyн-'нdlα'-gα.
pear, 'ei-ƙoudl-'αm-dα.
pecan nut, toun-'н'-'ei-bα.
pecan tree, toun-'н'-'н'-dα.
Pecos river, Pα'-'eidl-syнn.
pen, writing table, kuαt-н'-dα.
pendant hanging down back,
    goum-hн'-gyн.
penis, sou-p.
people, ƙyнkoum-gα.
pepper, tsoue-sei-'ou-gyн.
peppery, sour (to be), dei-sнdl.
persimmon tree, 'Ӕhyнdl-'нdlα'-
    p'eip.
prsn. of the present head chief of
    the Kiowas, 'H'-piн-t'α'.
prsn., 'H'-tae-'eitdei.
prsn., Hн-e-tsi-k'iн.
prsn., Kα'α'-piн-t'αn.
prsn., Mα'-k'α'p'eidl.
prsn., Seit-'eim-ƙiн'-н.
prsn. of the culture hero, Sei-n-
    dei.
person (man), ƙyнkoum-ƙiн.
person (woman), ƙyнkoum-mн.
petal, 'н'k'i'н-'нedei-gα.
peyote, cactus, sei-gα.
phlegm, k'iн-n.
ᵗᵒ pick (e. g. fruit), sei-t.
ᵗᵒ pick up, gather, convene,
    tou-dα.
pie, 'ei-tнt-bα'-t.

to pierce, t'н . . .

pig, seit-tseiou.

pigeon (domestic), ĩɑ'k'ɑe-kyнe-sɑ̃'-dei.

pinacate, poudl-k̃ɑ̃'ĩɑ̃'ę.

pineapple, fig, sęį-ĩɑ̨ę-t'нdl.

pine tree sp., zǫ̣ụ-dɑ, zǫ̣ụn-'н'-dɑ.

pinworm, ĩeidl-poudl.

pipe, sɑ̃'-tou-p.

pipestone, sɑ̃'toudl-ĩsou.

pit, grave, -t'ǫ̣ụ-n.

pitch (pine gum), zǫ̣ụ-k̃ɑdl.

pitiable, k'ɑ̨'-.

pitiable (to be), k'ɑ̨'-'ɑ̨n.

pit marked (to be), pou-dɑ.

to pity, k'ɑ̨'-t'н̨'.

to place foremost, ahead (to be), ĩɑ̨m-dou'.

plain, prairie, pн'-gyн, pн'-gyн-p.

plain (to be), 'ɑ-hįн.

plainly, hн-y-ǫ̣ụ-dei.

plane, 'н'-ĩɑ̨ę-'ɑ̨'-bɑ.

plant, gou-p.

plant sp., 'н'-sęį-'ǫ̣ụ-gɑ̃'-t.

plant sp., bǫ̣ụę-'ei-gɑ.

plant sp., dęįsнdl-'н'-dɑ.

plant sp., k'ɑek̃į(н)hн'-'ei-p'eip.

plant sp., mɑ̨nĩsǫ̣ụ-'н'p'eip.

to plant, 'ei-k̃oup.

planted (to be), 'ei-k̃uɑdl.

planted field, 'ei-k̃uɑ.

planting machine, -'ei-k̃uɑ-bɑ.

to play, yн-e- . . ., yнe-'ɑ̨'męį.

to play (a game), gamble, 'ɑ.

to play arrow-throwing game, kɑ̨m-ɑ.

to play cards, 'нdl-ɑ, ĩɑ̃'k'ɑe-'нdl-ɑ.

to play flute, tǫ̣ụbн-dɑ̃'p̃н'egɑ.

to play hand game, tou-'ɑ.

to play shinny, kǫ̣ụm-'ɑ.

to play with, yнe-dou'.

to play women's awl game, tsǫ̣ụ-'ɑ.

playing card, 'н-ĩ-dɑ.

plcn., 'H'-tɑe-'eiĩdei-p̃ɑ.

plcn., "H-tɑ̨n-p̃ɑ'.

plcn., 'H'-tou'н'-p̃ɑ'.

plcn., K̃oup-'ou-t'н'-bɑ.

plenty to eat (to have), pei-dн.

plow, dɑ̨m-sн'-bɑ.

plum fruit (wild), 'нdl-ɑ̃'-gɑ.

plum bush (wild), 'нdlɑ̃'-p'eip.

pneumonia, k'ɑhyoudl-k'ouþ-dн.

point, -tsн-t, mɑ̨'-tsнt.

to point, mɑ̨n-kɑ̨m . . ., mɑ̨n-kɑ̨m-dou'.

to point with the lips, beidl-mɑ̨n-kɑ̨mdou'.

pole mattress, 'ou'-gɑt-н'.

pollen (particle of), 'нe-p'iн-bei-gɑ.

Ponca man, 'Ɑdlt'ęį'm-'ɑdlk'ɑe-k̃į(н)hн'-k̃iн.

poor man, k'ɑ̨'ɑ̨n-k̃iн.

porcupine, p'iн.

porcupine quill, p'iн-t'ǫ̣ụn.

potato, 'нep̃iн-'ei-gɑ.

potato bug, 'нep̃iн-'ei-poudl.

potato plant, 'нep̃iн-'ei-goup.

pottery vessel, tsęįn-dɑ'нĩ-dɑ.

to pound up, ĩɑ-p'н'-d . . .

pounding stone, hammer, ĩsou-t'н-'e.

prairie, plain, pн'-gyн, pн'-gyн-p.

prairie (on the), pн'-yɑ'.

prairie chicken, t'н'-kiнdl.

prairie dog, tsн.

to pray, dɑ̃'-tsнe.

precipitous (to be), k̃ɑ'dɑ.

pregnant (to be), 'iн-bouĩ-dɑ.

pregnant woman, 'iн-bouĩ-mн̨.

to prepare food, *pįн-'ɑ̨'męį.

pricky-pear fruit, sęį-'нdlɑ̃'-gɑ.

privy, sɑ̃-tou.

prohibitive particle, pou-e.

to project, p'iнhouĩ-dɑ.

pubic hair of man, sou-p'ɑĩ-dɑ.

pubic hair of woman, *beidl-p'ɑ̃'-, p'ei-p'ɑĩ-dɑ.

puckery (to be), p'н̨-n-k̃i'н-t.

Pueblo man, Pou-boudl-ʜ'-k̑iʜ, Teiguɑ-k̑iʜ.
to pull, tei̯-m.
to pull (out), k'uɑ-t, k'u-e-, k'ue-zǫyn.
puller, -k'ue-tsǫyn.
pump, windmill, t'ǫy-pɑ'-t'out.
pupil of eye, tʜ'-k'ǫy-gyʜ.
puppy, tsei̯hiʜ-'iʜ, t̑sei̯hiʜ-syʜn.
purse, 'ɑdlhɑ̯'-bi̯ʜmk'ɑe.
to push, 'ou-t'ɑ'-gɑ.
to put one in, erect one, tsei.
to put several in, erect several, sɑ.
to put several in, 'outk'ɑe-sɑ.
to put on the fire, tʜ'-t̑seip.
to put one to sleep, dei̯-t̑seip.
to put several to sleep, dei̯-k̑oup.
to put out, drive out, 'ʜdl-t'eip.

q

quail, pei̯-syʜn.
quiet (to be), tou-b . . .
quill of feather, 'ʜ'-goup, 'ʜ'-goup̭-t'ei̯'m.
quilt, pʜdl-k'ɑe.
quinine, sʜdl-dɑe.
quiver, sɑ'-bi̯ʜ.
quotative particle, 'ǫy.

r

race, t̑sʜ-n-gyʜ.
to race, run, t̑sʜ-n-dei.
race horse, t̑sʜngyʜ-tsei̯.
raccoon, seit-kuɑt.
ragweeds, 'ʜ'sɑhyei-dei̯sʜdl.
railroad train, hɑ̯-'ǫnk'iʜ-gɑ.
rain, sei-p.
to rain, fall; descend (e. g. a hill), sei-p.
rainbow, tsou-e-kuɑ-t.
rain cloud, sei̯p̭-p'ʜn.
rain water, sei̯p̭-t'ǫy.
Rainy Mountain, plcn., Seip-yʜdl-dɑ.

to raise self up higher, dʜdl-t̑ʜ'-dou'.
to raise selves up higher, dʜdl-t'ʜ'-dou'.
rattlesnake, sʜ'nei̯-hi̯'ʜ.
raven, mɑ̯'-sɑ.
rawhide box, 'oudl-tsʜ'-dɑ.
real, right, very, -hi̯ʜ.
rectum, zʜdl-sei-k'ǫye̯.
red, colored, guɑ-dl.
red clay, dɑ̯m-guɑdl, tsei̯n-guɑdl.
to redden tr., guɑdl-ɑ̯'mei̯.
red-neck, red-necked person, k̑oudl-guɑdl.
red-necked (to be), k̑oudl-guɑdl-dɑ.
Red river, plcn., Pei-p̑ɑ'-'eidl.
relative, teip̭-dei; relatives, followers, tou-dɑ.
relative (male), teip̭dei-k̑iʜ.
relative (female), teip̭dei-mʜ.
to remove tr., depart, separate oneself, go away, open (door), hei̯-dɑ.
to remove tr., pɑ'-hei̯dɑ.
to remove skin whole, k'ɑe-k'uɑt.
to repeat, 'ʜdldʜ-'ɑ̯'mei̯.
repeated sun dance, 'ʜdldʜ'-k̑ɑ'-tou.
repeatedly, 'ɑ'-bɑ.
to resemble, pɑ-'ei-dou'.
to return from defecating, sɑ'-p'ɑ̯'-tsʜn.
to revive intr., pei-guɑ, pei-sei̯-hʜ'.
rib, guɑ-dɑ, guɑ-t'ei̯'m, guɑ-t'ǫy-bɑ.
rib (lowest), k̑ʜtʜe-guɑ-dɑ.
rice, 'ei-'oukuɑ-'ei-gɑ.
rich man, 'ǫy-dei-k̑iʜ.
ridged (to be), p'iʜ-dʜt-gyʜ.
right (dexter), 'ɑ̯m-hyy'-m-dei.
right side up, on back, tsou-yʜ-p.
to rile, make muddy, p'ʜe-'ɑ̯'mei̯.
riled (to be), p'ʜe-dɑ.

Rio Grande, Pɑ̄'-'eidl.
ripe, cooked (to be), tʜ'.
ᵗᵒ rise, bɑ̄'-dʜ.
river, also name of a game, p̄ɑ'.
roadrunner, t̄sou-t̄ęinęįt-tseiou.
roan, 'ɑ'-sǫʉ.
ᵗᵒ roast, cook, tǭ' . . .
roast beef, tsęįn-kiʜ.
roasting ear, 'ei-p̄ɑ̄'-gyʜ.
rock crystal, t̄sou-bǫʉę.
Rocky Mountains, T̄sou-k̄oup.
ṛoof of the mouth, k'ǫ-houdl-.
root, k̄ɑ'tęįnįʜ-bɑ.
rootlet, k̄ɑ'tęįnįʜ-syʜ̄'-dɑ.
room, tou-'e.
rough, guɑ-p̀-gyʜ.
rough (to be), guɑp̀gyʜ-dɑ.
round, -'ʜ-dl-, -'ʜ-t-, -'ʜ', t̄ǫę-
    pout-gyʜ, -pou-t̄-gyʜ.
ᵗᵒ round up, 'ʜdl-tou-dɑ.
rotten (to be), bǫʉ-n-dɑ, bǫʉ-n-
    gyʜ.
ᵗᵒ rub, stroke, mǫn-seip̀gɑ.
rubbish pile, mǭ'-p̄ʜdl.
rug, 'ǫn-bʜ-pʜdl-k'ɑe,    tou-
    dǫʉ'mdei-k'ɑe.
rump, t̄ei-dl, t'ou-dl-, zʜ-dl.
ᵗᵒ run, 'ʜ-e, k'oup̀bei-'ʜe, k'oup̀-
    bei-tɑ̄'-'ʜe.
ᵗᵒ run, race, t̄sʜ-n-dei.
ᵗᵒ run away, t̄ǫʉm-'ʜe.
ᵗᵒ run one's best, pei-d . . .
ᵗᵒ rule, k̄iʜ-gǭ'-m.
rule, kingdom, k̄iʜgǫ'm-dʜ,
    k̄iʜgǫ'm-gyʜ.

### s

saddle, t'ɑ̄'-gyʜ.
Saddle Mountain, T'ɑ̄'-k̄oup.
sagebrush, t'ʜ̄'-gɑ̄'-t.
salamander sp., mǫn-t̄ou-gu'ɑ.
salt (grain of), 'ɑt'ʜ-t̄ʜę-mǫ.
ᵗᵒ salt, 'ɑt'ʜt̄ʜę-'ǭ'męị.
Salt Fork of Red river, Tʜ̄'mʜ̄'-
    t'ǫn-'ʜ'-p̄ɑ'.

Salt Fork of Red river sun dance,
    Tʜ̄'mʜ̄'t'ǫn-'ʜ'-p̄ɑ̄'-k̄ɑ̄'tou.
salty, 'ɑ-t'ʜ̄.
salty (very, to be), 'ɑt'ʜt̄ʜę-'ǫʉ.
sand (grain of), pei-gɑ̄'-t.
sand bur, t'ɑ̄'gue-sęį-gɑ.
sandstone, pei-t̄sou.
Satanta, prsn., Seit̄-t̄ʜę-dei.
Saturday (on), dɑ̄'k'iʜ-syʜ̄n-gyʜ.
ᵗᵒ save, k'iʜ-bǫʉm.
saved (to be), k'iʜ-bǫʉ-dɑ.
saw, 'ʜ̄'-t'ʜ̄'-bɑ.
ᵗᵒ say, talk, tǫʉ-ę.
scab, k̄ǫ-n.
scalp, 'ɑt̄-k̄ɑ̄'-gɑ̄'-t, 'ɑt̄-t'ʜt̄-dɑ.
ᵗᵒ scalp, *'ɑt̄-k̄ɑ'.
ᵗᵒ scalp, skin, 'ɑ̄'-yʜ-t.
scalp dance, 'ɑdl-dɑ̄'-kuɑn-gyʜ.
scalp lock, kyʜe-p̄ǭ'-dɑ.
school bell, kuɑt-hǭ'k̄oudlp'ʜ̄'-gɑ.
schoolhouse, kuɑt-tou.
scorpion, t'ǫʉn-sęįnhʜ̄'y-iʜ.
ᵗᵒ scowl, wrinkle forehead, k̄ǭ'-n.
ᵗᵒ scrape, t̄ǫʉ . . .
scraper (for skins), t̄ǫʉ-dɑ, t̄ʜp̀-
    t̄ǫʉ-dɑ, p'ɑ̄'-t̄ǫʉ-dɑ.
scrotum, k̄ǭ'mǫn-biʜmk'ɑe.
scum (green), sei-kǫn.
scurf, filth on the skin, boudl-
    kuɑt̄-gyʜ.
ᵗᵒ seat, sɑ-e, t'ɑ̄'-dɑ . . ., t'ɑ̄'-iʜ.
ᵗᵒ seat oneself, sit down, sɑ̄'-gyʜ.
second (ordinal numeral), niʜn-
    yʜt̄-dei.
second time, yɑ-guɑ-t-.
secret action (referring to), sęį-m-.
ᵗᵒ see, bǫʉ.
ᵗᵒ see in dream, 'ʜ̄'-bǫʉ.
ᵗᵒ see stars, be dizzy, tʜ̄'-hęị'm.
seed, dǫʉ-gɑ̄'-t.
seed, fruit, -'ei-bɑ, 'ei-gɑ, -'ei-
    gɑ̄'-t.
seed⸴ (for planting), 'eik̄uɑ-'ei-
    gɑ̄'-t.
ᵗᵒ seek, hunt for, dǫʉ-n

Seindei, name of the culture hero, Sęi-n-dei.
to sell, kǫ'dɑ-'ǫ.
semen, egg, 'iн, 'iн-t̂нę.
to send, tou-t.
to send to get, k'ɑ'-toudɑ.
to separate and travel off angry, t̂ǫ'-hou-t̂нt.
septum of nose, mǫ'-k'yнt̂-dɑ.
to set (of luminaries), yн-'e.
to set to boil, sǫn-tsei.
seven, p'н-n-sęi.
seven (in an old Kiowa count), p'н'ou-dl.
seven by seven, p'нnsęi-n.
seven places (in), p'нnsęi-dou.
seventeen, p'нnsęi-t'н.
seventh (ordinal), p'нnsęin-dei.
seventy, p'нnsęi-k'iн.
to sever one, cut one, t̂н-t.
to sever several, cut several, t'н'.
severed (to be, ss.), t̂н-dl t̂н-t-gyн.
severed (to be, tpls.), t'н'-dɑ, t'н-t̂-gyн.
to sew, mend, sou . . .
shade, shadiness, t̂ou-p'ou-t.
shadow, shade, kɑþ-k'ǫų-gyн.
shady (to be), t̂ou-p'out̂-dɑ.
to shake tr., zн-n-gɑ.
shallow, knee-deep, waist-deep, zǫųn-yį'н.
to sharpen, pн'- . . .
sheep (domestic), kyн'boudl-iн.
sheep ranch, kyн'boudliн-hǫ'̂tн'-dei-'eidl.
shell (of mollusk), zou-t.
shield, k'yų-'ę.
shield bag, k'įн-bįнmk'ɑe.
shin, t'ǫų-bout.
shine, pн'-pɑ'-dн.
shinny game, kǫųm-'ɑ'-gyн.
shinny player, kǫųm-'ɑ'-ḱiн.
shinny stick, kǫųm-'ɑ'-t'ǫųę.
shirt, article of clothing, clothes, hou-dl-dн, t̂ǫų-gyн.

to shoot, t'ɑ-t̂-gɑ.
to shoot up, *dǫ-m-gyн.
shore, t'ǫų-'ɑ'-ḱou-.
short of food (to be), to famish, hęi-m.
Shoshone man, Sǫųn-tou-ḱiн.
shot up (to be), dǫmgyн-dɑ.
shoulder, k'ɑ'-t'ǫų-.
shoulder blade, dǫ-n.
"shoulder bread," k'ɑ't'ǫų-'ei-gɑ.
to shout, hн'-dɑ.
shower comes, 'н'-hout-н.
to shut, shut in, t̂н'dɑ.
to shut in smoke, 'нesęi-t̂н'dɑ.
to shut in with a door, tsнt̂-t̂н'dɑ.
to shut out, tsнt̂-t̂seip.
shut in, t̂н'-dei.
shut in (to be), t̂н'dei-dɑ, tsнt̂-t̂н'dei-dɑ.
sick (to be), houdl-dɑ.
sickness, -houdl-dн, houdl-gyн.
sickness (referring to), hou-dl-.
silent man, tǫų-hęi-ḱiн.
sinew, tęi-hyų-ę.
sinew, thread, cord, tęi-gɑ'-t.
sinew (plaited, used in game), mнędei-ḱiн.
sinew game, to play, mнędei-ḱiн-'ɑ.
to sing, dɑ-, dɑ'-, dɑ'-dɑ, dɑ'-þн'egɑ, pɑ-dl-, pɑdl-dou'.
singer, dɑ'-ḱiн, pɑdl-dei, pɑdl-dou'-ḱiн.
singing hall, singing house, dɑ'-tou.
singing woman, medicine woman, dɑ'-mнyįн.
sister, þiн.
sister, brother, tǫ'.
to sit, 'н'-gyн.
sitting room, k'iнpн'-tou'e.
six, mǫ-sɑ'.
six by six, mǫsɑ'-t.
six places (in), mǫsɑ'-dou.
sixteen, mǫsɑ'-t'н.

sixth (ordinal), mɑsɑ'-dei, mɑsɑt-dei.
sixty, mɑsɑ'-k'iн̥.
to sizzle, k̯'-poụ̥e.
skin, k̄ɑ'-gyн, 'ɑ'-, tei-t̂-.
skin, cloth, mat, k'ɑ-e.
skin (dim.), rind, pod, bark, k'ɑ̥-ẹ.
skin scraper, t̂нр̀-t̂oụ-dɑ.
to skin, scalp, 'ɑ'-yн-t.
skunk, tн-dl.
skunk sp., tнdl-tou'ekuɑt.
skunkberry, tн̥-ẹ-pei-'ei-gɑ.
skunkberry bush,tн̥ẹ-pei-'ei-p'eip.
sky, cloud, p'н̥-n.
to slant tr., tou-hɑ'-'q̯'mẹi.
sleep (referring to), dẹi-.
sleepy (to be), dẹi-pн'dlei'.
sleeping room, dẹi-tou'e.
sledge hammer, hq̯'t̂sout'н'e-'eit-dɑ.
sleet (particle of), t̂ẹin-p'н'-gɑ'-t.
to slide down, doudlei-'out.
sliding (referring to), dou-dl-ei-.
sling, t̂sou-k̄iн-k'ɑe.
small, child, syн̥-n.
small, tiny, p'н'-syн̥n.
smallpox, t'нdl-k'ouр̀-gyн.
smallpox (to have), t'нdl-k'ouр̀-dɑ.
to smell intr., sẹi.
to smell tr., doụ-n-gyн-e, sẹi-mн̥ẹ, sẹi-yiн̥.
smoke, 'н'-gyн, 'нe-sẹi-gyн.
to smoke tr., 'н'-k̄ou-t.
to smoke (tobacco), hн'-b . . .
smoke hole, k'oụmpɑ'-gyн.
Smoky, Enoch, prsns. of, 'Ɑ'piн̥guɑdl, Mq̯'sou-dɑe, T̂soụ-t'нdliн.
smoky (to be), 'нe-sẹi.
smooth, sleek, t̂ɑ̥-ẹ, 'ɑ-t̂ɑ̥ẹ.
snail, teiguɑ-t'eibei.
snake, sн̥'-nẹi.
snake sp., pei-sн̥'nẹi.
to snap fingers, mq̯n-poudl-t'ɑt̂gɑ.

to sneeze, guɑdl-k'iн̥n.
snow, t̂ou-dl.
snow water, t̂oudl-t'oụ.
to soar, t̂soudl-touhɑ'-'q̯m-dou'.
soft (to be), tou-dl.
soft, excrement, t̂ei-t.
soldier, soudlei-k̄iн.
sole of foot, 'q̯n-doụ-bн, 'q̯n-doụ-bн̥-e.
somebody, pн'-hq̯ndei; somebodies, some (people), pн'-bн, pн'.
sometimes, pн'-hн'-gyн.
son, 'iн; son, voc., bou-dl.
son-in-law, yнt̂-k̄iн.
song, dɑ'-gyн, dɑ'-p̄н'e-gyн.
soon, houdl-dei, miн-n.
sore (to be), pн̥'-dɑ.
to sound, 'q̯-n, 'q̯n-koụ'm, toụ-'q̯n, poụ-ẹ.
to sound belchingly, bout-q̯n.
sour (?), -'н-'q̯'-.
sour, spoiled (to be), boudl-dɑ.
south, pнe-bei-, sнdl-dq̯m-.
south (in the), pнe-bei-bн, sнdl-dq̯m-gyн.
south (to the), pнe-bei-guɑ, sнdl-dq̯m-guɑ.
Southerner (man), Sнdl-t̂ɑ'k'ɑe-k̄iн.
spade, shovel, peidei-dq̯mku'ɑ.
to sparkle, boụ-hн'beip.
to speak, talk, toụ-ẹ.
to speak of, toụ-k'q̯'m.
to speak to, toụ-t'нe.
spear, guq̯-sei-dɑ.
spear (feathered along edge), kɑ-'ɑ.
to spend night on road, k'oụ-t̂ɑ'.
spider, k̄q̯'nq̯'-t'q̯'.
spider web, k̄q̯'nq̯t'q̯'-p'ou.
spirit country, k'oụmtou-dq̯m-gyн, k'oụmtou-gyн.
spirit man, ghost, k'oụmtou-k̄iн.
spirit woman, k'oụmtou-mн̥.

spittle, ȶout-kʻyн-dl.
ᵗᵒ splice, ȶei-dн-tsei.
ᵗᵒ split with wedge, ȶɑ-sн'-.
spoon, ȶɑ̜, ȶɑ̜'-tʻɑ̜n.
ᵗᵒ spot, ȶoue-guɑt.
spotted, pʻou-p.
spotted (coarsely), ȶou-, ȶou-e-, ȶoue-kuɑt.
spotted (to be), pʻoup̣-dɑ.
spotted coarsely (to be), tou-'e-kuɑt.
spotted (to be), 'ɑ-k̄ɑ-pɑ̄'-dɑ.
spring of water, tʻo̜u-tʻei-p.
spy, k̄ou-k̇iн.
ᵗᵒ stab, sei-bɑ.
stallion, ȶɑ-k̄ɑ̄'-dei.
stamen, 'н'kʻi̜'н̜-pʻɑ̄'-gyн.
ᵗᵒ stand, dei, pʻɑ̜'-ko̜u'm.
ᵗᵒ stand (tpls.?), dei-yɑ'.
ᵗᵒ stand, be in (ss.), tsei-dl.
ᵗᵒ stand up, pʻɑ̜.
ᵗᵒ stand up, get up, hн', *ɑ̜n-hн'.
ᵗᵒ stand straight up with the heat (ss.), sнȶ-dнdl-ȶɑ̄'-dou'.
ᵗᵒ stand straight up with the heat (tpls.), sнȶ-dнdl-tʻн̄'-dou'.
standing up (referring to), dн-dl-, dн-t-.
star, tн̜'.
ᵗᵒ stay, live, be about, ȶɑ'.
ᵗᵒ stay a while, temporarily, 'ɑ̄'-ȶɑ'.
steam, sнdl-hɑ̜'tʻo̜ugyн.
stem, -tʻo̜u-bɑ, goup̣-tʻo̜u-bɑ.
stick, wood, 'ɑ̄'-dɑ.
stick, club, tʻo̜u-e̜.
stick, stake, tipi stake, tou-p.
stick (hidden in hand in hand game), k̄iн-tsei-bɑ.
stick of firewood, k̄iн-bɑ.
stiff, hard, chapped, -k̄ɑ̜-n-.
stiff, hard, chapped (to be), k̄ɑ̜n-dɑ.
stiff leg, peidei-tʻo̜u-dei.
stiff-legged man, peidei-tʻo̜u-k̄iн.

stingy (to be), 'ɑ̄'-gyн.
ᵗᵒ stink, bo̜u-se̜i.
ᵗᵒ stir, mɑ̜-ku̜e̜.
stirring stick, 'ei-mɑ̜ku̜e̜gyн-'н̄'-dɑ.
stomach, tʻe̜in-tʻo̜u.
stone, ȶsou.
stone house, ȶsou-tou.
stone pipe, ȶsou-sɑ̄'toup.
ᵗᵒ stop working, sɑ̄'dei-pʻнȶgyн.
ᵗᵒ store away several, *'ɑ̄'-k̄oup, 'ɑ̄'-sɑ.
storeroom, 'ɑ̄'k̄uɑ-tou'e.
story, myth, he̜i-dei-gyн.
stove, hɑ̜'-pʻiн-dɑ.
straight, pʻɑ̜'-hei.
straight, stiff, pei-dei.
straight, stiff (to be), peidei-dɑ.
straight (very, to be), pei-'o̜u.
ᵗᵒ strain, toubн-'ou-p.
strainer, bo̜uebн-toubн-hɑ̜ndei-gɑ.
straining (referring to), tou-bн-.
strawberry, pou-'ei-gɑ.
ᵗᵒ stretch tr., kʻyн.
stretcher, pнdl-'н̄'-syн̜'-dɑ.
string, rope, yн-e-bɑ.
ᵗᵒ string, sou-dou-p.
ᵗᵒ strip, dɑ-e-gɑ.
striped on the back (to be), go̜um-ȶн̜e.
strong, bou'.
strong, hard, kou-t.
strongly, te̜i-m.
stuck in (to be), k̄iн-gyн-e.
ᵗᵒ suck, ȶн̜ . . ., 'ɑ̄'-ȶн̜ . . .
ᵗᵒ suckle, ȶн̜'-me̜i.
ᵗᵒ suffer, kʻoup̣-tʻн̜.
sugar, panocha, honey, pe̜in-hн'.
sugar cane, pe̜inhн'-'н̄'-dɑ.
sulphur, guɑtk̄ou-dɑe.
summer, sun, pн-e.
summer, pнe-dн.
summer (in), pн̄y-ɑ'.
sun, summer, pн̜-e.

sun dance, k̃ɑ'-tou.
sun-dance house, k̃ɑ'tou-tou.
Sunday, dɑ'-k'iɴ.
sunflower sp., hou-sɑ̨m-'ɴ'-dɑ.
sunflower sp., t'eip̀-sɑe-ɴ'-dɑ.
sun perch, k'ɑe-k̃i(ɴ)hɴ'.
supper, tei-pi̧ɴ.
surely, tsou-hɑ'.
surely, really, 'ou-bɑe-.
swallow, toudl-k̃ɑ̨'-dei.
to swallow, 'oubɴ-k'yɴe.
to swap, gɑ̨p-ɴe-goup.
sweat, sɴdl-t'ǫ̧ɥ.
to sweat, sɴdl-t'eip.
to sweep, k̃ɑ̨ę-p'iɴt.
sweet (to be), pȩinhɴ'-dɑ.
sweet, savory (to be), -'ɑ̨', 'ɑ̨'-,
 k̃oudl-ɑ̨'.
sweetbread, k̃ɑ̨'-dɑ.
to sweeten, k̃oudlɑ̨-'ɑ̨'mȩi.
sweetgrass plant, 'ɑ'-sǫɥ-dɑ.
sweet potato, sȩi-'ei-gɑ.
swift (to be), sɑ-'e.
to swim, bathe, kɑ'-k̃ɑ-'e, kɑ-k̃ɑ-
 'ɑ̨m-dɑ, kɑ'-zei . . .
swimming (referring to), k̃ɑ'-.
swing, 'out-bɴ-tsɴe-you-p.
to swing in swing, 'out-bɴ-tsɴy-
 iɴ-'ɴe.
sycamore tree, 'ɴ'-k̃ɥȩ-mɑ.
syphilitic (to be), p'ouk̃ɑt-dɑ.

t

tadpole, kɑdl-sȩim-'ɑ'-k'yɴ'dlei.
taemei (sacred fetish), t'ɥ-ȩ-mȩi.
tail, t'ǫɥ-n.
tail feather, t'ǫɥn-k̃i̧ɴni̧ɴ.
to take, hɑ'-d . . ., hɑ'-gyɴ.
to take a handful, mɑ̨n-k'ɑ̨n-hɑ'-
 gyɴ.
to take along, pɑ'-hɑ'.
to take care of, kyɴȩbɴ'dɑ, k̃yɴȩ-
 bɴ'-p̃ɴ'egɑ.
to take in, carry in, hei-bɑ, pɑ'-
 heibɑ.

to take out, pull out, take off,
 zǫɥ-n.
to take out, go out, t'ei-p.
to talk, speak, tǫɥ-ȩ.
to talk about, talk, tǫɥ-zɥnmɥ
 (curs.).
to talk about, talk plain, tǫɥm-
 k'i̧'ɥ.
to talk Kiowa, kɑe-tǫɥzɥnmɥ
 (curs.).
talkative person, tǫɥ-pɴedl.
talkative man, tǫɥpɴedl-k̃iɴ.
tall, long, k̃i̧ɴ-ni̧ɴ.
Tall Trees creek, plcn., 'ɴ'-
 -k̃i̧ɴmi̧ɴ-p̃ɑ'.
tanned (with the sun, to be),
 sɴdl-tɴ'.
tapeworm, bout-poudl.
tar, k'ǫɥ-k̃ɑdl, k'ǫɥ-k̃ɑdlsei.
tarantula, k̃ɑ̨'nɑ̨'t'ɑ̨'-k'ǫɥ-'eidl.
tassel (of corn), 'ɴ'-t'ɥn.
to taste intr., 'oubɴ-dɑ.
to taste good, be sweet, k̃oudl-ɑ̨',
 'ɑ̨'-guɑ-dou'e-gyɴ.
to taste of, k̃oudlɑ̨'-bɴ-'ɑ̨'nȩi.
tea, tsoue-guɑdl.
tea particle, tea leaf, tsoue-guɑtdɑ.
tear, tɴ'-bɴ.
telegraph, typewriter, hɑ̨'-tǫɥ-
 kuɑt, hɑ̨'-kuɑt.
telegraph pole, hɑ̨'kuɑt-'ɴ'-dɑ.
to tell, tei-t.
to tell a story or myth, hȩi-tei-t.
temple (anat.), p'ɑ-'ɴ', p'ɑ-ɴt-
 bɴ, p'ɑ-'ɴt-bɴ-e.
temporarily, a while, 'ɑ'-.
ten, kɑ'-k'i̧ɴ.
ten by ten, kɑ'douk'i̧ɴ-n.
ten places (in), kɑ'k'i̧ɴ-dou.
tendril, gyɴ̀-tɴ'-bǫɥnmɑ̨ȩ.
tenth (ordinal), kɑ'k'yɴn-dei.
testicles, k̃ɑ̨'-mɑ̨-n.
Texan (masc.), Teihɥ'nȩi-k̃iɴ.
Texas, Teihɥ'nȩi-dɑ̨m.

thank you, 'ʜ-hou'.

that, dem. stems, 'α-, 'αp-, 'ou, 'ou-p-.

that, 'α̅'-dei, 'αp̣-dei, *'ou-dei, 'ouei-dei, *'oup̣-dei; also 'αhα̅'-dei, 'αhyα̅'-dei, etc.

their, his, your, prefixed to certain relationship terms, 'ʜ-.

then, again, pou-e.

there, 'α-hα', 'αhy-α', 'αp-hα', 'ou, 'ouhy-α', 'ou-e, 'ouehy-α', *'oup̣-hα'; also 'α̅'-bʜ-hα', 'α̅'-dei-hα', etc.

there, enough, that is all, 'oudei-hα', 'oudei-hịʜ.

therefore, pei-dou.

thick, t͡sei.

thief, seịm-k͡iʜ.

thief, mouse, seịm-hʜt.

thigh, pα̅'-, pα̅'-t'ọu-dei.

thigh (flesh of), pα̅'-kiʜ.

thigh (top of), pei-t͡soudl.

thigh vein, pα̅'-p'iʜ.

thin (to be), p'ʜ-t̨-gyʜ.

to think, *'α̅'-dα, peidl-dọun.

to think about, peidl-dou', peidl-p̄ʜ'egα.

thinking (referring to), pei-dl-.

third (ordinal), p'ʜ̨'out-dei, p'ʜ̨'-ouyα̅'-dei.

thirsty (to be), t'ọu-heị'm, t'ọu-pʜ'dlei.

thirteen, p'ʜ̨'ou-t'ʜ̨.

thirty, p'ʜ̨'ou-k'ịʜ̨.

thirty-one, p'ʜ̨'ouk'ịʜ̨ pʜ'tʜ̨.

this, dem. stems, 'eị-, 'eị-m-, 'ịʜ-.

this, 'eị-dei, 'eịm-dei, 'ị(ʜ)-dei; also 'eịhα̅'-dei, eịmhα̅'-dei, etc.

this way, thus, 'eịdei-tsou.

this way (in this direction), 'eịmgα-t'αp.

thorn, seị-gα̅'-t.

thought, pei-gyʜ.

thought-tired (to be), peigyʜ-dʜ̨mgyʜ, peigyʜ-dʜ̨mgyʜ-dα.

three, p'ʜ̨-'ou.

three (in an old Kiowa count), p'ʜ̨'ou-k̄ou.

three by three, p'ʜ̨'ou-t.

three places (in), p'ʜ̨'out-dou.

throat, 'ou-sei.

throat, neck, 'ou-.

through, -kα̅'-gα.

through the middle of, -k'ou-p̄α̨-'e̩-guα.

to throw, k̄iʜ-gyʜ.

to throw (away), dance, guα-n.

thrown away thing, kuα-n.

thumb, mα̨n-sα.

thunder, p̄α̅'-sou-t.

thus, so, that way, tsou-dl-hα'.

tick, 'α̅'-t͡sọu.

to tie, *p'ʜ̨-e̩.

to tie cloth, k'αe-p'ʜ̨e̩.

to tie load on, 'oudl-p'ʜ̨'e̩.

to tie in a hard knot, p'ʜ̨msα-p'ʜ̨e̩.

tied (to be), p'ʜ̨.

tied in a bundle (to be), p'ou-p'ʜ̨.

Timber Bluff, plcn., 'ʜ̄'-yʜdldʜ.

Timber Bluff winter, 'ʜ̄'-yʜdldʜ-sʜe.

timbered hill, also plcn., 'ʜ̄'-bαdlhα'.

tipi pin, t̄α̨m-toup.

tipi pole, guα-n,, guα̨n-hịʜ̨.

to tire tr., dʜ̨'-m.

tired (to be), dʜ̨-m-gyʜ, dʜ̨m-gyʜ-dα.

to, toward, -guα.

to (the region of), -bei-guα.

toad (frog?) sp., dα̨m-t'ʜdl.

toadstool, p̄α̅'sout-sα̅'-gyʜ.

tobacco (particle or piece of), t'ʜ̄'-bα̅'-t.

tobacco plant, t'ʜ̄'bʜ'-goup.

toe, 'α̨n-t'ʜdl.

toenail,'α̨n-t͡sọu.

together, k'α-dl-hei-, pʜ'-, pʜ'-gue-gα, pʜ'-yα'.

tomato (wild and garden sps., fruit of), k̄α̨'.

tomato soup, k̄ǫn-tsoue.

told as a story (to be), hei̯teiṭ-dɑ.

tomorrow, k'yн̯-hi̯'н̯-gɑ, k'yнhi̯-'н̯-gɑ-tsou.

tomorrow morning, k'yн̯hi̯'н̯-'oue.

tongue, de̯i-n.

tonsil, k̄iн-'нṭ-dɑ'-dei.

tool, sɑ'dei-hǫndei.

tooth, zǫy̯.

topweed fruit, top (toy for spinning), se̯i-'н̯'-toudl-'ei-gɑ.

topweed plant, se̯i-'н̯'-toudl-'ei-goup.

toward, to, -guɑ.

trail, road, hy̯'ǫn.

train, -'ǫn-k'iн̯-gɑ.

transparent, bǫy̯ -e̯.

trap, snare, fishhook, p'ou.

to trap, p'ou-te̯i'.

to travel, hou-bн, houdɑ-'н̯, tsн̯'-dei.

to travel, to travel off, hou-'ǭ'-zǫy̯-n.

to travel off apart, hou-k̄iн-t.

traveler, hou-k̄iн.

tree, stick, wood, 'н̯'-dɑ.

tree sap, 'н̯'-t'ǫy̯.

tree sp., bou-'ɑt-н̯'-dɑ.

tree sp., k̄ɑdl-н̯'-'ei-p'eip.

tree sp., k'i̯'н̯-guɑdl-'н̯'-dɑ.

tree sp., pǫy̯-'н̯'-dɑ.

tree sp., seiṭ-k̄нdlt'ǫn-'н̯'-dɑ.

tree sp., toudl-kout-'н̯'-dɑ.

tree squirrel, zǫy̯n-t'н̯'bei.

to tremble, shiver, yǭ-m-gɑ.

turkey, pe̯i'.

turnip, k̄н̯e̯-k̄ɑ'dнdlei.

to turn back, pнdl-k'ou-'ei-gyн.

to turn over tr., mǭ-tɑ'dei.

to turn somersault, p'oue - k̄eidl-нdldн̯'-guǫn.

turquoise, k̄sou-sɑhyei.

turtle          (hard - shelled),          t'ǫy̯-k̄ǫnk'iн̯.

turtle          (soft-shelled),          k̄ǫn-k'iн̯, k̄ǫnk'iн̯-p'нt-gyн.

twelve, yiн-t'н̯.

twenty, yiн-k'iн̯.

twenty places (in), yiн-k'iн̯-dou.

twenty-one, yiнk'iн̯ pн̯'-t'н̯.

twin, p'н̯-dɑ-'iн.

to twist, turn crank, mǭ'-k̄uǫn-gɑ.

twisting machine, coffee grinder, mǭ'k̄uǫn-gɑ'-t.

two, yiн.

two (in an old Kiowa count), yi(н)-kɑdl-k̄н̯e̯.

two bits, t'oubeitsei.

two by two, two abreast, niн-hyн.

two hundred, yi(н)-kɑ'dou-k'iн̯.

two places (in), yiн-dou.

typewriter, telegraph, hǭ'-kuɑt, hǭ-tǫy̯-kuɑt.

typhoid fever, sнdl-kyy̯-'e̯.

## u

udder, milkbag, 'ɑ'-zн-'e.

Udder-angry Traveler Off, trbn., 'Ɑ'zн'-k̄ǭ'-hou-k̄iн.

unable (to be), 'ɑ-'ɑ'-dɑ.

unable to do (to be), mɑ-'ɑdǭ'mǭ'.

uncle (maternal), sister's child, sei-gyн; my or our ———, sei-gyн-'e.

under, -dǫy̯'-m, -dǫy̯-bн, -dǫy̯-gyн, -bouk̄-dǫy̯-gyн.

unreal particle, 'ǭ-kɑ-dl.

to untie, *yн-t.

up, above, mн̯, mн̯-e̯, mн̯-m, mн̯-n, mн̯e̯-gɑ, mн̯m-gɑ.

up, above, -mн̯, -mн̯-e̯, -mн̯-m, -mн̯-n.

up close to, -bн-gɑ'-bei.

up, upper, roof, mн̯m-dei.

upslope, hei-t'н- b̯-tsou.

urine, sн̯'-tsoue.

urine bladder, sн̯'tsoue-bi̯нmk'ɑe.

Ute man, 'Iнtн-k̄iн.

uvula, 'ou-pнk̄-k̄ɑdl.

vein, p'iн.

venereal disease (to have), toudl-
ꞣyн.

ᵗᵒ vent wind, p'ou-t'ɑtgɑ.

vertex, top of head, tꞧ-n-, tꞧn-
p̌ɑ̨'ę-gyн, ꞇɑ-p̌-gɑ'-t.

very, very much, very many,
pretty, kou-dou-, -'ǫy̨, -hį̨н,
-hi'ꞧ, kiн-t'ɑ'-hį'ꞧ, k'oup̌-dei.

vine, gou-p, p'ei-p.

vinegar, dęisнdl-t'ǫy̨.

vomit, zou-dl-gyн.

ᵗᵒ vomit, zou . . ., hiн-dɑ.

vomit water, thin vomit, zoudl-
t'ǫy̨.

vulva, p'ei.

w

wagon, wheel, ꞣɑ'-dнdl.

wagon, harness, ꞣ'ue-p'ꞧ, ꞣɑ'-
dнdl-k'uep'ꞧ.

wagon tongue, ꞇoup̌dei-'н'-dɑ.

ᵗᵒ wake intr., tн-e.

ᵗᵒ wake tr., 'ꞧ'-n-ęį.

Waldo, James (prsn. of), Guɑt-
k'ɑe-dei, (recent prsn. of),
ꞣougɑe-t'ɑdl.

ᵗᵒ walk, go, travel, start, 'ǫ̨'-zǫy̨n.

ᵗᵒ walk off, fly away, k'i'нba.

walnut nut (wild), p'ǫy̨hǫy̨n-ei-gɑ.

walnut tree (wild), p'ǫy̨-hǫy̨-n-
'н'-dɑ.

ᵗᵒ want, 'ǫ̨n-dɑ, *kǫ̨-m, t'ęin-dɑ.

ᵗᵒ want to get, k'ɑ'-ꞇɑ', k'ɑ'-
t'ęindɑ.

ᵗᵒ want to kill, dɑ'-t'ęindɑ.

ᵗᵒ want to see, pǫy̨-' ǫ̨ndɑ, pǫy̨-
t'ęindɑ.

war, kyнe-gyн.

war, enemy (referring to), kyнe-.

war bonnet, dorsal fin of fish,
'н-ꞇɑ-hɑ-'e.

warrior, kyнedɑ'-ꞣiн.

warrior, soldier, member of a society, yнꞇ-bн-hei, yнꞇ-bн-hei-
ꞣiн.

war club, ꞣoup-guɑp̌-gɑ'-t.

war dance, 'ou-hǫy̨-mǫ̨-kuɑn.

wart, ꞣǫ̨'-p'oudl.

ᵗᵒ wash, p̌ǫ̨-'ǫ̨-ę.

washwoman, 'ɑdl-p̌ǫ̨'ǫ̨-mꞧ, p̌ǫ̨'ǫ̨-
mн.

water, t'ǫy̨, (?) 'ɑ'-.

water, liquid, soup, coffee, tea,
tsou-e.

water cress, t'ǫy̨-'ei.

water insect, t'ǫy̨-poudl.

water jug (of clay), t'ǫy̨-'oudl-
p'ꞧ'-gɑ.

waterfall (to be), zout-syꞧn-goup.

watermelon, 'ei-sɑhyei-gɑ, tн'hęį-
pįꞧ-gɑ.

water moccasin snake, t'ǫy̨-sꞧ'nęį.

waves (to have), *zouꞇ-badlhɑ'-
-hн'.

way down under, -dǫy̨-bei-hįꞧ.

way over there, 'ou-hįꞧ, 'ouei-hįꞧ.

weasel, tsн'-ꞇǫ̨-dei.

ᵗᵒ weave, p'ou-sou . . .

wedge, 'н'-ꞇɑsн'-hǫ̨'-gyн.

well, 'ɑ'-gɑ.

well, nicely, ꞇн'gyн-e.

west, pнe-yiнyн-.

wet, t'ꞧ'-dн'-.

wet (to be), k'yнdl-dɑ, t'ꞧ'-dн'-
dɑ.

wet through (to get), k'yнdl-hǫn.

what? hǫ̨-n.

what? something, hǫ̨n-dei.

what? what kind of? something,
thing, hн'-dei.

wheat, wheat flour, 'ei-tǫ̨'.

wheat plant, 'ei-tꞧ'-goup.

wheat planting machine, 'ei-tǫ̨'-
'eiꞣuɑ-bɑ.

wheat seed, 'eitǫ̨'-dǫy̨-gɑ'-t.

wheel, circular thing, wagon, ꞣɑ'-
dн-dl.

when? sometime, hʜ'-'ou-e.
when, if, whenever, -tsẹị.
where? somewhere, hʜ'-bʜ, hʜ'-bei, hʜ'-bei-tsou.
where? somewhere, sometime, perhaps, hʜ'-gyʜ.
where to? in which direction? somewhere, hʜ-yʜ'.
which one? someone, hʜ'-gyʜ-e.
to whip, t'ꞑ'-hou-goup.
whipsnake, sꞑ'nẹị-t̂c̨ẹ.
whirlwind, mꝗ'-t'ou-'i(ʜ)-gyʜ.
whisk broom, p'ʜẹ-p'iʜdl-'ʜ'-dα, p'ʜẹ-p'iʜt-dα.
whisky, t'ǫʉ-'αdlk'αe.
to whistle, sẹịm-hʜ'dα.
white (to be), t̂ʜ-ẹ.
white earth (particle of), t'ei-t̂-dα.
white man, T̂α'k'αe-k̑iʜ, Beidl-p'α'-k̑iʜ, P̂'ei-p'αt̂-k̑iʜ.
white wolf, kue'-t̂ʜẹ.
white woman, t̂α'k'αe-mʜ.
white of eye, tʜ'-t̂ʜẹ.
who? somebody, hʜ'-dei-dl.
whole, all, tei.
whore, 'ƙ-'oudl-k̑α'-dei.
why? hc̨n-dou.
wide, kα't-eit, k'ou-'eit.
widow, mꝗ'dα-mʜ.
widower, mꝗ'dα-k̑iʜ.
wife, woman, t'ʜ'.
wife (to have), t'ʜ'-dei.
wild goose sp., kc̨.
wild goose sp. (white), kc̨-t̂ʜẹ.
wild grape, t̂ei-dei-'ei-gα.
wild grape vine, t̂ei-dei-'ei-p'eip.
wild grape mush, t̂eidei-'ei-kuα'n.
wild onion sp., sou-t̂-dα.
wild tomato, tomato, k̑c̨'.
willow sp., 'ʜe-p̂iʜ-gα.
willow sp., sẹị-'ʜ'-dα.
to win, hc̨'-n.
wind, air, gǫʉ-m-gyʜ.

10559°—28——16

window, 'α'gα-sc̨m.
windpipe, hꝗ'-tsǫʉ-n.
windshield (of smokehole), chimney, k'ǫʉm-pα'-gα.
wing, t̂sou-t̂-dα.
winged ant, 'ẹịmhꞑ'mẹị-t̂soudl-sα.
winter, year, sʜ-e, sʜ'-dʜ.
winter (in), sʜy-α'.
to wipe, brush, p'iʜ-t.
wise (to be), guα, peigyʜ-sα'-'ǫʉ.
wise, smart (to get), guα-'c̨mgyʜ.
with, by, in, -dou.
with, along, (denoting accompaniment), t'ʜ-e-.
without end, forever, 'αþk'c̨n-hẹị.
wolf, ku-e'.
wolf cub, kue'-'iʜ.
woman, mꞑ-y-ịʜ, -mʜ.
woman, wife, t'ʜ'.
womb, 'iʜ-k'c̨ẹ.
wood-gathering rope, k̑iʜ-yʜe-bα.
wood, stick, 'ʜ'-dα.
wooden arrowpoint, *'ʜ'-sei-sei-gα.
Wooden Arrowpoint creek, plcn., 'ʜ'-seisei-p̂α'.
wooden bowl or dish, 'ʜ'-k̑α'-ʜt̂-dα.
wooden club, 'ʜ'-t'ǫʉ.
wooden flute, 'ʜ'-tǫʉ-bα'-t.
wooden house, 'α'-tou.
wooden leg, wooden-legged, 'ʜ'-t'ǫʉ-dei.
woodpecker sp., 'αdl-guαdl.
woodpecker sp., 'ʜ'-bʜ-k̑ʉẹ.
woodpecker sp., mꝗ'-t̂α-ku'α.
woodpecker sp., kyʜe-'αdlguαdl.
Woohaw, prsn., Gu(α)hα'dei.
wool, kyʜ'boudliʜ-p'α'-gyʜ.
word, language, tǫʉ-gyʜ.
work, sα'-dei.
to work, sα'dei-dα, sα'dei-p̂ʜ'egyʜ.
workman, sα'dei-k̑iʜ.

worm, bug, pou-dl.

worm that bores holes in wood, poudl-k'iн-dei.

ᵗᵒ wrap, mǫ-tsң̇ę.

ᵗᵒ wrestle, kouṫ-pн'egα.

wrestler, kouṫ-p̱н'egyн-k̇iн.

wrist, mǫn-kα'e-gα.

ᵗᵒ write, tǫy-guαt.

writer (man), author, tǫy-guαt-k̇iн.

writing book, kuα-t.

writing place, guαṫ-yα'.

writing table, guαt-н'-yα'.

writing table, pen, kuαt-н'-dα.

## y

ᵗᵒ yell, give whoop, tsн-ṫ-.

yellow, guαṫ-k̇ou.

yellow horse, 'ouyαdl-ṫң̇ę.

yellow jacket, ṫeidl-seip.

yellow-jacket honey, ṫeidlseip̱-pęįnhн'.

yes, hα'.

yesterday, yesterday morning, k'iн-deidl.

yet, still, hei-dα.

you, your, spl., 'н̇-m.

young animal, pet, colt, tsei-ou.

young female animal, calf, ṫsн-dl-iн.

young man, tou-guαdl.

young skunk, tнdl-iн.

young woman, yα-gα-e.

your, 'н̇-m; your, his, their, prefixed to certain relationship terms, 'н-.

yucca plant, k̇α'gyн-ṫsout'н'e.

yucca root used as soap, soap, 'αdl-p̱ǫ'ǫ.

# APPENDIX A

## Pronoun Tables

### I. Subjective Series

| | |
|---|---|
| I | 'n̥- |
| we dpl. incl | bn̥- |
| we dpl. excl | 'èi- · |
| you | 'ę̀ịm- |
| ye d | mǹ̥- |
| ye tpl | bn̥- |
| he an | ——— |
| they d. an | 'ę̀ị- |
| they tpl. an. maj | { 'n̥- ——— |
| they tpl. an. min | { 'éi- ——— |
| they tpl. inan. coll | { gyn̥- ?̣- |

237

## II. TRANSITIVE SERIES [1]

| | you an. | ye d. an. | ye tpl. an. |
|---|---|---|---|
| I | { 'ęim- | mǫ́- | bǫ́- |
| we dpl. excl | gǫ́- | mǫ́- | bǫ́- |

| | him an. | them d. an. | them tpl. an. maj. | them tpl. an. min. | them tpl. inan. coll. |
|---|---|---|---|---|---|
| I | { gyꜧ- | nęin- | dėi- | dėi- | { gyꜧt- |
| we dpl. incl | bꜧ- | bėit- | béit- | béit- | bꜧt- |
| we dpl. excl | 'éi- | 'éit- | 'éit- | 'éit- | 'éit- |

| | me an. | us dpl. an. |
|---|---|---|
| you | { 'ęi- | dǫ́- |
| ye d | mꜧ- | dǫ́- |
| ye tpl | bꜧ- | dǫ́- |

| | him an. | them d. an. | them tpl. an. maj. | them tpl. an. min. | them tpl. inan. coll. |
|---|---|---|---|---|---|
| you | { 'ꜧ- | męin- | bęi- | bėi- | bꜧt- |
| ye d | mꜧ- | męin- | męi- | męin- | męn- |
| ye tpl | bꜧ- | bꜧit- | bęi- | bėit- | bꜧt- |

[1] Transitive verbs used intransitively (e. g. boꭓ, to see), and some other verbs (e. g. k'ouꝑbei'ꜧe, to run) employ the forms of this series indicating inanimate collective object, e. g. gyꜧt-k'ouꝑbei'ꜧe, I ran.

| he or they d | me an. | us dpl. an. | them tpl. inan. coll. |
|---|---|---|---|
| he or they d | 'ę́į- | dǫ̀- | gyᴴ- |
| they tpl. an. maj | H-² | dǫ̀- | 'ę́in- |
| they tpl. an. min | 'éi- | dǫ̀- | gyᴴ- |
| they tpl. inan. coll | | | 'éit- |
| | | | 'éit- |

| he or they dpl | you | ye d. | ye tpl. |
|---|---|---|---|
| he or they dpl | gǫ̀- | mǫ̀- | bǫ́- |

| | him an. | them d. | them tpl. maj. | them tpl. min. | them tpl. an. |
|---|---|---|---|---|---|
| he | 'ę́į- | 'ę̀į- | 'ę̀įm- | 'éi- | gyᴴ- |
| they d | H- | 'ę̀įn- | 'ę̀įn- | 'ę̀įn- | 'ę̀įn- |
| they tpl. an maj | 'éi- | 'éit- | 'ę̀įm- | 'éit- | gyᴴ- |
| they tpl. an. min | | 'éit-³ | 'éit- | 'éit- | 'éit- |
| they tpl. inan. coll | | | | | 'éit- |

² Also they tpl. mountains.—me, where one would expect 'ę́į-.
³ But 'éi- for they tpl. horses—them tpl. mountains.

### III. REFLEXIVE SERIES [1]

| | |
|---|---|
| I | dèi- |
| we dpl. incl | béi- |
| we dpl. excl | 'éit- |
| | |
| you | bèi- |
| ye d | méį- |
| ye tpl | béi- |
| | |
| he an | 'èįm- |
| they d. an | 'éįn- |
| they tpl. an. maj | 'éįm- |
| they tpl. an. min | 'éit- |
| they tpl. inan. coll | 'éit- |

[1] The forms of this series are the same as those of the transitive series indicating third person tpl. an. maj. object, e. g. dèi-houdl, 1. I killed them tpl. an. maj.; 2. I killed myself. Thus the tpl. an. maj. object is felt to signify both they indefinite (=somebodies) and self.

## IV. SUBJECTIVE-REFERENTIAL SERIES [1]

| | he | they d. | they tpl. maj. | they tpl. an. min. [2] | they tpl. inan. coll. |
|---|---|---|---|---|---|
| for me ⎱ for us dpl. incl. and excl. ⎰ | 'ę́i-dɔ̨- | nę́i-déit- | nɔ̨-dɔ̨t- | nɔ̨-dɔ̨t- | yɔ́n-gyн́t- |
| for you | gyн | nę́in-méin-béit- | gɔ̨-mɔ̨n-bɔ̨t- | gɔ̨-mɔ̨n-bɔ̨t- | yɔ́n-mɔ́m-bн́t- |
| for ye d. | mɔ̨- | | | | |
| for ye tpl. | bɔ̨- | | | | |
| for him | 'н́-méi-béi- | 'ę́in-méin-béit- | 'ɔ̨-méin-béit- | 'ɔ̨-méin-béit- | 'ɔ́n-mę́in-béit- |
| for them d. | | | | | |
| for them tpl. an. maj. | | | | | |
| for them tpl. an. min. | | | | | |
| for them tpl. inan. coll. | | | | | gyн-? [3] |

[1] Only with third person subject.

[2] Also 1 mountain—for me.

[3] piн-hęi gyн-dɔ'męi', they were without food, is hardly this form.

## V. TRANSITIVE-REFERENTIAL SERIES [1]

| | him | them d. | them tpl. maj. | them tpl. an. min. | them tpl. inan. coll. |
|---|---|---|---|---|---|
| I—for you --------- | {him gyʜ | nę́in- | nę́in- | gᴐ́- | yᴜ̨n- |
| I—for ye d -------- | mę̆- | mę́in- | {mę́in- / mᴐ̨n- | {mᴐ̨n- | mᴜ̨n- |
| I—for ye tpl ------ | bᴐ́- | béit | {béit- / bᴐ́t- | {bᴐ́t- | |
| we dpl.—for you --------- | gᴐ́- | déit- | déit- | gᴐ́t- | gyʜt- |
| we dpl.—for ye d -------- | mᴐ̨- | mę́in- | {mę́in- / mᴐ̨n- | {mᴐ̨n- | mᴜ̨n- |
| we dpl.—for ye tpl ------ | bᴐ́- | | béit- | | |

[1] Only with third person object. Not all the forms of this series were obtained. Apparently certain verbs, e. g. 'ʜ'nei̢, to wake intr., employ the forms of this series indicating inanimate collective object.

| | him | them d. | them tpl. an. maj. | them tpl. an. min. | them tpl. inan. coll. |
|---|---|---|---|---|---|
| I—for him | { gyǻ-<br>mę́į-<br>gyн- | nę́įn-<br>mę́įn-<br>nę́įn- | nę́įn-<br>mę́įn-<br>déi- | gǻ-<br>mę́įn-<br>déi- | yǻn-<br>mę́įn-<br>gyнt-<br>béit- |
| I—for them d. | | | | | |
| I—for them tpl. an. maj. | | | | | |
| I—for them tpl. an. min. | | | | | |
| I—for them tpl. inan. coll. | | | | | |
| we dpl. incl.—for him | bн'н-<br>mę́į-<br>bн- | béidèi'èi-<br>mę́įn-<br>béit- | { béidèi-<br>bádà'à-<br>mę́įn-<br>béi- | } bádà'à-<br>mę́įn-<br>béit- | bнgıн-<br>mę́įn-<br>bнt- |
| we dpl. incl.—for them d. | | | | | |
| we dpl. incl.—for them tpl. an. maj. | | | | | |
| we dpl. incl.—for them tpl. an. min. | | | | | |
| we dpl. incl.—for them tpl. inan. coll. | | | | | |
| we dpl. excl.—for him | 'èi-<br>mę́į-<br>'èi- | 'éidèi-<br>mę́įn- | { 'éidèi-<br>'éidà-<br>mę́įn-<br>'éit- | } 'éidà-<br>mę́įn-<br>'éidèi-<br>'éit- | 'éigıн-<br>mę́įn-<br>'éidèi-<br>'éit- |
| we dpl. excl.—for them d. | | | | | |
| we dpl. excl.—for them tpl. an. maj. | | | | | |
| we dpl. excl.—for them tpl. an. min. | | | | | |
| we dpl. excl.—for them tpl. inan. coll. | | | | | |

V. TRANSITIVE-REFERENTIAL SERIES—Continued

| | | | | | |
|---|---|---|---|---|---|
| you—for me | 'ę́i-dc̨c̨- | nę́i-déit- | nę́i-déit- | nc̨c̨-dc̨c̨t- | yн̇-gyн̇t- |
| you—for us dpl | | | | | |
| ye d.—for me | mḁ'н̇-dc̨c̨- | mę́inę̀i'ę̀i-déit- | mę́inę̀i'ę̀i-déit- | mc̨nc̨'c̨c-dc̨c̨t- | mḁnì'н̇-gyн̇t- |
| ye d.—for us dpl | | | | | |
| ye tpl.—for me | bн̇'н̇-dc̨c̨- | béidę̀i'ę̀i-déit- | béidę̀i'ę̀i-déit- | bc̨dc̨'c̨c-dc̨c̨t- | bн̇gì'c̨c-gyн̇t- |
| ye tpl.—for us dpl | | | | | |
| you—for him | 'н̇-mę́i | 'ę́in-mę́in- | 'ę́im-mę́in- | 'c̨c-mę́in- | 'н̇n-mę́in- |
| you—for them d | | mę́in- | bę̀i- | {bèit- bę̀i- | }bн̇t- |
| you—for them tpl. an maj | 'н̇- | | | | |
| you—for them tpl. an. min | | | | | |
| you—for them tpl. inan. coll | | | | | |
| ye d.—for him | mḁ'н̇- | mę́inę̀i'ę̀i- | mę́inę̀i'ę̀i- | mc̨nc̨'c̨c- | mḁn- |
| ye d.—for them d | mḁ- | mę́in- | mę́in- | mę́in- | |
| ye d.—for them tpl. an. maj | | mę́in- | mę́i- | | |
| ye d.—for them tpl. an. min | | | | | |
| ye d.—for them tpl. inan. coll | | | | | |

| | | | | | |
|---|---|---|---|---|---|
| ye tpl.—for him<br>ye tpl.—for them d.<br>ye tpl.—for them tpl. an. maj.<br>ye tpl.—for them tpl. an. min.<br>ye tpl.—for them tpl. inan. coll. | bʜ'ʜ-<br>bʜ- | béit- | béidèi-<br>mɛ́jn-<br>béi- | béit- | bʜt- |
| he—for me<br>he—for us dpl. | 'ɛ̀i-<br>dɑ̀- | nɛ́i-<br>déit- | nɛ́i-<br>déit- | nɔ́-<br>dɑ̀t- | yʜ-<br>gyʜt- |
| they d.—for me<br>they d.— for us dpl. | 'ɛ̀i'ɛ̀i-<br>dɑ̀- | 'éinɛ̀i'ɛ̀i<br>déit- | 'éinɛ̀i'ɛ̀i-<br>déit- | 'éinɑ̀'ɑ̀-<br>dɑ̀t- | 'éinɛ̀i'ɛ̀i-<br>gyʜt- |
| they tpl. an. maj.—for me<br>they tpl. an. min.—for me<br>they tpl. inan. coll.—for me | 'ʜ'ʜ- | déi'èi- | déi'èi- | dɑ̀'ɑ̀- | gyʜ'ʜ- |
| they tpl. an. maj.—for us dpl.<br>they tpl. an. min.—for us dpl.<br>they tpl. inan. coll.—for us dpl | dɑ̀- | déit- | déit- | dɑ̀t- | gyʜt- |

## V. TRANSITIVE-REFERENTIAL SERIES—Continued

| | | | | | |
|---|---|---|---|---|---|
| he—for you | gↄ́- | déit- | déit- | gↄ́t- | gyↄ́t- |
| he—for ye d | mↄ́- | méin- | méin- | méↄn- | méↄm- |
| he—for ye tpl | bↄ́- | béit- | béit- | bↄ́t- | bↄ́t- |
| they d.—for you | | | déit- | | |
| they d.—for ye d | | | méin- | | |
| they d.—for ye tpl | | | béit- | | |
| they tpl. an. maj.—for you | | | déit- | | |
| they tpl. an. min.—for you | | | | | |
| they tpl. inan. coll.—for you | | | | | |
| they tpl. an. maj.—for ye d | | | méin- | | |
| they tpl. an. min.—for ye d | | | | | |
| they tpl. inan. coll.—for ye d | | | | | |
| they tpl. an. maj.—for ye tpl | | | béit- | | |
| they tpl. an. min.—for ye tpl | | | | | |
| they tpl. inan. coll.—for ye tpl | | | | | |

| he— | | | | |
|---|---|---|---|---|
| he—for him | | | 'éim- | méin- |
| he—for them d | | | méin- | béit |
| he—for them tpl. an. maj | | | 'éim- | gyʜ- |
| he—for them tpl. an. min | | | | |
| he—for them tpl. inan. coll | | | | |

| they d.— | | | | |
|---|---|---|---|---|
| they d.—for him | 'éi'èi- / méin- / 'éi- | | | |
| they d.—for them d | 'éinèi'èi- / méin- / 'éin- | 'éinèi'èi- / méin- / 'éin- | 'éind'ɔ̆- / méin- / 'éin- | 'éinl'ʜ- / méin- / 'éin- |
| they d.—for them tpl. an. maj | | | | |
| they d.—for them tpl. an. min | | | | |
| they d.—for them tpl. inan. coll | | | | |

| they tpl.— | | | | |
|---|---|---|---|---|
| they tpl. an. maj.—for him | 'ʜ'ʜ- | déi'èi- | déi'èi- | dɔ̆'ɔ̆- | gyʜ'ʜ- |
| they tpl. an. min.—for him | | | | |
| they tpl. inan. coll.—for him | | | | |

| they tpl.— | | | | |
|---|---|---|---|---|
| they tpl. an. maj.—for them d | méi- | méin- | méin- | méin- | méin- |
| they tpl. an. min.—for them d | | | | |
| they tpl. inan. coll.—for them d | | | | |

## V. TRANSITIVE-REFERENTIAL SERIES—Continued

| | 'ʜ- | 'èit- | 'ẹim- | 'éit- | gyʜ- |
|---|---|---|---|---|---|
| they tpl. an. maj.—for them tpl. an. maj. | | | | | |
| they tpl. an. maj.—for them tpl. an. min. | | | | | |
| they tpl. an. maj.—for them tpl. inan. coll. | | | | | |
| they tpl. an. min.—for them tpl. an. maj. | | | 'éit- | | |
| they tpl. an. min.—for them tpl. an. min. | | | | | |
| they tpl. an. min.—for them tpl. inan. coll. | | | | | |
| they tpl. inan. coll.—for them tpl. an. maj. | | | | | |
| they tpl. inan. coll.—for them tpl. an. min. | | | | | |
| they tpl. inan. coll.—for them tpl. inan. coll. | | | | | |

VI. Reflexive-Referential Series[1]

I—for you myself _____ nę́in-

I—for ye d. myself _____ {mę́in-
                                                     {mę̀n-

I—for ye tpl. myself _____ {béit-
                                                    {bǽt-

we dpl.—for you ourselves _____ déit-

we dpl.—for ye d. ourselves _____ {mę́in-
                                                     {mę̀n-

we dpl.—for ye tpl. ourselves _____ béit-

I—for him myself _____ nę́in-

I—for them d. myself _____ mę́in-

I—for them tpl. an. maj. myself _____ dèi-

I—for them tpl. an. min. myself _____

I—for them tpl. inan. coll. myself _____

we dpl. incl.—for him ourselves _____ {béidèi-
                                                    {bǽdɑ̀'ɑ̀-

we dpl. incl.—for them d. ourselves _____ mę́in-

we dpl. incl.—for them tpl. an. maj. ourselves _____ béi-

we dpl. incl.—for them tpl. an. min. ourselves _____

we dpl. incl.—for them tpl. inan. coll. ourselves _____

we dpl. excl.—for him ourselves _____ {'éidèi-
                                                    {'éidɑ̀-

we depl. excl.—for them d. ourselves _____ mę́in-

we dpl. excl.—for them tpl. an. maj. ourselves _____ {'éidèi
                                                     {'éit-

we dpl. excl.—for them tpl. an. min. ourselves _____

we dpl. excl.—for them tpl. inan. coll. ourselves _____

you—for me yourself _____ nę́i-

you—for us dpl. yourself _____ déit-

ye d.—for me yourselves _____ mę́inèi'èi-

ye d.—for us dpl. yourselves _____ déit-

---

[1] The forms of this series are the same as those of the transitive-referential series indicating 3d person tpl. an. maj. object, e. g. nę́in-houdl, 1. I killed them tpl. an. maj. for him, 2. I killed myself for him. Verbs employing the transitive-referential series use the reflexive-referential series when the indirect object is unexpressed, e. g. gyń-k̑ingyн, I threw it at him (tr.-rfr. ser.), but nę́in-k̑ingyн, I threw it, I threw it for myself.

ye tpl.—for me yourselves_____ béidèi'èi-
ye tpl.—for us dpl. yourselves_____ déit-

you—for him yourself_____ 'ę́įm-
you—for them d. yourself_____ mę́įn-
you—for them tpl. an. maj. yourself_____ bèi-
you—for them tpl. an. min. yourself_____
you—for them tpl. inan. coll. yourself_____

ye d.—for him yourselves_____ mę́įnèi'èi-
ye d.—for them d. yourselves_____ mę́įn-
ye d.—for them tpl. an. maj. yourselves_____ mę́į-
ye d.—for them tpl. an. min. yourselves_____
ye d.—for them tpl. inan. coll. yourselves_____

ye tpl.—for him yourselves_____ béidèi-
ye tpl.—for them d. yourselves_____ mę́įn-
ye tpl.—for them tpl. an. maj. yourselves_____ béi-
ye tpl.—for them tpl. an. min. yourselves_____
ye tpl.—for them tpl. inan. coll. yourselves_____

he—for me himself_____ nę́į-
he—for us dpl. himself_____ déit-

they d.—for me themselves_____ 'ę́įnèį'èi-
they d.—for us dpl. themselves_____ déit-

they tpl. an. maj.—for me themselves_____ déi'èi-
they tpl. an. min.—for me themselves_____
they tpl. inan. coll.—for me themselves_____

they tpl. an. maj.—for us dpl. themselves_____ déit-
they tpl. an min.—for us dpl. themselves_____
they tpl. inan. coll.—for us dpl. themselves_____

he—for you himself_____ déit-
he—for ye d. himself_____ mę́įn-
he—for ye tpl. himself_____ béit-

they d.—for you themselves_____ déit-
they d.—for ye d. themselves_____ mę́įn-
they d.—for ye tpl. themselves_____ béit-

they tpl. an. maj.—for you themselves_____ déit-
they tpl. an. min.—for you themselves_____
they tpl. inan. coll.—for you themselves_____

they tpl. an. maj.—for ye d. themselves_____ mɛ́ịn-
they tpl. an. min.—for ye d. themselves_____
they tpl. inan. coll.—for ye d. themselves_____

they tpl. an. maj.—for ye tpl. themselves_____ béit-
they tpl. an. min.—for ye tpl. themselves_____
they tpl. inan. coll.—for ye tpl. themselves_____

he—for him himself _____ 'ɛ́ịm-
he—for them d. himself_____ mɛ́ịn-
for them tpl. an. maj. himself_____ 'ɛ̀ịm-
he—for them tpl. an. min. himself_____
he—for them tpl. inan. coll. himself_____

they d.—for him themselves_____ 'ɛ́ịnɛ̀ị'ɛ̀ị-
they d.—for them d. themselves_____ mɛ́ịn-
they d.—for them tpl. an. maj. themselves_____ 'ɛ́ịn-
they d.—for them tpl. an. min. themselves_____
they d.—for them tpl. inan. coll. themselves_____

they tpl. an. maj.—for him themselves_____ déi'èi-
they tpl. an. min.—for him themselves_____
they tpl. inan. coll.—for him themselves_____

they tpl. an. maj.—for them d. themselves_____ mɛ́ịn-
they tpl. an. min.—for them d. themselves_____
they tpl. inan. coll.—for them d. themselves_____

they tpl. an. maj.—for them tpl. an. maj. themselves_ 'ɛ́ịm-
they tpl. an. maj.—for them tpl. an. min. themselves_
they tpl. an. maj.—for them tpl. inan. coll. themselves_____

they tpl. an. min.—for them tpl. an. maj. themselves_____ 'éit-
they tpl. an. min.—for them tpl. an. min. themselves_
they tpl. an. min.—for them tpl. inan. coll. themselves_____
they tpl. inan. coll.—for them tpl. an. maj. themselves_____
they tpl. inan. coll.—for them tpl. an. min. themselves_____
they tpl. inan. coll.—for them tpl. inan. coll. themselves_____

## APPENDIX B—TEXT

### 'ɑ'zнîɋ'нoup [1]

#### The Udder-Angry Travelers Off

Dictated by Delos Lonewolf (Kiowa names 'Ẹ̀ịmнɑ'н̥', He Ca tured Them and K'ọц'eidl, Great Dark), adopted son of the late chief Lonewolf (Kiowa name Kue'pн'gɑ'e, Lone Wolf). Ḍelos is one of the councilmen (tọцgɑ, lit. talkers). For this story cp. Mooney, op. cit., pp. 153–154.

'н̥hou'н̥'heidl [2]   nɋ [3]   hн'deidl [4]   îнp [5]   houdlheidl. [6]   'н̥peịnẹị' [7]
They were traveling along   and   somebody   an antelope   killed.   They butchered it

nɋ   ƙyнtнeƙiн [8]   tsн̥mheidl. [9]   îнp   peịndɑ'dei [10]   bọцheidl [11]   gɑ [12]
when   the chief   came up.   The antelope   butchered   he saw   and

'ɑ'zн'e [13]   'ẹ̣ihɑ'heidl. [14]   nɋ   ƙiнgyн [15]   kɑ'dei [16]   ƙyнtнeƙiн
the d. udders   he took.   Then   later   the other   chief

tsн̥mheidl   gɑ   'ɑ'zн'e   k'ɑ'îɑ'dei'. [17]   nɋ   kɑ'dei   ƙyнtнeƙiн
came up   and   the d. udders   he wanted.   But   the other   chief

hɋ'nẹị [18]   tọцnẹị', [19]   hɋn [20]   'ɋ'nɋ'heidl. [21]   nɋ   ƙɑ'dei:   'ɋ'deiþgɑ [22]
"No"   said,   not   he granted.   And   the other one:   "Half

nɋ̇'ɋ'!'' [23]   tọцnẹị'.   nɋ   kɑ'dei   hɋ'nẹị   tọцnẹị'.   nẹịgɑ [24]
give me!"   he said.   And   the other one   "No"   he said.   And already

'ẹịdei [25]   sɋ̇'ɋ'deiheidl, [26]   gɑ   heigɑ [27]   'ɋ'gɑ'dei [28]   ƙyн̥hyoup [29]   gɑ
this one   was angry   and   now   own   men   and

mн̥youp [30]   teip'ɑe [31]   'ẹ̀ịmtouda [32]   gɑ   heigɑ   mhouîнdlheidl. [33]
women   all   he gathered   and now   they traveled off apart.

'ɑhyɑ'gɑ [34]   hн̥yн' [35]   mhou'ɋ'zọцnheidl. [36]   nẹịgɑ   hɋn
Those (are the ones that)   somewhere   traveled off.   And now   not

gyн̥hнegɑ' [37]   hн̥yн'   'н̥bн'gyн'dei'. [38]   mɋn [39]   hн'gi [40]   'н̥îɑ'. [41]
it is known   where   they went.   Maybe   somewhere   they are staying.

"'ɑ'zнîɋ'нoup"   'н̥n [42]   'ẹ̣imk'ɑ'mɋ. [43]   hн'gi   'н̥îɑ'dei' [44]   Kɑeguɑ. [45]
"The udder-angry travelers off"   always   they call them.   Somewhere   there are   Kiowas.

'oudeihɑ' [46]   gyн̥heịteiîdɑ. [47]
That is all   the story.

#### Free Translation

The people were traveling along and somebody killed an antelope. They butchered it, when the chief came up. He saw the butchered antelope and took both the milkbags for himself. Then later the other chief came up and wanted the milkbags. But the first chief refused and did not grant him. And the other chief said: "Give me

252

half." But the other refused. And now the former got angry; he gathered his own men and women together and they traveled off apart.

Those are the ones that traveled off somewhere. And it is not known where they went to. I guess they are staying somewhere. "Those who traveled off angry because of the milkbags" they call them. Somewhere there are Kiowas. Thus it is told.

### Notes

[1] 'Œ'zнⁱ꜒'houḰiн (an. I; 'Œ'zнⁱ꜒'houp, tpl.), udder-angry traveler off ['α'zн-, milkbag; -ⁱ꜒'-, prepound form of ⁱꜱ-n, to be mean, ugly, cp. '꜒'-dei, to be mean, note 26; hou-Ḱiн, traveler off (an. I; hou-p, tpl.), hou-, referring to traveling, -Ḱiн, man].

[2] hou-'ḥ, to come traveling, to travel along [hou-, referring to traveling; 'ḥ, to come]. 'ḥ-, they tpl. an. maj., sbj. series.

[3] nꜳ, and. Cp. neiᵢgα, and now, note 24; gα, and.

[4] hн'deidl, interrogative and indefinite pronoun, who? somebody [hн'-, interrogative pronoun stem, cp. hн-yн', where? note 35, hн'-gyн, where? note 40; -dei-dl, pronoun postfix: -dei, pronoun postfix; -dl, noun and pronoun postfix].

[5] ⁱнp (an. II) means either deer or antelope, but here refers to an antelope, as was confirmed by Mrs. Pedrick. When referring to deer (and possibly sometimes also to antelope) the decl. is an. II, the form remaining unchanged in the tpl.; but for antelope a coll. tpl., ⁱα'-seidl, herd of antelope, is used and is treated as an an. singular (e. g. ⁱα'-seidl gyȟ-bọụ, I saw a herd of antelopes). Cp. ⁱαp-, which refers to buffalo as well as to deer and antelope.

[6] houdl, to kill. houdlheidl, infer. ——, he —— it, tr. series.

[7] peᵢin, to butcher. peᵢineᵢi', infer. 'ḥ-, they —— it, tr. series.

[8] ḰyнтнеḰiн (an. I; Ḱyнтн'e, tpl.), chief [Ḱyнтне-, unexplained; -Ḱiн, man].

[9] tsḥn, to arrive, come up. tsḥnheidl, infer. ——, he, sbj. series.

[10] peᵢin-dα, to be butchered, from peᵢ-n, to butcher plus dα, to be; -dei, participial postfix, the one who, tpl. correspondent -gα.

[11] bọụ, to see. bọụheidl, infer.

[12] gα, and. Cp. nꜳ, and, note 3 above.

[13] 'α'zн'e (an. II ᵇ; 'α'zн'e, 'α'zн, d.; 'α'zн'dα, 'α'zн'gα, tpl.; 'α'zн-in comp.), udder. The antelope has four teats but is thought of by the Kiowa as having two "milkbags," hence the dual gender of the present word as shown by the accompanying verb, 'ęi-hα'heidl. Cp. 'ḥm mèᵢin-hα', you get both (the milkbags)!

¹⁴ hɑ'gyн, to get, take.  hɑ'heidl, infer.  'è̜i-, he —— them d., tr.
series.

¹⁵ ǩiнgyн, adv., afterwards, later.

¹⁶ kɑ'dei (kɑ'gɑ, tpl.), pron., the other.

¹⁷ k'ɑ'ɫɑ', to want to get, want to take [k'ɑ'-, prepound form of
hɑ'-gyн, to get; -ɫɑ', unexplained, app. identical in form with ɫɑ',
to be about].  k'ɑ'ɫɑ'dei', infer. ——, he, sbj. series; cp. 'ɑ'zн'e
'н̜-k'ɑ'ɫɑ', I wanted the (spl.) milkbag(s).

¹⁸ hǫ'ne̜i, neg. particle, no (e. g. in ans. to question) [cp. hǫ-n, not,
note 20; -'e̜i, unexplained].

¹⁹ tǫųe, to say.  tǫųne̜i', infer. ——, he, sbj. series.

²⁰ hǫn, adv., not [cp. hǫ'-n-e̜i, no, note 18].

²¹ 'ǫ, to give.  'ǫ'nǫ'heidl, infer. neg. ——, he, sbj. series; 'ǫ,
which usually takes the tr. series, is here used with the sbj. series
and means to grant, yield (as nearly as I could understand the
informant).  Cp. note 23.  Cp. 'нdl-ǫmgyн, to grant.

²² 'ǫ'deiþgɑ, tpl. form of 'ǫ'deiþdei, half here used to agree with
the reversed decl. of 'ɑ'zн'e; cp. 'ɑ'zн'e déi-bǫų, I saw the "milkbag."
Another word meaning half is zнedei.  When these two words were
compared, 'ǫ'deiþdei was said to mean "the other half" and zнedei.
"half."

²³ 'ǫ', imp. of 'ǫ, to give.  n&-, you —— me — it (an. min. s.),
tr.-refer. series.

²⁴ ne̜igɑ, particle, from nǫ heigɑ, and now.  Cp. geigɑ, from gɑ
heigɑ, and now.  heigɑ from hei, now, already; -gɑ, adverbial.

²⁵ 'e̜idei ('e̜igɑ, tpl.), dem. pron., this one.

²⁶ sǫ-'ǫ'dei, to be angry [sǫ-, unexplained verb prefix; 'ǫ'dei, to be
mean, cp. ɫǫn, to be mean, note 1].  sǫ-'ǫ'deiheidl, infer.

²⁷ heigɑ, now, already.  Cp. ne̜igɑ, from nǫ heigɑ, and now, note
24 above.

²⁸ 'ǫ'gɑ'dei, own ['ǫ'gɑ, own; -dei, pronoun postfix].

²⁹ ǩyн̜hi̜'н̜ (an. I; ǩyн̜hyoup tpl.), man [cp. -ǩiн, man; -hi̜'н̜,
real].

³⁰ mн̜yin̜ (an. I; mн̜youp, tpl.), woman [for mн̜-e̜-in̜: mн̜-e̜- as in
-mн̜-e̜-mǫ, woman; w. -in̜ cp. -hin̜, -hi̜'н̜, real].

³¹ teip'ɑe, all, = tei, all [-p'ɑ-e, unexplained].

³² toudɑ, to pick up, gather together.  'e̜im-, he —— them tpl.
an. maj., tr. series.

³³ hou-ɫнt, lit. to travel-sever, with refl. to break oneself away
and travel off.  houɫнdlheidl, infer.  m-, from 'e̜im-, they tpl.
an. maj. —— themselves, refl. series.

³⁴ 'ɑhyɑ'dei ('ɑhyɑ'gɑ, tpl.), that he ['ɑ-e-, dem. stem.; -hɑ',
postp., at; -dei, pronoun postfix].

³⁵ hн̜yн', where? somewhere.  Cp. hн̜yн' 'e̜im-bн'ɫɑ', where are
you going to go?  [hн̜-, interrogative pron. stem, cp. hн'-deidl, who?

note 4; -yн', postp., at. Cp. hн'-gyн, where?, somewhere, note 40 below].

³⁶ hou-'ʠ'zǫ̨ṇn, lit. to travel go [hou-, referring to traveling; 'ʠ'zǫ̨ṇn, to walk: 'ʠ'-, with the foot; zǫ̨ṇ-n, to pull out]. hou'ʠ'zǫ̨ṇnheidl, infer. m- from 'ę̨im-, they tpl. an. maj.—themselves, refl. series.

³⁷ hнegyн, to know. hнegɑ', punct. neg. Here used impersonally; cp. gyн̀-sнdl, it is hot (weather). gyн̀-, it inan. coll., sbj. series.

³⁸ bн, to go. bн'gyнdei', infer. 'н̨-, they tpl. an. maj., sbj. series. Cp. hǫ̨n yн̨-hнegɑ' 'н̨-bн'gyн, I don't know where they went.

³⁹ mǫ̨n, particle expressing uncertainty, perhaps, maybe, I guess. Cp. mʠ', like.

⁴⁰ hн'gyн, interrogative and indefinite adv., where? somewhere [hн'-, interrogative pron. stem; -gyн, postp., at]. Cp. hн-yн', where?, somewhere, note 35 above.

⁴¹ t̂ɑ', to stay, live. 'н̨-, they tpl. an. maj., sbj. series.

⁴² 'нn, adv., always; with neg. never.

⁴³ k'ʠ'm, to call tr., name. k'ʠ'mǫ̨, curs. 'ę̨im-, they tpl. an. maj. —— them tpl. an. maj., tr. series.

⁴⁴ t̂ɑ', to stay. t̂ɑ'dei', infer.

⁴⁵ Kɑek̂iн (an. I; Kɑeguɑ, tpl.; Kɑe- in comp.), Kiowa man. Cp. Kɑemн̨, Kiowa woman; the tpl., Kɑeguɑ, is common gender [Kɑ-e-, unexplained; -k̂iн, man; -mн̨, woman; -guɑ, tpl.]. From the tpl. are corrupted Sp. Caigua, Eng. Kiowa.

⁴⁶ 'oudeihɑ' gyн̀hę̨iteitdɑ, that is all the story. 'oudeihɑ', adv., that is all, enough [*'ou-dei, that; -hɑ', postp., at]. Cp. 'ou-bн-hɑ', enough.

⁴⁷ hę̨iteit-dɑ, to be told as a story or myth, from hei-tei-t to tell a story or myth plus dɑ, to be. Cp. pę̨in-dɑ, to be butchered, from pę̨i-n, to butcher plus dɑ, to be, note 10 above. hę̨i-teit is from hę̨i-, unexplained, referring to a story; tei-t, to tell. gyн̀-, it inan. coll. spl., sbj. series.

O

Printed in the United States
131292LV00003B/259/A